Austrian Law and Economics
Volume II

Economic Approaches to Law

Series Editors: Richard A. Posner

Judge, United States Court of Appeals for the Seventh Circuit and Senior Lecturer, University of Chicago Law School, USA

Francesco Parisi

Oppenheimer Wolff and Donnelly Professor of Law, University of Minnesota Law School, USA and Professor of Economics, University of Bologna, Italy

Wherever possible, the articles in these volumes have been reproduced as originally published using facsimile reproduction, inclusive of footnotes and pagination to facilitate ease of reference.

For a full list of published and future titles in this series and a list of all Edward Elgar published titles visit our website at www.e-elgar.com

Austrian Law and Economics Volume II

Edited by

Mario J. Rizzo

Department of Economics
New York University, USA

ECONOMIC APPROACHES TO LAW

An Elgar Research Collection
Cheltenham, UK • Northampton, MA, USA

Published by
Edward Elgar Publishing Limited
The Lypiatts
15 Lansdown Road
Cheltenham
Glos GL50 2JA
UK

Edward Elgar Publishing, Inc.
William Pratt House
9 Dewey Court
Northampton
Massachusetts 01060
USA

A catalogue record for this book is available from the British Library

Library of Congress Control Number: 2011922856

MIX
Paper from
responsible sources
FSC   FSC® C018575
www.fsc.org

ISBN 978 1 84542 753 5 (2 volume set)

Printed and bound by MPG Books Group, UK

Contents

Acknowledgements

The editors and publishers wish to thank the authors and the following publishers who have kindly given permission for the use of copyright material.

Association of Private Enterprise Education for article: Edward Stringham (2002), 'The Emergence of the London Stock Exchange as a Self-Policing Club', *Journal of Private Enterprise*, **17** (2), 1–19.

Cambridge University Press for article: Anthony Ogus (1999), 'Competition Between National Legal Systems: A Contribution of Economic Analysis to Comparative Law', *International and Comparative Law Quarterly*, **48** (2), April, 405–18.

Campbell Law Review for article: Roy E. Cordato (1996), 'Time Passage and the Economics of Coming to the Nuisance: Reassessing the Coasean Perspective', *Campbell Law Review*, **20**, 273–92.

Cato Institute for articles: Peter Lewin (1982), 'Pollution Externalities: Social Cost and Strict Liability', *Cato Journal*, **2** (1), Spring, 205–29; Mario J. Rizzo (1985), 'Rules Versus Cost-Benefit Analysis in the Common Law', *Cato Journal*, **4** (3), Winter, 865–84.

Elsevier for article: Edward Stringham (2003), 'The Extralegal Development of Securities Trading in Seventeenth-Century Amsterdam', *Quarterly Review of Economics and Finance*, **43** (2), Summer, 321–44.

Hofstra Law Review Association for article: Mario J. Rizzo (1980), 'The Mirage of Efficiency', *Hofstra Law Review*, **8** (3), Spring, 641–58.

Independent Institute for article: Randall G. Holcombe (2004), 'Government: Unnecessary but Inevitable', *Independent Review: A Journal of Political Economy*, **VIII** (3), Winter, 325–42.

Institute of Economic Affairs for excerpts: Karol Boudreaux and Paul Dragos Aligica (2007), 'The Evolutionary Path', in *Paths to Property: Approaches to Institutional Change in International Development*, Chapter 6, 71–9, references; Karol Boudreaux and Paul Dragos Aligica (2007), 'An Intellectual Toolbox for the Creation of Property Rights', in *Paths to Property: Approaches to Institutional Change in International Development*, Chapter 8, 84–99, references.

Liberty Fund, Inc. for excerpt: James M. Buchanan (1969), 'Private and Social Cost', in *Cost and Choice: An Inquiry in Economic Theory*, Chapter 5, 70–83.

Ludwig von Mises Institute for article: Edward Stringham (1999), 'Market Chosen Law', *Journal of Libertarian Studies*, **14** (1), Winter 1998–1999, 53–77.

Mario Rizzo and Douglas Glen Whitman for their own work: (2003), 'The Camel's Nose is in the Tent: Rules, Theories, and Slippery Slopes', *UCLA Law Review*, **51** (2), December, 539–92.

Mohr Siebeck Tübingen for article: Walter Block and Thomas J. DiLorenzo (2000), 'Is Voluntary Government Possible? A Critique of Constitutional Economics', *Journal of Theoretical and Institutional Economics*, **156** (4), December, 567–82.

NYU Journal of Law and Liberty for articles: Mario J. Rizzo (2005), 'The Problem of Moral Dirigisme: A New Argument Against Moralistic Legislation', *NYU Journal of Law and Liberty*, **1** (2), 789–843; Richard A. Epstein (2006), 'Intuition, Custom, and Protocol: How to Make Sound Decisions with Limited Knowledge', *NYU Journal of Law and Liberty*, **2** (1), 1–27; Douglas Glen Whitman and Mario J. Rizzo (2007), 'Paternalist Slopes', *NYU Journal of Law and Liberty*, **2** (3), 411–43.

Oxford University Press via the Copyright Clearance Center's Rightslink service for article: Peter T. Leeson (2008), 'How Important is State Enforcement for Trade?', *American Law and Economics Review*, **10** (1), Spring, 61–89.

Sage Publications, Inc. via the Copyright Clearance Center's Rightslink service for article: John Hasnas (2003), 'Reflections on the Minimal State', *Politics, Philosophy and Economics*, **2** (1), 115–28.

Springer Science and Business Media for articles: Todd J. Zywicki (1998), 'Epstein and Polanyi on Simple Rules, Complex Systems, and Decentralization', *Constitutional Political Economy*, **9** (2), June, 143–50; Peter T. Leeson (2006), 'Efficient Anarchy', *Public Choice*, **130** (1–2), 41–53; Peter J. Boettke, Christopher J. Coyne and Peter T. Leeson (2007), 'Saving Government Failure Theory from Itself: Recasting Political Economy from an Austrian Perspective', *Constitutional Political Economy*, **18** (2), June, 127–43; Peter T. Leeson (2008), 'Coordination Without Command: Stretching the Scope of Spontaneous Order', *Public Choice*, **135** (1–2), April, 67–78; Douglas Glen Whitman (2009), 'The Rules of Abstraction', *Review of Austrian Economics*, **22** (1), March, 21–41.

Taylor & Francis Books UK for excerpts: David A. Harper (2003), 'Institutions I: Rule of Law, Property and Contract', in *Foundations of Entrepreneurship and Economic Development*, Chapter 4, 57–88, references; David A. Harper (2003), 'Institutions II: Money, Political and Legal Decentralisation and Economic Freedom', in *Foundations of Entrepreneurship and Economic Development*, Chapter 5, 89–126, references.

University of Chicago Press for articles: Mario J. Rizzo (1980), 'Law Amid Flux: The Economics of Negligence and Strict Liability in Tort', *Journal of Legal Studies*, **9** (2), March, 291–318; Peter T. Leeson (2007), 'Trading with Bandits', *Journal of Law and Economics*, **50** (2), May, 303–21; Peter T. Leeson (2007), 'An-*arrgh*-chy: The Law and Economics of Pirate Organization', *Journal of Political Economy*, **115** (6), 1049–94.

In addition the publishers wish to thank the Library of Indiana University at Bloomington, USA for their assistance in obtaining these articles.

Part I
Common Law, Balancing
and Efficiency

[1]

LAW AMID FLUX: THE ECONOMICS OF NEGLIGENCE AND STRICT LIABILITY IN TORT

MARIO J. RIZZO*

T<small>HE</small> economic efficiency approach to the analysis of the common law, particularly the law of torts, has been growing rapidly in recent years and shows no sign of abatement. Nevertheless, some very fundamental analytic problems have not even been recognized in this literature, much less solved. It is the purpose of this essay to raise these problems in the context of the perennial conflict between negligence and strict liability. The first and major part of this paper will consist of a detailed study of the efficiency rationale for negligence law. Next, we shall analyze some of the economic aspects of a system of strict liability. The overall conclusion is that efficiency, as normally understood, is impossible as a goal for tort law. The law cannot and should not aim toward the impossible. Consequently, both the normative and positive justifications for the efficiency approach to tort law must be rejected. Our reasons for this conclusion can be divided into static and dynamic considerations. The most important by far, however, are the dynamic factors: Precisely because we live outside of general competitive equilibrium and in a world of unpredictable flux, the efficiency case for negligence must fail. In such a world, it is impossible to compare alternative liability systems in terms of judicial cost-benefit analysis or "fine tuning." Instead, they must be analyzed in terms of institutional efficiency—the certainty and stability that these rules impart to the social framework. A static world of general equilibrium would make an efficient tort law possible, and yet render it unnecessary; in such a world, markets would be universal. A dynamic world, however, demands the certainty and simplicity of static law.

I. Negligence

Traditional, noneconomic definitions of negligence are generally based on such intrinsically vague concepts as the lack of "due care" or the absence of

* Assistant Professor of Economics, New York University. I am indebted to the Institute for Humane Studies and the Scaife Foundation for financial support of my research. I am also indebted to Michael Becker, Richard Epstein, William Landes, Richard Posner, and Paul Rubin for comments on previous versions. Responsibility for errors remains mine alone.

the level of care that *would* be undertaken by the "reasonable man." The economic efficiency approach attempts to make this concept more rigorous. Negligence can be defined in economic terms as the behavior of the utility-maximizing individual when he bears less than the full social costs of his activity. To make such a definition operational the analyst must be able to measure, with tolerable accuracy, the relevant social costs. This is no simple task; and if our thesis is correct, it is fundamentally intractable. Nonnegligence refers to the behavior that *would* be undertaken by the rational agent if he were made to bear the full social costs associated with his conduct. This formulation brings into sharp relief the counterfactual nature of the predictions involved. Hence, the kind of evidence that would shed light on these counterfactual hypotheses is, at best, indirect.

The efficiency approach requires not only the testing of hypotheses about the defendant's negligence, but also investigation into the (contributory) negligence of the plaintiff. If, however, the doctrine of contributory negligence is to be interpreted as a lesser-cost avoider defense,[1] our task is still not complete. If we find that both defendant and plaintiff have been negligent, we must still determine which party could have avoided the accident at less cost. Therefore, we are driven to compare two counterfactual hypotheses: if A were required to bear the full social costs attached to his behavior he would have avoided the accident at $X, and if B bore the full costs he would have avoided it at $Y. Now if $X is less than $Y, the efficiency framework implies that A ought to be made liable for the harm resulting from the accident. The issue is not to compare or evaluate what *has* happened but, rather, to speculate about what *might* have happened in two alternate worlds and then to compare the outcomes.

In purely formal terms, the efficiency reformulation of the law of negligence seems to make it more precise, but the *operational* precision of this approach hinges on the ease with which the empirical counterparts to the theoretical categories can be determined. Even so committed an efficiency theorist as Harold Demsetz has recently admitted that "it is so difficult to know what the underlying efficiency considerations are . . . ."[2] If, therefore, the promise of adding greater precision to the concept of negligence is to be realized, there must be some method of *testing* the relevant hypotheses. Although the recent literature has not formulated the central question in these terms, testing is, nevertheless, crucial. Let us briefly consider three possible methods of testing hypotheses about efficient liability assignment.

[1] Richard A. Posner, Economic Analysis of Law 123-24 (2d ed. 1977).

[2] Harold Demsetz, Ethics and Efficiency in Property Rights Systems, in Time, Uncertainty, and Disequilibrium: Exploration of Austrian Themes 97, 106 (M. Rizzo ed. 1979). Demsetz apparently believes, however, that it is still possible to at least approximate efficient outcomes.

The first and second we shall examine in greater detail later in this essay, and the third has been analyzed in depth elsewhere.[3]

The most attractive method of testing claims about negligence and cheaper-cost avoidance is to let the economic agents "speak" for themselves. Suppose that A may have been negligent in not undertaking certain precautions while driving; in economic terms, the (expected) value of the costs of such precautions may fall below the (expected) social benefits. The best way to test this hypothesis is to place liability for the harm which may ensue on A. A will be forced to internalize the relevant costs and to make a cost-benefit calculation based on information that his own self-interest has led him to acquire. However, testing the defendant's negligence precludes testing the plaintiff's negligence; this method will work only when, on other grounds, the nonnegligence of one party has already been established. These are the pure adaptation problems which we shall subsequently discuss.

The second method is probably far too loose and unsystematic to deserve designation as a testing method at all. It consists simply of looking at a situation and guessing what the underlying efficiency considerations might be.[4] Strictly speaking, this is merely the first step of a test—a conjecture which is in need of corroboration or refutation. It may be argued, however, that these are not merely wild guesses, but are based on common, everyday empirical observations. This is the crux of the problem: such data are totally insufficient and misleading. The serious *conceptual* problems in identifying an efficient assignment of liability make this kind of observation without much merit. Furthermore, the whole notion of efficiency has often been used so imprecisely as to inject a large arbitrary element in the specification of an efficient outcome. Both of these important points will later be elaborated.

The final method does not guide us in choosing the efficient liability assignment, but claims that *whatever* method is initially used only the efficient rules will survive.[5] This rests on the contention that inefficient rules will be litigated and, therefore, altered because of the utility-maximizing decisions of private litigants. Once a rule becomes efficient, however, litigation will cease. The test thus consists of imposing liability in a particular way and then observing whether the rule survives. If it does, it was efficient; if it does not, it was inefficient. A number of very significant objections, however, have been raised against this view.[6] In particular, it is clear that litigation of

[3] Mario J. Rizzo & Frank S. Arnold, The Tendency toward Efficiency in the Common Law (1978) (unpublished manuscript, New York Univ.)

[4] See Posner, *supra* note 1, *passim.*

[5] George L. Priest, The Common Law Process and the Selection of Efficient Rules, 6 J. Legal Stud. 65 (1977); and Paul H. Rubin, Why Is the Common Law Efficient?, 6 J. Legal Stud. 51 (1977).

[6] William M. Landes & Richard A. Posner, Adjudication as a Private Good, 8 J. Legal Stud. 235 (1979); and Rizzo & Arnold, *supra* note 3.

a legal rule depends on whether change in the rule is expected to be toward greater or lesser efficiency, which in turn, depends on the attitudes of the judiciary. To the extent that their "bias" is toward efficiency, many efficiency-enhancing litigation opportunities will emerge.[7] Therefore, the ability of a judge to recognize an efficient rule has an impact on this process, by providing, as it were, the proper environment for efficiency-enhancing litigation to occur.[8] Even this conclusion, however, is based on several stringent assumptions, including agreement of both plaintiff and defendant on the probability of a win or a loss in the given case.[9] In any event, we shall take as our working hypothesis that the "Darwinian" mechanism cannot be solely, or even mainly, relied upon to produce efficient legal rules. Therefore, the informational problems in identifying empirically optimum liability assignments are of crucial importance.

II. Simple Negligence: Adaptation

This section will analyze some economic aspects of the simplest negligence cases: the pure adaptation problems,[10] which concern only the existence of a duty and not its location.[11] To be more precise, the only question is whether the defendant ought to have been more careful, not whether the plaintiff ought to have done anything differently. The issue is restricted in this way ultimately because of asymmetrical information. Suppose the court can more easily determine the negligence or nonnegligence of the plaintiff than of the defendant.[12] In some contexts, the costs of ascertaining whether due care had been undertaken might be lower with respect to the plaintiff's conduct.[13] When this is so and the plaintiff is considered nonnegligent, placing liability on the defendant can both yield valuable information and provide the economically proper incentives. We shall illustrate these points in four important cases.

In *Bolton v. Stone*[14], a woman was struck on the head by a cricket ball as she was walking just outside of her house. The ball had emanated from a nearby cricket field which had never before been the source of such an

---

[7] See Rizzo & Arnold, *supra* note 3, at 12-13.

[8] As Priest denies. See Priest, *supra* note 5, at 72.

[9] See Rizzo & Arnold *supra,* note 3, at 20-21.

[10] Abraham Harari, The Place of Negligence in the Law of Torts 147-67 (1962).

[11] *Id.* at 101.

[12] The assumption that the court can easily determine the economic nonnegligence of any party is one that is made provisionally and only in this section. Later our critique becomes more fundamental and this assumption is accordingly dropped.

[13] Obviously, the ascertainment costs can be lower with respect to the defendant. However, this type of case is not being considered here.

[14] [1951] A.C. 850.

LAW AMID FLUX 295

accident. Although treated by the court as an ordinary negligence question, it is more precisely an adaptation problem.[15] The woman is clearly viewed as a virtually passive bystander who could not conceivably be characterized as negligent. The only question is: should the defendant have done anything differently? Lord Reid's analysis here is particularly interesting. In determining whether the defendant had been negligent, it is proper to examine "not only how remote is the chance that a person might be struck but also how serious the consequences are likely to be if a person is struck."[16] This is merely the expected value of the harm and is perfectly consistent with one-half of the famous Hand formula.[17] However, Lord Reid continues immediately, ". . . . but I do not think that it would be right to take into account the difficulty of remedial measures. If cricket cannot be played on a ground without creating a substantial risk, then it should not be played there at all."[18] The question of whether the "remedial" or precautionary measures cost more than their expected benefits (prevention of the harm) is not one with which the court should concern itself. If there is a "substantial risk," then the owner of the cricket field ought to make the cost-benefit calculation himself. If he is held liable for the harm, he may decide to put up a higher fence or even to stop playing cricket there at all. While Reid indicates that he would have held for the plaintiff had the risk been substantial, the fact that the risk was "extremely small" means that the plaintiff is not entitled to recover. The defendant's behavior was completely nonnegligent.

There are two inconsistent lines of thought in this decision. First, within the class of substantial risks the defendant ought to be made liable regardless of the "difficulty of remedial measures." Here the onus of the cost-benefit analysis is his. The second line of thought (and the actual holding) is that within the class of small risks, the plaintiff cannot recover. From this perspective, the court determines the reasonableness of the behavior.

In pure adaptation cases like this, placing liability on the defendant (the causal agent), regardless of degree of risks, provides a means of testing the hypothesis of nonnegligence. If the defendant had been held liable and continued to behave in the same way, the court's hypothesis would have been corroborated. If, however, the defendant began to increase his level of care, the hypothesis would have been falsified. A "strict liability" approach here would have obviated the need for a judicial cost-benefit analysis and, paradoxically, would have tested the claim of nonnegligence.

---

[15] Harari considers this a coordination problem rather than one of adaptation. See Harari, *supra* note 10, at 172.

[16] Bolton v. Stone, [1951] A.C. at 867.

[17] See U.S. v. Carroll Towing Co., 159 F.2d 169 (2d Cir. 1947); Richard A. Posner, A Theory of Negligence, 1 J. Legal Stud. 29 (1972).

[18] Bolton v. Stone, [1951] A.C. at 867.

Re Polemis is another important example of the adaptation issue.[19] Longshoremen, servants of the defendants, were unloading cargo on the plaintiff's ship. One of them dropped a plank into the ship's hold which contained benzine vapor. A spark created by the plank ignited the vapor, and the ship was destroyed by flames. The court held that the handling of the plank was negligent because *some* harm to the ship was foreseeable. Although the burning of the ship itself was not foreseeable, it was nonetheless the "direct" consequence of a negligent act. Therefore, the defendants were fully liable for the destruction of the ship. From the efficiency point of view, the decision would seem incorrect. Liability would not increase the defendants' precautionary activity because unforeseeable contingencies will not motivate behavior. The defendants should have been held liable for, say, a dent in the hold because against that contingency they would have exercised due care, but nothing would be accomplished by holding them liable for the fire.

Although the court couched its decision in terms of the "directness" of the harm, this case can be viewed as an effort to test the negligence hypothesis.[20] As long as there is any indication that the defendants were negligent, because of, say, the foreseeability of a dent in the hold, liability ought to be imposed on them for the ship's destruction by fire. The assertion that the fire was unforeseeable was only an *hypothesis* and, as such, is quite possibly incorrect. Whether the fire was foreseeable is something for which a test can be provided. If the defendants must pay, then they can strike the cost-benefit balance and determine for themselves the category of foreseeable harms. What is unforeseeable to the court may possibly be foreseeable to defendants anxious to avoid liability.

Vincent v. Lake Erie Transportation Co. raises the important adaptation issues in a somewhat different context.[21] The steamship Reynolds was held fast to a dock by the defendant's servants during a violent storm. The force of the wind and the waves constantly drove the ship against the dock. This resulted in $500 worth of injury to the plaintiffs' dock. *Vincent* was not treated as a negligence case, nor as one in which the behavior of the defendant inflicted *net* social costs. Indeed, "the defendant prudently and advisedly availed itself of the plaintiffs' property for the purpose of preserving its own more valuable property."[22] The court, nevertheless, held that the defendant was liable for damages. The reasonableness of the defendant's behavior did not prevent recovery by the plaintiff.

---

[19] *In re* Polemis and Furness, Withy & Co., [1921] 3 K.B. 560.

[20] Remember that there was never any question of the plaintiff behaving differently with respect to the harm.

[21] 109 Minn. 456, 124 N.W. 221 (1910).

[22] *Id.* at 460, 124 N.W. 222.

LAW AMID FLUX 297

Although *Vincent* is generally classified as an intentional tort case, its implications go far beyond the narrow confines of that category; indeed for our purposes here, the distinction between intentional and negligent torts is largely illusory. In cases of the former variety, the harm inflicted may have a certain value of, say, $500; in the latter cases it may have an *expected* value of $500. Suppose the "offsetting" benefit of the activity is hypothesized to be worth more than $500. In the (intentional tort) characterization of *Vincent* that hypothesis is subject to a test. Let the defendant bear the costs of his activity, and he will decide whether the benefits were truly offsetting. In a negligence characterization of similar facts, however, the court's assertion of the defendant's reasonableness would remain untested.

The differential treatment of similar patterns of facts in the laws of negligence and intentional harms gives rise to an unfortunate structure of incentives which has rarely been recognized. Consider that a rational defendant would substitute an expected harm of $1,000 for a certain one of $500 when the corresponding two different kinds of activities can achieve the same result worth $5,000. This is because in the first case the defendant's behavior is nonnegligent (and therefore he is not liable) while in the second case he must pay in any event.[23]

Vincent can be seen, then, as an attempt to place the burden of the cost-benefit analysis on the defendant. As a pure adaptation problem (no one ever suggested the possibility of plaintiff negligence), liability ought to be placed on the causal agent of harm.[24]

Rylands v. Fletcher raises similar adaptation problems in the context of traditional strict liability.[25] In this case, the defendants erected a reservoir on their land, unaware that the coal under the land had been mined out. Due to this "defect," the water of the reservoir burst into the old shafts, eventually entered the plaintiff's nearby mine, and damaged it. The decision of the court was well-summarized by Lord Cranworth: "If a person brings, or accumulates, on his land anything which, if it should escape, may cause damage to his neighbour, he does so at his peril."[26] Clearly, *Rylands* is a pure adaptation case; there is no question of the plaintiff being able to avoid the accident at lesser cost.[27] Hence, the imposition of liability enables us to test either the direct negligence of the defendant or the defendant's possible negligence in choosing those who erected the reservoir. Paradoxically, a rule

---

[23] This assumes that in both the intentional and accidental cases the harm is a *byproduct* of the desired result; injury to the plaintiff is not the defendant's goal. An early recognition of the incentives problem can be found in Warren A. Seavey, Negligence—Subjective or Objective?, 41 Harv. L. Rev. 1, 8 n.7 (1927).

[24] This case will be dealt with again. See p. 316 *infra*.

[25] 3 H.L. 330 (1868).

[26] *Id.*

[27] See Harari, *supra* note 10, at 147-67.

of "strict liability" in adaptation cases can reveal the reasonableness or un-reasonableness of the defendant's behavior. A *Rylands* analysis, then, can obviate the need for a negligence analysis.

A number of important conclusions can be drawn from the foregoing discussion. First, the conventional efficiency criterion does not yield a determinate result in cases like *Bolton, Vincent,* and *Rylands* where both the defendant and plaintiff acted reasonably. Furthermore, the efficiency criterion cannot explain the result in *re Polemis.* The defendants here were not economically negligent with respect to the harm that actually came to pass and hence ought not to have been held liable. Second, the imposition of liability can test the hypothesis of (economic) nonnegligence in cases in which one need not test the nonnegligence of the plaintiff.[28]

III. Statics of Negligence

A. *Incomplete-Markets Argument*

A fundamental prerequisite for economy-wide optimality in the sense of Arrow and Debreu is the existence of a separate market for every commodity, where the commodities are defined, not only by their usual properties, but also by the time and circumstances in which they are enjoyed.[29] Unless the economy is characterized by a complete set of markets (including futures markets), Pareto efficiency cannot be assured.

Much of the efficiency-based economics of law literature sees the tort law as an attempt, however crude, to approximate the outcomes of hypothetical markets.[30] Suppose, for example, there were a perfect market in accidents between automobiles and pedestrians. Then the driver of a car who was in a great hurry to get somewhere could pay pedestrians and other drivers for permission to subject them to increased risk of injury. Absent this market, it may seem that the law of torts ought to balance the costs and benefits and decide when driving has been "negligent." Yet even if this were done, it is not sufficient to deal only with the hypothetical accident market. There are a whole array of externalities that the law of torts must, on this view, consider. Often external costs (or benefits) cannot be measured in a way "which is acceptably objective and non-arbitrary." Calabresi and Melamed have called these costs "moralisms."[31] How, for example, can we accurately mea-

---

[28] It ought to be stressed that answering the question of whether the plaintiff ought to have done things differently need not proceed on economic grounds. There may be reasons of ethics or custom for insulating the plaintiff against liability that the law may wish to enforce.

[29] See generally Kenneth J. Arrow & Frank H. Hahn, General Competitive Analysis (1971).

[30] See Posner, *supra* note 1, at 119-59.

[31] Guido Calabresi & A. Douglas Melamed, Property Rules, Liability Rules, and Inalienability: One View of the Cathedral, 85 Harv. L. Rev. 1089, 1111-12 (1972).

sure the revulsion that some people would feel if others were allowed to make voluntary "slavery" contracts? How is the distaste for allowing the purchase and sale of babies revealed? How can the envy that my neighbor feels when I prosper be measured? These externalities cannot be dismissed merely because they are hard to measure. Minimization of social costs differs from the minimization of private costs precisely because there is an absence of complete markets, and this absence is exactly what makes measurement so difficult.

In general, economists explain behavior *as if* it were the minimization of certain costs. In particular, as we have seen, some of the economics of law literature has attempted to explain common law *as if* it aimed at the minimization of social costs. In view of the many difficulties of measurement, how does the analyst decide what constitutes a "social cost"? If we are willing to *postulate* the existence of certain costs, we can "explain" anything as the minimization of those costs. We would succeed in developing a construct to "predict" successfully the same body of legal rules we set out to explain. However, new forms of costs and benefits would have to be "discovered" continually to explain rules outside of that original set. In essence, we would have only constructed an elaborate tautology. The costs that we use to explain certain legal rules must be measurable outside of the "market" that produces those rules. This is the crux of the problem: in many cases the relevant social costs are revealed with any degree of accuracy only through the legal system they are relied upon to explain.

From a normative perspective, the difficulties in determining the relevant social costs to be minimized threaten arbitrarily to override *actual* market transactions. For example, restrictions on the sale of pornography can be justified in a social cost-benefit framework by the disgust some people feel at even the thought of others reading this material. If it could be shown that the "prudes" were willing to pay more to have the "perverts" stop reading pornography than the latter would pay to read it, then the attempt to duplicate a result on a hypothetical market would override an actual one. Frequently, however, quantification of such costs is not feasible, and it is not very useful to view the whole matter in a cost-benefit framework. The normative case for deciding these matters on efficiency grounds then fails because the measurement difficulties will preclude any clear-cut solution.

B. *Time Frames*

In the previous section, we discussed the difficulties that the efficiency framework must face in deciding what will be considered a "social cost" and what will not. A related question is addressed here: if we place liability on the cheaper-cost avoider, within what time frame do we measure the relative avoidance capabilities of individuals? In this section, we will examine two examples of the tension in the law that arises out of the practical difficulties in choosing among time frames. The efficiency framework in many cases cannot yield a determinate implication as to the correct time perspective.

1. *The Last Clear Chance.* The doctrine of the last clear chance provides an exception to the classical rule that contributory negligence by the plaintiff completely bars his recovery. Consider the following simplification of the facts in *Kumkumian v. City of New York.* [32] Suppose that the defendant was negligently operating a subway train while at the same time the plaintiff was negligently wandering on the tracks. Although "the accident might [have been] prevented at low cost if the trespasser [had] simply stay[ed] off the track, *at the moment* when the train is bearing down on him it is the engineer who can avoid an accident at least cost, and this cost is substantially less than the expected accident cost."[33] The trespasser is the longer-run, lesser-cost avoider, the trainman is the immediate-run, lesser-cost avoider. In principle, the choice between the runs might be determined by the liability assignment that minimizes the sum of deaths and other costs. The choice is not obvious, however, for it depends on several very difficult-to-measure quantitative relationships. It will be necessary to know how many additional plaintiffs would walk on the subway tracks if relieved of liability, how many of them would be saved by subsequently more cautious engineers, and how many of the additional trespassers saved would have wandered onto the tracks, even if they were liable. If the sum of the latter two factors exceeds the first, then fewer lives would be lost. This cannot, however, be determined *a priori.* Furthermore, the savings in lives would have to be measured against the additional costs of the engineer acting more cautiously at the first sign that something *might* be wrong. It is hard to see how in practice such data will be available to the courts or anyone else. Thus, cost minimization is unlikely to determine the choice between time frames.[34]

2. *Negligence of Third Parties.* The second example of the time-frame

---

[32] 305 N.Y. 167, 111 N.E.2d 865 (1953).

[33] See Posner, *supra* note 1, at 129 (emphasis added).

[34] Harold Demsetz, on the other hand, apparently thinks that the last clear chance rule is clearly efficient. This is because he believes that without the rule very few (if any) additional plaintiffs would wander onto the tracks. Hence, "[r]ecognizing that not much deterrent is lost by the last clear chance rule, the law weighs the likelihood of saving a man's life, and the value of doing so, as sufficiently great to warrant holding the railroad liable if it fails to take the last clear chance at warning the trespasser." See Demsetz, *supra* note 2, at 109. His low estimate of the deterrent value of this rule rests on the imperfect ability of the legal system to make whole the victim of physical injuries. *Id.* This, of course, proves too much. In the law of torts as a whole, the recovery obtained by the plaintiff is the cost imposed on the defendant. If recoveries are imperfect and hence have low incentive value, then the costs imposed on defendants will have suboptimal deterrent value. This then amounts to a general argument against the position that tort law can encourage defendants to undertake close to the optimal level of precautionary activity.

problem gives rise to what, from an efficiency framework, appears to be exactly the same set of issues. Yet in this case the law adopts a different position. The rule we wish to discuss has been succinctly summarized by Hart and Honoré: "In general the negligent act of a third party is not held to negative causal connexion."[35] Consider, for example, a situation in which the defendant negligently permitted gasoline to pour out on the street. A bystander lit a match, threw it down, and the gasoline ignited. The resulting explosion injured the plaintiff.[36] If the act of the third party were negligent rather than intentional, then the defendant would still be liable: the causal chain remains unbroken. Here again there are different cheaper-cost avoiders depending upon the time frame chosen. At the moment of the gasoline spill, the bystander is the cheaper-cost avoider. Prior to the spill, however, the defendant assumes that role. If the logic underlying the efficiency explanation of the last clear chance rule were to apply similarly to this time-frame problem, the bystander should be liable for the plaintiff's injuries. Yet the law has switched time frames and is now concerned with the longer-run avoider. The problems of determining the cost-minimizing solution in this case are conceptually identical to the previous one. The law's confusion as to the proper time frame reflects the enormous practical difficulties of choosing among them on cost-minimization grounds.

C. *Second Best*

The general theory of second best poses, perhaps, the most profound of the static informational difficulties for those arguing that the tort law maximizes economic efficiency.[37] As should be obvious from many of the examples already discussed, most accidents occur in the course of otherwise productive activity. Suppose now that the price of output (X) from one such activity is below its true social marginal cost because the producer is not liable for these accidents. Consider, for simplicity, the case where the producer is the cheaper-cost avoider. In a world of other distortions from general equilibrium prices, a simple application of the theory of second best states that imposing liability will not necessarily be an efficiency-improvement. It could even reduce efficiency. To see this, imagine two other outputs $(Y$ and $Z)$ which are each complementary to X. Suppose that due to either monopoly or excise taxes, their prices *exceed* social marginal cost by

---

[35] H. L. A. Hart & A. M. Honoré, Causation in the Law 143 (1959).

[36] Watson v. Kentucky & Indiana Bridge & Ry. Co., 137 Ky. 619, 216 S.W. 146 (1910).

[37] See generally R. G. Lipsey & Kelvin Lancaster, The General Theory of Second Best, 24 Rev. Econ. Stud. 11 (1957).

different proportions. Now raising the price of X to marginal cost through the imposition of liability may create further distortions. The supramarginal cost price of Y and Z reduces the output of X below its optimum (due to complementarity). To restore some semblance of the optimum output of X its price should be lower than the social marginal cost.[38] This is precisely the case when liability is "imperfect."[39]

Calabresi has attempted to minimize the importance of the second-best arguments by arguing, in effect, that if we hold constant the output of X, or if there is a very good substitute, then the whole issue boils down to a simple question: shall X be produced with greater or fewer accidents?[40] We cannot *always* assume, however, that there will be good substitutes, but this is an obvious objection. Putting it aside, Calabresi's reformulation of the issue is still misleading. Second-best arguments are relevant in a different way. Without producer liability in our previous example, the price of factor (A), which if used to a greater extent could reduce the number of accidents, would be below its true social marginal product. If there are distortions in the prices of other factors $(B$ and $C)$ such that their prices will exceed the social marginal products (perhaps because of negative externalities), and if each of these factors are, on an economy-wide basis, complementary to A, then to use more of A in the production of X will not be an improvement. Too many of the other factors are being used and hence, at a price equal to its social product, too many units of A would also be used. Now, if the marginal product of A facing the producer of X is reduced (by eliminating liability) fewer units of A, and consequently B and C, will then be used. This, of course, is clearly the direction of the desired change. Thus, the absence of liability can be a second-best optimum.

The purpose of the discussion in this section has not been to demonstrate that the absence of producer liability *is* a second-best optimum. Instead, we have sought to emphasize the enormous informational requirements in even fairly simple models for ascertaining whether (in the presence of other distortions) a given change is an efficiency improvement.[41] Further, the informational problems discussed here cannot be dismissed as merely limiting the *perfect* attainment of optimality while still permitting an approximation of that state. Far from approximating the results in a world of complete markets, judicial cost-benefit tinkering may well move us farther from it.

---

[38] See generally E. J. Mishan, Cost-Benefit Analysis 102 (2d ed. 1976).

[39] The degree to which it ought to be lower will approximate the weighted average of Y and Z's excess of price over marginal cost.

[40] Guido Calabresi, The Costs of Accidents 87 (1970).

[41] The formal requirements are developed by H. A. J. Green, The Social Optimum in the Presence of Monopoly and Taxation, 29 Rev. Econ. Stud. 66 (1961).

IV. Dynamics of Negligence

A. *Foreseeability: Legal Background*

In 1961, the famous case known as *The Wagon Mound* (No. 1)[42] overruled the "directness" test of *Polemis* and replaced it with a test of foreseeability of consequences. If some consequences of a defendant's negligence are reasonably unforeseeable, he ought not to be held liable for them. This result appears broadly consistent with the efficiency rationale for tort law. However, the issue is not as clear-cut as it may at first seem; questions of foreseeability are, unfortunately, extremely complex.

In an important English decision the following year, the court limited its opinion in *Wagon Mound. Smith v. Leech Brain & Co. Ltd.*[43] attempted to reconcile the foreseeability test with the thin skull rule by distinguishing between the *type* of injury and the *extent* of injury of a given type. Individuals ought to be held liable only for foreseeable types of injury but, within a foreseeable type, they must be liable for the complete extent of harm, however unforeseeable. Consider the facts of this case. Due to the defendant-employer's negligence, the plaintiff's deceased was burned on the lip at work by molten metal which splashed beyond its confines. The deceased had a predisposition toward cancer which was aggravated by the accident. He later did get cancer and died. The court allowed full recovery, citing the foreseeability test in *Wagon Mound* and the thin skull rule. Since the type of injury—the burn—was clearly foreseeable, it did not matter that the amount of damage suffered as a result of the burn—dying of cancer—was not foreseeable. Similarly, in *Hughes v. Lord Advocate*,[44] the defendant's servants placed paraffin warning lamps around a manhole which they had been using and then left the area unguarded. The plaintiff, an eight-year old, knocked one of the lamps into the manhole while he was playing in the area. As a result of atypical circumstances, the lamp exploded and hurt the plaintiff. The court held that the injury due to the explosion was a foreseeable type of harm. Although "it is said that, while a paraffin fire . . . was a reasonably foreseeable risk so soon as the pursuer got access to the lamp, an explosion was not. To my mind the distinction drawn between burning and explosion is too fine to warrant acceptance."[45] Here exploding is viewed as a mere variant of a clearly foreseeable type of risk: burning. The plaintiff was thus allowed to recover.

---

[42] Overseas Tankship (U.K.) Ltd. v. Morts Dock & Engineering Co., Ltd., [1961] A.C. 388 (P.C. Aust.).

[43] [1962] 2 Q.B. 405.

[44] [1963] 1 All E.R. 705.

[45] *Id.* at 710.

Doughty v. Turner Manufacturing Co., Ltd.[46] will come as somewhat of a shock to those who accept the decision in *Hughes*. An object was negligently knocked into a vat of very hot solution of sodium cyanide. Although no one was hurt by the splash, the object later caused a chemical reaction that resulted in an explosion, hurling the dangerous solution at the plaintiff. The plaintiff, however, could not recover. "So it is said here that a splash causing burns was foreseeable and that this explosion was really only a magnified splash which also caused burns and that, therefore, we ought to follow *Hughes v. Lord Advocate* and hold the defendants liable. I cannot accept this. In my opinion, the damage here was of an entirely different kind from the foreseeable splash."[47] The reader has every right to be confused at this point. Consider that a burn and cancer are the same type of injury and that an explosion and burning are the same kind of risk. Yet a splash and an explosion resulting in a "splash" are "entirely different." It is doubtless an understatement to conclude that the classification of injuries and risks into different types or different extents of the same type contains a large element of arbitrariness. Merely by reclassifying a harm, the foreseeability requirement can be dispensed with or reinstated virtually at will.[48]

B. *Foreseeability: Economic Reconstruction*

An economic analysis of the important issues underlying foreseeability will clarify, not only the prerequisites for an efficient system of liability, but also the enormous obstacles to achieving such a system. As an example of the judicial attitude toward the foreseeability principle, the elusive nature of the type and extent of injury distinction discussed previously is paradigmatic.

For discrete notions of probability the distinction between the type of injury and the extent of injury is without economic significance.[49] Suppose, as in *Smith*, that the burn was foreseeable but that the extent of injury—cancer—was unforeseeable. From an efficiency perspective nothing is gained by holding the defendant liable for the unexpected cancer damages: no additional precautions will be undertaken. Efficiency demands that he be liable only for the foreseeable degree of harm.

The case law makes more economic sense when foreseeability is conceived in terms of continuous probability distributions. For each type of harm let us postulate a (continuous) probability distribution of the possible extents of

---

[46] [1964] 1 Q.B. 518.

[47] *Id.* at 529, Harman, L.J. concurring.

[48] As a consequence, judicial application of the foreseeability doctrine does not lead to predictable results.

[49] Mario J. Rizzo, Uncertainty, Subjectivity, and the Economic Analysis of Law, in Time, Uncertainty, and Disequilibrium, *supra* note 2, at 71, 76-77.

that harm. Further assume that there exists a one-to-one correspondence between these possible extents and the scenario or mechanism by which the harm occurs. Now due to the paradox of continuous distribution the probability of each scenario is zero. However, the probability of certain *intervals* of harm-extents (for example, the probability that the harm will be between $200 and $500) or of certain classes of mechanisms is obviously greater than zero.

From the economic efficiency perspective one could not refuse to hold the defendant liable because the precise scenario which actually occurred was unforeseeable. If this were done, the defendant would find himself immune to *all* liability and no precautions whatever would be taken against harmful outcomes. (Since only one event will actually occur, its probability is necessarily zero.) Thus, the defendant must be held liable even though the exact scenario will always be unforeseeable: liability must encompass unforeseeable extents of harm.

An unforeseeable type of harm, however, is one for which the individual does not "envisage" a probability distribution of extents.[50] These kinds of harm are not within the universe of perceived possibilities. To hold a defendant liable for unforeseeable kinds of damage will not encourage him to abstain from the harm-producing activity or to undertake any avoidance measures. Therefore, liability under such circumstances is genuinely without efficiency-enhancing value.

The foregoing discussion is probably the strongest argument that can be made for the efficiency rationale of the type-extent distinction, but even this is not sufficient to obviate the critical problems that distinction raises. Certain extents of a given type of harm may be unforeseeable in that a probability distribution is not defined over these quantities. Liability for these cannot be justified by the efficiency standard. Yet how can the court distinguish between truly unforeseeable events and those which have a zero or low probability because of the paradox of continuous probability distributions? It is hard to imagine a practical solution to this problem.

The difficulty of determining the degrees of harm that are foreseeable is, of course, only a subcategory of the problem of determining the reasonably foreseeable types of harm. The latter is no more tractable. Recall that the distinction between the two is largely arbitrary. By dubbing an injury a "degree" or an "extent" the law can obviate altogether the foreseeability requirement. By renaming all unforeseeable types of injury "mere extents," the courts could maintain a facade of foreseeability while having actually

---

[50] This corresponds to what Shackle and Loasby have referred to in a different context as unlistable outcomes. See generally, G. L. S. Shackle, Epistemics and Economics 365-67 (1972); and Brian J. Loasby, Choice, Complexity, and Ignorance 7-10 (1976).

abolished it. It all depends on how the harm is described, and there is no principled way to do it. Foreseeability, like its twin "cheaper-cost avoider", is not the unambiguous scientific concept many implicitly claim it is. To examine it is to watch it dissolve.

C. *Coordination Problems*

The foreseeability test would not be necessary in a stationary world, for all events would mechanically repeat themselves and there would be no uncertainty. The concept of foreseeability arises precisely because events occur under dynamic conditions. It is ironic, then, that foreseeability cannot act as a test of liability outside of stationary equilibrium. Without established patterns of behavior we cannot say that harm is foreseeable from a particular act or omission.[51] Under conditions where the behavior of more than one individual can affect the outcome in a given situation, the question of coordination assumes considerable importance. Each individual must make some assumption about the behavior of others. This is especially true when "due care" exercised by any one of several people will be sufficient to prevent an accident. Therefore, if each party assumes that the others will be nonnegligent, it will not be possible to say that a given harm was the foreseeable result of a specific party's conduct. Accordingly, no one could be held liable for failure to exercise due care. If, however, each individual assumes the negligence of the other parties too much avoidance will be undertaken.[52] An individual's assumption of negligence or nonnegligence by other parties depends on the existence of established patterns of behavior. A prior pattern of responsibility or coordination is essential to the successful use of the foreseeability test. However, the very existence of that pattern makes the test redundant.

Suppose that three cars are driving along. A, because of his carelessness, swerves in front of B. B, as a result, loses control of his car and in turn hits C. B could have avoided loss of control, and thus also avoided crashing into C, had he not also been driving carelessly. C could have avoided being hit had he engaged in a proper level of caution. The entire three-car accident could have been avoided by any *one* driver exercising adequate care. With respect to whose conduct can we say that harm was foreseeable? If A, B, and C each make the assumption that the others will be nonnegligent, then none could

---

[51] See Harari, *supra* note 10, at 108.

[52] Landes and Posner claim that the assumption of negligence by other parties does not constitute an equilibrium under joint and several-party liability for concurrent negligence. This, however, requires not only that the due care standards be efficient but also that the relevant parties *believe* (or act as if they believe) them to be efficient. See William M. Landes & Richard A. Posner, Joint and Multiple Tortfeasors: An Economic Analysis, 9 J. Legal Stud. (forthcoming).

have foreseen injury due to his own conduct. There is thus no foreseeability basis for imposing liability on anyone.

U.S. v. Carroll Towing Co. is another interesting example of a coordination problem.[53] Due to the absence of a bargee during daylight hours, a barge broke away from her moorings and damaged some other boats in the harbor. In his famous analysis, Judge Hand held that the expected cost of damage was greater than the cost of taking adequate precautions. Therefore, the bargee should have at least been on board during the day to prevent the harm. This solution, however, avoids the coordination problem. Could any individual be held negligent if proper precautions (say, a bargee) on the other boats could have avoided the accident?[54] It would seem impossible to say that harm was reasonably foreseeable (that is, the expected value of the harm was significant) to any individual apart from an assumption that none of the others would exercise due care.[55]

D. *Technology and the Cheaper-Cost Avoider*

Could courts, convinced of the merits of the efficiency argument, place liability for accidents on the cheaper-cost avoider? In an earlier section of this essay, the problems of applying the correct time dimension, even in a static framework, were discussed. In the dynamic framework now under consideration, the problem of determining the time frame in which a given party is the cheaper-cost avoider becomes even more severe. A world in which technological change is permitted involves infinitely greater informational problems.

Consider a situation in which the expected loss arising out of a certain activity is $100. A can avoid the accident at $50 and B at only $25. If courts place liability on B they will relieve A of the incentive to find cheaper avoidance methods.[56] In the longer run, A would possibly be the cheaper-cost avoider because he could reduce those costs to $10, whereas B would have only been able to reduce his to $20. Therefore, by imposing liability incorrectly the court did not minimize the total social costs of accidents. Obviously, this is not merely a question of finding the correct rate of discount to balance present and future cost savings (although that is obviously in-

---

[53] 159 F.2d 169.

[54] Richard A. Epstein, A Theory of Strict Liability, 2 J. Legal Stud. 151, 156-57 (1973) [hereinafter cited as Epstein, Strict Liability].

[55] Perhaps Learned Hand was a bit wiser than some of his disciples. He *implicitly* recognized these coordination difficulties in his reference to custom: "We need not say whether, even in such crowded waters as New York Harbor a bargee must be aboard at night at all; it may be that custom is otherwise . . . and that, if so, the situation is one where custom should control." [159 F.2d 169, 173].

[56] See Posner, *supra* note 1, at 138.

volved). It is more fundamentally a question of predicting the future course of technology under alternative incentive arrangements. Clearly, this is an impossibility because the growth of technology is essentially the growth of knowledge, and future knowledge, by definition, cannot be obtained in the present.[57]

It is perfectly possible to agree with what has been said above and yet to claim that all is not lost because we can apply probabilistic methods to the solution of the problem. In principle, it might seem reasonable to associate with each actor an *expected* value of cost savings due to technological advance under alternative incentive structures. Then, appropriately discounting future benefits, the court might place liability on the party able to avoid the accident at cheaper cost in the expected present value sense. Even if this option were feasible in view of the limited capacity of the court system, a conceptual difficulty makes the scheme implausible. The application of probabilistic methods assumes that all of the possibilities are known beforehand.[58] This may be plausible in situations like games of chance in which the rules set limits to the possible outcomes or in other more or less "static" contexts. Technological change, however, essentially involves unknown possibilities. Novel ideas or genuine surprises are not possibilities over which a probability distribution can be drawn: the sample space is incomplete and incompletable.

These informational difficulties are clearly quite severe. There is no cost-benefit formula that can solve them. Even Richard Posner has admitted that trying to determine who has the greater long-run accident-avoidance potential is "an intractable question, in most cases."[59] Consequently, the overall

---

[57] Karl R. Popper, The Poverty of Historicism vi-vii (1957); Ludwig M. Lachmann, Professor Shackle on the Economic Significance of Time, 6 Metroeconomica 64, 71 (1959).

[58] See generally G. L. S. Shackle, Decision, Order, and Time in Human Affairs 47-113 (1961).

[59] Richard A. Posner, Economic Analysis of Law 93 (1st ed. 1973). See, however, Posner, *supra* note 1, at 139, where in the second edition he omits this phrase.

There is, of course, a possible counterargument. If a system which tries to place liability on the lesser-cost avoider does not always give the proper long-run incentives neither does the unassisted market (which lets losses fall where they may). (See Posner, *supra* note 1, at 138.) The implication is clearly that an efficiency-motivated negligence—contributory negligence standard will approximate optimality more closely since it enables us to make use of the information we do have. This is a defective argument for at least two reasons. First, the assertion of the superiority (in this respect) of a system of negligence cannot be falsified. Technologies never developed because of the lack of proper incentives cannot be compared with those actually developed. Hence it is not possible to say, for example, that by placing liability on A a lower-cost method of accident avoidance was developed than *would* have been the case had liability been placed on B. Second, to the extent that there are opinions as to the likely course of technological change, the courts have no method of choosing among them. It is doubtful that a court will be able to determine the *reasonably* foreseeable course of technological development when even the experts will disagree. Knowledge about these matters will not be homogeneous so that "society's" best guess can be chosen.

efficiency rationale for placing liability on (short-run) cheaper-cost avoiders must fail as we extend the time frame of analysis.

E. *Disequilibrium Costs*[60]

Suppose that in order to avoid an accident with an expected cost of $100, A must spend $80 on resources which are disequilibrium-priced. B, on the other hand, must spend $90 on similarly priced resources if he is to avoid the accident. If the court responds only to existing market prices and seeks to place liability on the cheaper-cost avoider, A will be held liable. However, existing market prices do not reflect true social opportunity costs when they are not at their general equilibrium values. The mere clearing of markets (Marshallian partial equilibrium) is inadequate because the quantity of resources produced may be either excessive or deficient relative to a state where returns are equalized (adjusting for risk) across all industries. Consequently, the imposition of liability on A may not minimize social opportunity costs. This will be the case, for example, if the general equilibrium (GE) price of A's resources is $95 while that of B's (different) resources is $85.[61] The divergence of actual market prices from their true social opportunity costs need have nothing to do with the issue of externalities: prices can deviate from their GE values because of imperfect adjustment to changes in the underlying economic data.

Consider, now, a variation on the first illustration in this section. In order to avoid the $100 accident, either of two firms (A or B) must forgo some portion of its output. Assume further that all of the avoidance costs are in terms of output forgone evaluated at $80 and $90 respectively in current market prices. Clearly, the courts will value the outputs at these prices, which are quite likely not GE prices. If so, A will once again be liable on the cheaper-cost avoider rule. Suppose, however, A believes that the market has significantly undervalued its output so that the true GE value of its output forgone would be $95, and B thinks that the market has overvalued its output such that its forgone output is really worth only $85. For purposes

---

[60] See the previous treatment of this issue in Rizzo, *supra* note 49, at 78-82; see generally James M. Buchanan, Cost and Choice 49-50 (1969).

[61] It may be argued, nevertheless, that placing liability on A merely duplicates what would be the market outcome if transaction costs were not prohibitive. If liability were on B, he could pay A $81 to undertake the precautions and save $9 in the process. So A will do the avoiding anyway and the same resources will be utilized. This argument clearly presupposes that the courts can identify the relevant costs. If they cannot or if they are quite likely to make mistakes, then the argument must be reevaluated. (Our next example in the text will demonstrate one possibility in this regard.) However, even if the ability of the courts correctly to determine costs is conceded, the argument fails for another reason. What is the virtue of duplicating the market when it makes mistakes? Surely, the economic case for the market does not consist of elevating its mistakes but rather lies in the ability of competitive processes to *eliminate* error.

of illustration, we shall assert that both A and B are correct in their estimates. If these firms' market prices are expected to approach the GE values,
then A may well be willing to pay B to avoid the accident.

The moral of the story is that costs are not easily measured by outside
observers, especially where there is a subjective expectational component to
the evaluation of the forgone outputs. [62] This has two implications: (1) judicial cost-benefit analysis cannot duplicate what the market result would have
been merely by following objective market prices, and (2) if these market
prices are not "correct" GE prices then the courts may push us *farther away*
from optimality by imposing liability on the party which only appears to be
the cheaper-cost avoider.

It may seem possible to argue, however, that market prices are society's
best guess of general equilibrium values, and so to follow them will enable us
at least to approximate an optimal allocation of liability. This counterargument is clearly wrong. Market prices are only the *marginal* buyers and
sellers' best estimate of the worth of resources or final outputs. The market
itself consists of divergent estimates. Even if each agent rationally bases "his
anticipations on all the information at his disposal . . . this may include a
great many facts and observations not available to others."[63] Markets are
valuable precisely because the divergence of estimates gives rise to incentives
to make correct predictions. If society places divergent and inconsistent
estimates of the value of a good in the factor and in the commodity markets,
opportunities for pure profit will emerge. [64] For example, if the relevant
factors of production are underpriced and undercapitalized with respect to
the values of their outputs, there will be arbitrage returns to those who
narrow the gap. In general, economic agents will attempt to outguess market
prices rather than follow them mechanically. The ability to know the extent
to which market prices are incorrect is fundamentally an entrepreneurial
skill, and the courts are not populated by entrepreneurs.

V.   STRICT LIABILITY

The recent literature contains several notions of strict liability each of
which has different premises and different economic implications. In this
section, we shall focus on the most highly developed system of strict liability,

---

[62] The problem of the subjectivity of costs is, of course, more severe where only nonpecuniary
values are at stake as when the crops in the famous crops-sparks example have only "sentimen-
tal" value.

[63] Kenneth J. Arrow, The Future and the Present in Economic Life, 16 Econ. Inquiry 157,
164 (1978).

[64] See generally Israel M. Kirzner, Perception, Opportunity, and Profit (1979).

that analyzed and advocated by Richard A. Epstein.[65] At the outset of this discussion, it ought to be emphasized that the case for strict liability, as presented by Epstein, does *not* rest on its economic implications. The purpose of analyzing those here, however, is to show how such a system minimizes the problems encountered in our study of negligence and, despite its disdain for judicial cost-benefit calculation, may, in fact, promote efficiency by providing an institutionally more stable environment in which economic decision making can take place. In this context "efficiency" must be understood in a more general, long-run sense than in previous sections of this essay. Accordingly, use of the term "institutional efficiency" will emphasize that distinction.

A. *Causal Paradigms*

Epstein divides his discussion of causation into four paradigms of causal relations: A hit B, A frightened B, A compelled B to hit C, and A created a dangerous condition which resulted in harm to B.[66] Liability in his system is established *prima facie* simply by showing the existence of one of these relationships. We shall examine each of them separately.

1. *A hit B.* Suppose a man (B) is minding his own business reading in a library. A comes up and punches him in the face. Who is the cause of the injury? Obviously, A is: A hit B. Implicit, however, in our statement that A was the cause of the injury is a notion that B's failure to prevent the accident is, *prima facie,* irrelevant. Clearly, B's failure may be considered a condition *sine qua non* of his injury. Had B not been sitting in the library reading in the first place, he probably would not have been injured. In a causal analysis, we take certain things like B's sitting in the library as constant or fixed and then observe the "marginal product" of A's behavior. The key question, of course, is what can be taken as fixed for the purpose of analysis? Inherent in our concept of man is a notion of the physical integrity of the individual which serves to mark off where one individual begins and another individual ends. It is clear that A's pushing of physical particles toward B is a violation of B's physical integrity. It is furthermore a violation of B's rights for A to act in this way, but it is not a violation of A's rights for B to sit in the library.[67]

---

[65] See Epstein, Strict Liability, *supra* note 54; Richard A. Epstein, Defenses and Subsequent Pleas in a System of Strict Liability, 3 J. Legal Stud. 165 (1974) [hereinafter cited as Epstein, Defenses]; Richard A. Epstein, Intentional Harms, 4 J. Legal Stud. 391 (1975) [hereinafter cited as Epstein, Intentional Harms].

[66] See Epstein, Strict Liability, *supra* note 54, at 166-89; see also Mario J. Rizzo, Introduction in Richard A. Epstein, A Theory of Strict Liability: Toward a Reformulation of Tort Law (Cato Institute reprint 1980).

[67] See generally Richard A. Epstein, Nuisance Law: Corrective Justice and Its Utilitarian Constraints, 8 J. Legal Stud. 49, 50-53 (1979). But see Richard A. Posner, Epstein's Tort

Hence, B's conduct is taken as given or fixed, and A is the cause of the injury.

Consider the famous case of the railroad operating near a farmer's land. The farmer has decided to let crops grow right up to the edge of his property even though this means that the sparks emitted by the train will destroy some of the crops. Should the farmer be allowed to recover for the damage to his crops? In a system of strict liability, there is no need for a problematic cost-benefit analysis of the value of more food versus the value of faster train service. The railroad's use of its property oversteps the *physical* bounds of that property by the emission of particles in the form of sparks. The farmer's use does not similarly overstep the physical bounds of his property, and his conduct can be taken as constant.

2. *A frightened B.* To the extent that the reactions of B "are in no sense volitional"[68] this causal paradigm raises no issues of principle that are different from "A hit B." The purely mechanical nature of the reaction provides the rationale for viewing B's behavior as "fixed" and hence the "product" (fright) as attributable to A's conduct. The only question worth touching on briefly is one already mentioned by Epstein—the case of the extrasensitive plaintiff.[69] Should a plaintiff be allowed to recover if he is frightened by an act of the defendant, even though most other people would not have been so affected? The answer, consistent with the thin skull rule, must be that he can recover. The defendant takes his victim as he finds him. There may be evidentiary problems here, but they ought not to be used to legitimate a general defense of extrasensitivity. In some cases, the preexisting sensitivity of the victim may be well documented.[70]

3. *A compelled B to hit C.* In a sense, this is not an independent causal paradigm but can be derived from the first. B hit C so, on the reasoning developed above, C has a *prima facie* case against B. It is also clear that A compelled B (say, by threatening him with a gun) to incur losses by hurting C. This is as much an interference with B's individual integrity as the relationship "A hit B." Therefore, C is entitled to recover against B, B is entitled to recover against A, and, by a transitivity argument, C can recover directly against A.[71]

From the efficiency perspective, this is indeed a difficult matter. B's be-

---

Theory: A Critique, *id.* 457, 465-71. For a reply see Richard A. Epstein, Causation and Corrective Justice: A Reply to Two Critics, *id.* 477, 498-502.

[68] See Epstein, Strict Liability, *supra* note 54, at 172.

[69] *Id.* at 172-73 n.65.

[70] The fact that it might be impossible to document most of the time, if true, should not be used to deny recovery when it can be substantiated. For some additional arguments on this subject see Rizzo, *supra* note 66.

[71] See Epstein, Strict Liability, *supra* note 54, at 174-76.

havior assumes a critical importance: *given* the conduct of A in compelling B, we want B to engage in the optimal amount of resistance. B ought to weigh the costs to himself and the benefits to C of refusing fully or partially to go along with A's commands. The situation can thus be analyzed in a negligence framework. If B failed to exercise due care in resisting A, then placing liability on B for C's injuries would provide the correct economic incentives. B is left, however, without a cause of action against A; for if B could, after paying C, turn around and collect from A, the incentive to engage in optimal resistance would disappear. Then A would not be made to bear the costs of *his* activity, and there would be "too much" compulsion. In principle, the courts could impose liability so as to minimize the number and severity of injuries. The identification of this optimal solution will depend on whether many injuries could be avoided by B's resistance which, in turn, will depend on just how severe A's compulsion is. The informational requirements will no doubt be substantial, and therefore such a system will likely impose significant uncertainty costs on society.

In a system of strict liability, not only would the *prima facie* case be much more straightforward but the equities of compensation would apparently work out more satisfactorily. If C sues B and B is judgment-proof, then C can always sue A. He has a greater chance of recovering for his injury. In an efficiency framework, if B were nonnegligent and if the optimal solution were to hold A liable, a judgment-proof A would be the end of the story for C.

4. *A created a dangerous condition that resulted in harm to B.* This is the most complex of the causal paradigms. Many of the important issues, including those relating to intervening factors, have been discussed elsewhere.[72] The question which we shall address, however, is whether "a dangerous condition" can be defined in a way that does not readmit issues of negligence. Consider a typical defective products situation. Negligence in a products liability context depends in part on two probability distributions of outcomes. First, there is the probability distribution of defective products given a certain production (construction) technique. Second, given that a product is defective in some way or to some degree, there is a probability distribution of injuries. Suppose, for simplicity, that the likelihood of a defective product can be summarized by a probability "p" which may be so small that no negligence is involved in the current production methods. On the other hand, the defective product, once produced, can result in harm. Suppose that possibility could be summarized by the conditional probability

---

[72] *Id.* at 180-89; for a general theory of multiple causation and apportionment see, Mario J. Rizzo & Frank S. Arnold, Causal Apportionment in Tort Law: An Economic Theory (1980) (unpublished manuscript, New York Univ.).

"*q*." Liability, however, need not be dependent on *either p* or *q*. The producer (A) of a product could have created a dangerous condition even though he was unlikely to have done so. Furthermore, that condition—a defective product—could result in harm even if *q* were low. Low values for *p* and *q* are still consistent with a causal relationship between A's activities and B's injury.[73] The irrelevance of both low avoidance costs and high probabilities of harm mean that we have not simply retraced the negligence analysis.

B. *Defenses*

The defenses in a system of strict liability have two important characteristics: they are relatively simple and hence minimize, if not totally avoid, most of the difficulties encontered in our study of negligence, and they enter in a strict staged fashion so assertions and counterassertions are brought up only if and as they are relevant.[74]

Defenses are causal or noncausal. Causal defenses are merely adaptations of one or more of the other causal paradigms to overcome the one that constitutes the *prima facie* case.[75] These defenses have a strict order of priority as the following example will illustrate:

(1) A hit B (good *prima facie* case)
(2) B compelled A to hit B (good defense)
(3) A frightened B into compelling . . . (sufficient plea to overcome defense).

The result is clear and simple compared to the impossible task set by the efficiency criterion. There is no issue of reasonableness or of relative costs of avoidance. B can recover from A. Case closed.

The noncausal defenses are, for our purposes, more interesting and so we shall concentrate attention on them. The way in which these defenses relate to the issues brought up in the traditional negligence analyses is important and will be the focus of the following discussion.

1. *Assumption of risk.* The unilateral form of this defense rests "on the ground that the plaintiff decided he would take the risk of a known and perceived danger in order to pursue some objective of his own."[76] The individual has voluntarily given up his right to be free from certain types of invasions of his integrity. This defense and the concept of negligence both deal with the possibility of harm in an uncertain world. In view of this, to

---

[73] Probabilities have a valid role in cases of *concurrent* causation. See Rizzo & Arnold, *supra* note 72.

[74] Richard A. Epstein, Pleading and Presumptions, 40 U. Chi. L. Rev. 556 (1973); Epstein, Defenses, *supra* note 65, at 166-67.

[75] *Id*. at 174-85.

[76] *Id*. at 187.

what extent do the problems in determining what is foreseeable reoccur in determining what risks were assumed; or, is not assumption of risk merely a form of (contributory) negligence? Three considerations reveal the important differences between these two modes of analysis.

First, the reasonableness of the particular risk that an individual assumes is immaterial. Therefore, the courts will not be forced into a cost-benefit analysis with its attendant uncertainties. There is no need to wonder whether a hypothetical construct (the reasonable man) would have, in similar circumstances, assumed the risk that the plaintiff did. It is clear from an efficiency framework that people have different degrees of risk preference, and it is suboptimal to compel an individual to assume only the level of risk a standard or reasonable man would assume.

Second, in a negligence system issues of risk arise twice: once in the *prima facie* case, and again in the defense of contributory negligence. A system of strict liability, however, minimizes such discussion because it is irrelevant to the *prima facie* argument. If A hit B, whether he did so under conditions of certainty, foreseeability or unforeseeability is immaterial. The case is made on the paradigm of force. Under most circumstances the assumption-of-risk defense will not even arise.

Finally, in a system of strict liability the (unilateral) assumption of risk defense is a narrow one, to be used only where the assumption is clear and obvious.[77] If it is not, then the *prima facie* case of plaintiff against defendant should be allowed to stand.

A system of strict liability thus minimizes the number of situations in which the complex problems of risk must be faced and, when they must be addressed, it considerably simplifies the subissues involved.

2. Trespass. The final defense we shall consider is that of the plaintiff's trespass. This is not an absolute defense in the sense that, once it is shown, it is totally impossible for the plaintiff to recover. Instead, consistent with the staged pleas of a system of strict liability, it acts "as an independent ground to *shift back* to the plaintiff the risk of accidents that occurred on the defendant's land, when *prima facie* he had no business being there at all."[78] Showing that the defendant intended to harm the plaintiff, and not merely to expel him, however, would be sufficient to shift liability back to the defendant.[79]

Let us examine from the efficiency perspective two famous cases that relate to plaintiff's trespass, one which was not decided in accordance with the principles of strict liability and another which was. *Ploof v. Putnam* is

---

[77] Carr v. Pacific Telephone Co., 26 Cal. App. 3d 537, 103 Cal. Rptr. 120 (1972).

[78] Epstein, Defenses, *supra* note 65, at 202 (emphasis added).

[79] Epstein, Intentional Harms, *supra* note 65, at 403.

the classic example of the former.[80] During a violent storm, the plaintiff moored his boat, which had been at sea, to the defendant's dock to protect his life and property. The defendant, in an act of expulsion, unmoored the boat, which was later driven out to sea. The boat was destroyed and the plaintiff injured. The court held that he could recover. *Vincent v. Lake Erie Transportation Co.* did not concern trespassing in the contemporary sense of the word (there was a contract between defendant and plaintiff in this case), but did involve "unauthorized" damage or trespass to the plaintiff's dock. This case was decided in accordance with the principles of strict liability. The defendant was liable for the damages he caused, regardless of the reasonableness of his behavior.

Richard Posner has attempted to reconcile these two cases by claiming they are both necessary to promote economic efficiency.[81] In *Ploof*, the value of being able to trespass was great to the plaintiff, but the cost of that trespass was low to the defendant. Since the act of trespass was value enhancing (to "society" but obviously not to the defendant), the plaintiff should be allowed to recover his damages. This, presumably, would provide an incentive for dock owners to allow such trespass in the future. On this rationalization, it is hard to imagine what the outcome in *Vincent* could possibly add. Given *Ploof*, is liability for damages to the dock "appropriate to encourage dock owners to cooperate with boats in distress"?[82] The dock owner will cooperate to the point where his expected costs equal the expected benefits (to the boat) because he is fully liable for the harm. Similarly, under *Vincent* the dock owner will be fully compensated for any losses he might incur by the trespass of the ship in trouble so it is hard to imagine why he would undertake the effort of expulsion in the first place. On efficiency grounds it may appear there is nothing to choose between these two approaches. The rule in *Vincent*, however, is superior, even on efficiency grounds, because here there will be some incentive for the shipowner (or other kinds of trespassers) to choose the least-cost method of ensuring its safety. This *may* not have been much of a problem in *Ploof*, but the principle is important. Merely to hold the dock liable for injuries to the ship places *all* of the burden on the dock owner.

The most important difference between *Ploof* and *Vincent* is not to be found on efficiency grounds. These cases really represent two vastly divergent philosophies: the former implicitly accepts the pseudo cost-benefit analysis or judicial "fine tuning," against which we have argued, while the latter represents an application of the principles of a system of strict liability.

[80] 81 Vt. 471, 71 A. 188 (1908).

[81] See Posner, *supra* note 1, at 129.

[82] *Id.*

VI. Institutional Efficiency of Strict Liability

If we are correct in the central thesis of this paper that efficiency in the form of judicial cost-benefit analysis represents an impossible *raison d'être* for the law of torts, then it would seem that, *even on economic grounds,* a system of strict liability is to be preferred to one of negligence. In a dynamic world in which the uncertainties of technological change, the ambiguities of foreseeability, and the absence of a unique objective measure of social cost all conspire to make the efficiency paradigm a delusion, the importance of certainty in the legal order is clear. Strict liability obviates or minimizes the need for courts to grapple, if only implicitly, with such impossibly elusive problems as foreseeability, cheaper-cost avoider, social cost, and second best. It provides a series of basically simple, strict presumptions. The *prima facie* case is based on straightforward commonsense causal paradigms, whereas the defenses and later pleas minimize the number of issues which must be considered in a given case.

Having said farewell to the fleeting and sometimes superficial guesses about efficiency and having adopted the simple static framework of strict liability, we should find that there is considerably greater certainty about the locus of responsibility in accidents. This greater certainty promotes efficiency in the basic institutional sense because property rights, in effect, become more clearly or definitely defined.

It has been suggested, however, that the simplicity of strict liability may also be its undoing. While admitting that strict liability would simplify "the issues in a trial" and remove "an element of uncertainty," Richard Posner believes that it would increase "the scope of liability" and, hence, the absolute number of claims might rise.[83] It is a fundamental mistake to believe that strict liability would necessarily increase the scope of liability. The following example should make this clear. Consider:

1. A created a dangerous condition on his land that resulted in harm to B (*prima facie* case).
2. B entered on A's land (defense).

Unless B has a good reply (for example, A gave his permission or A compelled B to enter), the case is closed without any examination of the "reasonableness" of A's behavior: B cannot recover. The scope of liability is in these circumstances decreased, not increased. The primary effect of strict liability is to change both the instances and the rationale for liability. In addition, by simplifying the grounds on which cases are decided, the parties to a dispute are more likely to agree on the probabilities of the outcome. This

---

[83] Richard A. Posner, Strict Liability: A Comment, 2 J. Legal Stud. 205, 209 (1973).

will ensure less litigation and more out-of-court settlements.[84] Administrative costs will, therefore, be lower.

A more formal analysis of the certainty-enhancing aspects of strict liability would undoubtedly be worthwhile. Yet it already seems clear that since the "fine-tuning" paradigm is a mere delusion, the only basis on which the "efficiency" of systems can be compared is on a fundamental institutional level. The *central* question is then: which legal framework provides a more stable environment for individuals to pursue their own ends in harmony with each other? Ironically, it is precisely because we live in a dynamic world where the information needed by the "fine-tuners" is not available that the answer must be the antiquated and static system of strict liability.

[84] See Landes & Posner, *supra* note 6, at 272.

[2]

THE MIRAGE OF EFFICIENCY

*Mario J. Rizzo**

In recent times economists have typically attempted to make clear the distinction between normative and positive economics. Nevertheless, since economic efficiency has frequently been hailed as a normative ideal, studies that show the efficiency properties of certain activities are sometimes interpreted as endorsing those activities. This, unfortunately, has occurred in the economic analysis of common law. To demonstrate that many aspects of the law can be explained as if some simplified notion of efficiency were the goal need not amount to advocating that goal. However, because the precise mechanism by which the law might have become efficient is far from clear, some theorists have sought to demonstrate the desirability of efficiency. If this could be shown, it would then be plausible to assume that judges seek, at least implicitly, to create efficient law.

The purpose of this Article is to show that if the normative case for common law efficiency has any validity at all, it can only be for concepts of efficiency for which the information requirements are exceedingly high. This is true not only in the usually analyzed partial-equilibrium context, but even to a greater extent in a general-equilibrium framework.[1] In fact, partial efficiency is insufficient as a basis for constructing any persuasive normative argument. If, for example, a liability rule is efficient as between two potential litigant-classes, it can be inefficient once third-party or spillover effects are taken into account. Clearly, if there is to be a

* Assistant Professor of Economics, New York University. B.A., 1970, Fordham University; M.A., 1973; Ph.D., 1977, University of Chicago. I am indebted to the financial support of the Scaife Family Charitable Trusts and the New York University Challenge Fund. I have also benefited from discussions with Frank S. Arnold of Harvard University, Michael A. Becker of New York University, and A. Mitchell Polinsky of Stanford University. Responsibility for errors is mine alone.

1. By "partial equilibrium" economists mean the equalization of planned supply and demand in a single (small) market so that there are neither surpluses nor shortages. Furthermore, a state of affairs is efficient from a partial-equilibrium standpoint when there are no opportunities for improvement in the *single* market under discussion. By "general equilibrium" economists mean the simultaneous clearing of *all* markets in the entire economic system. Accordingly, efficiency in this sense means the absence of opportunities for improvements anywhere in that system.

social basis for the efficiency norm these indirect effects must be considered. Any attempt, however, to incorporate such factors into the analysis raises the information requirements of the system to such an extent as to make the whole enterprise unmanageable.

An illusion of manageability has been created by the overly simple models within which much of the economic analysis of law takes place. Even if the desirability of overall efficiency or wealth maximization were uncontroversial,[2] it would not follow that pursuit of a simplified partial-efficiency norm is also desirable. Under many circumstances such a restricted efficiency criterion is not an approximation to its general-equilibrium counterpart but, rather, may lead us farther from it. While in principle all of the spillover effects of alternative legal rules might[3] be totaled and the socially value-maximizing set of rules specified, the information requirements for such an achievement are well beyond the capacity of the courts or anyone else.[4] Therefore, if we cannot determine with any reasonable degree of accuracy when an overall efficiency improvement has occurred, the normative attractiveness of that goal must be thrown into serious doubt. Unless the empirical counterpart to a theoretical standard can be identified, advocacy of the latter cannot lead to any change in or validation of existing law.

The focus of this Article will be on elucidating the tremendous information requirements that make pursuit of the efficiency norm impractical. The first section concentrates on the dangers of tautological reasoning in the efficiency analysis of common law, and the second section demonstrates the impossibility of assigning basic rights on the basis of their ability to maximize wealth. Next the difficulties of making even marginal changes in the law in accordance with this criterion are explored. Finally, the notion of ex ante com-

---

2. Which it is not. *See, e.g.*, Dworkin, *Is Wealth A Value?*, 9 J. LEGAL STUD. 191 (1980).

3. There are, however, many situations in which the efficiency or wealth-maximization criterion will fail to give an answer, even in principle. *See* pp. 646-47 *infra*.

4. This ought not to be construed as an argument against all uses of partial-equilibrium analysis in positive economics. In such contexts the appropriateness of ignoring economy-wide interdependencies can be tested by reference to the explanatory power of the hypothesis. If a partial-equilibrium theory can explain much of a phenomenon, then perhaps the interdependencies are not quantitatively significant. In normative analysis, on the other hand, we are frequently trying to deduce, or "predict," something different from the current state of affairs. Hence we need independent evidence as to the significance of the general-equilibrium effects. For more on the difference between normative and positive analysis, see pp. 644-48 *infra*.

pensation is analyzed and shown to be an insufficient ground for inferring consent to the wealth-maximization principle.

TAUTOLOGIES AND MORALISMS

Both the normative and positive efficiency analysis of law must answer two closely related questions: (1) What ought to be included in wealth? and (2) What are the appropriate shadow prices[5] of the various components of wealth?[6] Answers to these questions are the source of falsifiable content in the efficiency hypothesis. Any instance of behavior is "explicable" in terms of a maximization process if the commodity space[7] and shadow prices are judiciously postulated. This, of course, is just an example of the purely formal character of the maximizing framework. Falsifiability, on the other hand, requires both economy in the postulation of goals[8] and measurement of the relevant costs and benefits in a way that is independent of the phenomenon under investigation.

The theoretical definition of wealth as "the value in dollars or dollar equivalents . . . of *everything* in society"[9] is unfortunately inadequate for either positive or normative empirical analysis. So broad a definition would not foreclose inventing new goals or commodities to "explain" any discrepancy with the efficiency hypothesis. Hence it is necessary to work with a more restricted notion of wealth. One possibility is to use that notion which is most successful in explaining the law.[10] Similarly, when implicit or shadow prices are difficult to measure independently, there is an understandable tendency to be satisfied as soon as they are measured sufficiently to rationalize the phenomenon in question.[11] This

---

5. In this context "shadow prices" refer to the prices society *would* assign in perfect markets to commodities for which, in reality, no market exists.

6. The first question logically collapses into the second, because "items" with a zero shadow price ought not to be included as part of wealth. For heuristic purposes, however, it is useful to separate these questions.

7. A "commodity space" is the set of all commodities deemed relevant for the purpose of analysis.

8. *See* Michelman, *Norms and Normativity in the Economic Theory of Law*, 62 MINN. L. REV. 1015, 1036-1037 (1978).

9. Posner, *Utilitarianism, Economics, and Legal Theory*, 8 J. LEGAL STUD. 103, 119 (1979) (emphasis added).

10. This bears an obvious similarity to Milton Friedman's defining the empirical counterpart to theoretical money in a way that best predicts nominal income. Friedman & Schwartz, *Money and Business Cycles*, in THE OPTIMUM QUANTITY OF MONEY 189, 208 n.16 (M. Friedman ed. 1969).

11. On strict positivist grounds the proper procedure would be to test the ade-

method of giving specific content to the wealth-maximization hypothesis will, at the very least, enable us to "predict" those common law doctrines already known. The data will reveal whether the goals or shadow prices have been postulated correctly and indicate any adjustments that need to be made in the model. Under certain conditions, the apparatus may predict some common law doctrines not yet known (either those of the future or those hidden from the analyst's sight). In any event, the wealth-maximization model would be tied to the law as it exists. It would not permit us to stand outside of it and recommend changes or make any normative judgments.

Perhaps mindful of the need to maintain falsifiability, William Landes and Richard Posner use a restricted notion of "efficient" in their positive analyses. In a recent article they define an efficient liability rule as one that induces potential injurers and victims to undertake "efficient levels of care—i.e., the levels that minimize L [the sum of expected accident and accident-avoidance costs]."[12] This definition is more interesting for what it ignores than for what it includes. First, all relational and distributional goals,[13] or what Calabresi and Melamed call "moralisms," are excluded. Moralisms refer to public goods, the costs or benefits of which "do not lend themselves to collective measurement which is acceptably objective and nonarbitrary."[14] Suppose, for example, ex post compensation

---

quacy of the measurement technique independently. This, however, is not very often done—especially in the literature here under discussion.

    12. Landes & Posner, *Joint and Multiple Tortfeasors: An Economic Analysis*, 9 J. LEGAL STUD. 517, 522 (1980). This definition implicitly assumes that the parties are risk neutral because only mathematically expected costs matter and not the dispersion or variance around the expectation. Another example of the narrow view of efficiency can be found in Shavell, *Strict Liability versus Negligence*, 9 J. LEGAL STUD. 1, 1 (1980).

    13. These terms are borrowed from Michelman, *supra* note 8, at 1036. My use of the word "distributional" here does not imply that, for example, the tort system ought to be used to effect changes in wealth distribution that are unrelated to corrective justice. If it is merely desired that the poor be provided with better housing, medical care, etc., then the tax system is a better tool to accomplish that. "Distributional" refers in this context to making plaintiff whole after, say, a tort has been committed; "relational" refers to the desirability of requiring the defendant, rather than someone else, to compensate the victim. Posner does not distinguish between these two senses of distributional goals and hence concludes that the common law is not well-equipped to serve such goals. *See* Posner, *The Ethical and Political Basis of the Efficiency Norm in Commmon Law Adjudication*, 8 HOFSTRA L. REV. 487, 504-05 (1980).

    14. Calabresi & Melamed, *Property Rules, Liability Rules, and Inalienability: One View of the Cathedral*, 85 HARV. L. REV. 1089, 1111 (1972).

of victims, regardless of whether defendant had been negligent, is a public good; then the exclusion of this consideration from decisions about the proper liability arrangement would ensure an inefficient outcome. One cannot arbitrarily limit the goods that enter into the domain of social wealth and then proclaim an outcome as efficient or inefficient. Second, Landes and Posner streamline the form of the litigants' utility function by assuming risk neutrality (because only expected costs are taken into account). This permits them to deal with the simpler notion of expected wealth rather than the more complex expected utility.[15] Third, the theory of second best[16] is completely ignored. In the presence of other economic distortions, especially those produced by legislatively enacted policy, the creation of "efficient" liability rules may well decrease overall efficiency. In other words, there can be negative spillover effects into other sectors.[17] The hypothetical markets that incorporate such effects are apparently not to be counted.

Landes and Posner justify their particular variant of the utility-maximization hypothesis by reference to its alleged explanatory or predictive power. In principle, they cannot be faulted for claiming that the omission of moralisms, risk preferences, and second-best considerations is warranted by the hypothesis' ability to explain the common law without them. This is just economy in the construction of hypotheses.[18] On the other hand, there is no justification for using whatever degree of corroboration is gained for the positive hypothesis to lend credence to a normative variant of the wealth-maximization doctrine. Moralisms and risk preferences, for example, cannot be left out of a normative analysis merely because it is possible to generate corroborated predictions about common law doctrines without them. If they are omitted for that reason, then the principle of explanation—or, better, of prediction—would

---

15. To make the concept of expected utility operational it is necessary to know the precise form of the utility function.

16. *See generally* E. MISHAN, COST-BENEFIT ANALYSIS 98-108 (2d ed. 1976); Lipsey & Lancaster, *The General Theory of Second Best*, 24 REV. ECON. STUD. 11 (1957).

17. For a more detailed discussion, see pp. 648-49 *infra*. *See also* Rizzo, *Law amid Flux: The Economics of Negligence and Strict Liability in Tort*, 9 J. LEGAL STUD. 291, 301-02 (1980).

18. Economy in the construction of hypotheses is a cardinal feature of the positivist methodology. It would be beyond the scope of this Article to enter into an evaluation of that notion here. For some of the author's doubts about unflinching positivism, see Rizzo, *Praxeology and Econometrics: A Critique of Positivist Economics*, in NEW DIRECTIONS IN AUSTRIAN ECONOMICS 40 (L. Spadaro ed. 1978).

646   *HOFSTRA LAW REVIEW*   [Vol. 8: 641

also be the standard of evaluation. Therefore, whatever *is* would also be efficient. Clearly, such a crude Panglossian fallacy could not be taken seriously.

From the normative perspective what is needed is an independent method of determining both the components of wealth and the shadow prices of these components. To the extent that, say, moralisms—by assumption or by hypothesis—reveal themselves and their prices mainly through the common law, an insoluble problem arises. There is no way, then, to stand outside of the law and see how it measures up against an external standard. Where is the price that reveals what people are willing to pay to avoid exposing children to pornography? How can the monetary value of corrective justice be measured? On what pseudo or implicit market is the societal distaste for voluntary slavery demonstrated? To my knowledge, efficiency theorists are not significantly concerned with the answers to these questions. Yet, unless we claim that whatever cannot be (easily) quantified does not exist,[19] they are indeed crucial. Typically, moralisms reveal themselves in the writings of legal scholars, philosophers, and others, as well as in the opinions of the man-on-the-street. However, none of this is even remotely capable of revealing the willingness to pay.[20] From the efficiency point of view, such expressions of preference have no weight. Our very inability to monetize the social value of moralisms serves effectively to deny their relevance. The problem is further compounded by the realization that even if we could discover a moralism's price it would have to be its general-equilibrium price. If a partial-equilibrium price is used, then the prices or weights of the various moralisms cannot be compared or added since they would be inconsistent with each other. A wealth-maximizing set of legal rules cannot be constructed on the basis of such inconsistent prices.

The difficulty in measuring what we have every reason to believe are relevant variables is not, however, an argument for disregarding them; rather, it demonstrates the essential limitations of the wealth-maximization criterion. Moralisms cannot be treated as a form of wealth without *in practice* making the hypothesized com-

---

19. This would hardly be a comfortable position for most of the efficiency-of-law analysts because their evidence of costs or benefits is rarely more than casual.

20. When we restrict attention to costs like the sum of accident and accident avoidance the task is easier. There are parallel markets (*e.g.*, in car damage, brakes, repair, etc.) through which a better estimate of the relevant costs might be obtained.

ponents of wealth nonfalsifiable. Thus to the extent that moralisms are to be considered it must be within a framework other than wealth maximization. Attempts, then, to narrow the meaning of efficiency merely to make a model more tractable must be viewed suspiciously in a normative context. What appears to be an efficient outcome in a "streamlined" model might well be inefficient in the context of a more inclusive notion of efficiency (and vice versa). The former does not include everything valued by society and for which people would be willing to pay. Hence the ethical appeal of legal rules that are efficient in a narrow sense is considerably less than the appeal of rules efficient in a broader sense.

The measurability of private or public goods' prices on hypothetical markets spans a continuum from the completely unmeasurable to perhaps the easily measurable. As such, can it not be claimed that efforts to use the wealth-maximization norm permit us to approximate more closely an efficient set of legal rules than would be the case if we used some other norm? As the analysis of subsequent sections will demonstrate the answer is no.[21] In many situations wealth maximization cannot yield a determinant implication for the assignment of rights or liabilities. In other cases the theory of second best tells us that efficiency improvements in one sector might make us worse off overall. In fact, unless we can acquire a great deal of information about interrelations between markets, we cannot know if such improvements bring us closer or farther from optimality. Furthermore, even if it could be confidently claimed that despite measurement difficulties we could still attain a crude approximation of optimality by applying the wealth-maximization standard, it would not follow that we ought to do so. If the ultimate normative basis for efficiency is the inferred consent of potential litigants,[22] this basis is seriously undercut by the inability of the courts to achieve a reasonable approximation of efficiency. It is not at all clear that individuals would give their consent to a system of liability that was efficient in a very crude or narrow sense in preference to one that embodied other important but difficult-to-measure social values.[23]

---

21. *See also* Rizzo, *Uncertainty, Subjectivity, and the Economic Analysis of Law*, in TIME, UNCERTAINTY, AND DISEQUILIBRIUM 71 (M. Rizzo ed. 1979).

22. *See* Posner, *supra* note 13, at 492-97.

23. It might be argued that as long as judges trade off one value against another there is an implicit price attached to that value. This is true. However, the issue under discussion in the text is whether we can determine the rates of trade-off of the potential litigants and not those of the judges.

In summary, an attempt to include in wealth maximization all goods for which people are willing to pay carries with it the problem of generating tautological reasoning.[24] An attempt, on the other hand, to maintain falsifiability by restricting the commodity space reveals the inherent limitations of the efficiency criterion.

THE ALLOCATION OF FUNDAMENTAL RIGHTS

This section elucidates the reasons why the wealth-maximization principle cannot be used to produce or validate a theory of fundamental rights or of nonmarginal changes in the law. None of the arguments advanced here are new in the context of welfare economics. However, their absence from discussion in the efficiency-analysis-of-law literature has led to many oversimplifications and misleading hopes. Perhaps a brief review of these issues will help remedy the problem.

Pure Wealth Effects

It has been long recognized that with respect to rights constituting a large fraction of an individual's full wealth, efficiency considerations may be unable to determine their proper allocation.[25] For example, if A is assigned the right to determine when and where he can travel, he may be willing to pay up to $50,000 to retain it. If, on the other hand, it is assigned to his master B instead, A may be willing or able to pay only $25,000 to acquire it. This is because A's wealth is substantially increased or decreased depending on whether he has this right in the first instance.[26] If we further suppose that B would be willing to pay $30,000 to acquire the right or would be willing to accept a minimum of $25,001 to part with that right, then the efficiency principle will not yield a unique allocation. When A is initially assigned the right it is wealth maximizing for him to retain it; when B is initially assigned the

---

24. *See, e.g.,* Calabresi & Melamed, *supra* note 14, at 1112 n.43.

25. *See, e.g.,* E. MISHAN, *supra* note 16, at 133-38. For a recent reemphasis, see Demsetz, *Ethics and Efficiency in Property Rights Systems,* in TIME, UNCERTAINTY, AND DISEQUILIBRIUM 97, 98-100 (M. Rizzo ed. 1979). Although Posner seems to recognize this problem, *see* Posner, *supra* note 9, at 108, he proceeds as if it did not exist. *See id.* at 125, 127, 135; Posner, *Some Uses and Abuses of Economics in Law,* 46 U. CHI. L. REV. 281, 291 (1979). However, he may have recently come to realize that the difficulties in assigning basic rights on economic grounds are indeed significant. *See* Posner, *supra* note 13, at 500-02.

26. Although we assume here that the right to travel freely is a normal good, wealth effects of the sort discussed here are possible even if the good were inferior.

right it is wealth maximizing for her to keep it. Thus whatever allocation of rights happens to exist will also be efficient.

Although most of the literature has concentrated on such wealth effects in a single hypothetical market, the impact of changes in wealth may spill over into other hypothetical rights markets. If, for example, a group of "perverts" has spent a fortune in a hypothetical market for the right to read child pornography, will it have enough wealth left over to buy the right to travel? The determination of an optimal set of rights requires that an individual's wealth constraints not be exceeded. While in principle a court could conceivably keep a running total of the wealth already "expended" on basic rights, it appears highly unlikely that such a problem would be manageable at reasonable cost.

Relative Price Effects

Variations in wealth brought about by different assignments of a single right might affect the shadow prices of other rights. If, for example, a certain class is given the right to own the labor of others, then the relative value of freedom from arbitrary search and seizure may change. In such a world it may be optimal to place fewer restrictions on the government's ability to search homes, if only to make the hiding of slaves on their way to a free zone more costly. This may have effects on still other markets which, in turn, may then reverberate in the original market. There is thus no assurance that the system will converge to a unique set of rights. Even if this convergence does occur, however, there is every possibility that it will not be independent of the precise sequence in which the rights are affirmed.[27] Suppose that first the government is prohibited from engaging in the search of homes under almost all circumstances. If the issue of slavery is decided after this assignment, then it may be optimal not to permit it. This is because the expected value of such ownership rights will be relatively lower because the freedom from search will increase the probability of successful escapes. Therefore, merely by changing the order in which issues of basic rights are decided the final outcome can be dramatically altered.

Relative prices of all sorts, not just those of other rights, may be affected by different assignments of fundamental rights. The

27. The probability of this is greater the more significant the changes in relative prices due to changes in wealth distribution.

most famous problem arising out of this phenomenon is the Scitovsky Paradox.[28] On one set of relative prices right X ought to be granted to individual A. Once this is accomplished, however, relative prices may change as a result and, on the new set, right X ought to be given to B. Hence in any conflict between two classes of individuals, A and B, it can be efficient both to reassign a right from B to A and then, after having made that move, to allocate the right back to B.[29]

Measurement

The final problem we shall discuss is the difficulty of comparing two alternative societies with different sets of rights. Even if there are no wealth effects of the type examined above, it is still not clear that one society can be viewed as unambiguously wealthier than another. Typically, wealth is computed on the basis of shadow or actual prices, which are marginal valuations. It is probably more accurate to make comparisons of large or nonmarginal differences in societies on the basis of total consumer surplus[30] instead. Valuations at the margin ignore the importance of the inframarginal units, which are relevant when making "lumpy" comparisons. The problem here is that the measurement of consumer surplus throughout many different hypothetical and actual markets is an enormously more formidable task than the computation of shadow prices. In the former case the entire area under the relevant portion of an actual or hypothetical demand curve must be estimated; in the latter, only a value on the margin must be computed.

If relative prices differ between the two societies, then the comparison of consumer surpluses is even more difficult. It is then necessary to add or subtract portions of the areas under the rights-demand curves in accordance with the relative price differences among substitute or complementary goods.[31]

---

28. *See* Scitovsky, *A Note on Welfare Propositions in Economics*, 9 REV. ECON. STUD. 77 (1941).

29. For a diagrammatic exposition of the Scitovsky Paradox, see E. MISHAN, *supra* note 16, at 395-96.

30. Consumer surplus is the difference between the maximum price people are willing to pay for a unit of a good and the actual price they must pay. Consumer surplus is zero on the last unit an individual buys (the marginal unit) but positive on all the others he or she has purchased (the nonmarginal units).

31. For more detail on how to perform calculations of this variety, see E. MISHAN, *supra* note 16, at 40-45. The measurement problem discussed in this subsection is not the same as the problem of precisely determining which of two soci-

The preceding analysis indicates that the efficiency norm is incapable of uniquely assigning fundamental rights. Pure wealth effects make it possible to find that any existing allocation of rights will be efficient. The Scitovsky Paradox, moreover, means that both a given change and, later, its opposite may prove to be wealth maximizing. Even the order in which changes in rights occur may affect the final equilibrium set (if one exists). Finally, it is far from clear that nonmarginal changes in legal rules can even be compared in terms of their wealth-generating properties.

MARGINAL CHANGES IN LEGAL RULES

Although it is impossible to assign basic rights in accordance with the efficiency norm, it can be argued that such a norm is effective in prescribing small or marginal adjustments in the law.[32] Indeed, since common law judges are constrained by precedent, all changes resulting from judicial decisionmaking will take place in small steps. Therefore, efficiency may not be a manageable goal for those concerned with major changes, such as legislatures and constitutional conventions, but it is a manageable one for the courts.

Unfortunately, it is not very clear what "marginal" means in this context. A change in the law can be marginal in the sense that it is perceived as deviating only slightly from precedent. It can also be marginal insofar as it changes the distribution of wealth, and perhaps relative prices, to a minor degree. The two senses need not coincide. Precedents from one area are sometimes applied in another with novel fact patterns through the use of analogous reasoning. Suppose this latter area is a new industry, such as atomic power, with highly undeveloped liability rules. A court decision in this context may be both marginal, because an entire body of established law is used, and nonmarginal, because it is used in an area that is unexpected. This may bring about significant wealth effects of the type discussed above.

Aside from the merely routine cases that face the lower courts on a daily basis, it is not evident which decisions ought to be considered marginal. The positive or descriptive efficiency literature has always emphasized its ability to rationalize the major or land-

---

eties is wealthier in an overall sense. Here we are concerned with determining which set of legal rules is more efficient. Therefore, we must be able to attribute the greater wealth of one society to the legal structure as opposed to physical capital, etc.

32. This is the implication in Posner's argument. See Posner, *supra* note 13, at 500-02.

mark cases in the common law. Presumably, from a normative perspective these are also the cases to which the efficiency stamp-of-approval would be given. It is not at all obvious that these decisions had only negligible wealth-altering effects. In so far as these effects were significant, the ability of the efficiency theory to explain or justify its own set of data is seriously compromised.

Second Best

Different, but no less serious, problems exist when we consider those decisions that produce insignificant wealth effects: decisions that are marginal in the economic sense. The general theory of second best[33] demonstrates that if there are distortions from competitive equilibrium throughout the economy due to taxes or monopoly, for example, a change that can be viewed as value maximizing in one small sector may actually decrease value overall. Suppose, for example, that the price of X is raised to its true social marginal cost by the imposition of liability to internalize negative external effects in its production.[34] Suppose, further, that Y and Z, each complements of X, have prices in excess of their true marginal costs because of taxes. Under these circumstances, the higher price of X may make matters worse from the general-equilibrium viewpoint. Consider that the prices of Y and Z are too high and hence their outputs too small. A lower price of X, on the other hand, would encourage (via complementarity relationships) more production of these commodities. Hence, although a price of X equal to marginal cost would maximize value in that sector, it may decrease value in other sectors by more. Therefore, the liability rule that maximizes overall value, subject to the tax constraint, may be no liability at all.

The problem of determining an efficient legal rule in a second-best context is even more difficult than the above illustration may indicate. It is necessary to know the degree of complementarity or substitution among goods, the value produced in each of the relevant sectors, the direction of the distortions elsewhere in the economy, and the sectors that ought to be viewed as constrained for the purpose of analysis. While in principle the necessary conditions for second-best optima can probably be derived (and have

---

33. *See generally* E. MISHAN, *supra* note 16, at 98-108; Lipsey & Lancaster, *supra* note 16.

34. Assume that the producer is the cheaper cost avoider of the negative externality.

been for simple models),[35] the information needed in practice to make those conditions operational is extremely unlikely to be forthcoming.[36]

If we assume, as it seems safe to do, that the courts cannot achieve wealth maximization in the general-equilibrium sense, then the normative case for common law efficiency must rest on partial-equilibrium maximization. However, the normative attractiveness of this is highly dubious. Of what value is partial efficiency when one of the major purposes of legal rules is to take account of third-party effects? If incorporating spillover effects in complementary and substitution markets decreases net value, it is small comfort indeed to know that value was maximized as between the two litigants.

Finally, it ought to be clear that failure to consider the problem of second best cannot be justified by claiming that we are only interested in "approximate efficiency" rather than mathematically precise results. Unless we have a great deal of information, the availability of which is doubtful, it is not possible to say whether pursuit of partial efficiency leads us closer to or farther from overall efficiency.[37]

Myopia

Let us assume that A and B are two systems of basic rights which, as we demonstrated previously, cannot be compared on wealth-maximization grounds. Suppose, however, that it is feasible

---

35. See, e.g., Green, The Social Optimum in the Presence of Monopoly and Taxation, 29 REV. ECON. STUD. 66 (1961).

36. The entire second-best argument decreases in importance as the sector affected by the particular common law decision becomes larger, i.e., the larger the unconstrained sector. However, if this is very large, then there are likely to be significant wealth effects, thus bringing into play the problems discussed in the section on the Allocation of Fundamental Rights, pp. 648-51 supra.

37. The second-best argument outlined in the text presupposes complementarity (or substitution) interconnections between output markets. However, even if these were zero, second-best analysis of a different sort would apply. Suppose again liability for negative externalities is placed on the producer of X. If more of A, a factor in the production of X, will be needed to produce with fewer externalities, liability will increase the utilization of A (assuming the plant does not shut down). Suppose further that B and C are complementary factors and that they are priced below their social marginal cost because of subsidies. Now increased use of A will cause still greater overutilization of B and C. Hence there will be a suboptimal mix of factors to produce X and higher marginal cost. The second-best optimum will be for the amount of A used to be less than the amount corresponding to full liability, the assumed first-best optimum.

Austrian Law and Economics II

HOFSTRA LAW REVIEW [Vol. 8: 641]

to compare small changes in the system of rights on these grounds. In this context, common law adjudication may be making marginal adjustments away from *A*, the initial point, and towards *B*. While each marginal change is comparable in wealth terms with the prior state of affairs, the sum of these changes once we reach *B* cannot be so evaluated. There is no way in this framework of comparing the starting and finishing points. This produces a troublesome result: efficiency-motivated courts will, after a period of years, bring about systems of rules that cannot be judged desirable or undesirable on efficiency grounds. To the extent that people wish to evaluate changes in rights, therefore, recourse must be made to another principle. If, initially, rights were assigned in some nonarbitrary way, then, presumably, *that* principle ought to be used in evaluating the change. In any event, insofar as nonefficiency-based ideas are introduced into the analysis of nonmarginal changes, it would seem appropriate to use those same ideas to evaluate the marginal moves.[38] The adoption of a dichotomized system of comparison must indicate the existence of some third principle by which efficiency is chosen over individual autonomy, for example, in the marginal case. Unless and until that principle is elucidated this two-stage normativity will fail to be persuasive.

EX ANTE COMPENSATION

Both Richard Posner[39] and Gordon Tullock[40] argue that while individual decisions in an efficiency-based common law will ex post make at least one party worse off, ex ante, efficient rules benefit everyone. Posner then goes on to claim that such ex ante compensation (for the ex post loss[41]) provides the ultimate basis for the

---

38. In a pure corrective justice system initial rights are assigned on the basis of some principle, and then causal analysis is used to identify the source of the rights violation. Causal analysis does not introduce an independent principle for making marginal adjustments or fine tuning the system to cope with conflicts. *See generally* Epstein, *Nuisance Law: Corrective Justice and Its Utilitarian Constraints*, 8 J. LEGAL STUD. 49, 50-65 (1979).

39. *See* Posner, *supra* note 13, at 492-97.

40. *See* Tullock, *Two Kinds of Legal Efficiency*, 8 HOFSTRA L. REV. 663 (1980).

41. If negligence is more efficient than strict liability and the negligence system is in effect, the ex post loss is the failure to compensate victims when defendants take due care. If, however, strict liability is more efficient and this is in effect, then the ex post loss falls on the defendant who must compensate plaintiff. Defendant is worse off ex post than under the alternative system. Posner discusses only the first case. *See* Posner, *supra* note 13, at 492-96.

wealth-maximization norm. If each individual had to choose between an efficient legal rule and an inefficient one he would, under
allegedly reasonable conditions, choose the former. Hence efficiency is attractive as a norm in common law adjudication because
it rests on the inferred[42] consent of the litigants.

This section will analyze the extremely rigid and arbitrary assumptions necessary to conclude that efficient rules compensate individuals ex ante. Furthermore, the previously discussed difficulties in identifying an efficient rule make it unlikely that such
compensation will occur even if the necessary assumptions are
made about potential litigants.

Pure Ex Ante Compensation

In a world in which there is neither first-party accident nor liability insurance, everyone would choose a more efficient tort-
liability rule if each person were (1) risk neutral, (2) identical to all
others, and (3) symmetrically distributed in defendant-plaintiff
roles.[43] In the more efficient system the sum of expected accident
and accident-avoidance costs will, by definition, be lower. In addition, there will be no distributional considerations because all individuals are identical and symmetrically distributed. For each person, then, the choice comes down to a rule with higher expected
costs versus one with lower expected costs. If everything worth
considering is included in these costs, and if people are risk neutral, they will unhesitatingly choose the more efficient rule.

Although a more efficient system of liability will be characterized by a lower sum of expected accident and accident-avoidance
costs, it is not necessarily true that the number of accidents will be
smaller. Expected losses through accidents could be larger as long
as there was an overcompensating fall in accident-avoidance costs.
Since accident costs are the risky component of the total and accident avoidance is the certain component, a rise in accidents
implies a trade-off between risky and certain costs.[44] If people are
risk averse they may not choose the rule with lower expected total
costs because the amount of risk they will have to bear is now

---

42. We are abstracting from the question of whether inferred consent is as good
as actual consent.

43. In this subsection we abstract from the issue of identifying the more efficient rule.

44. If the individual will face a very large number of the same kind of accidents, ex ante and in the aggregate he will be certain about his accident costs.

greater. Hence under such conditions, risk-averse potential litigants will choose the more inefficient rule.

On the other hand, if the expected number of accidents and accident costs are lower under the more efficient rule, risk-preferring individuals may actually choose the less efficient one. The trade-off for risk-preferrers favors giving up certain costs in exchange for risky costs in accordance with their degree of risk preference. Hence these individuals would rather face lower accident-avoidance costs even if it means higher expected accident costs.

Consequently, in order to determine the kind of rules to which people would give their consent ex ante it is necessary to know, among other things, the nature of people's attitude toward risk and whether a more efficient rule would result in higher or lower expected accident costs. Unless the requirement of risk neutrality is met, there is no assurance that the more efficient liability rule will be chosen.[45]

Ex Ante - Ex Post Compensation

If people are risk averse and they fully insure against both first-person accidents and liability, then there is no reason to be concerned about the interaction between risk attitudes and expected accident costs. All of the relevant risk would be eliminated by insurance.[46] Therefore, each individual chooses on the basis of accident and liability insurance premiums and avoidance costs. The sum of these three will be lower under the more efficient system. Whether an individual would therefore choose the more efficient system depends on the presence of at least two crucial assumptions.

If an individual is asymmetrically distributed between his or her future defendant-plaintiff roles, he or she may never choose

---

45. One can, of course, include in wealth "the dollar value (or cost) that people who are not risk neutral attach to uncertain outcomes." Posner, *supra* note 13, at 499 n.32. *See generally* Posner, *supra* note 9, at 105 n.11. This means that the wealth-maximizing solution will be different depending upon the degree of risk aversion or preference. Unfortunately, this is not a solution to our problem but merely a way of disguising it. To identify the efficient outcome would then require knowledge of the precise form of the utility function—merely adding to the complexity of an already difficult problem.

46. Not all risks are insurable, however, due to the problems associated with moral hazard, adverse selection, and disagreements between insurer and insuree about the relevant probabilities. For a good summary of the first two problems, see P. LAYARD & A. WALTERS, MICROECONOMIC THEORY 382-86 (1978).

the more efficient liability rule. Suppose, for example, that a negligence rule is more efficient than one of strict liability. Nevertheless, an individual who expected generally to be in the role of plaintiff might find that her costs were minimized by strict liability and hence would choose that system. The greater the asymmetry the more private and social costs will diverge.[47]

Individuals may have different accident-avoidance capabilities, just as they have different skills in ordinary market contexts. In general, there will be a different efficient solution for each level of avoidance capability. A rule that is optimal for the average individual may not be for any given person. Hence it may be perfectly rational to choose the rule that is on average less efficient because it is individually cost minimizing.

Even if these and other objections to the ex ante compensation doctrine are admitted, it may seem reasonable to assume that in the aggregate or over the long run many efficient rules will benefit everybody.[48] While some people will lose on certain rules they will no doubt gain through others. The net result, then, will be a gain for everyone.[49] Unfortunately, to the extent that the aggregation required for this result is relatively large, all of the problems discussed earlier will reappear. That analysis demonstrated that nonmarginal aggregations of legal rules cannot be unambiguously compared with one another on wealth-maximization grounds. Aside from this objection, the aggregation argument is seriously incomplete, even on its own terms. If we are going to say that the benefits of some legal rules will offset the losses arising from others, we are invoking a kind of general-equilibrium argument. In the same spirit, it would seem natural to examine the interrelation between efficient legal rules and constrained inefficient sectors. Here again the theory of second best applies. If the overall effect of an "efficient" set of common law rules is wealth reducing, then the normative case for the efficiency standard cannot rest on inferred consent. Unless potential litigants are deceived into thinking that the rules are efficient in the general-equilibrium sense, there is no reason for them to give their consent. The fact that people may

---

47. There may also be asymmetry over time. If all of the costs for particular individuals occur during the near future and the benefits during the more distant future the net present value of the rule may be negative for them.

48. *See* Tullock, *supra* note 40, at 663-64.

49. For the important assumptions necessary to achieve this result, see Polinsky, *Probabilistic Compensation Criteria*, 86 Q.J. ECON. 407 (1972).

choose to do something out of ignorance or deception ought not to be elevated to the status of an ultimate justification for crude efficiency notions.

CONCLUDING REMARKS

The purpose of this Article has been to demonstrate that the substantial information requirements that must be satisfied in order to identify efficient legal rules make efficiency impractical as a standard. Unless the efficiency theorists can show how courts can overcome the difficulties outlined here they will continue to argue for a norm that has little operational content. It is all too easy to show that efficiency leads to desirable results within simplified constructs; it is quite another thing to show what this has to do with the world in which we live.

[3]

Private and Social Cost

Equality between *marginal private cost* and *marginal social cost* is the allocative criterion of Pigovian welfare economics,[1] and the principle remains acceptable to most modern welfare economists. Corrective taxes and subsidies are deemed to be required in order to satisfy the necessary conditions for optimality when external effects are observed to be present. The subject of discussion here is limited to the cost conception that is implicit in the Pigovian policy criterion; for this reason, there is no need to review recent works in the theory of externality, as such, some of which place major qualifications on the Pigovian norms.[2] The purpose of this chapter is to demonstrate that the Pigovian principle embodies a failure to make the distinction between costs that may influence choice and costs that may be objectively measured.

---

[1] The companion criterion, equality between marginal private product and marginal social product, reduces to the cost criterion when the latter is stated in opportunity cost terms. The failure to take action that exerts external benefits can be treated as analytically equivalent to the taking of action that exerts external costs. In his own formulation, Pigou used the product terminology almost exclusively, although he referred to both types of divergence. See A. C. Pigou, *The Economics of Welfare* (4th ed.; London: Macmillan, 1932), esp. pp. 131–35.

[2] Notably, R. H. Coase, "The Problem of Social Costs," *Journal of Law and Economics*, III (October 1960), 1–44; Otto A. Davis and Andrew Whinston, "Externality, Welfare, and the Theory of Games," *Journal of Political Economy*, LXX (June 1962), 241–62.

SUMMARY ANALYSIS

Consider a standard example where the behavior of one person (or firm) exerts marginal external diseconomies on others than himself. These represent the loss of "goods" to others for which they are not compensated through ordinary market dealings. Application of the Pigovian norm suggests that the costs imposed externally on those who are not party to the decision-making should be brought within the calculus of the decision-maker. These costs should be added to the decision-maker's own internal costs, costs that he is presumed to take into account. The device often suggested is the levy of a tax on the performance of the externality-generating activity, a tax that is equated to the external costs per unit that the activity imposes. Other devices sometimes advanced are institutional arrangements designed to internalize the externality. In all cases, the purpose is to bring the costs that inform or influence the decision-maker into conformity with true "social" costs. The models remain individualistic in the sense that "social" costs are computed by a simple summation over individuals in the relevant community or group.

A CLOSER LOOK

According to the Pigovian theory, the change in "costs" which results from an explicitly recommended levy of a tax modifies the behavior of the acting person so that "efficiency" results. But what is meant by "costs" here? This Pigovian framework provides us with perhaps the best single example of confusion between classically-derived objective cost concepts and the subjective costs concepts that influence individual choice.

Consider, first, the determination of the amount of the corrective tax that is to be imposed. This amount should equal the external costs that others than the decision-maker suffer as a consequence of decision. These costs are experienced by persons who may evaluate their own resultant utility losses: they may well speculate on what "might have been" in the absence of the external diseconomy that they suffer. In order to estimate the size of the corrective tax, however, some objective measurement must be placed on these external costs. But the analyst has no benchmark from which plausible estimates can be made. Since the persons who bear these "costs"—those who are externally affected —do not participate in the choice that generates the "costs," there is simply no means of determining, even indirectly, the value that they place on the utility loss that might be avoided. In the classic example, how much would the house-wife whose laundry is fouled give to have the smoke re-moved from the air? Until and unless she is actually con-fronted with this choice, any estimate must remain almost wholly arbitrary. Smoke damage cannot be even remotely approximated by the estimated outlays that would be neces-sary to produce air "cleanliness." "Clean air" can, of course, be physically defined; the difficulty does not lie in the impos-sibility of defining units in a physically descriptive sense. Regardless of definition, however, "clean air" cannot be *exchanged* or *traded* among separate persons. Each person must simply adjust to the degree of air cleanliness that exists in his environment. There is no possibility of mar-ginal adjustments over quantities of the "good" so as to produce an equilibrium that insures against interpersonal differences in relative evaluations.

Figure 1 illustrates my argument. There is no way in which the analyst can objectively determine whether the housewife is at position A, B, or C on the diagram, yet it is clear that the utility loss, both at the margin and in total, may be significantly different in the three cases. There is no behavioral basis for observing evaluations here. Figure 1 also suggests that if individual preference functions have the standard properties, the valuations of separate persons probably vary directly with private-goods income. The affluent housewife will value clean air more highly than the poverty-stricken. The reason is obvious. The external dise-conomy, "smoke damage," cannot be "retraded" among per-sons. If it could be, the poverty-stricken housewife might be quite willing to take on an extra share of the damage in

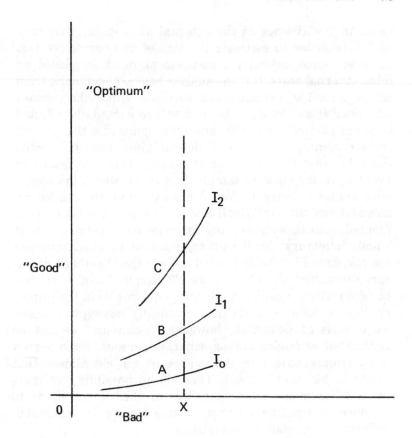

FIGURE 1

exchange for some monetary payment from her affluent neighbor. But since such a trade cannot take place, she must simply adjust to the degree of "bads" in her environment.

Objective measurement of externally-imposed costs seems more feasible in cases where the removal of the damaging agent results in changes in the production function of firms. If the damaged units should be producing firms, not individuals, there would seem to be no need to get into the complications of evaluating utility losses. A change in the rate of "pollution" can be observed to change the rate of outlay required for producing marketable goods and services. Since these goods and services command prices in markets, objective measurement of their value can be made.[3]

If a corrective tax, equal to the costs that are imposed externally upon others (which we shall now assume to be objectively measurable despite the problems noted above), is to generate the behavioral changes predicted by the Pigovian analysis, the internal costs as faced by the decision-maker must also be objectively measurable, at least indirectly. The analysis assumes implicitly that, in the absence of the corrective tax, choices are informed by money outlays made in purchasing inputs in ordinary market transactions. As an earlier discussion has shown, however, there is no logical support for this presumption in the general case. Observed money outlays need not reflect choice-influencing costs, the genuine opportunity costs that the decision-maker considers.

There is an obvious inconsistency. The Pigovian norm aims at bringing marginal private costs, *as these influence choice*, into line with social costs, *as these are objectively measured*. Only with objective measurability can the proper corrective devices be introduced. But under what conditions can objectively-measurable costs, external and internal, be taken to reflect, with even reasonable accuracy, the costs that the effective decision-maker may take into account. In conditions of ideal competitive equilibrium, the costs that can be measured by the observer provide a reasonable proxy for the subjective evaluations of decision-makers. However, almost by definition, external effects are not imposed in such a setting.

---

[3] It seems likely that this helps to explain the source of the confusion. Marshall and Pigou developed the externality notion within the context of interfirm models, implicitly assuming competitive structures. As we shall see, the relevance of objectively-measurable costs is limited even in this model, but the errors are of a different order of magnitude from those that arise when the externalities refer to an interpersonal interaction or to an interfirm interaction where utility functions are employed. The possibility of objectively measuring external costs does not, of course, ensure that the policy of levying a corrective tax is desirable. Under competition, this policy can be plausibly defended within certain limits. In noncompetitive structures, by contrast, the attempt to levy corrective taxes on an externality-generating firm may do more harm than good. On this elementary point, see my "External Diseconomies, Corrective Taxes, and Market Structure," *American Economic Review*, LIX (March 1969), 174–77.

INTERNAL COSTS, EQUILIBRIUM, AND QUASI-RENTS

The conditions under which these outlays may be taken to measure, even indirectly, the subjective barrier to choice must be carefully specified. These are as follows: (1) The individual, or firm, must be in full competitive equilibrium with respect to the activity that generates the external diseconomy; (2) at this equilibrium level of activity, and only at this level, losses are avoided and no profits are made; and (3) there are no profits in prospect of being made anywhere else in the economy. Under such conditions, the costs that may be *avoided* are simply the outlays that must be made. The individual, or firm, has available only one alternative loss-avoiding course of action which is that of not acting. In the latter, he avoids the outlay that the decision to act, considered in total or at the margin, requires. Not acting is clearly the most attractive alternative course of behavior here since all other alternatives must yield net losses.

It is important to note that quasi-rents cannot exist in the competitive equilibrium required in this model. The device of capitalizing differential resource capabilities into quasi-rents so as to equalize costs among separate firms cannot, therefore, be utilized. If it is to exist at all, the bridge between choice-influencing costs and objectively-measurable outlays depends critically on the absence of quasi-rents. If such rents exist, either with respect to the personal behavior of an individual or with respect to the productive activity of a firm, there can be no presumption that anticipated outlay measures subjective opportunity costs, those that must influence actual choice behavior. The indirect linkage between subjective-opportunity costs and objectively-measured outlays which such equilibrium establishes is shattered. The reason is that in the presence of "quasi-rents," the individual or the firm has available more than one loss-avoiding alternative course of action. "Quasi-rents" or their equivalent provide a cushion which allows subjectively-relevant elements of the decision calculus to become meaningful. As Frank Knight recognized, even if imperfectly, in his 1935 papers,[4] the allowance for any non-pecuniary aspects in the choice calculus of an individual or a firm plays havoc with the use of measurable outlays as surrogates for the opportunity costs that do, in fact, influence choice behavior. For our purposes at this point, the allowance of "quasi-rents" or their equivalent destroys the underlying logic of the Pigovian policy norms. There is simply no means to make an effective translation between the subjective-opportunity costs that influence decision and the objectively-measurable outlays that both the decision-taker and others who are externally affected undergo as a result of decision.

AN ILLUSTRATIVE EXAMPLE

Much of the critical analysis may be clarified by a simple illustrative example. Let us suppose that I enjoy foxhunting and that I maintain a kennel of hounds near my residence. I am considering adding one more hound to my already-large pack, and I know with reasonable accuracy the market price for hounds. This price is, let us say, $100.

My neighbor lives within sound range of my kennel, and he (and his family) will suffer some predictable utility loss if I decide to purchase the additional dog. For purposes of analysis here, let us say that this external damage can be reasonably evaluated at $45, presumably by an expert observer and also by both my neighbor and myself. Now let us suppose that I anticipate that the incremental benefits of the additional dog at $160. This substantially exceeds the price of $100. Let us also assume that there are no alternative spending outlets where I can secure net marginal benefits. In such circumstances, the opportunity costs arising from the enjoyments that I must avoid by the fact of making the outlay can roughly be measured at $100. However, in addition to these costs, I may well, in my calculus of decision, place some value on the enjoyments that my neigh-

---

[4] F. Knight, "Notes on Utility and Cost" (Mimeographed, University of Chicago, 1935). Published as two German articles in *Zeitschrift für Nationalökonomie* (Vienna), Band VI, Heft 1, 3 (1935).

bor must also forego as a consequence of my purchasing the dog. His anticipated suffering, as well as my own, can be an obstacle to my decision.

Suppose that I try as best I can to place a value on this expected loss in utility for my neighbor and that I arrive at a figure of $45, which, as noted above, does roughly represent the value that he himself places on the action. The obstacle to my choice, my choice-influencing cost, will embody two elements. First, there is the evaluation of the alternative uses of the anticipated $100 outlay, which, under the conditions postulated, we measure at $100. Second, there is the evaluation that I place on the anticipated enjoyments that my neighbor must forego, in this case $45. Under such circumstances, I will proceed to carry out the purchase since the anticipated marginal benefits, $160, exceed the evaluation of foregone alternatives, $145.

Note that in the behavior postulated, I am acting in accordance with the Pigovian criterion, treated here as an *ethical norm for private behavior*. Quite literally, I am treating my neighbor as myself, and my internal decision calculus accurately reflects "marginal social cost" as the obstacle to decision, despite the absence of any corrective tax. Note also, however, that for the discrete choice in question, I shall be observed to impose an external cost on my neighbor for which I do not compensate him. If a Pigovian-trained economist should be called in to advise the government, he would likely recommend that I be subjected to a corrective tax, levied in the amount of the external costs, in this example $45. It is clear that, unless the components of my subjective opportunity costs are directly modified by such a tax, the effect will be to change my decision. Costs that a positive decision embody will now be approximated at $190. Facing these, I shall refrain from purchasing the hound despite the "social" or allocative distortion that my failure to do so generates. In this example, the corrective tax tends to convert a socially desirable choice outcome into a socially undesirable one.

My internal opportunity-cost components may be modified by the imposition of the tax. If I am fully aware that I am being taxed for the express reason that my behavior

exerts the external economy, I may reduce the valuation
that I place on my neighbor's foregone enjoyment of silence.
This reaction may be especially likely if the proceeds of the
tax are earmarked for direct transfer to my neighbor. Such
a direct linkage, and more importantly such a consciousness
of the purpose of corrective taxes, has not been emphasized
in the Pigovian literature and does not seem remotely descriptive of choice behavior. At best, we may acknowledge
some substitution between the tax and the subjective valuation of the "external" component of opportunity cost;
surely there is no reason to expect anything like a full offset.

In the simplified example, it is assumed that I value the
foregone alternatives of others more or less equally with my
own. This extreme altruism need not, of course, be assumed
in order to reach the conclusion that the corrective tax
produces inefficient outcomes. In the discrete choice discussed in the example, even if I place a valuation of *only $16*
on the foregone enjoyment of my neighbor, the corrective
tax of $45 will cause me to choose the inefficient outcome
($100 + $16 + $45 = $161 > $160). This valuation figure
becomes even smaller as the personal "quasi-rent" or "marginal surplus" is reduced. Suppose, for example, that my
estimate for marginal benefits is only $146, and that I place
only a $2 valuation on the foregone enjoyment of my neigh-
bor. My choice-influencing costs after the tax are then $147
($100 + $2 + $45), which exceed my anticipated marginal
benefits. I shall be led to the inefficient social choice, although the differential inefficiency here will be lower than in
those cases where I place a somewhat higher valuation on
the prospective utility losses of others.

PIGOVIAN ECONOMICS AND
CHRISTIAN ETHICS

The example above suggests that a defense of the Pigovian
policy norm's applicability may lie in the behavioral assumption that each person acts strictly in accordance with
his own narrowly-defined, materialistic "private" interest.
His own behavior may be assumed to be wholly uninfluenced

by the effects it exerts on other persons. Under such conditions, it might be argued, the demonstrated conflict between the corrective policy and the achievement of allocative efficiency would not arise. As the following section will show, even this restrictive assumption will not rescue the Pigovian analytics. At this point, however, the legitimacy of the assumption itself must be more carefully examined.

Initially, the behavioral assumption seems nothing more than an extension of the "economic man" who roams throughout predictive economic theory. Closer examination reveals, however, that the requirement here is much more restrictive than this. In the traditional neoclassical theory of markets, the implicit behavioral assumption is that of "nontuism," first clarified by Wicksteed. This is merely the assumption that, by and large and on the average, individuals or firms engaged in market-like behavior leave out of account the direct interests of those who are on the opposing side of the trading contract. The "economic man" of Wicksteed can adhere to a Christian ethic without neurosis, since he can, if he so chooses, incorporate in his behavior pattern some recognition of the interests of all his fellows except those with whom he is directly trading. He may continue to "love his neighbor," as long as his neighbor is not trading with him. In the externality relationship, by definition, trade does not take place. It seems reasonable to think that it is precisely in this kind of relationship that genuinely benevolent behavior patterns might be witnessed. Indeed, it might plausibly be argued that in almost all of our nonmarket behavior, there is potential externality and that the ordinary functioning of civil society depends critically on a certain mutuality of respect. When property rights are not well defined and, hence, market-like arrangements are difficult to establish, the very forms of behavior seem to pay at least lip service to something other than narrowly-defined self-interest. "May I smoke?" provides a classic illustration.

The departures from behavior patterns based on narrowly materialistic utility functions seem to be almost universal only when *personal* externality relationships exist. That is to say, the argument against the narrow self-interest assumption applies fully only when the potential externality relationship is limited to a critically *small number of persons.* In large-number groups, by comparison, there may be little or no incorporation of the interests of "others" in the utility calculus of individuals. Here the individual really has no "neighbors," or may have none in any effective behavioral sense, despite the presence of "neighborhood effects." Under the latter conditions, the Pigovian logic and its policy implications are at least partially restored. The person who litters the nonresidential street in the large city probably does not worry much about the effects of his action on others. This suggests that, for such cases, the corrective devices implied by the Pigovian analysis should not generate conflicts with standard allocative norms provided, of course, that all of the other conditions required for their applicability are met.[5]

NARROW SELF-INTEREST AND ALTERNATIVE-OPPORTUNITY QUASI-RENTS

The preceding section indicated that one means of rescuing the Pigovian policy logic lies in making the explicit assump-

[5] It is perhaps worth noting here the interesting difference in emphasis between political scientists and economists, both of whom discuss essentially the same behavioral interactions. In politics, primary emphasis has traditionally been placed on political obligation, on the duty of the individual to act in the "public interest." This represents an attempt to improve results through modifying the individual's utility function in the direction of causing him to place a higher valuation on the utilities of others. Relatively little attention has been given until quite recently to the prospects of making institutional changes that will channel private choice in the direction of producing more desirable social results.

In economics, by contrast, institutional or policy changes have been the center of attention, and relatively little discussion has been devoted to norms for individual behavior. As our analysis shows, economists have implicitly assumed that individuals act in accordance with quite narrowly-defined self-interest, and they have developed policy norms which may prove inapplicable if this underlying behavioral postulate is not descriptive of reality.

For an earlier discussion of this difference between the two disciplines, see my "Marginal Notes on Reading Political Philosophy" included as Appendix I in James M. Buchanan and Gordon Tullock, *The Calculus of Consent* (Ann Arbor: University of Michigan Press, 1962; Paperback Edition, 1965).

tion that no factor involving "regard for others" influences the choices of the person who exerts external costs. Even with this constraint on individual utility functions, however, conflicts between applications of the policy norms and efficiency criteria will arise if prospective "quasi-rents" exist for alternative courses of action. This can also be shown in terms of the simple illustrative example already discussed.

In the earlier use of the example, we assumed that no "profit" prospects exist for any other spending opportunities. In this case and only in this case will the expected money outlay on resource inputs, $100, reflect at all accurately the internal component of genuine opportunity costs, and the expected marginal tax, $45, the comparable externally-imposed component. In such a model, the added assumption that the choosing-acting person places no evaluation on either the utility levels attained by others or the changes in these levels that are the results of his own behavior will restore the consistency between the Pigovian policy logic and overall efficiency norms. What we now must show is that, even if we retain the narrowly-defined self-interest assumption about individual behavior, any relaxation of the assumption about "profits" or "quasi-rents" in alternative courses of action will undermine the whole policy apparatus.

Consider the situation where there are anticipated "profit" prospects in alternative spending opportunities. Suppose that in considering the purchase of the additional foxhound, from which I estimate a marginal benefit of $160, I expect the outlay on resource inputs measured at $100, but that I also anticipate that I could invest $100 in some other line of activity yielding an expected marginal benefit which I subjectively value at $115. In this case, $115, and not $100, is the figure that best represents my choice-influencing opportunity cost, the barrier to choice, before the imposition of the tax. Suppose now that the corrective tax of $45 is levied on the marginal purchase, and, as before, let us accept that this accurately reflects my neighbor's own evaluation of the external damage that he will suffer from my action. It follows that "social costs"—those costs that must be borne by all members of the group and which are the result of the marginal choice—are best measured at $160. This figure reflects my own marginal opportunity costs, now measured at $115, plus the external costs borne by my neighbor, measured at $45. Because both the social costs and the social benefits of my acquiring another foxhound are measured at $160, the standard allocative norms suggest that I should be indifferent in the decision. Note, however, that this indifference will *not* be realized in my own choice calculus once the corrective tax is imposed on my marginal purchase. As I now confront the alternatives, my choice-influencing costs will be $166.75, not $160. Not only must I value the expected outlay on inputs in terms of the foregone alternatives, *i.e.*, $115, but also, I must value the expected marginal tax outlay in terms of foregone alternatives which payment will make impossible to achieve. If the expected "profit" on the $100 outlay in an alternative course of action is $115, we should expect the choice-influencing costs of the expected $45 tax to be roughly $51.75. The choice is no longer marginal in my own decision calculus; the corrective tax has caused choice-influencing opportunity costs—*private* costs—to exceed marginal social costs. I shall overadjust my behavior, even considering the most restrictive self-interest arguments in my utility function.

CONCLUSION

I should emphasize that this chapter is not designed as a general critical analysis of the Pigovian policy norms. Such an analysis would have required the treatment of many interesting issues that have been ignored here. My purpose has been to utilize this familiar branch of applied economic theory to demonstrate the desirability of clarifying the basic notions of opportunity costs. To those who fully accept and understand the London-Austrian contributions, the internal inconsistencies in the Pigovian logic will be apparent. To those who have been trained in the neoclassical paradigms of opportunity cost, recognition of the inconsistencies may require a working out of elementary examples. It is not easy to question long-accepted precepts, and in the several versions of this chapter, I have found it difficult to prevent the analysis from lapsing into the kind of conventional methodology that I have often used in other works. The result may give the appearance of complexity despite the elementary nature of the points being made. In effect, the incorporation of the London conception of opportunity cost amounts to transforming one of the foundation stones of economic theory. Only when this basic modification is completed can real progress toward changing the superstructure be attempted on a large scale. Meanwhile, only the most exposed aspects of this superstructure—the Pigovian welfare analytics, for example—can be related directly to the particular flaw in one of the theory's cornerstones.

[4]

POLLUTION EXTERNALITIES: SOCIAL COST AND STRICT LIABILITY

Peter Lewin

Introduction

This paper critically considers the neoclassical social-cost approach to problems of pollution. This traditional approach, when subjected to close scrutiny, is found to be seriously wanting in applicability and consistency. A less ambitious alternative based on notions of strict liability is offered.

The social-cost approach is an offshoot of the "new welfare economics" developed during the last four decades. In its modern manifestation it entails the use of notions of economic efficiency to determine basic rights, including the right to pollute. This efficiency approach is surveyed in the next section. In the final section I will offer the strict liability alternative as a preferred approach.

The methodological basis of the criticism of social cost comes from a revived and growing tradition in economics known as subjectivism. I contend that most economists would agree that the subjectivist approach is the correct one, but they are unwilling to live with its implications. For that reason the implications are seldom drawn. This inconsistent behavior may be responsible for much ill-conceived policy. It is my purpose in this paper to foster an awareness of these problems in the hope of promoting more careful policy responses.

The Efficiency Approach

Pollution as an Externality

In by far the majority of cases, modern economists writing about

Cato Journal, Vol. 2, No. 1 (Spring 1982). Copyright © Cato Institute. All rights reserved.

The author is Assistant Professor of Economics and Political Economy at The University of Texas at Dallas, Richardson, Texas 75080.

CATO JOURNAL

pollution do so within a theoretical framework that sees pollution as a result of some sort of "market failure." If property rights of ownership and exchange of resources were always well defined, and as a consequence, the exchange process did not generate any "externalities,"[1] market failure could not exist. Thus, if a factory located next to a laundry spews smoke into the air, thereby increasing the laundry's production costs, this is because the "market fails" to charge the factory for its use of the air as a dumping ground. Similarly, if two firms are located on a river, one upstream, one downstream, and the former discharges waste into the river that impacts adversely on the latter, this is only an externality problem if no one owns the river and can regulate and charge for its use.

In the absence of market failure in a fully competitive, stationary economy (one devoid of monopoly elements and distorting taxes), relative prices will reflect accurately the (private) costs as seen by the individual economic agents. Such a situation will be a Pareto optimum, that is, a situation characterized by the property that any change will make at least one agent worse off. In the presence of externalities the marginal costs as seen by the private agents — marginal private cost — may diverge from the marginal costs to "society" — marginal social cost. Thus, the polluting factory mentioned above does not reckon as part of its incremental cost of production the cost to "society" of the additional deterioration of the atmosphere that it causes. Its marginal private cost is below the marginal social cost. Such a situation will not be Pareto optimal.

Economists often suggest that a judicious combination of taxes and subsidies (ignoring administration costs) can move the society to a new situation in which both a polluting factory and society are better off; the factory, because it is paid not to pollute (or pollute less), society because it has cleaner air. If so, the new situation is Pareto superior. A potentially Pareto superior position exists if the value of cleaner air to society is greater than the value of lost production to the factory. Thus, a policy to reduce pollution may be a move to a potentially Pareto superior position (sometimes identified as a Kaldor-Hicks move) even if no compensation is actually paid to the factory. Obviously, these concepts apply not just to our factory example, but to all pollution externalities.

Naturally, the question arises: If a potential Pareto improvement exists, why do the affected parties not negotiate a mutually beneficial deal voluntarily? The amount that smoke pollution vic-

---

[1] An externality is an effect "external" to the transacting parties.

tims are willing to pay to reduce (eliminate) the pollution is, by definition, sufficient to bribe the factory to go along. The short and obvious answer (to which I will return later) is that the costs of transacting such a deal are prohibitive, particularly if there are a large number of pollution victims or if the negotiating parties engage in strategic behavior.[2] If there are a large number of pollution victims, pollution acquires the characteristics of a public good (or, more accurately, a public "bad"). Public goods are those goods like radio, television, national defense, and widespread pollution from whose benefits or harms it is difficult (impossible) to exclude additional consumers. More intuitively, pollution removal may be something which automatically (i.e., at no extra cost) benefits all the pollution victims so that the familiar "free rider" problem emerges.

From the perspective of this theoretical framework then, pollution is equivalently a problem of a divergence between private and social costs, an inability or reluctance to adequately define and enforce property rights, or a problem of the existence of (sometimes public goods-type) externalities. And the general solution is somehow to "internalize" the externality (for example, by establishing and enforcing new property rights or by tax-subsidy policies to achieve equality between private and social costs, etc.). Such policies will involve potential Pareto improvements. A move involving a potential Pareto improvement is sometimes called an "efficient" move.

Alternative Solutions

The efficiency approach to pollution outlined in the previous section seems to provide, in spite of its formidable terminology of externalities, market failure, Pareto optima, public goods, etc., a coherent and consistent framework for analyzing pollution problems. Its attractiveness lies in its apparent ability to "solve" the pollution problem by identifying the "optimal level" of pollution[3] and adopting the most attractive policy to achieve it. The economics literature, nevertheless, evidences considerable debate as to which policy would best achieve the desired result.

[2] See, for example, A. Mitchell Polinsky, "Controlling Externalities and Protecting Entitlements: Property Rights, Liability Rule, and Tax-Subsidy Approaches," *Journal of Legal Studies* 8 (January 1979): 1-48, for a rigorous treatment of the questions of strategic behavior in this context.

[3] For a prototype, see Wildred Beckerman, *Pricing for Pollution* (London: The Institute of Economic Affairs, 1975).

CATO JOURNAL

It was in his influential *The Economics of Welfare* that Arthur Pigou[4] made popular the notion of a divergence between marginal social cost (MSC) and marginal private cost (MPC). A simple solution to this divergence would appear to be to impose an excise tax on the polluter equal to the divergence MSC-MPC. This would internalize the cost to the polluter whose marginal cost including the tax would be MPC + (MSC - MPC) = MSC. An alternative would be to subsidize the polluter not to pollute. If we ignore the implications of wealth effects and entry into the polluting industry in the long term, this should produce a result identical to that obtained with the excise tax. This is because for every increase in output that the polluter produces, he forgoes a subsidy equal to the increase in the value placed on the damage to the environment that he causes. However, the tax alternative is often preferred for two reasons. First, since it is the polluter who "causes" the damage, equity considerations entail that he should pay. Second, the subsidy alternative will encourage more polluting firms in the long run.[5]

The tax on pollution of the air and water (effluent charges) is seen to have a number of advantages over more direct systems of regulation. A system of direct regulation of pollution would have to choose among controlling the output of the polluting industry, the level of pollution it causes, the pollution avoidance measures it adopts, or the pollution avoidance methods adopted by the victims. As with all systems of direct quantitative controls, the danger of bureaucratic inefficiency looms large. The strong incentive to collect and use information relating to pollution in an efficient way is lacking. By contrast, using a tax preserves many of the features of a spontaneously adjusting price system. It reduces the range of decisions to be made by a pollution administration bureaucracy to the choice of tax rates, methods of collection, disbursement, etc., and it preserves the incentive of the firm to search for innovative, less expensive methods of pollution control.[6]

> Effluent charges always possess a further major attraction; their enforcement mechanism is relatively automatic. Unlike direct controls, they do not suffer from the uncertainties of detection, of the decision to prosecute, or of the outcome of that judicial hearing including the possibility of penalties that are ludicrously lenient.[7]

---

[4] A.C. Pigou, *The Economics of Welfare*, 4th ed. (London: Macmillan and Co., 1946).
[5] For example, Beckerman, *Pricing*, pp. 38-39.
[6] See generally Beckerman, *Pricing*; Allen V. Kneese, *Economics and the Environment* (Middlesex: Penguin Books, 1977), chaps. 1 and 5; and Stephen F. Williams, *Pollution Control: Taxes Versus Regulation*, ITER original paper, August 1979.

POLLUTION EXTERNALITIES

However, introducing complications into the analysis may cause one to modify the presumption in favor of taxes somewhat. In spite of their well-known disadvantages, direct controls may be preferred on the grounds that *if they can be enforced* (at reasonable cost) "they can induce with little uncertainty, the prescribed alterations in polluting activities."[8] The facts of uncertainty may, furthermore, entail some sort of hybrid program, particularly when some threshold level of pollution damage is to be avoided at all costs.

> Where threshold problems constitute a serious environmental threat and where levels of polluting activities may require substantial alteration on short notice, which is not a rare set of circumstances, a hybrid program using both fees and controls may be preferable to a pure tax subsidy program.[9]

The reference to changing conditions in the above quotation should give us pause. The efficiency framework of analysis, which lies in the background of the discussion of the optimal regulatory policy, is at its best in an unchanging, static environment. As long as the changes we admit into the analysis are easily predictable in a relative frequency sense (like the weather as an influence on pollution effects), we may preserve some of the neat properties of the framework and proceed (as do Oates and Baumol and others) to weigh advantages and disadvantages of alternative regulatory schemes in a fairly definitive way. But when the environment is a radically dynamic one, in the sense that intrinsically unforeseeable changes occur often, we may wonder whether an alternative approach is not called for. I will return to this at some length.

A major challenge from within the efficiency approach to the use of any regulatory device as a solution is provided by the property rights approach to resource usage. It is best to consider this first before attempting a more general critique. Early contributions by Frank Knight and Jacob Viner[10] served to weaken arguments in favor of administrative intervention and to strengthen the presump-

---

[7] Wallace E. Oates and William J. Baumol, "The Instruments for Environmental Policy" in Edwin S. Mills, ed., *Economic Analysis of Environmental Problems* (New York: National Bureau of Economic Research, 1975), p. 103. See also the highly readable Edwin G. Dolan, *Tanstaafl* (New York: Holt, Rinehart and Winston, 1969), chaps. 3 and 4.

[8] Oates and Baumol, "The Instruments," p. 106.

[9] Ibid., p. 108. See also E.J. Mishan, "What is the Optimal Level of Pollution?," *Journal of Political Economy* 82 (November 1974): 1287-99.

[10] Frank H. Knight, "Some Fallacies in the Interpretation of Social Cost," *Quarterly Journal of Economics* 38 (August 1924): 582-606; Jacob Viner, "Cost Curves and Supply Curves" in *Readings in Price Theory* (American Economic Association, 1953), pp. 233-42.

tion that unaided market forces could deal effectively with environmental problems.

Too ready a recourse to excise taxes or other controls was to be avoided. The identification of the "optimal" tax was an extremely difficult task, and the presence of monopolistic and other distortions elsewhere in the economy than in the polluting industry may imply perverse general equilibrium results from an optimal policy in the partial equilibrium context (about which more below). If, however, one characterizes pollution problems in terms of inappropriately defined (or enforced) property rights, the need for regulatory policy tends to disappear. Thus, dealing with Pigou's optimal tax solution to the congested highway problem, Knight characterized the problem as one of the overuse of the scarce highway space as a result of its being treated as a common property resource. From this perspective the correct solution was to treat the highway as private property. Its use would then tend to be automatically priced to reflect the marginal cost of congestion.

This major insight was not developed much further until the seminal contribution by Ronald Coase in 1960.[11] With this contribution the property rights approach was found to contain an impressive set of important and provocative policy implications all of which may not yet have been uncovered. Coase's argument starts with a basic proposition that has become popularly known as the Coase theorem. If there are not any (or negligible) wealth effects and there are no costs associated with transacting private environmental contracts, the optimal solution to any externality problem would be independent of the assignment of liability (or property rights) and would be automatically attained in the market place. Thus, in the factory-laundry example it makes no difference (in the absence of wealth effects and transactions costs) whether the right to pollute is awarded to the factory or the right to be free of pollution is awarded to the laundry. Following E.J. Mishan[12] we may designate the former assignment of rights an L law and the latter an $\bar{L}$ law.

Generally, an L law awards the right to the party generating the negative externality and an $\bar{L}$ law awards it to the party harmed by it.[13] Under the L law the laundry will have to pay (bribe) the factory

---

[11] Ronald H. Coase, "The Problems of Social Cost," *Journal of Law and Economics* 3 (October 1960): 241-62.
[12] E.J. Mishan, *Cost-Benefit Analysis* (London: George Allen and Union, 1971), chaps. 19 and 52; "Pareto Optimality and the Law," *Oxford Economic Papers* 19 (November 1967): 255-87.

POLLUTION EXTERNALITIES

not to pollute. It will do so only as long as the incremental gains from pollution reduction outweigh the incremental cost of the bribe. And the factory will accept the incremental bribe only if it outweighs its marginal loss in incurring (the lesser of) a reduction in production or an increase in pollution removal. Obviously an equilibrium will involve equality between the marginal benefits and marginal costs of pollution reduction as valued by the parties. At this point the optimum amount of pollution will be produced. The position will be efficient in the sense that both parties will have an incentive to adopt the least-cost alternatives. In this way the externality is automatically internalized; the social costs are automatically reflected in the parties' willingness to "pay for" pollution or its absence.

Under an $\overline{L}$ law the factory would have to compensate (bribe) the laundry to accept incremental units of pollution. It would do so only so long as the value to it of increases in pollution outweighed the lesser of the costs of removing the extra pollution or bribing the laundry. The equilibrium will be identical with that under the L law, with the marginal benefit to the factory of the last pollution unit equal to the marginal cost of that unit to the laundry (for which it is justly compensated). The two cases are exactly symmetrical with the equilibrium outputs of the factory's product, the pollution and the laundry's product unaffected by the choice of law. The distribution of wealth between them, however, will be so affected as well as by the bargaining power of the parties. The uniqueness of the solution arises, as I shall have occasion to emphasize, because the exchange values, at the margin, between the outputs of the factory (its product and its pollution) and of the laundry are independent of the liability assignment.

In summary, if, for any marginal change, the cost to the laundry of the pollution damage is less than the cost to the factory of not polluting (where "cost" refers to the least-cost method), the pollution will be tolerated whatever the law. Under an L law the laundry cannot bribe the factory; under an $\overline{L}$ law the factory can bribe the laundry. Similarly, if, at the margin, the cost to the laundry exceeds the cost to the factory, the pollution will be removed; under the L

---

[13] A strict interpretation of the Coase theorem requires, as we shall see in a moment, that the notion of "cause" be abandoned once we recognize the reciprocal nature of these problems. The pollution damage may thus be seen to be "caused" by the laundry in choosing to locate next to the factory. If so, the L and $\overline{L}$ law definitions lose meaning. However, in most contexts the activity to be regarded as the "nuisance" is very clear and there will be no ambiguity. Where it is not, it simply requires that we specify the content of the L law.

law, because the factory will be bribed; under the $\overline{L}$ law because the laundry cannot be bribed. The results generalize easily to all externality situations. In the absence of wealth effects and transaction costs all changes for which the benefits to the gainers outweigh the costs imposed on the losers will be undertaken; all changes for which the benefits of the gainers fall short of the losses imposed on the losers will not. All changes are thus potential Pareto improvements; all changes are efficient.

From the perspective of the Coase theorem, since resource allocation is unaffected by the assignment of liability, the question of responsibility for the pollution is blurred. Where we observe externalities persisting uncorrected it must be because of the existence of prohibitive transactions cost. Pollution is thus no longer a phenomenon attributable to a particular economic agent. Rather it reflects an inability (or unwillingness, given the costs) of all of the affected parties to negotiate externality away.[14] To the alternatives of simply tolerating the pollution or attempting to regulate it must be added that of attempting to redefine property rights so as to reduce transaction costs. The question of "who causes the pollution?" becomes irrelevant if not meaningless, and an appropriate common law response to questions of this nature then becomes: Award the right to whichever party would have been prepared to buy it in the absence of transactions costs.

It is this implication of the Coase theorem, namely, that the courts should respond to disputes involving externalities by awarding rights to those who value them most (as in accident cases, assign liability to the least-cost avoider) that has spurred the large and growing literature on what has become known as the economic approach to the law.[15] Some of the implications arising out of recent debate over this approach will be considered in the next section.

The Coasian challenge to the established Pigouvian framework was taken up by Baumol, who sought to address the following: Coase argued that powerful market forces exist that tend to bring private and social cost into equality without the use of a tax (subsidy). But where transactions costs are high (as in the case of pollu-

---

[14]It is important to note that "[B]y extending the concept of transactions cost to encompass any inertia or lack of initiative in society, one comes uncomfortably close to the thesis that in economics, whatever is, is best." E.J. Mishan, "The Folklore of the Market," *Journal of Economic Issues* IX (December 1975): 699.

[15]See especially Richard A. Posner, *Economic Analysis of the Law,* 2d ed. (Boston: Little, Brown & Co., 1977). A particularly clear short statement is Harold Demsetz, "When Does the Rule of Liability Matter," *Journal of Legal Studies* 1 (January 1972): 13-29.

POLLUTION EXTERNALITIES

tion with many victims) some kind of interference is necessary. The Pigou solution is formally equivalent to the zero transaction-cost solution.

> Despite the various criticisms that have been raised against it in the large numbers case, which is of primary importance in reality and to which Pigou's analysis directs itself, his tax-subsidy programs are generally those required for an optimal allocation of resources. Moreover . . . where an externality is (like the usual pollution problem) of the public goods variety, neither compensation to nor taxation of those who are affected by it is compatible with optimal resource allocation. Pigouvian taxes (subsidies) upon the generator of the externality are all that is required.[16]

This proposition seems to have some degree of acceptance, even among property-rights theorists. For example, Demsetz has recently argued that

> when the gains or costs associated with particular interactions are not confined to a few parties, but instead are spread thinly over large numbers of individuals, then "high" transactions costs and "free rider" problems may be serious, even when utilizing the best of private property rights definitions, and some attenuation of private rights may be rationalized to achieve a more efficient solution to resource allocation problems. The traditional examples of providing national defense, national foreign policy, and cleaner air come to mind. . . .
>
> High transactions costs and free rider problems sometimes can be resolved by substituting private rights for communal property rights arrangements . . . But this is practical only when the cost of excluding nonpayers is not too high. When dealing with national defense and air pollution problems this does not seem to be the case, and when it is not, a rationalization for action by the state in the name of efficiency becomes available.[17]

Thus, while there may remain some disagreement among efficiency theorists about the policy (or policies) of choice in the face of externalities where small numbers of individuals are affected (although one gains the strong impression that the Coase property-rights approach has strong majority support), when it comes to public goods-type problems this disagreement disappears. The presumption in favor of a (court-encouraged) market solution

---

[16] William J. Baumol, "On Taxation and the Control of Externalities," *American Economic Review* 62 (June 1972): 307-22. But see Earl A. Thompson and Ronald Bathelder, "On Taxation and the Control of Externalities: Comment," *American Economic Review* 64 (June 1974): 467-71.

[17] Harold Demsetz, "Ethics and Efficiency in Property Rights" in Mario Rizzo, ed., *Time, Uncertainty, and Disequilibrium* (Lexington: Lexington Books, 1979), 97-116.

CATO JOURNAL

evaporates. One suspects that it is because public goods-type problems appear so difficult to deal with on a voluntary basis that we find even the most popular spokespersons for the market explicitly sanctioning a government-imposed tax system as apparently the only alternative to the much inferior regulatory agency approach.[18] The imposition of taxes (subsidies), it should be noted, is ironically advocated in the "name of efficiency"[19] and the market. And, in an ideal world, the ideal tax would strike that balance between "social" costs and benefits that yielded the "right" amount of pollution.

> The real problem is not "eliminating pollution" but trying to establish arrangements that will yield the "right" amount of pollution: an amount such that the gain from reducing pollution a bit more just balances the sacrifice of the other good things . . . that would have to be given up in order to reduce the pollution.[20]

We may call this general approach a *social-cost* approach.

Before concluding I should note that it is widely recognized that *as a practical matter* it is impossible to evaluate the optimal tax. In light of what is to follow it is worth quoting at some length from Baumol:

> . . . we do not know how to estimate the magnitudes of the social costs, the data needed to implement the Pigouvian tax-subsidy proposals. For example, a very substantial portion of the cost of pollution is psychic; and even if we knew how to evaluate the psychic cost to some one individual we seem to have little hope of dealing with effects so widely diffused through the population. . . .
>
> Unfortunately, convergence toward the desired solution by an iterative procedure of this sort requires some sort of measure of the improvement (if any) that has been achieved at each step so that the next trial step can be adjusted accordingly. But we do not know the socially optimal composition of outputs, so we simply have no way of judging whether a given change in the social tax values will even have moved matters in the right direction. . . .[21]

---

[18] Thus, Milton and Rose Friedman write: "Most economists agree that a far better way to control pollution than the present method of specific regulation and supervision is to introduce market discipline by imposing effluent charges." *Free to Choose* (New York: Harcourt Brace Jovanovich, 1979), 217-18.

[19] See Demsetz, "Ethics and Efficiency."

[20] Friedman, *Free*, p. 215. And Mishan (not particularly enamored with any aspects of the market solution) affirms, citing Baumol and Oates: "Certainly the use of taxes to enforce tolerable standards may yield significant social gains over and above the costs of enforcement." "The Folklore," p. 701.

[21] Baumol, "On Taxation," p. 316. The problem is compounded, explains Baumol, by the fact that where externalities are significant the likelihood of non-convexities and multiple optima increases, pp. 316-18.

POLLUTION EXTERNALITIES

> All in all, we are left with little reason for confidence in the ap-
> plicability of the Pigouvian approach, literally interpreted. We do
> not know how to calculate the required taxes and subsidies and
> we do not know how to approximate them by trial and error.[22]

This being the case, the argument is made in favor of a less
precise tax system designed to achieve some reasonable "set of
minimum standards of acceptability."[23] Even this may require
severe measurement problems but surely no worse than the next
best alternative of direct controls.[24] And besides, the tax alternative
alleviates the need to use the police or the courts and can be shown
"at least in principle, to achieve decreases in pollution or other
types of damage to the environment at minimum cost to society."[25]

It is important to note that if we regard the polluter as the active
agent, *the tax solution to a pollution problem implies an L law.* The
right to pollute, though attenuated by the imposition of a tax like
the many other rights, is given to the polluter. So, at least in the
public goods case, the social-cost approach implies unambiguously
the assignment of rights under an L law. I turn now to a critical
assessment of the efficiency framework and the social-cost approach it implies.

Wealth Effects and Second Best

Certain well-known problems with the efficiency framework exist, and these apply in a fairly static, unchanging world. It will be
remembered that one of the crucial assumptions necessary for the
Coase theorem was that wealth effects were absent (or, at least,
negligible). This assumption is often justified with the argument
that though the assignment of rights may affect the distribution of
wealth, as long as it does not affect the allocation of resources to
alternative uses, the distribution question should be kept separate.
(The concept of ex ante compensation, also relevant in this context,
will be examined in the next section.) But what if the assignment of
rights does affect resource allocation, as it plausibly will when
wealth effects are significant?

That it should do so is quite obvious upon reflection. The ability
to pay, by influencing relative prices, determines the allocation of
resources to their highest valued uses. Thus, unless individuals are

---

[22] Ibid., p. 318.
[23] Ibid., p. 318.
[24] Beckerman, "Pricing," p. 53.
[25] Baumol, "On Taxation," p. 319.

very similar in their expenditure patterns, any change in wealth will affect relative prices and, therefore, resource allocation. But if relative prices are not variant with respect to the distribution of wealth, they will be affected by the assignment of property rights. As shown originally by Scitovsky,[26] and reiterated many times since by writers on welfare economics, the lack of invariance of relative prices with wealth distributions implies that the Kaldor-Hicks criterion of allocative improvements may yield ambiguous (actually contradictory) results. If situation A is allocatively superior to situation B in that everyone could be made better off by a movement from B to A, a movement from A to B may yield the same result. This apparent contradiction results from the fact that the relative prices that are used to value the outputs in the two situations are different. At one set of prices the goods and services in situation A are valued higher than those in situation B, while at another set of prices the ranking is reversed.

The consequences of this are particularly noteworthy in the context of pollution. The importance of wealth effects on the outcome of any rights assignment can be assumed negligible only if the impact of the assignment on people's overall utility is small. This is often not the case for pollution externalities. As Mishan puts it, "What a person in a noisy environment is willing to pay for continuing quiet may be only a fraction of the minimum sum he is willing to accept to put up with the existing noise, or with the additional noise expected to be generated by a highway or airport to be built near his home."[27] In these cases the choice between an L or an L law will have more than a negligible effect and may indeed imply the difference between the *existence* of a pollution externality and its total absence and that *both situations are, from the property rights viewpoint, efficient.*

The other important assumption underlying the efficiency approach is the absence of significant distortions elsewhere in the economy. The calculation of social costs and benefits is profoundly affected if this assumption is violated. In a world of distortions, where prices are not general equilibrium competitive prices that reflect marginal costs, the imposition of a Pigouvian tax or a liability that would achieve efficiency if distortions were absent may *reduce* efficiency. Assume a polluting factory is producing more than the optimal amount of pollution. Assume further that there are

---

[26] Tibor Scitovsky, "A Note on Welfare Proposition in Economics," *Review of Economic Studies* 9 (November 1941): 77-88.
[27] Mishan, "The Folklore," p. 701.

POLLUTION EXTERNALITIES

two outputs in the economy complementary to our factory's output and that because of monopoly or taxes (or both) their prices *exceed* their social marginal costs by different proportions. In such circumstances the factory's output *should* be priced below its marginal social cost (to offset the high-priced complements) so that a Pigouvian tax will reduce efficiency. Distortions in the factory market may be even more intractable.[28] These problems of second-best point to the high probability that any attempt at a finely tuned solution is bound to face hopeless information problems in the real world.

It might be thought that it would nevertheless be possible to approximate the general equilibrium outcome by a series of partial adjustments. The remarks of Baumol, quoted above,[29] should dispel that hope. In more general terms, outside of equilibrium there is no way to know if any move is efficiency-enhancing or not.[30] In fact, as we shall see now, the notion of efficiency makes little sense outside of general equilibrium.

The Elusiveness of Efficiency

The concept of efficiency is an appealing one. To be efficient would seem to be a noble aim, achieving any given goal at minimum cost. And when some goals are shared by the members of society, the minimization of "social cost" commends itself. Yet when we move from the perspective of the individual, where the concepts of efficiency and cost make some sense, to that of the society, a careful examination reveals that the efficiency cost-minimizing framework is seriously misleading. This has emerged from a number of recent critical articles on the efficiency of the common law.[31] Though not all of these contributions are relevant to my topic, it is impossible to report on even all those that are. Some

---

[28] See Mario Rizzo, "Law Amid Flux: The Economics of Negligence and Strict Liability in Tort," *Journal of Legal Studies* 9 (March 1980): 301-02; and idem, "The Mirage of Efficiency," *Hofstra Law Review* 8 (Spring 1980): 652-53.

[29] At note 21.

[30] See Mario Rizzo, "Uncertainty, Subjectivity, and the Economic Analysis of Law," in Rizzo, ed., *Time*, pp. 84-85.

[31] Mario Rizzo at note 28 as well as various articles in the symposia editions of *Journal of Legal Studies* 9 (March 1980) — "Change in the Common Law: Legal and Economic Perspectives," *Hofstra Law Review* 8 (Spring 1980) — "Symposium on Efficiency as a Legal Concern," and 8 (Summer 1980) — "A Response to the Efficiency Symposium." Also, Murray Rothbard, "The Myth of Efficiency," and John B. Egger, "Comment: Efficiency Is Not a Substitute for Ethics" in Rizzo, ed., *Time*, chaps. 4 and 5, respectively.

CATO JOURNAL

brief remarks on the essential points, nevertheless, are of immediate relevance.

In my remarks so far I have been treating the efficiency approach
(to the law and to Pigouvian taxation) as a normative theory, a
theory of optimal policy. In the literature there has been a tendency
to move from normative proposition to assertions about the actual
evolution of the law in practice, claiming, with greater or lesser
confidence, that the common law tends to be efficient.[32] Any problems relating to the efficiency concept as a normative ideal will be
seen to apply with equal force to the concept of efficiency as an empirical standard.

Efficiency is understood here to mean the maximization of social
wealth as measured by ability to pay.[33] Any administrative
decision-maker, whether it be a judge imposing a liability or an
agency imposing a tax, to maximize social wealth must calculate the
social benefits and costs consequent upon its actions. If we treat
social costs as the social benefits forgone, we may talk simply of
maximizing social benefits or minimizing social costs. This
presumes that social cost is (at least in principle) an identifiable
entity. The notion of cost in general bears further examination.

Most, if not all, economists would agree that when the term
"cost" is used it should refer to what is often loosely called "opportunity cost." The implications of a rigorous opportunity-cost concept for much of modern economic theory would, however, be too
devastating to bear, so that most economists are thoroughly inconsistent when it comes to applying the concept of cost. Opportunity
cost correctly understood[34] refers to the *individual* decision-making

---

[32] See Richard Posner, "The Ethical and Political Basis of the Efficiency Norm in
Common law Adjudication," *Hofstra Law Review* 8 (Spring 1980): 487-508; Paul H.
Rubin, "Why is the Common Law Efficient?," *Journal of Legal Studies* 6 (1977);
George L. Priest, "The Common Law Progress and the Selection of Efficient Rules,"
Journal of Legal Studies 6 (1977); among others.

[33] See, for example, Ronald M. Dworkin, "Is Wealth a Value?," who writes "Wealth
maximization as defined is achieved when goods and other resources are in the
hands of those who value them most, and someone values a good more only if he is
both willing and able to pay in money (or in the equivalent of money) to have it."
Journal of Legal Studies 9 (March 1980): 191. I should add that though Dworkin is
highly critical of the efficiency approach, this definition is not contested by those he
is criticizing. This is clear from Richard Posner, "Utilitarianism, Economics, and
Legal Theory," *Journal of Legal Studies* 8 (January 1979): 119-120.

[34] For a most complete statement see James M. Buchanan, *Cost and Choice* (Chicago:
Markham, 1969). Also relevant to this reviving tradition is James M. Buchanan and
G.F. Thirldry, eds., *L.S.E. Essays on Cost* (New York: New York University Press,
1973). I have treated this in P. Lewin, "Perspectives on the Costs of Inflation,"
Southern Economic Journal 48 (January 1982).

POLLUTION EXTERNALITIES

process. In making a rational choice at a point of time, the individual must weigh the perceived alternatives. The cost of choosing any one alternative is related to the opportunities sacrificed by forgoing all the others and may be expressed as the utility forgone on the next best alternative. From this perspective three propositions about cost follow. 1) Cost is borne exclusively by the decision-maker. Obviously, one person's decision may influence the costs borne by another but, if understood correctly, any cost must attach to an individual out of choice. 2) Cost is inherently subjective. First, it is expressed in utility terms making it noncomparable across individuals if adherence to an ordinal utility concept is to be maintained. Second, cost implies subjective expectations. It refers to the *perceived* alternatives; it relates to an *imagined* future. The alternatives at any point of time exist only in the mind of the decision-maker, and although there may be some degree of consensus concerning hypothetical imagined future prospects, there almost certainly will remain a divergence of expectations. Thus, costs cannot be measured by an outside observer. 3) Cost is unrealizable. Once a choice is taken the hypothetical imagined future evolves with time into the *actual* future and the displaced alternatives cease to exist. There is no way to verify if they were really alternatives. Stated differently, the fact that the concept of costs involves counterfactual alternatives renders it unrealizable.

This insistence on a thoroughgoing, subjective opportunity-cost concept may strike the reader as excessively purist. Its importance may be sharpened, however, if we attempt to relate it to the notion of cost more common in everyday speech (and in applied economics).

Once a decision is taken, certain consequences, like money outlays, follow. These are not, strictly speaking, costs. They are choice-induced, not choice-influencing; they do not represent forgone opportunities in any direct way. In a very restricted sense and in very constrained circumstances, the money outlays and market prices that we observe can represent costs. If there are no nonpecuniary elements unique to individuals involved in the choices concerned, and if full competitive equilibrium prevails in an unchanging environment so that there is no uncertainty about future outcomes (i.e., imagined future alternatives can be taken to represent actual alternatives), then market prices will represent individuals' evaluations, at the margin, of the traded goods and services in terms of each other (and money). Of course, in terms of utility these costs are still not objectifiable, but in the postulated

CATO JOURNAL

conditions, they do represent an accurate reflection of traders' preference orderings and could be used to interpret, explain and perhaps predict hypothetical decisions. But these objective costs are the *results* of choices that occur in equilibrium (where plans and outcomes coincide). They cannot reflect perceived alternatives outside of this equilibrium. Outside of equilibrium, perceptions of alternatives differ and cost is inescapably subjective.

In any actual dynamic economic process, where the future is, in some respects at least, radically different from the past (such as is often the case with technological changes that could not have been anticipated), expectations will diverge. A strict application of the opportunity-cost concept is thus bound to lead one to the conclusions that costs are individual and private and cannot be "social." The social-cost concept requires the summation of individual costs, which is impossible if costs are seen in utility terms. The notion of social cost as reflected by market prices (or even more problematically by hypothetical prices in the absence of a market for the item) has validity only in conditions so far removed from reality as to make its use as a general tool of policy analysis highly suspect.

In externality situations where the disputing parties are small in number, the efficiency approach would favor a common law solution requiring the court to simulate a market condition by awarding the right in question to the party who would have bought it if a market devoid of transactions costs had existed. In light of the forgoing discussion on the nature of costs, one may ask not only how this is possible but, more pertinently, what notion of efficiency is being served here. In making such a determination the court would have to weigh the consequences of alternative resource allocations and somehow estimate and evaluate their effects. Among the problems that exist are the following:[35] 1) The time frame is arbitrary. Over how long a timespan are the forgone alternatives projected? As the doctrine of "the last clear chance" applied to accidents illustrates,[36] the "efficient" solution may vary with time frames. Also, the longer the horizon chosen, the more uncertain the outcomes. How is one to know which timespan "the market" would have chosen?

2) Often what is being disputed is the very nature of the external effects. Where, for example, eminent scientists may disagree about

---

[35] In addition to the articles by Rizzo, Rothbard and Egger referred to above, see Gerald P. O'Driscoll, "Justice, Efficiency, and the Economic Analysis of Law: A Comment on Fried," *Journal of Legal Studies* 9 (March 1980): 355-66.
[36] Rizzo, "Law Amid Flux," p. 300.

POLLUTION EXTERNALITIES

the effects of low-level radiation and acid rain, how are the courts to decide? Where it is possible to attach a probability to the likelihood of a harm of a specified market value occuring, such as in insurance situations where the events in question are part of a homogenous class of repeatable events, the notion of "least-cost insurer" may be meaningfully applied in pursuit of an efficiency standard.[37] But where the events in question are inherently unforeseeable in that they are in no meaningful sense part of a class of repeatable events over which a probability distribution could be defined, no efficiency criterion is possible. Whatever the court does could be construed as efficient given its own (subjective) probability assignment. In this category of events would fall all those harms (including irreversible environmental catastrophes) whose long-term effects are uncertain (sometimes because they are so new that experience is totally lacking). If one adopted the principle that no harm will be assumed unless and until relevant information is available, one applies an L law by default. Mishan has observed that "such a principle amounts to the methodological rule: When in doubt, continue to pollute."[38]

Even if the effect of the externality could be accurately identified, it would still be impossible to determine the least-cost method of pollution reduction in a dynamic setting; for what is least-cost with today's technology may be relatively expensive with tomorrow's.[39] And whose cost are we talking about? The cost of any option will vary among individuals insofar as their value scales and expectations of future technological development differ. A new pollution control device may be invented by the factory if the right to be free of the pollution is awarded to the laundry, but the incentive to do so is diminished if pollution rights are awarded to the factory. While the laundry then has the incentive to do so, it may be at a serious disadvantage being unfamiliar with the factory's production process and unable to learn about it except at considerable cost. As Rizzo has remarked, what is involved is "fundamentally a question of predicting the future course of technology under alternative incentive arrangements. Clearly this is an impossibility because the growth of technology is essentially the growth of knowledge, and future knowledge, by definition, cannot be obtained in the present."[40]

---

[37] Where events that cause harm are recurring with predictable frequency in large populations, assigning liability for harm to the least cost insurer would be efficient in the long run in that the "optimum" level of precautions would be taken.

[38] Mishan, "The Folklore," p. 701.

[39] Rizzo, "Law Amid Flux," p. 307.

CATO JOURNAL

All this applies with even greater force to the case of an externality affecting many parties. Here the notion of social cost is even more obscure. If it is an administrative agency that is charged with the responsibility of implementing the efficient policy, it will face the same problems of having to choose among time frames across disparate individual evaluations in the face of an inherently uncertain technological future. It is important to emphasize that it is precisely where administrative action is called for that it is least able to apply an efficient rule. For an efficient rule implies simulating the market, but market data on which to base a decision are absent owing to the "market failure" that motivated the administrative action in the first place.

The foregoing suggests that any perception of efficiency at the social level is illusory. And the essential thread in all the objections to the efficiency concept, be it wealth effects, distortions, or technological changes, is the refusal by economists to make interpersonal comparisons of utility. Social cost falls to the ground precisely because individual evaluations of the sacrifice involved in choosing among options cannot be compared. If we were willing by a leap of faith to compare hypothetical satisfactions (accepting at the same time the policy-maker's projections for the future), the notion of social cost might be salvaged, but only if it is understood as a metaphor for the real or hypothetical decision-maker's cost. Our reluctance to compare utilities reflects a very basic theoretical conviction that individuals should be taken to be the best judges of their own welfare. Thus, we consider market transactions as welfare-enhancing (assuming no spillovers) because they are entered into voluntarily. The principles of autonomy and consent come to mind. From this perspective it is difficult to see how any involuntary transaction (one that does not occur through the market) could be judged efficiency-enhancing.

Posner has attempted to deal with this problem by suggesting that an efficient legal system, by reducing social costs, would provide everybody with an equal chance to gain sometime, somewhere from the "better" system.[41] So an individual harmed without compensation by an externality may, nevertheless, be considered to

---

[40] Ibid., p. 308. There is a related point. If there is uncertainty as to who is the long-run, least-cost avoider of a harm, and if the court is known to be operating under an efficiency standard of liability, then there is necessarily uncertainty about who is likely to be held liable. This will inhibit the operation of the "correct" incentives in which proponents of the efficiency approach put such store.

[41] Posner, "The Ethical," pp. 491-94.

POLLUTION EXTERNALITIES

have consented to it on the grounds that the shoe might have been on the other foot and probably will in some future situation. As a result of the more efficient system, the pie is bigger and all have a chance of sharing it. In this sense compensation has been made ex ante. "If there is no reliable mechanism for eliciting express consent, it follows, not that we must abandon the principle of consent, but rather that we should look for implied consent, as by trying to answer the hypothetical question whether, if transactions costs were zero, the affected parties would have agreed to the institution. This procedure resembles a judge's imputing the intent of parties to a contract that fails to provide expressly for some contingency."[42]

Even if one is willing to forgo the objection (of which Posner is aware) that implied consent is not express consent on the grounds that it is too "costly" to obtain express consent, how is one to infer implied consent for a more efficient system when, as I hope I have shown, the very concept of efficiency as applied to society is meaningless? As Kronman pertinently asks, "[H]ow are we to distinguish those cases in which there has been ex ante compensation from those in which there has not?"[43]

One is left with the strong impression that if efficiency means anything, then *rights are logically prior to efficiency*. Efficiency is a result of maximizing social wealth, and social wealth is evaluated by individuals expressing their ability and willingness to pay. But ability and willingness to pay depend on wealth, and wealth depends on prior rights assignments. Thus, the way in which individuals would evaluate any resource depends on the prior assignment of rights. To attempt to base an entire system of law on such a flawed concept as social wealth seems to be an exercise in futile circularity. Yet, as we shall see, the utilitarian impulse is a difficult one to avoid, especially in the context of pollution externalities.

Strict Liability

If Not Efficiency, Then What?

An alternative basis on which to deal with pollution-type questions may be provided by a strict liability approach to rights.

---

[42] Ibid., p. 494.
[43] Anthony T. Kronman, "Wealth Maximization as a Normative Principle," *Journal of Legal Studies* 9 (March 1980): 227-42. See also the penetrating critique of Posner's "ex ante compensation" concept by Ronald Dworkin "Why Efficiency," *Hofstra Law Review* 8 (Spring 1980): 573-90. Also see Rizzo, "The Mirage," pp. 654-58.

CATO JOURNAL

Recently Richard Epstein in a series of articles has attempted to provide a systematic account of how the principles of strict liability could be applied to various circumstances.[44] Such a system is designed not to assign but to discover rights (on the basis of certain, sometimes unstated, ethical presumptions) or to discover when rights have been invaded in order to apply "corrective justice."

Epstein suggests basic common sense be used as an aid to determining the correct nature of causes and responsibilities. Causal principles are needed to identify the source of any invasion of rights. "A is liable, at least prima facie, if he is the cause of B's harm, regardless of A's ability or inability to avoid the harm . . ."[45] Esptein defines his causal ideas in terms of four simple paradigms: 1) A hit B; 2) A frightened B; 3) A compelled B to hit C; and 4) A created dangerous conditions that resulted in harm to B. Of these, 4) and 1) seem to hold the most relevance to pollution problems.[46]

If, as I have argued above, the efficiency arguments emanating from the Coase theorem fail in their attempt to provide a consistent basis for the conduct of policy to deal with pollution, it seems natural that causal principles should re-enter the picture. By definition, he who violates the rights of another causes him harm. So, once again, rights must be defined prior to any legal analysis. Epstein appears to favor a basic libertarian, natural-rights view that everyone is the unambiguous owner of his (her) body and of property acquired through voluntary exchange or original appropriation.[47] And in most cases involving a small number of individuals, applying this notion of rights to the four basic paradigms provides unambiguous criteria for establishing a prima facie case of harm. The only relevant question is, did A violate B's rights or cause C to

---

[44] Richard A. Epstein, "A Theory of Strict Liability," *Journal of Legal Studies* 2 (January 1973); "Defense and Subsequent Pleas in a Theory of Strict Liability," *Journal of Legal Studies* 3 (January 1974); "Pleadings and Resumptions," *University of Chicago Law Review* 40 (Spring 1973); "International Harms," *Journal of Legal Studies* 4 (June 1975); "Nuisance Law: Corrective Justice and Its Utilitarian Constraints," *Journal of Legal Studies* 8 (January 1979).

[45] Mario J. Rizzo, "Foreward" in Richard A. Epstein, *A Theory of Strict Liability* (San Francisco: Cato Institute Reprint, 1980), p. xi.

[46] Epstein, "Nuisance Law," p. 56. As Rizzo remarks (ibid., p. xi) these paradigms presuppose an ability to recognize an instance of any one of them and are perhaps better thought of as *classes* of causal relation.

[47] Epstein, "Nuisance Law," p. 52. "Each person owns his own body as a natural right. . . . It is more difficult to obtain agreement about the correct rules that in principle govern the acquisition of land or chattels. But for the purpose of tort law it is sufficient that the system has, in fact, settled upon the criterion of first possession . . . . coupled with rules that govern the transfer and alienation of the property rights so created."

POLLUTION EXTERNALITIES

do so? This involves a two-step procedure: 1) Identify an event or series of events that harmed B; and 2) connect this to an act or acts of A. Though there may be considerable uncertainty involved in both steps, purely economic considerations apparently do not enter into this phase of the analysis at all. It is necessary in the first step to specify the type of conduct that will be considered a violation of a plaintiff's rights. Some cases are clear-cut, like physical violence, extortion, and simple trespass. But some cases are more problematic. Among these are those that are classified as nuisances. "Nuisances are invasions of the plaintiff's property that fall short of trespasses but which still interfere in the use and employment of land. The cases make it quite clear that the forms of nontrespassory invasions are protean: Fumes, noises, smells, smoke, gases, heat, vibrations, and kindred activities."[48] In this sense pollution would appear to be a nuisance type invasion.

Having identified a nuisance, it is then necessary to link it to the defendant's actions. The ability to demonstrate fulfillment of steps 1 and 2 will then establish a prima facie case. In Epstein's scheme defenses can be made on the same paradigmatic grounds as the complaint. So, "B compelled A to hit him" is a valid defense against "A hit B." Other defenses exist as well: They are trespass and assumption of risk (either consensual or unilateral by the plaintiff). But if the plaintiff prevails, damage must be assessed, and some type of economic reasoning cannot be avoided. Summarizing, under this view, the investigation of the rights involved would appear to be prior to any examination of damage. Once an invasion has been established and a party found responsible, the question of relief can be addressed as a separate issue.

It should be emphasized that whenever the court would have to estimate the compensation necessary to make the plaintiff whole (whether injunctive relief was used or not) it would face the same difficulties discussed above in connection with the attempt to achieve an efficient outcome. Counterfactual assumptions cannot be avoided whenever a harmful event (which might not have occurred) is analyzed. The damage assessed must then be related to

---

[48] Ibid., p. 53. But compare Murray M. Rothbard, "The vital fact about air pollution is that the polluter sends unwanted and unbidden pollutants . . . . *through* the air and into the lungs of innocent victims, as well as onto their material property. All such emanations which injure person or property constitute agression against the private property of the victims. Air pollution, after all, is just as much aggression as committing arson against another's property or injuring him physically. Air pollution that injures others is aggression pure and simple." *For a New Liberty* (New York: Collier Macmillan, 1978), p. 256.

the difference between the state of the world as it actually is and as it *would have been* had the event not occurred. And since the parties have opposing incentives influencing the value they place on the harm, the court cannot but impose its own. In doing so it is necessarily attempting to empathically identify with the plaintiff and arrive at the pecuniary equivalent of the utility lost. This would appear to be an unavoidable ingredient of any justice system.

Still, a system of strict liability seems to preserve the advantage that though damage remains, to a greater or lesser extent depending on the complexity of the case, an uncertain element, the rights involved are clearly delineated and do not depend on any counterfactual determinations. The system should always apply an $\overline{L}$ law rather than an L law and should always be inclined to grant injuctive relief against violations of rights; so that apart from the estimation of damages, the system does not contain that element of arbitrariness in the assignment of rights that inheres in the efficiency arguments.

Two difficulties, however, remain. The first is that it is not always obvious when a right has been violated, although from a libertarian standpoint, common sense goes a long way. Thus, the blocking of a view, the blocking of light, and the creation of aesthetically displeasing structures are among a similar class of actions that do not constitute a violation, while the shining of light, creation of noise, etc., do. The physical invasion by a particle or wave of light, noise, or matter would seem to make the difference. Pollution occurs when many such invasions take place, creating direct harm or dangerous conditions.[49]

The second difficulty is much more important. An invasion may occur where the damage is small and/or the transactions and/or litigation costs (including the costs of administering the system) are high. In such cases there is a temptation to use economic criteria to implicity redefine and attenuate rights. This is particularly true in public goods situations where, for example, there are many pollution victims. "The nuisance law, unlike the law of accidents, does present abundant situations in which . . . utilitarian constraints militate in favor of redefinition of property rights and liability rules without explicit compensation."[50]

The problem seems to be that certain situations, while being clear cases of rights violations under a strict liability standard, are judged by most people to be generally (socially?) beneficial. Epstein

---

[49] Epstein, "Nuisance Law," pp. 56, 60-65.
[50] Ibid., p. 82.

POLLUTION EXTERNALITIES

presents some "rules" by which the strict liability outcome may be mitigated, among which are the "live and let live rule" and the "locality rule."[51] These rules can be briefly summarized as follows: 1) Live and let live: ". . . those acts necessary for the common and ordinary use and occupation of land and houses may be done, if conveniently done, without submitting those who do them to an action . . . It is as much for the advantage of the owner as of another, for the very nuisance the one complains of, as the result of the ordinary use of his neighbor's land, he himself will create in the ordinary use of his own, and the reciprocal nuisances are of a comparatively trifling character."[52] 2) Locality rule: "The function of the locality rule is to relax the basic nuisance rules where parallel uses by nearly all concerned insure the existence of implicit in-kind compensation."[53]

It should be clear that the ethical basis for these rules is similar to that advanced by Posner in justification of an efficiency standard, namely ex ante compensation and, therefore, implicit consent. As such, it is subject to the same objections. Instead of just deciding whether an invasion of rights has occurred, the court must now decide whether the appearance of such a violation is actually belied by the presence of ex ante compensation. And the latter thus calls for a judgment as to the social value of certain activities *in the process of determining rights*. Might it not be better to maintain as pure a theory of corrective justice as possible when determining rights and leave such speculations to the damages? In the conditions pertaining to the two rules in question this would imply that the incentive to litigate would be negligible and the problem would thus take care of itself. On the other hand, where (as in the "live and let live" situation) "the reciprocal nuisances are of a comparatively trifling character," the expected benefits of litigation are small. On the other hand, where large numbers are involved, unless the expected payoff is large, the transactions costs of joint litigation are likely to be prohibitive. This last consideration is mitigated to the extent that class action litigation is possible. But the conditions necessary to provide a basis for class certification are unlikely to apply in very many situations of this type.[54]

---

[51] Ibid., pp. 82-90.
[52] Ibid., p. 83, quoting Baron Bramwell's opinion in *Bramford* v. *Turnley* 3 B. & S. 55, 122 Eng. Rep. 27 (1862) at 83-84.
[53] Ibid., p. 90.
[54] In fact, as Rothbard points out (*For a New Liberty*, p. 258), class action suits are prohibited for air pollution cases.

CATO JOURNAL

An alternative (or complementary) approach is to use the concept of *homesteading* to define rights. What this implies is that the first occupier and user of a resource acquires a property right in that resource. One would extend this line of reasoning to air pollution, noise pollution, and so on.[55] Thus, where a producer acquires land and has preceded his neighbor in emitting air pollution, the neighbor has "come to the nuisance" and has not suffered any legal harm. Similar easements in a certain level of noise emission could be acquired.[56]

This approach implies the establishment of an $\overline{L}$ law but with stringent standards of proof to be borne by the plaintiff. But sometimes it appears impossible to establish an $\overline{L}$ law. Epstein gives the examples of highway traffic delays and automobile air pollution. The damages are "public" and private law mechanisms are apparently incapable of dealing with them. "When these conditions occur direct public regulation is the only possible way both to reduce harmful outputs and to equalize treatment across individual cases."[57] We are back to a Pigouvian tax and an implicit L law.

What Epstein fails to emphasize is that the root of the problem is that the highway and the air are not privately owned. Technically, there is no problem imagining private ownership of highways. And Rothbard has argued,[58] for example, that there are no "true" public goods of any kind, certainly not in water or on the land, which can, in principle, be parceled out. But what about the air? Rothbard suggests that allowing class action suits (under an $\overline{L}$ law) would provide the remedy.[59]

But having said this, two final difficulties remain: 1) Although one may agree that the bounds of human ingenuity in devising schemes of private property rights have hardly been stretched, there do appear to be situations that defy all such schemes. Examples are of the multiple tortfeasor type, like automobile air pollution. Here one may have to reluctantly agree that public regulation seems inevitable.[60] 2) A related point. Even it if were possible *in principle* to establish comprehensive property rights, in practice this will not be done. Our current difficulties in this regard may simply reflect our

---

[55] For a detailed argument see Murray N. Rothbard, "Law, Property Rights, and Air Pollution," *Cato Journal* 2 (Spring 1982): 55-99.

[56] Ibid.

[57] Epstein, "Nuisance Law," p. 7.

[58] "For a New" pp. 255-259.

[59] Ibid., p. 259.

[60] See Dolan, *Tanstaafl,* chap. 3, for an automobile pollution control scheme that preserves many of the features of the market.

POLLUTION EXTERNALITIES

refusal to do so in the past.[61] Automobiles would not have been made the same way if manufacturers had been enjoined from producing pollution damage in the distant past. Too many activities now common would be subject to injunction. How does one proceed, under a system of corrective justice, in such an imperfect world? I may conjecture that it would not entail the abandonment of corrective justice principles but merely the recognition that since they cannot be (or will not be) implemented, second-best alternatives must be considered. But if we can avoid making a virtue out of the need to compromise, we may succeed in the future in reducing the need to compromise.

---

[61] Although not necessarily. Sometimes our current difficulties may reflect the changing state of knowledge. We may at one time adopt a technology that we believe to be perfectly safe and only later (when it is already firmly integrated into the industrial infrastructure) learn that it is hazardous and invasive.

[5]

TIME PASSAGE AND THE ECONOMICS OF COMING TO THE NUISANCE: REASSESSING THE COASEAN PERSPECTIVE*

Roy E. Cordato**

I. Introduction

The doctrine of coming to the nuisance, or "first come first serve," in tort law suggests that the time sequence of events should be considered when making judgments in nuisance cases, i.e., cases involving harmful external effects. In the classic example of a railroad casting off sparks and setting fire to crops growing on adjacent farmland, a strict adherence to the doctrine suggests that if the railroad was there first, i.e., prior to the planting of crops by the farmer, then its owners should not be liable to the farmer for damages. In such circumstances, the plaintiff, in this case the farmer, has "come to the nuisance."

The arguments both for and against invoking the criteria when considering defenses in nuisance cases have been made on fairness and economic efficiency grounds. This paper reexamines the efficiency arguments that are made regarding coming to the nuisance and argues that the entire discussion has been cast in an inappropriate analytical framework. A problem that by definition involves the passage of time has been forced-fit into a static equilibrium framework of analysis. It will be argued that time pas-

---

* Earlier drafts of this paper were presented at the 1993 Eastern Economic Association Meetings in Washington, D.C. and the 1996 Austrian Scholars Conference in Auburn. Al. The author would like to thank Dr. Donald Boudreaux, and Professors E.C. Pasour, and John Moorhouse for some helpful comments on these earlier drafts.

** Dr. Roy E. Cordato is Lundy Professor of Business Philosophy at Campbell University.

sage automatically implies that the standard cost/benefit approach, an application and extension of Coase's classic 1960 article "The Problem of Social Cost,"[1] is inappropriate to this issue[2] and leads to the asking of fundamentally unanswerable questions.

A non-cost/benefit based alternative framework is offered which focuses on the efficiency of market activities as they unfold through time, rather than on static allocative effects. This alternative perspective is rooted in the works of F.A. Hayek[3] and other economists of the Austrian school[4] and gives rise to a unique set of conclusions with regards to the efficiency properties of first come first serve.

II. The View From Coasean Analysis

The most extensive and coherent discussion of the economics of coming to the nuisance was done by Donald Wittman. Wittman describes his task as follows:

---

1. Ronald H. Coase, *The Problem of Social Costs*, J.L. & Econ., Vol. 3 (October) (1960).

2. *See* Roy E. Cordato, *Subjective Value, Time Passage, and the Economics of Harmful Effects*, 12 Hamline L. Rev. 229 (1989); Cordato, Welfare Economics and Externalities in an Open-Ended Universe: A Modern Austrian Perspective (1992); Cordato, *Knowledge Problems and the Problem of Social Costs*, 14 The Journal of the History of Economic Thought 209, (1992). All three of these references elaborate much more generally and fully on criticisms of Coase's analysis discussed in this paper.

3. F.A. Hayek won the Nobel Prize for economics in 1974. Much of his work focuses on the role of the price system in disseminating information to market participants. It is this analysis of Hayek's that forms the basis for much of the analysis in this paper. *See* Cordato, *Knowledge Problems and the Problem of Social Costs*, *supra* note 2.

4. The term "Austrian school" refers to a tradition in economics that developed first in the late 19th century and early 20th century in Vienna, Austria, with the writings of its founder, Carl Menger and several of his students. (*See* Carl Menger, Principles of Economics (1981). The Austrian school of economics focuses on the implications of subjective preferences and expectations, imperfect knowledge, and the passage of time for understanding economic behavior. The modern Austrian school has developed primarily in the United States and to a lesser degree at the London School of Economics. Twentieth Century Austrian school economists have included Ludwig von Mises, F.A. Hayek, Murray Rothbard, and Israel Kirzner. (*See* Karen Vaughn, Austrian Economics in America (1994); *see also* Cordato, Welfare Economics and Externalities in an Open-Ended Universe: A Modern Austrian Perspective, *supra* note 2.

It is first necessary to establish the proper sequence of inputs into the productive process (including the production of negative externalities);[5] one must consider who should have been first instead of who was first. . . . Once the efficient sequence is determined, the next step is to determine the liability rule or property rule that promotes the efficient sequence.[6]

The efficiency properties of a rule of coming to the nuisance as a guide to resolving disputes in tort law have generally been considered in terms of a "Coasean" framework of analysis.[7] In evaluating guidelines for the implementation of tort law, the efficient or social welfare maximizing rules are those that would maximize the net social value of production, measured in terms of the pecuniary value of output. Within this context the criteria for evaluating coming to the nuisance described by Wittman, would be appropriate. The efficiency question that should be considered by a judge in evaluating a defense of coming to the nuisance is indeed "who should have been there first." In other words, whose use of the resource, the first or second user, would maximize the net social value of output? The factual question of who *was* there first only becomes relevant as a benchmark in determining whether the actual sequence of events was indeed the efficient sequence.

Wittman's approach is readily recognized as an extension of Coase's analysis to the area of coming to the nuisance. As Coase argued, in efficiently resolving conflicting resource uses of the kind that might give rise to a nuisance, what needs to be determined is the "arrangement of rights [that] may bring about a greater value of production than any other."[8] In a clear application of Coase's prescription to coming to the nuisance, Wittman argues that "the determination of who should have the right depends on the costs and benefits of the entire income stream, not just those costs and benefits after the second party came."[9] In this setting, a defense of coming to the nuisance should be recognized in cases where the defendant's use maximizes the income stream associated with the exploitation of the resource under consideration.

---

5. "Negative externality" is the term in economics for costs that are imposed on third parties as a result of production or consumption processes. A typical negative externality problem would be air pollution.

6. Donald Wittman, *First Come First Serve: An Economic Analysis of Coming to the Nuisance*, 9 J. Legal Stud. 557, 559 (1980).

7. Coase, *supra* note 1.

8. *Id.* at 16.

9. Wittman, *supra* note 6 at 558.

A. An Economic Analysis of Pendoley v. Ferriera

Wittman illustrates the procedure with a 1963 case, *Pendoley v. Ferriera*.[10] While a defense of coming to the nuisance was not part of this case, it does provide an effective scenario for an economic analysis of the issue. *Pendoley*[11] involved a conflict between an established pig farmer, in what was initially a rural area, and members of a subsequently established residential community located nearby. The complaint regarded the smells associated with the pig farm.

Wittman assumes two locations, one of which is categorized as "good" and the other as "bad." He then examines the use of these locations by the residents and the farmer over two periods, with the presence of the farmer on one of these locations in period one and the arrival of the residents in period two.

From this Wittman derives four scenarios, exhausting the possible efficient sequences of the use of "good" and "bad" land in the two periods.[12] The actual efficient scenario depends on assumptions that are made regarding the relative magnitudes of the farmer's profits and the residents' utility functions[13] with respect to the use of the good and bad land. Property and liability rules are then examined to determine how the application of these rules would promote the efficient sequence of events, i.e., the efficient use of the two categories of land over the relevant time frame.

B. Problems with Coasean Methodology

For our purposes there is no need to delve more deeply into Wittman's analysis. The problem is with the Coasean methodology and not this particular application. These problems are general in that they plague much if not most of the analysis in law

---

10. Pendoley v. Ferriera, 187 N.E. 2d 142 (Mass. 1963).

11. *Id.*

12. "(1) The Polluter is on the good land for both periods and the pollutee is on the bad land for period 2. (2) The polluter is on the good land for both periods and the pollutee is on the good land for period 2. (3) The polluter is on the bad land for both periods and the pollutee is on the good land for period 2. (4) The polluter is on the good land for period 1 and on the bad land for period 2 and the pollutee is on the good land for period 2." Wittman, *supra* note 6 at 560. Wittman rules out scenarios involving the possibility of moving in the middle of one of the time periods as always being less efficient.

13. A utility function is a mathematical representation of a person's preferences. The assumption behind this kind of representation is that individual preferences are objective, specifiable, and measurable.

and economics. They stem from fundamental methodological assumptions that were made by Coase that have been inappropriately carried forward into discussions of many real-world negative externality problems. While Wittman poses a two period scenario, his analysis is completely static in that it abstracts from all of the economically relevant problems associated with the passage of time. This is necessary if one insists on staying within the traditional Coasean framework of analysis, which assumes a state of the world that is always in a perfectly competitive general equilibrium, i.e., that all observed prices are competitive prices.[14] Coase's methodology is inappropriate to the task at hand.

III. Time Passage, Market Processes, and General Equilibrium Analysis

> As soon as we permit time to elapse, we must permit knowledge to change. . . . The state of knowledge of society cannot be the same at two successive points of time, and time cannot elapse without demand and supply shifting. The stream of knowledge produces ever new disequilibrium situations, and entrepreneurs continually manage to find new price-cost differences to exploit.[15]

The essence of time passage is change; change in preferences, change in technology, change in population, etc. The significance of these changes for economics is that they are either the product of, or they lead to, changes in human knowledge. Furthermore, the process by which knowledge changes is an imperfect one of trial and error, which itself, is time dependent. By implication, then, at any point in time some actions will be taken that are based on erroneous information. In other words, people will make plans that are inconsistent with the goals that they are pursuing. In a market setting, such actions are penalized with losses. These losses provide incentives to discard erroneous information and reassess and redesign plans in hopes that future activity will be based on accurate information and be rewarded by profits. This is an ongoing process of plan formulation and revision in light of new information. Knowledge is never perfected. As problems are fixed new ones are revealed by the continuous generation and flow of new information.

---

14. Coase makes this assumption throughout the analysis in his classic 1960 article, *see* Coase, *supra* note 1.

15. Ludwig Lachmann, *On the Central Concept of Austrian Economics*, 126-132 (Edwin G. Dolan, ed., The Foundations of Modern Austrian Economics 1976).

This is the nature of economic activity as it proceeds through time. It is a process that is never in general equilibrium. Furthermore, from the perspective of market participants, it is a never ending, open ended process. The economic assessment of any time dependent phenomena needs to make this process the central focus of its analysis. To abstract from the process by assuming that the world is in a perfectly competitive general equilibrium or that the state of knowledge is "perfect" or simply "given" is to move to a level of abstraction that bears little resemblance to the real world which, consequently, yields non-operational conclusions with respect to public policy.

This is why Coasean analysis is fundamentally inappropriate to the task of assessing the efficiency properties of coming to the nuisance. The cost-benefit approach derived from Coase's work only becomes intelligible as a guide to rule making within the context of a static, competitive equilibrium. Once the analyst steps out of this framework and into the world of imperfect knowledge that serious consideration of time passage implies, much of what Coase's analysis, and by implication Wittman's analysis, preordains must be done cannot be done.

IV. THE IMPLICATIONS OF TIME PASSAGE AND OPEN-ENDEDNESS FOR SOCIAL COST-BENEFIT ANALYSIS

The use of social cost-benefit analysis as an analytical tool is contingent upon making the simplifying assumption that all markets, not just those under consideration, are in a perfectly competitive general equilibrium (PCGE). While Wittman, and others who discuss the economics of coming to the nuisance much less extensively, do not make this assumption explicit, it is necessarily implied.[16]

The PCGE assumption allows several key analytical stumbling blocks to be finessed. As Buchanan[17] and others[18] have sought to emphasize, opportunity costs and benefits are subjective

---

16. This is not unusual. As is typically the case, when such simplifying assumptions are consistently made in a particular analytical framework, after a period of time they simply become a part of the implicit background information. Such assumptions tend to be made explicit only in text books in the field and in the earlier, seminal articles. *See* COASE, *supra* note 1.

17. *See* JAMES BUCHANAN, COST AND CHOICE: AN INQUIRY IN ECONOMIC THEORY (1969).

18. *See* LUDWIG VON MISES, HUMAN ACTION (1966); Karen Vaughn, *Does it Matter that Costs are Subjective?*, 46 SOUTHERN ECONOMICS JOURNAL (1980).

and therefore unquantifiable. Both costs and benefits are concepts rooted in individual satisfaction. Benefit is the satisfaction received from the taking of a particular action while cost is the satisfaction foregone by choosing not to take other actions. Strictly speaking, costs and benefits are *intra*personally perceived. There is no *inter*personal scale upon which they can be unified and ranked and therefore they cannot be interpersonally aggregated. There is no economically meaningful way to talk about costs and benefits to society, apart from the individuals who experience them. Yet all social cost benefit analysis, by definition, makes this abstraction.

To get around this problem, economists typically assume that all markets are in a PCGE. In such a setting, prices equate both marginal social cost and marginal social benefit and therefore can be invoked as a means of making objective the non-objective and measuring the unmeasurable. But this assumption, invoked in abstract analysis, does not change the nature of real world costs and benefits. Since an efficiency analysis of coming to the nuisance involves the assessment of behavior through time, the possibility that we are dealing with a general equilibrium world should be ruled out. Furthermore, even from the perspective of static analysis, the assumption that there is a nuisance problem in the first place, i.e., an externality problem, is by definition an assumption that a competitive equilibrium is not being obtained. Therefore, to assume a PCGE, a world that is free of externality problems, poses an internal contradiction in the theory.

The answer to "who should have been their first," in terms of social costs and benefits, can only be arrived at if interpersonal cost-benefit comparisons can legitimately, i.e., scientifically, be made. As Wittman noted, "the efficient sequence cannot be established without assigning relative magnitudes to profit and utility functions."[19] The assumption is that utility functions can indeed be specified and aggregated and furthermore that it is scientifically meaningful to make comparisons between utility functions and profit functions. But utility functions, in principle, cannot be specified. Furthermore, profit functions can only be specified in terms of accounting costs and not utility based opportunity costs. In reality no meaningful comparison between profit and utility functions is possible.

---

19. Wittman, *supra* note 6 at 560.

If the PCGE assumption is not made then a host of new problems arise for both the economic analyst and any policy maker attempting to implement the efficiency enhancing solution. In order to ascertain a property rights or liability rule that would facilitate the efficient sequence of events, the relevant PCGE would first have to be identified. From the perspective of social costs-benefit analysis the efficient solution is the one that would occur in a competitive general equilibrium. Coase's efficiency criteria is only intelligible within this context.[20] Consequently, in evaluating coming to the nuisance the sequence of events that would arise under conditions of competitive general equilibrium must be known. In reality though, empirical identification of such an equilibrium is impossible for even a point in time. Once it is made clear that a judge or jury considering a defense of coming to the nuisance is attempting to determine the efficient allocation of resources *through* time, the PCGE efficiency benchmark loses its relevancy even as a conceptual guide.

The analytical issue centers around what has come to be called "the knowledge problem," which is the central theme of F.A. Hayek's theoretical case[21] against the possibility of efficient resource utilization under central planning.[22] In order to identify a PCGE for a point in time one must have access to information that is fundamentally unobtainable. This includes utility functions for all market participants together with complete knowledge of all resource scarcities and production functions, including the economic significance of all technologies. This information must be known for the economic system as a whole. Clearly this task is beyond human capabilities, if not comprehension.

To complicate matters, when dealing with events taking place through time, an analyst trying to construct an equilibrium solution is faced with a moving target. Even if a PCGE could be identified for a point in time, its relevance would only be historical. As indicated by Lachmann's observations, continuous changes in

---

20. *See* CORDATO, WELFARE ECONOMICS AND EXTERNALITIES IN AN OPEN-ENDED UNIVERSE: A MODERN AUSTRIAN PERSPECTIVE, *supra* note 2 at Ch. 5.

21. The implications of the knowledge problem for Coasean type analysis in law and economics have been extensively analyzed in Cordato, *Knowledge Problems and the Problem of Social Cost, supra* note 2.

22. *See* F.A. Hayek, *Socialist Calculation I: The Nature and History of the Problem, in* INDIVIDUALISM AND ECONOMIC ORDER 119; *Socialist Calculation II: The State of the Debate, in* INDIVIDUALISM AND ECONOMIC ORDER 148; Socialist *Calculation III: The Competitive Solution, in* INDIVIDUALISM AND ECONOMIC ORDER 181 (1972).

knowledge, i.e., preferences, scarcities, technologies, etc., dislodge the relevance of any particular general equilibrium from moment to moment.

With regards to coming to the nuisance, if one could determine who "should have been there first" in light of the relevant data, i.e., utility and profit functions, for the beginning of time period one, there is no justification for concluding that the data and therefore the solution will not change by the beginning or the end of time period two. In fact, the most reasonable assumption to make is that it will change. It will be argued below that it must in order for the nuisance problem even to arise.

V. TIME PASSAGE AND EFFICIENCY

When considering a time dependent issue such as coming to the nuisance, efficiency analysis based on the normative benchmark of a PCGE is not useful. To assume that observed market prices are competitive equilibrium prices as a means of circumventing the problems associated with subjective costs and benefits is to make an assumption that *cannot* be true. In fact, to do so is to assume away the most fundamental efficiency problem associated with the passage of time, namely how best to deal with changing circumstances in a world of imperfect information. Furthermore, to try and construct the competitive equilibrium solution from empirical data is also a futile and ultimately an inappropriate undertaking.

A. *Efficiency Problems in Time Dependent Settings*

In a time dependent setting the efficiency problem facing market participants is not simply one of allocating resources to their highest valued use with all the relevant knowledge given. First, from the individual's perspective, efficiency relates to the accomplishment of one's goals under conditions where the relevant information can never be known completely and, furthermore, where the state of that information is changing. The passage of time implies the addition of information that did not previously exist and the discarding of information that has become irrelevant. As noted earlier, this leads to a market process that is characterized by trial and error, with activities based on both accurate and erroneous perceptions being brought to light by the system of profit and loss. This process is generated by the experiences of all market participants—consumers, entrepreneurs, workers, pig farmers, and home builders.

Given the nature of this process, "efficient" outcomes of the type that are typically pursued in the law and economics literature cannot be identified. Since aggregation of costs and benefits across individuals is not conceptually possible, people's individually determined goals must be taken as given when assessing social welfare. Social cost benefit analysis as a judicial decision making tool is an attempt to decide whose goals are relatively more important to society. But the concepts of social costs and social benefits, as typically invoked, are, from the perspective of economic analysis, neither operational nor conceptually meaningful. Therefore, efficiency must be construed strictly in terms of the welfare of individual members of society, as they, and not some outside observer, perceive it.

B. Social Efficiency

The relevant question for "social efficiency" is what institutional setting would best allow individual market participants to discover, assimilate, and act on accurate information that will be useful in the accomplishment of their goals. As this author[23] and others[24] have argued, this requires a legal environment where individuals are allowed the widest possible latitude for pursuing their own interests while not being allowed to violate the similar rights of others.

Maximum possible social efficiency, in this regard, requires that individuals have exclusive rights to resources and the fruits of their labor. The pursuit of goals and the formulation of plans cannot proceed without access to the physical means necessary for this process to take place. The implication, first, is that property titles need to be clearly defined and strictly enforced. In such a setting, conflict over the use of resources by two or more individuals with inconsistent plans with respect to the same resource, will be minimized. Such conflicts are an important source of inefficiency and serve as the fundamental source of all negative externality problems.[25]

---

23. *See* CORDATO, WELFARE ECONOMICS AND EXTERNALITIES IN AN OPEN-ENDED UNIVERSE: A MODERN AUSTRIAN PERSPECTIVE, *supra* note 3, Chs. 3 & 4.

24. *See* ISRAEL KIRZNER, MARKET THEORY AND THE PRICE SYSTEM, Ch. 2 (1963).

25. *Id.*

C. *Property Rights and Efficiency*

In a general sense, from this normative perspective the content of property rights can be specified. The individual resource owner should be allowed to utilize his property in any way he perceives to be consistent with his own ends. This ensures that the full force of people's preferences, perceptions of resource scarcities, and knowledge will come to bear on the utilization of resources. As a subset of this general principle, and particularly important to the enhancement of market and therefore social efficiency, is the right to contract and freely exchange property. This ensures not only that people will be able to mutually pursue otherwise conflicting plans through the exchange process, but it is also a necessary condition for the price system to perform its information enhancing functions. In this setting where property rights are clearly defined, strictly enforced, and freely exchangeable, relative prices will capture as much information about preferences and relative scarcities as possible, while weeding out erroneous information through the system of profit and loss, i.e., trial and error.

1. *Institutional stability requirement*

An additional requirement, one that is particularly relevant to the issue of coming to the nuisance, institutional stability,[26] argues that a dynamic market process requires that rules defining the scope of legitimate activity be stable. If efficiency, as discussed here, requires that individual market participants have accurate information regarding the relationship of means to ends, then a fundamental cause of inefficiency is error. Indeed, to assume perfect knowledge is to assume away the entire efficiency problem that individuals face in a time dependent setting. Uncertainty with respect to property rights can be an important source of error in the plan formulation process.

Again, this is an issue that arises because of the passage of time. Plans are made and executed sequentially through time. Plans that are made with respect to the use of resources of any kind cannot be implemented unless one has the "right" to do so at some point in the future. Uncertainty about what one's rights may be with respect to the use of resources at different points in the future, or false certainty in the face of future alterations of

---

26. *See* Mario Rizzo, *Law Amid Flux: The Economics of Negligence and Strict Liability*, 9 J. LEGAL Stud. (1980).

one's rights (and obligations), will generate errors and therefore inefficiencies.

2. *Certainty of legal rights*

Furthermore, uncertainty with respect to legal rights and obligations will have a negative impact on markets as a whole. In a time dependent setting, expectations about the future are incorporated in relative price movements. In implementing plans, market transactions are made which affect price movements. To the extent that exchanges are made based on erroneous expectations, relative prices will reflect inaccurate information, sending false signals to other market participants. False price signals can facilitate the formulation of inefficient plans in a far flung and unpredictable manner.

Since market processes take place through time, it is necessary to consider the impact of institutional instability on economic efficiency. Economic analysis of coming to the nuisance has disregarded this entire issue by assuming a world devoid of any of the characteristics of real time passage. Because of this, rules that appear to be efficient within the traditional static framework could generate a great deal of inefficiency when imperfect knowledge and institutional uncertainties are considered.

3. *Predictability for efficiency in planning future activities*

Wittman, for example, argues that the conclusions he reaches regarding allocative efficiency also have efficiency enhancing incentive effects with regards to planning future activities. In a footnote he points out that "the court case is more important in its precedent-setting effects than in the effect on this particular set of actors."[27] He claims that implementation of the efficient rule "can serve as a useful guide for the future." Concluding that:

> cost-benefit calculations in . . . legal rulings . . . will encourage those who come first to predict the probable uses of the land in the future. If the most efficient alternative is for the farmer to use the inferior land from the beginning, the farmer will in fact make this choice if he can reasonably predict the future uses of the land.[28]

This analysis calls on potential first users to have prospective information regarding relative utility and profit functions concerning people they do not know and situations that have yet to

---

27. Wittman, *supra* note 6, at 561.
28. *Id.* at 562.

occur. From this information they are to draw conclusions about the efficient allocation of resources. As we have argued, all this is conceptually unknowable even retrospectively. Furthermore the first user is called upon to have probabilistic information regarding "future uses of the land" by people other than himself which must be based on unknowable information about the efficient allocation of resources.

This prescription calls on the first user of a resource to play "central planner" with respect to not only the area that he is occupying directly but all of the relevant surrounding resources. Since the first user of a resource cannot possibly know the most productive pattern of resource use over time he is simply being asked to make guesses about what the cost-benefit analysis invoked by some future court might conclude regarding a yet-to-materialize externality problem. Neither the first user nor the future court could objectively determine the "efficient" resource allocation as defined in the standard analysis. In reality, the entire scenario simply calls for one person to guess what a future court will guess at some unspecified point in the future.

Wittman's analysis rejects out-of-hand any of the information problems discussed here. He asserts that, except for the level of certainty (in a probabilistic sense), no distinction should be made regarding ex ante and ex post knowledge. He states that it is a "fallacy" to argue that "since the homeowners knew the pigsty was there, they are the responsible party as they willingly accepted the conditions of the sty when they initiated building."[29] This is because "the farmer knew (in a less certain way) that the homeowners would want to build there. Therefore he is equally at fault."[30]

In putting the burden of accomplishing what is fundamentally an impossible task on first users of resources, a great deal of additional uncertainty is introduced into the formulation of plans, which detracts from efficient decision making. The probability that the first user will make decisions that enhance allocative efficiency, *ex ante*, would be decreased. The first user of a resource would be more uncertain about his future rights and obligations. This, in turn, would increase the probability that his expectations regarding future resource utilization will be erroneous. Uncertainty with regards to future rights must be considered when

---

29. *Id.*
30. *Id.*

assessing the efficiency properties of coming to the nuisance. It has been ignored because it does not exist in the traditional Coasean framework of analysis.

VI. THE ROLE OF COMING TO THE NUISANCE

What would be the role of coming to the nuisance in this time dependent setting where efficiency dictates that property rights be stable, clearly defined, and provide for the widest possible range of resource utilization by owners consistent with the same rights of others?[31] The question "who should have been there first?" is conceptually flawed and non-operational.

Furthermore it requires that the analyst make comparative value judgments between the conflicting ends of market participants. It does not take people's ends as given but suggests that we must decide whose goals, in Wittman's example, the pig farmer's or the home owners', are more important to society. As discussed, cost-benefit analysis cannot be scientifically invoked as a criterion for making this decision.

Ultimately, the assessment must be based on a question that is not even recognized in most of the standard literature, namely, who has title to the resources under dispute? This is consistent with the conclusion reached above, that market efficiency in a change laden, time dependent setting, requires that property rights be clearly defined and strictly enforced. In this setting, not only is it irrelevant to ask "who should have been there first" but it is equally unhelpful to ask "who was there first." If we assume that all property titles are clearly defined and had been throughout the relevant time period, the question of who was there first becomes muddy at best and possibly vacuous. This question only becomes meaningful in the absence of clearly delineated property titles.

A. Question of Ownership

With respect to the pig farmer in Wittman's example, we assume that he initiated the farming activity on land that he had legitimate title to, i.e., that he legally acquired (purchased, inherited, etc.) from someone else. Over some period of time the farmer

---

31. Implicitly, this is the same question asked by Richard Epstein in his article, *Defenses and Subsequent Pleas in a Theory of Strict Liability*, III J. LEGAL STUD. 197-201 (1974). However his concern was one of corrective justice and not economic efficiency.

makes use of adjacent property (by allowing the spillover of odors) that someone else has title to. For whatever reason, the owner of the adjacent property did not mind that the farmer made use of his property in this way and either implicitly or explicitly gave the farmer his blessing.

Given this arrangement, it is simply not accurate to say that the farmer was there first. The farmer was there with his smells only because of the implicit or explicit permission of the owner. So long as the adjacent property was owned by somebody when the farm was built, it was the owner of the adjacent property who was there first and continued to be there, making use of his property in such a way that allowed the farmer to emit the pig odors onto it. The plans of the adjacent property owner with respect to the use of his property were consistent with the presence of the odors. He felt no conflict with respect to the use of the resource during the relevant time frame and therefore continued to allow the farmer to enjoy what was essentially a windfall use of his property.

When Wittman's example is viewed as a sequence of activities through time it is clear that plans that were made with respect to the use of the adjacent property, by its owners, have changed. This might be because the same owners simply have had a change in their preferences or the market has changed in such a way that the land became more valuable in alternative uses. Also, it may be because new owners, who prefer alternative uses of the land, have acquired the property.

In either scenario there is no efficiency case to be made in support of allowing a defense of coming the nuisance in a tort action that may be brought by the owners of the adjacent land.[32] In the first instance, it would be difficult to argue that the farmer was even there first. By assumption the adjacent land was owned at the time that the pig farm was built and the smells started leaking onto the adjacent property. The owner simply did not mind if his neighbor, the farmer, made use of his property in that particular way. There is no way to argue from an efficiency perspective that, having made that decision in the first place, he forfeits the right to change his mind at future points as personal preferences and external circumstances may warrant. To argue

---

32. Economic analysis of this scenario that takes into account the implications of time passage leads to a conclusion also reached by Epstein. In examining the ethical implications of this same issue, Epstein argued that "[t]he enjoyment of a past windfall does not create the right to enjoy one in the future." *Id.* at 198.

otherwise is to make the specifically anti-efficiency argument that markets and the price system should not be allowed to respond to such changes and reallocate resources accordingly.

The second scenario is, in principle, the same. The original owner, who didn't mind the smells from the pig farm, sells the property to someone who, for whatever reason—possibly because he plans to build a home or housing development on the property—does mind. What has happened is that the relative value of the property to the original owner has declined and he decides to sell. Again, from an efficiency perspective, there has been some change in circumstances and relative evaluations of the property.

The efficiency of the market process should be gauged by the extent to which prices can accurately incorporate the new information regarding these changes, reflected in the sale price of the property. Furthermore, it seems safe to presume that when selling the property it was offered for sale publicly and that the farmer had the right to put in his bid. In other words, he could have secured his future rights to emit smells onto the property by outright purchase. Indeed, the farmer could have made offers at any point prior to the property officially going on sale to secure similar future rights. In a general sense, the efficiency of a market process to incorporate information regarding preferences, scarcities etc., depends on the extent to which resource owners are allowed to bring their utility functions and perceptions of the world to bear on decisions regarding the exchange of their property. Restrictions on this right will impair the extent to which prices can perform their knowledge communicating functions. Ultimately, without this fundamental right there is no market process.

Viewing the pig farmer-home owner example from this alternative perspective, reinforces earlier arguments regarding the relationship of coming to the nuisance to dynamic disequilibrium analysis. It should be clear that the reason a problem arises for the farmer is that with the passage of time, something—preferences, resource scarcities, etc.—has changed. If there were no change from the original set of circumstances, there would have been no conflict to resolve.

It is the passage of time that instigates this change. Static, general equilibrium analysis is, therefore, inherently inappropriate to the problem at hand. To assume that there is a "given" cost-benefit scenario at the beginning of "t_1" that remains constant to the end of "t_2" is inconsistent with any conflict ever arising.

B. *Implications when Ownership is in Question*

An efficiency justification *can* be made for considering a defense of coming to the nuisance when, unlike the previous scenario, title to the resource involved in the dispute is unclear or when the resource has been previously unowned. In this instance, one of the criteria for an efficiently functioning market process is not present. That is, property rights are not clearly defined. The question then is who should have the right to use a previously unowned resource. If the time sequence of use is detectable then it can be argued that an allocation of rights based on first use, if consistently applied, would enhance market efficiency.

1. *The first use rule*

In the example, as unlikely as this scenario would be in modern times, let's assume that the farmer built his pig farm on property that was adjacent to unowned, virgin wilderness, possibly in the 19th Century when parts of the country were still being homesteaded. At some future point, new arrivals stake a claim on the adjacent property and begin to build houses. As part of this the new arrivals claim that the smells from the pig farm are a nuisance and ask for either an injunction or damages from the farmer.

In this case it *is* clear who arrived first in time. Furthermore, if generally invoked as a well understood and consistently applied rule, application of the "first use" principle would enhance efficient plan formulation and the overall efficiency of markets and the price system. First, such a rule would remove a great deal of uncertainty and therefore reduce error in the formulation and execution of individual plans. In the example at hand, the pig farmer, by being first to "use" the adjacent property, can be confident that his continued right to do so for the established purpose (emit odors) will be upheld in the face of future nuisance claims. This will increase the probability that his perceptions of the future are accurate and that plans that are currently being made will ultimately be fulfilled.

Such a rule would send important signals to potential comers to a nuisance. In the example, those considering making use of the adjoining property would do so in full knowledge that the farmer has preceded them and, as such, has certain rights with respect to its use. This knowledge, and the certainty about future rights and obligations that it would generate, would be factored into any decisions that are made with respect to the use of the adjacent land, ex ante. Anyone planning to build a house on the land would do so in full knowledge that they would either have to put up with the odors from the pig farm, incur the costs of insulating themselves from the odors, or negotiate a "Coasean" type bargain with the farmer.

With regard to the price system and market efficiency, all of this information regarding the farmer's property rights and obligations, and the rights associated with the use of the adjacent land would tend to be accurately reflected in relative prices. Any transactions that are part of plans made for future use of the adjacent land would be based on expectations of returns that incorporate the farmer's right to emit odors from the farm onto the land.

For example, if someone planned to lay claim to this previously unowned land and build homes on it with the expectation of selling these homes to future residents of the area, his expectations about the potential market price of those homes would probably include some discount for the odors. This discount would be included in the price he is willing to pay for labor, construction materials, etc. In this manner, the certainty that is generated by a consistently applied first use rule would enhance the efficiency and orderliness of the entire market process. Furthermore, such a rule would reduce the extent to which nuisance suits in such cases are even brought. In the example, with the knowledge that the farmer would probably win in court based on a defense of coming to the nuisance, it is more likely that the housing developer or home owners would never file suit.

2. Modern applicability of the first use rule

As already noted, the scenario presented in this example is not a likely one, given that nearly all land is owned by someone and the days of homesteading land are long over. On the other hand, this analysis does suggest that if a case similar to the pig farm example were to arise, even within a context where titles to property seem to be clear, it would be important to investigate the history of those title claims before dismissing a defense of coming to the nuisance. For example, if the pig farm, or maybe another kind of farm that emitted foul odors, was established 125 years ago and the adjacent land was homesteaded and titles began changing hands 100 years ago, a defense of coming to the nuisance might indeed be appropriate. Beyond this example, the analysis suggested here could have other modern applications. For example, conflicts regarding users of rivers, streams, or the air, where rights to the these resources have not been clearly defined, could possibly be resolved based on a principle of first use.

The point to be emphasized here is that from the perspective of a time dependent market process, the only setting where a defense of coming to the nuisance will have efficiency enhancing attributes is where titles to property have not been previously established. In such cases, if applied as a general rule it would reduce uncertainty in both individual plan formulation and in market-oriented entrepreneurial activities.

VII. Conclusion

The efficiency properties of "coming to the nuisance" are intricately tied to the economic analysis of disequilibrium market processes as they unfold through time.[33] In light of this, it is clear that the perspective from which the issue has traditionally been analyzed is inappropriate. Social cost-benefit analysis cannot be meaningfully applied in a world where no general equilibrium solution can be identified, where knowledge is imperfect and errors are made, and where information is in a continuous state of flux. Yet, this is the context in which coming the nuisance should be assessed. Standard analysis examines an issue that is dependent on the time sequence of events and assumes away the essential characteristics of time passage.

As many economists who have sought to emphasize the passage of time in their analysis have argued,[34] the efficiency problem facing both the individual and society in this setting is a "knowledge problem." As Hayek suggested:

> the economic problem of society is . . . how to secure the best use of resources known to any members of society, for ends whose relative importance only these individuals know. . . . It is a problem of the utilization of knowledge that is not given to anyone in its totality.[35]

Where the "relative importance of ends" cannot be known by any outside observer, cost benefit analysis, when examining a conflict over the use of resources, has no role. The answer to who *should* have been there first, when the normative standard refers

---

33. *See* Gerland O'Driscoll & Mario Rizzo, The Economics of Time and Ignorance (1985) (overview of perspective on economic analysis).

34. *See* F.A. Hayek, *The Use of Knowledge in Society, in* Individualism and Economic Order 77 (1972); Gerland O'Driscoll & Mario Rizzo, *supra* note 31; Israel Kirzner, Market Theory and the Price System, Ch. 4 (1963).

35. *See* F.A. Hayek, *The Use of Knowledge in Society, supra* note 32, at 77-78.

to the sequence of events "that may bring about a greater value of production than any other,"[36] is unknowable.

Efficiency analysis in this setting should focus on the overall institutional setting that governs the plan formulation process which, in turn, impinges on the overall ability of the price system to utilize and disseminate accurate information. As a general principle, in this setting property rights should be clearly defined and strictly enforced, but beyond this the nature of those rights can also be specified. Efficiency from this perspective requires the maximum possible freedom with respect to the use of one's property in the plan formulation and implementation process. The only restraint is that the individual not violate the same rights of others.[37]

If this is the starting point for the economic analysis of coming to the nuisance then a unique set of conclusions are reached with regards to its efficient implementation. If all property titles are clearly delineated and had been so throughout the time period under consideration then there is no argument for allowing a defense of coming to the nuisance. Indeed, in this setting it is not clear as to what it means for one or the other party to claim that they had "been there" first. The only time that a rule of coming to the nuisance would be useful is when property titles are not clearly delineated. As an example one might consider conflicts over the use of "publicly owned" waterways such as rivers, streams, or lakes.

The overall purpose of this article has been to assess the traditional framework for analyzing the issue of coming to the nuisance and to suggest and draw out some conclusion of a possible alternative approach. The fact is that this alternative analysis has implications that run much wider than the analysis of coming to the nuisance. All economic analysis of issues in tort law is essentially analysis of events that happen through time. Furthermore, time elapses from the period over which the nuisance takes place to the period over which a claim is brought and a judgment is rendered. Given this, the appropriateness of static, general equilibrium analysis for many other issues related to the economics of tort liability is questionable.

---

36. Coase, *supra* note 1, at 16.
37. *See* KIRZNER, *supra* note 22, at Ch. 2.

[6]

RULES VERSUS COST-BENEFIT
ANALYSIS IN THE COMMON LAW

Mario J. Rizzo

> When they speak so resonantly of "public policy," do lawyers have
> the slightest idea what they're talking about?
>
> —B. A. Ackerman[1]

I. Introduction

The relation between economic liberty and the judiciary is far
broader than that evident from those areas of law that are explicitly
concerned with policy. Everyone recognizes this interrelation in
antitrust, securities regulation, environmental policy, labor law, and
countless other areas. In each of these it is universally accepted that
as long as we have law it must be based on specific policy goals. The
idea of economic legislation that is policy-neutral is a contradiction
in terms. In the 20th century this emphasis on policy considerations
has spread to all areas of the law including the classic common law
fields (Prosser and Keeton 1984, pp. 15–20). Economic policy factors
(as well as other forms of policy) are said to be relevant to the formulation of society's contract, property, and tort rules. The fundamental purpose of this paper is to demonstrate that this need not be
the case. The common law, that is, judge-made private law, can be
policy neutral in the sense that it need not impose a specific hierarchy
of values on society. It can restrict itself to the provision of abstract
rules that enhance the possibilities of an order in which individuals
can pursue and attain their own goals. In other words, the purpose

Cato Journal, Vol. 4, No. 3 (Winter 1985). Copyright © Cato Institute. All rights
reserved.

The author is Associate Professor of Economics at New York University. He wishes
to thank the Earhart Foundation and the Sarah Scaife Foundation for financial support
in preparing this paper. He also acknowledges the Civil Liability Program at the Yale
Law School for providing him with a congenial atmosphere during the spring of 1984
in which to think about the issues discussed in this paper.

[1]Ackerman (1984, p. 22).

of this paper is to show that we can eliminate, or at least drastically reduce, consideration of specific public policy questions even in those areas where we must have law. The judiciary can promote economic and other forms of liberty by returning to the classic common law adherence to abstract rules and eschewing the now-fashionable balancing of economic or social interests.

The remainder of this paper is organized as follows. In Section II we argue that there is a lack of appreciation of the principle of spontaneous order among many economists and most legal theorists. This principle is central to understanding the nature of a policy-neutral legal system. In Section III we show that the function of the pure common law is to promote such a spontaneous order of individual actions. Section IV demonstrates that the common law is itself a spontaneous order that is not the result of conscious direction.[2] Section V elucidates the concept of an abstract or general rule by contrasting it with the idea of interest balancing. Section VI illustrates the tension between rules and balancing in the law of negligence, while Section VII demonstrates the superior rule-orientation of strict liability in tort. In Section VIII, we offer a brief discussion of a recent and important explanation for the decline in the common law's emphasis on rules, and in Section IX, we present some concluding remarks.

II. Decline of Spontaneous Order in Economics and Law

The concept of spontaneous order is a general principle of social organization that once commanded widespread recognition in economics and significant adherence in legal theory. In economics it has been best known in the form of Adam Smith's "invisible hand." The system of natural liberty—the free interaction of individual producers, merchants, and consumers—would tend to yield socially beneficial outcomes, as if by an invisible hand. During most of the 20th century, however, the principle of spontaneous order has been out of favor with the majority of the economics profession.

In recent years there has been a revival of interest in spontaneous ordering forces, but most economists still remain skeptical. Among general equilibrium theorists, especially, these forces have been given an interpretation that renders the principle entirely useless. Frank Hahn, for example, identifies the invisible hand with the

[2]Sections II and III draw heavily on, and in some respects expand, the seminal work of F. A. Hayek (1973, 1976, 1979).

formal model of general equilibrium developed by Kenneth Arrow
and Gerard Debreu (Hahn 1973, p. 324):

> When the claim is made—and the claim is as old as Adam Smith—
> that a myriad of self-seeking agents left to themselves will lead to
> a coherent and efficient disposition of economic resources, Arrow
> and Debreu show what the world would have to look like if this
> claim is to be true. *In doing this they provide the most potent avenue
> of falsification of the claims* [emphasis added].

The Arrow-Debreu general equilibrium construct is based on
extremely stringent assumptions: perfect information and foresight,
complete futures markets, perfect divisibility, and a host of other
technical requirements. When these assumptions are met, it can be
shown that an unregulated system results in a Pareto-efficient allocation of resources. In the real world, however, the assumptions are
not even remotely satisfied, and hence an "efficient" disposition of
resources is not possible. Thus, argues Hahn, the claims of Adam
Smith and other spontaneous order theorists must be false, because
the necessary conditions for the realization of these claims are absent.[3]
Hahn's argument is held together, though, by a weak logical link:
the identification of the principle of spontaneous order with the
Arrow-Debreu formal construct. On the contrary, the principle has
little to do with and is far broader than its general equilibrium representation. The lesson to be drawn from Hahn's remarks is not the
illusory character of the spontaneous order principle, but rather the
intellectual aridity of the general equilibrium style of thought (Coddington 1975; Demsetz 1969).

The concept of spontaneous order has never dominated legal theorizing to the extent it once dominated economics. Even so staunch
an advocate of economic liberty as Jeremy Bentham thought of law
solely in terms of conscious design. Law, for Bentham, was "a command issuing from the requisite source" (Bentham 1973a, p. 155) or,
more specifically, "the will of the sovereign in a state" (Bentham
1973b, p. 157). In modern times the Benthamite banner was held,
although in far more sophisticated fashion, by the great legal realist
Roscoe Pound. Pound thought of law as an instrument for the satisfaction of specific human desires and for the rational balancing of
those desires when they conflict. He believed that the instrumental
character of law could be more perfectly attained "if we have a clear
picture before us of what we are seeking to do and to what end" and

---

[3]Hahn is guilty of a logical error. The assumptions of the Arrow-Debreu construction
are merely sufficient conditions for an efficient allocation of resources (Hausman 1981,
p. 152). The absence of these conditions does not imply inefficient resource allocation.

insofar "as we consciously build and shape the law" (Pound 1954, p. 45). Pound saw the entire history of law as a gradual unfolding of this vision (p. 47):

> For present purposes I am content to see in legal history the record of a continually wider recognizing and satisfying of human wants or claims or desires through social control: a more embracing and more effective securing of social interests; a continually more complete and effective elimination of waste and precluding of friction in human enjoyment of the goods of existence—in short, a continually more efficacious social engineering.

F. A. Hayek, on the other hand, has seen the development of the law as a manifestation of spontaneous ordering forces. For Hayek the idea of consciously building and shaping law completely misconstrues the nature of the common law process (however accurately it may describe administrative law). The common law is a system that is grown or evolved, not a system that is made. It is an order quite unlike the changeless equilibrium of Arrow and Debreu or the system of conscious compromises produced by Pound's realist judges. The common law is a dynamic order that allows for and even promotes change. It is also an abstract order that is unbound by the specific value hierarchies or compromises of its judges. The purpose of the law is to promote "that abstract order of the whole which does not aim at the achievement of known particular results but is preserved as a means for assisting in the pursuit of a great variety of individual purposes" (Hayek 1976, p. 5).

Hayek applies the principle of spontaneous order to the legal system in two different but interrelated ways. First, he uses it to explain the function of a pure common law system; second, he uses it to elucidate the process by which that system grows or adapts to change. There is thus both a functional and dynamic aspect to Hayek's theory, and each aspect is necessary for understanding his concept of a legal rule. These aspects of the spontaneous order approach are explored in the following two sections.

III. Function of the Common Law

Authority and Legitimacy of the Common Law

Hayek's fundamental model of the common law is one of purely private rule creation. The law and the courts are not creations of the sovereign but rather are evolved institutions within which all individuals, including the sovereign, must operate. The common law antedates legislation, and it draws on preexisting implicit societal rules or customs, as well as on previous judicial decisions (Hayek

1973, p. 72). It is by deference to this preexisting opinion that the common law judge can lay claim to authority and legitimacy. People respect his judgments because, in part, they see in those judgments the crystallization of commonly held moral views.

The legitimacy of the law is also enhanced by the abstract character of the rules that the judges draw upon and that is manifest in their opinions. A defendant is not subject to a particular judgment because of his personality or individual circumstances, but because his conduct belongs to a certain general class that is deemed legally relevant. Jones, for example, may be prima facie liable to Smith for the latter's injuries because Jones hit Smith, and thus his behavior is subsumed into a general class of causal relationships, A hit B (Epstein 1973, pp. 166–71). All who act in this way—not only Jones—are subject to liability. On the basis of their perception of the general rule, people grow to expect a certain outcome in a particular class of cases. These expectations are then reinforced by the continual application and reinforcement of the rule in future cases (Hayek 1973, p. 98).

Nature of the Order

Because the common law is abstract (that is, in all cases of a given type, independent of particulars, a certain consequence follows), it gives rise to expectations that are similarly abstract. Suppose we say that valid contracts require consideration. This rule does not assist us in predicting the specific content of future contractual relationships. It does, however, help us in forming reasonable expectations about the overall character of these relationships. By voluntarily complying or failing to comply with this and other contractual rules, an individual can widen or narrow the range of his protected domain. Inasmuch as he validly contracts, his claims on others become, as it were, an extended "property right" (just as their claims on him become part of their extended property rights).

The order thus engendered by common law rules is an abstract order, one in which only general features of individual interaction are constant through time. The abstract order of expectations consequently enhances, but does not guarantee, the coordination of individual plans. Or, to put matters another way, the order coordinates the *pattern* of plans and activities, rather than the particulars of those plans and activities (O'Driscoll and Rizzo 1985, chap. 5).

An abstract order ensures certain expectations, but permits others to be disappointed. Individuals may (forward) contract today for 1986 soybeans in the hope that the spot price at that future time will be higher than the contract price. The common law does not seek to ensure anyone's expectations about the future price of soybeans.

"The task of rules of just conduct can . . . only be to tell people which expectations they can count on and which not" (Hayek 1973, p. 102).

Even if it were in some sense desirable to ensure all expectations, it would be impossible to do so. The necessary condition for the fulfillment of some expectations is the disappointment of others (Hayek 1973, p. 103). For example, we could not be continually supplied with the products we want (and expect) if producers refused or could not change their behavior in the light of new circumstances. It might even be physically impossible for them to continue as before if resource constraints significantly change. Paradoxically, change of the particulars within an abstract order is vital to the maintenance of that order. "It will only be through unforeseeable changes in the particulars that a high degree of predictability of the overall results can be achieved" (Hayek 1973, p. 104). For Hayek, then, uncertainty with respect to certain features of our environment is necessary for certainty with respect to other features.

The most we can expect from a system of abstract rules is that, on balance, individuals will be able to pursue their own purposes more effectively within the system than outside of it. The role of the common law, therefore, is not to enshrine any particular hierarchy of specific ends, but rather to "maximize the fulfillment of expectations as a whole," and thus to promote the achievement of as many individual ends as possible (Hayek 1973, p. 103).[4] The pure common law system is "purposeless" and does not seek to achieve specific social goals or to balance them when they are in conflict.

IV. The Common Law Process

Hayek has both a micro and macro analysis of the common law process. The macro story, based on a Darwinian survival mechanism, is not extremely relevant to understanding those aspects of legal rules in which we are interested, and so we do not pursue it here.[5] The micro story, on the other hand, does shed considerable light on our subject by elucidating the judicial decision-making or reasoning process that gives rise to common law rules.

---

[4]In the second volume of *Law, Legislation and Liberty* Hayek clarifies somewhat this idea of maximizing the fulfillment of expectations. "A policy making use of spontaneously ordering forces . . . must aim at increasing, for any person picked out at random, the prospects that the effect of all changes required by that order will be to increase his chances of attaining his ends" (Hayek 1976, p. 114).

[5]Hayek argues that a society based on a system of abstract rules will prosper relative to those societies that do not rely on such ordering mechanisms (Hayek 1979, pp. 153–76).

THE COMMON LAW

The process or, perhaps more exactly, the method of arriving at decisions in a common law system does not rest on deduction from a closed and limited set of explicit premises. It is based instead on "trained intuition" that draws on the unarticulated rules of society and adapts the reasoning and results of previous cases (Hayek 1973, pp. 116–17). The common law judge makes decisions in new cases on the basis of analogies with earlier cases (Levi 1949) and with simpler hypothetical situations in which there is a clear right answer.

The process of common law reasoning has important implications for the nature and function of the rules it generates. To see this clearly, it is useful to trace the evolution of rules in a specific area of law. One important area that is currently undergoing significant change is that of negligent infliction of emotional distress.[6]

The doctrine that originally prevailed in the 19th century was the "impact rule." To recover for his emotional distress, the plaintiff also had to be physically injured by the defendant. Without such physical impact, no recovery was allowed. In time the courts began to interpret the impact requirement more and more liberally. Eventually, even the slightest physical contact could be construed as sufficient to allow recovery for emotional distress. This loosening of the impact requirement transformed it into what many felt was a meaningless formality. Still worse was the apparent injustice of permitting recovery for emotional distress to one who had been simply scratched and denying such recovery to one who had narrowly escaped being killed by a truck.

Consequently the impact rule gave way to the "zone of the physical danger" doctrine. Under this approach, if the plaintiff had been in danger of physical injury, he could recover for his emotional distress even if he escaped actual physical harm. The logic of the new rule, however, seemed to be that only emotional distress arising out of fear for one's *own* safety could be compensable. Suppose, for example, the plaintiff had been in a situation where he narrowly escaped physical injury and, at the same time, saw his children physically injured. Could he recover for fear of his *children's* safety? By the strict logic of the zone rule, he could not. The courts were then faced with the impossible task of apportioning the plaintiff's distress between the two sources: fear for his own safety and fear for that of his children. Most courts, of course, never even tried to do this. As a consequence it began to appear rather awkward for plaintiffs, who were themselves in the zone of danger, to recover for their distress over the safety of

---

[6]For a survey of the development of the law in this area see Epstein, Gregory, and Kalven (1984, pp. 1049–83).

others, while plaintiffs not in personal danger could not recover. The distress was, after all, the same in both cases. Accordingly, some states (for example, California, Hawaii, and Massachusetts) shifted to a broader "bystander rule." Mothers, fathers, and possibly other close relatives could now recover for the emotional distress suffered upon seeing their child or relative physically injured in an accident. In California the bystander rule requires that the plaintiff contemporaneously observe the accident, be physically close to it, and be a close relative of the person injured. As should be apparent, this rule also contains the seeds of its further development. How should the courts decide, under the bystander rule, a case in which the mother of a child happens on the scene of an auto accident three minutes after her child is killed? The image of a mother seeing her child in a pool of blood may provide ample "justification" for extending the rule to cases of "almost contemporaneous" observance.

Our story could go on, but doubtless the reader can now imagine possible extensions himself. The important point to appreciate is that analogous reasoning provides a dynamic whereby the law develops, changes, and adjusts. While the problem of recovery for emotional distress is extremely difficult and current developments may well be unfortunate, this brief doctrinal history is a vivid illustration of two important and related theoretical insights. The pure common law process is both incremental and purposeless. Observe that in none of the developments sketched above was there a sharp break with what had been the previous rule. The process of change is as close to a continuous development as one is likely to see in human affairs.

The purposelessness of the process, although somewhat more difficult to appreciate, is nonetheless the crucial element in our analysis. The current state of the law of emotional distress could not have been predicted or directed when the impact rule was the prevailing doctrine. There are two reasons for this (Hart 1977, p. 125). First, and primary, is the indeterminacy of judges' aims. Judges do not start out with a clear objective function to which they then fit the facts of each case. Instead, they reason by analogy or similarity with already decided cases. Second, due to our inability to predict future fact patterns, even if judges had tentative policy goals, they could not foresee the full consequences of any rule they might adopt. These consequences would obviously differ in different concrete situations and judges would be forced, at least in large part, to adhere to rules irrespective of their specific consequences in order to ensure the stability of the legal order. These two factors in effect guarantee that a common law system will tend to be dominated by what to outsiders must seem to be myopia. This "myopic" vision is really the working of the

THE COMMON LAW

spontaneous order principle and a manifestation of the purposeless of the common law.

V. Rules versus Balancing

The abstract character of the common law is intimately related to the tension between rule-oriented methods and cost-benefit or balancing methods of resolving disputes. The more abstract a legal order is, the more heavily it depends on rules. Recall that the function of an abstract order is to maximize the fulfillment of individual expectations and plans rather than to impose upon society a particular hierarchy of ends. When the legal system engages in the balancing of interests or, equivalently, of social costs and benefits, it produces at best a particularistic order that supplants the ends sought by individuals with the ends desired by the courts. Rules, on the other hand, enable the legal system to adopt a more neutral position on the pursuit of private interests.

The need for rules is predicated on our ignorance (Hayek 1976, pp. 8–11). A utilitarian or balancing framework would require us to trace the full effects of each (tentative) judicial decision, and then evaluate it against the particular utilitarian standard adopted. It is, however, no mean feat to determine these effects in view of the substantial information problems and uncertainties likely to face a court (Hayek 1976, pp. 19–20; Rizzo 1980a, 1980b). There also are substantial interactive effects among decisions and rules that are often impossible to discern. Rules must therefore be applied in particular cases regardless of the hypothesized or "guessed-at" consequences. The very unpredictability of these consequences requires adherence to the given rule (Hayek 1976, pp. 16–17). If the law cannot systematically achieve specific social goals, then the best it can do is provide a stable order in which individuals are free to pursue their own goals. The unpredictability of a rule's effects in a concrete situation is the price we must pay so as to achieve predictability of the abstract order.

Much of the above discussion of rules versus balancing is couched in stark terms of contrast. This is because we are comparing, as it were, the ideal typical rule with ideal typical balancing. Admittedly, real-world legal systems simply tend to move in the one direction or the other. All legal doctrines are an admixture of rules and balancing. Both ideal types cannot be achieved in practice for what are surprisingly the same reasons. A thoroughgoing cost-benefit approach to law is impossible because, as we have seen, we are not always able to determine adequately the consequences of specific judgments.

Similarly, an unflinching rule-oriented approach will inevitably break down because unfamiliar factual situations will make the meaning of any previously announced rule unclear. At the same time, attempts to apply a rule rigidly to novel situations may appear patently unjust from the perspective of the more basic implicit (or unarticulated) rules that guide society. Thus the critical question concerns the direction in which the system tends—either toward more rules or more balancing.

VI. Negligence: Rules and Balancing

In this section and the following section, an analysis of two alternative theories of tort liability is used to illustrate the difference between a rule-oriented system and a system that rests on interest balancing. In the present section the tension between rules and balancing within a theory of negligence is explored; in the next section the analysis is extended to encompass the role of rules in a system based on strict liability. The purpose in both sections is to clarify the precise nature of an abstract legal order and the kind of rules it generates.

Negligence Congealed into Rules[7]

At its core the concept of negligence in tort is far more compatible with the balancing approach to dispute settlement than with the rule-oriented approach. Nevertheless, the late 19th century and early 20th century law and legal theory struggled to put reins on negligence liability. While notions of "due care" or "the care undertaken by the reasonable man" invite the weighing of costs and benefits according to some social calculus, many theorists were prone to interpret these generalities in ways that minimized discretion. As Oliver Wendell Holmes recognized, when "the elements are few and permanent, an inclination has been shown to lay down a definite rule" (1963, p. 102). Under static conditions it is possible to interpret the due care standard in terms of simple rules of thumb. Thus what was formerly a factual matter of jury determination becomes, in effect, a matter of law or a legal rule. Henry Terry made the point succinctly: "[A]lthough negligence is . . . always in its own nature a question of fact, a number of positive rules of considerable generality have been evolved, that certain conduct in certain circumstances is or is not negligent per se . . . When one of these rules applies, the question of negligence is really one of law" (1915–16, p. 50). Illustrative of these rules is the

---

[7]This subsection and the following two subsections are strongly influenced by the work of G. E. White (1980).

exhortation to "stop, look, and listen" at railroad crossings. Failure to do so could easily be construed as "negligence per se." The acknowledged function of these evolved rules of negligence was to promote certainty in the legal order by reducing the case-by-case discretion of juries. "[T]he tendency of the law must always be to narrow the field of uncertainty" (Holmes 1963, p. 101).

In addition to rules of thumb for negligence determination, the turn of the century saw efforts aimed at developing rules of proximate causation. Subsequent to a showing that the defendant's conduct fell below the due care standard, it still remained to demonstrate that his negligence was the legal cause of the plaintiff's injuries. If the method by which causation was established left room for a substantial amount of discretion, then most of the certainty that had been won at the initial stage through the use of rules would be lost at the subsequent stage. Joseph Beale and others tried to extract from the common law decisions certain rules or patterns of causal reasoning so as to constrain the use of discretion in later cases (Beale 1919–20). Among Beale's rules for determining the proximate consequences of an act were:

> [A] direct result of an active force is always proximate [p. 644].
>
> Though there is an active force intervening after defendant's act, the result will nevertheless be proximate if the defendant's act actively caused the intervening force [p. 646].
>
> [W]here defendant's active force has come to rest in a position of apparent safety, the court will follow it no longer; if some new force later combines with this condition to create harm, the result is remote from defendant's act [p. 651].

Rules such as these in the form of a judge's instructions to the jury, it was supposed, could reduce the range of their discretion. "The law does not place in the hands of the jurors power to decide that the causal relation may be inferred from any state of facts whatever. . . . It is for the judge to say whether the jury *can* reasonably so find" (Smith 1911–12, p. 306).

Assumption of Risk

The rule of assumption of risk functioned to narrow still further the scope for discretion generated by negligence liability. A plaintiff who had voluntarily assumed the risk of the type of injury he actually suffered could not recover even from a negligent defendant. Under 19th century evidence law, the burden of proof was on the plaintiff to show that he had not assumed the risk of his own injury (Warren 1894–95, p. 461). If he were not able to meet this burden, he would be barred from bringing a suit based on the negligence of the defendant. In fact, under such circumstances, there can be no negligence on the part of the defendant: There is no duty of care owed to those who assume the risk of injury (Warren 1894–95, pp. 458–59).

The plaintiff's assumption of risk effectively barred recovery whether it was "reasonable" or "unreasonable." Unlike the defense of contributory negligence where the reasonableness of the plaintiff's conduct is crucial, assumption of risk is a strict rule (Epstein 1974, pp. 185–201). It does not require any balancing of the social costs and benefits of the plaintiff's activity. All that matters is whether the risk was knowingly encountered and assumed.

The assumption of risk rule, taken in conjunction with the allocation of the burden of proof to the plaintiff, completely eliminated the need for any balancing whatsoever in a significant number of negligence cases. The plaintiff's case for recovery could be extinguished without any serious determination of the defendant's negligence simply by the plaintiff's failure to prove that he had not assumed the risk. Thus it is quite likely that a coal miner, who presumptively knows the risks of his occupation, would be barred from seeking compensation for a "typical" mining accident. Similarly, the plaintiff who sees defendant's automobile precariously wobbling at the edge of a cliff and yet decides to have a picnic on the grass below would be unsuccessful in an attempt to recover if the car hit him. In both of those cases the issue would be settled without worrying about the reasonableness of either party's behavior.

The general and abstract character of a strictly applied assumption of risk rule was clearly seen by many legal theorists at the turn of the century. Francis Bohlen, for example, summarized the dominant view: Assumption of risk "is a terse expression of the individualistic tendency of the common law, which . . . regards freedom of individual action as the keystone of the whole structure. Each individual is left free to work out his own destinies [sic]; . . . the common law does not assume to protect him from the effects of his own personality and from the consequences of his voluntary actions or of his careless misconduct" (Bohlen 1906–7, p. 14). The rule of assumption of risk thus makes any view of the social value of the plaintiff's actions or goals completely irrelevant to the resolution of the dispute.

Particularistic Negligence

Rule-oriented negligence was based on an abstract universal conception of duty (White 1980, pp. 16–18; Terry 1915–16, p. 52). The duty of care owed by the reasonable man was, with few exceptions, to everyone in the community. Thus, the utility of the defendant's general class of conduct was balanced against the general class of harms it might cause, and not merely the particular harm it did cause. From this perspective, certain types of conduct could be viewed as negligent in a broad category of circumstances; it would be unnecessary to reconsider the negligence of these types of conduct in each and every set of circumstances in which they recurred. The rules of thumb discussed above are consequently intimately related to the abstract universal conception of negligence.

In more recent times, however, a particularistic concept of negligence has emerged. This has been fundamental to the breakdown of a rule-oriented approach. In *Palsgraf v. Long Island Rail Road*,[8] Cardozo applied particularistic negligence to what was to become one of the most discussed set of facts in modern legal history. Two men were late for a train and ran to catch it as it was leaving the station. The first reached the train with no mishap; the second, who was carrying a package, seemed as if he was going to miss it. At that point one guard on the train pulled him aboard, while another guard on the platform pushed him onto the train. In the process the package he was carrying became dislodged. Unbeknownst to the guards it contained fireworks, and exploded upon hitting the ground. The force of the explosion tipped over some scales at the other end of the platform, injuring Mrs. Palsgraf.

Cardozo focused on the defendant's conduct relative to the particular harm that occurred, the injury to Mrs. Palsgraf. The conduct of the defendant had to be balanced against the likelihood of harm to the plaintiff. Since the ex ante likelihood of injury to Mrs. Palsgraf was undoubtedly miniscule, Cardozo found no negligence *relative to her*. The abstract view of negligence, on the other hand, would balance the defendant's conduct against the likelihood of harms to all members of society. Thus, possible harm to the man carrying the package, other trainmen, and those in the immediate area, as well as persons standing in Mrs. Palsgraf's position, would be considered. Consequently the conduct would be found either negligent or not relative to a large number of possible harms. Hence such a determination could be applicable to possible future cases with similar fact patterns. To single out, as Cardozo did, the particular harm that did occur fragments the entire process of negligence determination. Now the question becomes the utility of the defendant's conduct relative to each harm that occurs, *taken separately*. The rule orientation that Holmes and others had hoped to inculcate in the law of negligence was seriously compromised.

[8] 248 N.Y. 339, 162 N.E. 99 (1928).

It is possible to preserve, at least formally, the abstract quality of negligence while undermining it through the doctrines of proximate causation. Consider the view, expounded by Arthur Goodhart, that liability for negligent acts should extend only to the foreseeable consequences of those acts (Goodhart 1931, p. 114). This idea accomplishes at the causation stage exactly what Cardozo's analysis accomplished at the duty stage. While the defendant might have violated a duty of care because of the general class of harms that could stem from his behavior, Goodhart's proximate cause doctrine would require a particularistic causal analysis. After establishing that the defendant had indeed been negligent (in the abstract universal sense), we would then proceed to determine whether the particular harm that occurred was foreseeable to the reasonable defendant. Since "foreseeability" generally refers not only to foresight but to a complete cost-benefit balancing, we are in effect balancing the utility of defendant's conduct against the prospect of a particular harm to a specific plaintiff (for example, Mrs. Palsgraf). Thus, by a circuitous route, we have returned to the particularistic concept of negligence.

The price of adopting this concept indirectly, however, is a loss of analytical coherence. What sense does it make to perform the cost-benefit balancing twice—once with respect to the general class of possible harms and then with respect to the specific harm alleged? (Hart and Honore 1959, pp. 234–48). Presumably the latter is contained in the former and is one of the reasons that the defendant's conduct was found negligent (if indeed it was). Nevertheless, the bifurcation of the balancing process clearly directs the analysis away from the overall potential consequences of an act to the specific, more nearly unique, consequences. The critical determination of liability turns on the foreseeability of those consequences.

Today, while many courts and tort theorists might refuse to go along with Cardozo's and Goodhart's formulations of particularistic negligence, they do accept their emphasis on the dominance of balancing considerations. Prosser and Keeton, for example, take a totally policy view of proximate causation, and hence, ultimately, of the entire law of negligence. "The real problem, and the one to which attention should be directed, would seem to be one of social policy: whether defendants in such cases should bear the heavy negligence losses of a complex civilization, rather than the individual plaintiff" (Prosser and Keeton 1984, p. 287). The solution to this problem, in their view, depends on such policy considerations as risk spreading, relative avoidance costs, and the desirability of promoting or retarding certain kinds of industrial development. The rules of proximate causation have all been tried and found wanting. "There is no substitute," we are told by Prosser (1953, p. 32), "for dealing with the *particular facts*" (emphasis added).

VII. Strict Liability as a System of Rules

While theorists and judges in the late 19th and early 20th centuries attempted to reduce the scope for discretion in negligence law, they were constrained in their efforts by the simple fact that negligence fundamentally involves the balancing of interests. Strict liability principles, on the other hand, fit far more naturally into a rule-oriented approach. These principles, long a fundamental part of the common law, have been developed into a general theory of tort liability by Richard Epstein (1973, 1974, 1975). His theory seeks to extract from the common law those traditions that are most consistent with rule-based protection of individual domains.

This brief discussion is not intended to constitute a comprehensive analysis of strict liability, but to merely demonstrate that, in its broad outlines, Epstein's system appears to be precisely the kind of rule-based abstract order about which Hayek has written.

Prima Facie Case

Under strict liability the plaintiff's prima facie case is established when he shows that the defendant has injured him in any of four patterns of causal relationship. These "causal paradigms" are (1) *A* hit *B*, (2) *A* frightened *B*, (3) *A* compelled *C* to hit *B*, and (4) *A* created a dangerous condition that resulted in harm to *B* (Epstein 1973). Unlike negligence, strict liability does not require implicit or explicit balancing in the prima facie case. The plaintiff is not claiming that, weighing the costs of avoidance against the likelihood of harm, the reasonable person would not have injured him. Instead he is merely asserting the fact of his injury at the "hands" of the defendant. The causal claims of the prima facie case function to protect, in a strict fashion, existing individual domains defined generally in terms of clear physical boundaries.

Causal Defenses

The causal paradigms that constitute plaintiff's case against the defendant can also be used as defenses against that case (Epstein 1974, pp. 174–85). The very strictness of the causal claims, prima facie, implies that these claims, when raised against the plaintiff, provide a sufficient answer. A causal defense means in effect that the plaintiff really injured himself.

Consider the following simple situation: (1) *A* hit *B* (prima facie case); (2) *B* compelled *A* to hit *B* (defense). The defense of compulsion, if proved, means simply that the plaintiff's own conduct compelled the blow. *A* was therefore merely an instrument of *B*'s injuring himself (Epstein 1974, pp. 174–75). Note that in both the prima facie case and defense no balancing of social costs and benefits takes place. There is simply a factual assertion of the defendant's invasion of the plaintiff's domain, answered by another factual assertion that the "invasion" was self-inflicted. The other causal paradigms also can be used in a similar way as defenses. Since the same underlying principle of strict defenses with no balancing is at work in these cases as well, the analysis is not pursued here.

Trespass as a Defense

There are also noncausal defenses under strict liability. One of them is assumption of risk in its strict form, unrelated to contributory negligence (discussed above in the analysis of a rule-oriented negligence system). The other noncausal defense is trespass (Epstein 1974, pp. 201–13). The ancient action of trespass functioned to protect the plaintiff's proprietary interests in his own body, his movable possessions, and his land. As such it was simply the corollary of individual autonomy. In a system of strict liability, trespass to land, for example, states a sufficient prima facie case. The plaintiff has a right to expect the defendant to keep off his land regardless of the costs of avoidance. Thus the trespass action is strict. Used as a defense it is an assertion of exclusive possession that shifts the risk of injury to the plaintiff.

Consider the following situation: (1) *A* created a dangerous condition that resulted in harm to *B* (prima facie case); (2) *B* trespassed on *A*'s land (defense). This defense is sufficient to overcome the prima facie allegation. Thus, if the crane on the defendant's land fell on the plaintiff as he trespassed, the latter's action for damages would fail. The plaintiff had no right, prima facie, to be on the defendant's land. Had he stayed off, there would have been no injury and hence no prima facie case at all. The trespass defense also is strict in the sense that the plaintiff's inability to stay off the land is an insufficient reply to the defense. An infant trespasser, for example, cannot successfully plead his diminished ability to avoid the defendant's land. In general the plaintiffs have no right to shift the burden of their problems or deficiencies to the defendant. While it may not be the "fault" of the infant that it trespassed, it is certainly not the "fault" of the defendant either.

The strict quality of the trespass defense means that there is no question of balancing the costs of trespass avoidance with those of greater safety precautions by the defendant. His property right does

THE COMMON LAW

not depend on whether he or the plaintiff were the "cheaper cost avoider" of the accident. Under strict liability principles, property rights are protected by rules and are not subject to the compromises of balancing considerations.

White (1980, p. 229) argues that Epstein's system implicitly introduces a form of balancing in the sense that, for example, the right to be free of trespass is accorded a higher status than the right to be free of the effects of the defendant's dangerous condition. Of course, all decision making involves the balancing or weighing of alternative courses of action; consequently, so long as there is any kind of dispute settlement, there will be weighing in this sense. This is not the sense, however, in which the term "balancing" is customarily used. Rather, the term is used to refer to two kinds of activity. First, there is the particularistic or case-by-case weighing of social costs and benefits, which is the essential thrust of the modern law of negligence. Second, even where there is an attempt to apply "rules," the balancing approach evaluates them by reference to specific (particularistic) social goals. Thus, the increasing tendency to impose liability on defendants in product cases has been interpreted as an attempt to achieve a greater degree of risk spreading (since manufacturers are assumed to pass liability costs on to all purchasers of the product). Rules in this area of law, such as defendant liability for "foreseeable misuse" of products, are therefore to be evaluated with respect to the risk-spreading goal. In other areas of law, however, there may be different goals and consequently different standards of evaluation. In all cases, then, balancing is a particularistic form of weighing because it often requires a case-by-case analysis of costs and benefits and because these costs and benefits are defined in terms of the pursuit of specific social goals.

The evolution of an order of priority among abstract rules is part of the overall process in which the rules themselves develop. In fact a rule is not fully defined unless its priority with respect to other rules is also determined. A rule is best viewed as a *complex* of pleadings and counterpleadings that ultimately establish a result. The system of law thus evolves as a whole in which the various parts interact with each other. Therefore, the order of priority among rules or pleadings, like the overall system itself, is not specific-goal directed; it is "purposeless." Judges do not know the particular outcomes produced by a given hierarchy of rules. All they know (and need to know) is that there is a *meta-rule* by which, for example, trespass is a sufficient defense to the allegation that the defendant created a dangerous condition that resulted in harm.

The function of a clearly defined priority of rules is identical to the function of the system itself. A complex of pleadings and counter-pleadings with no clear relationships in the form of an adequate prima facie case, sufficient defense, and sufficient reply to the defense, etc. would not produce an abstract order of expectations. Property owners, for example, would be unsure about whether trespassers could impose costs on them if something untoward were to happen on their land. The answer would all hinge on the outcome of a balancing endeavor. "The most frequent cause of uncertainty is probably that the order of rank of the different rules belonging to a system is only vaguely determined" (Hayek 1976, p. 24). In contrast, a system of strict liability implies a legal framework in which both the prima facie case and subsequent pleadings are all strict and accordingly largely free from the vagaries of cost-benefit balancing.

VIII. Common Law Process and Rules Revisited

Earlier in this paper it was argued that the pure common law process produces abstract rules that do not impose a particular hierarchy of ends on society, but simply facilitate the attainment of various individual ends. To some readers this may appear at odds with the recognition that contemporary doctrines in common law areas have been formulated increasingly in terms of interest balancing. The resolution of this paradox lies in understanding that we do not have a pure common law system. Indeed, as Hayek himself recognizes, it may be impossible to avoid certain legislative adjustments or "corrections" of evolved rules (Hayek 1973, pp. 88–89). Nevertheless, the degree to which the common law system is "contaminated" by outside influences is crucial to understanding the kinds of doctrines that have developed. While a detailed analysis of this issue is outside of the scope of this paper, it is important to at least mention a recent interesting, and probably correct, explanation of the change in the common law.

Ackerman (1984, pp. 9–18) argues that the rise of the administrative state in general and New Deal legislation in particular transformed a more nearly rule-based common law into one that became increasingly reliant on the balancing of social interests. Specific-goal-oriented legislation, passed in an ad hoc piecemeal fashion, destroyed the idea of law as a seamless web. Judges, lawyers, and litigants now had to be content with heterogeneous pockets of law with different, and frequently conflicting, policy goals. Indeed, many pieces of legislation were themselves each motivated by conflicting policies and so tradeoffs became a way of life. The growth of administrative agencies and of administrative law necessarily introduced a level of bureaucratic discretion that the law had not known before. This discretion is precisely in the form of balancing costs and benefits of one kind or another. That the legislature could delegate discretionary authority to various agencies means that, in a real sense, the agencies both interpret and "evolve" a type of law that is quite alien to the common law tradition. This tradition now found itself to be only one part of a triune legal system that also included heavy reliance on statutes and bureaucratic discretion.

Inevitably pressure mounted for a consistent mode of analysis in all three areas. Any legal system that continued to adhere to a rigidly dichotomized method of reasoning would, in the long run, incur the extremely heavy costs of increased complexity. There is little doubt that both the statutory/administrative and common law domains would have to interact because, while the law may not be a seamless web, society and the order of actions governed by law are so constituted. Consequently the balancing mode of reasoning and specific-goal orientation quickly rose to prominence in the "abstract common law."

IX. Concluding Remarks

In this paper it has been argued that it is possible to have a policy-neutral common law. This claim has been elucidated by contrasting rule-oriented and balancing approaches to law in the context of negligence and strict tort liability. Finally, it was suggested that the rise of the administrative state is at least partly responsible for the decline in legal rules.

References

Ackerman, B. A. *Reconstructing American Law*. Cambridge, Mass.: Harvard University Press, 1984.

Beale, J. H. "The Proximate Consequences of an Act." *Harvard Law Review* 33 (1919–20): 633–58.

Bentham, J. "What a Law Is." In *Bentham's Political Thought*. Edited by B. Parekh. New York: Barnes and Noble, 1973a.

Bentham, J. "Source of a Law." In *Bentham's Political Thought*. Edited by B. Parekh. New York: Barnes and Noble, 1973b.

Bohlen, F. "Voluntary Assumption of Risk I." *Harvard Law Review* 20 (1906–7): 14–34.

Coddington, A. "The Rationale of General Equilibrium Theory." *Economic Inquiry* 13 (December 1975): 539–58.

Demsetz, H. "Information and Efficiency: Another Viewpoint." *Journal of Law and Economics* 12 (April 1969): 1–22.

Epstein, R. A. "A Theory of Strict Liability." *Journal of Legal Studies* 2 (January 1973): 151–204.

Epstein, R. A. "Defenses and Subsequent Pleas in a System of Strict Liability." *Journal of Legal Studies* 3 (January 1974): 165–215.

Epstein, R. A. "Intentional Harms." *Journal of Legal Studies* 4 (June 1975): 391–442.

Epstein, R. A.; Gregory, C. O.; and Kalven, H. *Cases and Materials on Torts.* 4th ed. Boston, Mass.: Little, Brown and Company, 1984.

Goodhart, A. "The Palsgraf Case." In his *Essays in Jurisprudence and the Common Law*, pp. 129–50. Cambridge, England: Cambridge University Press, 1931.

Hahn, F. H. "The Winter of Our Discontent." *Economica* 40 (1973): 322–30.

Hart, H. L. A. *The Concept of Law.* 1961. Reprint. Oxford, England: Clarendon Press, 1977.

Hart, H. L. A., and Honore, A. M. *Causation in the Law.* Oxford, England: Clarendon Press, 1959.

Hausman, D. M. *Capital, Profits and Prices: An Essay in the Philosophy of Economics.* New York, N.Y.: Columbia University Press, 1981.

Hayek, F. A. *Law, Legislation and Liberty: Rules and Order.* Chicago, Ill.: University of Chicago Press, 1973.

Hayek, F. A. *Law, Legislation and Liberty: The Mirage of Social Justice.* Chicago, Ill.: University of Chicago Press, 1976.

Hayek, F. A. *Law, Legislation and Liberty: The Political Order of a Free People.* Chicago, Ill.: University of Chicago Press, 1979.

Holmes, O. W. *The Common Law.* 1881. Reprint. Edited by Mark DeWolfe Howe. Boston, Mass.: Little, Brown and Company, 1963.

Levi, E. H. *An Introduction to Legal Reasoning.* Chicago, Ill.: University of Chicago Press, 1949.

O'Driscoll, G. P., and Rizzo, M. J. *The Economics of Time and Ignorance.* Oxford, England: Basil Blackwell, 1985.

Pound, R. *An Introduction to the Philosophy of Law.* 1922. Reprint. New Haven, Conn.: Yale University Press, 1954.

Prosser, W. L. "Palsgraf Revisited." *Michigan Law Review* 52 (November 1953): 1–32.

Prosser, W. L. , and Keeton, W. P. *Prosser and Keeton on the Law of Torts.* St. Paul, Minn.: West Publishing Company, 1984.

Rizzo, M. J. "Law amid Flux: The Economics of Negligence and Strict Liability in Tort." *Journal of Legal Studies* 9 (March 1980a): 291–318.

Rizzo, M. J. "The Mirage of Efficiency." *Hofstra Law Review* 8 (Spring 1980b): 641–58.

Smith, J. "Legal Cause in Actions of Tort II." *Harvard Law Review* 25 (1911–12): 303–27.

Terry, H. "Negligence." *Harvard Law Review* 29 (1915–16): 40–54.

Warren, C. "Volenti Non Fit Injuria in Actions of Negligence." *Harvard Law Review* 8 (1894–95): 457–71.

White, G. E. *Tort Law in America: An Intellectual History.* New York: Oxford University Press, 1980.

Part II
Rules

[7]

NYU JOURNAL OF
LAW & LIBERTY

INTUITION, CUSTOM, AND PROTOCOL: HOW TO MAKE SOUND DECISIONS WITH LIMITED KNOWLEDGE

Richard A. Epstein

It is my very great pleasure to be asked on this occasion to deliver the first Friedrich von Hayek lecture at the New York University School of Law. One need look no further than NYU's new Journal of Law & Liberty to have some sense of the enduring influence that Hayek has had on the intellectual temper of modern times. It is no mean feat for a native Austrian to migrate to England and then to the United States, while composing along the way some of the most influential works of the twentieth century. Like so many individuals of enduring greatness, Hayek defied the usual conventions that separate one academic discipline from another. Trained as an economist, he gravitated away from technical subjects to the more ethereal realm of political theory. Moreover, his work in this area was tempered by a real appreciation for the power of legal institutions to shape human behavior. A cross between the economist, the philosopher, and the lawyer, he addressed a wide range of issues that escaped writers who were tightly bound to a single discipline. He is generally regarded as the single most

2   *NYU Journal of Law & Liberty*   [Vol. 2:1

important figure in the revival of classical liberalism in the twentieth century.[1]

    All the more remarkable, he did his best work by writing against the grain. At a time when central planning was regarded as the solution to the ills of a chaotic and disorganized market economy, Hayek marshaled his intellectual firepower to explain that the failures of central planning were not unfortunate lapses that could be cured by a more careful application of the socialist program.[2] He showed that the inability of any one person or bureau to assemble all information about everyone's (indeed anyone's) needs and desires doomed any system that relied primarily on the centralized distribution of goods and services to satisfy the full range of human needs.

    I think his vindication on this frontier marks the most positive portion of the Hayekian legacy, and it is surely enough for one lifetime. But the great political successes should not be allowed to conceal the other side of the story. If socialism is wrong, then how do we find out what kind of system should be put into place? How do we figure out what social norms should be, and how do we decide which of these—all, some, or none—should be converted into legal norms? In dealing with this question, Hayek showed great disdain for what he termed the "constructivist" fallacy, by which he meant the idea that scholars outside the social system are able to generate a grand theory that unifies all of social experience under a single tent.[3] Hayek was deeply suspicious of anyone's effort to formulate overarching principles that explained social life.

---

[1] For a full collection of his works, see *The Friedrich Hayek Scholars' Page*, http://www.hayekcenter.org/friedrichhayek/hayek.html (last visited Oct. 23, 2005).

[2] F. A. Hayek, *Socialist Calculation: The Competitive 'Solution,'* 7 ECONOMICA 125 (1940); F. A. Hayek, *The Use of Knowledge in Society*, 35 AM. ECON. REV. 519 (1945). The objects of his criticism were OSKAR LANGE & FRED M. TAYLOR, ON THE ECONOMIC THEORY OF SOCIALISM (Benjamin E. Lippincott ed., 1938) and HENRY D. DICKINSON, ECONOMICS OF SOCIALISM (1939); and, somewhat later, BARBARA WOOTTON, FREEDOM UNDER PLANNING (1945).

[3] 1 F. A. HAYEK, LAW, LEGISLATION AND LIBERTY 27 (1973).

Neither a libertarian nor utilitarian be was in one sense the guiding principle of his work.

Yet what is put in the place of the two political philosophies that, for all their failings, have done enormous amounts of good in organizing and taming social behavior? Hayek took refuge in what could be termed a theory of social evolution. He believed we come to a form of "spontaneous order" that leads us to the right social answers through the accumulation of a large number of trial and error decisions made by individuals on the ground. His major illustration was his (oversimplified) account of how the law merchant evolved over time and across cultures independent of formal legal intervention: it is for that reason that he chose the title "Reason and Evolution" for the first chapter of *Law, Legislation and Liberty*.[4] The law merchant (which he did not fully understand) was treated as an outgrowth of this spontaneous process and strong evidence of the evolution of legal norms prior to the intervention of the state.[5] Even on this point, he overstated the extent of decentralized development relative to judicial pronouncement, but the challenges that the law merchant poses to the usual dichotomy between positive and natural law is not the main focus of this talk. Rather my concerns travel along a different path. To what extent does this system of spontaneous order, achieved by evolutionary change, give a sensible account of legal and social institutions?

In order to attack that question, I would like to examine the three sorts of devices that could be used to set up rules and procedures under which individual and collective choices are made. My main focus is on the processes by which knowledge is acquired, which then leads to the further question of what legal rules best harness the knowledge so acquired. In answering this inquiry I do

---

[4] *Id.* at 8.

[5] For a recent symposium on this subject see Symposium, *The Empirical and Theoretical Underpinnings of the Law Merchant*, 5 CHI. J. INT'L L. 1 (2004) My contribution is Richard A. Epstein, *Reflections on the Historical Origins and Economic Structure of the Law Merchant*, 5 CHI. J. INT'L L. 1 (2004).

not think that we can come up with a univocal source for all decisions, so I will then distinguish three related ways of looking at knowledge: intuition, custom, and protocol.

To set the stage, let me adopt a form of indirect utilitarianism (which Hayek was loath to do) that helps us examine these methods of knowledge. One common view of utilitarianism is that it seeks to maximize net social benefits over social costs. Often utilitarian theorists take less care than they ought on the question of *whose* benefit or *whose* cost. But since in this context we are talking about broad rules of constant application, the distributional issue tends to drop out of the equation. All gains and losses are roughly proportional for individuals that operate behind some Rawlsian veil of ignorance (which is why that metaphor offers such a powerful heuristic). But the great insight is that the rules that work best by utilitarian standards do not have to be couched in utilitarian terms; nor do they have to be motivated by a conviction that they will maximize the greatest good of the greatest number. Rather, in many cases, these desirable social ends are best achieved by responses done for independent reasons at the micro level that generate beneficial results at the macro level. But by the same token, the path of aggregation is sufficiently perilous that we have to be cautious that these multiple processes will achieve that result.

So what key insight drives this form of indirect utilitarianism? I think that much of what is at stake here is captured in flawed but instructive form by Malcolm Gladwell's recent book *Blink: The Power of Thinking Without Thinking*,[6] whose major theme is that we are able to make accurate decisions, often in the blink of an eye, by systematically filtering out information that looks to be relevant but in fact generates more trouble than it is worth. Gladwell's basic insight is that we have limited capacities and are better off concentrating on key features that are capable of quick assessment than running on at great length, seeking to juggle lots of

---

[6] MALCOLM GLADWELL, BLINK: THE POWER OF THINKING WITHOUT THINKING (2005).

different observations into some grand whole. Although Gladwell never draws the connection, it should be obvious that his thesis is much like the Hayekian norm in which social evolution generates a spontaneous order without central planning.

The difficulty with this thesis, I think, is that it fails to observe the differences in the three terms that I placed in series in the title of the lecture: intuition, custom, and protocol. All of these embody the basic proposition that less is more in decision theory as in architecture. But they do so in different ways. No single approach that confuses each device with the other will do the job.

Intuition

The first of these elements is ordinary human intuition, which in many instances has played a powerful role in social theory. I will pass by any detailed discussion of the theory of self-evidence as it worked its way into the Declaration of Independence and note that the first half of the twentieth century witnessed the result of a strong theory of ethical intuitionism, associated with G.E. Moore[7] and W.D. Ross,[8] by which individuals were said to have certain "prima facie rights," chiefly to bodily integrity and the enforcement of promises. Modern utilitarians like to deride this low-tech theory and prefer to explain the emergence of these rules as an effective means to secure and promote social well-being. But the rational reconstruction does not explain clearly why these more primitive norms have such a powerful draw on the minds of ordinary people, most of whom find their quest for moral guidance frustrated by the more learned utilitarian reformulation. This point was brought home to me by an incident some years ago at a Liberty Fund Conference, where at lunch I waxed on about some functional explanation for a given social rule—it matters not which. My interlocutor was an English professor from Wofford College who confessed that he did not follow the fine points of the argument. But

---

[7] *See generally* G.E. MOORE, PRINCIPIA ETHICA (1903).

[8] *See generally* W.D. ROSS, THE RIGHT AND THE GOOD (1930).

6 *NYU Journal of Law & Liberty* [Vol. 2:1]

he said with complete confidence that he thought that a videotape of our conversation would allow him to secure my civil commitment in any state in the union. The jargon about social optimality fell on deaf ears.

It turns out, or so my friends in psychology say, that there is some reason to believe that most people exhibit a tone-deaf response to moral arguments that rely explicitly on generalized conceptions of social welfare. In this context I rely on an instructive review article by Jonathan Haidt.[9] Individuals have to make decisions all the time, and they could not wait for the formulation of expected utility theory to get on with the business of their lives in caves and other prehistoric conditions. They had huge numbers of interactions that they had to process, and they would not succeed in their own productive labor if they had to calculate expected utilities for each activity undertaken. So they had to develop and internalize some quick rules of thumb that would give them a leg up in the business of life. Perfection and refinement is not the goal in such a system. Passable reliability, better than random outcomes, is all that can be expected. If the psychologists are to be believed, ordinary people are hard-wired, so that they have strong predispositions that allow them not only to judge others, but also to restrain themselves. The natural lawyers took this same basic view of human behavior. Some of these thinkers clothed the natural set of dispositions in their divine origins and took the position that the utility of man's basic nature was evidence of the benevolence of divine creation. But that religious orientation was not part of the original Roman view on the subject, which was much more naturalistic in origin.[10] The basic model was that cooperative human behavior could not emerge in any social regime unless individuals had some bulwark against the relentless forces of Hobbesian self-interest. Any

---

[9] Jonathan Haidt, *The Emotional Dog and Its Rational Tail: A Social Intuitionist Approach to Moral Judgment*, 108 PSYCH. REV. 814 (2001). For my take on its implications for state of nature theory, see Richard A. Epstein, *The Theory and Practice of Self-Help*, 1 J. L., ECON. & POL'Y 1 (2005).

successful barrier against aggressive impulses could not depend on conscious decisions to adopt honorable behavior. Any such decisions could not withstand the temptation to which human beings are routinely subject. Basic behaviors have to be internalized, almost as a matter of stimulus and response, driven by deep hormonal instincts.[11] It was of course in tension with naked self-interest, and at times it would yield to desire. But that inborn instinct also allows individuals, chiefly through gossip, to articulate the relevant norms of behavior as they evaluate disputes that arise within their circle of friends and acquaintances. The social context is strong enough that they have to be able to persuade other individuals to go along with them. The relevant norms here do not kick in with the power of autonomic reactions, such as breathing, but their responses are highly structured nonetheless. The word "visceral" is a literal term in describing reactions to certain forms of improper conduct. Do it this way and you will have a knot in your gut, a pang of conscience, or whatever.

Just what were the dominant norms in cases of this sort? Jonathan Haidt summarizes them as follows. There is a norm of reciprocity, a norm of nonaggression, and a norm against disgust. These norms are not just philosophical abstractions, but are concrete guides to behavior as well.[12] For example, individuals who adopt the norm of reciprocity have to show trust toward other individuals. Similarly they have to be able to figure out, often in the blink of an eye, whether other people are worthy of their trust. Likewise, they learn to detect, and hence to avoid, individuals who exhibit aggressive or, broadly conceived, socially destructive

---

[10] See JUSTINIAN, INSTITUTES, bk. 1, tit. 1 (Peter Birks & Grant McLeod trans., Cornell Univ. Press 1987) (533).

[11] For a popular summary of modern research, see Robert Lee Hotz, *Anatomy of Give and Take*, L.A. TIMES, Mar. 18, 2005, at A1, describing experiments on trust in which the participants could not bring themselves to cheat on cooperation in the final round although it was in their narrow self-interest to do so.

[12] *See generally* Leda Cosmides & John Tooby, *Knowing Thyself: The Evolutionary Psychology of Moral Reasoning and Moral Sentiments, in* 4 BUSINESS, SCIENCE, AND ETHICS 91 (2004).

behavior. Stated more generally, individuals are in general drawn to others who do not violate these particular norms, which helped to establish the norms in small communities that had only the weakest centralized institutions associated with the Austinian vision of law as the command of the sovereign.

And how should we interpret these norms? As the foundation of much of the common law system of basic entitlements. It does not take a legal genius to see how the nonaggression principle morphs into the law of tort; how the reciprocity principle, down even to the doctrine of consideration, morphs into the law of contract; and how the norm against disgust evolves into the system of social prohibitions against various sexual and bodily practices, which bore a close relationship to procreation, on the one hand, and sexually transmitted diseases on the other.

There is little doubt in my mind that the nineteenth century political synthesis embraced all these norms, for the police power, as it was generally termed, made it clear that the state could regulate liberty (of contract) and property in the name of morals, a position that held firm until its reversal in the twentieth century and its revival in the twenty first[13] with the succession of states that have enacted bans of gay marriage. These norms have real clout and they fit into the system of strong intuitions. Let yourself imagine a situation in which there is a violation of one or another of these norms, and your hard-wires send off all sorts of alarms. The system of prima facie rights has a tight normative connection to the psychological underpinnings of human behavior.

And it is just here that some of the shortfalls of intuitionism assert themselves. The two most important have a close relationship

---

[13] For the traditional account, see ERNST FREUND, THE POLICE POWER (1904). For discussion, see WILLIAM NOVAK, THE PEOPLE'S WELFARE: LAW AND REGULATION IN NINETEENTH-CENTURY AMERICA (1996). For the modern view that gave sexual relationships the preferred position of "intimate associations," see Griswold v. Connecticut, 381 US 479 (1965); Lawrence v. Texas, 539 U.S. 558 (2003), *overruling* Bowers v. Hardwick, 478 U.S. 186 (1986).

with each other. The first of these asks this simple question: if we use the term "prima facie right" to account for these intuitive relationships, how then do we flesh out the rest of the picture? There are two difficulties here, each of which has been faced by every legal system from the Roman law to the present.[14] The first concerns the coverage of the basic prohibitions. Here are two obvious examples: does the prohibition against killing also extend to cases where someone lays traps for his victim, or sets poison in front of him? It seems clear to anyone who *reflects* about the issue that the original prohibition will lose much of its bite if these easy circumventions work. So the holes have to be plugged. But the question is, how far can one move from the original case before the analogies looked strained?

The second difficulty is every bit as great. One reason why we call the rights protected by these prohibitions prima facie rights is that on *reflection* it is clear that they are stated too broadly. All killings are not regarded as wrongful; some could be justified or excused by insanity or self-defense. And, therefore, any system has to ask how these corrections are worked into the basic pattern without undermining the force of the original prohibition altogether. Put these two points together and you have a hermeneutical project that required centuries of arduous labor to complete. But it is not just a coincidence that the inclination to undertake that kind of close examination of both text and structure is more a characteristic of ancient legal systems than of modern ones. They have fewer structural questions—infrastructure, interoperability, taxation—to worry about than we do. The corrective justice arguments that work so well in dealing with one-on-one cases often fall short when dealing with today's provision of public goods and organization of network industries.

---

[14] For the Roman approach, see the discussion of the Lex Aquilia in 1 JUSTINIAN, DIGEST, bk. IX, tit. 2 (Alan Watson ed. & trans., Univ. of Penn. Press 1998) (533); for my analysis, see generally Richard A. Epstein, *A Common Lawyer Looks at Constitutional Interpretation*, 72 B.U. L. REV. 699 (1992).

10   *NYU Journal of Law & Liberty*   [Vol. 2:1

Without question, the classical scholars did a superb job in executing their long-standing program of correcting and refining these basic moral intuitions. Anyone who teaches ancient legal subjects, as I do, is always impressed with the deft treatment of particular cases, and the slow and orderly development of the law. For example, the basic classifications in such areas as bailments or finders developed by the classical lawyers remain the accepted rules today. Modern scholars have little desire to undo the results of these earlier efforts. Yet at the same time, there is, in general, a deep suspicion that the classical lawyers did not supply a *justificatory* apparatus equal to its assigned task. At every critical juncture in the argument, we are told that natural reason or natural justice is the explanation for the decision at hand.[15] There is a clear sense in which these terms are intended to evoke some connection between the basic personality and temperament that nature endows in all human beings, for the biological element is certainly prominent in much of this early thought. Yet at the same time, there is little effort to explain how the preferred legal rules discharge their appropriate social function. The modern task of reinterpreting ancient legal rules is usually meant to supply, in anti-Hayekian style, some functional reason why the individual who takes first possession of some natural object becomes its owner. The various efforts to defend this rule sound very tinny all the way through Adam Smith, who envisioned the implied consent of mankind as the glue that holds us all together.[16] The effort failed because it takes categories that do have relevance—consent is a powerful source of contractual obligations—and uses them in a somewhat fictional sense to cover situations where consent is in principle needed but in practice not available.

The modern notion of social improvement, in the Paretian sense of the term, really took much longer to emerge, and was not clear until the late nineteenth or even mid-twentieth century. Once

---

[15] *See, e.g.*, JUSTINIAN, *supra* note 10.

[16] *See* ADAM SMITH, *Of Occupation, in* LECTURES ON JURISPRUDENCE 14 (R.L. Meek et al. eds., Oxford Univ. Press 1978) (1766).

developed, it then tended to reinforce the old rules in many of their key applications. At this point if we look back at our three fundamental norms, the first two have fairly clear content, but the last one is much more complex. The prohibition against aggression is meant to cut out those negative sum games; that is, those in which the gains on the one side are not large enough to compensate for the losses on the other. Stopping these cases is critical because there is no cure, no magic offset, in large numbers. The more these destructive cycles take place, the greater the cumulative losses. If A kills B, the situation is not set aright if C kills D by way of vengeance, inviting further retaliation. The utilitarian justifications for that prohibition are so strong under every conceivable variation of the theory that the legal rules and their endless refinements show little movement in the last 2,000 or so years. Even rule adaptations that are attributable to technical innovations—death by laser beam or nuclear attack—are analyzed under the traditional framework. The advantage of the utilitarian approach is that it gives some help in figuring out the various exceptions and how they should be interpreted. Self-defense, or the threat thereof, is a way to reduce the initial incidence of aggression. But it is itself subject to sufficient abuse that the terms and conditions under which it is allowed are heavily circumscribed, just as the traditional law had it.

Parallel problems of explication also arise with respect to the obligations of reciprocity. The attractiveness of that norm lies in the win/win situations that it produces. The difficulty with the norm lies in the two major adjustments needed to translate that intuition into a desirable social state. The first of these addresses the defects in the process of contract formation. If that is defective, then it undermines our confidence that the win/win condition will hold. The second relates to possible negative external effects that can dwarf the private gain to the contracting parties. This last point is worthy of at least one brief elaboration. Contracts *magnify* the ability of individuals to do what they want: after all, gains from trade just mean that the combined efforts of two individuals yield an outcome that is greater than the sum of their individual efforts. So, if the negative effects of certain conduct (e.g. murder) are large, then the contracts in service of that end will produce mutual gains to the transacting parties that will, regrettably, generate high social losses as well. Increasing the private gain simultaneously increases the social loss. For those contracts, we have negative words: combinations, conspiracies, trafficking, aiding, abetting, and the like. But notwithstanding these difficulties, the classical synthesis, which relied on working out the implications of the early intuitions, stands us in good stead today.

The last intuition on morals and distaste is in fact the hardest to harmonize with more modern functional norms. The fear of contagion, the inability to determine parentage, and the like did pose a serious threat to social organizations. Hence, there are a powerful set of taboos that grow up around some practices. Those taboos resonate powerfully today with some people, as with red-state opposition to gay marriage. But there is a second point of view which takes a more libertarian view of matters, and insists that all cases in this third category should be decomposed into cases that fall into either of the first two categories, so that gay marriage becomes in modern times a protected win/win transaction instead of an "offense against nature," which is the instructive early term. So intuition ends up as a guide through this moral thicket, useful but limited. And in modern thought it is more likely to be displaced as two features come together: first, as the factual patterns in particular cases move further away from those that generated our bedrock intuitions, and second, as we develop more powerful functional theories. The point here is not unfamiliar—intuitions yield to protocols in many areas of life.

Custom

Let me now move on to the second area of discussion, that of custom. There is little doubt that this particular element of the Hayekian synthesis played a very powerful role in early thought. The natural lawyers did not place all their eggs in a single basket that defended natural reason. They also placed great stock in the idea that the rules of nature were of broad application so that they could be found in virtually any society on the face of the globe.[17] The implication was that any rule that could survive in so many different circumstances had to have tapped a sensitive nerve. Survival, therefore, was a crude proxy for utility. It may not pick the best of all rules to govern any situation, but it will certainly rule out the worst. It is, moreover, for that reason that the customary norm appealed to Hayek. It did not offer the false optimism that perfect optimality is attainable in setting up social institutions. It did, however, set up the more modest and defensible claim that its decentralized tendencies, more often than not, lead toward some form of efficient solution. The point here was that individuals who did not understand the mechanisms of efficient market organization could stand aside, and in many cases watch, as the right solution unfolded before their eyes in specific contexts. That local excellence managed to persist in relative isolation even when other sectors of social life became highly dysfunctional. Custom was in effect an invisible hand that shepherded organizations through their rough spots.

There are, moreover, two particular contexts in which it played a large role. One is in setting out (customary) property rights. Here we cannot rely on ordinary two-party contracts because all property relationships take place between a given individual owner who has exclusive rights to possess, use, and dispose, and the rest of the world, which is duty-bound to forbear from interfering with these rights. Custom takes center stage because real contracts fail because it is not possible for large numbers of dispersed individuals to enter into voluntary contracts. Custom thus becomes the loose surrogate for contract in which others respect the rights of owners, and, by those nice hard-wired instincts, have a better than even chance that others will respect

---

[17] GAIUS, THE INSTITUTES OF GAIUS, bk. I, ¶ 1 (Francis de Zulueta trans., 1946) (170) ("[W]hat natural reason establishes among all men and is observed by all peoples alike, is called the Law of Nations, as being the law which all nations employ.").

their rights as well. Once one person takes possession of a thing, others tend to back off from challenging their supremacy.

Yet here too we have to be aware of the question of the just-so story about the smooth evolution of customary norms. We need to pay some attention to several difficulties with the great weight we place on custom. The first is that frequently, discontinuous changes with respect to the external environment make it impossible to rely on any incremental system to achieve collective well-being. That is in one sense the moral of Harold Demsetz's account of the switch in property rights among the Indian tribes in Quebec.[18] The huge external demands required that the hunters back off the first possession rule that was long sanctioned by common practice, and adopt a system of territories in order to deal with the problem of over-consumption. It is quite correct to think that non-government groups can respond to these changes in at least some circumstances. It is wrong to assume that they respond to them by speeding up the process of incremental change. In most cases, some coercive action by tribe or by state is needed to work the shift. Whether we speak of the change in property regimes in the Demsetz setting, or the highly divisive situation of the English enclosure, it behooves us to remember that the transitions in question are often bloody, and sometimes bloody-minded. And most importantly, one byproduct of these transitions is massive wealth shifts that provoke intense political outcry, precisely because no one is able to either compute the needed side payments or secure the political will to make the transfers. The role of custom in the generation of property rights is important, but it is no panacea. At some point, collective, purposive intervention has to take place. The sharp increase in demand for beaver pelts, for example, led to a centralized response to the common pool problem that the increased demand created. The Hayekian model is displaced by more systematic and centralized means, fraught with dangers as they are.

---

[18] Harold Demsetz, *Toward a Theory of Property Rights*, 57 AM. ECON. REV. 347 (1967).

The same drift can be seen in the law of contract, which has within it a strong customary base. In one sense, there is much to commend about customs: if there is a standard way in which traders do business, then it would be most unwise for an outsider to decree that other transactional modes are better for the welfare of the parties. The Hayekian point was that the outsider may not understand how the insiders work; yet the insider might not be able to explain his own conventions to the doubter who stands outside the system. One role of custom in contract is that it asks courts and other outsiders to defer to the explicit terms that insiders write into contracts for use for their own businesses. It is also said that custom is the preferred way to fill gaps within written contracts, which allows the participants to save time in drafting and negotiating by following these background norms. This last point is somewhat trickier than the former, because it is always an open question whether the gap-fillers that courts use are as uniform as a system of customary law presupposes. But here the argument is quite simply one of second best: there is no opposition to freedom of contract. There is only an effort to make do until some explicit written term emerges that obviates the need for the judicial inquiry. Customary practices are weak, but they are better than nothing, and certainly better than judicial efforts to construct from whole cloth a default efficient set of arrangements.

Custom therefore can be used in two senses: it can refer to the standard terms that are written into contracts or to the usual background terms that govern in the absence of explicit terms. But an appeal to custom in either of these two senses in discrete transactions overstates its power in the area of its greatest strength: commercial transactions. The most powerful evidence for this point is that the economic role of contracts is not fully understood when they are treated as dyadic arrangements that govern only the relationships of the immediate parties to them. That understanding will work for goods that are bought for consumption, but not for goods that are purchased to be resold, or for the currency that is used to purchase these goods, which is then reused by sellers when they enter the market as buyers. The entire system of trade depends critically on the ability to string transactions in cash and goods together, and this requires a degree of standardization to make discrete transactions interoperable, to use the modern phrase. That pressure toward standardization rears its head in both ancient and modern times. The ancient law had a wide range of contracts (e.g. mutuum) which presupposed a definition of *fungible* goods.[19] The introduction of any system of weights and measures, of cash, or the definition of a barrel or cartload requires some degree of standardization, which is exceedingly hard to obtain by the decentralized trial and error methods associated with custom. These standardized devices moreover are not collusive or anticompetitive. Rather, the ability to make efficient comparisons facilitates both monopoly and competition by making both forms of business more efficient than they would be in the absence of standardization.

More generally, we know that the cycle of standardization is much more complex than this Hayekian model presupposes. Nothing is more common in emerging industries with rapid technology change than to have individuals whose functions are to establish, first, "best practices" for certain kinds of common tasks, and, second, precise standards for communication between machines whose interoperability is essential to technical advances. The use of these institutions, which can create problems of their own, is meant to both build on and displace the customary process. The advantage of these standards organizations is that they are often funded and organized outside the earshot of the government, so the dominance of one single player is minimized.

Typically, such organizations favor a single open form of architecture, so that the new standard is best understood as a common highway to which all industry participants have equal

---

[19] The contract of mutuum is a loan for consumption that obligates the buyer to return the same type of good, without interest, that he borrowed. *See* GAIUS, *supra* note 17, bk. III, ¶ 90 (defining "mutuum").

access. There is in this context always the risk that individual participants in these industry meetings will take advantage of this collaborative process, for example, by steering the collective body toward a standard that requires people to use their own undisclosed patents.[20] Matters of this sort can precipitate major lawsuits. But the key point here is not to determine how to resolve the individual cases, but to note that the entire process of commerce generates, by conscious design, these second-order organizations that build the common platforms on which the primary activities take place. Hayek was right to see that nongovernmental bodies often take over and discharge standard-setting functions associated with the state. But he was wrong to think that social drift is the dominant force behind these forms of behavior. Conscious design figures much more centrally into standard-setting than his account would allow.

There is, moreover, good reason why in the end standard-setting has to take this form. Recall that the initial set of human intuitions that were hard-wired stressed the importance of reciprocity. That element remains central in understanding the role of standard-setting organizations. But the intuition at most explains why merchants, either in isolation or in firms, participate on a cooperative basis in these activities. But the intuition as to which bus, port, or wire to use in some modern computer setting does not come from nature. It comes from an intimate and detailed knowledge within the field, knowledge that is attained only after years of hands-on experience. So the older sources of information give out, and more rational methods have to be used to supplement and update what went before. Choosing the right people and the right institutional frame will have a large role to play.

Protocols

There is next the question of what kinds of standards and rules groups will adopt in particular institutional settings. And this

---

[20] *See* Rambus, Inc. v. Infineon Techs. AG, 318 F.3d 1081, 1085 (Fed. Cir. 2003).

Austrian Law and Economics II

question leads me back to a theme that I have stressed for so many years. The more complex the world, the simpler the rules needed for it to operate successfully. The increased size of an economy means people have to transact at low costs with strangers. The uniquely tailored arrangements that are suitable for family connections do not work in this context. People have to be able to come together in much the same fashion as electrical outlets. There is a standard form of connection, but the appliances that attach can differ widely. The outsider looks at the connection, and the insider adapts the functionality free from external complications.

Institutions therefore look very different on the ground from the way in which lawyers think about difficult cases that make it through the entire system for appellate resolution. The objective of sound management in all lines of business is to make sure that simple tasks are correctly discharged. These tasks are usually highly repetitive, and they must be done correctly for the business to function. Establishing the right protocols is critical for the work to go forward: unless the simple tasks are regimented, the more complex matters of design and judgment can never be addressed. There are protocols for computers, for medicine, for improvisation, credit-scoring,[21] and countless other areas. It is important in dealing with these protocols to see how they relate to the basic intuitions and customary rules that we have spoken of before. And they do have both critical similarities and differences.

The similarity goes to the way in which information is organized and presented. The word information literally means data points of one kind or another put "in formation" so that

---

[21] *Credit Scoring*, FTC Facts For Consumers: Focus on Credit (August 2005), *available at* http://www.ftc.gov/bcp/conline/pubs/credit/scoring.pdf ("Credit scoring is based on real data and statistics, so it usually is more reliable than subjective or judgmental methods. It treats all applicants objectively. Judgmental methods typically rely on criteria that are not systematically tested and can vary when applied by different individuals."). For discussion, see Wendy Edelberg, *Risk-based Pricing of Interest Rates in Household Loan Markets* (Dec. 5, 2003), *available at* http://www.federalreserve.gov/pubs/feds/2003/200362/200362pap.pdf.

patterns emerge that allow for their successful manipulation. The intuitionist program has as one of its key elements the belief that the amount of information that we have to collect from certain situations consists of a smaller set of data points than we might have thought. Protocols may be generated in a different fashion from intuition, given the hard work involved. But they rely on the same technique of paring down the information used in making particular decisions. The point of Hayek and the modern blink types is that too much information gets in the way of making sound decisions, so we strip out many bits of *relevant* information, and, by using less, we get more.

But the way in which that culling takes place differs radically by context. Thus we know for example that little or no instruction is needed to reinforce the norms of reciprocity and nonaggression. The great risk is that people will migrate away from these norms even after they have proven their value. But protocols are the antithesis of intuition in the mode of their formation and in the particular tasks that they address. They pick up where intuitions drop off, and they only work when they are followed slavishly. Protocols are the antithesis of discretion. Here are two definitions of the term protocol, one from computers and one from improvisation, which tell the same tale from the vantage points of very different disciplines. The computer-based account reads:

> An agreed-upon format for transmitting data between two devices. The protocol determines the following:
>
> - the type of error checking to be used;
>
> - data compression method, if any;
>
> - how the sending device will indicate that it has finished sending a message;
>
> - how the receiving device will indicate that it has received a message.

The commentary then continues: "There are a variety of standard protocols from which programmers can choose. Each has particular advantages and disadvantages; for example, some are simpler than others, some are more reliable, and some are faster."[22] Note that protocols that are machine-based can tolerate a greater level of complexity than those that are applied directly by human beings, where simplicity earns a higher premium.

Here is what is said about improvisation:

> Protocols—"long-established codes" determining "precedence and precisely correct procedure"—may seem antithetical to popular notions of improvised creativity. Interdisciplinary research into improvisation shows, however, that it typically occurs either within, or in close relation to, voluntary constraints. Pressing, for example, writes: "To achieve maximal fluency and coherence, improvisers, when they are not performing free (or 'absolute') improvisation, use a referent, a set of cognitive, perceptual, or emotional structures (constraints) that guide and aid in the production of musical materials." Attali writes extensively on the "codes" found in the production of music: "rules of arrangement and laws of succession" which provide "precise operationality"[23]

The critical point is that protocols and intuitions are generated by wholly different processes. Malcolm Gladwell's *Blink* presents an instructive example.[24] Gladwell describes the heroic efforts of Brendan Reilly of Cook County Hospital to implement

---

[22] Webopedia, *What Is a Protocol?*, http://www.webopedia.com/TERM/P/protocol.html (last visited Oct. 24, 2005). Note the accurate description of the trade-off between simplicity and reliability on the one hand, and sophistication and error on the other. The empirical observation is that there is no dominant solution to these questions, but that the presumption should be set in favor of simplicity and reliability.

[23] Marshall Soules, *Improvising Character Jazz, the Actor, and the Protocols of Improvisation*, http://www.mala.bc.ca/~soules/shepard/character.htm. (last visited Oct. 24, 2005).

[24] GLADWELL, *supra* note 6, at 125.

some simple protocols that Dr. Lee Goldman had developed for physicians to sort cases of potential coronary disease. The recounted story is, however, the antithesis of the *Blink* thesis that it is supposed to support. The difficulty in this particular area is that intuitions, even those that experienced physicians hone over years of practice, just do not do a very good job in sorting out the cases. The doctors involved made all sorts of leaps and relied on all sorts of hunches to make their choices. Goldblum and Reilly relied on a triage method developed only after "hundreds of cases" were fed into a computer, which led to a three-part algorithm that asked whether the pain felt by the patient counted as unstable angina, whether there was fluid in the patient's lungs, and whether the patient's systolic blood pressure was below 100. Ignore everything else, and just stick to the protocol, which was designed to eliminate intuitive judgments. Here was a case of not thinking, period. Empirical tests showed that Goldblum's algorithm triumphed "hands down" over the intuitions that it displaced. It did better in reducing false positives by not holding for special treatment patients who were not having a heart attack. It also excelled in predicting those who have heart attacks with an accuracy rate of 95 percent, as opposed to 75 to 89 percent by the old methods. That improvement is impressive in its own right, but it is all the more astounding when one considers that the doctors were able to achieve their high percentages under the intuitive method by heavily over-admitting patients. It is a matter of total dominance when one decision procedure simultaneously reduces both forms of error.

The emergence of this successful protocol supports the Hayekian view that a few simple factors are dispositive in complex situations. Simultaneously, it casts doubts on the ability of intuitions to work in difficult and complicated situations. The work to get the right three steps took years to accomplish, but the number of lives saved is very large. We need simple rules for a complex world, but we have to be sure that these rules are applied in discrete settings and that we have our attention fastened onto the right simple rules. Rules of thumb that work well at sea may not work well on land.

Legal Implications

The previous discussion of protocols did not deal with legal situations, where the usefulness of simple rules is always challenged by the need to successively *refine* the outcomes that these rules generate. It is therefore not appropriate to conclude that all legal rules, regardless of context, can be as simple as intuitions and protocols. But simplicity should often be preferred nonetheless, although practice usually runs the other way. Here the most obvious area in which to see the difficulty is the legal rules that purport to regulate the transmission of information by penalizing those who do not supply what is required. We have a broad law of misrepresentation and add to it a set of complex obligations for disclosure. These embrace a number of areas, of which it is useful to mention a few here: the duty to warn in product liability cases, duty to disclose in security cases, and duty to disclose in informed consent situations. The older law on this question was quite minimalist on required disclosures, and usually put some portion of the burden on the recipient of the information to make further inquiries if more information were required. But one tendency in modern law is to permit the compilation of long lists of material information, and then to consider presumptions that could be introduced to help the plaintiff over the hump of deciding whether the particular information that was not supplied would have made some difference in the plaintiff's choices. This view treats the information that is missing as more important than the large amounts of information that is available from all sources.

One case that merits some particular attention was the open-and-obvious rule, which held that, for example, machine tools that did not have guards may be dangerous but that disclosure rather than redesign or extensive warnings was sufficient.[25] The repudiation of that rule, which imposed a hard stop on liability in many cases, was paired with an understanding (which still holds today) that stringent liability is prima facie proper when concealed defects result in harm. The older open-and-obvious rule strongly applied to any situation where there was asymmetrical information; that is, the seller knew of some condition but the buyer did not. But most product cases do not involve intentional concealment, so here the strong liability for latent defects was justified on the ground that the seller had better ways to prevent or correct these. Yet the general protection against liability for open and obvious conditions allowed for a greater range of goods to be sold, some of which could in turn be subject to downstream adaptations by users, or in workplace settings, by their employers. It in effect put the decision on the party best able to prevent the harm in question. And it did not create any real incentive to corrupt the original manufacturing process, because the higher risk, if any, is known and will reduce the willingness to purchase.

The next generation of criticism questioned the belief that information transmission was the sole goal and argued that design changes should be imperative when warnings did not suffice. Harper and James, in a very influential passage, wrote shortly after *Campo*:

> The bottom does not logically drop out of a negligence case against the maker when it is shown that the purchaser knew of the dangerous condition. Thus if the

---

[25] *See, e.g.*, Campo v. Scofield, 95 N.E.2d 802, 804 (N.Y. 1950) ("If a manufacturer does everything necessary to make the machine function properly for the purpose for which it is designed, if the machine is without any latent defect, and if its functioning creates no danger or peril that is not known to the user, then the manufacturer has satisfied the law's demands. We have not yet reached the state where a manufacturer is under the duty of making a machine accident proof or foolproof. Just as the manufacturer is under no obligation, in order to guard against injury resulting from deterioration, to furnish a machine that will not wear out, so he is under no duty to guard against injury from a patent peril or from a source manifestly dangerous.") (citation omitted).

> product is a carrot-topping machine with exposed moving parts, or an electric clothes wringer dangerous to the limbs of the operator, and if it would be feasible for the maker of the product to install a guard or safety release, it should be a question for the jury whether reasonable care demanded such a precaution, though its absence is obvious. Surely reasonable men might find here a great danger, even to one who knew the condition and since it was so readily avoidable they might find the maker negligent.[26]

This argument influenced the New York Court of Appeals twenty-five years after *Campo* to jettison the open and obvious rule[27] in a decision that states the now-dominant position found in the Restatement (Third) of Torts: "The fact that a danger is open and obvious is relevant to the issue of defectiveness, but does not necessarily preclude a plaintiff from establishing that a reasonable alternative design should have been adopted that would have reduced or prevented injury to the plaintiff."[28]

Note here the new levels of complexity introduced into the situation which allow wiggle room, albeit less under the Restatement than under John Wade's well-known formulation that made liability turn on a long list of factors.[29] Now one has to ask

---

[26] 2 FOWLER HARPER & FLEMING JAMES, JR., THE LAW OF TORTS § 28.5 (1956).

[27] Micallef v. Miehle Co., 348 N.E.2d 571, 577 (1976) ("Apace with advanced technology, a relaxation of the *Campo* stringency is advisable. A casting of increased responsibility upon the manufacturer, who stands in a superior position to recognize and cure defects, for improper conduct in the placement of finished products into the channels of commerce furthers the public interest.").

[28] RESTATEMENT (THIRD) OF TORTS: PRODUCTS LIABILITY § 2, cmt. d (1998).

[29] John W. Wade, *On the Nature of Strict Tort Liability for Products*, 44 MISS. L.J. 825, 837–38 (1973) ("If there is agreement that the determination of whether a product is unreasonably dangerous, or is not duly safe, involves the necessary application of a standard, it will, like the determination of negligence or of strict liability for an abnormally dangerous activity, require the consideration and weighing of a number of factors. I offer here a revised list of factors which seem to me to be of significance in applying the standard:

(1) The usefulness and desirability of the product — its utility to the user and to the public as a whole.

about feasibility, which in turn requires a calculation of costs and benefits. Yet no awareness is shown that the same piece of equipment might be used in different ways for different jobs (as is common with many machine tools), so that customization at the buyer level will trade off safety and efficiency better than any one-size-fits-all solution that a manufacturer could design into the product before sale. Moreover, if the original manufacturer is the cheaper installer, then he could offer the original buyer a set of options, with downstream selection, wholly without legal intervention. Yet, once the new standard is in place, then the list of factors is essentially unbounded on either side. This is best captured by the complex formula offered in the Wade risk/utility test, which has exerted immense influence over judicial decisions, but its main consequence is to sharply limit the number of cases where a defendant can obtain summary judgment. The reliability and complexity tradeoffs that are apparent to designers of computer protocols are lost on judges, who see only one half of the problem at most. Yet in the end, the Wade position cannot be sustained because of the utter lack of guidance that it gives in any situation where there are countless permutations of the safety/effectiveness tradeoff.[30]

---

(2) The safety aspects of the product — the likelihood that it will cause injury, and the probable seriousness of the injury.

(3) The availability of a substitute product which would meet the same need and not be as unsafe.

(4) The manufacturer's ability to eliminate the unsafe character of the product without impairing its usefulness or making it too expensive to maintain its utility.

(5) The user's ability to avoid danger by the exercise of care in the use of the product.

(6) The user's anticipated awareness of the dangers inherent in the product and their availability, because of general public knowledge of the obvious condition of the product, or of the existence of suitable warnings or instructions.

(7) The feasibility, on the part of the manufacturer, of spreading the loss by setting the price of the product or carrying liability insurance.") (citations omitted).

[30] For my criticism, see Richard A. Epstein, *The Risks of Risk/Utility*, 48 OHIO ST. L.J. 469 (1987).

Hence, there is in many cases a creep back towards the older position in which the question of obviousness tends to loom quite large in the decision, even in courts that think it sensible to then ask the defendant to explain why leaving the obvious choice was the best design decision.[31] There is a huge reluctance to treat the decisions as something to be made privately, once the information transfer has been completed. The legal evolution on this question is marked by a collective failure of nerve, which hardly shows the inexorable movement of common law judges to ever more efficient liability rules. The hard open and obvious rule will make mistakes in some cases. The more fluid rules of reasonableness carry with them the illusion that all these errors can be avoided. There is, moreover, no question that if the subtler risk/utility analysis were flawlessly performed it would replicate the open and obvious test in many cases, and deviate from it in at most a few. But in real-world settings, reliability in the broad run of cases counts for far more than some hypothetical ability of a heavily nuanced rule to get all the cases right—a postulate that it is easy to state in theory but hard to generate in fact. Quite simply, we are better off with a simple rule that gets 90 percent of the cases right than with a more complex rule that aspires to get 100 percent of them right only to miss on more than 10 percent. There is no reason to favor expensive rules that yield weak results. I have no doubt that the logic of protocols works to support the traditional rule over its modern alternative.

The more general proposition that follows from this illustration is that the usual sophisticated modern rules in all areas of life tend to do badly over the broad run of cases relative to simpler and sensible rules. The literature on intuition, custom, and protocol is not meant to say that social cost/benefit calculations are illegitimate. It is only meant to say that the indirect utilitarian approach trumps the more conscious effort at multi-factor decision-making, whether by courts or administrative agencies. Hayek did

---

[31] Linegar v. Armour of America, Inc., 909 F.2d 1150 (8th Cir. 1990).

not coin the phrase "simple rules for a complex world," but his own thought, suitably refined, was one of the key factors that led me in that direction. We must always be aware of the limitations of intuitions, customs, and protocols. But by the same token, we should never lose sight of the huge benefits that they provide.

[8]

Rev Austrian Econ
DOI 10.1007/s11138-008-0064-2

The rules of abstraction

Douglas Glen Whitman

Abstract Friedrich Hayek's work on spontaneous order suggests that the emergence of a spontaneous order requires the existence of *abstract* rules of conduct. But how much abstraction is required? Abstraction exists on a gradient, from the highest specificity (pertaining to particular persons and narrowly defined circumstances) to the highest generality (pertaining to all persons in all circumstances). If rules create order by coordinating expectations, either end of the spectrum is undesirable; the most specific and the most abstract rules fail to provide decision makers with useful guidance. This article argues that rules that foster coordination must be characterized by an *intermediate* degree of abstraction. This conclusion will be explained and applied to law, language, and etiquette in order to draw out the similar character of rules across various contexts. The article concludes by discussing four properties that rules of intermediate abstraction must also possess to foster spontaneous order.

Keywords Abstraction · Spontaneous order · Rules · Law · Language · Etiquette

JEL codes B53 · K0 · Z1

Friedrich Hayek's work on spontaneous order, particularly in *The Constitution of Liberty* (1960) and *Law, Legislation and Liberty, Volume 1: Rules and Order* (1973), emphasizes the crucial role of abstract rules of conduct in creating the conditions for such an order. Although Hayek focuses mostly on legal rules that create fertile ground for the emergence of a market economy, he strongly implies that abstract rules are a key ingredient of *any* spontaneous order. He specifically cites language, manners, and morals as areas in which people learn, often unconsciously, an abstract set of rules that guide their behavior (1973, p. 19).

D. G. Whitman (✉)
Department of Economics, California State University, 18111 Nordhoff St., Northridge,
Northridge, CA 91330-8374, USA
e-mail: glen.whitman@gmail.com

But what sort of abstraction is required? How abstract must a rule be to satisfy Hayek's criterion? Is abstractness a necessary or sufficient condition for rules to foster a spontaneous order? And if abstractness is not sufficient, then what other conditions must the rules satisfy?

In this article, I hope to offer a partial answer to these questions. Hayek's work offers numerous hints about the properties of the abstract rules of a spontaneous order, but the hints are scattered. Moreover, in the passages where Hayek is clearest about the necessary properties of rules, he is usually addressing the specific case of law—and not just any law, but the kind of law that creates a free society.[1] My goal here is to extract from Hayek's work the characteristics of abstract rules that facilitate any kind of spontaneous order. To do so, I will need to draw on orders other than law and markets, especially etiquette and language.

The primary insight that emerges is the notion of an *intermediate degree of abstraction*. It is not enough for rules to be abstract, for they must have *neither too little abstraction nor too much*. In much of his work, Hayek is concerned with countering the modern movement toward command-and-control regulatory systems, which often err in the direction of too little abstraction. "The nature of these abstract rules that we call 'laws' in the strict sense," Hayek says, "is best shown by contrasting them with specific and particular commands" (1960, p. 149). He therefore places great emphasis on the need for high-level abstraction; for instance, he says that law in its ideal form "is directed to unknown people and…is *abstracted from all particular circumstances of time and place* and refers only to such conditions as may occur *anywhere and at any time*" (1960, p. 150; emphasis added). The possibility of excessive abstraction gets little attention, although in some passages, Hayek does seem to recognize its importance by implication.[2]

The problem of too much abstraction is just as serious as that of too little, I will argue, because it is in many respects *the same problem*: both extremes offer decision makers too little guidance about how they should act. If abstractness exists on a spectrum from total specificity to total abstraction, then the ends of the spectrum share similar problems, and the "sweet spot" for abstract rules lies somewhere in the center. In fact, an intermediate degree of abstraction seems to be a characteristic of *most* entities that go by the name of "rules," whether or not they encourage the growth of a spontaneous order.

The purpose of this article was to explore the relationship between abstraction and the rules that foster spontaneous order. Part 1 of this article will explain the principle of intermediate abstraction in rules. Part 2 will apply that principle to law and language. Finally, part 3 will examine four additional features that (intermediately) abstract rules for a spontaneous order must satisfy: purpose independence,

---

[1] For instance: "There is only one such principle that can preserve a free society: namely, the strict prevention of coercion except in the enforcement of general abstract rules equally applicable to all" (Hayek 1960, p. 284).

[2] For instance: "Such rules, presumed to have guided expectations in many similar situations in the past, must be abstract in the sense of referring to a limited number of relevant circumstances…" (Hayek 1973, p. 86). That the rules must refer to a *limited* number of circumstances—neither referencing every particular circumstance nor abstracting from all circumstances—seems to indicate that abstraction must be intermediate in character.

extensibility to novel cases, tolerance for small deviations, and openness to the generation of new rules.

1 Intermediate degree of abstraction

1.1 Simple illustrations of the principle

One simple illustration of intermediate abstraction can be found in the rules of etiquette at the dinner table. One rule is to say "Please" when requesting a service from someone, such as handing you the butter; another is to say "Thank you" after a service has been performed; another is to keep your mouth shut while chewing; and so on. Now, imagine if we replaced all these rules with a single, highly abstract directive: "Be polite." That directive would not provide much useful guidance. Lacking more information, the decision maker would have to decide for each and every table interaction what would be the "polite" thing to do.

On the other hand, what if we had a different prescription for every possible table interaction? One directive for when someone passes the butter, another for when someone passes the salt, another for when someone serves food onto your plate, and so on. The decision maker's problem would be very similar to that which he encountered under the abstract "Be polite" rule. Any time he encountered a novel situation—and arguably, every situation is novel in at least some infinitesimal degree[3]—he would have to decide the correct action, without much assurance that it is correct (would it be okay for him to use the passing-the-butter response the first time someone passed him I-Can't-Believe-It's-Not-Butter?).

So far, we have only discussed dinner table etiquette. But we could imagine the highly abstract rule (Be polite) being applied to all types of interactions, from proper treatment of the opposite sex to proper behavior in an elevator. Or we could imagine having a different highly specific rule of etiquette for each and every different activity or interaction, however minutely defined. But we have neither of these. The actual rules of etiquette possess an intermediate degree of abstraction, neither so broad as to include all situations nor so narrow as to differ for each and every specific situation.[4] They identify abstractly defined types or kinds of situation.

The same analysis applies to legal rules. A rule of tort liability that said "Do the right thing" or "Be careful" would not be very helpful in guiding behavior, unless the decision maker had some strong notion of what other people think is right in more narrowly defined categories of situation. But if the categories were too narrow, depending too much on the particular characteristics of the particular situation, the decision maker's dilemma would be the same. A more useful rule of tort liability tells the decision maker how to act in situations with an intermediate degree of abstraction, e.g., "Always yield to cars already on the freeway when merging." This

---

[3] O'Driscoll and Rizzo (1996, pp. 61–62) argue that even if two situations are identical in all externally visible respects, they will still differ because the passage of time causes the memories and expectations that people bring to those situations to differ. However, this is a subset of the point I'm making here, which is simply that no two situations are exactly identical.

[4] There are exceptions, which will be discussed later.

rule picks out some relevant features of a situation (who is merging versus who is already on the freeway), while ignoring countless other features of the situation (relative speeds of the cars, types and models of cars, colors of cars, ages of drivers, number of occupants, ultimate destinations, and so on ad infinitum).

Actual tort law, and law generally, does rely on rules with an intermediate degree of abstraction. But there is a spectrum from perfect specificity to perfect abstraction, which means that intermediateness lacks clear boundaries. Although the law generally does not incorporate directives at either extreme, it does sometimes rely on modes of decision making that veer in one direction or the other. In the direction of highest specificity, we have case-by-case decision making: the notion that judges ought to consider the particulars of each case, decide based on those features, and refrain from drawing conclusions that stray too far from the particular facts before them. In the direction of highest abstraction, we have the ubiquitous standards of the common law—such as "reasonable man" tests, which direct judges and juries to decide a wide range of cases according to whatever factors would be relevant to a typical, decent person with rational faculties, and "balancing" rules, which ask judges and juries to decide based on an array of relevant factors without necessarily specifying the weight that should attach to each factor.

The virtues and demerits of such abstract decision making guidelines have been discussed extensively in the legal literature on rules-versus-standards, which will be addressed later. For now, it is worth noting that standard-based decision making and case-by-case decision making have much in common; arguably, they are the same thing. In order to make decisions on a case-by-case basis, decision makers are likely to appeal, at least implicitly, to broad principles in order to decide what is relevant and what is not. In order to apply standards, decision makers end up having to decide each individual case based on its particular merits. Moreover, both forms of decision making lack the certainty of rules with an intermediate degree of abstraction; this impedes the ability of agents subject to the law to know how to behave in their own situations. To predict the effect of either pure case-by-case or pure standard-based decision making, the agent must possess and process an untenable amount of information and predict the behavior of an untenable number of other agents. The informational burden and cognitive load are simply too great.

Examples aside, I will now attempt to lay out the general problem. Although the word "rules" is sometimes used broadly to refer to any kind of directive for decision making, or any regularity of behavior, it also has a less general connotation. Rules are *those directives that help people make decisions with some degree of certainty about which behaviors are acceptable (or expected) and which are not.* That is, the primary function of rules is to lend predictability to one's own choices as well as the choices of others (including their responses to one's own choices).[5] Predictability results from a reduction in the amount of information individuals must collect and

---

[5] Roger Koppl (2002, p. 533) adopts a similar notion of ruleness: "The object [such as an agent] follows a rule if its behavior exhibits invariance across some states but variance across others. It follows a rule if only a subset of variables determining the larger system influence the behavior of the object. The rule-bound object processes less information than it otherwise would. Similarly, the observer needs to process less information than the object unbound by any rule." In other words, rule-governed behavior responds to some *but not all* aspects of the environment, thereby minimizing information costs.

process, and it is desirable because it enhances individuals' ability to make plans and to coordinate with each other.[6] This does not mean that predictability is the *only* function or value that rules serve. Rather, what distinguishes rules from *other kinds of directives*, such as case-by-case or standard-based decision making, is their effect on predictability.

This predictability—which is, of course, never perfect—is achieved by attaching specific outcomes or behaviors to *classes* of situations. The breadth of these classes corresponds to the degree of abstraction of the rules. If the classes are defined very narrowly, the rules lose some of their rule-like quality because of the difficulty of discerning which class includes one's own situation. When class definitions depend on a virtually infinite number of characteristics of a situation, the human mind may fail to grasp them all. Some of the characteristics might be difficult to measure, and others might simply be forgotten or not conceived in the first place. As a result, the decision maker faces greater uncertainty when assessing the acceptability of his actions and in projecting their likely results. In addition, other agents will face greater uncertainty about how the decision makers will act (for instance, potential litigants will find it harder to predict both each other's actions and judges' actions).

Virtually the same problem emerges if the classes are defined too broadly; again, the rules start to lose their rule-like quality. This occurs because very broadly defined classes generally correspond to broader sets of possible outcomes in order to allow a better match between outcomes and the particular features of the situation (the possibility of very broad classes corresponding to narrow outcome sets will be considered later). Here, the decision maker has little difficulty discerning the class into which his situation falls, but he still faces a knowledge problem: he does not know exactly how the general principles will govern in his case. He does not know which factors will be deemed relevant, and he does not know the precise values to be attached to these factors. In short, the decision maker still faces great uncertainty in determining the acceptability or likely outcome of his decisions.

Figure 1, below, depicts the emerging relationship between abstraction and "ruleness," where ruleness refers to the quality of directives that guide behavior by reducing uncertainty of application. The straight line shows increasing ruleness (from left to right). The circular curve shows increasing abstraction (in a clockwise direction); the endpoints of extreme specificity and extreme abstraction approach each other.[7] Those directives which are most rule-like will generally display an intermediate degree of abstraction, as shown at the right edge of the abstraction curve.

Figure 2 illustrates three different degrees of abstraction. The left panel is characterized by a very low level of abstraction (innumerable distinctions being

---

[6] There is a close affinity between my approach here and Heiner's (1983) model in which regularity of behavior (and thus predictability) is a means of coping with a gap between the competence of the decision maker and the difficulty of the decision problem (the "C–D gap"). In Heiner's approach, a larger C–D gap corresponds to greater uncertainty. Both case-by-case and standard-based decision making would tend to increase the difficulty of the decision problem.

[7] An alternative figure showing the same relationship would place abstraction on the horizontal axis, ruleness on the vertical axis. The relationship would then take the form of an upside-down U-shaped curve. I have chosen the circular representation to emphasize the similarity of extreme specificity and extreme abstraction.

🍂 Springer

26   D.G. Whitman

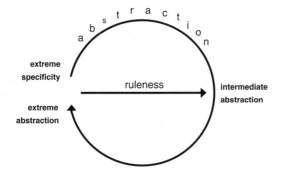

Fig. 1 Abstraction and Ruleness.

made among cases), the right panel a very high level of abstraction (no distinctions made among cases), and the middle panel an intermediate level of abstraction (a few distinctions made among cases). The spaces between lines can be understood as the classes defined by rules. The uncertainty generated by a proliferation of low-abstraction rules corresponds to the difficulty of determining which space one's own case falls into; there are so many spaces, delimited by so many relevant factors, that it becomes difficult to distinguish one space from another—and therefore difficult to determine the acceptability of one's decision. That source of uncertainty does not exist in the case of extreme abstraction, but it is replaced by something very similar: although you know what class your case falls into (because there is only one), that is not sufficient to determine acceptability of your decision, as cases within this large class are treated differently based on all conceivably relevant factors.

1.2 Why we rely on abstraction

The reason why most rules worthy of the name rely on intermediate abstraction is closely related to the reason why we use abstraction in general. Abstraction is a device that allows our minds to cope with literally limitless amounts of information. As Hayek puts it, "[A]bstract concepts are a means to cope with the complexity of

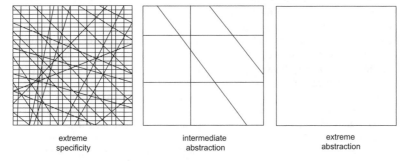

Fig. 2 Degrees of Abstraction.

the concrete which our mind is not fully capable of mastering" (1973, p. 29). We deal with that complexity by filtering it, deeming some features relevant while ignoring others. Hayek again: "We never act, and could never act, in full consideration of all the facts of a particular situation, but always by singling out as relevant only some aspects of it..." (1973, p. 30). The more we abstract, the more features we choose to ignore in order to focus attention on the remaining features deemed relevant. But there is a limit to the usefulness of the process because at some point, abstracting further means excluding some features that could be important for some purposes. Indeed, this is true even at the lowest level of abstraction, but the steepness of the trade-off increases as the level of abstraction rises. Statements at the highest level of abstraction will often have a tautological or vacuous character, as they no longer allow us to make useful distinctions.

Consider, for example, the use of abstraction in social scientific modeling. Koppl and Whitman (2004), drawing on the ideal-type analysis of Schutz (1932), observe that models of human behavior can be placed on a spectrum of "anonymity." A model with low anonymity makes very specific assumptions about the characteristics of the people modeled; the least anonymous model would attempt to predict the behavior of just one person—say, Napoleon (Koppl and Whitman 2004, p. 302). A model with very high anonymity makes very generic assumptions about people's characteristics; the most anonymous model would only make assumptions literally true of every single human being. An example of a highly anonymous ideal type would be Ludwig von Mises's model of a human being as someone who acts "to substitute a more satisfactory for a less satisfactory state of affairs" (Mises 1949, p. 13, cited in Koppl and Whitman 2004, p. 304). The analogy to the level of abstraction in rules should be clear: highly specific ideal types are analogous to highly specific directives, highly anonymous ideal types to highly abstract directives. And it turns out that the advantages of rules with an intermediate degree of abstraction correspond to the advantages of ideal types with an intermediate degree of anonymity.

The use of ideal types allows us to make predictions about entire groups or classes of people, economizing on mental effort. But there is a precision-versus-accuracy trade-off involved in moving to higher levels of abstraction; as our models become more abstract, the kind of things we can say about any abstractly defined group become less precise (Koppl and Whitman 2004, p. 305). In the extreme, we can abstract so much that we can say almost nothing at all. The Napoleon ideal type is not useful for predicting the behavior of anyone but Napoleon. The Misesian ideal type is not useful for predicting much behavior at all, except in the very broadest of terms, without filling in more specific details about the type of people whose behavior we wish to predict (e.g., that they prefer leisure to work, that they discount the future, etc.). The highly specific end of the spectrum is all precision, no accuracy; the highly abstract end is all accuracy, no precision. But these turn out to be very similar! If your point is to be able to say something useful, to make a prediction about behavior, then both have the same problem. The highly abstract end of the spectrum requires us to get more information to make a sufficiently precise statement. The highly specific end also requires us to get more information to determine which model to use—Napoleon or Idi Amin or George W. Bush? So the most useful social scientific models will be those in the intermediate range (although more and less anonymous models will be useful for some purposes). By settling on models with intermediate levels of anonymity, we can be reasonably (though not perfectly) confident about which ideal type applies in understanding any given social situation.

Rules with intermediate abstraction provide an analogous benefit. Adopting rules that abstract from specifics and focus on a few relevant factors allows us to make predictions for entire groups and classes. For those classes, we can make reasonably confident predictions about "correct" behavior. But if the rules become too abstract, the classes become larger, and we become less confident about our ability to determine "correctness" for any given member of a class.

Why, if rules with an intermediate degree of abstraction have the advantages I have stated, are such rules occasionally displaced by either more abstract or more specific directives? This question is best answered by reference to examples from law, language, and etiquette. But first, we need some additional terminology.

1.3 Input sets and output sets

As noted earlier, we can imagine a very abstract rule whose effects are nonetheless easy to predict. If every case within the entire class will be treated *exactly* the same way, then the breadth of the class poses no problem at all. It is easy to determine what class one's case falls in, and it is easy to predict the outcome. In writing, an example of this kind of rule would be, "Always end a sentence with a period." The rule would be clear and easy to apply. Of course, it would also rule out the use of question marks and exclamation points. But there would be little or no problem of uncertainty. In tort law, an example would be, "The plaintiff shall always win and receive damages in the amount of $1 million." This rule might produce all sorts of problems, but it would be highly predictable in its application. So there is no *necessary* connection between high-level abstraction and uncertainty. I will argue, however, that there is a *systematic and empirical* connection.

Borrowing from Pierre Schlag, I will use the word "directive" broadly to refer to any mode of assessing appropriateness or determining outcomes, whether a command, rule, or standard. As Schlag puts it, "The formula for a legal directive is 'if this, then that.' A directive thus has two parts: a 'trigger' that identifies some phenomenon and a 'response' that requires or authorizes a legal consequence when that phenomenon is present" (1985, p. 381).[8] The same is true of non-legal directives as well.

Any system of directives creates a *mapping* from situations to outcomes. The mapping divides the set of all cases into a number of *input sets*; these sets may be wide or narrow, as illustrated earlier in Fig. 1. Thus far, I have implicitly defined the abstraction of rules solely in terms of the breadth of input sets. But the mapping also designates an *output set* corresponding to each input set. The output sets may also be wide or narrow. So a system of directives creates a mapping from input sets to output sets.

---

[8] According to Schlag, the breakdown of a directive into these two components is conventional in the rules-standards literature (1985, p. 381, n11).

Fig. 3 Input Sets and Output Sets. **A** Case-by-Case, **B** Rules, **C** Standards.

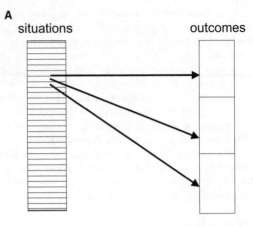

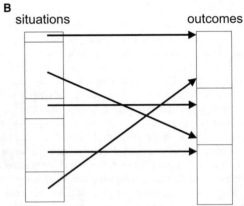

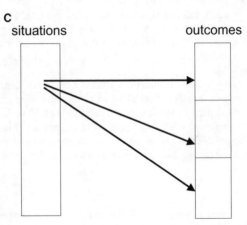

Figure 3A–C illustrates the input sets and output sets of case-by-case, rule-based, and standard-based decision making, respectively. In each figure, the system of directives is illustrated by arrows leading from situations (cases) to outcomes. Within the "situations" column, the divisions separate input sets, so having more divisions means having more (and narrower) input sets. Within the "outcomes" column, the divisions separate different outcomes (for simplicity of presentation, I have assumed only three possible outcomes). The divisions do *not* distinguish output sets. For any given input set, the corresponding output set is *all* outcomes with arrows from that input set.

For a directive system with a low level of abstraction—that is, very narrow input sets as shown in Fig. 3A—uncertainty is likely to result regardless of the size of the corresponding output sets. Even if each input set maps to a singleton output set (only one outcome, as in the figure), the decision maker has to determine which input set his case falls in. If other "nearby" input sets that differ only in minute details nevertheless map to different outcomes, then the decision maker cannot effectively predict the outcome.

For a directive system with a high level of abstraction, the breadth of output sets matters. It is relatively easy to determine the relevant input set, but uncertainty can arise from a too-broad output set. In Fig. 3C, there is only one input set, but it maps to all possible outcomes (a wide output set). We can imagine a version of Fig. 3C in which there is just one arrow, leading from the only input set to one possible outcome. But in reality, that sort of directive is rare, and wide output sets are more common. For instance, the standards observed in law—such as balancing and reasonable man tests—are characterized by the vagueness of their recommendations. They specify relevant factors, not particular outcomes. In language, and specifically in writing, style guidelines like "be concise" and "avoid run-on sentences" are similarly vague in their specification of outcomes; they identify some relevant factors to consider in one's speech and prose, but their application to particular cases is not apparent a priori (for instance, was the previous sentence a run-on?).

The directives we most often think of as rules have intermediate-sized input sets with relatively small output sets. In Fig. 3B, there is only a handful of input sets, thereby minimizing uncertainty about where one's own situation falls, and each input set maps to a single outcome (a singleton output set), thereby minimizing uncertainty about the rule's application.

Although we can imagine directives with very wide input sets and very narrow output sets, such beasts are rarely found in the world. When input sets are large, output sets tend to be large as well. As we shall see in the next section, this fact results from the desire to achieve a desirable match between situations and outcomes.

2 Applications in law, language, and etiquette

2.1 Rules versus standards in the law

The issues raised here have been most extensively considered in the legal literature on rules versus standards. Although the literature is large, legal scholars do not seem to have noted explicitly the importance of intermediate abstraction in rules. On the contrary, rules and standards are typically characterized as the poles of a spectrum. Duncan Kennedy's seminal article on the subject, for instance, says, "At the opposite pole from a formally realizable rule is a standard or principle or policy" (Kennedy 1976, p. 1688). Spencer Overton, in a recent application of the rules-versus-standards debate in the context of *Bush v. Gore*, says, "[T]he form that legal directives may take is actually relative: directives may fall anywhere on a graduated continuum between the extreme poles of rule-like and standard-like" (Overton 2002, p. 73). Vincy Fon and Francesco Parisi, in developing a model of optimal specificity in the law, say, "Standards and rules can be visualized as two extremes in a one-dimensional space representing the degree of precision of laws" (2007, p. 148). The present analysis indicates that in fact, ruleness does not reside at one end of a spectrum, but somewhere in the center.

Nevertheless, the rules–standards literature does draw attention to the leading reason that directives mapping from very wide input sets to very narrow output sets do not persist—and the reason is closely related to the reason that intermediately abstract rules sometimes get replaced by more or less abstract directives. While bright-line rules have the advantage of clarity, and thus the salutary effect of reducing uncertainty in a wide range of cases, they also create problems of over- and under-inclusion relative to other values. Kennedy uses age-of-majority laws as an example:

> The choice of rules as the mode of intervention involves the sacrifice of precision in the achievement of the objectives lying behind the rules. Suppose that the reason for creating a class of persons who lack capacity is the belief that immature people lack the faculty of free will. Setting the age of majority at 21 years will incapacitate many but *not all* of those who lack this faculty. And it will incapacitate some who actually possess it (Kennedy 1976, p. 1689).

Because rules are abstract, they will necessarily neglect a variety of details, and those details will sometimes appear important. The rules will therefore be perceived as creating injustice or unfairness in some cases. Although Kennedy is friendly toward the use of general standards, even those who strongly prefer rules recognize this point. Richard Epstein identifies the demand for "perfect justice" as one of the "enemies of simplicity" in the law: "[Perfect justice] aspires to rooting out error in every individual case. Simple rules do not meet that exacting standard. At best they are only tests; and tests are rules of thumb that work most of the time, but are known and expected to fail some of the time" (Epstein 1995, p. 38).

If the desire to avoid one-size-fits-all (or all-in-the-class) outcomes is the reason for the rejection of rules that map from intermediate input sets to narrow output sets, then it should also be obvious why a mapping from very broad input sets to narrow output sets won't do: it will produce even more errors of over- and under-inclusion than would a mapping with intermediate input sets. I will refer to the desire to avoid such errors as the "matching principle": ideally, we would like a system of directives to produce a perfect match between situations and outcomes, as determined by some external set of values.

Pursuit of the matching principle creates a tendency to slide toward either case-by-case decision making or standard-based decision making. In the rules-versus-standards literature, the slide is typically characterized as movement away from the pole of rules and toward the more abstract pole of standards. Yet the explanations given for the sliding, interestingly enough, often illustrate movement in the direction of *lower* abstraction. Carol M. Rose, who uses the metaphor of "crystals" and "mud" to mirror the dichotomy between rules and standards, draws attention to the tendency

 Springer

of strictly enforced property rules of the sort that prevailed in the nineteenth century to generate cases in which sympathetic plaintiffs suffered great losses as a result of seemingly small errors. "It is this booby trap aspect of what seems to be clear, simple rules—the scenario of disproportionate loss by some party—that seems to drive us to muddy up crystal rules with the exceptions and the post hoc discretionary judgments" (Rose 1988, p. 597). Rose describes a process by which bright-line rules are transformed into standards through the accumulation of exceptions. Yet the creation of specific exceptions seems a move in the direction of more *specific* rules, not more abstract ones. Eventually, the mass of exceptions "congeal" into standards that name all the relevant factors without demarcating clear boundaries. Once again, we see how the ends of the abstraction continuum approach each other.

Kennedy, on the other hand, describes a process by which standards devolve into case-by-case decision making:

> Finally, the application of a standard to a particular fact situation will often generate a particular rule much narrower in scope than that standard. One characteristic mode of ordering a subject matter area including a vast number of possible situations is through the combination of a standard with an ever increasing group of particular rules of this kind. The generality of the standard means that there are no gaps: it is possible to find out something about how judges will dispose of cases that have not yet arisen. But no attempt is made to formulate a formally realizable general rule. Rather, *case law gradually fills in the area with rules so closely bound to particular facts that they have little or no precedential value* (Kennedy 1976, p. 1690; emphasis added).

Kennedy's argument here again supports the thesis that case-by-case decision making and standard-based decision making have much in common; the ends of the spectrum approach each other. Under a standard, the need for some basis of decision making will generate a tendency to create rules—but the rules may end up being highly specific instead of intermediately abstract.

Thus, the legal literature on rules-versus-standards has implicitly recognized the central thesis of this article, although the impulse to cast rules as one end of the spectrum has impeded making the thesis explicit. In Rose's terminology, bright-line rules are crystals and standards are mud; but then what is case-by-case decision making? Take crystals and crush them to make smaller and smaller crystals, and eventually you get sand. As it turns out, mud and sand have much in common.

2.2 Regular versus irregular verbs in language

The issue of levels of abstraction in behavioral directives can also be found in linguistics, perhaps most obviously in the distinction between regular and irregular verbs—a topic that Steven Pinker uses as the leading example throughout his book *Words and Rules* (1999). Most verbs in the English language form their past tense and participle simply through the addition of -*ed*.[9] Yet there exist 150 to 180 verbs in

---

[9] This rule is not quite as simple as it seems, since the pronunciation of this suffix depends on the preceding sounds in the verbs to which it attaches, as illustrated by the different sounds at the end of *jumped* and *loaded*.

the English language that form their past tense and past participle in some other way: *go/went/gone, run/ran/run, sting/stung, bear/bore/borne*, and so on (Pinker 1999, p. 16); they are exceptions to the general rule. This phenomenon is not unique to English; other languages also have regular and irregular forms.

Note that the standard rule for forming the past tense possesses an intermediate level of abstraction; it applies only to verbs, and only when you wish to form the past tense or participle. For a wide input set, the rule specifies a singleton output set. Different rules apply to the inflection of nouns—and nouns, too, come in regular and irregular forms. But the irregular forms are loopholes, exceptions made for specific cases. We can tolerate these words that live by their own rules, but their presence in the language does create difficulties for people searching for the right word when writing and speaking—especially those learning the language, like children and non-native speakers. This is a problem of uncertainty, an inability of decision makers (speakers) to know what is appropriate behavior (speech) under particular circumstances. Too many irregular words would be intolerable. As Pinker says, "One can imagine a language in which every verb picked its own substitution of vowels and consonants from among the thousands that are logically possible. But generations of learners have passed down an English language that is very different from that possibility" (p. 91). This imaginary scenario would constitute a case of extreme specificity or too low abstraction, and it is clearly untenable. Yet the opposite extreme would also be untenable: a language whose only rule for verbs was "form the past tense in a way that is easily pronounced and understood" would fail miserably at coordinating the expectations of speakers, and for essentially the same reasons.

Abstraction is justified in language for the same reason it is justified in general: it allows humans to manage complexity by focusing on some features while ignoring others. Pinker points out the gains in terms of economizing on mental effort and space: "The advantage of a rule is that a vast number of forms are generated by a compact mechanism. In English the savings are significant: The rules for *-ed, -s,* and *-ing* (the three regular forms of the verb) cut our mental storage needs to a quarter of what they would be if each form had to be stored separately" (p. 18).

The advantage of clear rules of intermediate abstraction is clear, so why have irregular words at all? One obvious (and true) explanation is history; most irregular forms are simply remnants of older rules of inflection (Pinker 1999, pp. 67–68). They do, however, also have some advantages over regular forms, the most salient being ease of pronunciation: "A sequence of sounds that encodes a concept precisely and efficiently may be unresolvable by the ear or unpronounceable by the tongue" (p. 18). Regular inflection can produce words and phrases that are difficult to speak and to hear, thus sometimes requiring a modification. *Ice cream* is now the accepted term for what used to be *iced cream; ice tea* does not (yet) have the same acceptance, but both phrases illustrate how the usual rules can be set aside to ease pronunciation. *Sixths* and *edited* are examples of difficult-to-pronounce words created by the regular inflection rules; "Monstrosities like these are never found among the irregulars, which all have standard Anglo-Saxon word sounds such as *grew* and *strode* and *clung*, which please the ear and roll off the tongue" (p. 19). That irregular forms are typically euphonious points to the role of evolution in selecting rules, and exceptions, to fit the needs of speakers.

As in the case of law, then, we can see that rules can create bothersome outcomes that apparently conflict with underlying values—whether fairness in the law or ease

 Springer

34   D.G. Whitman

of pronunciation in language. As Frederick Schauer argues, any rule is likely to create errors of both over- and under-inclusion relative to the real or perceived functions of the system: "Just as the factual predicate [of a rule] may sometimes indicate the presence of the justification [for the rule] in cases in which it is absent, so too can the factual predicate occasionally fail to indicate the justification in cases in which it is present" (1991, p. 32). As a result, rules are necessarily suboptimal when measured against the yardstick of ideal decision making (Schauer 1991, p. 100). Similarly, Ronald Heiner considers suboptimality a defining feature of rule-governed behavior: "If we use the jargon of standard economics, rule-governed behavior means that an agent must ignore actions which are actually preferred under certain conditions" (Heiner 1983, p. 568). The matching principle urges us to create exceptions or to allow greater discretion in order to reduce the divergence between our values and the output of rules. Seeking a perfect match in every case, however, can reduce clarity and, paradoxically, undermine the pursuit of those values.

2.3 Generalities versus minutiae in etiquette

The issue of levels of abstraction arises in etiquette as well, though the literature on etiquette is not as well developed as that of law and linguistics. Two popular commentators on etiquette, Amy Vanderbilt and Judith Martin (a.k.a. "Miss Manners") both affirm the predictability-generating character of the rules of etiquette. Vanderbilt says that "The rules of etiquette give us something to lean on in a world that grows increasingly large and complex" (1968, p. 98). Notably, Vanderbilt does *not* call for the rules to become more complex as society grows more complex. The rules are valuable because they help manage complexity, not because they reflect it. Similarly, Martin says, "In its symbolic function, etiquette provides a system of symbols whose semantic content provides for predictability in social relations, especially among strangers" (1993, p. 354).

   Both authors recognize the hostility that some people have toward etiquette. Vanderbilt attributes the hostility to their having effectively given up; in essence, they say, "I don't know anything about it. I'm not going to try. I might make a mistake" (1968, p. 98). Presumably, the fear of making a mistake derives from a sense that etiquette is dominated by *minutiae*—that is, directives that apply to very specific situations, such as differences in how to hold a tea cup versus a demitasse. Directives like these err on the side of too much specificity and thus leave people uncertain about whether their actions are appropriate. The alternative to the etiquette of minutiae might seem to be a general statement of purpose, such as the aforementioned "Be polite." But this, too, would be problematic. The notion that people should simply be nice to each other leaves us, as Martin puts it, with "the Jean-Jacques Rousseau School of Etiquette, with its charmingly naïve directive that we should all behave like (noble) savages" (1993, p. 350). Whether presented with directives that are too specific or too general, people still do not know how to behave.

   The more useful rules of etiquette, through their intermediate abstraction, serve to divide up social interactions into broad classes. Martin explains:

   Once learned and correctly interpreted, the symbols of etiquette permit one
   person to recognize such essential attributes of other persons as their intentions,

 Springer

status, friendliness or hostility, and thus to deal appropriately with a wide range of social situations and relationships (1993, p. 354).

Notice that the "symbols" of etiquette simultaneously provide useful information while nevertheless allowing the user to deal with a broad range of circumstances; this is the key feature of intermediate abstraction. Martin gives the instructive example of someone reaching out to shake your hand, which indicates that this person will likely treat you better than someone who spits at your feet (1993, p. 354).

What, then, drives a system of etiquette away from intermediate abstraction? Again, the answer is the matching principle: a fixed rule will generate outcomes that do not perfectly match the goals of people using the system. Martin says the functions of etiquette include "communal harmony, dignity of the person, a need for cultural coherence, and an aesthetic sense" (1993, p. 351). Perhaps more importantly, etiquette can function to distinguish insiders from outsiders. A secret handshake allows people within a select group to recognize each other. This is a special case of the broader function of distinguishing classes of people who will treat you differently. But because rules are both under- and over-inclusive, the symbols of an etiquette system may fail to send the precise signals that people want to send. A handshake, for instance, only distinguishes the tolerant from the actively hostile. More complicated (and specific) practices can develop to show gradations of friendship. In some social situations, it is now necessary to choose whether to perform a standard handshake, three consecutive hand clasps, or a fist bump. The expansion of options allows a more finely tuned message, but it also can create uncertainty and discoordination—such as when someone meets an attempted hug with an attempted handshake. While etiquette generally is supposed "to soften personal antagonisms and thus to avert conflicts" (Martin 1993, p. 352), crossed signals like these can actually foment conflict.

As with law and language, we see that the desire to achieve a perfect match between goals and actions creates a tendency to make exceptions to rules or to replace them with more open-ended standards. But if too many exceptions accumulate, or if the standards become too open-ended, the resulting uncertainty can undermine the achievement of those same goals.[10]

3 Other rules conducive to spontaneous order

Are rules of intermediate abstraction a *necessary* condition for the emergence of a spontaneous order? Apparently not, given the existence of both standards and case-by-case decision making in the law and the existence of irregular forms in language. Somehow, we are still able to coordinate our economic behavior and to communicate effectively. However, more and less abstract modes of decision making like these

---

[10] See Heiner (1983, p. 564): "[A]llowing flexibility to react to information or to select [more] actions will not necessarily improve performance if there is uncertainty about how to use that information or about when to select particular actions. Thus, an agent's overall performance may actually be improved by restricting flexibility to use information or to choose particular actions."

 Springer

seem to exist in the context of an overall system that is mostly populated by rules of intermediate abstraction. As long as such a background exists, it seems that a spontaneous order can tolerate some degree of exception making (in the form of more specific directives) and vagueness (in the form of broader standards).

Intermediate abstraction of rules also does not guarantee the emergence of a spontaneous order. As Hayek repeatedly observes, not just any kind of abstract rules will do.

> [I]t is evident that in society some perfectly regular behaviour of the individuals could only produce disorder: if the rule were that any individual should try to kill any other he encountered, or flee as soon as he saw another, the result would clearly be the complete impossibility of an order in which the activities of the individuals were based on collaboration with others (1973, p. 44).

To understand spontaneous order, we need to identify the other characteristics that abstract rules must have. "The question which is of central importance as much for social theory as for social policy," says Hayek, "is thus what properties the rules must possess so that the separate actions of the individuals will produce an overall order" (1973, p. 45). In this section, I will attempt a partial listing of those properties.

3.1 Purpose independence

The characteristic most clearly identified by Hayek—other than abstraction—is that rules need to be *purpose-independent*, meaning they apply without reference to the specific goals of specific people. The rule governing a situation does not change depending on who is doing an activity or why he is doing it; as Hayek puts it, "[T]he rules governing a spontaneous order must be independent of purpose and be the same, if not necessarily for all members, at least for whole classes of members not individually designated by name" (1973, p. 50). Purpose independence is important for two reasons.

First, purpose independence allows the order to persist even when a particular goal has been accomplished or is no longer relevant. Because the rules can accommodate a wide (though not unlimited) range of goals, new members of the community will find it in their interest to continue using them to coordinate behavior. A language persists, for instance, because people always have communicative needs—but the needs can change dramatically from person to person and from time to time. The abstract rules of language can assist in any activity from the writing of a contract to the planning of a terrorist attack. Similarly, the market economy persists in large part because it responds to the ever-changing needs of economic actors. The rules of just conduct that foster the market process need not make reference to specific resources, products, services, and technologies; this is one of the advantages of (intermediate) abstraction. Instead, the rules generally refer to broad classes and types of situations, from transfer of control over resources (movable and immovable) to accidents between strangers. Because these classes of interaction occur regardless of the particular people and goals involved, the system provides a means that can serve innumerable different ends.

 Springer

Second, purpose independence allows for the continual incorporation of new knowledge by allowing individuals to respond to a changing environment. A changing environment guarantees that *no* system can satisfy all expectations; it is therefore a given that some expectations will be dashed. "The protection against disappointment of expectation which the law can give in an ever changing society will always be only the protection of some expectations but not all" (Hayek 1973, p. 102). If the system aimed, in the face of an ever-changing environment, at the satisfaction of all expectations of specific individuals, it would necessarily have to obstruct the discovery and use of new ideas and information by other individuals. The inability to respond to change would lead to ever greater disappointment of expectations of other people. Purpose independence substitutes satisfaction of certain kinds of expectations across persons for the satisfaction of all expectations of a few.

3.2 Extensibility to novel cases

A closely related characteristic of rules of intermediate abstraction is their *extensibility to novel cases*—that is, their capacity to be extended to cover new and unforeseen activities and interactions. This provides a degree of certainty to people in new and unfamiliar situations. As long as those situations possess some of the features identified as relevant by existing rules, it is possible to make some predictions about how the situations will be treated.

In language, the existence of regular rules of inflection facilitates the entry of new words into the language, often in the presence of new activities people wish to communicate about. As Pinker observes, when the new verbs *fax*, *mosh*, and *spam* entered the lexicon, there was no doubt about how to form their past tenses: *faxed*, *moshed*, and *spammed* (1999, p. 13). The same is true when a word is repurposed into a different part of speech; if we decided to *verb* a noun, we would know the noun had been *verbed*. Interestingly, even irregular forms can exert some control over the formation of new words. When words are formed by adding a prefix to an existing irregular word, such as *understand* from *stand*, we know that the past tense will be formed in the same manner as the root word: *understood*, not *understanded*. If we invented new words based on irregular stems, such as *withset* or *overhold*, we would automatically know their past tenses as well (*withset* and *overheld*; Pinker 1999, p. 45).

The fact that even irregular verbs can plant the seeds of patterns illustrates two related points. First, when exceptions are made to rules, often, the exceptions themselves will take the form of rules. As long as there are not too many exceptions, the intermediate abstraction of the system of rules can be maintained and its beneficial properties—like extensibility to novel cases—preserved. Second, logical consistency is *not* a necessary component of a system of rules. As Rizzo (1999) argues in the context of legal rules, *logical consistency* and *praxeological consistency* are not the same thing. Praxeological consistency refers to whether the rules allow individuals to coordinate their actions with others by making mutually compatible plans (Rizzo 1999, p. 502). If two classes, A and B, are treated by two different rules, even though logically A and B would seem to be the same, individuals can still rely on those rules to guide their behavior so long as they can tell whether a case falls in A or B. The distinction between the two classes need not be logically relevant, so long as it is visible. For instance, if English units of measure are used for most everyday purposes, but metric units are used for medical and scientific purposes, the system is not logically coherent. But if people can nevertheless coordinate their measuring activities (because they can easily distinguish everyday from medical/ scientific contexts), then the system is praxeologically coherent. The system can tolerate at least some degree of logical inconsistency.

3.3 Tolerance for small deviations

Any system of abstract rules will produce occasional failures in satisfying the customary functions of the order, such as communicating ideas or coordinating economic behavior. This fact creates an endogenous impulse to make exceptions or appeal to vague standards—the matching principle at work. To resist extreme applications of the matching principle, a system of rules must have a means of accommodating it to some degree.

Commonly, the process involves turning exceptions into general-purpose rules. In the field of etiquette, an example is provided by queuing norms. In a study of ticket queues for football matches in Australia, Mann (1969) observed that queue members followed a general rule of first-come-first-served; however, the rule had exceptions that lessened the burden of waiting by allowing people to leave the queue from time to time—to eat, use the bathroom, and even play games. The two most common exceptions were (a) that one person could hold up to four spots for people in his group and (b) that an object (such as a cardboard box) could hold a spot for a single person for two to three hours (Mann 1969, pp. 344–345). Notably, these exceptions took the form of rules with relatively well-defined boundaries. They allowed better satisfaction of the matching principle without creating great uncertainty (although some uncertainty remained, as we will see below).

The same process is evident in the common law, where judges often refuse to make exceptions unless they can find some principle that will tell them when to make similar exceptions in the future. Of course, there is some danger in this approach. If too many exceptions accumulate, the list of relevant factors that distinguish them can morph into a vague standard such as a balancing test, which asks judges simply to weigh all the relevant factors in specific cases. Alternatively, a proliferation of narrow exceptions can move the system toward the pole of extreme specificity. Either way, the intermediate abstraction of rules gets eroded. Fortunately, as observed earlier, a spontaneous order can tolerate some degree of such erosion in the rules.

3.4 Openness to generation of new rules

A dynamic system governed by abstract rules will continually generate situations that expose vagueness in the rules (even when the rules appear very clear) or conflict among different rules (even when no conflict was apparent initially). Hayek, in explaining the role of common-law judges, observes that the exposure of residual vagueness may require the creation of new rules to supplement the old:

> Since new situations in which the established rules are not adequate will constantly arise, the task of preventing conflict and enhancing the compatibility

of actions by appropriately delimiting the range of permitted actions is of necessity a never-ending one, requiring not only the application of already established rules but also the formulation of new rules necessary for the preservation of the order of actions (Hayek 1973, p. 119).

The emergence of cases that expose conflict or vagueness may well result from the intermediate degree of abstraction. Sufficiently specific directives are likely to have "cracks" between them because they are not abstract enough to cover every new kind of case. Sufficiently abstract directives, on the other hand, are unlikely to have cracks because they are broad enough to encompass everything—but their corresponding vagueness in terms of output (that is, the breadth of their output sets) will create the need for more specific rules. Intermediately abstract directives will have more cracks than highly abstract ones, but fewer than highly specific ones.

In language, the existence of conflicting rules can put words "in play" with regard to their proper inflection. Consider, for example, the verb *know/knew*. The formation of the past tense by means of this specific vowel change applies to a whole class of irregular verbs, including *grow/grew* and *throw/threw*, all of which involve stems that end in a vowel sound and start with a consonant cluster. How did *know/knew* end up in this group even though it begins with a single consonant sound? Originally, the *k* was pronounced, but then English began to lose the pronunciation of *kn* and *gn* at the beginning of words. So the emergence of a new rule (no more *kn* and *gn* consonant clusters) created conflict with an old one (inflection for this group of words). As it turned out, the old rule won out, with *know* keeping its old past tense *knew* (Pinker 1999, pp. 71–72).

In etiquette, Mann's football queues provide a nice example of how vagueness gets exposed. The rule that an object can hold a spot has an uncertain time limitation. In one football queue in 1966, "irate latecomers, who noticed that many people in the middle of the queue had not made an appearance for most of the day, spontaneously seized their boxes and burnt them," and the result was a melee (Mann 1969, p. 346). This is a notable example of how uncertainty can undermine the basic function of the system—in this case, avoiding interpersonal conflict. To avoid such a conflict, it would be necessary to create new rules or clarify the old ones.

One commonly followed rule of etiquette says, "Always hold a door open for a woman"; another common rule says, "Always allow a woman to enter first." These two rules generate a conflict in cases where a door opens *into* the place to be entered, because there is a leverage problem in trying to hold open such a door without actually walking in. In practice, a different rule had to evolve to govern this case (enter just enough to open the door). But what is to be done in the case of a revolving door? A conflict emerges here as well; one writer on etiquette suggests that "man first" governs the revolving-door situation (Post 2008), but custom may still be evolving on this point (the emergence of a clear rule in this case may have been slowed by weakening of the old norm of deference toward the "weaker sex"). For an example of where etiquette had to develop a new rule for a novel situation, consider the emergence of "ATM distance," the appropriate distance to stand behind someone at an automatic teller machine. Prior rules of social distance addressed distance for regular conversation, flirting, standing in a subway, etc., but not for standing in line at an ATM.

 Springer

The need to generate new rules for cases of vagueness and conflict among rules highlights a significant role that high-level abstraction can play in the maintenance of a spontaneous order. Although I have argued throughout this article that a system cannot be based entirely on directives at very high levels of abstraction, such directives can be very helpful in *supplementing* rules of intermediate abstraction. The intermediately abstract rules cannot, by their nature, provide the solution or answer to their own contradictions and omissions. Rules do not explain themselves; they do not include their own justifications. Standards, however, can provide a list of the relevant factors that could enter into the creation of new rules or resolution of conflicts among existing rules. This matters for two reasons. First, it means standards are useful in allowing the system of rules to grow and change—as it must to accommodate a changing environment. Second, standards can lend a degree of certainty when agents have to make decisions in situations where the rules are unclear, even *before* the new rules congeal. The certainty will not be as great as when the rules for one's case already exist, but it will be certainly be greater than when there is neither a rule nor a standard to rely on.

4 Conclusions: On structure and content

The rules that encourage the growth of a spontaneous order will, taken as a whole, tend to display an intermediate degree of abstraction. A system governed by rules that are too specific or too abstract will fail to coordinate expectations of people working within the order that emerges, whereas rules of intermediate abstraction economize on mental space while minimizing vagueness. Intermediate abstraction is not enough; however, the rule set also needs to be purpose-independent, extensible to novel cases, robust to small deviations, and open to emergence of new rules.

It is useful to distinguish between the rules that create the conditions for a spontaneous order and the spontaneous order itself. A market economy is a spontaneous order that emerges from certain regularities of human economic behavior, some of which result from the rules of just conduct embodied in the law. That does not mean the law itself is a spontaneous order, although it might be. Hayek points out that "[I]t is possible that an order which would still have to be described as spontaneous rests on rules which are entirely the result of deliberate design" (1973, p. 46). The rules of language set the stage for a spontaneous order of human communication; in principle, the rules of the language could have been designed, like Esperanto or Klingon. The rules of hypertext markup language (HTML) provide a partial basis for the spontaneous order of the Internet, yet HTML itself was deliberately designed.

Nevertheless, it turns out in practice that the rules that facilitate spontaneous order are often themselves the product of spontaneous order (or some process of evolution without design). The rules of law, language, and etiquette emerged spontaneously, albeit with numerous attempts at central direction by governments, grammarians, and guardians of manners. The discussion in part III of the properties that abstract rules need to satisfy helps to explain why. In order for the system of rules to be extensible to novel cases, robust to small deviations, and open to creation of new rules, the rules themselves must be capable of some amount of evolution in response to changing needs and new circumstances.

 Springer

Imagine a designer of rule systems who wishes to create a spontaneous order. He might start by creating rules characterized by an intermediate degree of abstraction and then set the system in motion. But there is no way the designer can foresee all possible novel cases, conflicts, and changes in circumstances a priori, so the rule set will assuredly have to change. So the designer faces a choice: either he can maintain constant watch over the system and make every rule change deliberately or he can find a way to allow the system to evolve on its own. The latter will, of course, require less effort on the designer's part; moreover, the changes that occur in the rules will have to result from changes that occur in the system. In short, an ongoing spontaneous order seems to require an ongoing evolution of the rules that help generate it. To the extent that the evolutionary process responds to the human need for predictability, we should expect the resulting rules to possess an intermediate degree of abstraction.

References

Epstein, R. A. (1995). *Simple rules for a complex world*. Cambridge: Harvard University Press.
Fon, V., & Parisi, F. (2007). On the optimal specificity of legal rules. *Journal of Institutional Economics, 3* (2), 147–164.
Hayek, F. A. (1960). *The constitution of liberty*. Chicago: The University of Chicago Press.
Hayek, F. A. (1973). *Law, legislation and liberty, vol. 1: Rules and order*. Chicago: The University of Chicago Press.
Heiner, R. A. (1983). The origin of predictable behavior. *American Economic Review, 73*, 560–595.
Kennedy, D. (1976). Form and substance in private law adjudication. *Harvard Law Review, 89*, 1685–1778.
Koppl, R. (2002). Custom and rules. *American Journal of Economics and Sociology, 61*, 531–537.
Koppl, R., & Whitman, D. G. (2004). Rational-choice hermeneutics. *Journal of Economic Behavior & Organization, 55*, 295–317.
Mann, L. (1969). Queue culture: The waiting line as a social system. *American Journal of Sociology, 75*, 340–354.
Martin, J. (1993). A philosophy of etiquette. *Proceedings of the American Philosophical Society, 137*, 350–356.
O'Driscoll, G. P., & Rizzo, M. J. (1996, 1985). *The economics of time and ignorance*. London: Routledge.
Overton, S. (2002). Rules, standards, and *Bush v. Gore*: Form and the law of democracy. *Harvard Civil Rights-Civil Liberties Law Review, 37*, 65–102.
Pinker, S. (1999). *Words and rules*. New York: Basic Books.
Post, P. (2008). Revolving doors. GoodHousekeeping.com. Retrieved Feb. 17, 2008 from http://magazines.ivillage.com/goodhousekeeping/etiquette/peggy/qas/0,,284571_431459,00.html.
Rizzo, M. J. (1999). Which kind of legal order? Logical coherence and praxeological coherence. *Journal des Economistes et des Etudes Humaines, 9*(4), 497–510.
Rose, C. M. (1988). Crystals and mud in property law. *Stanford Law Review, 40*, 577–610.
Schauer, F. (1991). *Playing by the rules: A philosophical examination of rule-based decision-making in law and in life*. Oxford: Clarendon.
Schlag, P. (1985). Rules and standards. *UCLA Law Review, 33*, 379–430.
Schutz, A. (1932). *The phenomenology of the social world* (translation by G. Walsh and F. Lehnert). Evanston, IL. Northwestern University Press.
Vanderbilt, A. (1968). Bad manners in America. The changing American people: Are we deteriorating or improving? *Annals of the American Academy of Political and Social Science, 378*, 90–98.

 Springer

[9]

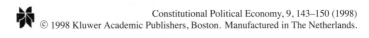 Constitutional Political Economy, 9, 143–150 (1998)
© 1998 Kluwer Academic Publishers, Boston. Manufactured in The Netherlands.

Epstein and Polanyi on Simple Rules, Complex Systems, and Decentralization

TODD J. ZYWICKI
Mississippi College School of Law, Jackson, MS 39201, USA

1. Introduction

Conventional wisdom holds that as a system becomes more complex, the rules governing that system also must become more complex. Thus, it is argued that as the American economy and society becomes more complex, legal rules and regulations must become more complex as well in order to reflect the new realities. The invention of toxic waste, pervasive pollution, computers, automobiles, and air travel are just a few of the many variables which make society and the economy more complex than they were in bygone eras. In turn, these new pressures are believed to call for increasingly complex rules to regulate those phenomena.

With *Simple Rules for a Complex World*, Richard Epstein has dealt a blow to this syllogism. So long as the incentives created by alternative rules are identical, the law should choose the rule which is simpler—i.e., the rule which minimizes administrative and error costs.[1] This creates "a simple rule of thumb: When in doubt, choose the simpler of two alternatives."[2] "The more complicated the legal rule, the greater the likelihood that these administrative costs, including error costs, will be high."[3] The administrative and error costs associated with complex rules creates a presumption in favor of simple rules, one which can be overcome by showing that an increase in those costs will be offset by an improvement in the incentives of those governed by the rule.

By forcing us to consider the trade-offs between administrative costs, error costs, and incentive effects, Epstein has done a marvelous service. But what of the argument stated at the outset—that there is correlation between the complexity of a system, and the rules which govern that system? Is it true in some general sense that a more complex economy with more complex dangers *necessitates* more complex legal rules? In other words, is there some underlying dynamic driving the legal system toward complexity that is not captured in Epstein's three-variable equation?

Epstein rejects this view. He concludes that "As a normative matter, the conventional view of the subject has matters exactly backward. The proper response to more complex societies should be an ever greater reliance on simple legal rules. . . ."[4] And he also suggests a link between complex systems and the need for decentralization for these systems to function.[5] But he makes those observations only in passing, and does not draw any systematic connections between complex systems and decentralization on one hand, and their link to his central theme of simple rules on the other.

In the remaining portion of this essay I will sketch out some of the connections between simple rules, complex systems, and decentralization, which Epstein identifies but does not fully explore. In particular, I will provide support for the general proposition that the conventional wisdom that complex systems require complex rules is not only incorrect, but completely *backward*. Thus, this article is primarily a supplement to Epstein's analysis, not a criticism. It expresses some themes which seem to be present, but also seem to be somewhat muted, in Epstein's book.

Instead, complex systems can thrive only where they are organized according to a high degree of decentralization; in turn, a decentralized system can be best organized only according to simple rules. Thus, complex systems *demand* simple — not complex — rules.

2. Complex Systems and Decentralization

To elucidate this link between simple rules, decentralization, and complex systems, I will draw on the ideas of Michael Polanyi.[6] And while Polanyi himself does not explicitly explore all the connections between these concepts, his work provides insights for understanding Epstein's intuition that a link exists between simple rules, decentralization, and complex systems.

Consider first the observation between decentralization and complex systems. Polanyi distinguishes two types of organizational structures.[7] On one hand, we have hierarchical corporate order.[8] On the other, we have spontaneous order systems. Consider them in turn.

A corporate order is organized according to the principle of one superior officer, who is responsible for continuously redirecting the operation of the organization. In practice, this means that the chief executive of the operation is responsible for assigning tasks to his subordinates with an aim towards efficiently accomplishing the organization's ends.

Polanyi observes that the organizational structure of such corporations is determined by the "span of control" of the chief executive. Because the chief can give orders directly to only a handful of subordinates, any enterprise larger than the chief's immediate span of control must be coordinated through devolution to successive tiers of subordinate officials.[9] In turn, each of these subordinates can supervise only a handful of subordinates, requiring successive tiers of administration until the lowest level is reached, where the job is actually performed. The directions of the chief executive pass downward through this administrative apparatus; this same apparatus is used to transmit information upward from the base to the peak.

In a hierarchic order of this kind, each person's primary task is assigned to him by direction from above and his principal communications regarding the progress of his work are transmitted to his immediate superior. The chief executive has sole responsibility for making major decisions on behalf of the enterprise. Those in subordinate tiers lack such authority, and any attempt to exercise such authority would disrupt the smooth functioning of the system. Instead, subordinates are supposed to execute faithfully the assignments delegated to them by their immediate superiors. The actions carried out at the base of this pyramid can be said to be "centrally directed" or "centrally planned" because each of the subordinates actions are coordinated with one another by the explicit assignment and re-assignment of tasks by those further up the pyramid. Coordination is imposed from above: the chief executive assigns certain tasks to his subordinates, who do the same to their subordinates, and so on down the line. Polanyi provides as example of corporate order the crew of a small craft riding a heavy sea, where each man's actions are coordinated to the others' by a captain's commands.

Polanyi contrasts corporate order with a system of spontaneous order. A spontaneous order differs from a corporate order, in that coordination results from *ongoing mutual* adjustment among the members of the enterprise. "When order is achieved among human beings by allowing them to interact with each other on their own initiative — subject only to laws which uniformly apply to all of them — we have a system of spontaneous order in society."[10] The defining characteristic of a spontaneous order is decentralization, with most decision-making authority dispersed to those at the base of the organization.

Polanyi illustrates the concept of spontaneous order through the example of five forwards in a soccer game, charging at the opposite goal and coordinating themselves by mutual adjustment.[11] Through a series of mutually responding to the actions of one another, as well as those of the defense, these forwards form a pattern without the need for any superior (e.g., a coach) to tell them what to do.

Two implications result from Polanyi's distinction between corporate and spontaneous orders. First, spontaneous order systems generally will be able to adapt more quickly to changes in circumstances than will corporate orders. Second, systems organized as spontaneous orders can be larger and more complex than corporate orders. Spontaneous order systems on average will be able to adapt more quickly to changes in circumstances than a corporate order. In a spontaneous order all members of the enterprise continually and simultaneously adapt to each other's actions. By contrast, in a corporate order, such as the sailing crew in a storm, no one member can make adjustments until the captain determines who should be assigned or re-assigned to each task and then issues those orders to his subordinates. Thus, a spontaneous order system on average will be able to adapt more readily to changes in circumstances than will corporate orders.[12] More importantly for present purposes, larger and more complex organizations can be run most efficiently if organized according to spontaneous order principles. In a corporate body, an increase in size has no effect on the per capita number of relations which any member can undertake. Thus, the effective span of control for any one member of a corporate order remains constant regardless of its size. The chief, for instance, can still only direct a handful of subordinates. If the number of subordinates under his direct control becomes too large, then he has to add an additional tier of administration to return his span of control to a workable level.

The span of control of a spontaneous order, by contrast, increases *proportionally* with the increase in the number of its members. Each member of the spontaneous order can respond directly to the actions and decisions of each other member of the order. Thus, to return to our soccer example, *each* of the five forwards can respond simultaneously to the actions of all four of the other members of the team. Increasing the size of the team to eleven players increases the span of control of each player by many multiples, as each player will respond to the actions of every other player. By contrast, increasing the centrally-directed size of the sailing crew does *not* increase the span of control of the captain significantly, as each member of the crew will continue to react only to the captain's orders, not to one anothers' actions. Thus, Polanyi observes,

> An authority charged with replacing by deliberate direction the functions of a large self-adjusting system, would be placed in the position of a man charged with control-

ling single-handed a machine requiring for its operation the simultaneous working of thousands of levers. Its legal powers would avail it of nothing. By insisting on them, it could only paralyse a system which it failed to govern.[13]

Or, as Fuller describes the problem, trying to replace a system of spontaneous order with corporate order "is like trying to set an intricate ballet to the music of a Sousa march."[14]

As a result of these differing spans of control, it becomes apparent that complex systems which require flexibility to adapt quickly to changing circumstances will be governed most effectively by spontaneous order principles.[15] In practice, this means a large degree of delegation of decision-making authority to the most dispersed levels. Note, however, that a system may be large without being complex. Thus, Polanyi observes,

> [C]orporate organizations will as a rule not grow to large sizes so long as they are performing closely co-ordinated, complex and flexible operations. Where we meet large hierarchic organizations which can apparently be extended indefinitely, like railways or post offices, they turn out to be rather loose aggregates performing standardized functions.[16]

Complex systems, therefore, must be organized according to a decentralized, spontaneous order model of organization. The classic example, of course, is a market economy, and the central point of Polanyi's essay was to demonstrate the impossibility of centrally planning the economy.[17] Polanyi also describes the common law system as a spontaneous order system, as it involves a continuous "sequence of adjustments between succeeding judges, guided by a parallel interaction between succeeding judges, guided by a parallel interaction between the judges and the general public."[18]

But what of simple rules? Given that complex, flexible systems must be organized as spontaneous order systems, does this allow us to draw any conclusions about the types of rules which are most compatible for governing those systems? Is there any connection between the degree of complexity of a system and the degree of complexity of the rules which govern that system? In other words, given that a complex system like the economy will have to be organized according to decentralized spontaneous order principles, and that the degree of decentralization will have to increase as the economy's complexity increases, are simple legal rules or complex rules more compatible with organizing a decentralized spontaneous order? As suggested at the outset, it appears that there is actually an *inverse* relationship between a system's complexity and the degree of complexity of the rules which govern that system. In other words, complex systems require simple rules, *ceteris paribus*.

Legal rules perform a social function of "condition[ing] the ways in which individuals pursue their various ends."[19] Or, as Hayek has written, "laws "are intended to be merely instrumental in the pursuit of people's various individual ends.... They could almost be described as a kind of instrument of production, helping people to predict the behavior of those with whom they must collaborate, rather than as efforts toward the satisfaction of particular needs."[20] Those who postulate that legal rules must become more complex as the economy becomes more complex have lost sight of law's social function of coordinating the interactions of *individuals*, and have instead claimed a relationship between law and an artificial abstraction (e.g., the "economy").

Once it is appreciated that when we refer to legal rules we are referring to inputs into *individual* decision-making, it becomes evident that the more decentralized and complex a system is (such as the economy), the more critical it is that rules become simpler. A highly decentralized system necessitates simple rules, so that dispersed individuals performing many different tasks can understand and incorporate these rules into their plans and decision-making. Individuals have to be able to understand legal rules in order to act in accordance with them.

Spontaneous order systems require each individual to make large numbers of adaptations on an ongoing basis. Just as individuals are required to constantly react to changes in circumstances caused by market changes or the actions of others, changes in legal rules force them to also make adjustments. Simple organizing rules allow maximum attention to be spent on making adjustments on other margins. Complex rules, by contrast, require ongoing adaptations by individuals to legal rules, thereby distracting them from spending energy and attention on more productive matters.

Complex rules are also usually the result of hierarchical decision-making processes, and thus are likely to be incompatible with decentralized spontaneous order systems. [21] Thus, a rule promulgated by the EEOC, or OSHA, or EPA, will tend to be extremely complex in an attempt to anticipate all possible situations. Because of their complexity and the attempt to regulate all matters, these rules also will tend to allow little discretion for the regulated to respond according to local needs and circumstances. At the same time, the distance between the rule-makers and rule-followers will tend to result in ill-fitting rules designed on the basis of incomplete information and unawareness of the application of those rules to specific fact situations.[22] Moreover, the process for amending these rules will likely be cumbersome and difficult, as complaints will have to be relayed back up the same pyramid structure. Thus, the rules promulgated by the center of this hierarchy, despite their complexity (and partly because of their complexity), are unlikely to fit with the needs of those at the periphery.

Complex rules will also tend to become obsolete more quickly, requiring constant rewriting in order to keep up with changes in circumstances. The very specificity of complex rules in trying to regulate all contingencies means that those rules will have to be constantly rewritten to deal with changing circumstances.[23] By contrast, simple rules of general application will create long-term stability and predictability.[24] As a result, not only will complex rules be more difficult for individuals to understand and to incorporate into their decision-making, they will also be subject to constant change, requiring ongoing monitoring. Rather than providing a stable and simple background basis for decision-making and individual planning, complex rules thrust themselves into every aspect of decision-making. As a result, the benefits of a decentralized system suffer under the weight of complex rules.[25]

3. Simple Rules, Complex Systems, and Decentralization

Complex rules, therefore, are incompatible with the long-term efficiency of a spontaneous order system.[26] Decentralized, complex systems require simple rules, which will allow individuals to focus on making the many other mutual adjustments which they must make in order for the system to function. Given this, it should not be surprising that when Polanyi finally refers to the substantive legal rules necessary to govern an economic system, his list bears a strong resemblance to Epstein's list of simple rules. Polanyi writes:

> Spontaneous economic systems are ... governed ... by institutions of property and exchange. Dominant over these is the code of private law. In the Code Civil of France (leaving out of account the law of the family) Duguit finds only three fundamental rules and no more—freedom of contract, the inviolability of property, and the duty to compensate another for damage due to one's own fault. Thus it transpires that the main function of the existing spontaneous order of jurisdiction is to govern the spontaneous order of economic life. A *consultative* system of law develops and enforces the rules under which the *competitive* system of production and distribution operates. No marketing system can function without a legal framework which guarantees adequate proprietary powers and enforces contracts.[27]

Similarly, he adds later,

> Generally speaking, the mutual adjustments required for the establishment of a competitive economic order must be initiated by individual agents empowered to dispose of resources and products, subject to general rules; these mutual adjustments are bargains concluded through the market; the application of general rules to conflicts between bargainers constitutes the legal order of private law, which is itself a system of mutual adjustments. Economic liberty and an important range of juridical independence thus jointly form the institutional basis for the social performance of an economic task of a polycentric character.[28]

Thus, Polanyi and Epstein end up at similar points—prescribing simple rules for a complex world. Or, as Epstein sums it up, "Complex rules for a complex world are an invitation to disaster."[29]

Notes

1. Richard A Epstein, *Simple Rules for a Complex World* 32(1995).
2. Id. at 33.
3. Id. at 31.
4. Id. at 21.
5. See id. at 48.
6. Michael Polanyi, *The Logic of Liberty: Reflections and Rejoinders* (University of Chicago Press, Chicago 1951). This is certainly not meant to suggest that Polanyi is unique in recognizing these connections. F. A. Hayek is probably the most famous expositor of the concepts which will be discussed here, but Lon L. Fuller addressed many of the same themes in his article, Freedom—A Suggested Analysis, 68 Harv. L. Rev. 1305 (1955). Fuller recognizes slight differences in terminology and analysis from Polanyi, but admits that his insights build on Polanyi's contributions. See Fuller, Freedom, at 1320 n.7 ("This criticism of one chapter of Polanyi's book does not imply a criticism of the book as a whole. On the contrary, I consider it one of the greatest works I have encountered and certainly the most perceptive analysis of intellectual and economic liberty that I know of. Michael Polanyi's book, along with the writings of Frank H. Knight, have probably influenced the thought of this essay more than anything else I have read."). This short essay, however, will focus on Polanyi's underappreciated contributions.

7. Fuller refers to these concepts as "organization by common ends" and "organization by reciprocity." See Fuller, Freedom, supra note 6, at 1317–19.

8. Polanyi, supra note 6 at 112–14. Although Polanyi refers to this structure as "corporate order," it is applicable to organizations and systems other than prototypical corporations, as the discussion will soon demonstrate.

9. Polanyi estimates that the span of control for a "delicate and rapidly changing task" usually cannot exceed three to five subordinates. Id. at 112. The exact number of subordinates who fall under the "span of control," however, is not important.

10. Polanyi, supra note 6, at 159. Fuller notes that the use of the term "spontaneous order" should not be read to "imply[ ] that they have come into existence without purposive human effort. In fact, . . . they are produced by the coming together of countless individual purposive acts." Fuller, Freedom, supra note, at 1322.

11. Polanyi's example will strike many as being somewhat anachronistic, as few soccer teams in the modern era use five forwards, favoring instead either two or, at most, three forwards.

12. Polanyi, supra note 6, at 118.

13. Id. at 119. See also id. at 156 ("It is clear that the intervention of any human agency which attempted to take over the task of such internal forces would be entirely inadequate. If the particles had to wait to be picked out and placed into position individually, the authorities assuming responsibility for ordering them would, in fact, merely compel them to remain in disorder indefinitely. This seems to suggest that when very large numbers are to be arranged carefully, it can be achieved only by the spontaneous mutual adjustment of the units, not by assignment of the several units to specifically prescribed position.").

14. Fuller, Freedom, supra note 6, at 1320.

15. Id. at 122 ("This shows once more the comparatively small span of control exercised by corporate authority and that if any attempt were made to replace a spontaneous system by a corporate order, it would result in cutting down to a tiny faction the operation of any large system of that kind.").

16. Id. at 114. Thus, primitive or static economies (such as a medieval guild economy) may be governed by highly complex rules, which assign specific tasks to all individuals. Because there would be no need for continuous adjustments among the members of such a system, a hierarchical structure of complex rules assigning specific duties would be workable. See Polanyi, supra note 6, at 190, 190 n.3.

17. See id. at 126–137. Of course, Polanyi was not alone in predicting the eventual abandonment of central planning experiments and the downfall of Communist economies. See id. at 122–23 (discussing von Mises's critique of socialism); id. at 181 (discussing Hayek's analysis of collectivist economic planning).

18. Id. at 162. Polanyi continues, "The result is the ordered growth of the Common Law, steadily reapplying and re-interpreting the same fundamental rules and expanding them thus to a system of increasing scope and consistency. Such coherence and fitness as this system possesses at any time is the direct embodiment of the wisdom with which each consecutive judicial decision is adjusted to all those made before and to any justified changes in public opinion." Id. Polanyi also classifies the process of science as a spontaneous order. See id. at 163–65. Fuller provides as examples such things as "language, economic markets, scientific theory, the common law, and on a homelier plane, a footpath through a woodland." Fuller, Freedom, supra note 6, at 1322.

19. Todd J. Zywicki, A Unanimity-Reinforcing Model of Efficiency in the Common Law: An Institutional Comparison of Common Law and Legislative Solutions to Large-Number Externality Problems, 46 Case Western Reserve L. Rev. 961, 978 (1996). See also Lon L. Fuller, The Morality of Law 74 (1969) (defining law as "the enterprise of subjecting human conduct to the governance of rules"); Richard A. Posner, Economic Analysis of Law 242 (4th ed. 1992) (describing law as a "set of prices" giving individuals incentives to behave in certain ways).

20. Friedrich A. Hayek, (1944) *The Road to Serfdom* 72–73.

21. Indeed, I have argued that the decentralized process of the common law provides a better mechanism than centralized legislative processes in many cases for regulating environmental pollution. See Zywicki, supra note 6, at 1016–31. Epstein, however, argues that environmental pollution provides an example where centralized regulation is necessary, even though he advocates the use of decentralized methods (such as tradable pollution permits) as a mechanism for carrying out that regulation. See Epstein, supra note, at 275–305.

22. Fuller, Freedom, supra note 6, at 1316.

23. See Bruno Leoni, Freedom and the Law 74–75 (expanded 3d ed. 1991); F. A. Hayek, 1 *Law, Legislation, & Liberty: Rules and Order,* 117–18 (1973).

150   TODD J. ZYWICKI

24. See Zywicki, supra note 19, at 995–1004; F. A. Hayek, 1 *Law, Legislation, & Liberty: Rules and Order* 118 (1973) ("To be legitimized, new rules have to obtain the approval of society at large—not by a formal vote, but by gradually spreading acceptance.").

25. Of course, because complex and changing rules make it difficult for average citizens to understand the law and keep up with changes, this increases the demand for lawyers in the economy. See Epstein, supra note 1, at 2.

26. See Epstein, supra note 1, at 245.

27. Polanyi, supra note 6, at 185; compare Epstein, supra note 1, at 53 ("the simple rules are self-ownership, or autonomy; first possession; voluntary exchange; protection against aggression; limited privilege for cases of necessity; and takings of property for public use on payment of just compensation").

28. Polanyi, supra note 1, at 186. See also id. ("[T]he task of allocating a multitude of resources to a large number of productive centres for the purpose of processing them into products of such variety as is usual to-day and distributing the latter rationally to consumers numbering tens of millions, requires for its social management a system of civil law which establishes rights of (marketable) property and enforces contracts.").

29. Epstein, supra note 1, at 140.

Part III
Slippery Slope Analysis

[10]

THE CAMEL'S NOSE IS IN THE TENT: RULES, THEORIES, AND SLIPPERY SLOPES

Mario J. Rizzo[*]

Douglas Glen Whitman[**]

Slippery slopes have been the topic of a spate of recent literature. In this Article, the authors provide a general theory for understanding and evaluating slippery slope arguments and their associated slippery slope events. The central feature of the theory is a structure of discussion within which all arguments take place. The structure is multilayered, consisting of decisions, rules, theories, and research programs. Each layer influences and shapes the layer beneath: Rules influence decisions, theories influence the choice of rules, and research programs influence the choice of theories. In this structure, slippery slope arguments take the form of meta-arguments, as they purport to predict the future development of arguments in the structure of discussion. Evaluating such arguments requires knowledge of the specific content of the structure of discussion itself. This Article then presents four viable types of slippery slope arguments; draws attention to four different factors that, other things equal, tend to increase the likelihood of slippery slopes; and explores a variety of strategies for coping with slippery slopes.

[*]   Department of Economics, New York University.
[**] Department of Economics, California State University, Northridge.
    We are indebted to the James M. Buchanan Center at George Mason University, the Pierre and Enid Goodrich Foundation, and the W.B. Earhart Foundation for financial support. We are also indebted to the following groups for their comments and suggestions: the participants of the Liberty Fund Colloquium on Slippery Slopes and the Austrian Economics Colloquium at New York University. Many individuals have provided valuable suggestions, especially Peter Boettke, Mark Brady, William Butos, Young Back Choi, Adam Gifford, David Harper, Tsutomu Hashimoto, John Hasnas, Sanford Ikeda, Israel Kirzner, Roger Koppl, Elisabeth Krecké, Chidem Kurdas, Ejan Mackaay, Robert Murphy, Edna Ullmann-Margalit, Joseph Salerno, Eugene Volokh, and Douglas Walton. Responsibility for errors remains ours alone.

> *"The question of questions for the politician should ever be—'What type of social structure am I tending to produce?' But this is a question he never entertains."*
>
> —Herbert Spencer, *The Coming Slavery*

INTRODUCTION

"If you accept a seemingly appropriate argument now, you will be more likely to accept an inappropriate argument later. And if you accept such an inappropriate argument, you will be more likely to make a bad decision or perform a dangerous act." This is a common, general form of the so-called slippery slope argument. More specific slippery slope arguments occur in public policy (instituting a price ceiling on milk will lead to price controls on the sale of cows[1]), in law (forbidding the Nazis to march in Skokie will lead to the forbidding of valuable speech that hurts the feelings of religious or ethnic groups[2]), in ethics (acceptance of the abortion of a month-old fetus will lead

---

1.   For an explanation of how price controls on milk can lead to further controls on the prices of inputs into milk production, see LUDWIG VON MISES, *Middle-of-the-Road Policy Leads to Socialism*, in PLANNING FOR FREEDOM AND SIXTEEN OTHER ESSAYS AND ADDRESSES 22–24 (4th ed. 1980). See more generally LUDWIG VON MISES, HUMAN ACTION: A TREATISE ON ECONOMICS 762–64 (3d ed. 1966), for a description of the process by which price controls on some goods and services lead to demand for price controls on other goods and services.

2.   *See, e.g.*, Collin v. Smith, 578 F.2d 1197, 1205–06 (7th Cir. 1978).

to acceptance of the abortion of third-trimester fetuses or even to infanticide[3]), and, indeed, in almost every arena where decisions must be made.

Slippery slope arguments have been used by thinkers from across the political spectrum. These arguments can be found in the writings of twentieth and twenty-first century civil libertarians, opponents of euthanasia, opponents of some frontier medical procedures including genetic engineering and cloning, and advocates and opponents of abortion rights. A shared characteristic of these arguments is that they are used to oppose some type of change in the status quo. In that sense, and only in that sense, slippery slope arguments are usually employed for "conservative" purposes.

The scholarly literature on slippery slopes and their related arguments is not extensive. Recently, however, there have been some important contributions. Sanford Ikeda has analyzed tendencies toward expansion that inhere in the state's intervention in the economy.[4] Eugene Volokh has produced a wide-ranging study of various possible slippery slope mechanisms in both judicial decisionmaking and legislative action.[5] And Douglas Walton has critically analyzed the various forms of slippery slope arguments used in many types of public debate.[6] None of these authors, however, has attempted to construct a unified framework in which such arguments can be studied and related to actual or potential slippery slope events. This is what this Article attempts to provide.

Sometimes slippery slopes appear to involve only actions: One action leads to another. But in the cases of law, ethics, and public policy, the actions usually require justification. Hence, first and foremost, *slippery slopes are slopes of arguments*: One practical argument tends to lead to another, which means that one justified action, often a decision, tends to lead to another. When we say that one argument (and its supported action) tends to lead to another, we mean that it makes the occurrence of the subsequent argument more likely, not that it necessarily makes it highly likely or, still less, inevitable.[7] Hence the transition between arguments is not based on strict logical entailment.

---

3.   "Infanticide (killing of newly born children), also called neonaticide, follows abortion like night follows day." TENNESSEE RIGHT TO LIFE, HUMAN LIFE ISSUES, *at* http://tennesseerighttolife.org/ human_life_issues/human_life_issues_infanticide.htm. For a more objective analysis of slippery slope arguments in the context of abortion, see, for example, DOUGLAS WALTON, SLIPPERY SLOPE ARGUMENTS 45–50 (1992).

4.   SANFORD IKEDA, DYNAMICS OF THE MIXED ECONOMY: TOWARD A THEORY OF INTERVENTIONISM (1997).

5.   Eugene Volokh, *The Mechanisms of the Slippery Slope*, 116 HARV. L. REV. 1026 (2003).

6.   *See generally* WALTON, *supra* note 3.

7.   "A slippery slope argument claims that permitting the instant case—a case that it concedes to be facially innocuous and that it linguistically distinguishes from the danger case—will nevertheless lead to, or *increase the likelihood* of, the danger case." Frederick Schauer, *Slippery Slopes*, 99 HARV. L. REV. 361, 369 (1985) (emphasis added).

The ubiquity of slippery slope arguments should not lead us to believe they are unproblematic or simple in structure. First, there is no single paradigm of a slippery slope argument. Walton has distinguished four types: sorites, precedent, causal, and full (a complex combination of the first three).[8] Our concerns do not exactly parallel these distinctions. In particular, our concerns do not extend to the purely causal argument. This is not to say that the causal mechanisms by which one external event leads to another are irrelevant, but that they must be mediated by arguments. We are interested in those realms of decisionmaking in which justification is the essence. Thus we are concerned with arguments about arguments—also known as *meta-arguments*. To put it another way, these are arguments about accepting or rejecting arguments for actions. They involve intellectual commitments that, as it were, take on a life of their own.

Second, there is the perplexing question of whether slippery slope arguments invoke some form of irrationality. Can purely rational thought produce a progression from the acceptance of a correct or persuasive argument to the acceptance of a clearly incorrect or unpersuasive argument? Slippery slope arguments appear to be vulnerable to the following three objections from the perspective of rational choice:

1. If the future decision (the "danger case," as Schauer calls it[9]) is bad, but the prior decisions are good, why not simply refrain from making the bad decision down the road? The slippery slope argument seems to rob our future selves of the ability to make reasoned decisions. It treats future decisionmakers as automata who cannot resist doing the wrong thing. We call this the *automaton objection*.

2. If the consequences of a sequence of decisions are undesirable overall, then why are we tempted to defect from the right path now? Suppose, for instance, that undesirable future decisions will somehow flow with high probability from the present decision. Unless we are simply ignorant of the causal chain, the undesirability

---

8.   WALTON, *supra* note 3, at 3–7. A sorites argument claims that, with respect to a critical characteristic, it is impossible to say where the dividing line is between the clear presence of the characteristic and its clear absence. A precedential argument is based on the notion that a decision in a particular case commits one to decide the same way in future similar cases. A causal argument claims that an initial event causes further events leading to an ultimate bad outcome, similar to a domino effect. To see the interaction of all three in a full argument, consider a rule that would make the termination of "biologically unworthy" life permissible. This is obviously a vague concept without a clear cut-off point. Initially, it might be applied to cases of infants born without some important part of their brains. If such a decision were to become a precedent, then it could be applied in other, somewhat different, cases. For example, the termination of grossly mentally defective life might lead over a series of events to the termination of the lives of those with grossly deformed facial features.
9.   Schauer, *supra* note 7, at 365.

of the final outcome should be imputed backward to the initial decision,[10] and the initial decision should thus not appear desirable after all. The slippery slope argument seems to violate the assumption, taken for granted by many economists, of rational expectations. This we call the *imputation objection.*

3. The mere fact that the ultimate decision appears undesirable from today's vantage point does not mean it will appear undesirable tomorrow. After all, if we take that final step when the time arrives, it must look desirable at that time. The slippery slope argument appears to privilege the current over the future point of view, ruling out the possibility that new values will exist at the moment of decision. We call this the *presentism objection.*[11]

Because of these and similar objections, some analysts have concluded that slippery slope arguments are questionable or even fallacious. Nonetheless, slippery slope arguments can constitute a valid form of argumentation. In this Article, we provide a general theory of slippery slope arguments that allows us, among other things, to evaluate their validity and explore strategies for avoiding the events they describe. In Part I, we outline the essential features of a slippery slope argument, and clarify terminology. In Part II, we present a rubric for understanding the structure of discussion in which slippery slope arguments—and all other arguments, for that matter—are made. This structure provides us with a foundation for analyzing particular types of slippery slope arguments. In Parts III and IV, we discuss four different processes that could provide the basis for slippery slopes: the sorites with precedent process, the altered economic incentives process, the separately validated propositions process, and the Humean beneficence process. In Part V, we respond to the three objections to slippery slope arguments presented above, explaining why

---

10.   Some clarification of the idea of "somehow flow[ing] with high probability" is in order. In order to differentiate this objection from the automaton objection, we do not focus on the (in)voluntariness of the future decisions. Instead, we treat the high probability of undesirable future decisions as emanating from the inability of decisionmakers to find relevant dissimilarities between a future case and the current one. Thus, the imputation is epistemic rather than causal. It is the joint consequence of the decisionmaker's adherence to a principle of universalizability ("treating similar cases in a similar way") and his inability to discern a relevant dissimilarity. "If we judge X to be right, and we can point to no relevant dissimilarities between X and Y, then we cannot judge Y to be wrong." TOM L. BEAUCHAMP & JAMES F. CHILDRESS, PRINCIPLES OF BIOMEDICAL ETHICS 120 (2d ed. 1983).

11.   "Presentism" refers to the stipulation that the individual never acts counter-preferentially. He always acts to maximize the satisfaction of his current preferences, including his current preferences about the future. So at t = 0 the agent wishes mightily to avoid the "danger case," but when the choice arrives at t = 1, with changed preferences, he embraces it (if he has not previously bound himself against it). Presentism excludes the possibility that the agent may avoid certain choices simply because of previous preferences or a commitment to oneself based on them. *See* JED RUBENFELD, FREEDOM AND TIME: A THEORY OF CONSTITUTIONAL GOVERNMENT 103–30 (2001).

we think they are not (always) valid. In Part VI, we offer several propositions about factors that make slippery slopes more likely. Finally, in Part VII, we discuss various strategies employed by individuals and systems for dealing with or reducing the likelihood of slippery slopes. We conclude with some general observations about the validity and invalidity of slippery slope arguments.

I. DEFINITIONS AND CLARIFICATIONS

A. Essential Characteristics of a Slippery Slope Argument

Although there is no paradigm case of *the* slippery slope argument, there are characteristic features of all such arguments. The key components of slippery slope arguments are three:

1. An initial, seemingly acceptable argument and decision;
2. A "danger case"—a later argument and decision that are clearly unacceptable;
3. A "process" or "mechanism"[12] by which accepting the initial argument and making the initial decision raise the likelihood of accepting the later argument and making the later decision.

The "processes" invoked as the link between the initial case and the danger case can be quite varied. It is useful for our purposes to distinguish processes that, in principle at least, can be generated by a single individual in isolation from the activities of others—in other words, a Robinson Crusoe process. We call these *microprocesses*. For example, Robinson Crusoe might be susceptible to a slippery slope from accepting the virtue of relaxation from work to accepting the vice of laziness. (This slope might occur as a result of, for example, Crusoe's commitment to reasoning by analogy from past choices to present ones.) Note that the defining feature of a microprocess is not that it must be generated by a single individual, but that it could be; this point will become clearer later.[13] In contrast, other processes, by their very nature, require the interaction of many

---

12. In this Article, we choose the term "process" over "mechanism." Although mechanism is, in some respects, more precise, it may convey a sense of automaticity or deterministic reaction as in the common use of the word "mechanistic." We wish to avoid that connotation. In what follows, we do not intend to suggest that the processes discussed are completely deterministic.

13. The results of the microprocesses are usually unexpected. The source of this is the aggregation of individually plausible premises and arguments. These individually plausible statements may not be collectively consistent. The "paradoxical" conclusions reached by a decisionmaker are the results of prior intellectual commitments. *See generally* NICHOLAS RESCHER, PARADOXES: THEIR ROOTS, RANGE AND RESOLUTION 65–70 (2001). Microprocesses can therefore be set in motion by a single mind that is not fully aware of the consequences of the aggregation of its accepted arguments. In this sense, they are generated by individual action or decisions but not by individual design. *See generally* FRIEDRICH A. HAYEK, *The Results of Human Action but Not of Human Design, in* STUDIES IN PHILOSOPHY, POLITICS AND ECONOMICS 96 (1967).

individuals to generate the final result. These we call *macroprocesses*. For example, certain kinds of government regulation may distort the incentives of particular agents, as when retail price controls encourage suppliers to limit production. This may produce unintended consequences for consumers who then try to remedy the situation by voting for controls on the input prices faced by suppliers.[14] In this Article, we examine slippery slope processes of both micro and macro varieties.

B.   Slippery Slope Arguments and Slippery Slope Events

Considerable confusion can be forestalled by distinguishing between slippery slope arguments and slippery slope events. A slippery slope argument (SSA) is an argument about how the acceptance of one argument (regarding a decision, act, or policy) may lead to the acceptance of other arguments (regarding other decisions, acts, or policies). It has a hypothetical form: if this, then that—with increased likelihood. A slippery slope event (SSE) refers to the actual manifestation of the events (decisions, acts, or policies) described in the SSA.

It is possible that the persuasiveness of an SSA may preclude the occurrence of an SSE. For example, if (on the basis of some initial argument) decisionmakers are persuaded that allowing first-trimester abortions will lead with high probability to infanticide, they may never accept the initial argument for permitting first-trimester abortions. Thus, acceptance of the SSA may help prevent the more easily observable SSE.

To understand better the distinction between an SSA and an SSE, it is important to recognize that there are two distinct types of ideas in the social sciences: *constitutive ideas* and *speculative ideas*.[15] Constitutive ideas are ideas that motivate the actions of individuals. Speculative ideas, on the other hand, are ideas that observers—such as social scientists or policy analysts—have about the actions individuals will take and the results that will follow. For instance, ideas that consumers have about the desirability of goods and services are constitutive ideas, as they affect consumers' buying decisions. The ideas that

---

14.   In general, macroprocesses are those that stem from the existence of social systems and systems effects. The defining characteristics of systems are interconnections between decisions and emergent outcomes. *See generally* ROBERT JERVIS, SYSTEM EFFECTS: COMPLEXITY IN POLITICAL AND SOCIAL LIFE 3–25 (1997). In these cases, the aggregation of the actions of many individuals is the essence of the process. The consequences of this aggregation are beyond the anticipation and intention of the actors because of the cost of such knowledge, the effects of bounded rationality, or the lack of intellectual insight and alertness. Thus, in a second sense, these are the results of individuals' actions but not of individuals' designs. *See supra* note 13.

15.   F.A. HAYEK, THE COUNTER-REVOLUTION OF SCIENCE: STUDIES ON THE ABUSE OF REASON 61–65 (2d ed. 1979).

economists have about the effect of consumers' decisions on market outcomes (such as the prices and quantities of goods sold) are speculative ideas. Although constitutive and speculative ideas are usually distinct, it is possible for a speculative idea to *become* a constitutive idea. For example, if economists predict that a recession is looming, and consumers believe them, then consumers may respond by altering their buying decisions. Thus, the economists' speculative idea that a recession is coming becomes the consumers' constitutive idea, insofar as it motivates consumers to reduce unnecessary expenditures in the expectation of possible unemployment.

SSAs are typically speculative ideas. They are predictions, made by observers, about how acceptance of some ideas (and resulting actions) can lead to acceptance of other ideas (and resulting actions). But an SSA can become a constitutive idea, if the SSA is accepted by individuals and affects their actions. Indeed, the person who formulates an SSA may do so with the intention of persuading others to change their behavior—that is, with the intention of making it a constitutive idea. For instance, those who argue against voluntary euthanasia, on grounds that it will increase the likelihood of involuntary euthanasia, presumably hope their argument will persuade the public to oppose policies allowing voluntary euthanasia.

In short, an SSA is by nature an idea about other ideas. Like the theories and models used by social scientists, it makes a prediction about the behavior of people who are motivated by their own ideas.

II. THE STRUCTURE OF DISCUSSION
AND ARGUMENT: THE MICROANALYTIC FOUNDATIONS
OF SLIPPERY SLOPES

A distinctive feature of most, perhaps all, SSAs is that they are arguments about arguments. That is, they are meta-arguments. The SSA relies on the notion that the argument (and decision) we take now will, at some time, make people more likely to accept another argument.

Consider the illustrative case in which the Village of Skokie, Illinois, made it a misdemeanor to disseminate material promoting or inciting racial or religious hatred. This included, in the words of the local ordinance, the "public display of markings and clothing of symbolic significance." Accordingly, Skokie tried to stop a Nazi group from demonstrating peacefully, in uniforms and with banners, in front of the village hall. In *Collin v. Smith,*[16] the Seventh Circuit struck down the ordinance. The court explained that if it were permissible to graft an exception onto the First Amendment for a demonstration

---

16.   578 F.2d 1197 (7th Cir. 1978).

that might inflict "psychic trauma" on certain people (such as Holocaust survivors), it might also be permissible to halt any speech that generates "anger," "unrest," or "dispute."[17] At that point nothing would remain of the First Amendment. In our terminology, the court is stating that, if it accepts an argument about the permissibility of the Skokie ordinance, it would also have to accept (or would at least be more likely to accept) future arguments about further speech restrictions. These arguments might allow, perhaps *seriatim*, restrictions on the kind of speech that generates anger, then unrest, and then simple dispute. Having accepted the initial Skokie argument, the court would find the others "indistinguishable in principle." It would then be led to accept an ultimate argument that, in today's view, is clearly wrong.

In essence, the court makes an SSA that claims that if Argument 1 is accepted, then so will be Argument 2, and then Argument 3, and so on to, say, Argument 10 that would justify some clearly unacceptable outcome. Now, it cannot be the case that Arguments 1 and 10 are identical; otherwise the SSA would be redundant. If Argument 10 were clearly bad, and Arguments 1 and 10 were identical, then Argument 1 would be unacceptable on its face. Therefore, on what basis can the analyst predict that *different* arguments will be made and accepted? How can he predict what he himself or later decisionmakers will find similar or close to a previous argument? Only, it seems, if he understands the theoretical framework in which the judicial decisionmakers operate.

To understand an SSA, then, it is necessary to think more carefully about the structure in which decisions are made. Our object in this part is to lay out a rubric for thinking about the structure of decisionmaking. We start by offering a discussion of the key concepts within this structure: rules, theories, research programs, and arguments.

A. Rules

A rule is a mapping from a type of factual situation or event to a desirable action. A rule's mapping seeks "to change or channel behavior" relative to what it would be without the rule.[18] In political analysis, the factual situation may be a social problem and the desired action a governmental policy. In law, the situation may be a justiciable dispute and the action a ruling. In ethics, the situation may be a set of moral options and the action a moral decision.

Three clarifications are in order. First, it is important to distinguish our use of the word "rule" from other meanings of the term. There is a difference

---

17.   *Id.* at 1205–06.
18.   FREDERICK SCHAUER, PLAYING BY THE RULES: A PHILOSOPHICAL EXAMINATION OF RULE-BASED DECISION-MAKING IN LAW AND IN LIFE 2 (1991).

between rule-conforming and rule-guided behavior.[19] In the case of rule-conforming behavior, agents need not understand that they act or make decisions in accordance with a rule. They simply exhibit a regularity, which the rule describes. Much animal behavior, such as the tendency of birds to migrate, conforms to rules in this way. The laws of physics, such as Newton's Law that bodies tend to move toward each other, are also of this nature. In rule-guided behavior, a rule is prescriptive in nature, as agents use the rule as a reason or justification for their decisions. It is the latter sense of the word "rule" that we employ here.

Second, it is worth noting that rules are often stated along with their rationales, that is, as part of arguments. But a rule in its pure form is simply a mapping. It is also true that rules can map situations to more than one desirable action. But, for simplicity, we shall think of rules as issuing in one fairly specific action.[20]

Third, any rule works by reference to a set of characteristics that describe a situation, and this set is necessarily a subset of all those characteristics that might be construed as describing it "fully." Rules are unavoidably abstract, as they omit or abstract from a potentially infinite number of characteristics that could be used. Consider a legal rule that says, "Whenever a car rear-ends another car, the car that came from behind is liable for damages." This rule identifies one characteristic of the situation (which car came from behind) while effectively ignoring an endless number of other characteristics (the color of the cars, the time of the accident, the number of people in each car, whether the occupants were listening to their radios, ad infinitum).[21] Of course, actual rules can be, and generally are, more complex. They may identify a very large number of characteristics. But no matter how many characteristics are identified, an infinite number of other characteristics are ignored. The choice of which characteristics to include, if it is not arbitrary, must be made on the basis of a higher-order conceptual entity; that is, a theory.

---

19. Edward F. McClennen & Scott Shapiro, *Rule-Guided Behavior*, in THE NEW PALGRAVE DICTIONARY OF ECONOMICS AND THE LAW 363, 363 (Peter Newman ed., 1998).

20. Compare, however, Joseph Raz:

The distinction between rules and principles of obligation both in law and outside of it turns on the character of the norm-act prescribed. Rules prescribe relatively specific acts; principles prescribe highly unspecific actions . . . . The distinction is . . . one of degree, since there is no hard and fast line between acts that are specific and those which are unspecific.

Joseph Raz, *Legal Principle and the Limits of Law*, 81 YALE L.J. 823, 838 (1972).

21. "A rule withdraws from the decisionmaker's consideration one or more of the circumstances that would be relevant to [a] decision according to a standard." Isaac Ehrlich & Richard A. Posner, *An Economic Analysis of Legal Rulemaking*, 3 J. LEGAL STUD. 257, 258 (1974).

B. Theories

A theory is a system of ideas based on general principles designed to organize thought and to explain or justify something. A theory can be positive, normative, or both.[22]

The most important role of theory, at least in the present context, is as a source of justifications for rules and decisions. In normative terms, a theory can justify a rule.[23] The normative and positive elements of a theory interact to produce arguments about how rules should be chosen and how decisions should be made. As suggested earlier, a rule itself does not necessarily carry with it any justification; it could be entirely arbitrary in the characteristics it identifies as relevant. But often, rules have their basis in theories about what kinds of characteristics are positively and normatively relevant in a given context.

For instance, the rule "whenever a car rear-ends another car, the car that came from behind is liable for damages" might be justified by a theory that emphasizes the capacity of law to promote accident prevention. Thus, if the driver of the rear car has greater control over whether a rear-end accident takes place (a positive judgment), and it is desirable to minimize the sum of expected accident and accident prevention costs (a normative judgment or standard), then the theory, at least prima facie, justifies the rule.

Theories are closely related to the notions of relevance and similarity. The application of these notions, far from being a matter of direct insight, is theory-laden. What is relevant according to one theory may be irrelevant according to another. For example, an orange is similar to a banana, and a banana is similar to a cigar; therefore, can we say an orange is similar to a cigar? To answer affirmatively would be an example of invalid reasoning because the similarity relations are not the same.[24] The first similarity relation presumably derives from a theory that identifies an object's use or origin in nature as a relevant characteristic, whereas the second similarity relation presumably derives from a theory that identifies an object's shape or length as a relevant characteristic.

One implication of the theory-laden nature of relevance and similarity is that a theory can be either implicit or explicit. Even if someone claims not to have a theory in some context, his statements about similarity and relevance

---

22.   A positive theory explains or predicts an event or state of affairs without reference to the value judgments of the theorist. A normative theory establishes an analytical ideal against which some aspect of the world is evaluated by the theorist or observer.

23.   "Rule-based decision-making . . . is a form of decision-making arising *within* some theory of justification and existing only relative to it." SCHAUER, *supra* note 18, at 86.

24.   WALTON, *supra* note 3, at 131–32.

in that context belie his claim. He must have a theory, even if he does not realize what it is. Karl Popper notes:

> Generally, similarity, and with it repetition, always presuppose the adoption of a point of view: some similarities or repetitions will strike us if we are interested in one problem, and others if we are interested in another problem. But if similarity and repetition presuppose the adoption of a point of view, or an interest, or an expectation, it is logically necessary that points of view, or interests, or expectations, are logically prior, as well as temporally (or causally or psychologically) prior, to repetition.[25]

In short, there cannot be any theory-free identification of "similarity." It can be identified only by use of a (possibly implicit) theory.[26]

C. Research Programs

"Research program" is a term we have borrowed from philosopher of science Imre Lakatos, who uses it to refer to a broad set of basic assumptions, premises, and methods shared by a group of scientists working in the same scientific tradition.[27] A research program is sufficiently loose that it can encompass multiple theories held by different scientists, and those theories may contradict each other. The research program places constraints on the types of theories scientists can use without losing credibility in their community of scholars.[28] We use the term "research program" here in much the same way,

---

25.   KARL R. POPPER, THE LOGIC OF SCIENTIFIC DISCOVERY 421–22 (10th ed. 1980).

26.   This point has not always been recognized, even by distinguished legal scholars. Edward Levi, for example, believed that the "basic pattern of legal reasoning is reasoning by example." EDWARD LEVI, AN INTRODUCTION TO LEGAL REASONING 1–2 (1949). The pattern consists of three steps. First, "similarity is seen between cases; next the rule of law *inherent* in the first case is announced; then the rule of law is made applicable to the second case." *Id.* (emphasis added). This deceptively simple procedure involves theory at every stage. "Similarity," as we have seen, is dependent on a theoretical construct. Extracting the "inherent" rule of law depends on a theory that correctly identifies a set of factors. To apply a rule requires that we distinguish relevant and irrelevant characteristics of the new case. Furthermore, since a rule is first established in a particular factual context (never exactly repeated), it must change, even slightly, as it is applied. A theory establishes the framework of allowable changes in rules justified by the theory.

27.   Imre Lakatos, *Falsification and the Methodology of Scientific Research Programmes, in* CRITICISM AND THE GROWTH OF KNOWLEDGE 91 (Imre Lakatos & Alan Musgrave eds., 1970). For a summary of the components of a research program, see *id.* at 132–35.

28.   There is an obvious similarity with Thomas Kuhn's idea of a scientific paradigm. *See generally* THOMAS S. KUHN, THE STRUCTURE OF SCIENTIFIC REVOLUTIONS (2d ed. 1970). We prefer the concept of a research program to that of the paradigm, however, for reasons identified by John Worrall:

> Although Kuhn's detailed development of [the paradigm]—especially his emphasis on inarticulable skills, "disciplinary matrices", and the like—can be challenged (and certainly stands in need of clarification), he was surely pointing in the direction of an important and then relatively neglected aspect of mature science. Imre Lakatos, with his notion of research programme complete with "positive heuristic", and Larry Laudan, with his notion of a research

but without the emphasis on science.[29] In law, the relevant community may include judges, legal scholars, and private actors subject to the law. In ethics, the relevant community may be much broader, including everyone within the same moral community.

A research program is not a theory in the usual sense, as it does not have enough content to provide meaningful predictions or explanations in applied contexts. Instead, it is a meta-theory, a theory about theories. A research program in the law places broad limits on what legal theories can assume, how they can differ, and what sorts of conclusions they can reach. In other words, a research program defines the structure of allowable change and difference among theories, thereby indirectly affecting rules and decisions.

As an example of the sort of guidelines that may characterize a research program, consider Melvin Eisenberg's claim that replicability in legal decisionmaking requires that "the courts employ a consistent methodology across cases."[30] The use of a common methodology, Eisenberg argues, enables "private actors, within limits, to determine before they enter into a transaction the legal rules—including the 'new' legal rules—that will govern the transaction if a dispute should arise."[31] Perhaps this conclusion is too strong, because a research program or "methodology" is an incompletely defined structure. It cannot, therefore, provide a great deal of guidance for private actors attempting to predict outcomes in specific disputes. Nonetheless, the use of a common methodology places limitations on how far a legal decisionmaker's approach may differ from the approaches of others in the legal community at large.[32]

One example of a legal research program is the economic efficiency approach. The normative premise of this research program is the notion that legal rules should be chosen so as to maximize economic efficiency, understood

---

tradition, both later underlined this same point in slightly different (*and considerably sharper*) ways.

John Worrall, *Philosophy and the Natural Sciences*, in PHILOSOPHY 2: FURTHER THROUGH THE SUBJECT 203 (A.C. Grayling ed., 1998) (emphasis added).

29.   This usage may appear awkward in the case of law, since it seems that a research program should have something to do with research. Law, in fact, is generated by an intellectual framework with assumptions, premises, and methods. So in this sense, legal decisions *are* the result of "research," or the development of theories, rules, and arguments within a "research program."

30.   MELVIN ARON EISENBERG, THE NATURE OF THE COMMON LAW 11 (1988).

31.   *Id.*

32.   As Gerald Postema notes:

Classical common law jurisprudence resolutely resisted the theoretical pressure to identify law with canonically formulated, discrete rules of law. Law, on this view, is not a set of rules or laws, but a practised framework of practical reasoning, and this practised framework provides a form of social ordering. Its rules and norms can be formulated, perhaps, but no such formulation is conclusively authoritative.

Gerald Postema, *Philosophy of the Common Law*, in THE OXFORD HANDBOOK OF JURISPRUDENCE AND PHILOSOPHY OF LAW 596 (Jules Coleman & Scott Shapiro eds., 2002).

as social wealth maximization.[33] There are a variety of assumptions inherent in this approach, mostly drawn from the field of economics, including: Agents have relatively stable and well-defined preferences; agents change their behavior in response to legal incentives; wealth maximization is a relevant standard for measuring social welfare; and so forth. But within the economic efficiency approach, there exist differing theories. Richard Epstein, for instance, has emphasized the importance of simple, well-known rules that serve to guide the expectations of litigants in a wide range of cases.[34] Richard Posner, on the other hand, has placed more emphasis on the selection of rules that induce wealth-maximizing choices in specific circumstances.[35] Their differing theories have yielded differing conclusions about which rules should be used in specific areas of law; for instance, Posner has generally supported negligence rules in the law of tort, whereas Epstein has leaned toward strict liability rules.[36] More generally, legal efficiency analysts can reach different conclusions because of their differing perspectives on issues such as the magnitude of transaction costs, the relevance of administrative costs, the elasticity of litigants' behavior with respect to expected punishments, or the frequency of efficiency-relevant parameters across cases.

D. Arguments

For our purposes, an argument is a reason or sequence of reasons, usually defeasible, for acting in a particular manner. Often, an argument will take the form of a deductive justification:

> If *E* occurs and has characteristics *X*, *Y*, *Z*, then one should do *D* (major premise).

---

33.   Social wealth maximization may be seen as a generalization of the more specific standard of the minimized sum of expected accident and accident prevention costs mentioned *infra* Part II.B. Minimization of the latter does not necessarily imply maximization of the former in a model with more than two cost variables.

34.   *See generally* RICHARD A. EPSTEIN, SIMPLE RULES FOR A COMPLEX WORLD (1995).

35.   *See generally* RICHARD A. POSNER, ECONOMIC ANALYSIS OF LAW (5th ed. 1998).

36.   Over the years the differences between Posner and Epstein have narrowed considerably, coming down to an important matter of emphasis. Posner stresses the multidimensionality of the choice between negligence and strict liability. He believes that there are many efficiency considerations: some more applicable in some contexts than in others, including the levels of care and of activity, and the response to court errors in applying the negligence standard. "Because of these differences between negligence and strict liability, we would not expect the tort system to opt all for one or all for the other. Nor would we expect the balance between the two regimes to be the same at all times." POSNER, *supra* note 35, at 196. Epstein, on the other hand, has concluded that because of high administrative costs in making the judgments required in a negligence system (such as, the costs of untaken precautions and the probabilities of unique accidents), strict liability is generally more efficient than negligence. "But this implicit acquiescence in cost/benefit thinking does not require making cost/benefit analyses as part and parcel of the legal rules. Quite the opposite, achieving the efficient social outcome often requires that the legal rules *consciously* avoid making any explicit reference to cost/benefit analysis." EPSTEIN, *supra* note 34, at 97.

Event E has occurred and has characteristics X, Y, Z (minor premise).
Therefore, one should do D.

This argument provides a normative major premise for reaching a conclusion, and a decisionmaker who wishes to apply the argument must verify or support the minor factual premise.

Again, some clarifications are in order. First, we employ the word "argument" in the sense of a *justification* for taking some action or accepting some proposition. This is distinct from other sorts of arguments, such as the use of empirical data to test a scientific theory. Second, it is important to distinguish a justificatory argument from a causal explanation of some agent's action. Simply because the foregoing syllogism is valid, and even if its premises are true, the agent need not act in accordance with the conclusion. He obviously can ignore his duty to do what he "should" do. Nevertheless, the argument provides a structure for the justification of an action—a reason or set of reasons for acting in a certain way.[37]

We reach the definition of argument last, because arguments can take place on different levels of analysis. The structure we have outlined here consists of four levels:

1. Decisions
2. Rules
3. Theories[38]
4. Research Programs[39]

At each level, there are arguments among the different items at that level, and some of those arguments consist of applying items at the next higher level. At the decisions level, there are arguments made about which decision to make, and some of those arguments involve the application of rules. At the rules level, there are arguments about which rule to select, and some of those arguments involve the application of theories. At the theories level, there are arguments about which theory to employ, and some of those arguments involve the application of research programs.

---

37. Not all arguments are deductive in form. A deductive argument such as that in the text presupposes that there is no problem interpreting an existing normative rule as the generalization in the major premise. It also presupposes that there is sufficient legal or normative warrant for the major premise in the first place. In a context in which there are no explicitly stated rules, one must go beyond the "problem of interpretation" to determine whether there is sufficient warrant in the appropriate sources for the generalization (the "problem of relevance"). Establishing the correct interpretation or finding sufficient warrant for a rule is not arrived at by deductive argument. Other methods, such as analogous reasoning, must be used. *See* Neil MacCormick, Legal Reasoning and Legal Theory 19–72 (H.L.A. Hart ed., 1978).

38. Theories can exist at multiple levels; a low-level theory might be a relatively specific normative standard. See the discussion *infra* Part II.F.

39. Research programs may include relatively general or abstract normative standards.

E.   Example: Make-Up Exam *Meshugas*[40]

Suppose a student asks his professor, "Why did you refuse to give me a make-up exam?" The professor responds, "Because there is a rule that, absent a doctor's note, you may not be given a make-up exam. You don't have a doctor's note, so you don't get a make-up exam." This is an argument at the decision level; it is a reason for deciding not to give a make-up exam. It is also the application of a rule.

Now suppose the student responds, "But my great aunt Polly died. One purpose of the rule was to allow exceptions for students who have a good reason for missing the exam. A death in the family is a good reason, so the rule should have an exception for that."[41] This is an argument, but it is no longer at the decision level. Instead, it is at the rules level. The student contends that the rule should be something other than what it is. To bolster his argument, he appeals to the justification for the rule, and in doing so he is applying a theory about how to select rules. He hopes the professor will share his normative judgment (that a death in the family is a good reason to miss an exam) as well as his understanding of one purpose of the make-up rule (to allow exceptions for good reasons). In short, the student hopes the professor will share his theory.

The professor might at this point advance theoretical arguments against the student's position. For instance, he might agree that one purpose of the rule is to make exceptions for good reasons, but respond that the death of a distant family member is not a good enough reason to expand the rule to include the present case. This argument, like the student's, is about the correct application of the theory. That is, the student and professor are having a rules-level discussion, in which appeal is made to a shared theory.

On the other hand, the professor might argue that a purpose of the rule is not merely to allow exceptions, but also to constrain the professor's discretion. In making this argument, the professor posits an alternative theory of the justification for rules, and he thereby raises the discussion to the theories level within a research program.[42]

---

40.   "Meshugas" is Yiddish (and New Yorkese) for craziness. For a humorous discussion of the use of Yiddish in court decisions, see Alex Kozinski & Eugene Volokh, *Lawsuit, Shmawsuit*, 103 YALE L.J. 463 (1993).

41.   Relatedly, in a humorous article, Mike Adams observes that a "student's grandmother is far more likely to die suddenly just before the student takes an exam than at any other time of the year." Mike Adams, *The Dead Grandmother/Exam Syndrome and the Potential Downfall of American Society*, CONN. REV., Summer 1990, at 70, 70, *available at* http://biology.ecsu.ctstateu.edu/People/ConnRev. The author facetiously concludes: "Family members literally worry themselves to death over the outcome of their relatives' performance on each exam." *Id.* at 72.

42.   When there is discussion at a certain level, it may employ items derived from a higher level. A discussion at the decision level will employ rules (that are effectively taken for granted). The

It would not be terribly surprising to hear any of the arguments made so far. But it would certainly be surprising to hear the professor say, "The rationale of the theory underlying the rule is to maximize my personal satisfaction, and I don't want to administer make-up exams." If he did, he would be raising the discussion to the research programs level. A professor with this point of view would stand outside the research program in which most professors, students, and other members of the educational community operate.[43]

The different levels at which arguments can be made are not hermetically sealed off from each other. As the example indicates, the different levels of argument can mingle, even within a single conversation. And sometimes, the level at which an argument is made may not be clear. For instance, suppose the student argues, "You should let me take a make-up exam anyway, because my great aunt died." If the professor agrees, has the professor changed the rule (operating at the rules level), or has he simply chosen not to apply the rule in the present case (operating at the decisions level)? After all, arguments may be defeated, so the choice not to apply a rule does not necessarily imply a modification of the rule. The argument for the application of the rule may be simply incorrect. But we contend that, at least in principle, it is possible to distinguish between levels of argumentation.

The structure we've described consisting of four levels (decisions, rules, theories, and research programs) is a simplification. What we've called the theories level may actually consist of multiple layers. Some theories are broader and more abstract, others narrower and more applied. In a discussion about choosing among theories (not merely applying them to choose rules), the arguments need not appeal to the research program, but merely to a higher level of theory.

Our broader point is simply that discussion and argumentation can take place at many different levels of analysis. Those things that are taken more or less for granted at a lower level can become objects of questioning and analysis at higher levels.

F. Arguments About Arguments

A distinguishing feature of an SSA is that it relies on the future acceptance of arguments not yet made or appreciated. But in order to predict, even roughly, the arguments that may be accepted, an SSA must go beyond the level

---

discussion at the rules level will employ a theory (that is taken for granted). A discussion at the theory level will employ a research program (again taken for granted).

43.   Presumably the more common research program would include the normative standard of maximizing the joint welfare of students and professors or, less plausibly, the welfare of students alone.

at which the initial argument is constructed. It must go at least one step up in the decisions–rules–theories–research programs structure.

Consider the following hypothetical argument against socialized healthcare: "In a socialized system of healthcare, people are not confronted with the monetary costs of their risky behavior; consequently, a moral hazard problem is likely to result. People will take greater health risks than otherwise. In the aggregate, such behavior will drive up the costs of the system as a whole, fueling demands by taxpayers and legislators to restrain the behaviors that increase costs. Thus they will end up supporting the regulation of lifestyle choices, such as 'unsafe' sexual practices, indulgence in dietary fat and sugar, and so forth, on the grounds that some choices cost society more in healthcare expenses than others."

The above argument may or may not be persuasive; that is not the issue here. The issue is the form of the argument. The proponent of the SSA is claiming that the acceptance of an argument (that we should have socialized healthcare) will "cause" people to accept another argument (that lifestyle choices should be regulated) that they would otherwise be less likely to accept. The proponent shifts our attention away from the initial argument itself to the transition between arguments. In this sense, he is making an argument about arguments, or a meta-argument.

The two decisions, whether to socialize healthcare and whether to regulate lifestyles, could be made in isolation. But the proponent draws a connection between them, and the connection is made by a meta-argument. He claims that an affirmative answer to the first question about socialized healthcare will lead to (or make more likely) an affirmative answer to the second regarding lifestyle restriction. On what grounds can this claim be supported? Socialized medicine will result in consequences—such as higher external costs of gluttony—that will make other arguments applicable to the question of lifestyle regulation more persuasive.

What would the proponent need to know to make this claim with reasonable support? He would need to know what arguments are likely to be made in the lifestyle debate, which factors increase or decrease their likelihood of acceptance, and so on. In short, he must have knowledge of the structure of discussion and argument. The arguments people will make in the future depend upon their rules, theories, and research programs, as well as the factual situation.

An SSA relies on a model of how people construct, evaluate, and apply arguments. The validity of the argument depends on the accuracy of the model. Obviously, some models are correct and others not. The validity of the argument against socialized healthcare depends, in large part, on whether taxpayers and legislators do in fact consider the monetary costs of lifestyle choices to the community.[44] In the next few parts, we outline some specific slippery slope processes, or models that sometimes prove accurate. We divide our discussion into consideration of microprocesses, which can in principle be generated by the actions of a single agent, and consideration of macroprocesses, which require the interaction of decisions of more than one agent.

III. A MICROPROCESS: SORITES WITH PRECEDENT

In this part we consider one kind of process that could, in principle, be the result of the actions of a single individual. *Sorites* refers to a particular type of logical paradox that occurs in the presence of vague words and phrases. The term "sorites" derives from the Greek *soros* for "heap," a reference to a classic example of the paradox: "If there is a heap of sand, you can always remove one grain of sand and still have a heap." If this premise is applied repeatedly (a heap of premises), we eventually must conclude that even just one grain of sand is also a heap.[45] Similar reasoning can lead to conclusions such as there are no bald men, pygmies are tall, and so forth.

The root of the paradox is the existence of vague or fuzzy concepts like "heap," "bald," and "tall."[46] While clear cases of heaps and nonheaps do exist, there is a gradient of cases in between that are neither clearly heaps nor clearly nonheaps. The gradient creates the possibility of a chain of reasoning, seemingly valid, that links the ends of the spectrum and effectively erases the distinction between them.

---

44.   Evidence for this proposition is provided by California's motorcycle helmet law. Starting in 1992, all motorcycle riders have been required to wear helmets in an attempt to reduce the number of injuries and fatalities arising out of motorcycle accidents. One reason the state legislators adopted the law was to save taxpayer money. The taxpayers bore most of the cost of the accidents because fewer than half those hospitalized had private medical insurance. *See* Wendy Max et al., *Putting a Lid on Injury Costs: The Economic Impact of the California Motorcycle Helmet Law*, 45 J. TRAUMA: INJURY, INFECTION & CRITICAL CARE 550 (1998) ("During the first 2 years of implementation of California's helmet law, there were reduced costs for injuries and fatalities and large dollar savings to the state and other payers compared with the previous year."). Note also that recent lawsuits against the tobacco and gun industries have relied on the notion that the use of tobacco and guns increases public health costs. *See* Douglas Glen Whitman, *Legal Entrepreneurship and Institutional Change*, 12 J. DES ECONOMISTES ET DES ETUDES HUMAINES 257 (2002).

45.   Strictly speaking, the premise need not be applied repeatedly. By mathematical induction, the result can be achieved by recognizing that adding or subtracting one grain *never* matters. *See* STEPHEN READ, THINKING ABOUT LOGIC: AN INTRODUCTION TO THE PHILOSOPHY OF LOGIC 174–75 (1995); *see also* "Sorites," *in* THE DICTIONARY OF PHILOSOPHY 524 (Dagobert Runes ed., 2001) ("In a statement of a sorites all conclusions except the last are suppressed, and in fact the sorites may be thought of as a single valid inference independent of analysis into constituent syllogisms.").

46.   "Vagueness is a widespread feature of our thought. Consider the following list: 'child', 'book', 'toy', 'happy', 'clever', 'few', 'cloudy', 'pearl', 'moustache', 'game', 'husband', 'table.'" R.M. SAINSBURY, PARADOXES 26 (2d ed. 1985).

Suppose we begin, following Nicholas Rescher, with two "observable facts": first, that one grain of sand does not make a heap and, second, that a million grains of sand do make a heap.[47] So long as we accept the "seemingly evident general principle"[48] that it is *always* true that adding only one grain to a nonheap still yields a nonheap, we shall end up contradicting our belief that a million grains of sand make a heap.[49]

The sorites paradox is relevant to the present discussion because it can act as a slippery slope process,[50] particularly in systems where precedent plays an important role in the decisionmaking process. If the actual and potential cases in which decisions need to be made are distributed along a spectrum according to some relevant factor, a series of logical steps can link highly disparate cases, leading to the erroneous or undesirable conclusion that unlike cases should be treated alike. To put the problem in mathematical terms, imagine that all cases are arranged on a gradient from zero to one. One is the clearest possible case for taking some action A. Zero is the clearest case for not taking action A. According to whatever theory is used by decisionmakers, two cases are "similar" if the difference between their numbers on the scale is less than 0.1. A case arises with a value of 0.95 on the scale, and this falls within the realm of clear cases for taking action A, so action A is taken. In a subsequent case with value 0.9, the decisionmaker observes that it is similar to the first case, and so he follows precedent by taking action A in the present case as well. Then there arises a case with value 0.85, then 0.8, and so forth. Through a series of decisions based on similarity and precedent, we eventually conclude that case n with a value of 0.1 should also result in action A, even though case n is, or is similar to, a clear case for not taking action A.

---

47.   RESCHER, *supra* note 13, at 78–79.
48.   Logicians often call this the "tolerance principle." *See, e.g.*, MARK SAINSBURY, LOGICAL FORMS: AN INTRODUCTION TO PHILOSOPHICAL LOGIC 275 (1991).
49.   Philosophers and linguists have attempted to resolve the sorites paradox in a variety of ways. *See, e.g.*, TIMOTHY A.O. ENDICOTT, VAGUENESS IN LAW 77–98 (2000); RESCHER, *supra* note 13, at 77–83. We do not attempt to add to this literature. It is worth pointing out, however, that one unsuccessful method of resolving the paradox involves trying to create a third category, the "unsure" or "ambiguous" category. For example, in the case of collections of grains of sand, we might say there are clear heaps, clear nonheaps, and cases that are neither. The problem with this approach, and the reason it does not resolve the paradox, is that the borderline between clear cases and unclear cases is itself vague—and therefore susceptible to sorites reasoning. If you start with a collection of sand that is clearly a heap and remove one grain of sand, you still have something that is clearly a heap. Apply this premise repeatedly, and we eventually conclude that there are no unclear cases. Alternatively, one could insist that there is a definite borderline between the clear cases and the unclear cases—but this is just as problematic as asserting that there is a definite borderline between the cases where the original vague term applies and cases where it does not. Just as there is no specific minimum number of grains of sand that constitutes a heap, there is also no specific minimum number of grains of sand that constitutes a *clear* heap. The transition from clear to unclear is itself indeterminate. *See* WALTON, *supra* note 3, at 50–51.
50.   *See* WALTON, *supra* note 3, at 37–68.

It should be noted that the character of the slippery slope is crucially dependent on the initial precedents; it is a path-dependent process. Suppose we started from the other direction, that is, with situations that are clear cases for not taking action A. Then the momentum for the sorites slope would move toward a situation that results in inaction for something that would otherwise have been regarded as a clear case for taking action.[51] From an external point of view, the strict logical error in the numerical example above is that similarity, as defined in the example, is not a transitive relation.[52] If case *x* is similar to case *y*, and case *y* is similar to case *z*, that does not necessarily mean that case *x* is similar to case *z*.[53] While this may be apparent from an external point of view, it may not be apparent to decisionmakers operating within the system. The root of their difficulty is that it is *plausible* that *x* is similar to *z*; indeed it may even be true in some instances,[54] but it is costly to determine this. If the agent's decisions are made by reference to precedent and plausible similarity, then the sorites chain can occur. To recognize and possibly avoid the slippery slope, one must be willing to raise the discussion to a higher level that considers the *cumulative* effect of many marginal decisions.[55] In other words, the SSA—the argument that draws attention to how a chain of seemingly correct decisions can lead to an undesirable outcome—is a meta-argument.

The meta-argument nature of the sorites SSA may be better appreciated by generalizing the progression illustrated above in the following way:

α^1 is an acceptable argument (to do or decide action A^1)
α^2 is close to or similar to α^1
Therefore, α^2 is an acceptable argument

. . .

α^{10} is close to or similar to α^9
Therefore, α^{10} is an acceptable argument (to do A^{10})
But α^{10} (A^{10}) is, in fact, unacceptable

---

51.   If the cases arise in a mixed way, that is, some near one and others near zero, then the decisive factor may be the location of the burden of proof or standard of persuasion. For more on how burdens of proof or standards of persuasion can impede slippery slopes, see *infra* Part VII.

52.   For a brief discussion of the nontransitivity of similarity in a related context, compare SAINSBURY, *supra* note 48, at 329.

53.   This problem is not created by a shifting definition of similarity, as in the example of saying a banana is similar to a cigar, because the same similarity relation is used in every step here.

54.   *See* RESCHER, *supra* note 13, at 15–20.

55.   The resister of a slippery slope argument "should demand that the argument be looked at in a holistic way, and point out that, because of the vagueness of the key term, it is arbitrary to fasten on any particular point in the reapplication sequence." WALTON, *supra* note 3, at 59. There is, however, the important economic question of whether any particular decisionmaker has an incentive to take account of the cumulative effect.

In this generalization of the sorites SSA, the progression is generated by an overall perceived similarity[56] of arguments that is often—but not always—rooted in the vagueness of a central concept. For example, an argument that justifies state subsidization of school lunches may be seen as similar to the argument that justifies state subsidization of education in the first place—perhaps because the education of the mind and the health of the body are empirically related.[57]

If the law sometimes manages to resist slippery slopes in the presence of vague terms, it is because the legal profession has adopted various stratagems for resisting them. Such stratagems include the establishment of clear (though arbitrary) rules and the selective use of higher standards. We will delay our discussion of these slope-resisting strategies until later. For now, we will observe that there do not seem to be any foolproof methods of resisting slippery slopes, only methods that have been more or less successful than others.

IV. MACROPROCESSES

In this part we consider processes that involve, in an essential way, the interaction of more than one decisionmaker.

A. Altered Economic Incentives

Some slippery slopes involve, as an essential feature of the process, changes in the real-world costs and benefits faced by decisionmakers. We refer to these as *altered economic incentive processes*, or *incentive slopes* for short. Like all SSAs, the incentives slope argument points out that accepting some Argument 1 will increase the likelihood of accepting some other Argument 2. The crucial difference is that the transition between arguments is eased by some change in incentives resulting from the earlier argument's acceptance.[58]

---

56. The judgment of "closeness" or "similarity" depends on a theory, including its empirical presuppositions.

57. For a critical analysis showing that this connection was being made in the late nineteenth century, see HERBERT SPENCER, *The Coming Slavery*, in THE MAN VERSUS THE STATE 44 (Liberty Classics 1981) (1884).

58. A.V. Dicey makes a closely related analysis of the growth of government during the latter part of the nineteenth century. *See* A.V. DICEY, LECTURES ON THE RELATION BETWEEN LAW AND PUBLIC OPINION IN ENGLAND DURING THE NINETEENTH CENTURY 303 (1981). The utilitarian argument for laissez-faire became a utilitarian argument for state intervention because of certain doctrinal and institutional reforms wrought by the Benthamite liberals. They fought to overthrow the doctrine of natural rights, promote the idea of Parliamentary sovereignty, and improve the efficiency of government administration. All of these lowered the cost of state regulation when utility might be (or appear to be) directly enhanced. This, in turn, made the acceptance of such arguments more likely. "The effect actually produced by a system of thought does not depend on the intention of its originators; ideas which have once obtained general acceptance work out their own logical result under the control mainly of events." *Id.* at 310.

The incentive slopes in which we have the greatest interest are those generated by interventions in complex social systems. Such systems are characterized by two fundamental properties: first, the interaction of individuals' actions and plans; and second, the existence of emergent properties resulting from the interactions of these individual behaviors. In these systems, there is an absence of linearity: The effect of the sum of two or more factors is not necessarily equal to the sum of the individual effects arising from them. Furthermore, agents cannot predict outcomes simply by knowing the initial data, because the path of decisions taken will influence which outcome actually occurs. Even outside of systems—where consequences are foreseeable in principle—they may be unforeseeable in practice, because they follow from changes in incentives that are obscure and not immediately apparent to a decisionmaker subject to, for example, high information costs or bounded rationality.[59]

Economists have long emphasized that decisions, especially policy decisions, often have consequences neither intended nor expected by the decisionmaker.[60] Often, the unintended consequences result from changes in incentives wrought by new policies. Simply pointing to the unanticipated and unintended consequences that result from altered incentives, however, does not create an SSA. But when these consequences affect the way future decisionmakers (or the same decisionmaker under different constraints) will form and evaluate arguments in some systematic way, then the foundation for an SSA exists. The sliding takes place not because the arguments made at the various stages are similar (as in the sorites process) but because the stages are causally interlinked, inasmuch as the first step lowers the cost or increases the benefit of taking the next step relative to what it otherwise would have been.[61]

More concretely, when unanticipated consequences are caused by a government restriction on individual behavior, an SSE can occur if the initial restriction makes further restrictions more likely. This may happen if the experience of unanticipated consequences is conjoined with an argument that further restrictions are curative or, at least, ameliorative. If this scenario is likely to occur, or is perceived likely, some observers or analysts may construct SSAs on this basis.

---

59. Even if some individuals happen to *foresee* consequences, they will not have an incentive to act on this foreknowledge if they cannot affect the consequences. But the inability to affect outcomes is a good reason that a rational individual will not even try to anticipate consequences in the first place (unless he is an academician!).

60. *See, e.g.*, FRÉDÉRIC BASTIAT, *What Is Seen and What Is Not Seen, in* SELECTED ESSAYS ON POLITICAL ECONOMY (George B. de Huszar ed., Seymour Cain trans., 1964).

61. For a more extensive discussion of "cost-lowering" slippery slope mechanisms, see Volokh, *supra* note 5, at 1043–47. Note that the change in incentives does not ensure that a particular chain of events will occur, but makes it more likely than otherwise.

Note that even in this "causal" process, theoretical constructs are utilized at every stage of both the event and the argument. Beginning with the argument, the observer recognizes a causal relationship between the government policy and the undesirable and often unanticipated consequences. There are at least four types of theory operative here. First, there is the positive theory that links the initial intervention with its real-world consequences. Second, there is the normative theory that deems the consequences undesirable. Third, there is the further positive theory (typically held by someone other than the observer, such as legislators or voters) that sees the second intervention as ameliorative.[62] Finally, there is the further normative theory (typically held by one or more decisionmakers) that sees amelioration as beneficial, all things considered. With respect to the SSE, however, it is not necessary that the economic agents (legislators and voters) understand the connection between policy and the undesirable outcome. It is sufficient that they find it undesirable and believe that further intervention is the answer (that is, they hold the last three theories above).[63]

The socialized healthcare hypothetical, previously mentioned, is a simplified case of the altered economic incentives process. Recall that there is a moral hazard problem resulting from changes, at the margin, in incentives to make risky decisions. Although merely pointing to moral hazard does not create an SSA or describe an SSE, claiming that the moral hazard problem will increase support for regulation of lifestyle choices is to make an SSA or to point to an SSE. The key to the SSA and possible SSE in this case is the notion that voters believe it is possible to lower their tax burden by (further) restrictions on individual autonomy ("No food with a saturated fat content beyond x may be sold!"). This is a belief derived from positive theory. They also believe that it is morally *acceptable* to so restrict individual autonomy for the purpose of lowering their tax burdens. This is derived from a normative theory, if only an implicit one, held by the voters (though not necessarily shared by the person making the SSA).

This incentive slope produces results that may be unacceptable from the initial point of view of those who decide to implement a program of socialized healthcare. These same agents may put into effect the very regulations that they previously disliked, because of the unpredicted change in their own incentives. Their underlying preferences have not changed but their actions have,

---

62. In other words, given the initial intervention, the cost of the second is perceived to be lower, perhaps so much lower that it creates a perceived net benefit. Thus, the argument urging acceptance of the second intervention is more likely to be persuasive.

63. A contemporary illustration of this phenomenon is the vast network of price controls in Zimbabwe under the rule of Robert Mugabe. As each control was imposed it created conditions that the government interpreted as suggesting the desirability of further controls. *See Economic Focus: The Zimbabwean Model,* ECONOMIST, Nov. 30, 2002, at 68.

because they must now bear costs they previously did not. Whether this new outcome is of such lower utility that agents would choose not to adopt socialized healthcare, if they knew the full consequences in advance, cannot be determined a priori.

B. Separately Validated Propositions

In this process, propositions that have been validated separately result in a conclusion or overall outcome that would not have been validated if considered by itself. To see how this is possible, consider decisionmaking by majority rule. It is a well-known fact that if a majority approves of policy A, and a majority also approves policy B, it does not follow that a majority would also approve the union of A and B. The reason is that the majorities supporting the separate policies may not be the same. If 51 percent support A and 51 percent support B, it is possible that as few as 2 percent support both. This fact may not be relevant for our purposes if policies A and B are totally unrelated, but it takes on special significance if the policies are logically or practically related. If that is so, then separate validation of the two policies could result in an overall "coherent" policy outcome that would not itself be validated and could constitute an SSE.

For example, consider the question of whether a nation should institute a more generous welfare system. Suppose that a majority of the population supports this position. Suppose also that a different but overlapping majority believes that a more restrictive immigration policy should accompany a more generous welfare system, so that natives will not have to support new arrivals. Both policies could be implemented, even though as few as two percent of the population might initially support that outcome. Separate implementation of the two policies leads to an outcome desired only by a small fraction of the public.[64]

As with the altered economic incentives process, there are unanticipated consequences in this process. In the former process, decisionmakers fail to predict the results of a change in the economic incentives of the people affected by the policy. In the present process, decisionmakers fail to predict the likely behavior of other decisionmakers. For the second step in the process to occur, it must be the case that at least 51 percent of the population prefers the option "generous welfare with restrictive immigration policy" to the option "generous welfare without restrictive immigration policy." Note that these preferences are consistent with having preferred the status quo over either or both policies;

---

64. We are not, of course, claiming that the actual preferences of voters in the United States or any other country are like those described in this example. The example is purely hypothetical.

for example, one's first preference might be "neither generous welfare nor restrictive immigration policy." The outcome of the voting process could be "generous welfare with restrictive immigration policy" even if it were the preferred option of as few as 2 percent of the public. These preferences are summarized in Table 1. From the table, it can be seen that 51 percent of the population (Groups A and C) would prefer generous welfare (GW) to the status quo. Given the existence of generous welfare, a different 51 percent (Groups B and C) would impose greater restrictions on immigration (RI), yet 98 percent of the population (Groups A and B) would have preferred the status quo ante over the combined regime.

TABLE 1

HYPOTHETICAL POPULATION PREFERENCES LEADING
TO SEPARATELY VALIDATED PROPOSITIONS

	Percentage of Population	First Preference	Second Preference	Third Preference
Group A	49%	GW	status quo ante	GW + RI
Group B	49%	status quo ante	GW + RI	GW
Group C	2%	GW + RI	GW	status quo ante

Unanticipated consequences are involved in this process. The members of Group A, who initially supported generous welfare, did not foresee the voting behavior of Groups B and C. If they had, they might not have supported generous welfare in the first place. This is not, however, the incentives slope process as defined earlier, since it is not a change in the economic incentives of the people affected by the policy that brought about the slope.[65]

Readers familiar with the literature on social choice will no doubt recognize the figures above as an instance of Condorcet's paradox,[66] which can occur when voters have preferences that are not "single-peaked."[67] This implies that majority voting on pairs of policies can generate nontransitive "social

---

65.   However, the two slope processes may be combined. For instance, members of Group B, who favor restrictive immigration once generous welfare is in place, may take that position because they believe generous welfare will encourage a larger than normal amount of immigration, leading to an expanded tax burden.

66.   For a discussion of Condorcet's paradox or the "paradox of voting," see, for example, P.A. MCNUTT, THE ECONOMICS OF PUBLIC CHOICE 61–66 (1996).

67.   In this case, a single-peaked preference means that all three groups are in agreement that a particular alternative is the worst. A multi-peaked preference means that, from the point of view of the individual groups, there are at least two, possibly three, least preferred alternatives. See MICHAEL J.G. CAIN, *Social Choice Theory, in* THE ELGAR COMPANION TO PUBLIC CHOICE 107 (William F. Shughart II & Laura Razzolini eds., 2001).

preferences."[68] Eugene Volokh provides more examples of this nature.[69] We wish to add two observations. First, although it is often suggested that the intransitive nature of the voting process will lead to cycling (policy A is replaced by B, which is replaced by C, which is replaced by A again, ad infinitum),[70] that need not be the case. Often policy reversal involves high costs that effectively prevent a return to the original policy. Thus, it is easier to fall down the slope than to climb back up. Second, the separately validated propositions process does not *require* non-single peaked preferences like those above, as majority rule is not the only social means of making decisions. In law, the authoritative opinions of one or a few courts can be sufficient to validate a proposition. Distinct legal propositions may be validated through separate precedent-setting decisions, and later cases may reveal the unanticipated consequence of combining them. Unless the courts deciding such cases are willing to break at least one precedent, they may find themselves validating additional propositions even if they seem undesirable.

The issue of fetal personhood[71] is an excellent demonstration of how separately validated propositions have the potential to combine to reach conclusions that are (at least to some observers) unpalatable. The issue is whether, and under what circumstances, fetuses should be treated as legal persons. According to the line of reasoning followed in the U.S. Supreme Court's *Roe v. Wade*[72] decision, a fetus is not regarded as a legal person with respect to the issue of abortion. But in a number of cases unrelated to abortion, American courts have been willing to treat fetuses as persons, especially in criminal cases involving an intentional or accidental fetal death caused by someone other than the mother, such as an attacker or drunk driver.[73] The apparent conflict between the lines of reasoning has not yet been resolved, but some slippery slope possibilities are apparent. From the perspective of a proponent of abortion rights, the danger is that the recognition of fetal personhood in criminal cases could, in combination with the Fourteenth Amendment's protection of the life, liberty, and property of all persons, eventually undermine *Roe v. Wade's* protection of abortion rights. From the perspective of abortion opponents, of

---

68.   Nontransitivity means that if the voting process generates the outcomes "A is preferred to B" and "B is preferred to C," it could, nonetheless, generate the outcome "C is preferred to A," without any change in the utilities of the voters. The latter outcome would be inconsistent with the logical (transitive) implication of the first two because A "should be" preferred to C. For further discussion of transitivity in this context, see DENNIS C. MUELLER, PUBLIC CHOICE III 586–88 (2003).

69.   Volokh, *supra*, note 5, at 1048–75.

70.   *See* MUELLER, *supra* note 68, at 38–49.

71.   For a full discussion of the fetal personhood issue, see Aaron Wagner, Comment, *Texas Two-Step: Serving up Fetal Rights by Side-Stepping* Roe v. Wade *Has Set the Table for Another Showdown on Fetal Personhood in Texas and Beyond*, 32 TEX. TECH. L. REV. 1085 (2001).

72.   410 U.S. 113 (1973).

73.   Wagner, *supra* note 71, at 1103.

course, this would be a desirable slope. But there is also the potential for a slope in the other direction: The denial of fetal personhood in abortion cases could, in combination with the traditional definition of murder as the wrongful killing of a person, result in a situation in which the deliberate killing of someone else's unborn child could only be prosecuted as battery, not murder. Thus, both advocates and opponents of abortion rights have reason to fear the effect of consistency in the law.[74]

SSAs based on the separately validated propositions process highlight the likelihood that certain arguments, if accepted now, will interact with other arguments to increase the likelihood of accepting different arguments in the future. In the case of more generous welfare policy, opponents might warn potential advocates that accepting the policy would increase the likelihood of persuasive arguments for immigration restrictions they do not support. In the case of fetal personhood, abortion rights advocates might warn against allowing charges of murder against a person who caused the death of another's fetus, since it might reinforce persuasive arguments against *Roe v. Wade*. As with previous types of SSA, this argument requires a model (implicit or explicit) of how decisionmakers (judges, voters, and legislators) accept arguments. Specifically, the model in the welfare/immigration example states that some percentage of voters are willing to "vote their pocketbooks" and accept arguments for immigration restriction. The model in the fetal personhood

---

74. In Michigan, however, the court of appeals argued that fetal personhood is "not pertinent" to the question of whether a pregnant mother has the right to use deadly force to repel an assault on her "nonviable" (outside the womb) seventeen-week old fetuses. People v. Kurr, 654 N.W.2d 651, 657 (Mich. Ct. App. 2002). It reached this conclusion by interpreting the "defense of others" doctrine in light of Michigan's Fetal Protection Act. *Id.* at 654 (interpreting MICH. COMP. LAWS § 750.90a (2003)). The court argued that it is reasonable to extend the meaning of "others" to include a fetus or embryo because the state had enacted protections for the fetus against assault or gross negligence. *Id.* at 653–54. Thus a mother has the right to use deadly force to protect her fetus, only while still in the womb, whether viable or not, against assault even when her own life is in no danger. *Id.* at 655. "Any other result would be anomalous given the express policy of this state as declared by the Legislature in the fetal protection act." *Id.* at 657. The more important anomaly, however, would seem to be with *Roe v. Wade*. This is because the state is offering a level of protection from assault to unviable fetuses that is, in principle, indistinguishable from that provided to *persons* under the law. Consider that the pregnant woman is able to use (1) deadly force (2) even when her own life is in no danger to protect her fetus deemed "other" for the purposes of the defense of others doctrine. (One is tempted to ask: What does "other" or "another" mean to the court—another *what*? Since the defender in this case, the mother, is a person, it seems reasonable to conclude that the "other" is a person as well.) This is in sharp contrast to the settled law that anti-abortionists cannot use even less than deadly force to protect fetuses when they are endangered by their mothers. There may be other, doctrinally more consistent, ways to protect the right of abortion while granting some protection to the fetus against assaults by anyone besides the mother. But the Michigan Court of Appeals chose to provide protection to the fetus to the same degree as a person and chose to consider it within the scope of a doctrine plausibly (and heretofore) applicable only to persons. This belies the court's statement that whether the fetus is a person is "not pertinent" to its decision. It decided the case *as if* an unviable fetus were a person. Thus, the legal tensions discussed in the text remain.

example says that judges are inclined to accept, on grounds of precedent or consistency, arguments that follow logically from others already accepted.

To evaluate the models empirically, it is necessary to examine (a) the preference distribution of voters and (b) the power of consistency in the formation of legal doctrine, respectively. Voters may not have preferences like those hypothesized. And although systemic consistency[75] does have influence in the law, it is not an absolute value; courts may rule inconsistently by creating a special doctrine or area containing certain factual or legal presuppositions that are at variance with those in other doctrines or areas. The crux of the matter is how much emphasis the legal system places on consistency among legal doctrines. Ultimately, the persuasiveness of an SSA relying on the described processes depends on the credibility of the underlying models.

There is one more aspect of the separate validation process that bears emphasis. In the structure of discussion and argument, we observed that conclusions at one level are often applied as arguments at the next lower level. Research programs provide arguments in the choice of theories, theories provide arguments in the choice of rules, and rules provide arguments in the making of decisions. In the discussion of the sorites process, we assumed that discussants shared the same theory, as exemplified by identical similarity relations. But here, no such assumption is necessary. Proposition A might result from the influence of theory X, proposition B from the influence of theory Y. Indeed, the process may even *require* the existence of multiple theories, as it seems unlikely that people would disagree with conclusions that follow from propositions arrived at through the same theory—unless the theory is internally inconsistent or incomplete.[76]

---

75. Systemic consistency is the notion that "rule A, should be adopted in preference to a competing rule, rule B, because *neither applicable social propositions* [for example, moral norms or policy goals] *nor any deep doctrinal distinction* would justify adopting rule B while adhering to some other previously announced rule." EISENBERG, *supra* note 30, at 93 (emphasis added).

76. Consider a series of cases: A . . . m, n . . . B where A is innocuous and B is danger. Now suppose:

> Different judges . . . hold different theories about the correct ground for the distinction [between A and B]. But they have to accept each other's decisions as part of the law. This may be illustrated as follows. Judge X may think that n and B are similar and that the line should be drawn between m and n, while Judge Y thinks that the line should be drawn between n and B. If Judge Y upon this basis has accepted n, then Judge X, respecting the precedent created by Y, will make the further step toward the acceptance of B. Though neither Judge X nor Judge Y would have made the step from A to B directly, their combined activity leads to an acceptance of B.

Wibren van der Burg, *The Slippery Slope Argument*, 102 ETHICS 42, 50 (1991).

C. Humean Beneficence

David Hume argues that private benevolence is a "natural virtue," as distinct from justice, which is an "artificial virtue."[77] Whereas acting on a feeling of benevolence toward specific individuals in difficult situations produces an immediate and direct positive feedback, for most people, acting in accordance with the general rules of justice does not produce positive feedback in every case. The social utility of the rules of justice[78] is based on the convention that if one actor adheres to the rules, so will the other. The utility of justice is thus derived from the "whole plan or scheme"[79] and not from a single application of justice. The rules are acquired primarily through socialization and immersion in the norms of the society. This is not, to Hume, an argument against the fundamental nature of the rules of justice; on the contrary, he contends that the general, inflexible pursuit of justice is indispensable to the general happiness of society.[80] But its artificial character makes it more difficult to act upon than benevolence.[81]

Therefore, and of special importance to SSAs, there will sometimes—even often—arise conflicts between justice and beneficence. The principle underlying beneficent action is one that takes note of special circumstances and the particular character of individuals, whereas justice is deliberately blind to such factors. In this sense benevolence is a concrete virtue and justice is an abstract virtue.[82] As a result, a benevolent person focused on particular circumstances will become aware of many seemingly undesirable consequences of specific acts of justice. As Hume argues:

> All the laws of nature, which regulate property, as well as all civil laws,
> are general, and regard alone some essential circumstances of the case,

---

77. On benevolence as a natural virtue, see DAVID HUME, A TREATISE ON HUMAN NATURE 369–70 (David Fate Norton & Mary J. Norton eds., 2000) (1740); on justice as artificial, see *id.* at 307–11, 319.

78. For Hume, substantive justice consists, most fundamentally, of the rules that function to preserve existing property rights in a "general, inflexible" manner. See DAVID HUME, AN ENQUIRY CONCERNING THE PRINCIPLES OF MORALS 171 (Tom L. Beauchamp ed., Oxford University Press 1998) (1751). But since "possession and property should always be stable, except where the proprietor agrees to bestow them on some other person," rules regarding the transference of property by consent (contract law) are implied. See HUME, *supra* note 77, at 330.

79. HUME, *supra* note 77, at 319.

80. *See id.* at 368–71.

81. *See id.* at 370–71.

82. *Cf.* 1 HERBERT SPENCER, PRINCIPLES OF ETHICS 156 (Liberty Classics 1978) (1897). Spencer argues:

> The motive causing a generous act has reference to effects of a more concrete, special, and proximate kind, than has the motive to do justice; which, beyond the proximate effects, usually themselves less concrete than those that generosity contemplates, includes a consciousness of the distant, involved, diffused effects of maintaining equitable relations.

Id.

Rules, Theories, and Slippery Slopes 569

> without taking into consideration the characters, situations, and connex-
> ions of the person concerned, or any particular consequences which may
> result from the determination of these laws, in any particular case which
> offers. They deprive, without scruple, a beneficent man of all his posses-
> sions, if acquired by mistake, without a good title; in order to bestow them
> on a selfish miser, who has already heaped up immense stores of superflu-
> ous riches.[83]

As a result, decisionmakers will sometimes find themselves torn between the
demands of justice, on the one hand, and the demands of pity, compassion, and
benevolence on the other.[84]

The conflict between justice and beneficence creates the potential for a
slippery slope. In a specific case, a judge or other decisionmaker may be tempted
to depart from the rules of justice to make a special exception. It may seem
undesirable, for instance, to enforce a contract against a well-meaning person
who simply failed to think through the consequences of his decision to sign.
Or it might seem harsh to extract large liability damages from a poor person who
accidentally caused harm to another. Now, the mere act of making an exception
does not itself constitute a slippery slope. But if the exception in some way makes
future exceptions more likely than they would have been otherwise, then there is
the potential for a slippery slope.

But why would one exception increase the likelihood of further exceptions? Consider a simple model of judicial decisionmaking, in which judges
weigh their personal preferences about the disposition of cases versus a concern
for their reputations. The reputation of a judge is determined primarily by the
perception that he abides by precedents set by other judges.[85] The more a
judge's decision appears to depart from the pattern established in prior cases,
the greater will be the negative impact on the judge's reputation. Now, suppose
a judge faces a case that he would prefer to decide in a beneficent manner, but
there is a general rule established by prior cases against deciding in that way.
Other things equal, he will be more inclined to decide the case beneficently
(instead of according to the general rule) when there exist at least some "nearby"
cases also decided in that way, because such cases reduce the appearance of

---

83. HUME, *supra* note 78, at 171 (footnotes omitted).

84. For an analysis of Hume on justice and benevolence, see, for example, JAMES BAILLIE,
HUME ON MORALITY 153–59 (2000). For Hume's claim that neither public nor private benevolence
can be the foundation of justice, see HUME, *supra* note 77, at 309–11.

85. A number of analysts have modeled judges in this way. *See* William M. Landes & Richard
A. Posner, *Legal Precedent: A Theoretical and Empirical Analysis*, 19 J.L. & ECON. 249, 273–74 (1976);
Thomas J. Miceli & Metin M. Cosgel, *Reputation and Judicial Decision-Making*, 23 J. ECON. BEHAV. &
ORG. 31 (1994); Georg von Wangenheim, *The Evolution of Judge-Made Law*, 13 INT'L REV. L. & ECON.
381 (1993); Douglas Glen Whitman, *Evolution of the Common Law and the Emergence of Compromise*, 29
J. LEGAL STUD. 753 (2000).

renegade behavior. The judge can more plausibly claim that his case follows the pattern of previous cases.

Early on, few or no exceptions may have been made, and so judges who wish to indulge their feelings of benevolence have little support from precedent. Only the most "compassionate" judge, one whose desire to act beneficently is large enough to overcome his desire to safeguard his reputation, would be willing to make an exception. But the few early cases in which exceptions are made establish the basis on which further exceptions can be made later. As more exceptions are made, the margin moves, so that judges who previously had not been willing to make exceptions become more willing to make them. The more exceptions that have been made, the easier it is for further exceptions to be justified as consistent with the body of prior cases, and thus the reputational constraint gradually becomes less binding. The process is comparable to the mathematical description of the sorites slippery slope, in which the movement along a scale from zero to one is made possible by intermediate judgments of similarity. But in the present story, the choices of decisionmakers result not from "blind" application of precedent, but from a weighing of concern for precedent versus a desire to act beneficently in the instant case.

The Humean process, described above, has two welfare consequences. The first is that there is a weaker enforcement of "justice" than any decisionmaker at the outset dares to implement. In terms of *initial* preferences, most judges would find the later decision unsatisfactory or suboptimal, but some—those with extreme benevolence preferences—would approve of it and would actually be better off. The second is that, *at any time* during the slippery slope process, most judges believe the *system* to have more beneficence and less justice than is desirable given their concurrent preferences. This is because acting in a beneficent manner creates a negative externality. There is an immediate positive feedback to the individual judge but a weakening of the security of property and contract (with its attendant social costs) in the system as a whole.

V. RESPONDING TO THE OBJECTIONS

We now return to the objections we presented at the beginning of this Article, to explain why they do not always present a problem for SSAs.

The Automaton Objection. The automaton objection is that, if the future decisions in question are "bad," then we can simply choose not to make those decisions when the time comes. Three replies are in order.

First, the decisions we make now can change the incentives we face in the future. We do possess free will (we stipulate), and thus we could in principle refuse to make the "bad" decisions in the future. However, our present decisions can make certain future decisions harder to resist by lowering their perceived costs or increasing their relative benefits. In the socialized healthcare example, we could refuse to engage in lifestyle regulation—but the moral hazard created by socialized costs would give us a stronger incentive to regulate than we would have without socialized costs.[86]

Second, even in the absence of changes in direct incentives to action, arguments do not exist in isolation. They exist in the context of a structure of discussion. The acceptance of some arguments can lead, logically or by force of precedent, to the increased likelihood of other arguments also being accepted. Again, a person can in principle refuse to accept an argument, perhaps by resisting its logical relationship or similarity to another, but the point is that the acceptance of certain arguments is eased by the acceptance of others.[87] In making this point, we are asserting that (at least some) people choose what arguments to accept in the same way they decide what clothing to buy, what products to produce, and so on: They weigh the costs and the benefits. Policies that alter costs and benefits do not remove the capacity for choice, but they do push the choices in one direction or another, and that is as true for the acceptance of arguments as it is for any other kind of choice.

Both of these replies are related to the third and most important reply: It is misleading to say that "we" are capable of making correct decisions in the future. The process by which arguments are accepted and decisions made is a social one that derives from the decisions of many individuals.[88] No single decisionmaker can control the evolution of the discussion. The person who makes an SSA does not necessarily claim that the listener himself will be the perpetrator of the future bad decision. Rather, he draws attention to the structure of the discussion that will shape the decisions of many decisionmakers involved in a social process.[89]

The Imputation Objection. The imputation objection raised against SSAs is that any bad consequences that flow from the future are imputed backward to the initial decision, and therefore the initial decision should not appear attractive after all. We have two replies.

First, this objection implicitly recognizes the persuasiveness of the SSA. If the current decisionmaker already understands the full consequences of his decision, *including its likely impact on future decisions*, then his assessment of his

---

86. Strictly speaking, the individual is confronted with a situation in which the costs of adhering to an *argument* such as "lifestyle choice should be unrestricted because it is so important to individual identity" have increased, perhaps greatly so. If he now rejects this argument, his actions will change.

87. In effect, we are appealing to the internal or psychological costs of accepting an argument. If the human brain has any desire for consistency, it will be psychologically costly for the individual to resist a similar or entailed argument given previous arguments.

88. Schauer, *supra* note 7, at 373–76.

89. This reply is most appropriate, of course, for macroprocesses. But it can also be true of a microprocess involving a sequence of individuals with identical theories.

current decision should indeed be correct. But the whole point of the SSA is to draw attention to a class of consequences that are typically ignored. Decisionmakers in the real world frequently do not clearly see all the likely results of their decisions. The SSA, like many other forms of argument, tries to emphasize the importance of some set of costs or benefits that the decisionmaker may have failed to consider adequately. Since real-world decisionmakers may exhibit myopic behavior,[90] an SSA could make a real contribution in terms of illuminating distant costs and benefits. In other words, SSAs may be valid precisely because they can become constitutive ideas that encourage the consideration of distant costs.

Second, this objection, like the last one, pays insufficient regard to the social nature of the discussion. The single decisionmaker may not have incentives or interests aligned perfectly with those of the society at large. The Humean beneficence process outlined earlier provides an example of how this can be the case. A single judge may be tempted to make exceptions in specific cases because he gets the personal benefit of performing an act of "compassion." Even if the judge also has a regard for the good of the system as a whole (either directly or through the effects on his reputation), this may not be enough to overcome his other concerns.

The Presentism Objection. The third objection is that a current judgment that some future decision is "bad" may reflect a bias for the present perspective, hence disregarding our future values. Again, we have two responses.

First, the fact that some future decision will seem desirable in light of future circumstances does not imply that the circumstances themselves are desirable. Present decisions often have the capacity to alter the environment in which future decisions will be made. The point of the SSA is not necessarily that the future decisions are bad, in the context of today's point of view, but that we can affect the future context in positive or negative ways by our present

---

90.   By "myopic behavior" we mean the phenomenon of excessively discounting future costs relative to the preferences expressed by the agent *prior* to the decision that constitutes the first step on the slippery slope. For example, an individual may believe and accept an SSA that claims that taking decision A will significantly increase the probability of the danger case D. Further, he may accept the argument that, all things considered, the costs of D will exceed in present value the benefits of A (and any other intermediate steps). Nevertheless, when it comes time to decide A or not-A, the individual is "myopic" and chooses A. For an examination of this apparent "preference reversal," see the literature on "hyperbolic discounting," especially JON ELSTER, ULYSSES UNBOUND: STUDIES IN RATIONALITY, PRECOMMITMENT, AND CONSTRAINTS 29–34 (2000), and David I. Laibson et al., *Self-Control and Savings for Retirement, in* BROOKINGS PAPERS ON ECONOMIC ACTIVITY 91, 92–100 (William L. Brainard & George L. Perry eds., 1998). For a compact survey of the empirical evidence, see Shane Frederick et al., *Time Discounting and Time Preference: A Critical Review*, 40 J. ECON. LIT. 351, 360–63 (2002). Not all economists, however, believe that the assumption of inconsistent intertemporal preferences is useful or warranted by the more basic assumption of rationality. *See, e.g.*, Gary S. Becker & Casey B. Mulligan, *The Endogenous Determination of Time Preferences*, 112 Q.J. ECON. 729, 736–37 (1997).

decisions. Thus, no judgment against the *values* in play at some future time is necessarily involved.[91]

But second, there is no reason the discussion cannot involve a normative component. If the decisions to be made now have consequences in terms of what values will be held or accepted later, our normative theory need not be indifferent to the outcome. Alternative futures may involve alternative sets of preferences, but that does not mean we have no means of choosing among them. We may have meta-values that are relevant to our choices. Thus it may be rational to avoid the initial decision, or to make that decision but somehow prevent our future selves[92] or future decisionmakers from acting on the then-transformed values. Unfavorable changes in future values are normally dealt with by the prior imposition of constraints.[93] Judges, for example, may try to create precedents or stopping rules that impose constraints on future judges, thereby reducing the likelihood that they will act on the new values.[94]

Nevertheless, there is one sense in which we are guilty of presentism. The traditional view of rationality is such that the decisionmaker always attempts to maximize his utility relative to the values and constraints (present and future) that he perceives now at the moment of decision.[95] Thus all his actions are based on that present perception. This is a version of presentism that is perfectly consistent with the theory of rational choice, and thus would not constitute a challenge to slippery slope argumentation from that point of view.

---

91.   In other words, simply because there is an undesirable change in *context* does not imply that there has been a change in values.

92.   There is an alternative way to model our future selves that makes no reference to meta-values. A single individual decisionmaker can be modeled to have a change in values. In this analysis, rationality obliges him to be *unbiased* between present and future values (or present and future selves). He thus simply discounts future utility by a rate reflecting its uncertainty. Therefore, the decisionmaker's actions will strongly favor the present only when future utility has a large uncertainty discount. *See* Richard A. Posner, *Rational Choice, Behavioral Economics and the Law*, 50 STAN. L. REV. 1551, 1568 (1998) ("What is true is that any personal discount rate higher than necessary to adjust for the risk of death is suspect from the *narrowest rational-choice standpoint*, as it implies an arbitrary preference for present over future consumption.") (emphasis added). *But see* RUBENFELD, *supra* note 11, at 118–19.

93.   *See generally* JON ELSTER, ULYSSES AND THE SIRENS: STUDIES IN RATIONALITY AND IRRATIONALITY (1979).

94.   *But cf.* EISENBERG, *supra* note 30, at 76 ("[T]he legal standing of every rule announced in a binding precedent depends not simply on the fact that it was announced, but on whether the rule is congruent with [current] applicable social propositions, considered either explicitly or tacitly."). Applicable social propositions include current widely shared moral norms. To the extent that Eisenberg is correct in his characterization of the common law process, present courts will be less able to bind future courts. Thus initial decisions perceived as likely to lead to undesirable results later may not be taken in the first place.

95.   JAMES M. BUCHANAN, COST AND CHOICE: AN INQUIRY IN ECONOMIC THEORY 42–44 (1969).

VI. FACTORS AFFECTING THE LIKELIHOOD OF SLIPPERY SLOPES

Once introduced in an argument, slippery slopes can be difficult to eliminate. This is, in large part, because the slippery slope eliminated at one level of analysis often reemerges at a higher level of analysis. For instance, a commitment to following bright line stopping rules might avoid sorites-style events at the level of decisions, but then the choice of the rule itself may be subject to slippage. This difficulty is exacerbated in the law, where the judges often have the responsibility of both applying rules *and* choosing them. Any temptation to make exceptions to the rules at the decision level can be recast as a temptation to change the rules at the rules level. This became apparent in the "Make-Up Exam *Meshugas*" example, where the same position could be cast as a decision-level argument ("Make an exception to the make-up exam rule") or as a rules-level argument ("The make-up exam rule should include an exception for cases like mine").

Still, there are factors that can affect the likelihood and severity of SSEs and hence the persuasiveness of the associated arguments. In this part, we suggest four such factors. We argue that the probability of slipping down a slope is positively related to all of the following, other things equal:

1. The degree of disagreement among decisionmakers in their (lower level) theories.
2. The degree of vagueness in the generally accepted theory.
3. The degree of "empirical vagueness" created by the accepted theory.
4. The degree of looseness of the research program in determining the future development of theories.

We address each of these factors in turn.

The degree of disagreement among decisionmakers in their (lower level) theories. The decisionmakers in a system need not share the same positive or normative theories. Different theories will often lead to different conclusions about how to make decisions and how to select rules. It might seem that disagreement would simply make the system unpredictable or unreliable, but not necessarily more subject to slippage. But slippage can indeed be a problem when multiple theories compete, because multiple theories create a greater potential for problems of nontransitivity in similarity relations. The separately validated propositions process discussed earlier relies on the existence of differing theories that lead to differing judgments about arguments. One argument might be accepted through the efforts of adherents of one theory, a second argument through the efforts of adherents of another theory. The propositions together may encourage the acceptance of yet other arguments that possibly fit neither original theory.

This problem is exacerbated when courts use "analogous reasoning." As the number of acceptable theories becomes greater, relationships of similarity are increased and hence the range of plausible legal doctrines or rules can be extended. For any characteristic *a* of an established case, there is a greater chance it will be found similar to another characteristic *b* of a newly arisen case. Furthermore, characteristics may be connected in similarity by groups of jointly incompatible theories: *a* is similar to *b* on theory X; *b* is similar to *c* on theory Y; and *c* is similar to *d* on theory Z, where X, Y, Z are incompatible in whole or part. When courts reason by analogy, the theoretical context for the similarity relation is not always made explicit. As a result, statements of similarity may be made without recognition of their conflicting bases. Hence, "like cases that will be treated alike" may not be truly alike according to a consistent principle or theory. Nevertheless, the rule of a precedent may be expanded[96] beyond the most general intention as manifested in the theory of the original decisionmakers.[97]

Furthermore, the existence of multiple theories creates an indeterminacy in the sort of arguments that are viable in a system. Decisionmakers looking for an excuse to decide in a particular way are more likely to find a justification when multiple (and potentially contradictory) justifications exist.[98] If multiple theories have intellectual currency, it is easier to find acceptable reasons to support any given position on a particular case. Thus, for example, the existence of multiple theories creates more room for the Humean beneficence process to operate.

Finally, the existence of multiple theories can lead to the adoption of political, legal, and ethical doctrines that are deliberately vague. For instance, politicians will sometimes pass intentionally vague legislation in order to avoid having to make tough decisions, thereby passing the buck to bureaucratic agencies.[99] Balancing "rules" in the common law, which direct judges to weigh a

---

96. In addition to finding cases similar according to inconsistent theories, courts may also distinguish cases (that is, make exceptions) according to inconsistent theories.

97. Joseph Raz recognizes the possibility of conflicting analogies in the law. His emphasis is on a single court choosing sides, as it were, in a conflict over policy goals, for example. He does not seem to appreciate that the existence of incompatible analogies can produce a chain of similarities (or differences) across different courts or in the same court at different times. *See* JOSEPH RAZ, *Law and Value in Adjudication, in* THE AUTHORITY OF LAW: ESSAYS ON LAW AND MORALITY 180, 205 (1979).

98. Some legal scholars think that this is always the case. "According to the moderate thesis [of American realism] . . . [i]n reality, judges at every level are able to select or disregard precedent to suit the conclusion already arrived at." MARK TEBBIT, PHILOSOPHY OF LAW: AN INTRODUCTION 31 (2001). More radically, the Critical Legal Studies movement believes "*All* rules will contain within them, deeply embedded, structural premises that clearly enable decision makers to resolve particular controversies in opposite ways." MARK KELMAN, A GUIDE TO CRITICAL LEGAL STUDIES 258 (1987).

99. Bryner provides an example:
Some laws provide competing objectives that give administrators broad latitude. Under the Emergency Petroleum Allocation Act [15 U.S.C. Sec. 753(b)(1)], for example, regulations were to be issued for the allocation of petroleum products that "protected the public health, maintained public services and agricultural operations, preserved a sound and competitive petroleum industry, allocated crude oil to refiners to permit them to operate at full capacity,

variety of factors when deciding cases, are arguably a means of finessing the differences among judges' theories. Vague constructs such as the reasonable person may not reflect a consensus among judges about acceptable behavior, but in fact just the opposite: a divergence of opinion about how to identify acceptable behavior. These doctrines can lay the groundwork for sorites-style reasoning, which, as discussed earlier, thrives on the existence of vague words with fuzzy boundaries. Even if vague terms are not deliberately adopted to cover up differences of opinion, they may nonetheless have the same effect. For instance, a precedent for voiding contracts in cases involving "coercion" may turn out to be vague when many different notions of what constitutes coercion exist, even if the judge who first used the coercion standard thought the meaning of coercion to be unambiguous.[100]

The degree of vagueness in the accepted theory. Setting aside the existence of multiple theories, it is possible that a single theory can be inherently vague. A theory of ethical behavior, for instance, might rely on the use of terms such as "commitment," "promise," "force," and the like. The meaning of these terms is not self-evident. The theory might provide further definition of these terms, but the definitions themselves may rely on yet other vague terms. Much like "heap," "bald," and "tall," the terms used in political, legal, and ethical discourse may not have clear and obvious boundaries of application.[101] And in the presence of such vague terms, there is again the potential for sorites-style slopes.

---

resulted in an equitable distribution of supplies to all parts of the country, promoted economic efficiency, and minimized economic distortion."
GARY C. BRYNER, BUREAUCRATIC DISCRETION: LAW AND POLICY IN FEDERAL REGULATORY AGENCIES 7 (1987).

100.   However, there are, within the common law, resources to resist the proliferation of theories. For example, Raz believes:

[A] modified rule can usually be justified only by reasoning very similar to that justifying the original rule. Not only will its justification show the reason for applying the ruling to a subclass of the cases to which it was originally applicable, it will also show the relevance of all the operative conditions set out by the original rule.

RAZ, *supra* note 97, at 187–88. This point is by no means uncontroversial. *See, e.g.,* EISENBERG, *supra* note 30, at 52. To the extent that Raz is incorrect, multiple theories will be more widespread and the "problem" noted in the text more severe.

101.   One of the vaguest (and hence one of the most elastic) terms in ethical and legal discussions is "addiction." This is not simply a consequence of the way the word is used but also of the lack of clarity in the underlying theory of "autonomous behavior" that addiction is supposed to overwhelm:

The mere fact that a person is physiologically dependent and uses a drug to relieve withdrawal symptoms does not entail that his use of that drug is nonautonomous. In addition, the pain of withdrawal must be sufficiently severe so that it is unreasonable to expect him to endure it. Only then might it be said that an addict is powerless to quit . . . .

Social conventions create a vague and imprecise threshold of pain or discomfort that adults should be able to withstand for the sake of avoiding an evil.

DOUGLAS N. HUSAK, DRUGS AND RIGHTS 108–09 (1992). Even more troubling is the inconsistency in the application of the threshold. On the one hand, heroin use is considered sufficiently painful to stop that it is labeled "addictive." On the other hand, the level of pain experienced by

The degree of "empirical vagueness" created by the accepted theory. Some theories do a reasonably good job of avoiding conceptual vagueness. The notion of wealth maximization employed in the economic analysis of law, for instance, is a relatively well-defined theory.[102] But the fact that an idea is well defined in theory does not guarantee that it is easily applied in practice. We use the phrase "empirical vagueness" to refer to indeterminacy in the application of a theory, typically created by lack of knowledge on the part of agents and decisionmakers who are expected to apply it.

Consider the question of efficiency (wealth maximization) in the context of tort law. A simple application of the usual economic approach suggests that a rule of negligence plus contributory negligence, with optimally set due-care levels, is the most efficient rule to adopt.[103] The story becomes substantially more complex when it is recognized that the rule adopted must be applied not just to a single case, but to a whole class of cases that will not have identical characteristics. What would be efficient care in one case (considered in isolation) is not necessarily what would be efficient in another. The judgment about what is the efficient *rule* to apply to the class of cases depends, then, on the distribution of relevant characteristics over both plaintiffs and defendants. Yet this is not information that a single court could reasonably be expected to possess, since (a) each court sees only a subset of all the cases that arise, and (b) the cases that reach the legal system are a biased subset of the class of all the relevant situations that will be affected by the chosen rule.[104]

Thus, even if there is broad agreement among decisionmakers about what theory to use, and even if the theory is internally consistent and well defined, the theory may be vague in application. If courts are directed to hold

---

heroin users who do not get their fix is not sufficient to excuse them from even minor crimes committed to sustain their addiction. *Id.* at 113. To see the possibilities for a large expansion in the use of the term "addictive," consider the following news report:

> Caroline Goddard, director of the Obesity Treatment Center Medical Group in Sacramento, is among those who contend there is an addictive quality to foods high in fat and sugar because of their ability to stimulate pleasure centers in the brain . . . .
>
> Among her patients is Virginia Lee, who has struggled for years to stay under 300 pounds. Lee says she feels incapable of ordering a cheeseburger without the fries, and that when she gives in and goes to a McDonald's, she finds herself compelled to go back the next day. And the next.

Will Evans, *Vets of Tobacco Wars Take Aim at Fast Food: Lawsuits Blaming Restaurants for Obesity Appear to Represent a New Trend*, SACRAMENTO BEE, Feb. 24, 2003, at A1, *available at* http://www.sacbee.com/content/news/story/6169959p-7125099c.html.

102. It is relatively well defined, but not perfectly. The Scitovsky objection is a well-known source of indeterminacy in the Kaldor-Hicks (wealth maximization) approach. *See* MARK BLAUG, ECONOMIC THEORY IN RETROSPECT 589–90 (4th ed. 1985). In the context of law and economics, see, for example, Mario J. Rizzo, *The Mirage of Efficiency*, 8 HOFSTRA L. REV. 641, 649–51 (1980).

103. We abstract from problems relating to the activity levels of plaintiffs and defendants. *See* STEVEN SHAVELL, ECONOMIC ANALYSIS OF ACCIDENT LAW 21–32, 41–46 (1987).

104. *See generally* Gillian K. Hadfield, *Bias in the Evolution of Legal Rules*, 80 GEO. L.J. 583 (1992).

a party liable for actions that are "inefficient," that can be just as vague as telling the court to hold a party liable for actions that are "unreasonable." In practice, decisionmakers will likely have to rely on the precedent set by other courts to decide what is efficient, because they do not have the necessary information to make a direct judgment of efficiency. But following precedent in the context of vague terms is a recipe for the occurrence of sorites-style slopes. The applied boundary between "efficient" and "inefficient" may slide in one direction or the other. The fact that the boundary is sharp in theory does little to prevent the slope, because empirical vagueness creates the problem.

The degree of looseness of the research program in determining the future development of theories. The research program is a broad set of principles that shape the development of theories in a particular area of discussion. Some research programs are relatively tight, putting substantial constraints on the development of theories, while others are relatively loose, allowing more room for divergence among theories consistent with the program. In a loose research program, there is a greater ease of transition from one theory to another, and a greater capacity for individual participants to introduce new theories that are at odds with existing theories. Given the preceding discussion of multiple theories, it follows that a looser research program is more susceptible to the emergence of slippery slopes.[105]

VII. COPING WITH SLIPPERY SLOPES

In this part we explore the methods or techniques available, in various decision contexts but especially in the law, to resist or deal with potential slippery slopes. We do not argue that the methods are always used consciously for these purposes but that, at the very least, they respond to the threat of slippery slopes to greater or lesser degrees of success, and that some may have the effect of reducing the likelihood of sliding.

---

105.   The clash of research programs or paradigms characteristic of great transitional phases in the law accentuates the proliferation of incompatible theories. In the "Progressive" and post–World War I period the first wave of Legal Realists sought to balance and partially integrate the competing research programs of formalist liberalism and pragmatic welfarism. No coherent synthesis was achieved. *See* David Ingram, *The Sirens of Pragmatism Versus the Priests of Proceduralism: Habermas and American Legal Realism, in* HABERMAS AND PRAGMATISM 83–98 (Mitchell Aboulafia et al. eds., 2002). The Realists reconstructed "judicial reasoning as an impartial process of reconciling or balancing different perspectives, values and interests through open and public 'conversations' with scientific experts, affected parties and the broader community." *Id.* at 98. In this context tentative theories abounded and the myth of deducing the one appropriate rule for a situation took its final blow.

A. Accepting the Trade-Off

Suppose that a decisionmaker has just been exposed to a persuasive SSA. The SSA convinces him that making some desirable decision now will lead to some undesirable decision later. So what should he do? The simplest response is to accept the trade off: The desirable and the undesirable cannot be separated, so they must be accepted or rejected as a package. The good must be weighed against the bad to make a decision. If the bad outweighs the good, then the SSA averts the SSE by preventing the initial decision. If the good outweighs the bad, then the potential SSE becomes an unpleasant but expected consequence of the initial decision.[106]

Although accepting the trade-off is one possible response to the SSA, it is not a satisfying one, so decisionmakers are inclined to seek other strategies. Probably the most common strategy is to attempt to create a rule that will prevent the SSE from taking place.

B. Stipulating an Arbitrary Stopping Rule

The decisionmaker may attempt to establish a clear rule, a line between the cases in which future decisionmakers should take a particular action and cases in which they should not. For instance, consider the question of executing murderers who are mentally retarded. Although many people would agree that retarded persons should not be executed for their actions, this question is susceptible to a sorites-style slope because of the vagueness of the concept "retarded." IQ is often considered a summary statistic or proxy for intelligence, although it clearly does not capture everything we mean by intelligence. Nevertheless, IQ is a characteristic located on a continuum, and it is not clear where the line should be drawn to separate those whose IQ is high enough to allow execution from those whose IQ is too low. To resolve this problem, society might adopt a somewhat arbitrary rule saying that a murderer with an IQ of seventy-one or greater may be executed, while all others may not. The decisionmakers in actual cases are directed to decide according to this rule, rather than by analogy to similar cases.[107]

---

106. For example, the decisionmaker could accept that allowing physician-assisted suicide (PAS) for terminal illnesses would likely lead to PAS in severe but nonterminal cases like "Lou Gehrig's disease." But the latter, while undesirable, might not be so bad as to make the disadvantages of prohibiting PAS in terminal cases worth bearing.

107. It is quite interesting to note that the U.S. Supreme Court in *Atkins v. Virginia*, 536 U.S. 304 (2002), did not take the route of instructing states to follow a clear IQ rule. In its holding that the execution of "retarded" persons violates the Eighth Amendment to the U.S. Constitution, the Court did not specify a single (or even multiple) sharp criterion to distinguish the "retarded" from the "normal." The Court seems to quote with approval various psychiatric standards. Nevertheless, these

This approach could avoid the slippery slope at the level of decisions, but it could reemerge in another form. If the rule itself should ever be called into question, then the very process of rule selection could be susceptible to the same kind of sorites reasoning.[108] If all persons with IQs of seventy or greater may be executed, then why shouldn't the person with an IQ of sixty-nine get the same treatment? In response to this challenge, the rule could be moved by increments in much the same way the decisions were. To a certain extent, entrenched rules in general and an entrenched IQ rule in particular are arbitrary. This is because the rule maker refuses to change them even when they appear to be inconsistent with their underlying justifications. If the rule can be maintained, SSEs may be avoided here, but the very arbitrariness of the rule may weaken the rule maker's resolve to hold firm.

C. Appealing to a Higher Standard

In this approach, the decisionmaker appeals to a higher standard for judgment in cases in which the correct decision is unclear. This approach is

---

are quite vague, both theoretically and empirically. *See id.* at 309 n.3. From a theoretical perspective: "[C]linical definitions of mental retardation require not only subaverage intellectual functioning, but also significant limitations in adaptive skills such as communication, self-care, and self-direction that became manifest before age 18." *Id.* at 318. From an empirical perspective:

> To the extent there is serious disagreement about the execution of mentally retarded offenders, it is in determining which offenders are in fact retarded. . . . Not all people who claim to be mentally retarded will be so impaired as to fall within the range of mentally retarded offenders about which there is a national consensus.

Id. at 317–18. Furthermore, the underlying theory about why mental retardation is relevant in a criminal context is also vague.

> Mentally retarded persons frequently know the difference between right and wrong and are competent to stand trial. Because of their impairments, however, by definition they have diminished capacities to understand and process information, to communicate, to abstract from mistakes and learn from experience, to engage in logical reasoning, to control impulses, and to understand the reactions of others.

Id. at 318. As a result of this three-fold vagueness, any court attempting to apply legislation that embodies these criteria or standards will face slippery slope problems emanating from analogies with previously decided cases. The class of retarded may narrow or widen depending on the predilections of judges or other decisionmakers (for example, on their attitudes toward capital punishment in general). Furthermore, the capital punishment limitations for the retarded may extend to limitations on other forms of punishment as well if the rationale of the decision is generalized: Retarded persons' "deficiencies do not warrant an exemption from criminal sanctions, but they do diminish their personal culpability." *Id.* at 318. Limitation of personal responsibility, by the logic of this theory, cannot be limited to acts of murder.

   108.   *See,* for example, Endicott's argument:

> Higher-order vagueness is a threat because the [underlying] theory needs a notion of "admissible" sharpenings [bright line distinctions or rules]. The meaning of "tall" does not allow you to sharpen it so that no one less than nine feet tall is tall. So clearly tall people must be those who are tall on all *admissible* sharpenings. But "admissible" seems to be vague, just as "clearly tall" is vague . . . . We could [then] formulate a new form of the sorites paradox . . . .

ENDICOTT, *supra* note 49, at 80.

most natural when there is already a rule in place, but the rule itself includes a vague term. Consider the well-known example of a rule from H.L.A. Hart:[109] "No vehicles are permitted in the park." The word "vehicle" is inherently vague. It is entirely possible that a myopic analysis of the term "vehicle"—perhaps through a series of analogies—can rationalize the extension of this rule to motorized toy cars or wheelchairs. But if the courts were to make reference to the underlying original rationale (for example, protection of pedestrians from serious traffic accidents) instead of focusing on the meaning of the word "vehicle," the SSA and SSE might be avoided.

Or not. Appealing to a higher standard effectively changes the level of discussion from rules to theories. Whether appealing to a higher standard is an effective means of avoiding slippery slopes depends on the characteristics of the theory itself. In the "no vehicles in the park" rule, it seems likely, though not certain, that substantial agreement will exist about the theoretical rationale for the rule. The *clarity* of the standard helps to "nail down" the rule. But this need not always be the case. Choosing an appropriate standard involves the selection (perhaps implicit) of a theory, and raising the discussion to the level of theory can actually increase the likelihood of a slippery slope. This may be true for any of the reasons discussed in the last part: Theories may be inherently vague, theories may create empirical vagueness, or there may be disagreement among theories.

As an example of theoretical vagueness, consider the treatment of obscenity in First Amendment law. It is well established that obscene material does not enjoy First Amendment protection, while other material (that does not fall in another unprotected category) does. Uncertainty about the meaning of "obscene" prompted the Supreme Court to adopt a standard, in *Miller v. California*,[110] under which an allegedly obscene work must not, "taken as a whole, ... have serious literary, artistic, political, or scientific value" to lose its First Amendment protection. In essence, the Court directed lower courts to interpret a rule about obscenity by reference to a higher standard, or theory, that defines obscenity in terms of the social value of the expression. The problem, of course, is that judges and legal scholars who use the term "value" might very well possess different, perhaps radically different, theories of value in literature, art, politics, and science. If judges regularly made reference to the theory enunciated in *Miller*, we might worry that, little by little, the rule protecting nonobscene works from regulation would be eroded as the social value of the work is

---

109. H.L.A. Hart, *Positivism and the Separation of Law and Morals*, 71 HARV. L. REV. 593, 606–07 (1958).
110. 413 U.S. 15, 24 (1973).

increasingly taken into account.[111] If other areas of free speech jurisprudence relied on the alleged social value of individual acts of expression to the same extent as obscenity doctrine, without other buttressing justifications, it is not hard to imagine that courts would be left with an unacceptably weak First Amendment.[112] Freedom of speech becomes more resistant to slippery slopes when we treat it as an "entrenched abstraction"[113] or a generalization that is largely immune to exception-making. The fundamental difficulty with appealing to "social value" as the primary underlying standard for protection of free speech is that social value is an inherently vague term, susceptible to a variety of interpretations.[114]

As an example of empirical vagueness, suppose we are interested in the question of when contracts should be voided by the courts. According to one current economic theory, it is desirable for a contract to be voided when it is likely that the transaction did not make both parties better off in expected value than they would have been without the contract. This is an efficiency standard. One possibility is to examine each case individually to determine whether it fulfills the standard. This presupposes that the judge has sufficiently good data to make such an individual determination. In practice, however, the standard is empirically vague, and so courts will probably argue by analogies to clear cases.

Now, there presumably exists a spectrum here, from cases in which the contract clearly made both parties better off, to cases in which one party clearly suffers an ex ante loss because the contract was signed at gunpoint. In between, there are cases in various shades of gray. What if, for instance, one party threatened to withhold sexual favors? Or to inflict mental anguish by reminding him in graphic detail of his abusive childhood? Or to kill a beloved pet that

---

111.   We leave it to the reader to decide whether that has indeed happened, and if so, whether the slippage was desirable or not.

112.   This seems to be the implication of Schauer's characterization of Harry Kalven's First Amendment views: "[H]e applauds over-protection of speech as the only alternative to under-protection." Frederick Schauer, *Harry Kalven and the Perils of Particularism*, 56 U. CHI. L. REV. 397, 407 (1989) (reviewing HARRY KALVEN, A WORTHY TRADITION: FREEDOM OF SPEECH IN AMERICA (1988)).

113.   *Id.* at 403–04.

114.   *See, e.g.*, JOHN STUART MILL, ON LIBERTY 65 (Stefan Collini ed., Cambridge Univ. Press 1989) (1859). Mill stresses the difficulty the general public will have in estimating the social value of original ideas. "Originality is the one thing which unoriginal minds cannot feel the use of. They cannot see what it is to do for them: how should they? If they could see what it would do for them, it would not be originality." *Id.; see also id.* at 67 ("In other times there was no advantage in [exceptional individuals acting differently from the masses], unless they acted not only differently but better. In this age, the mere example of nonconformity, the mere refusal to bend the knee to custom, is itself a service."). Karl Popper observes that even wrong ideas will have social value. *See, e.g.*, KARL R. POPPER, *On the Theory of the Objective Mind, in* OBJECTIVE KNOWLEDGE: AN EVOLUTIONARY APPROACH 153 (rev. ed. 1981). "[A]voiding error is a poor ideal: if we do not dare to tackle problems which are so difficult that error is almost unavoidable, there will be no growth of knowledge. In fact, it is from our boldest theories, *including those then there which are erroneous*, that we learn most." *Id.* at 186.

belongs to the threatening party? Or to reveal potentially embarrassing secrets about his personal life? Some of these cases might appear quite similar to the contract signed at gunpoint. It is conceivable, furthermore, that a chain of cases could be found that connects the clear cases for upholding the contract to the clear cases for voiding the contract. As a result, courts following precedent in similar cases might be led to void contracts that should clearly be upheld (if the slope goes in that direction), or to uphold contracts that should clearly be voided (if the slope goes in the other direction).

Therefore, the level of discussion per se is of little significance for sliding. What is significant is whether we have moved to a more or less vague, or to an empirically more or less determinate, level of discussion. In some cases, theories will be particularly susceptible to sliding while rules will be less so; in other cases rules will be relatively susceptible while theories less so.[115]

D. Adopting an Open-Ended or Standard-Mediated Rule

This strategy represents a compromise between the previous two approaches. The decisionmaker accepts the first decision, and even some subsequent ones as well, but follows or imposes a rule on other decisionmakers that stops the process short of the danger case. Unlike the strategy of stipulating a somewhat arbitrary stopping rule, the rule here is chosen based on a factor that has a stronger theoretical rationale.

In the contract example above, this would mean specifying the conditions under which contracts may be voided. A rule embodying these conditions would

---

115. Bernard Williams distinguishes between "reasonable" and "effective" stopping points. *See* BERNARD WILLIAMS, *Which Slopes Are Slippery?, in* MAKING SENSE OF HUMANITY AND OTHER PHILOSOPHICAL PAPERS 214–15 (1995). Not everything reasonable is effective and not everything effective is reasonable. For an example of a reasonable but possibly ineffective stopping rule, suppose the issue of euthanasia is tentatively resolved by a distinction between acts of the patient and those of the doctor. For many purposes this distinction will be clear enough to prevent a slide from suicide to murder. But this reasonable stopping point might become ineffective when it is understood that some patients lack the physical ability to effect their own decision. Is physician assistance, under these circumstances, simply an aid to suicide or is it murder? For an example of a rule that may be effective but unreasonable, the law might impose a fourteen-day cut off point for fetal experimentation. "Fourteen days" is a quite clear but largely arbitrary stopping point. Is there much difference between a fourteen- and fifteen-day fetus in terms of morally relevant human characteristics? *See also* John D. Arras, *Slippery Slope Arguments, in* ENCYCLOPEDIA OF ETHICS 1594, 1594–95 (Lawrence C. Becker & Charlotte B. Becker eds., 2d ed. 2001). In terms of our framework, however, the problem is not a reasonable stopping point versus an effective one. The real difficulty is that a distinction at one level of analysis may be sharp but at a more theoretical level, it becomes vague. In the first case, the standard that people ought to be able to effect their *desires* regarding their own life and death is only implicit in the simple cases. Reference to it in more complex cases clouds a previously sharp distinction based on the external observation of acts. In the second case, the standard that fetuses that are also "persons" should not be experimented upon is only implicit as long as we do not question the fourteen-day rule. A sharp stopping point becomes vague by reference to the underlying standard.

likely refer to factors generally but imperfectly correlated with the likelihood of a value-decreasing contract. One such rule is that "a contract should be voided if it was formed in the presence of duress." A potential difficulty with this rule is the vagueness of the concept "duress."[116] Although there are clear cases of duress and clear cases of no duress, there is also a spectrum of cases in between. Is the infliction of severe mental distress a form of duress, or is some form of physical intimidation necessary?[117] Suppose that the courts (in their capacity as rule makers) take the latter approach, setting physical intimidation as a necessary and sufficient condition for voiding a contract on grounds of duress. This rule might be capable of preventing a slippery slope on the level of decisions, as courts deciding cases would only have to verify the existence of a physical threat.[118] But at the level of rule selection, the rule could be exposed to challenges based on the over- and under-inclusiveness of the rule relative to the underlying standard. Suppose that in case *x* one party threatened to yank the last hair on a (nearly) bald man's head, and in case *y* one party threatened to recount the details of the other party's abusive childhood (and evidence shows that this was indeed extremely frightening to him). The stated rule would void the contract in case *x* but not in case *y*, even though *y* appears to present the stronger case for voiding on the basis of a plausible theory of human motivation. Just as in the IQ example given earlier, a questioning of the rule relative to its underlying justification could be used to weaken, change, or move the rule in one direction or another.

As another example, consider the issue of abortion. Suppose the cost of remaining at a postulated status quo of no abortions under any circumstances is high. Suppose also that the cost of accepting the danger argument for infanticide is even higher. Does this mean that the decisionmaker will not take the first step if a persuasive SSA is made that "leads" from abortion to infanticide? Not necessarily. The idea behind the argument is that there is a simple gradient that connects zygote to infant child. But if there are important turning points

---

116.   The concept of duress has become increasingly vague over the past three centuries:
In Blackstone's time relief from an agreement on grounds of duress was a possibility only if it was coerced by actual (not threatened) imprisonment or fear of loss of life or limb. . . . [T]oday the general rule is that any wrongful act or threat which overcomes the free will of a party constitutes duress. This simple statement of the law conceals a number of questions, particularly as to the meaning of "free will" and "wrongful."

JOHN D. CALAMARI & JOSEPH M. PERILLO, THE LAW OF CONTRACTS 261–62 (2d ed. 1977) (citation omitted).

117.   One could include under "physical intimidation" only violence, threats of violence, imprisonment, and threats of imprisonment. This, absent the threat of imprisonment, is more or less the rule Blackstone believed was in effect in the seventeenth century. *See id.* at 337.

118.   Of course, there is some residual vagueness even in this rule, since the meaning of "physical intimidation" has fuzzy boundaries. Even when a relatively restricted Blackstonian conception is involved, terms such as "violence" and "threat of violence" are vague at the boundaries.

within that gradient, there may be an effective stopping rule that can serve to differentiate the cases and stop the process. The decisionmaker may focus, for example, on the development of a functioning cerebral cortex as a rule-like criterion. This would permit some early abortions while not permitting infanticide. Whether the stopping rule will hold depends, at least in part, on its being perceived as nonarbitrary. For this to be the case, an argument must be made at the level of theory. Some have claimed that there are good reasons to believe that the development of a functioning cerebral cortex is a non-arbitrary stopping point. The cerebral cortex is responsible for many of the functions or capacities that we usually conceive a human person to have.[119] So a rule that prohibits abortions beyond that stage will be consistent with a theory that privileges the human person rather than merely developing human life or tissue. The persuasiveness of this theory will be imputed downward to the rule and determine its effectiveness as a stopping point.

It seems, then, that neither the use of arbitrary rules nor underlying standards nor quasi arbitrary rules offers an infallible escape route from slippery slopes, because slippery slopes can emerge in the process of rule selection as well as in the process of rule application. Still, it is possible that these approaches can reduce the likelihood of slippery slopes.

E.   Altering the Scope and Power of Precedent

The reader may notice that we have taken a somewhat ambivalent position on the desirability of precedent. On the one hand, we have indicated that following precedent could encourage slippery slopes of the sorites variety. On the other, we have implied that the progressive weakening of precedent was responsible for the Humean beneficence slippery slope. The seeming contradiction dissipates once we realize that the role of precedent in retarding a slippery slope depends on the assumed location of the danger case and which decisions are regarded as precedent.

Consider the mathematical version of the sorites story, in which one end of a continuum (the "one" end) is the clearest case for taking action A, and the other (the "zero" end) is the clearest case for not taking action A. The slope, as we described it, involved action A being taken in more and more cases, so that eventually it is taken in some case where it clearly should not be—the danger case. If we suppose that action A makes an exception to some rule, the problem is that when an exception is made in a clear case for doing so, precedent allows and perhaps even requires that the exception be made in similar but less clear

119.   DANIEL A. DOMBROWSKI & ROBERT DELTETE, A BRIEF, LIBERAL, CATHOLIC DEFENSE OF ABORTION 11–12 (2000).

cases. If making an exception did not establish a precedent for further exceptions, there would be no problem of a slope in the direction of too many exceptions.[120] To put it differently, what if we supposed that the application of the rule (hence the refusal to do A) was treated as the only relevant precedent? Then the slippery slope, if any, would occur in the opposite direction, resulting in too few exceptions to the rule.

A similar set of observations can be made about the Humean beneficence process. In the early stage of that story, when few or no exceptions had been made to the established rule, precedent played a *restraining* role: Judges were loath to make exceptions because doing so would deviate too much from the established case law. But in the late stage of the story, when many exceptions had been made, precedent played an *enabling* role: Judges who wished to make further exceptions could easily find previous decisions to justify their own. If exceptions did not act as precedents, then as in the sorites story, there would have been no slippery slope in the direction of exception-making. The problem, if any, would have been the making of too few exceptions.

Thus, we can see that precedent has both an enabling and a restraining aspect.[121] Whether either aspect is desirable depends crucially on what outcome is identified as the danger case. When the danger case is making excessive exceptions to some rule, then the restraining aspect is SSE-retarding and the enabling aspect is SSE-encouraging. When the danger case is making too few exceptions, then the reverse is true.

Precedent is thus an imperfect attempt to enforce rules adopted for the purpose of avoiding slippery slopes.[122] The rules enforced may be arbitrary or standard-based. As indicated above, such rules can only provide a partial barrier to slippery slopes, in large part because disputes about the application of rules can reemerge as problems of rule selection. The problem is exacerbated by (a) the continual emergence of novel cases for which the application of rules

---

120. In the courts of chancery prior to the seventeenth century equity decisions were made in personam. *See* F.W. MAITLAND, EQUITY: A COURSE OF LECTURES 8 (1949). In these circumstances, an exception would not establish a precedent for further exceptions.

121. Compare, for example, Hayek:

> In certain conditions, namely when some basic principles of the law have been accepted for some time, they will indeed govern the whole system of law, its general spirit as well as every single rule and application within it. At such times it will possess great inherent stability. Every lawyer will, when he has to interpret or apply a rule which is not in accord with the rest of the system, endeavour so to bend it as to make it conform with the others . . . .
>
> The situation is entirely different, however, when a general philosophy of the law which is not in accord with the greater part of the existing law has recently gained ascendancy. *The same lawyers will, through the same habits and techniques, and generally unwittingly, become a revolutionary force, as effective in transforming the law down to every detail as they were before in preserving it.*

F.A. HAYEK, LAW, LEGISLATION AND LIBERTY, RULES AND ORDER 66 (1973) (emphasis added).

122. We do not wish to imply that this is the only function of precedent.

Rules, Theories, and Slippery Slopes 587

is unclear and (b) the mingling of rule application and rule selection functions in the legal sphere.

As a result, courts may find it very difficult to separate the restraining and enabling aspects of precedent. To do so, they would need to establish a distinction between decisions to be regarded as binding precedents and decisions to be regarded as mere exceptions.[123] How might this be done? Schauer observes that some areas of constitutional law, especially those involving First Amendment prohibitions on the reach of government regulation, incorporate "entrenched" abstractions as a fundamental part of their jurisprudence.[124] The law pertaining to First Amendment freedom of speech has made all manner of activities, such as marches, "speech."[125] Further, it inhibits examination of the empirically vague underlying theories or standards that would determine the social worth of speech relative to its social costs.[126] Once an activity falls under the abstract characterization "free speech," it becomes immune to examination at a deeper level.[127] This approach attempts to enhance the precedential power of decisions that favor freedom of expression, while muting the precedential effect of decisions that do not by characterizing them as narrowly defined exceptions.

With regard to constitutional prohibitions on government behavior, the expansive conception of certain abstractions operates to resist slippery slopes in the direction of excessive restrictions on private behavior. The entrenched abstraction limits the putative danger inherent in overextension of the category, justifiable restrictions on speech, by allowing the possible overextension of another category, desirable acts of expression. This makes perfect sense if the identified danger case is the excessive restriction of speech. But if the Court had identified excessive freedom of expression as the danger case, then far from being SSE-retarding, the entrenched abstraction could be regarded as SSE-encouraging.

---

123. The distinction between a rule and its exceptions is troublesome. The difficulty of maintaining the distinction gives exception-making its precedential value. Consider the argument made by Paul Ramsey:

> The effort to locate a *justifiable* exception can only have the effect of utterly destroying its exceptional character. The deed is found to be morally doable, it is repeatable, it is one of a *kind*. How rare or frequent is of no consequence to the moral verdicts we render. The same justifying features, the same verdict, the same general judgment falls upon the alleged exception, if it is justified; and so that act falls within our deepened or broadened moral principles.

Paul Ramsey, *The Case of the Curious Exception, in* NORM AND CONTENT IN CHRISTIAN ETHICS 67, 78 (Gene K. Outka & Paul Ramsey eds., 1968).

124. Schauer, *supra* note 112, at 403–04.

125. "Nazis became political speakers, a suburban community populated by Holocaust survivors became a public forum, and popularly inspired restrictions became government censorship." *Id.* at 408.

126. Note we say "inhibits," not "completely prohibits."

127. "A principle of free speech, according to which the mode of analysis shifts when an occurrence can be categorized as 'speech,' is incompatible with a principle of maximally contextual evaluation of all aspects of situations in which speech is present." Schauer, *supra* note 112, at 397–98.

F.   Establishing Presumptions, Burdens of Persuasion, or Levels
     of Scrutiny

Another possible means of protecting a rule against erosion is to privilege
certain crucial facts by a legal presumption. If a rule refers to some characteristic about a case, but the characteristic is theoretically or empirically vague, then
requiring the finder of fact to infer its presence from certain sharper "basic facts"
can make sliding less likely.

Consider again the example of executing retarded persons. "IQ of 70 or
below" is a simple rule for inferring mental retardation (a vague characteristic)
from one's IQ score (a sharper or more observable characteristic). As we
observed earlier, this rule could be subject to a slippery slope. But now suppose
the rule is treated as a *presumption* that an IQ of 70 or less indicates mental
retardation.[128] Under these circumstances someone (for example, a district
attorney trying to obtain an execution) may wish to claim that an IQ of 70 is
indistinguishable from an IQ of 71 (not retarded or "normal") and hence the
defendant with an IQ of 70 should be subject to capital punishment as well.
The presumption throws an obstacle in the way of the argument. At a minimum, the presumption requires the proponent of action to produce or come forth
with sufficient evidence that a defendant with an IQ of 70 should be regarded
as normal. He may not be able to do it. Furthermore, under the "reformist
approach,"[129] the presumption will shift the burden of persuasion on this issue to
the proponent, requiring him to prove by a preponderance of the evidence that
the defendant is of normal intelligence. This, *ex hypothesei*, he will not be able to
do. If all he can say is that there is no reason to differentiate 70 from 71 or from
69, for that matter, then he is saying that there is no *better* reason to consider 70
retarded as opposed to normal. Hence the preponderance standard cannot be
met.

The problem with this approach is very similar to that of the arbitrary rule.
Just as any dispute at the rule application level can be recast as a dispute at the
rule selection level, any dispute at the presumption-application level can be
recast as a dispute at the presumption-selection level. The proponent can ask,
why should the presumption apply to IQs of seventy and below, rather than
sixty-nine and below? Indeed, a presumption is really just a different sort of
rule, possibly a weaker one since it is explicitly defeasible. But paradoxically, the
presumption's greater defeasibility is also its virtue. Implicit in the presumption

---

128.   Obviously this is a simplification. Courts would mostly likely decline to use *only* an IQ score
to make such a determination. See elaborations on the concept of mental retardation cited by the
Supreme Court in *Atkins v. Virginia*, 536 U.S. 304, 309, at nn.3, 5 (2002).

129.   CHRISTOPHER B. MUELLER & LAIRD C. KIRKPATRICK, EVIDENCE § 3.8, at 134–35 (2d ed.
1999).

is a recognition of the arbitrary character of the rule, with an allowance for exceptions to be made in cases with sufficient proof. When exceptions are made, they do not constitute changes in the rule itself, nor do they necessarily set precedent for future cases. As a result, a presumption may provide less traction for arguments in favor of shifting the rule. In another example, the rule that sets eighteen as the age of legal majority is actually a presumption, because a person under eighteen can petition for emancipation under unusual circumstances.[130] The existence of a possible exception for very special cases may, oddly enough, add legitimacy to a rule that would otherwise appear excessively arbitrary.

In constitutional law, higher levels of scrutiny will be applied to certain categories of state action. Content-based restrictions on freedom of speech, for instance, are exposed to strict scrutiny, whereas content-neutral restrictions face a lower (intermediate) level of scrutiny.[131] Presumably, the Supreme Court has identified content-based restrictions as more perilous—that is, closer to the danger case. Nonetheless, exceptions are allowed in cases in which the state interest is especially compelling. This approach tips the scales against speech restrictions without prohibiting them entirely. A government that wishes to institute a policy favoring free speech will not be expected to justify its choice, whereas a government wishing to institute a policy restricting the content of speech will be expected to provide substantial justification. This approach probably generates fewer challenges to the rule itself (at the rule-selection level) than would a rule prohibiting all content-restricting policies without exception. By providing a safety valve for the most persuasive exceptions, it protects the rule against direct legal challenge.

It should go almost without saying that the presumption approach has its dangers. If the individual cases allowing exceptions (on grounds that the burden of proof or standard of persuasion has been met) are regarded as enabling precedents, so that similar cases with slightly less support are seen as within their orbit, then the presumption may encourage SSEs rather than inhibit them.

G.   Creating Supermajority Requirements and Constitutional Constraints

We have been discussing legislative and judicially created impediments to SSEs. Another approach is to constrain those forms of decisionmaking by supermajority requirements and similar forms of constitutional constraint. These constraints can assure that certain types of change will occur only if there is a sufficiently large amount of support for the change.

---

130.   *See, e.g.,* CAL. FAM. CODE § 7120 (West 1994). The conditions for emancipation in California include being at least fourteen years of age, living separately from a parent or guardian, managing one's own financial affairs, and not having an illegal source of income. *Id.*

131.   *See, e.g.,* Turner Broad. Sys., Inc. v. FCC, 512 U.S. 622, 642 (1994).

Consider the legal voting age. There is nothing special about the age of eighteen that makes it the uniquely correct minimum voting age. The arbitrariness of the rule becomes apparent when, for example, a high school senior whose birthday is November 9th cannot vote in the presidential election, whereas a high school drop-out whose birthday is one week earlier can. But no other voting age, at least within some range, would be any less arbitrary, so this rule may be as good (or bad) as many others. If voting privileges were determined individually—say, in legal proceedings—it is not hard to imagine that the voting age might slide, by increments, in one direction or the other. The imbedding of the voting age in the Constitution assures that this sliding cannot occur. Even if a majority of people agreed that eighteen-and-one-month-olds should not be able to vote, that would not be sufficient to change the rule. Only the passage of a constitutional amendment could achieve that, and amendments are notoriously difficult to pass.

In a sense, the differential barriers to the alteration of different types of law or policy reflect the different layers in the structure of discussion. The debate over what terms should be included in a constitution (say, at a constitutional convention) is likely to occur at the level of theory, as the discussion is explicitly focused on what the basic rules should be.[132] Once the constitution is established, the subsequent discussion takes place largely within the established rules. Some may make arguments against the rules adopted, but those arguments are *not* generally understood as arguments for and against decisions being made within the current rule structure. For instance, an argument against the presidential veto (because, say, it gives too much power to one man) would not be considered a reason to enforce a bill that was passed by Congress and vetoed by the president. Until the Constitution is changed, the veto remains in place.

This is, of course, an idealized view. In any actual constitution, there exist many vague terms, and so there will inevitably be debate about their meaning. Different theories will exist both about what the terms do mean and what they should mean. There will inevitably be some blurring of the distinction between arguments about rule application and arguments about rule selection. A well known, if controversial, position states that the U.S. Constitution is a "living document" whose content is determined by its interpretation, which changes over time in response to changes in society.[133]

---

132.   James Buchanan has emphasized choice among rules, as opposed to choice within rules, as the essence of constitutional-level thinking. *See, e.g.,* JAMES M. BUCHANAN, THE LIMITS OF LIBERTY: BETWEEN ANARCHY AND LEVIATHAN (1975); James M. Buchanan, *The Constitution of Economic Policy,* 77 AM. ECON. REV. 243–50 (1987).

133.   This is a position most often associated with Justice Brennan and the Warren Court. *See* Bruce Ackerman, *A Generation of Betrayal?* 65 FORDHAM L. REV. 1519 (1997); Michael Les Benedict, *Constitutional History and Constitutional Theory: Reflections on Ackerman, Reconstruction, and the Transformation of the American Constitution,* 108 YALE L.J. 2011 (1999); Jeffrey Goldsworthy, *Dworkin as*

It is the possibility for blurring that is the Achilles' heel of the supermajority/constitutional constraints strategy for retarding slippery slopes. We have previously observed that virtually any dispute about rule application can be recast as a dispute about rule selection. We now observe that often the reverse is also true: Disputes about rule selection can be recast as disputes about rule application. If the existing rules are sufficiently vague, skillful advocates can argue that the rules effectively give discretion to the decisionmaker, who can employ whatever normative and positive theories he thinks best.

CONCLUSIONS

The key feature that distinguishes SSAs from other forms of argument is that they are arguments about arguments. The proponent of an SSA claims to predict how acceptance of one argument will lead (with increased likelihood) to the acceptance of other arguments not identical to the first. Whether the speaker's prediction is correct depends crucially on the process that he claims will lead from earlier arguments to later arguments. To evaluate such a process, one needs to understand the structure of discussion in which arguments are made and accepted. In this Article, we have attempted to fill this need.

The primary tool of our analysis is the structure of discussion and argument outlined in Part II. This structure characterizes discussion and argument as occurring in a hierarchical fashion. The lowest rung of the hierarchy is the decision to be made. The next rung up is the rules, which are applied (sometimes) in the making of decisions. The next rung is theories, which are applied (sometimes) in the selection of rules. The highest rung is research programs, which are used to constrain the selection of theories. Arguments can take place at any level in the structure: to influence the making of rules, to influence the selection of rules, to influence the debate among theories, and so on.

The maker of an SSA purports (implicitly) to have some knowledge of the actual content of the structure of discussion—that is, the actual rules, theories, and research programs at work in the minds of the participants. To the extent that the speaker's purported knowledge is accurate, his argument may be a good description of the likely development of future arguments in the system. In short, the SSA is valid. If the description is not entirely correct, of course, the argument is less valid (or just plain wrong).

We have described several types of SSAs that we think can, at least under some circumstances, be valid. But in each case, we have emphasized that the evaluation depends crucially on the proponent's model of how people make

---

an Originalist, 17 CONST. COMMENT. 49 (2000). Our intention here is not to enter the debate over constitutional interpretation on the side of originalism, but rather to observe how the inevitable vagueness of constitutional terms creates a fuzzy boundary between the choice of rules and the application of rules.

and adopt arguments and other ideas. Even if readers reject one or more of these types of argument, or the specific examples accompanying them, they will hopefully find the overall structure useful in understanding the nature of slippery slope arguments in general.

Slippery slopes are slippery in more ways than one. Aside from sliding from one argument to another, there can also be sliding from one level of discussion to another. Slopes at the level of decisions can become slopes at the level of rule selection, and vice versa. It is this characteristic, we think, that makes them so difficult to deal with. Nonetheless, there exist a variety of imperfect means for resisting slippery slopes, which we have discussed in Part VII of the Article. There may be yet other means. If slippery slopes can indeed be a legitimate form of argumentation, as we suggest, then finding effective means of coping with them will hopefully become a priority in legal, political, and ethical debates.

[11]

NYU JOURNAL OF
LAW & LIBERTY

PATERNALIST SLOPES

Douglas Glen Whitman
Mario J. Rizzo

A growing literature in law and public policy harnesses research in behavioral economics to justify a new form of paternalism.[1] The thrust of the argument is straightforward: Human beings
are not fully rational, in the sense traditionally used in economic
theory, but in fact exhibit an array of cognitive problems, including
but not limited to: status quo bias, optimism bias, hindsight bias,
context dependence, susceptibility to framing effects, and lack of
willpower. These cognitive problems lead to errors in decision making, meaning that people systematically behave in ways that fail to
advance their own best interest. Insofar as actual behavior deviates
from optimal behavior, governments (as well as other people and
institutions) can potentially intervene in ways that will improve the
individual's well-being.

The leading contributors to the "new paternalist" literature
(as we shall call it) place great emphasis on the modesty of their
proposals. The policies advocated are said to be minor and non-

---

[1] Colin Camerer et al., *Regulation for Conservatives: Behavioral Economics and the Case for
'Asymmetric Paternalism,'* 151 U. PA. L. REV. 1211 (2003); Richard H. Thaler & Cass R.
Sunstein, *Libertarian Paternalism*, 93 AEA PAPERS AND PROCEEDINGS 175 (2003); Cass
R. Sunstein & Richard H. Thaler, *Libertarian Paternalism Is Not an Oxymoron*, 70 U.
CHI. L. REV. 1159 (2003); Christine Jolls & Cass R. Sunstein, *Debiasing Through Law*, 35
J. LEGAL STUD. 199 (2006); Jonathan Gruber & Botond Koszegi, *Is Addiction 'Rational'?
Theory and Evidence*, 116 Q. J. ECON. 1261 (2001); Ted O'Donoghue & Matthew Rabin,
Studying Optimal Paternalism, Illustrated by a Model of Sin Taxes, 93 AEA PAPERS &
AER PROCEEDINGS 186 (2003); Ted O'Donoghue & Matthew Rabin, *Optimal Sin Taxes*
(2003) (unpublished manuscript, on file with Cornell University, University of Cali-
fornia at Berkeley).

intrusive. A recent feature article in *The Economist* captures the tenor:

> Their aim is not the 'nanny state', a scold and killjoy forcing its charges to eat their vegetables and take their medicine. Instead they offer a vision of what you might call the 'avuncular state,' worldly-wise, offering a nudge in the right direction, perhaps pulling strings on your behalf without your even noticing.[2]

Christine Jolls and Cass Sunstein, for instance, repeatedly refer to their proposals for debiasing behavior through law as a "middle ground" between laissez-faire and more heavy-handed paternalism[3], one that is a "less intrusive, more direct, and more democratic response to the problem of bounded rationality."[4] Colin Camerer et al. characterize their "asymmetric paternalism" model as "a careful, cautious, and disciplined approach" to evaluating paternalistic policies.[5] In general, the new "soft" paternalism is presented as a kinder, gentler form of paternalism that avoids the problems of the older "hard" paternalism.

A distinct literature in law and public policy analyzes the validity of "slippery slope" arguments.[6] A slippery slope argument is one suggesting that a proposed policy or course of action that might appear desirable now, when taken in isolation, is in fact undesirable (or less desirable) because it increases the likelihood of undesirable policies being adopted in the future. Despite the poor reputation of slippery slopes as a form of argument, recent work by various authors has rehabilitated slippery slope reasoning by identifying the specific mechanisms and processes by which slippery

---

[2] *The Avuncular State*, THE ECONOMIST, April 6th, 2006, at 67-69.

[3] Jolls & Sunstein, *supra* note 1, at 208, 216.

[4] *Id.* at 201.

[5] Camerer et al., *supra* note 1, at 1212.

[6] DOUGLAS WALTON, SLIPPERY SLOPE ARGUMENTS (1992); SANFORD IKEDA, DYNAMICS OF THE MIXED ECONOMY: TOWARD A THEORY OF INTERVENTIONISM (1997); Eugene Volokh, *The Mechanisms of the Slippery Slope*, 116 HARV. L. REV. 1026 (2003); Mario J. Rizzo & Douglas Glen Whitman, *The Camel's Nose Is in the Tent: Rules, Theories, and Slippery Slopes*, 41 UCLA L. REV. 539 (2003); Eric Lode, *Slippery Slope Arguments and Legal Reasoning*, 87 CALIF. L. REV. 1469 (1999); Frederick Schauer, *Slippery Slopes*, 99 HARV. L. REV. 361 (1985).

slopes operate, as well as the circumstances in which the threat of such slopes is greatest.

The present article sits at the nexus of the new paternalist literature and the slippery slopes literature. The new paternalist approach exhibits many of the characteristics conducive to the occurrence of slippery slopes. Indeed, new paternalist policies, and the theories that support them, are *permeated* by these dangerous features. As a result, soft paternalism—even if initially modest and non-intrusive—has the potential to pave the way for harder paternalism, including some policies of which the new paternalists themselves would disapprove. We conclude that policymaking based on new paternalist reasoning ought to be considered with much greater trepidation than its advocates suggest.

In Part I, we offer a brief defense of slippery slope reasoning, in general and as applied to the new paternalism. In Part II, we discuss the primary factor that makes the new paternalism especially vulnerable to slippery slopes: theoretical and empirical vagueness, which create a natural gradient between softer and harder paternalist policies. In Part III, we apply several specific slope processes (or mechanisms) to new paternalist policymaking. The specific processes include altered economic incentives, enforcement needs, the *ad verecundiam* heuristic (i.e., deference to perceived authority), bias toward simple principles, and reframing of the status quo. Finally, in Part IV, we briefly discuss the implications of slippery slope risks for evaluating policy proposals.

Part I. A Defense of Slippery Slope Reasoning

Although the slippery slope literature does not speak with a single voice, we think the general conclusion is clear: while slippery slope arguments are not universally valid, they cannot simply be dismissed. Some slippery slope arguments are valid and others are not. The key to distinguishing them is to identify the specific processes or mechanisms by which slopes occur, as well as the circumstances that affect the likelihood of such slopes.[7]

Nevertheless, slippery slope arguments continue to suffer from a poor reputation. As Eric Lode notes, the slippery slope has

---

[7] *See* Volokh, *supra* note 6; Lode, *supra* note 6; Rizzo & Whitman, *supra* note 6.

even been classified as a fallacy in many introductory logic texts.[8] A short defense therefore seems in order.[9] The most common response to the slippery slope argument is that it immediately crumbles in the face of any logical or reasonable distinction between the (presumably good) policy under consideration and the (presumably bad) policy to which it will allegedly lead. "We can do the right thing now," the response goes, "and resist doing the wrong thing later." The main problem with this reply is that it trades on an ambiguity in the word "we." The present decisionmaker and the future decisionmaker need not be the same. Even if present decisionmakers are willing and able to make the relevant distinctions, future decisionmakers may be unable or unwilling to do so. The proponent of a slippery slope argument need not show that policy A logically entails policy B, only that adoption of A increases the likelihood of future decisionmakers adopting B—even if doing so would be illogical or mistaken.

Put somewhat differently, we ought to heed Bernard Williams's distinction between "reasonable distinctions" and "effective distinctions." Reasonable distinctions are those for which one can make a sensible argument, whereas effective distinctions can be defended "as a matter of social or psychological fact."[10] These need not be the same; some reasonable distinctions will not be honored in practice, while some arbitrary (non-reasonable) distinctions can be successfully defended. The critic of slippery slope argumentation focuses on the existence of reasonable distinctions; however, effective distinctions are the ones that truly matter.

Moreover, slippery slope arguments are especially apropos in addressing the new paternalism. Our approach here might seem unfair, inasmuch as we are criticizing the new paternalists *not* primarily for the actual positions they have advocated[11], but for the

---

[8] Lode, *supra* note 6, at 1474.

[9] For a short defense of slippery slopes in the context of a different policy debate, see Eugene Volokh, *Same-Sex Marriage and Slippery Slopes*, 33 HOFSTRA L. REV. 1155, 1163-1165 (2005).

[10] Quoted in Lode, *supra* note 6, at 1479.

[11] We do that elsewhere; *see* Mario J. Rizzo & Douglas Glen Whitman, Meet the New Boss, Same As the Old Boss: An Inquiry Into the New Paternalism (2006) (unpublished manuscript, on file with New York University and California State University,

unwarranted positions that ignorant or illogical people may adopt because of them. Recall, however, that the new paternalists' arguments rely on the existence of just such such ignorant and illogical people. New paternalist policies are justified precisely on grounds that many people have cognitive and behavioral biases that lead them to make systematic errors in their decisions. And as Eugene Volokh has argued, slippery slopes are closely connected to phenomena such as "bounded rationality, rational ignorance, [and] irrational choice behaviors such as context-dependence;"[12] this connection will become more apparent as the article proceeds. Thus, we suggest that the new paternalists' own arguments should drive them to fear the slope—perhaps even more than we do.

Furthermore, at least some new paternalists invite slippery slope arguments. Camerer, et al. do so explicitly: "The potential for such 'slippery slopes' commonly arises in policy debates and clearly arises here as well. But just as for other domains, the ideal way to deal with these possibilities is not to avoid policy changes altogether, but to consider the extent to which future policies are made to appear more or less attractive by the one under consideration."[13] That is what we aim to do.

Part II. Gradients and Paternalism

A. Gradients as fertile ground for slippery slopes

Slippery slopes thrive in the presence of a continuum created by vague words or concepts, a phenomenon recognized by various slippery-slope analysts.[14] When words and concepts have fuzzy boundaries, it becomes difficult to defend sharp distinctions. Each case differs from the next case by only a small increment, so that unlike cases can be linked by a series of cases that differ only by degree. The classic example is the *sorites* paradox, named after the Greek word for "heap." How many grains of sand does it take

---

Northridge); Glen Whitman, *Against the New Paternalism: Internalities and the Economics of Self-Control*, CATO INSTITUTE POLICY ANALYSIS NO. 563 (2006).

[12] Volokh, *supra* note 6, at 1035.

[13] Camerer et al., *supra* note 1, at 1251.

[14] *See* Rizzo & Whitman *supra* note 6, at 557-560; Volokh, *supra* note 6, at 1105-1114; Lode, *supra* note 6, at 1477.

to make a heap? If we already have a heap of sand and remove one grain, presumably we still have a heap. And the same is true if we remove another, and another . . . . Repeatedly applying the premise that a heap minus one grain is still a heap, we eventually conclude that a single grain is a heap. That is a paradox, but not *merely* a paradox; it illustrates the difficulty of drawing lines in the presence of a gradient. In legal and policy contexts, the line-drawing dilemma can emerge whenever vague words or concepts are employed to define rules or the exceptions to them. Where is the line between mentally able and retarded (for purposes of capital punishment)? Where is the line between reasonable and unreasonable force (in defense of property)?

The presence of a vague term does not guarantee a slippery slope, but it increases the likelihood. The best defense against a slope is the possibility of finding a clear (logical or practical) distinction among cases. Lacking such a distinction, decisionmakers will find it tempting to decide new cases or adopt new policies on grounds of their similarity to existing cases and policies. Analogical reasoning economizes on information-gathering and calculation, allowing the decisionmaker to decide more quickly and with less effort. Note that this approach will be most appealing to boundedly rational decisionmakers—who, as the new paternalists emphasize, are common. The danger is that a chain of analogical reasoning can lead from sound to unsound decisions.

Lode argues that judicial decisionmaking is relatively more susceptible than legislative or bureaucratic decisionmaking to slippery slope risks created by vagueness, and we are inclined to agree. The vulnerability of judicial decisionmaking to slopes results from the prevalence of analogical and precedent-based reasoning, as well as the tendency of judges "to place a premium both on drawing non-arbitrary, rationally defensible lines and on maintaining a coherent, consistent body of case law within a particular jurisdiction."[15] But we think legislative and bureaucratic decisionmaking can also be vulnerable, for slightly different reasons.

First, legislators will sometimes purposely pass laws with vague language in order to finesse disagreements and avoid making tough decisions. The resulting laws will have to be interpreted

---

[15] Lode, *supra* note 6, at 1494.

by judges or administrative agencies (and their associated administrative courts).[16] Jolls and Sunstein, contrasting the modesty of their proposals to more intrusive legislation, draw attention to consumer protection laws that give administrative agencies a choice between requiring product information and banning the product outright.[17] So even if legislatures are capable of drawing sharp (perhaps arbitrary) lines to prevent sliding, that does not mean they will.

Second, legislatures can be affected by the lobbying pressure of groups with an interest in further legislation in a given area. Such groups can exploit the existence of a gradient to seek incremental changes that will largely go unnoticed by less organized groups. For example, financial services firms will have an interest in the expansion of default or mandatory savings schemes, as well as in affecting the policy particulars (e.g., what kinds of savings plans are eligible?). But the special interests involved need not be financially motivated, as there exist more "traditional" paternalist groups that would always favor more intrusive laws. For instance, some religious groups favor greater restriction of personal choice for moralistic reasons.[18] Another example is the Center for Science in the Public Interest, which advocates legislation to induce more healthful choices, with little hint of the new paternalists' recognition that other values (such as sheer enjoyment) might outweigh health concerns for some individuals.[19]

Third, gradients create fertile ground for legislative change when policy changes can affect the attitudes of voters and legislators—a claim that we will explain further in Part III. *Ad verecundiam* heuristics (i.e., deference to perceived authority), bias toward sim-

---

[16] GARY C. BRYNER, BUREAUCRATIC DISCRETION: LAW AND POLICY IN FEDERAL REGULATORY AGENCIES 7 (1987) ("Most regulatory laws, however, give little guidance to agencies for the substance of their regulations and for the way in which the burdens they impose are to be distributed. The responsibilities that have been delegated to them often greatly exceed the provided resources, thus necessitating important administrative choices and setting of priorities. *Some laws provide competing objectives that give administrators broad latitude.*") (emphasis added).

[17] Jolls & Sunstein, *supra* note 1, at 207-8.

[18] *See* Lode, *supra* note 6, at 1513 ("...[P]eople with power and influence also may stand to gain economically from taking steps down the slope. In addition, they may think that it is better from a moral point of view to take such steps.").

[19] Jacob Sullum, *The Anti-Pleasure Principle*, REASON, July 2003, *available at* http://www.reason.com/issues/show/381.html.

ple principles, and reframing of the status quo are all processes that can alter political attitudes, thereby making a slide down a gradient more likely.

As Rizzo and Whitman note, vagueness in terms can arise from vagueness in the *theories* used to justify rules and policies, as well from vagueness in the *empirical application* of those theories.[20] It is in these respects that the new paternalist literature is most troubling.

B. Theoretical vagueness and hyperbolic discounting

Various paternalist policies have been justified by citing the notion of hyperbolic discounting. Traditional economic theory assumes that people's rate of trade-off or discounting between successive time periods is constant; that is, that the trade-off between benefits at time T1 and at time T2 depends only on their distance from each other, not on their distance from the present. This is known as exponential discounting. But real people have inconsistent rates of discount: they exhibit higher rates of discount between time periods the closer those periods are to the present. This is known as hyperbolic discounting.[21] The result is that people exhibit time inconsistency: they will make decisions about future trade-offs, and then reverse those decisions later.

Hyperbolic discounting is used to explain self-control problems. Intuitively, people's inconsistent behavior reflects their vulnerability to temptation when those temptations are near. This creates a bias toward getting benefits now and incurring costs later: people spend too much and save too little, they consume too much and exercise too little, and so on. New paternalists have proposed various policies to deal with such self-control problems. Some have advocated automatic enrollment of employees in savings plans.[22] Others have advocated sin taxes, including fat taxes, as a means of

---

[20] Rizzo & Whitman, *supra* note 6, at 574-578.

[21] *See* Richard H. Strotz, *Myopia and Inconsistency in Dynamic Utility Maximization*, 23 REV. OF ECON. STUD. 165 (1955-56); *see also* George Ainslie, BREAKDOWN OF WILL (2001).

[22] Thaler & Sunstein, *supra* note 1, at 176-77.

inducing people to "internalize" the costs of their present behavior to their future selves.[23]

The theory of hyperbolic discounting, when used as a normative justification for policies to encourage greater self-control, involves considerable vagueness. While individuals may exhibit inconsistent rates of time discounting, there is no clear answer to the question of which rate of discount is the correct one. The new paternalists have typically assumed that the longer-term rate of discount is the appropriate one, but this assumption has no basis in theory. The behavioral inconsistency could be "fixed" to resemble exponential discounting (which generates no inconsistencies) by forcing individuals' short-term rate of discount to equal their long-term rate; but it could also be "fixed" by making the long-term rate of discount equal to the short-term rate.[24]

The new paternalist might reply that even if favoring the long-term perspective is arbitrary, it is not vague—it is a clear and obvious choice. But that clarity is an illusion created by the simplistic dichotomy between "short-term" and "long-term." The illusion is magnified by behavioral economists' frequent use of the *quasi-hyperbolic* time discount function, which represents an agent's short-term bias by means of a single parameter that gives extra weight only to the present. A quasi-hyperbolic discounter only has two rates of discount, the present rate and the future rate. The quasi-hyperbolic model "has been adopted as a research tool because of its analytical tractability,"[25] not because of its accuracy. In reality, people exhibit true hyperbolic discounting, which means they display a range of different discount rates. For sufficiently distant choices, they may display no time discounting at all. There is thus no single future discount rate to favor by means of policy.[26] The decisionmaker who would implement policies to "fix" agents' intertemporal choices has to choose from a spectrum of possibilities, not just two. We can easily imagine decisionmakers sliding along the spectrum, initially enforcing only modest degrees of patience

---

[23] Gruber & Koszegi, *supra* note 1; O'Donoghue & Rabin, *supra* note 1.

[24] Whitman, *supra* note 11, at 5, 15 n. 17, 18.

[25] George-Marios Angeletos et al., *The Hyperbolic Consumption Model: Calibration, Simulation, and Empirical Estimation*, 15 J. ECON. PERSP. 47, 50 (2001).

[26] This follows from the form of the generalized hyperbolic discount functions most commonly employed in the psychology literature. *See id.* at 50.

(say, with low fat taxes and low mandatory savings rates) and later shifting to higher and higher degrees of patience.

C.   Theoretical vagueness and the correction of context-dependence

For some types of decision, people are subject to framing effects: one presentation of a decision problem will lead them to choose A over B, while another (logically equivalent) presentation of the same problem will lead them to choose B over A. One example of a framing effect is that medical patients will be more inclined to assent to a treatment described as having a 90% survival rate than one described as having a 10% death rate.[27] People also exhibit status-quo bias, a tendency to favor whatever is (or is presented as) the status quo or initial baseline situation.[28] An example is the persistent difference between willingness-to-accept (WTA) and willingness-to-pay (WTP)[29]—that is, the tendency of people to demand more money to part with an item than what they would pay to acquire the very same item, even when the item's value is low enough that it could create no significant wealth effects. Framing and status-quo bias are both forms of context-dependence—the tendency of people's decisions to change depending on seemingly irrelevant aspects of the decision contexts. Some paternalist policies have been justified by the existence of context-dependence. Sunstein and Thaler, for instance, argue for the creation of new default rules in employment contracts, such as a presumed right to be fired only "for cause" rather than at will.[30] While it would remain possible to write contracts that override the default, and thus the same options as before would remain open, the new default would reframe the context to induce "better" choices (specifically, making employees more likely to reject "at will" employment).

The main theoretical difficulty with context-dependence as a justification for paternalist policy is similar to the difficulty with hyperbolic discounting: it relies on an internal inconsistency of an

---

[27] Sunstein & Thaler, *supra* note 1 at 1161, 1179.
[28] Russell Korobkin, *The Status Quo Bias and Contract Default Rules*, 83 CORNELL L. REV. 608 (1998).
[29] Sunstein & Thaler, *supra* note 1, at 1177.
[30] *Id.* at 1187.

individual's preferences, but it gives no particular reason for favoring one preference over the other. The fact that someone has a higher WTA than WTP tells us that her attitudes are not consistent, but it does not tell us which figure is the correct one. The fact that a patient will assent to a medical procedure under description 1 but not under description 2 points to an inconsistency, but it does not tell us whether the medical procedure is worth doing—that would depend on preferences and attitudes toward risk.

Sunstein and Thaler emphasize that when people's choices are subject to context-dependence, the very meaning of "preferences" is unclear. "These contextual influences render the very meaning of the term 'preferences' unclear,"[31] they say; and "[i]f the arrangement of alternatives has a significant effect on the selections the customers make, then their true 'preferences' do not formally exist."[32] If there can be no appeal to true underlying preferences as the basis for favoring one frame of reference over another, then some other external standard must be employed. Sunstein and Thaler do not specify the appropriate standard; instead they say: "We are not attempting to say anything controversial about welfare, or to take sides in reasonable disputes about how to understand that term."[33] But the standard of value chosen is the very essence of the problem. The justification for deliberate reframing of decisions to induce "better" choices therefore rests on a gaping theoretical lacuna. Different decisionmakers will naturally approach the problem with widely varying notions of welfare and well-being.

Does this theoretical vagueness create a gradient with slippery-slope potential? We believe it does. Although proposals like Sunstein and Thaler's genuflect to the notion of preserving individual choice, the underlying theory does not necessarily place any weight on choice. For any given standard of value, much more heavy-handed policies might be justified. The question, then, is how much weight the social welfare function ought to place on individual choice, and that parameter is not clearly specified by theory. There is no particular reason to think subsequent decisionmakers will rely on choice to the same extent as present ones in making

---

[31] *Id.* at 1161.
[32] *Id.* at 1164.
[33] *Id.* at 1163, n.17.

their policy decisions. Given that individual choice plays no salient role in selecting the appropriate framing of decision problems, a gradient connects soft to hard paternalist policies. Policies that do not restrict individual choice differ only by degree from policies that mildly restrict individual choice, a point that Sunstein and Thaler recognize explicitly when they say, "[I]n all cases, a real question is the cost of exercising choice, and here *there is a continuum rather than a sharp dichotomy.*"[34] Thus, statutes or judicial precedents that create freely waivable default rules lay the theoretical groundwork for default rules that can only be waived at a cost, which in turn can lay the groundwork for default rules that cannot be waived at all.

D. Theoretical vagueness and context-dependence as a corrective device

Setting aside context-dependence as a justification for paternalist policy, some authors have suggested the use of context-dependence as a tool to solve problems created by other cognitive biases. Jolls and Sunstein cite research showing that consumers' optimism bias causes them to underestimate the risk of adverse consequences of certain products and services[35], and then suggest using the availability heuristic to address the problem. The availability heuristic is another variety of context-dependence in which the images and narratives presented with a decision problem affect the choices made, despite no objective difference in the facts of the situation. Jolls and Sunstein propose to make use of availability as follows:

> Specifically, the law could require firms—on pain of administrative penalties or tort liability—to provide a truthful account of consequences that resulted from a particular harm-producing use of the product, rather than simply providing a generalized warning or statement that fails to harness availability.[36]

---

[34] *Id.* at 1185 (emphasis added).
[35] Jolls & Sunstein, *supra* note 1, at 204-205.
[36] *Id.* at 212.

Put simply, firms would have to provide their customers with frightening stories to emphasize the seriousness of certain types of risk. But there is considerable vagueness about how frightening the narratives should be. Jolls and Sunstein are suggesting a switch from a bright-line rule (did the firm truthfully disclose the risk?) to a gradient standard (did the firm provide sufficiently scary examples?). They admit that showing customers worst-case scenarios can be counterproductive[37], which means there must be a means of distinguishing too-frightening from not-frightening-enough. "Of course there are line-drawing problems here," they say, "but the basic point is straightforward."[38]

In the presence of a slippery slope risk, line-drawing problems are of the essence, and neither the theory of optimism bias nor the theory of availability heuristics provides any clear guidance. There is no objective means, in practice or in theory, to distinguish between (a) customers who absorbed the relevant information and decided rationally to assume the risks and (b) customers who did not hear a compelling enough narrative about the risk. We can expect judges deciding new cases arising under "insufficient narratives" claims to make decisions by analogy with prior cases. Hindsight bias could play a role in making such decisions: given that an accident did occur, is it not obvious that the narrative was insufficient? The slope goes from missing narrative to mildly compelling narrative to worst-case-scenario narrative.

And does a narrative even have to be truthful? Jolls and Sunstein's policy description specifies a "truthful account of consequences," but nothing in theory requires that. Indeed, Sunstein and Thaler note the potential harm arising from some truthful information: "In the face of health risks, for example, some presentations of accurate information might actually be counterproductive, because people might attempt to control their fear by refusing to think about the risk at all."[39] Could a service provider (say, an HMO) be faulted for presenting such information? Once we have moved away from the notion of truthful information as the standard for liability, the

---

[37] *Id.* at 214.
[38] Jolls & Sunstein, *supra* note 1, at 214.
[39] Sunstein & Thaler, *supra* note 1, at 1183.

appropriateness of any information (or lack thereof) depends entirely on the *result* in terms of consumer behavior. But again, mere results cannot tell us how to distinguish between (a) rational assumption or avoidance of risk and (b) behavior based on inadequate information about risk. *There is no objective standard for the "right" framing of a decision problem.*

And if it is sometimes appropriate to withhold information, might it not also be appropriate to misrepresent information—that is, to lie? Once more, the theory provides no reason to draw a line here. There is a gradient leading from merely providing information to reframing information to hiding information to providing deliberately incorrect information.

E. Empirical vagueness

Suppose, for argument's sake, that the new paternalist theories present no problems of theoretical vagueness: we have a theoretically valid means of selecting among intertemporal discount rates, of choosing among different framings of decision problems, and so on. Even so, the making of actual decisions and policies can run into a problem of empirical vagueness, meaning "indeterminacy in the application of a theory, typically created by lack of knowledge on the part of agents and decisionmakers who are expected to apply it."[40]

Consider policies designed to deal with hyperbolic discounting. Even supposing there exists a correct rate of discount, this does not mean decisionmakers will have access to or be able to apply it. The correct rate will presumably differ from person to person, and possibly from situation to situation (undersaving or overeating?). In addition, different people will respond to corrective policies in different ways; some will exhibit the desired response to the policy, while others might cut back on their own self-corrective efforts, while yet others might be too strongly affected by the policy. All of these factors are relevant for deriving the optimal policy devices to make people act on the correct discount rate. As we argue more extensively elsewhere,[41] the informational requirements

---

[40] Rizzo & Whitman, *supra* note 6, at 577.
[41] Rizzo & Whitman, *supra* note 11.

for choosing optimal debiasing policies are virtually insurmountable. Lacking the relevant information, decisionmakers will have to rely on incomplete research, guesswork, and—most troubling in the present context—reasoning by analogy. What is the appropriate size of a fat tax? What is the right amount to require people to save (or have saved by default)? The answers to these questions are *empirically* vague; we simply have insufficient knowledge to give precise answers.

Mathematical modeling can create the illusion of precision. A closed mathematical model can generate precise decision rules, defined in terms of all parameters included in the model. Calibrating the model to match reality is another matter entirely, particularly since a closed model necessarily excludes some potentially relevant variables. Consider, for example, Camerer et al.'s criterion for good "asymmetric paternalism"[42]: If some fraction of the public p is irrational, irrational people will receive a per capita benefit of B, and rational people will suffer a per capita cost of C, then the policy is justified if

$$pB - (1 - p)C > 0$$

(We have simplified their model to exclude implementation costs and profits to firms). This criterion seems clear enough in theory (though we might ask troublesome questions about the theory of value that generates B and C, especially in the absence of well-defined preferences). But the problem is in the application. How shall B and C be measured? What fraction of the public is subject to the form of irrationality in question? Moreover, as Camerer et al. would surely admit, the model excludes any heterogeneity. Everyone is either rational or not (allowing no degrees of rationality), and everyone in either group gets the same benefit or harm. So what we have is, at best, a rule of thumb that is open to interpretation by specific decisionmakers—whether legislators, bureaucrats, voters, or judges.

In the context of their proposal to debias consumers via frightening narratives, Jolls and Sunstein admit that "the ultimate question of the optimal form of debiasing through the availability heuristic is an empirical one."[43] We have argued that important

---

[42] Camerer et al., *supra* note 1, at 1219.
[43] Jolls & Sunstein, *supra* note 1, at 213.

theoretical questions remain, but set aside that objection; there is still a matter of how to measure the appropriateness of framing. We lack a scale on which to measure fright, and we lack the knowledge to derive the right point on the scale. The answer will depend on the product or service in question, as well as the characteristics and personal histories of diverse consumers (what is frightening to me could be mundane to you). The specter of empirical vagueness looms large, and decisionmakers forced to decide in its presence will tend to rely on their own heuristics, including analogical reasoning. As suggested in the context of theoretical vagueness, hindsight bias could play a role here: when the one clear fact in the instant case is that someone was harmed by a product, it seems natural to place substantial weight on that fact alone.

To summarize: new paternalist proposals typically rely on models that are beset by theoretical vagueness, and that have the potential to create empirical vagueness. Vagueness makes the boundaries of key concepts fuzzy, creating gradients that connect good policies to bad, modest interventions to more intrusive ones. Decisionmakers who wish to economize on conceptual processing (in the presence of theoretical vagueness) and information processing (in the presence of empirical vagueness) will instead rely on other means of making decisions on new cases and policies. Those other means could easily involve the same cognitive biases and sources of error that the new paternalists have identified in regular people.

Part III. Applied Slippery-Slope Processes

A. Altered Economic Incentives Slopes

Slippery slopes can occur when the implementation of a new policy changes economic incentives (and thus behavior) in a way that makes other policies appear more desirable.[44] One simple example, offered by Rizzo and Whitman, is the effect that socialized medicine could have on regulation of lifestyle choices. To the extent that lifestyle choices (such as smoking, drinking, or risky sexual behavior) can increase healthcare costs, taxpayers under socialized

---

[44] Rizzo & Whitman, *supra* note 6, at 560-563.

medicine might be more inclined to support restrictions on lifestyle choices than they would under a system in which people bear (most of) their own health costs.[45]

New paternalist policies have the potential to alter economic incentives in ways that encourage further interventions in the future. We offer four examples:

The second-best problem. The second-best problem in economics refers to the fact that some market imperfections can, partially or totally, offset the effects of other market imperfections. As a result, correcting one imperfection without correcting another can actually exacerbate a problem.[46] For example, monopoly power will tend to increase the price of a good—which in general is undesirable. But what if production of the good involves negative externalities? In that case, policies that reduce monopoly power could result in more production of the good and thus greater negative externalities.

Gregory Besharov[47] demonstrates that a related problem applies *within* a person subject to cognitive biases: some biases can partially or completely compensate for others. As a result, attempts to fix one source of cognitive error can exacerbate others. For instance, overestimation of one's future consumption needs can compensate for undersaving due to hyperbolic discounting.[48] Or overconfidence might counteract lack of willpower.[49] In Besharov's illustrative model, feelings of regret—which might appear irrational because they create disutility over sunk costs—and overconfidence in one's abilities can induce someone to exert more present effort despite the existence of present-bias.[50]

Besharov's point is that intervention to correct one bias might actually reduce the individual's welfare. But set that point

---

[45] *Id*. at 556, 562.

[46] *See* Richard G. Lipsey & Kelvin Lancaster, *A General Theory of the Second Best*, 24 REV. OF ECON. STUD. 11, 11-12 (1956).

[47] *See* Gregory Besharov, *Second-Best Considerations in Correcting Cognitive Biases*, 71 S. ECON. J. 12, 12 (2004).

[48] *Id*. at 12-13 (citing Matthew Rabin, Comment, in BEHAVIORAL DIMENSIONS IN RETIREMENT ECONOMICS 247, 250-251 (Henry Aaron ed. 1999)).

[49] Besharov, *supra* note 47, at 13 (citing Roland Benabou & Jean Tirole, *Self-Confidence and Personal Motivation*, 117 Q. J. ECON. 871 (2002)).

[50] Besharov, *supra* note 47, at 15-16.

428   *NYU Journal of Law & Liberty*   [Vol. 2:411

aside, and focus instead on the implications for future policy changes. When a new paternalist policy designed to "fix" a cognitive error is introduced, the second-best theory indicates that other problems could get worse, thus generating support for policies designed to fix them. For instance, suppose a new policy is implemented to counteract overconfidence or excessive optimism about investment opportunities. In line with Jolls and Sunstein's debiasing proposal for dangerous products, the policy might expose potential investors to horror stories about lost savings. This policy might successfully reduce overconfidence, hence reducing the person's perceived benefit of saving and investing *at all*, and thereby exacerbating the undersaving problem created by hyperbolic discounting. This will tend to increase the demand for policies to counteract undersaving. And those policies might have yet other effects, as yet unforeseen, if hyperbolic discounting offsets still other cognitive biases.

Some new paternalists might actually be happy with the process described: the state's correction of one bias creates the incentive to correct other biases, until all the biases are corrected. But others, who might have been persuaded by the new paternalist's insistence on the modesty of his proposals, should be less sanguine. The second-best problem emphasizes the potential for increasing involvement of the state in cognitive correction efforts. What starts as a single targeted intervention could escalate into a far more ambitious project. There is also no reason to assume that subsequent corrective policies, whose purpose is to correct problems exacerbated by old ones, will necessarily fit the new paternalist mold. When a problem is relatively minor, decisionmakers will be inclined to support only modest intervention; when a problem looms larger, decisionmakers might support more intrusive interventions. Those who favor small interventions *considered in isolation* might reconsider that support in light of the bigger picture.

Offloading of taxes to the future. The advocates of sin taxes to correct for self-control problems assume that the affected person will respond to the taxes by reducing consumption. This conclusion does not necessarily follow when people are not perfectly rational, as they may have other self-control problems that impede their response to the tax. For instance, someone who is willing to impose health costs on her future self (by overeating now) might also be willing to impose financial costs on her future self (by reducing her saving, or by charging the snacks to a credit card). This person could simply offload the burden of sin taxes to the future.[51]

Here again, the attempt to correct one problem could make other problems worse. The slippery slope risk emerges if the worsened problem creates demand for further intervention. In this case, a corrective sin tax could exacerbate the problem of undersaving, thereby creating support for further intervention to manipulate savings behavior. Of course, the steps in the process are not given, and the slippery slope not guaranteed. Whether the sin tax leads to reduction of consumption or offloading of the tax—or some of both—depends on the characteristics of the specific individual's bias. The tax might succeed for some and fail for others. Even if it fails, that failure will not necessarily lead to further interventions. The broader point, arising from this point and the previous point on second-best problems, is that paternalist interventions will generate unintended consequences through their effects on economic incentives. The resulting changes in behavior can lay the groundwork for further interventions.

Reduced incentives to learn. The new paternalists' leading example of successful paternalism (notably, non-governmental paternalism) is default enrollment in savings plans, which substantially increases enrollment rates.[52] But as the new paternalists also admit, default enrollments have had an unintended consequence: those automatically enrolled stick with the default asset allocation as well.[53] Because of the generally low returns to the default allocations, Choi, et al. found that automatic enrollment produced offsetting effects: "While higher participation rates promote wealth accumulation, the lower default savings rate and the conservative default investment fund undercut accumulation," and in their sample the two effects were approximately equal in magnitude.[54] Under the original policy of enrollment by active choice, those who chose actively had an incentive to pick a good allocation as well. Under the

---

[51] *See* Whitman, *supra* note 11, at 11-12.

[52] Camerer et al., *supra* note 1, at 1227; Thaler & Sunstein, *supra* note 1, at 176-77.

[53] Camerer et al., *supra* note 1, at 1228 (citing Choi et al., *infra* note 54).

[54] James J. Choi et al., *For Better or For Worse: Default Effects and 401(k) Savings Behavior* (Pension Research Council, Working Paper No. 2002-2, 2002).

430   *NYU Journal of Law & Liberty*   [Vol. 2:411

new policy, that incentive is lessened, since default enrollment in some plan reduces the costliness of failing to educate oneself about better plans.

The direction of future policy changes is easy to anticipate. If default enrollment in a low-return savings plan proves insufficient to increase overall savings, the next step is to implement a new default plan that involves a higher rate of savings with less conservative investments. It is certainly possible to leave the allocation at the conservative, low-return level, but given the initial justification for having default enrollment at all—the desire to increase savings—further regulation follows naturally from the initial policy decision. A careful analyst will argue that the original goal was not to increase savings *per se*, but to correct a bias; once the bias is corrected, the job is finished. But here vagueness comes into play. Theoretically, in the presence of context-dependent preferences, we lack a clear standard for bias-free decisionmaking. Even if such an empirical standard did exist, real-world decisionmakers would have no means to apply it; the correct policy depends on knowledge they lack. The unchanged rate of overall wealth accumulation could easily be taken as evidence of remaining bias that requires correction (on the same grounds as the original bias).

The generalized moral hazard problem. This example illustrates a more important point: self-awareness and self-correction are skills that must be learned. People who know they will bear the consequences of their own cognitive errors have an incentive to learn self-management techniques. This does not mean they always succeed, but it does mean we should expect less learning to occur in the presence of policies that reduce the cost of failure. Default enrollment reduces the incentive to learn about good investment choices. Similarly, other policies that substitute for self-correction will tend to reduce self-correction skills, which can have impacts on other aspects of personal choice. For example, if people come to expect protection against their excessive optimism, they have less reason to acquire critical thinking skills that will guard against both optimism and other errors of information processing. If people come to rely on policies that substitute for willpower, they have less reason to develop that willpower to begin with. Jonathan Klick and

Gregory Mitchell refer to such effects as the "moral and cognitive hazards" of paternalistic intervention.[55] The slippery slope risk emerges because failure to learn self-management techniques can lead to more errors of judgment, which then are used to justify further interventions.

Furthermore, people's failure to learn self-control and self-correction skills can result in a "spillover" effect, as additional cognitive errors may occur not just in the area of the original policy, but in other areas as well. The reason, as Klick and Mitchell observe, is that some forms of learning are domain-general:

> For instance, developing effective self-control techniques in order to save for an automobile or home may generalize to effective strategies for retirement saving. Or, as demonstrated by empirical research on the endowment effect, people may learn to overcome consumer biases with greater market experience, and this learning may generalize across goods.[56]

If new paternalist policies decrease the need to engage in certain kinds of learning, the result could be poorer performance in other, as-yet-unregulated aspects of life. This effect might be considered a direct argument against the initial paternalist policies, but that is not our point here; we are concerned with the how implementing the initial policies increases the likelihood of implementing others. Decisionmakers who have bought the new paternalist line—that cognitive errors justify intervention—will then tend to support additional policies to deal with the newly emerging errors in choice and judgment.

B. Enforcement Need Slopes

Eugene Volokh points out the potential for slippery slopes when at least some decisionmakers view the (apparent) failure of one intervention as justification for further intervention. Often, the

---

[55] Jonathan Klick & Gregory Mitchell, *Government Regulation of Irrationality: Moral and Cognitive Hazards*, 90 MINN. L. REV. 1620, 1626 (2006).
[56] *Id.* at 1631.

432 *NYU Journal of Law & Liberty* [Vol. 2:411]

second intervention is justified on grounds of the need to enforce the first.[57] His leading example is marijuana policy: some people might not initially support making marijuana illegal, but once it is illegal, they take the position that the law ought to be enforced rigorously (perhaps to avoid disrespect for the law).[58]

Attaining the perceived goal. New paternalism is vulnerable to enforcement need slopes because some modest initial proposals will have only modest success at best at achieving their perceived goals. The problem with default savings plans leading to reliance on the default asset allocation, discussed earlier, might provide the seed of an enforcement need slope. If the initial goal is seen as increasing savings, and the overall savings rate fails to rise enough, then some decisionmakers will call for regulation of asset allocation. If that measure also fails—perhaps because people become more inclined to opt out when the contribution rate is larger—then some decisionmakers might suggest that the default plan become mandatory.

Crowding out. Another potential source of initial policy failure is that paternalist policies could "crowd out" self-correction efforts. This is similar to the earlier point about reduced incentives to learn self-correction techniques, but the economic mechanism at work is different. The literature on public goods reveals that state funding of public goods can crowd out private funding, which means the state cannot simply fill in the gap between current funding and optimal funding—it has to provide more and more funding as the private sector provides less and less.[59] James Buchanan[60] has made a similar point about Pigovian taxes designed to internalize negative externalities such as pollution: To the extent that the polluters already care about the ill effects of their behavior (even if they care less than they should), they will have already controlled their

---

[57] Volokh, *supra* note 6, at 1051-56.

[58] *Id.* at 1051-52.

[59] *See* Burton A. Abrams & Mark D. Schitz, *The 'Crowding Out' Effect of Governmental Transfers on Private Charitable Contributions*, 33 PUB. CHOICE 29 (1978); B. Douglas Bernheim, *On the Voluntary and Involuntary Provision of Public Goods*, 76 AM. ECON. REV. 789 (1986); Theodore Bergstrom et al., *On the Private Provision of Public Goods*, 29 J. PUB. ECON. 25 (1986).

[60] JAMES M. BUCHANAN, COST AND CHOICE 76-80 (1969).

behavior to some degree.[61] If a tax is imposed to deal with the same problem, the polluter might decrease his self-correction because he sees the tax as performing the same job.[62]

How would new paternalist policy lead to crowding out? Presumably, even hyperbolic discounters care at least *some* about their future selves (or about their long-run interests), although perhaps less than they should. That caring is implemented via willpower and self-imposed rules. Self-imposed rules can take various forms, including resolutions, limitations on refrigerator contents, and commitments to third parties (like family members or Alcoholics Anonymous). Policymakers devising policies to correct for self-control problems should, presumably, take these self-correction efforts into account. The problem, however, is that the individual may respond by reducing the extent of their "caring" and associated self-control efforts. If the individual regards internal correction and external correction as substitutes, as some research indicates to be the case,[63] the latter will tend to crowd out the former.

To the extent that crowding out occurs, the initial policy will be ineffective. The initial policy merely had to address the gap between the individual's level of self-correction and the policymaker's ideal. But if crowding out occurs, the gap will remain, thus providing a justification for still further intervention—in the form of a higher tax or more intrusive regulation designed to force compliance.

C. The *Ad Verecundiam* Heuristic

A key insight of behavioral economics is that people's attitudes are context-dependent. Susceptibility to framing is one example; status quo bias is another. Both effects can be traced, at least in some cases, to an attempt by uninformed and boundedly rational people to glean information. When one savings plan is chosen as the default over others, for instance, employees who would prefer not to spend energy researching investment options may assume

---

[61] *Id.* at 76-77.

[62] *Id.* at 77-78.

[63] Ayelet Fishbach & Yaacov Trope, *The Substitutability of External Control and Self-Control*, 41 J. EXPERIMENTAL SOC. PSYCHOL. 256 (2005).

434   *NYU Journal of Law & Liberty*   [Vol. 2:411

(perhaps unconsciously) that someone with expertise must have thought the default plan was a good one.

In the political and legal spheres, wherein most people are ignorant and lack strong incentives to become informed, the tendency to defer to experts can be even stronger. As one example, Volokh offers the proper scope of police warrants: regular citizens unfamiliar with the law or police tactics will be inclined to assume the experts (judges) have probably arrived at reasonable rules.[64] We can draw a general lesson from the example:

> We should expect attitude-altering slippery slopes to be more likely *in areas that are viewed as complex, or as calling for expert factual or moral judgment*. The more complicated a question seems, the more likely it is that voters will assume that they can't figure it out for themselves and should therefore defer to the expert judgment of authoritative institutions, such as legislatures or courts.[65]

We could also add scientists, economists, and legal scholars to the list of authorities. We will dub this tendency to defer to authorities, of whatever variety, the "ad verecundiam" heuristic (after the Latin for the "appeal to authority," a traditional fallacy of logic).[66]

New paternalist proposals, based on the insights of these academic authorities, may make policymakers, judges, and the general public more inclined to defer to the perceived wisdom of the experts in social science and cognitive science. We should therefore ask, what ideas may become entrenched because people internalize the perceived opinions of such experts?

One idea conveyed by the new paternalism is that experts have identified *objectively correct* notions of human welfare. This is distinct from the notion of *subjective* welfare that has historically reigned in economics, where individual preferences are generally

---

[64] Volokh, *supra* note 6, at 1080.

[65] Volokh, *supra* note 6, at 1082 (emphasis in original).

[66] ENCYCLOPEDIA OF RHETORIC 295-96 (Thomas O. Sloane ed., 2001) ("FALLACIES. . . . The British philosopher John Locke (1632-1704) introduced the *ad* arguments: *ad verecundiam* was, originally, the 'argument on shame,' because one should not dare to question the authority mentioned in the argument, but it is now used to refer to a fallacy that involves a wrong appeal to authority.").

treated as given, and to a lesser extent in law, where contract law, in particular, relies on advancing the interests and expectations of the parties as they perceive them (or perceived them at the time of signing).

Now, the new paternalists may not *intend* to send this message; in some passages, they seem only to want to advance the true subjective interests of the people affected—to give them, as the Spice Girls would say, what they *really* really want. Sunstein and Thaler define "inferior decisions in terms of their own welfare" as "decisions that they would change if they had complete information, unlimited cognitive abilities, and no lack of self-control."[67] But what would they in fact choose under those conditions—what do they actually prefer? As noted earlier[68], Sunstein and Thaler also emphasize repeatedly that when decisions are context-dependent, the very meaning of individual preferences is in doubt. There seems to be internal conflict among distinct and unrationalized preference sets, and in such cases the new paternalists do not hesitate to choose among them. Although there is no strong theoretical basis for that choice (as we argued in Part II, B and C), non-academics could hardly be blamed for thinking the choice must be justified somehow; these are the experts, after all.

In their specific policy proposals, the new paternalists regularly make judgments about which frame of reference is best by reference to the actual choice favored by it. Sunstein and Thaler rely on differences between willingness-to-pay and willingness-to-accept to explain the efficacy of changes in the default rules of contract, and then they implicitly assume that certain contractual requirements—greater vacation time, for-cause dismissal, specific safety measures, and so on—are the preferred outcomes.[69] This conclusion is by no means self-evident, once we realize that other contractual terms such as the pay rate will likely adjust to account for the added benefits and guarantees.

The analytical wedge that allows the new paternalists to say people are making cognitive errors is the existence of *within-person inconsistencies* of choice, usually identified in experimental or labo-

---

[67] Sunstein & Thaler *supra* note 1, at 1162.
[68] *See supra* notes 27 and 29 and accompanying text.
[69] Sunstein & Thaler, *supra* note 1, at 1174-1177.

436   *NYU Journal of Law & Liberty*   [Vol. 2:411]

ratory contexts. But in their writing, the new paternalists frequently refer to objective factors about choices (without any visible inconsistency) as *ipso facto* evidence of irrationality. Camerer, et al., in discussing default contributions to 401(k)'s, treat it as obvious that savings need to be increased, based on macroeconomic concerns as well as "people's self-reports that they save less than they would like."[70] Macroeconomic concerns do not demonstrate an individual decision failure; nor do survey responses, once we recall that talk is cheap. Similarly, Thaler and Sunstein point to obesity rates as evidence of decision failure:

> "However, studies of actual choices for high stakes reveal many of the same problems [as in experiments]. For example, the Surgeon General reports that 61 percent of Americans are either overweight or obese. Given the adverse effects obesity has on health, it is hard to claim that Americans are eating optimal diets.[71]

Overweightness and obesity *per se* cannot demonstrate an inconsistency of choice; for some people, the subjective gains from heavy eating could outweigh their health concerns. It is worth noting that obesity and overweightness have both increased during the same time period that many of the associated health risks, such as heart disease, have rapidly declined.[72] In a different paper, Sunstein and Thaler cite the same health statistics, but then admit our point:

> Of course, rational people care about the taste of food, not simply about health, and we do not claim that everyone who is overweight is necessarily failing to act rationally. It is the strong claim that all or almost all Americans are choosing their diet *optimally* that we reject as untenable.[73]

---

[70] Camerer et al., *supra* note 1, at 1227-1228.
[71] Sunstein & Thaler, *supra* note 1, at 1167.
[72] L.A.G. Ries, et al. (eds). *SEER Cancer Statistics Review, 1975-2003*, National Cancer Institute.
[73] Sunstein & Thaler, *supra* note 1, at 1168.

In this version of their argument they emphasize the subjectivity of the decision; yet they still rely on sheer numbers as evidence for the existence of irrationality. We consider it telling that in the earlier version they don't even include these caveats. It is easy to see how statements like these will tend to be perceived as an endorsement of health as the sole appropriate measure of welfare.

The new paternalists' assumptions about what is objectively best do not appear only in their verbal statements, but in their models as well. Jonathan Gruber and Botond Koszegi, in justifying the correction of "internalities" of smoking by means of cigarette taxes, assume (without argument) that "the agent's long-run preferences [are] those relevant for social welfare maximization."[74] That assumption is crucial to the objective conclusions of their mathematical model. Ted O'Donoghue and Matthew Rabin make the same assumption in their model of "optimal sin taxes."[75]

Again, we should emphasize that theory shows only the existence of internal inconsistency, not a means of choosing one preference set over another. Nevertheless, the experts, through both their words and modeling choices, seemingly assent to the notion of objectively correct preferences or objectively desirable goods. If new paternalist policies are implemented, these assumptions will become enshrined in law. The *ad verecundiam* heuristic will apply doubly: first because of the expertise of the academics, and second because of the added authority of policymakers, judges, and bureaucrats. That, in turn, could increase support for still more paternalist policies based on the notion that policy can and should promote objective goods and preferences, *whether or not there is any demonstrable inconsistency of individual choice*. The new policies justified by the inferred principle of objective goods need not be modest in character, as the principle in question can justify much more. The proponents of the new policies need only point to previously established policies to demonstrate the acceptability of favoring supposedly objective values.

[74] Gruber & Koszegi, *supra* note 1, at 1287.
[75] O'Donoghue & Rabin, *supra* note 1, at 5.

D. Preference for Simple Principles

Slippery slope analysts have often observed the tendency for subtle and complex principles to get pared down to much simpler principles. Eric Lode quotes Justice Cardozo's observation that "the half truths of one generation tend at time to perpetuate themselves in the law as the whole truth of another, when constant repetition brings it about that qualifications, taken once for granted, are disregarded or forgotten."[76] Frederick Schauer takes note of the "bias in favor of simple principles"[77] in law. Volokh observes a similar bias at work in the policy realm: "Sometimes, the debate about a statute will focus on one justifying principle. But as time passes, the debates may be forgotten, and only the law itself will endure; and then advocates for future laws B may cite law A as endorsing quite a different justification."[78]

Why do decisionmakers display this tendency? People will often look to existing policies and rules and infer the justifications directly from them. If they do look to the original debates, they will often try to summarize them quickly, drawing out what they see as the most salient details. But the process is imperfect. An original policy P1 might have been supported by a relatively narrow justification J1, while a broader justification J2 would have justified both P1 *and* P2. Looking back, the observer might incorrectly—or opportunistically—infer that J2 was the real reason for P1's enactment. The result is a broadening of the original principle.

The application to the new paternalism is straightforward. To justify their policies, the new paternalists point to the existence of internally inconsistent choices. But as observed earlier, their presentation of the argument is not always clear; they at least appear to endorse favoring some preferences over others. After the proposals have been implemented, and more intrusive policies are on put forward, what inference will be drawn from the less intrusive policies already in effect? A simplistic summary of the new paternalist argument would strip out all reference to internal conflict and focus instead on the notion that we can justifiably choose

---

[76] Lode, *supra* note 6, at 1516.
[77] Schauer, *supra* note 6, at 372.
[78] Volokh, *supra* note 6, at 1089.

among preferences. An even greater simplification would focus on the perceived goals of the new paternalist polices such as inducing greater savings, encouraging better health choices, and supporting certain desirable terms in contracts.

A variant of the bias toward simple principles is the tendency to pare multiple justifications down to one. An initial policy P1 might be supported by multiple justifications J1 and J2. A later proposal P2 might be supported only by J1. People looking back on the passage of P1 might simplify the decision by ignoring J2 and treating J1 as the sole justification.

New paternalist laws often draw additional support from the existence of other, non-paternalist arguments. For instance, laws designed to encourage healthier or less risky choices are attractive not merely because they might help the individuals making the choice, but also because they reduce the burden on public health systems. Helmet laws are justified in part by paternalism (protecting the motorcycle rider from his own foolish choices) and in part by the cost helmetless motorcycling imposes on public emergency rooms.[79] The prohibition is supported initially by a dual justification: "the activity imposes harm on others, and probably isn't good for the individual anyway." Later, however, the justification may be reduced to "it's okay to restrict the individual for his own good." That, of course, is a principle that can justify intervention even when the benefits to others are small or non-existent.

Purely rational, perfectly informed, and cognitively unbounded policymakers, judges, and voters would not make mistakes like these. They would evaluate each policy carefully, cogitate on the principle or principles that would justify it, consider their own independently-chosen values, and make a decision on the merits. But as the new paternalists remind us, people are not like that. Having limited information and bounded cognitive powers, they will economize by employing heuristics to decide on new policies and cases. As a result, they are likely to internalize principles embodied by the status quo—a point we made when discussing the *ad verecundiam* bias. Moreover, they will not necessarily internalize the

---

[79] *See* Wendy Max et al., *Putting a Lid on Injury Costs: The Economic Impact of the California Motorcycle Helmet Law*, 45 J. TRAUMA: INJ., INFECTION & CRITICAL CARE 550 (1998).

nuanced principles of their predecessors; instead, they will often internalize stripped-down and simplistic versions of those principles. The entrenchment of less-sophisticated principles lays the foundation for more intrusive and less desirable policies.

E. Framing Effects and the Shifting Status Quo

As discussed in the introduction, the new paternalists often draw attention to the moderate character of their proposals. References to the "middle ground" or "middle course" are common. A passage from Camerer, et al. (quoted more briefly in the introduction) captures the rhetorical flavor of the movement:

> For those (particularly economists) prone to rigid antipaternalism, the paper describes a possibly attractive rationale for paternalism as well as a careful, cautious, and disciplined approach. For those prone to give unabashed support for paternalistic policies based on behavioral economics, this paper argues that more discipline is needed and proposes a possible criterion.[80]

This form of argument exploits a cognitive bias of which the new paternalists are surely aware: the power of framing to change what is seen as moderate or extreme. Proposals are more likely to be accepted when presented in the context of more extreme positions on either side; Itamar Simonson and Amos Tversky dub this tendency "extremeness aversion."[81] Like Goldilocks choosing amongst the Three Bears' beds, people presented with soft, medium, and hard options will tend to choose medium.

This kind of framing effect can be used to indict market outcomes. For instance, in a study in which potential camera buyers were presented with two options, a low-end camera and a mid-level camera, half of the customers chose the low-end camera as the better deal; but when presented with three options, a low-end, a mid-level, *and* a high-end camera, many more customers chose the mid-

---

[80] Camerer et al., *supra* note 1, at 1212-1213.

[81] Itamar Simonson & Amos Tversky, *Choice in Context: Tradeoff Contrast and Extremeness Aversion*, 29 J. MARKETING RES. 281 (1992).

level over the low-end camera.[82] Marketers could take advantage of this effect to get customers to buy more expensive products, and this is presumably the kind of behavior that new paternalists would like to change. But the very same kind of framing effect can occur in political and legal contexts. Deliberately or not, the new paternalists have framed the discussion in a way likely to make their proposals more attractive.

More importantly, in the context of slippery slopes, the *implementation* of their policies would reframe the political and legal debate. As framed by the proponents, new paternalist policies lie at the "center" of the debate, between laissez-faire and more intrusive paternalism. But once passed, they would cease to be the center. Somewhat more intrusive proposals would take center stage, bookended by existing new paternalist policies on the left and yet more intrusive proposals on the right. The new "moderate" would no longer be soft paternalism, but (let us call it) medium paternalism.

The treatment of cigarette smoking is one area in which this kind of effect has occurred. When the first cigarette bans were introduced for airplanes and workplaces, they were the middle ground between laissez-faire and more extensive prohibition. Now, however, workplace and airplane bans are taken as given, and the focus has shifted to smoking bans in indoor restaurants and bars. Such bans are positioned as the middle ground between the extremes of "only" banning in planes and workplaces, on the one hand, and implementing wider-reaching bans on the other. In California, where the ban in indoor restaurants and bars is status quo, some localities are now considering (and passing!) bans on smoking in outdoor locations, including restaurant patios, sidewalks, and beaches. The progression of these bans aptly demonstrates how new policies can change the status quo, so that proposals once regarded as the extreme come to be regarded as the middle ground.

The smoking example also illustrates the bias toward simple principles. Bans in workplaces and airplanes were justified primarily by the non-paternalist argument that non-smokers were being exposed to second-hand smoke in an enclosed space, with great sacrifices needed for non-smokers to avoid the exposure: don't travel by plane, work someplace else. The bans in restaurants

---

[82] *Id.* at 290, *cited in* Volokh, *supra* note 6, at 1101.

442 *NYU Journal of Law & Liberty* [Vol. 2:411

and bars have been justified on similar grounds, even though much less severe sacrifices are required of non-smokers to avoid the exposure: non-smokers can go eat or drink somewhere else. For the beach, sidewalk, and patio bans, the sacrifice necessary to avoid second-hand smoke is the same, but the enclosed-space justification has been lost. The apparent direction of change is toward justifications that require smaller and smaller benefits to non-smokers, combined with the paternalist justification that the smokers shouldn't smoke anyway.

The general point is that the supposedly moderate character of new paternalist policies does not guarantee their staying power. The very passage of such policies reframes the political debate in way that makes further changes in the same direction more likely.

IV. Conclusion: Reasonable Expectations about Decisionmakers

The existence of a slippery slope risk does not, of course, constitute a knock-down argument against any and all new paternalist proposals. Sufficiently great benefits can justify the risks of the proposals, particularly if the risks can be minimized. There exist various means of mitigating slippery slope risks, though all such means are imperfect.[83] Exploring ways in which new paternalist policies could potentially be "immunized" against the slope risk is beyond the scope of this article; we will, however, make some broad suggestions about how recognition of the slope risk should affect our thinking about paternalism.

One lesson of behavioral economics is that it is naive to expect decisionmakers to perform extensive calculations, to collect all relevant information, to ignore irrelevant information, and to make reasoned decisions in all cases. This lesson is no less true when applied to policymakers, judges, and bureaucrats than when applied to consumers. Indeed, it is arguably *more* true when applied to these groups.[84] Private actors making choices for themselves, and bearing the costs and benefits of those choices, at least have the in-

---

[83] Rizzo & Whitman, *supra* note 6, at 578-591.

[84] Edward L. Glaeser, *Paternalism and Psychology*, 73 U. CHI. L. REV. 133 (2006); Bryan Caplan, *Rational Ignorance versus Rational Irrationality*, 54 KYKLOS 3 (2001); Bryan Caplan, *Rational Irrationality: A Framework for the Neoclassical-Behavioral Debate*, 26 E. ECON. J. 191 (2000).

centive to root out their errors and correct them. That does not mean they will always succeed. However, the effects of their errors are relatively localized, and they can select courses of corrective action (also possibly in error) that take account of their personal characteristics and special circumstances. Public decisionmakers, by contrast, do not face all the costs and benefits of their choices. They make choices that create costs and benefits for numerous people besides themselves, including future generations, and they have the capacity to impose these choices society-wide. Even traditional economic theory, with its rational-actor model, does not predict wise and efficient policymaking under these circumstances.

The new paternalists have thus far paid little attention to these factors. They apparently hope policymakers will dutifully study the economic, scientific, and psychological research that identifies the existence of cognitive biases, their extent, and their locus; and then carefully craft policies designed to target those individuals in need while minimizing harm to others. That is the basic prescription of "asymmetric paternalism," for instance.[85] This ideal of new paternalist decisionmaking stands in sharp contrast to the blunt-instrument approach exemplified by recent proposals to ban trans-fats in Chicago and New York[86], or to ban all smoking in public places in parts of California.[87]

If we are to resist slippery slopes, then, we need to employ more realistic models of how public decisionmakers behave. That means we cannot expect them to make fine distinctions, to implement nuanced decision rules, and to engage in careful balancing of empirically verifiable needs based on valid theoretical reasoning. To expect otherwise is to ignore the central findings of both traditional economic theory and behavioral economics.

---

[85] Camerer et al., *supra* note 1, at 1212.

[86] Thomas J. Lueck & Kim Severson, *New York Bans Most Trans Fats in Restaurants*, N.Y. TIMES, Dec. 6, 2006, at A1, *available at* http://www.nytimes.com/2006/12/06/nyregion/06fat.html?ex=1323061200&en=ae cf1ac963f8435d&ei=5088partner=rssnyt&emc=rss.

[87] Josh Gerstein, *A Coastal City Bans Outdoor Smoking in Public Places*, N.Y. SUN, Mar. 17, 2006, at 1, *available at* http://www.nysun.com/article/29317.

Part IV
Institutions

[12]

On Institutions

I

TO UNDERSTAND human action means to understand
the plan which guides the observable acts to which it
gives rise. The praxeological method, which aims at
enabling us to understand action, rests on the parallelism between action and plan, a fact which has no
counterpart in nature. The plan which gradually un-
folds in space and time contains, we saw, an orientation
scheme which must comprehend purpose, means, and
obstacles. Action is thus oriented to them.

We must now return to the second question which
we raised at the end of our first essay, that is, the
interrelationship between the actions of various
actors. We said there that *formally* for the actor there
is no difference between the action of others and any
other circumstances affecting the constraints bounding
his freedom of action. But we also pointed out that
materially a significant difference lies in the fact that,
since human action is more volatile than the conditions of nature, it is far less easy to predict. In a complex society such as our own, in which the success of
our plans indirectly depends on the actions of millions
of other people, how can our orientation scheme provide us with firm guidance? The answer has to be
sought in the existence, nature, and functions of
institutions.

An institution provides means of orientation to a large
number of actors. It enables them to co-ordinate their

actions by means of orientation to a common signpost. If the plan is a mental scheme in which the conditions of action are co-ordinated, we may regard institutions, as it were, as orientation schemes of the second order, to which planners orientate their plans as actors orientate their actions to a plan. To investigate the nature, functions, and structural relationships between institutions is the main task of this essay.

Whether we post a letter, wait for a train, or draw a cheque, our action is in each case orientated towards a complex network of human action of which we know enough to make it serve our ends, though we may know next to nothing about the internal working-order of these institutions. We know of course that such an internal working-order exists, but in our everyday life take no interest whatever in its details. We know very well that the Post Office works according to a general plan, but such knowledge as we have about it is usually quite irrelevant to the achievement of our purpose in posting a letter. Only a few aspects of this general plan, perhaps the times of collection and delivery of mail, need be of concern to us.

The existence of such institutions is fundamental to civilized society. They enable each of us to rely on the actions of thousands of anonymous others about whose individual purposes and plans we can know nothing. They are nodal points of society, co-ordinating the actions of millions whom they relieve of the need to acquire and digest detailed knowledge about others and form detailed expectations about their future action. But even what knowledge of society they do provide in highly condensed form may not all be relevant to the achievement of our immediate purposes. Economy of effort may induce us to ignore most of the time a good deal of the knowledge available to us.

ON INSTITUTIONS 51

Most banks proudly display their balance sheets in their branch offices, but a normal customer hardly ever looks at them.

The existence of institutions raises a large number of problems, only a few of which we are able to consider here. But three of them appear to occupy such a prominent place that we shall have to examine them in detail.

There is, in the first place, the problem of institutional change. If institutions are to serve us as firm points of orientation their position in the social firmament must be fixed. Signposts must not be shifted. On the other hand, it is hardly possible to imagine that banks, railways, and other institutions are totally exempt from change. It appears that such change need not interfere with the plans of users of institutions provided it is known in advance. But some changes will not comply with this condition. What happens then? Are situations possible in which institutions mislead rather than guide planned action?

There is, secondly, the problem of the *institutional order* and its unity. If institutions are to serve as instruments of co-ordination, do they not themselves have to be co-ordinated? If so, that is, if each institution forms part of a comprehensive structure, what is the nature of the forces which integrate it? And what would be the character of circumstances in which these forces ceased to work? In other words, what are the conditions of integration and disintegration?

From the confluence of these two problems there arises, thirdly, the question whether the forces of integration, supposing they do operate, would operate in all conditions of change. It goes without saying that the rise of new institutions, partly to replace older ones, but partly to fill 'gaps' in the institutional structure, raises questions which belong to this third category.

What is the general nature of the conditions in which such new institutions would 'fit' into the existing structure? And where these conditions do not exist, is it impossible for new institutions to arise? If not, does it mean that the existing institutional structure would have to change in such a way as to accommodate the new accretions, or that it will be undermined by them?

To enumerate these questions is only to give a very rough outline of the tasks confronting us. But before coming to grips with them we shall first have to turn aside and examine what Weber thought about them. In scrutinizing Weber's legacy, however, we shall soon have to learn that the construction of a theory of institutions designed to answer our questions on the basis of this legacy is anything but easy.

II

No general theory of institutions is to be found anywhere in Weber's work. To be sure, he has much to say about institutions and their modes of change. Even today his work is one of our richest mines of information on institutions and their changes throughout history. Certainly we are entitled to say that the whole range of institutions, religious, political, economic, legal, and educational which his powerful mind encompassed, and their modes of change under the impact of various social forces, were always in the forefront of his interests. For all this it remains true that he never formulated a General Theory of Institutions. Fragments of such a theory can be found and we shall of course have to examine them carefully.

ON INSTITUTIONS 53

But a coherent general framework within which these fragments would find their places is not part of Weber's legacy. It is possible to find reasons for this absence of a general framework which look superficially plausible but provide no real explanation. Three such reasons suggest themselves readily to the student of Weber's work.

The first is a linguistic one. Modern German has no word which corresponds exactly to the meaning of the English word 'institution'. The German word *Institution* has a narrower meaning, confined to organized institutions. In modern German usage the family is, but language is not, an *Institution*. Weber usually avoids the term altogether and speaks of *Anstalt*, a legal term denoting an organized association. Modern German sociologists, on the other hand, have adopted the term *Gebilde* precisely in order to render the meaning of the wider term, and Weber knew the word. Moreover, Menger in his *Untersuchungen* used the word *Institution* in exactly the same sense which it has in current English. The suggestion therefore that Weber, even had he wished to formulate a general theory of institutions, would have lacked the linguistic mould in which to cast his thought, fails to carry much conviction.

A second, and stronger, reason we might find in Weber's repeatedly expressed view that theory, while a necessary tool in the kit-bag of the historian, must never be allowed to become an end in itself. He certainly deprecated all theory for its own sake. In general he saw no reason for a higher level of abstraction than the nature of the concrete object of enquiry warranted. Thus he may have thought a general theory of institutions unnecessary.

But are we really to believe that a mind as powerful

54   ON INSTITUTIONS

as his, having mastered a well-nigh incredible number
of detailed facts about institutions of the most diverse
kind, from ancient Judaism to Tsarist Russia, from
China to modern America, never felt the need for a
framework of generalizations to be drawn from these
facts? How, indeed, is it possible even to order this
vast store of facts without establishing a certain
number of generalizations at some level?

Weber was not opposed to theory as such, but only
to unnecessary theory or, what is the same thing,
theory at a higher level of abstraction than the object
of enquiry warrants. We have attempted to show in
the first section of this essay why a general theory of
action such as Weber envisaged not merely warrants,
but actually requires, a general theory of institutions.
Moreover, the facts show that on occasion, especially
when the (usually polemical) context of the discourse
appeared to require it, Weber was by no means
averse to establishing generalizations of a fairly high
order of abstraction. We shall have to devote attention
to some of these. What remains a puzzle is thus not the
absence of generalizations in Weber's work, but his
failure to integrate what generalizations there are
into a coherent framework.

A third reason, which some will regard as a variant
of the second, might be found in the circumstances
surrounding Weber's early training in the Historical
School. Abstract theory, one might say, Weber did
not feel to be his *métier*. He did not deny the need for
it, but in general, except in cases of (polemical)
emergency, was inclined to leave it to others better
equipped than he to supply. Not for him the long
chains of deductive reasoning proceeding from a few
aptly, but always arbitrarily, chosen axioms. He felt
he could do his best work tilling other fields.

ON INSTITUTIONS 55

The trouble with this explanation is that, as we already know, Weber *did* take an interest in the place of abstract theory in social thought. How can one be interested in methodology without being interested in all the methods, however abstract some of them may be, which might be used in a discipline? To this question the reply may be that it is one thing to be a critic of methods, yet quite another thing to practise them.

The fact remains, however, that, especially in polemical argument, Weber did not shun levels of abstraction of which, were this explanation valid, he should have been wary. In any case we may feel sure that, if he had thought a General Theory of Institutions called for, neither the limitations of his training in economic theory nor anything else would have prevented him from creating it. In proffering our own hypothesis why he did not do so we therefore have to explain, in the first place, why he may not have thought it called for.

In the *Methodenstreit*, an interest in which, as we saw earlier, sparked off Weber's methodological studies, the origin, nature, and functions of institutions had occupied a prominent place. The German Historical School had taxed classical economists with ignoring the effects of the institutional environment on human action. Pointing to the variety and diversity of economic institutions in different societies and centuries, adherents of this school asked how one analytical model could possibly account for all the varieties of economic action in circumstances so diverse. It seemed to them that this diversity of institutions by itself invalidated that universal theory of the market economy which lies at the heart of classical economics.

L.M.W.—3

56   ON INSTITUTIONS

Facing this challenge, Menger decided to turn the flank of his enemy's position by a bold move.[1] He admitted the importance of institutions for economic action but distinguished between those which are the product of legislation ('the common will') and those which are not. He then raised the famous question 'How can it be that institutions which serve the common welfare and are extremely significant for its development come into being without a *common will* directed towards establishing them?', which he described as 'perhaps the most noteworthy problem of the social sciences' (p. 146).

His answer was, briefly, that 'those social structures which are the unintended result of social development' are all, more or less, like market prices and wage-rates in that in a long historical process they have come into existence as a result of men pursuing their interests. 'They present themselves to us as the unintended result of individual efforts of members of society, i.e. of efforts in pursuit of individual interests . . . they are . . . the unintended social result of individually teleological factors'. (p. 158) In the Marshallian idiom we might say that, while in the short run economic phenomena are indeed shaped by existing institutions, in the long run these institutions themselves are shaped by the very forces whose ubiquity and universal power the Historical School had denied. In this way Menger claimed to have wrested a most powerful weapon from the hands of his opponents. For they had failed to understand the true nature of institutions, 'a nature which has up to now been characterized merely by vague analogies or by meaningless phrases' (p. 158),

[1] Carl Menger, *Problems of Economics and Sociology*, edited with an introduction by Louis Schneider (University of Illinois Press 1963).

ON INSTITUTIONS 57

while he had shown that this nature is identical with that of such strictly economic phenomena as market prices, wage-rates, etc.

We have here, then, what we may call a *praxeological* theory of institutions, admittedly in rough outline, in which the existence of certain institutions is explained as the unintended result of the pursuit of individual plans by large numbers of actors—as a 'resultant of social forces', not a product of social design. In Menger's terminology, they are the institutions of *organic*, not *pragmatic* origin. We may note that in this part of his book Menger says nothing about what determines the human actions which have such undesigned social effects. The pursuit of individual interests is here a wide notion without any deterministic connotation. Within the constraints of the given situation men are presumed free to pursue their ends.

Alas, this voluntaristic trait of Menger's thesis was marred by his Appendix VI which bears the title 'The Starting Point and the Goal of all Human Economy are Strictly Determined' (pp. 216–19). Here Menger argues that all economic action is strictly determined by human needs and the resources available to satisfy them: 'Our direct need and the immediately available goods are in respect to any present moment given facts that are not within our discretion' (p. 217). He admits that human action as such, 'the way which can really be taken or actually will be taken by human agents . . . is by no means strictly determined *a priori* . . .'. But the reasons for this are 'Arbitry, error and other influences'. Without such influences therefore all human action would be determinate.

It is possible, to be sure, to see in this Appendix VI

58   ON INSTITUTIONS

a relapse into an earlier period of Menger's thought, a more rigid determinism oriented to the ideals of nineteenth-century natural science, to which Weber, as we know, objected. But a reader must be forgiven if he is baffled by the contrast between the two passages.

What was Weber's attitude towards this issue? As we see it, he disagreed with the Historical School and was quite willing to give Menger his carefully qualified blessing, but one can sense that he felt uneasy nevertheless about Menger's rather ambiguous position on determinism and found it possible to convince himself that Menger did not have the whole answer either. In these circumstances he may have thought it wise to leave the whole question open—an attitude which in any case would come naturally to a disciple of the Historical School. To Weber, with his aversion to 'unnecessary' theory, no general theory seemed to be called for in this situation.

Weber's rejection of the *Volksgeist* theory of institutions, espoused by some, though not all, adherents of the Historical School, is emphatic. In 'Roscher's Historical Method', the first paper he wrote after recovering from his illness,[1] he explicitly endorses Menger's criticism that Roscher and his followers, the Historical School of economists, had misunderstood the method of Savigny and the Historical Law School, by making far more of the *Volksgeist* than the latter intended. Weber points out that this notion, at best 'an auxiliary concept for the preliminary denotation of a multitude of concrete phenomena not yet logically worked out' and a 'resultant of innumerable cultural

[1] *Gesammelte Aufsätze zur Wissenschaftslehre* (Second Edition, 1951), pp. 1–42. All translations from the German text of these essays are ours.

ON INSTITUTIONS   59

effects' had been endowed by Roscher with a 'metaphysical character' and regarded as 'the *real cause* of the individual cultural manifestations of a people which *emanate* from it.'[1] Such metaphysics was distasteful to him.

Otherwise, however, his attitude to Menger and his theory of institutions is rather ambiguous. It is a curious fact that in his greatest paper on methodology, the Essay on the 'Objectivity of the Social Sciences' of 1904, Menger's name is not mentioned once,[2] though the whole essay is clearly directed against 'naturalism', i.e. the dogmatic belief that there is and can be only one truly scientific method. Menger's view on determinism in human action is here evidently relevant. Later on, however, in his *Sociology of Law*, Weber took over, with some qualifications, most of Menger's thesis on the origin of 'organic' institutions as the unintended results of individual action in the pursuit of interests, as a 'resultant of social forces'— at least in the field of legal institutions. On the other hand he was careful to point out that he did not regard this thesis as a complete explanation.

It seems legitimate to infer that Weber's ambiguous

[1] ibid., p. 10.

[2] There is a reference to Menger, though not by name. 'In spite of the fundamental methodological distinction between historical knowledge and the knowledge of "laws" which the creator of the theory drew as the first and only one, he now claims empirical validity, in the sense of the deducibility of reality from "laws", for the propositions of abstract theory.' (*The Methodology of the Social Sciences*, p. 87).

This is rather odd. Menger, while a strong defender of the abstract method of classical economics, can hardly be regarded as its 'creator' nor as the 'first and only one' to draw this particular distinction. In our view this strange passage confirms the extent to which Weber's mind was preoccupied with Menger's work.

60   ON INSTITUTIONS

attitude towards Menger was due to Menger's ambiguous attitude on the freedom of human action. Weber, uncertain to what extent Menger's praxeological theory of institutions, towards which he was quite sympathetic, rested ultimately on a deterministic premise, wanted to avoid a 'confrontation' with him. But had he tried his hand at a general theory of institutions, such a confrontation could not have been avoided. In this situation he did not feel the time was ripe for generalizations on such a precarious matter.

III

Whether or not our explanation is accepted, the fact remains that no general theory of institutions is to be found in Weber's writings. But we need such a theory, as without it the theory of action which is to give expression to the praxeological method would be incomplete. We thus face the arduous task of piecing together what generalizations on institutions, of a sufficiently high order of abstraction, we are able to lay our hands on in Weber's work, in order to see whether they can serve as a foundation for the building we have to erect.

Taking Weber's utterances in order of time, the first is one we already know: his rejection of the 'emanationist' interpretation of the origin of institutions in the 1903 paper on Roscher mentioned above. We may here perhaps note that when Weber describes the *Volksgeist* as nothing but a 'resultant of innumerable cultural influences' this expression is similar to one sometimes found in Menger, for example when institutions are described as 'resultants of social forces'.

ON INSTITUTIONS   61

The second statement by Weber which is of interest to us we find in the context of his criticism of the work of the legal philosopher Stammler in 1907, in the 'Paradigm of the Skat game'[1] (a German card game). Stammler, not given to a very careful use of terms, held that the outstanding characteristic of social life was its being governed by rules, and had spoken of the analogy of 'rules of the game'. Since a game may be regarded as an institution, what Weber says in the context of his polemic against Stammler throws some light on his general view on institutions.

His main point against Stammler is that though the players' action is of course oriented towards the rules of the game they are playing, and though we might therefore call the rules a 'presupposition' of any concrete game, this tells us nothing about the actual happenings in a concrete game. In our terminology, the rules of the game constitute a set of orientation points, limiting the range of action of each player but also permitting him, because his rivals' actions are equally subject to limitation, to guess with greater confidence what they will do. Within these limits human action here as elsewhere remains free. Weber's argument thus follows the general line of anti-determinism. Norms as such cannot determine a concrete outcome. But nothing has as yet been said about the origin of the rules of the game.

In 1913 Weber published an essay in which he elucidated the meaning of some of the fundamental concepts to be used in his *magnum opus Wirtschaft und Gesellschaft*, which at that time was still in its early stages. The last part of this essay is devoted to the *Anstalt*, the organized institution. Here he makes three points which are of special interest to us.

[1] Ibid., pp. 337–40.

62   ON INSTITUTIONS

Firstly, on the origin of such institutions, he stresses
that the norms which govern them arise 'only in the
rarest cases by autonomous agreement of all those
participating in future action from whom . . . loyalty
towards the norms is expected'.[1] Almost always some
people proclaim such norms and the others then
submit to them. Institutional norms, then, have their
usual origin in *Oktroyierung*, in the few imposing their
will upon the many. We find here, in rough outline,
an élite theory of the origin of institutions, and Weber
close to the position of Mosca and Pareto of whom, so
far as we know, he knew nothing.

Secondly, he points out that the same institution
often comes to mean different things to different
people, and why this is so. It is created by a first
group who impose it upon, or 'suggest' it to, others.
It is 'run' by a second group, namely of executives,
who may interpret its purpose differently from the
first. It is then used 'for their private purposes' by a
third group for whose members it is 'a means of
orientation of their (legal or illegal) acts because
certain expectations concerning the conduct of others
attach to them' (p. 472). A fourth group, 'and these
are the masses', simply learns by tradition certain
modes of conduct in respect of the institution 'mostly
without any knowledge of purpose and meaning, or
even awareness of the existence of the norms' (p. 473).
He shows that the same principle applies to money,
which is not an 'organized' institution, an *Anstalt*.
'How this has actually acquired its peculiar qualities
the money-user does not know—since even the
experts quarrel about it so violently.'

At the end of the essay he stresses once more the
significant function of institutions, which lies in the

[1] *Gesamelte Aufsätze zur Wissenschaftslehre*, p. 468.

ON INSTITUTIONS 63

fact that they enable us to orientate our action towards 'unambiguous expectations to which they give rise. And here rests the specific interest of rational capitalistic "enterprise" in "rational" norms whose practical functioning, in terms of chances, can be just as well calculated as that of a machine' (p. 474). We shall have to return later on to this significant point.

The most important generalizations, from our point of view, are to be found in the Sociology of Law.[1] To be sure, what is said here applies, strictly speaking, only to legal institutions. But the generalizations we encounter here are of such a fundamental nature that they are readily extended beyond the legal sphere.

It is hardly surprising that in this part of his work Weber was at his very best, if we remember that his original training was in law and legal history, and that it embodies a lifetime's experience. Weber himself must have felt this when he told his wife that it was the most 'complete' part of his work.

In the Sociology of Law we find certain themes, by now familiar, with a number of interesting variations added. Weber asks 'How do new legal norms originate?' and answers that, while today this largely happens by legislation, it has not always been so and need not be so. He again rejects the metaphysical explanation of institutions: 'Scientifically, however, this conception leads nowhere' (p. 67). He also rejects the view that changes in 'external conditions of existence' by themselves are causes of legal change. 'The really decisive element has always been a *new line of conduct* which then results either in a change

[1] *Max Weber on Law in Economy and Society*, edited by Max Rheinstein (Harvard University Press, 1954). Here referred to as: Sociology of Law.

L.M.W.—3*

of the meaning of the existing rules of law or in the creation of new rules of law' (p. 68).

He then cautiously adopts what is in essence Menger's praxeological theory of the origin of undesigned institutions. New institutional forms are most frequently created by individuals through 'invention' and then disseminated by imitation and selection: 'Not merely in modern times has this latter situation been of significance as a source of economic reorientation, but in all systems in which the mode of life has reached at least a measure of rationalization' (p. 68).

On the other hand, the systematic character of law, the postulate that all legal norms constitute a coherent system, the legal system, is a late product of our civilization. Weber, who in this whole chapter is, perhaps inevitably, more the legal historian than the sociologist, ascribes its evolution primarily to the mental habits of the academically trained continental lawyers who were naturally inclined to interpret the legal order as a 'closed' system (just as modern science does). He is aware that: 'Among the conditions for the development of a market economy, the calculability of the functioning of the coercive machinery constitutes the technical prerequisite as well as one of the incentives for the inventive genius of the cautelary jurists' (p. 72). But it does not seem to have occurred to him to link this development of 'calculability' to the necessarily formal character of a coherent legal system. On the contrary, he stresses several times the conflicts which are apt to arise between the 'formalism' of the logical thought of the lawyers and the needs of their clients and the public at large:

> It is by no means the peculiar foolishness of modern jurisprudence which leads to such conflicts. To a large

ON INSTITUTIONS 65

extent such conflicts rather are the inevitable consequence of the incompatibility that exists between the intrinsic necessities of logically consistent formal legal thinking and the fact that the legally relevant agreements and activities of private parties are aimed at economic results and oriented towards economically determined expectations. (p. 308)

To us this discrepancy merely reflects a more deep-seated problem of society.

To Weber, then, the systematic character of the legal order is a late product of modern history, like other manifestations of 'rationalization'.

To a youthful law, it is unknown. According to present modes of thought it represents an integration of all analytically derived legal propositions in such a way that they constitute a logically clear, internally consistent, and, at least in theory, gapless system of rules, under which, it is implied, all conceivable fact situations must be capable of being logically subsumed lest their order lack an effective guaranty . . . In the main, the 'system' has predominantly been an external scheme for the ordering of legal data and has been of only minor significance in the analytical derivation of legal propositions and in the construction of legal relationships. The specifically modern form of systematization, which developed out of Roman Law, has its point of departure in the logical analysis of the meaning of the legal propositions as well as of the social actions. (p. 62)

On the other hand,

The increased need for specialized legal knowledge created the professional lawyer. This growing demand for experience and specialized knowledge and the consequent stimulus for increasing rationalization of the law have almost always come from increasing significance of commerce and those participating in it. For the solution

66   ON INSTITUTIONS

of the new problems thus created, specialized, i.e. rational,
training is an indispensable requirement.

However,

> a body of law can be 'rationalized' in various ways and
> by no means necessarily in the direction of the develop-
> ment of its 'juristic' qualities. The direction in which these
> formal qualities develop is, however, conditioned directly
> by 'intrajuristic' conditions: the particular character of
> the individuals who are in a position to influence 'pro-
> fessionally' the ways in which the law is shaped, and only
> indirectly by general economic and social conditions.
> (p. 97)

Weber also noted by what social forces the systematic
character of the modern legal order is threatened:

> New demands for a 'social law' to be based upon such
> emotionally coloured ethical postulates as justice or
> human dignity, and thus directed against the very
> dominance of a mere business morality, have arisen in
> modern times with the emergence of the modern class
> problem. (p. 308)

IV

We must now turn to our task of constructing a theory
of institutions which fits into our conceptual scheme.
In examining the legacy which Max Weber left us we
have come across a number of generalizations which
may serve us well as building blocks, but we shall also
have to look for other building material. If we are to
conduct ourselves like wise and responsible heirs,
drawing our rightful usufruct but also adding to our
legacy by our own efforts, we cannot rest content with
Weber's generalizations as they are. We have to fit
them into the edifice we are about to construct, a
theory of institutions which can be linked to the

ON INSTITUTIONS   67

theory of action set forth in the first essay. We shall find that, as is often the case, as soon as we try to fit a number of hitherto isolated generalizations into a coherent framework, they begin to reveal certain problematical features, which without this test would probably have gone unnoticed.

In turning to our task we shall not have to spend much time in examining the needs theory of institutions to be found in Menger's Appendix VI. We must reject it. To be sure, no institution can exist for long unless it satisfies some need. But not every need generates an institution. The weakness of this theory lies in its failure to provide us with any criterion by which to distinguish between those needs which will find their satisfaction through appropriate institutions and those which will not. Menger was, here as elsewhere, too readily inclined to draw on the analogy of the market. In a market economy of course the price system acts as a 'centralized agency' for the distribution of goods and services. We have here a simple criterion by which to determine which needs will in fact be satisfied. In the market, in this sense, all needs are brought into harmony, provided we regard prices as objective indices of the needs which the goods bought at these prices are to satisfy. Where this provision does not hold, no comparison of needs is possible. Outside the sphere of the market not even such a unifying agency as the price system is to be found. We must therefore conclude that the needs theory of institutions fails to satisfy our need for a coherent theory of the origin and functions of institutions.

On the other hand, Menger's praxeological theory of the origin of undesigned ('organic') institutions is much better suited to our analytical needs. Here we

68   ON INSTITUTIONS

have a theory which explains the origin of such institutions in the same way as other innovations. Some men realize that it is possible to pursue their interests more effectively than they have done so far and that an existing situation offers opportunities not so far exploited. In concert with others they do exploit them. If they are successful their example will find ready imitators, at first a few, later on many.

Successful plans thus gradually crystallize into institutions. Within the sphere of freedom of action new institutions arise as additional orientation points, which may take the place of older institutions that became obsolete. Imitation of the successful is, here as elsewhere, the most important form by which the ways of the élite become the property of the masses. Once an idea originally grasped by an eager mind has been 'tested' and found successful, it can be safely employed as a means to success by minds less eager and lacking originality. Institutions are the relics of the pioneering efforts of former generations from which we are still drawing benefit. Drawing once more on the analogy of the market, we may say that the theory of institutions is the sociological counterpart of the theory of competition in economics. In both cases innovation and imitation are the complementary elements of what is virtually the same social process.

But even if we were to regard the answer just outlined as, by and large, a satisfactory answer to the question about the origin and functions of undesigned institutions, a new host of intricate questions would make its appearance on the horizon. Most of these cluster around the problem of the nature and permanence of the institutional order, a problem which will have to remain at the centre of our stage until the end of the book.

ON INSTITUTIONS   69

When different men, successfully pursuing different interests, shape types of action which, by multifarious imitation, gradually crystallize into institutions, how can we know that these undesigned products of individual pursuit will all be compatible with one another? Will they all come to form a coherent system? What problems will arise if this is not the case?

In trying to answer these questions we shall get as little help from invoking the analogy of the market mechanism as we did in the case of the needs theory of institutions. In a market economy a 'tendency towards a general equilibrium' of prices and quantities produced and exchanged can be shown to exist, subject to a number of conditions, which include absence of unexpected change that would disrupt plans. Outside the market sphere no such predominant tendency towards a general equilibrium can be meaningfully asserted to operate. In every conceivable situation there are 'destabilizing' as well as 'stabilizing' forces at work. Moreover, it is hard to imagine any kind of institutional change which would not upset at least some existing plans. To invoke the analogy of the market forces will not therefore help us much.

We also have to remember that besides the undesigned institutions so far discussed there are those of the designed variety, the products of legislation and other manifestations of the 'social will'. What reasons have we to believe that all institutions, designed and undesigned, will easily fit into a coherent whole, when already the undesigned by themselves leave us in some doubt?

In these circumstances we must clearly establish, as our next step, whether the coherence of the institutional structure as a whole is of great importance to us in our

70　　　　　　　ON INSTITUTIONS

task of constructing a theory of institutions. For if this were not so, if, for example, this coherence were to us a feature of secondary importance to the task at hand, we might perhaps safely ignore the difficulties which now appear on our horizon.

Unfortunately this easy way out is not open to us. The coherence and permanence of the institutional order are of paramount importance to those engaged, as we are, in tracing all the major conditions of rational action. In reducing the uncertainty of the future which enshrouds all human action, and helping us overcome the limitations of our ignorance of the present, such coherence and permanence are indeed of primary importance.

That this is so is most readily seen if we at first consider only legal institutions. Here it is indeed obvious that any act by which somebody commits himself for a period of significant length, if for example he grants a loan repayable after twenty years, involves the coherence and permanence of the whole legal order. That in any agreement between creditor and debtor coherence and permanence of the legal rules is involved is obvious enough, but it might be thought at first that this requirement applies only to the rules concerning loan contracts. Of course this is a fallacy. In the first place, there can be no permanence of a set of norms unless they are coherent. Secondly, it is impossible to separate the legal provisions governing loans from the rest of the legal order. Every concrete business transaction involves such a large number of legal rules that it would be impossible to enumerate them all and, hence, separate them from the rest of the legal order. That in our everyday lives we remain unaware of this fact is of course due to the relatively infrequent occurrence of legal disputes in the lives of

ON INSTITUTIONS 71

non-lawyers, since it is as a rule only in the case of legal dispute that these matters are called to our attention, and even in such a dispute only a few rules become the subject of litigation. Finally, in a legal system that lacked coherence it would be impossible to predict the outcome of a single case, as it would be impossible to determine the scope and nature of the 'gaps' in the system as well as of all the conceivable contradictions in it.

It is therefore wrong to see, with Weber, in the coherence and permanence of modern legal systems nothing but the sediment of a certain type of legal education, the product of lawyers whose minds, trained to logic and order, demanded an orderly arrangement of their tool-box. These features of our legal order are typically undesigned features of our type of civilization.

This is not to deny that there is solid merit in Weber's way of looking at this development. In tracing the history of an institution there is always a good deal to be said for stressing the intellectual propensity, the 'spirit', of the élite which has created it. Successful institutions often bear the unmistakable imprint of the spirit of their creators even after centuries of change. But the tendency to stress such spiritual origins is a virtue which, like other virtues, can be practised to excess. In this case the lawyers clearly also had to take their orientation from the needs of their clients for a coherent legal order.

The discrepancy, stressed by Weber and mentioned above (p. 64), between the need of business-men for simple rules and the complex characteristics of legal logic, does of course exist and often leads to conflict between the lawyers and the public. But the real conflict exists here rather between the short-term need

72   ON INSTITUTIONS

of the individual businessman for simplicity and the
long-term need of the business community as a whole
for a coherent legal order, which entails complex
logical rules. In this situation the lawyers merely act
as intermediaries.

The question now arises as to how the coherence
and permanence of the legal order can be reconciled
with the facts of annual legislation. How can we speak
of the uniformity and continuous existence of a body
of norms if every one of these norms can be changed
every year? The answer has to be that this is precisely
how the lawyer has to regard the legal system, very
much as the merchant looks upon his stock as a whole,
as it appears in his balance sheet, as consisting entirely
of easily replaceable parts. It is a legal fiction necessary
to lend coherence to the framework of legal thought.

But we have to look at the matter from the praxeological, as distinct from the legal, point of view, and
must disregard legal fictions. In the light of what has
been said above about the social function of institutions as signposts, it must be clear that the more often
the legal order is subjected to change, by legislation
or judicial interpretation, the more it loses its capacity
to serve as a means of orientation in relation to the
action of others. This fact has some bearing on the
whole question of the status of designed institutions
within our conceptual edifice. There must clearly be a
limit to the amount of annual designing and re-
designing of institutions which society can stand. The
legal order can absorb some changes, but not too
many of them, and they must not be of a fundamental
kind.

If we are now to extend our perspective from the
legal sphere to the institutions of society as a whole
we have to establish, first of all, the existence of

ON INSTITUTIONS 73

coherence and permanence in this wider sphere. We are no doubt entitled to speak of a legal order, but with what right may we claim to speak of an institutional order in general? Even if we succeeded in establishing the existence of such an order, it is likely that it would have to be a much looser and less coherent order than that of the legal sphere.

V

In our situation it might be tempting to invoke the support of one of the many 'social system' theories which now abound in the field of the social sciences. It would seem that if the network of social relationships is to lend itself to description in terms of a 'system' at all, institutions will largely have to provide its structure and thus have an important part to play in it. And since institutions have an important function in guiding social action, do they not thus lend themselves readily to treatment in terms of the 'structural-functional' variety of social-system theories?

There are a number of reasons why we should not rely on such support, and why we are compelled to seek to establish the existence of an institutional order by our own efforts. In the first place, there are substantial differences between these various theories, in particular as regards their level of abstraction. Some authors do not seem to mean by 'system' anything more than the existence of a set of social relationships. Others rely largely on functional specialization. The status of institutions within the context of these theories would require a considerable effort at clarification. It is clear that a good deal of 'structure' rests on them. Unfortunately, however,

ON INSTITUTIONS

most of these theories proceed on such a high level of abstraction that one never knows when the institutions referred to are meant to be concrete institutions, and when they are elements of an abstract system.

There is another reason, even more important to us, why we should not invoke the support of the social-system theories currently in fashion to help us in our endeavour. We are concerned with the legacy of Max Weber. As we pointed out in the Introduction, Weber's approach to social action is something very different from that of the structural-functional theories.[1] Weber was concerned with the meaning the actor attributes to his action. Most social-system theories ignore this aspect of action. As regards institutions in particular, when we speak of the 'function' of institutions in guiding and co-ordinating the actions of millions of individuals we are following Weber in using this word in a sense very different from the one it has in the words 'structural-functional'. The theory we are attempting to establish aims at the reduction of certain social phenomena to human mental acts as manifested in plans. Most of the theories mentioned, by contrast, aim at establishing their 'systems' in terms of recurrent patterns of action *without* reference to the meaning such action has to the individuals acting. We believe we are making legitimate usufruct of Weber's legacy. It follows that we can hardly hope to draw benefit from social-system theories of the type characterized.

We also have to remember that Weber, as he

[1] For a detailed critique of 'functionalism' in social theory from a point of view very close to Weber's see John Rex, *Key Problems of Sociological Theory* (Routledge and Kegan Paul, 1961), ch. IV. *See also* W. G. Runciman, *Social Science and Political Theory* (1963), CUP, pp. 110–22.

ON INSTITUTIONS   75

explained at length in his famous critique of Stammler,[1] attributed great importance to the distinction between legal norms and human conduct oriented to such norms, and emphasized that the former in no way 'determine' the latter. We thus have good reason to distinguish carefully between legal norms and those recurrent patterns of conduct which we call institutions. Are we, then, entitled to speak of an institutional order?

First of all, the mere fact that each institution denotes a recurrent pattern of conduct does not by itself entail the existence of an over-all institutional order. As was the case with the legal order, the criterion of existence of the wider institutional order, if such can be shown to exist, would have to be sought in its capacity to outlast its individual elements. The forms and character of its existence have therefore to be established separately from that of its component elements. In comparing the legal system with the wider institutional order we have to remember that the unity of the former lies in its character as a system of norms, while the unity of the latter will have to be sought elsewhere.

We shall now compare the legal system and the institutional order with respect to their degrees of coherence, and we shall do so by comparing them with regard to four of their characteristics: permanence, consistency, unity, and over-all complementarity ('gaplessness').

The first characteristic is evidently shared by both the legal system and the institutional order as a whole. We simply cannot speak of an aggregate as a 'whole' unless it outlasts its component elements. The importance of the permanence of the institutional order

---

[1] *Gesammelte Aufsätze zur Wissenschaftslehre* (1951), pp. 291–359.

76   ON INSTITUTIONS

in general, as well as for a theory of action such as ours, requires no comment.

As regards consistency, our second characteristic, the matter is already more complicated. In the case of legal institutions the range of required compatibility comprehends them all. No two legal institutions can be incompatible. With other institutions the requirement of compatibility is less strict since not all institutions are used by the same actors or figure in the same plans. The existence of military institutions based on absolute obedience to superior authority does not preclude the existence of other institutions in which orders may well and are expected to be questioned, even though the two principles are incompatible. But there must indeed always be some fundamental institutions with which all others are compatible.

The unity of the legal system rests on the logical character of its norms. It stems from the comprehensive nature of the range of required compatibility just discussed. Though we find no exact counterpart of this in the wider institutional sphere, nevertheless institutions here also display an 'order', they are not an aggregate of random composition. The Post Office could hardly take over the functions of the police, the clergy scarcely act as a Fire Brigade. The basis of this order, the characteristic property which bestows upon it what unity it has, is here evidently functional specialization.

The greatest difference exists with respect to our fourth characteristic: over-all complementarity. The legal system is a seamless web. It has no 'gaps'. A judge before whom a legal case is brought can never refuse to give a decision on the grounds that he knows of no legal norm to apply to it. He has to find

ON INSTITUTIONS   77

one. The legal order abhors a vacuum no less that nature does. In the wider institutional sphere we find no parallel to this characteristic. Some institutions will be complementary to one another in that they require each other's services, like Post Office and railways or airlines. In fact, such group complementarity is the inevitable result of the functional specialization of individual institutions. But here no inter-group complementarity need exist. 'Gaps' are ubiquitous.

As a result of our comparison we have to conclude that the legal system and the wider institutional order share the first characteristic of permanence, while the fourth, 'gapless' complementarity, is absent from the latter. As regards compatibility of institutions, the range is less comprehensive in the wider sphere than in the legal sector. Both display enough unity to claim the character of a structured whole, but in the case of the institutions of society this unity rests on functional specialization and is not of a logical nature. All in all we have to realize that the coherence of the wider institutional order, while it certainly exists, is weaker than that of that part of it which is formed by the legal institutions.

From the fact that the two spheres, the wider and the narrower, share the property of permanence it follows that they also share the noteworthy characteristic that the permanence of the whole does not entail the permanence of each of its parts. It is as true of the institutional order as of its legal part that the order as a whole lasts while each individual institution may change. We shall see that this coincidence of permanence of the whole with flexibility of its parts gives rise to a number of intricate problems.

Institutions rise and fall, they move and change. An

78   ON INSTITUTIONS

institution may last a long time, but during this time
assume new functions or discard old ones. We shall
find later on that these facts are likely to have
particularly far-reaching effects in the sphere of
political institutions.

These institutional changes no doubt often take
place in response to changing needs, but also often for
other reasons. An institution may cease to exist, for
example, because the services required for it are no
longer available, perhaps because, owing to a change
in the moral and intellectual climate of society, the
qualities of will and mind needed from those responsible for it have become an object of contempt or
derision, or perhaps because those whose skills are
required are now attracted into other avenues. The
importance of factors such as these on the 'supply side'
provides further illustration of the inadequacy of the
needs theory of institutions that we rejected earlier.
To bring a new institution into existence requires not
merely the existence of certain needs but also the
specific 'entrepreneurial' skill of the innovator, as well
as that of his successful imitators. But even to adjust
an existing institution to new uses requires specific
skills.

In every society we shall therefore at any moment
find institutions belonging to different historical
'strata', some of which were originally devised for
purposes very different from those for which they are
presently used, and which nevertheless together form
a coherent pattern—a pattern which, however, will
not last. As the present lay-out of an old town (in
which we find buildings erected over many centuries
and built in many different styles) owes no less to the
ingenuity of its present users than to the genius of the
original architects who had probably designed its

ON INSTITUTIONS 79

buildings for entirely different purposes, so the present pattern of the institutional order owes no less to the ingenuity of present users of these institutions than to that of their originators. Institutions change less as a result of 'changing circumstances' than as a result of human action designed to meet change.

But how much change of individual institutions is compatible with the permanence of our structure? The whole problem of 'flexibility versus coherence' now appears on the horizon. There must be some flexibility, some room for manœuvre if men are to pursue their various interests. But how much of it can we concede before the whole institutional structure is impaired?

Confronted with this dilemma we must remember that it is not change as such, but unexpected change, which jeopardises planned action. The position of each institution on the social firmament must be given, or be at least knowable. It need not be fixed, to be sure, but then its orbit at least must be known. Not movement as such, but irregular movement disqualifies an institution from serving as a point of orientation. The crucial requirement is for actors to be able to take their bearings by existing institutions, to be able to 'steer by them'.

A night at the theatre with the first act of *Hamlet* followed by the second act of *Macbeth* and the third act of *King Lear* might have its attractions, provided everybody in cast and audience knew the programme beforehand. Only if the stage management were to introduce it unexpectedly would chaos on the stage and bewilderment in the audience be likely to result. The reason such a programme might be feasible is of course that some actors and actresses have a repertoire of rôles sufficiently wide to permit it, and that the immediate plans of most theatregoers extend over a

80   ON INSTITUTIONS

few hours only. But in our society, especially in
modern industry, many plans (buildings, plant,
equipment) have to extend over a large number of
years and are therefore particularly susceptible to
unexpected change. The conclusion appears inevitable that the more important become long-term
plans which, once the planned course of action has
been set in motion, cannot be adjusted to subsequent
change, the more damaging institutional change
becomes. Since at any moment some such long-term
plan is bound to be in course of execution, the time
for painless institutional change will never arrive
unless prior notice of it is given to all interested
parties sufficiently far ahead to give any plan in
operation time for completion. It is thus almost
inevitable that all institutional change will upset some
plans in the course of execution.

Unfortunately we have not yet reached the end of
our difficulties. Such unexpected change is likely to
have further repercussions. In particular with respect
to the relationship between designed and undesigned
institutions we have to note that institutions can only
be designed to meet a certain known situation, or a
limited number of possible, i.e. conceivable, situations,
but not an unlimited number of unknown situations.
We therefore face not merely the problem of how
designed and undesigned institutions can supplement
each other in such a way as to form together a
coherent institutional structure. We now encounter
an even worse possibility, namely that unexpected
change of undesigned institutions may not merely
jeopardize the coherence of the institutional structure
as a whole, but in addition may obviate the very
design of the designed institutions.

Here we might contemplate the following way out.

ON INSTITUTIONS   81

In a society in which it is generally known that frequent change of undesigned institutions is inevitable, the designers of designed institutions may deliberately confine their activity to designing a framework which leaves room for a good deal (in principle an unlimited amount) of change which, since it will take place within the framework, will not affect the latter as such. This device would serve to solve our second problem, even though we could not be certain that the integration of the institutional structure as a coherent whole can be accomplished in this fashion.

This idea is not a mere figment of our imagination. The legal framework of modern Western societies has in fact achieved something similar to the model just envisaged by leaving a wide sphere of 'freedom of contract' to individuals acting in pursuit of their respective interests. The modern market economy would not be possible without it.

In such a society it might be said that the undesigned institutions which evolve gradually as the unintended and unforeseeable result of the pursuit of individual interests accumulate in the *interstices* of the legal order. The interstices have been planned, though the sediments accumulating in them have not and could not have been. In a society of this type we might then distinguish between the *external* institutions which constitute, as it were, the outer framework of society, the legal order, and the *internal* institutions which gradually evolve as a result of market processes and other forms of spontaneous individual action. It seems to us that it is within a scheme such as this that the praxeological theory of institutions which we are attempting to establish most readily finds its place. We also believe that Menger had a scheme similar to

82   ON INSTITUTIONS

this in mind when he set forth his ideas on institutions in the third part of his book.

But such a model of the character of the relationships between external and internal, designed and undesigned, institutions is not quite satisfactory for our purpose. It fails to take account of the complex nature of the relationships which obtain here. The implied contrast between firm outer structure and shapeless inner void could actually be highly misleading.

In the first place, the model rests on the assumption that undesigned institutions evolve while the designed form an outer structure, that is to say, that the former alter much more rapidly than do the latter. But designed institutions also change and we have no reason to believe that their speed of change will always be less than that of the undesigned variety. The problems of structural change of designed institutions will occupy us in a subsequent essay.

Secondly, the processes of change of the two classes cannot be regarded as being independent of each other. Changes in the legal order may affect the area for manoeuvre within which individuals may move and undesigned institutions evolve. On the other hand, the evolution of undesigned institutions also creates new problems for the legal order. Sooner or later some of them may have to be co-ordinated. The law may permit everybody to form companies with limited liability, or trade unions, but sooner or later, simply to reduce the amount of possible litigation, some legal rules about the relationship between directors and shareholders, branch secretaries and members, have to be promulgated.

Thirdly, it is always possible that the slow evolution of some institutions, even though at first taking place apparently within the interstices of an existing social

ON INSTITUTIONS 83

and legal order, will gradually lead to what we might call 'deformation of social space'. The coherence and permanence of the existing social order will then be jeopardized even without any change in the legal system. The danger will be much greater where the institutions growing up are in some respects in conflict with each other, so that only one or the other, but not both, can be integrated into the existing institutional structure. Quite serious problems can arise in this way.

The problems mentioned can be grouped under three heads:

(1) those which arise from the multiplicity of sources (interests)—coherence;
(2) those which arise from the lapse of time and the need to adjust existing institutions to new institutions—flexibility, change;
(3) those which arise from uncertainty as to which new institutions will exist at a future time— flexibility, change, adjustment to what?

We shall now give a topical example of destabilizing institutional change in which all these three categories are involved.

When in the years following the First World War most countries of the Western world adopted the British institutions of 'collective bargaining', sometimes in their pure British form, sometimes with the addition of institutions of compulsory arbitration in industrial disputes, not many voices of dissent were heard. Some economists showed themselves aware of the element of bilateral monopoly that 'industry-wide bargaining' for wage-rates and working conditions would entail, and pointed to the dangers inherent in such a situation.

84   ON INSTITUTIONS

But as a rule they, and anybody else expressing doubts
about the excellence of the new dispensation, were
simply regarded as 'reactionaries'. It seemed that a
problem which in the early decades of the industrial
age had baffled so many men of good will had now
at last found a solution: how to fit labour relations in
modern industry into the framework of the market
without results which appeared to deprive the
individual worker of all influence on the outcome of
the market process. 'Collective bargaining' after all
was bargaining, and was not bargaining of the
essence of the market?

Since in the world of 1920 the framework of the
market economy was simply taken for granted, it
appeared that even collusion between the bargainers
could only occur within narrow limits. With a
competitive price system in existence no single price
and hence no single wage-rate could get very far out
of line. In fact, the competitive price system by its
very existence set fairly narrow limits to the area
within which wage-rates could be determined by
bargaining. Any attempt by trade unions to induce
employers to accept wage-rates which were 'too high'
would adversely affect the volume of sales and thus
lead to unemployment. The institutions of collective
bargaining as seen in the perspective of 1920 appeared
to be embedded in an economic order sufficiently
strong and stable to vouchsafe their beneficial
character.

We are living in a different world. No economist
would deny today that the continuous inflation from
which the Western world has suffered for more than
two decades has something to do with the modern
methods of determining wage-rates. We now have to
ask what are the precise circumstances that have

ON INSTITUTIONS 85

turned institutions which in 1920 looked quite harmless into a source of a dangerous and de-stabilizing social processes which contemporary Western society, for all its wealth and vaunted efficiency, appears to be unable to stop. We have here a clear example of what we called above 'deformation of social space'.

Three kinds of change in economic institutions, as well as in the mental climate in which they flourish, appear to us as the main causes of this development, though no doubt it would be possible to enumerate a number of other factors contributing to the inflationary result.

There is, in the first place, the change in the monetary system from a metallic standard to a debt money system. Modern money consists of claims against banks, central banks, or governments. It is of the essence of such a system that the total number of such claims that might be created is in principle unlimited, though control by a public authority may limit it at any particular point of time. While in the world of 1920 it was possible to hold that the limited quantity of metallic money kept the price system within bounds and thus also set limits to the maximum wage-rates attainable by bargaining, no such 'ultimate determinant' exists at the present time. Today it would be almost more correct to say that the total quantity of money-claims is influenced by nothing so much as by the total amount of wage-claims that have been granted. This is what Sir John Hicks meant by the 'labour standard' which has replaced the old gold standard. In other words, the transition from a metallic to a credit standard, the adoption of a monetary system in which money can be created virtually at will, has removed an important external

86   ON INSTITUTIONS

restraint on the wage-setting power of the industrial
bargainers.

The second change concerns the price-setting power
of industrialists, who at the same time represent one
side in the bargaining process. Today most prices of
industrial goods are set by their producers, they are
typically list or catalogue prices. When employers
grant higher wage-rates they are virtually certain that
they will be able to recoup such increases in the costs
of production in the form of higher prices of the goods
they sell, in particular since they know that their
competitors will have to pay the same higher wage
rates.

This situation differs in important respects from
that which prevailed in the market economy of the
nineteenth century. In that period the most important
industrial goods (textiles, coal, furniture) were typically
produced by firms of fairly small size, while the market
for them was dominated by wholesale merchants
acting as intermediaries between producers and retail
sellers. These wholesale merchants, deriving their
profits solely from their turnover of goods, were
primarily interested in maintaining their rate of
turnover, but not at all interested in production
costs, which did not affect them directly. They had
to match supply with demand if their profits were not
to suffer. A fall in demand would induce them to
reduce their selling prices, and so their buying prices.
Production costs of goods had then to be adjusted
accordingly. Market prices determined wage-rates
and not the other way round.

Today the wholesale merchant as a price-setter has
all but disappeared and with him the flexible price
system characteristic of the nineteenth-century market
economy. At present prices are set by industrial

ON INSTITUTIONS 87

producers more interested in their profit margin than in their rate of turnover. A fall in demand will lead today to a fall in output and employment, but hardly ever to a fall in prices.

Yet these two institutional changes by themselves would not have sufficed to bring about the permanent inflation of our age. The most important economic characteristic of our age is surely that in our world prices can, in the long run at least, only rise but never fall. Our first two reasons serve to explain merely why in our world certain restraints on the rise of wage-rates, which in 1920 were still universally taken for granted, have disappeared. They do not yet explain why these wage-rates rise continuously and do not fall even in times of depression.

The third change which explains this very fact was not, strictly speaking, of an institutional but of a moral nature. In our world it has come to be accepted as an article of social faith that no money wage-rate must ever be allowed to fall, that wage- and salary-earners have a right to expect that their money incomes will rise, at least in the long run, and that this expectation must in no circumstances be disappointed. This means for all practical purposes that, since wage-rates can only rise and never fall, the same must apply to prices.

Whether this change in the social atmosphere in which the institutions of collective bargaining function has to be regarded as the true cause of the inflationary process, while the other two changes mentioned should perhaps only be regarded as necessary conditions, is a question we shall not discuss. All human action is of course oriented to the conditions of its success. The lesson we have to learn from our example is rather that a change in the mental climate may by itself,

L.M.W.—4

without the creation of any new institutions or the disappearance of old landmarks in the institutional landscape, turn out to be an important institutional change because it affects the way in which men use their existing institutions, An undesigned institution which originally was able to operate in one of several possible ways (wage-rates could either fall or rise or remain constant) may, when one of these ways becomes socially obsolete and other institutional changes occur concurrently, acquire an entirely new kind of impetus never dreamt of by its pioneers. It is thus possible for an institution, without any change in its outer form of appearance and without anybody, even among those who make daily use of it, noticing it for a long time, gradually to change its character, its *modus operandi* and its place in the whole institutional structure.

VI

The time has come for us to cast a backward glance at the road along which we have travelled and to attempt to draw some conclusions from what we have learnt.

We came to see that a theory of action which aims at intelligibility must rest on the parallelism between plan and action. Institutions serve to co-ordinate plans in large societies. To serve this purpose they must form a structure to which coherence and permanence can be attributed, as no institution stands by itself and all action extends into the future. But a changing world also requires flexibility of plans and institutions. We saw that undesigned institutions in particular can be regarded as successful plans which have crystallized into institutions through widespread imitation. It

ON INSTITUTIONS   89

seems therefore that the need for coherence and
permanence on the one hand and for flexibility on the
other cannot be easily reconciled. But we need not
despair of our theory of institutional structure.

On the one hand, it would hardly be surprising if
the range of possible disturbances of the institutional
order generated by the need for flexibility which is
disclosed by our analysis were to considerably exceed
the actual range we are likely to find in any given
society. An analytical scheme such as ours must
comprehend the whole range of possible, and not just
of probable occurrences. How many of these will
become actual is another matter. The seriousness of
the potential threat to institutional stability emanating
from the need for flexibility is very much a matter of
time. Slow change is less harmful than fast change.
Almost any change takes time and so do its repercussions. The amount of change possible per unit of time
is also limited. As regards designed institutions, there
is a limit to the annual activity of skilled designers.
Devices such as delegated legislation may widen these
limits but cannot erase them. In the case of undesigned
institutions it takes time for successful modes of action
to crystallize into institutions. It takes time even for
the participants to find out which action was successful
and which was not. It takes further time for such
knowledge to become diffused among potential
imitators. Apart from the time aspect of the matter,
the very looseness of the institutional structure we
discussed above tends to act as a protective device in
such cases. The lack of complementarity between
institutions of different classes means here that the
area over which any given change will have repercussions is limited.

On the other hand we clearly have to ask how

in reality societies continue to cope with such problems. How is the need for coherence and permanence reconciled with that for flexibility in the real world? While no doubt different devices have been employed for this purpose in different societies and at different times, four such devices appear to call for attention in the context of our investigation and to be entitled to a place in an analytical scheme such as ours.

We are already familiar with the first two of these from the model which we presented in the previous section. The first device consists in granting to individuals a fairly wide sphere of 'contractual freedom', a sphere in which change must be expected to be frequent and which may be regarded as the main source of undesigned institutions. The first device consists then, briefly, in having institutions which are frequently mutable in a definite sphere of action.

Its complement, our second device, consists in having a few 'fundamental' institutions which, by contrast, are not mutable at all. In our former terminology, these external institutions must provide a firm outer structure in the interstices of which the sediments of individual efforts in the 'free and mutable' sphere can accumulate. We must stress again that these two devices are complementary to each other. Frequently mutable and (almost) immutable institutions require and support one another. As the classical economists knew well, a market economy may adjust itself to changes of many kinds, but it rests unconditionally on the institutions of property and contract.

The third device, which is new to us, takes the form of meeting a situation requiring change not by the creation of a new institution, nor by replacing an old by a new, but by 'widening' an existing institution in such a way that it can serve new interests without upsetting the plans which have thus far made use of it. The widening of the concept of property in the modern company, in such a way that the relationships between directors and shareholders can be brought within its province, appears a good example.

The fourth, and for more than one reason we might say the ultimate, device of which every society disposes in order to defend itself against the desperate cases of dilemmas of this kind, is to prohibit change which threatens to upset the social order, and to act against the interests engendering it. Where institutional change prompted by the pursuit of interests threatens the unity of the institutional order, it is the latter which has to be defended.

No society can stand more than a certain amount of change within any period. No doubt the limit of tolerance varies between one society and another, or between one period and another within the same society. A good deal will clearly depend on the extent to which the devices enumerated (and possibly others) are available as alternatives.

But there can be little doubt that some limit of tolerance of institutional change exists everywhere, and that every healthy society is able to call upon social forces of considerable strength when this limit is being approached. In this simple fact we have to see a manifestation of 'the Rationality of Tradition'. Every social system is always jeopardized by the pluralism of contending interests and has to depend on the strength of its institutional order to defend it against such deformation of social space as would threaten its continued existence.

[13]

THE EVOLUTIONARY PATH

If institutions are evolving, dynamic arrangements, how can we best take into account the various 'moving pieces' within the structure? Customary law is evolved law, having changed over time to meet specific needs in specific environments. In many cases, particularly in Africa, customary law may provide a greater degree of tenure security than formal law. This raises the question: is the better path for securing property rights in Africa to somehow formalise customary rights and privileges (Alden Wiley, 2006)? There are no simple answers here either, as this approach is also fraught with complexity and uncertainty and not free from problems associated with rent-seeking behaviours (Durand-Lasserve, 2006).

While it is clear that communities often respond to increasing demands for property by moving towards greater individualisation of property rights, we should not, however, expect such movements to be free of controversy. When societies shift from communal to individualised rights, those persons who previously had responsibility for allocating rights are likely to lose power and status within their community. Some individuals, particularly those with greater clout in the society, are likely to receive rights to more valuable parcels, or to larger parcels, than more marginalised members of the society. These changes may engender conflict, but unless the society develops an effective alternative method for meeting the increased demand for land (via effective land markets, for example) it may experience even greater levels of conflict.

The evolution of property rights in Plateau, Nigeria

One example of how property rights evolve and how blocking that process by legislation can lead to conflict comes from Nigeria. The central part of the country is dominated by a plateau – a highland that was lightly populated until the twentieth century. In the nineteenth century this rugged area was home to a heterogeneous population composed of small ethnic groups living independently from their neighbour to the north, the Muslim Sultanate of Sokoto, and their neighbours to the south, Igos, Ijaws and Edos, among others.

Britain took control of Nigeria in 1900 and created Northern and Southern Nigeria. The British also created different formal property environments in these two regions. In the south, property could be owned individually. Land registries existed to facilitate individual sale. In the north, land was essentially nationalised, with the government granting long-term permits to occupy. In the Plateau region, it seems that customary law probably lasted longer than in the other regions with local chiefs acting as native authorities and acting through native courts, making use and allocation decisions over land (Falola, 1999: 70–72).

The ethnic groups in Plateau had an abundance of different customary land-law rules. Property rules included norms for excluding outsiders, for incorporating outsiders via adoption, for lending/borrowing land, for inheriting land and for pledging property in satisfaction of a debt. Other rules governed physical structures erected on land and valuable trees.[1] People living in Plateau had many sticks in a bundle of property rights and these sticks provided flexibility and opportunity to community members. Although community members typically did not hold the stick that allowed for the sale or transfer of property, the norm of pledging land could approximate a sale so long as the pledge went unredeemed.

Reports from British officials in Nigeria in the 1930s testify that, in the eastern part of Plateau, people who cultivated land held it under rules that resembled freehold property (Boudreaux, 2005b: 61–102).[2] Their property could be sold, but not leased or pawned. In the northern part of Plateau, in the Jos region, land could be leased for long periods but land sales were rare, except around Ganawuri, a town with fertile land. In the southern part of Plateau the Kofyar people adopted intensive permanent cultivation techniques and expended tremendous effort creating terraces on hillsides. These terraces were a costly investment and, not surprisingly, people who made these investments had highly individualised rights to the land. Writing in the 1960s about these hill farmers, anthropologist Robert Netting says:

> The Kofyar insist that every square inch of arable soil, both village and bush, has an owner, a single person to whom the land belongs and who alone may decide on its use. This is probably a direct outgrowth of intensive farming. Wherever land can be made to produce heavily and continuously over a long period of time, it increased in value to both the occupant and his heirs. (Netting, 1968: 159)

---

1   For a discussion of customary land law in Africa, see Olawale Elias (1962).
2   See Boudreaux (2005b) for an extended discussion of the relationship between insecure property rights and violence in Plateau State.

Interestingly, the Kofyar moved away from intensive cultivation in the 1950s, towards cash cropping and then, in the 1970s, back to permanent settlements with a renewed effort at intensive cultivation (Netting et al., 1989: 299–319). The key point is that customary land-law rules were flexible enough in Plateau to allow for the increasing individualisation of property rights in response to the increasing value of land. Indeed, property in Plateau existed on a continuum from traditional communal rights towards something closely approximating freehold.

Residents of Plateau were travelling on an evolutionary path to property that was blocked by the Land Use Act, which nationalised land in Nigeria. This 1978 legislation shifted land allocation decisions to state governors, who are empowered to issue certificates of occupancy. Although the statute was supposed to 'rationalise' the complex system of customary, statutory and common-law rules governing land in Nigeria, as well as curb land speculation, the law provides many opportunities for side payments and corruption as certificate-holders must seek approval from state governors to gift their certificates, sell them or otherwise use them (not to mention obtaining them in the first place). Combine problems of corruption with liberal use of compulsory acquisition by the government and the Land Use Act creates an insecure property-rights environment in which individuals have bundles of property rights that are relatively thin.

This centralised and politicised process for land allocation removed the power to allocate land from traditional authorities. Donald Williams argues that the Nigerian land law 'was designed to pose a direct challenge to alternative sources of societal authority by relegating all private transactions in land to government agencies' (Williams, 1992: 587). The legislative process for allocating land in Nigeria, which is open to corruption, may also exacerbate conflict between groups, such as farmers and pastoralists, who in the past managed to share land but who now compete for land as Nigeria's population rises and as desertification sends more people from northern Nigeria into the central part of the country.

We would expect that in a situation where the demand for land increases as population rises, and as heterogeneity (hence transaction costs) increases as well, communities would expend additional resources defining property rights more clearly and defending those rights against others. In Nigeria, this redefinition cannot take place because of the nationalisation of land (or it does not take place in any formal sense, it takes place de facto). Because it is so costly to establish property rights under the Land Use Act, people may turn to informal, extra-legal means to protect land when outsiders encroach on it. The Act creates a situation of tenure insecurity and in this situation people may choose personal justice – fighting – and de facto rights over the current system. In Plateau, as in other parts of Africa that suffer from resource conflict, thousands of people have lost their lives in battles over property.[3] This is one of the most important aspects of secure property rights: they reduce conflict by clarifying rights and by providing the means to enforce rights through peaceful means.

---

3   'Nigeria: Plateau state violence claimed 53,000 lives – report', *UN Integrated Regional Information Networks*, 8 October 2004, *www.irennews.org/reprt. asp?ReportID=43580.*

Land ownership and cocoa production in western Ghana

Ghana provides a different example of the evolutionary path to property in Africa. Land devoted to cocoa production is controlled by rules of customary law. The right to use it for agricultural purposes was traditionally given to family groups by local leaders. As the area available for planting cocoa trees has dwindled, owing to an influx of migrants and rising local population, land rules have evolved from a system of communal rights towards more individualised property rights. Quisumbing et al. write that:

> [In western Ghana] [u]ncultivated forestland is owned by the community or village, and the village chief serves as the custodian of forest area. In reality, village forest is open access for the community members, as was the case also for migrants when the forestland was abundant. Thus, the clearance of forest is easily approved by the chief, so long as forestland is available. Forest clearance requires a large effort, and those who clear forests are rewarded by relatively strong individual rights to land. Such individually rewarded land rights are further strengthened if land converters make long-term or permanent improvements in the land such as tree planting. (Quisumbing et al., 2001: 55)[4]

The authors go on to note that property rights weaken when land lies fallow for extended periods of time. Over time, rules

---

4   See Quisumbing et al. (2001: 55). The authors note (p. 56) that these changes may have been strengthened by the passage, in 1985, of the Intestate Succession Law, which allows wives and children to inherit land from husbands who die intestate, something that was not possible under older customary law. This may be a case of legislation reflecting changing social norms, though the opposite could also be true: the law may have pushed social norms towards greater individualisation of property rights.

regarding the transfer of land have also changed. In the past, when land was plentiful, property devolved to nephews and other male family members. But as property has become increasingly scarce, and valuable, more men are giving property directly to their wives and children with the consent of family members. These gifts of property occur during the man's life and are formalised in ceremonies. Once the gift is given, the new owners have individualised rights to the land.

Migrants to cocoa-producing areas have also developed more individualised rights to property over time. In their case, some property is acquired through gifts, but more is acquired through sales and rental arrangements. The latter call for migrants to clear forestland, plant it with cocoa trees and tend the trees for a period of time, after which the ownership of the land will be divided between the original owner and the migrant (ibid.: 62). '[L]and scarcity stimulates land market transactions,' Quisumbing et al. argue (ibid.: 55). And land markets will allow some individuals to consolidate holdings, a prospect that some will find undesirable but others will see as paving the way for productivity gains in cocoa production, with benefits for cocoa farmers, their families and, the authors argue, the local environment. In western Ghana and other areas, people will often plant trees in order to establish stronger individualised land rights. Land that people wish to transfer through a gift is most often planted with cocoa trees as a way of creating stronger rights for a relatively new class of property claimants: wives and children. As the authors note: 'It is a mistake to assume that incentives to invest in land governed by customary land tenure rules are universally very weak' (ibid.: 64). With a detailed understanding of the local property-rights environment, these authors were able to describe its evolutionary nature.

Individualisation and formalisation

Will communal property inevitably transform into individualised, freehold property? Probably not; in some situations it remains the case that the costs associated with this move are prohibitive. Communal property serves particular needs for some societies (social insurance and risk-sharing, among others). In addition: 'property conventions, norms, and customs are often more predictable and unchanging than statutory law itself' (Blocher, 2006: 173). There is no reason to expect an inexorable move from communal to individual property under customary systems. The shift should happen in response to changing conditions and changes in the relative value of resources. As a given community experiments with new ways to adapt, it may opt for more individualised property rights or it may not.

A related question is whether changes towards greater individualisation inevitably lead to the creation of legal titles to property. Platteau argues they may not, and for good reason: so long as rights to use and 'gift' or rent the land are secure and defendable, formal titles might be desirable but not necessary for economic development (Platteau, 1996: 27–86). Alternatives to formal land titling exist. For example in Uganda the government registers certificates of customary ownership. This less formal process of securing tenure is facilitated by technological advances. Countries may use a geographical information database/system (GIS) that captures details about land parcels, rather than a more elaborate cadastral system (Sanjak, 2004). Sanjak notes: 'These systems [GIS] have the potential to make information more reliable and easier to obtain, thus making it easier to understand and price risk. This is especially important where court systems are neither efficient nor equitable and where access to and quality of information on real property has been problematic.' Formal titling programmes and cadastral registries are costly to create and implement effectively, so their creation and management will involve difficult trade-offs for developing nations – trade-offs between the potential for increased legal certainty over the status of ownership and other desirable social goals.

Do these examples offer any lessons about the evolutionary path to property? The evolutionary path is not perfect – it can be usurped and used to benefit some groups or individuals over others. The process of rule change under customary law can be slow and frustrating, but the system does promote flexibility. Given that customary law is an organic system, it may reflect the customs and social norms of the group to which it applies more closely than legislation. If so, there would be less reason to be concerned about a gap between de facto property rights and *de jure* property rights. Reducing gaps between the two may help lessen conflict. Further, in societies with predatory centralised governments, an evolutionary path that relies on customary law to allocate and enforce property rights may provide an important counterbalance to political power.

REFERENCES

Alden Wiley, L. (2006), 'The commons and customary law in modern times: rethinking the orthodoxies', in *Land Rights for African Development*, Washington, DC: Consultative Group on International Agricultural Research.

Blocher, J. (2006), 'Note: building on custom: land tenure policy and economic development in Ghana', *Yale Human Rights and Development Law Journal*, 9: 173.

Boudreaux, K. C. (2005b), 'The human face of conflict: property and power in Nigeria', *San Diego International Law Journal*, 7(1): 61–102.

Durand-Lasserve, A. (2006), 'Informal settlements and the Millennium Development Goals: global policy debates on property ownership and security of tenure', *Global Urban Development*, 2(1): 1–15.

Falola, T. (1999) *The History of Nigeria*, Westport, CT: Greenwood Press.

Netting, R. M. (1968), *The Hill Farmers of Nigeria*, Seattle: University of Washington Press.

Netting, R. M., M. P. Stone and G. Stone (1989), 'Kofyar cash cropping: choice and change in indigenous agricultural development', *Human Ecology*, 17(3): 299–319.

Olawale Elias. T. (1962), *Nigerian Land Law and Custom*, London: Routledge and Kegan Paul.

Platteau, J.-P. (1996), 'The evolutionary theory of land rights as applied to sub-Saharan Africa: a critical assessment', *Development and Change*, 27: 27–86.

Quisumbing, A., J. B. Aidoo, E. Payongayong and K. Otsuka (2001), 'Agroforestry management in Ghana', in K. Otsuka and F. Place (eds), *Land Tenure and Natural Resource Management*, Baltimore, MD, p. 55.

Sanjak, J. (2004), 'Commentary and reaction to theme paper/ legal and regulatory requirements for effective rural financial markets', Paper presented at Paving the Way Forward for Rural Finance, Conference on Best Practices, available at: *www.basis.wisc.edu/rfc/documents/theme_legal_r1.pdf*.

Williams, D. C. (1992), 'Measuring the impact of land reform policy in Nigeria', *Journal of Modern African Studies*, 30: 587.

[14]

AN INTELLECTUAL TOOLBOX FOR THE CREATION OF PROPERTY RIGHTS

The international development community – policy analysts, economists, decision-makers, donors – quite often sees its role as 'fixing' economies and setting them on the path of growth, much as doctors cure patients, or engineers repair very complex machines. Whether we fully accept this analogy or not, it clearly implies that in order to fulfil such a task both theoretical and practical knowledge are needed. Those involved in designing development strategies should understand the specifics of the cases they address and also understand the conditions and instruments of institutional change.

In dealing with property-rights creation, as in many other cases of institutional change, the main challenge is to find a balance between general knowledge and local knowledge, between change via evolution with its (often) gradual shifts in informal rules and norms and change via legislation with its shifts in formal rules. As noted above, the available strategies are defined by the various combinations of the two extremes: the spontaneous, bottom-up, evolutionary route and the top-down, precisely targeted, fiat approach, taking into account the many factors that will impact the implementation and enforcement of rights. The real-life practice in policy and institutional design strategy requires us to position our approaches on this spectrum of possible positions, as there is no unique solution. Finding a balance between the two extreme types requires fine tuning and calibration on a case-by-case basis.

This does not mean, however, that we are left with arbitrary alternatives. There are ways to obtain discipline and focus. One can better marry design to reality when informed by a specific conceptual framework rooted in the accumulated experience of property-rights policies in international development. In other words, property-rights policies could deal with complexity and the difficult task of finding an appropriate balance between different approaches by making reference to a set of insights derived from the accumulated findings of scholarly research and practical experience. One could think of these both as lessons based on past experiences and as intellectual tools in the toolbox of the designer of property-rights systems.

The process view of property-rights systems

Some international development agencies have begun to recognise that all institutions, including property rights, are part and parcel of a dynamic system (USAID, 2007). The factors that determine the property-rights configurations are many, complex and volatile, and changes in these factors will have unmistakable consequences. Property rights transform, adapt and reconfigure. For example, changes in property-rights technology can alter the costs associated with defining, enforcing or transferring rights. In turn, changes in these costs may alter the structure of the property-rights arrangement. In similar ways, informal rules may be altered in response to increasing scarcity or owing to changes in the values and beliefs shaping them. One may also expect property rights to be affected by developments in knowledge and technology. The transition from public to private property or the move from common to more individualised property should not be seen as an isolated sequence of events but rather as elements of a larger process. The movement from public to private (whether individual or common property) simultaneously creates and destroys rights, and this creation and destruction will have distributional effects.

Even when a property-rights configuration has stabilised within the private-property category, there are still various arrangements and forms in that category that get continually shaped and reshaped by contextual factors. This is in no way a mechanical process: in many cases the various configurations of property rights are a matter of sequencing and path dependency. If public or regulatory property emerges first, then the incentives for the discovery of private-property-rights technology may be weakened (Yandle, 2001). The process moves on specific paths and not on others. If the above is correct, then it is a mistake to limit our view of property rights to a mere static configuration of rules and laws and an associated set of incentives. To sum up: a process view of property rights puts their nature in better perspective and is entirely justifiable.

Property rights are in fact elements of an ongoing social process proceeding as the technological, social and economic environment is changing – a fact that many advocates of property rights (in all their forms) tend to forget. They assume a static view, which assumes that arrangements are frozen in place or aims at creating such arrangements. But this may be both theoretically and practically misleading. The fundamental objective of the property-rights initiatives may get distorted. Seen through the process lens, the policy objective is not just to create a specific

AN INTELLECTUAL TOOLBOX FOR THE CREATION OF PROPERTY RIGHTS

configuration but to create an institutional structure able to respond dynamically to ongoing changes in costs, technologies, social circumstances, etc. In other words, the objective would be the fluidity of the property-rights bundles so that they were free to adjust as changes in costs thresholds or changes in public or individual preferences became evident.

These observations correspond with a more general point of social theory and institutional policy made by Norman Barry. As Barry puts it, there are two basic traditions competing in social and political theory: an 'end-state' (or final outcome) approach and a 'process' (a chain of causes and consequences) approach. The end-state social theory attempts an understanding of social phenomena through 'a description of the features of a society at a specified point in time' – especially the features predetermining the society's distribution of income, wealth, power, prestige, status and the structures of the economic and political systems. On the normative side, it creates an ideal, a final state or goal, and declares its implementation the final purpose of politics (Barry, 1998: 25). In contrast, there is the process theory, which supports a 'decentralised activity, interaction and co-ordination of social action and shuns away from the government direction or planning designed to produce a predetermined state' (ibid.):

> They may also be called procedural theories, since they are pre-eminently concerned with the nature of the rules in an orderly, regularized society; acting and choosing individuals who follow them can be said to generate certain end-states. Social scientists who analyse processes that produce end-states are especially interested in constitutions. Their evaluation will thus not be confined to the end-state itself but will focus essentially on the procedural rules and human actions that generated it. (ibid.: 26)

Seen from this perspective, one of the common fallacies in the strategies of creating or reforming property rights is to think exclusively in terms of end-states and neglect thinking in terms of process. As we have seen, when dealing with property rights we are dealing with complex dynamics involving a multitude of factors. A change of emphasis from end-states to process has important practical implications. Rather than being fixated with a particular, unchangeable configuration of rights, the change process itself becomes just as important as the favoured arrangement. Instead of unfreezing an institutional arrangement just to refreeze it in a new configuration, the goal becomes making the system flexible, adaptable and resilient, resonating closely with the preferences of individuals on the ground. Such an approach implies special attention to exchange, transfer and transactions factors, and to the communication and exchange of information needed for coordination among rights-holders or stakeholders (Yandle, 2001: 8). Transfers and transactions based on the voluntary decisions of the holders and stakeholders are the ways through which the readjustment intrinsic to a dynamic and responsive property-rights system takes place. The process view can therefore be operationalised by creating the institutional conditions to facilitate such exchanges.

Adopting the idea of process implies the acceptance of the irreducible tension between the process view and the end-state view and with it the paradox of process thinking. Whether we like it or not, even when advocating a process view, we explicitly or implicitly operate with an end-state in mind: the end-state is merely shifted at a meta level. It simply becomes the 'constitutional' framework that facilitates the property-rights process, a framework that defines the parameters of the optimal dynamics of the process. This observation draws on the work of Elinor Ostrom,

AN INTELLECTUAL TOOLBOX FOR THE CREATION OF PROPERTY RIGHTS

who introduces the distinction between the operational level, the collective-choice level and the constitutional level as a useful way of understanding the complexity of human action within institutional frameworks (Ostrom, 2005). *Constitutional-level* rules determine how a group may craft collective-choice rules that in turn govern the way future collective decisions are made. The *collective-choice level* is the level at which 'officials' determine, enforce or alter the basic framework within which actions take place. Legislation is a well-documented example of collective-choice rules (Hayek, 1973). Finally, the *operational level* is the level of everyday life decisions.

Under this schematic, the meta level (constitutive level) is the framework within which the rules governing future collective decisions are determined. The bottom or operational level consists of direct actions and rules depending on and directly reacting to everyday, concrete circumstances and expectations. The sphere of action and scope of decision-making at this level are established by the other, higher levels. These operational actions and decisions, however, affect the higher levels in an indirect and aggregate way. In the end, a feedback loop is always possible, leading to the gradual alteration of the meta level.

The daily activity in a market nicely illustrates such decisions. Public choice and constitutional rules are gradually changed as a result of the dynamics set into motion by the exchange process. If market relations *do* promote changes not only in the allocation and production of resources but also in norms and institutions, towards higher levels of social efficiency, fairness and trust, then expanding opportunities for trade may positively affect the different layers by making the property systems of a society more functional and secure.

The interplay of the formal and informal

For those interested in property-rights reform it is essential to understand whether or not the de facto property environment matches or tracks de jure rules. This is a recurring theme in both the institutionalist and land-tenure literature. Authors such as Ensminger point to 'the importance of *complementarities* between informal and formal institutions' (Ensminger, 1997: 166). She argues that: '[w]hen formal systems are imposed upon a society with which they are out of accord, self-enforcement may erode and externally engineered incentives may fail to yield the predicted results' (ibid.).

If, for example, the de facto environment, and the social norms that support it, are opposed to particular property allocations (such as women inheriting property or property rights shifting towards individualisation), the de jure creation of such allocations may be a fruitless exercise. If the institutional environment is weak and de jure property rights cannot be exercised (because it is too costly to do so), a gap exists and property reformers would be well advised to attend to the institutional weaknesses if they hope to create meaningful benefits for the de jure rights-holders.

Understanding the de facto property environment will help reformers understand who may gain and who may lose if rules change. With this knowledge, reformers will be better equipped to identify or create coalitions to support any legislative changes in favour of individualisation (if that path is desirable). And finally, with an understanding of the de facto situation, reformers will be better able to identify possible property-rights entrepreneurs or those who can push positive changes in norms.

It is relatively easy to initiate changes to a nation's legal code. Creating an environment in which property rights are both broadened (provided to more citizens) and made more secure, however, will take more than an addition to the appropriate section of the constitution, land law or other property statute. Creating such a secure property-rights environment will require policymakers to adopt an integrated approach that identifies related deficiencies in the judicial and police systems, reduces transaction costs for registering property claims, recognises and understands how social norms relate to the proposed change and works with the various stakeholders affected – those who stand to lose from the changes as well as those who stand to gain. Without this deep local knowledge of the de facto property rights and their environment, top-down legislative approaches are unlikely to succeed.

Incentives, costs and the critical role of economic thresholds

Those promoting reforms should keep in mind the important fact that property rights have an economic basis. In other words, there are economic thresholds beyond which it is cost-effective or economically rational to introduce property rights (Kagwanja, 2006). Conversely there are thresholds under which costs hinder their emergence. In some situations people have incentives to define, create and enforce property rights, while under different circumstances such incentives are lacking. It has already been pointed out that the standard narrative of the emergence of property rights begins with a situation illustrated by the 'tragedy of the commons' and ends with some proposed property-rights solution. This is a story of economic thresholds. The initial property arrangement may vary: common, public or private property rights. But in all cases, an investment in a costly mechanism to define, monitor and enforce the right is required. Irrespective of its specific form, a right requires instruments and costs to keep it in existence. Thus economic considerations are introduced into the picture. The threshold beyond which it becomes economically feasible to sustain the property rights in question is an indirect measure of the availability of those instruments. Only when it is cost-effective to claim, define, monitor and/or enforce a certain right is it possible for a property-rights arrangement to emerge (Demsetz, 1967; Anderson and Hill, 1975, 2001; Barzel, 1997; Libecap, 1989; Ostrom, 1990).

The notion of 'economic threshold' could be further elaborated as it usually implies the existence of several conditions (Yandle, 2001: 1–2). The demand dimension of the threshold is one of these. This threshold is reached when the resources at issue increase in value owing to growing demand. Increasing demand for a resource changes the opportunity costs of investing in the instruments needed to maintain the rights over it. But this is just one aspect of the problem. For the property-rights threshold to be met, cost-effective technologies for measuring, monitoring and enclosing must also exist. Without appropriate technologies the task of identifying units of the resource, so that they may be claimed and transferred, may be impossible. Even at a constant demand for resources, the declining cost of the technologies could lead to a breaking point. Once these technologies become available, the conditions for property rights to emerge are in place. This was the case in the American West with the invention of barbed wire, a low-cost technology available to enclose, and hence readily identify, property rights (see below).

An additional economic dimension is given by the problem

AN INTELLECTUAL TOOLBOX FOR THE CREATION OF PROPERTY RIGHTS

of wealth-distribution effects. People may accept or reject a property-rights arrangement based on how they perceive its distributional consequences. Only when the impact of the redistribution is mitigated in acceptable forms is it likely that a property-rights arrangement will be relatively stable (Libecap, 1989: 11–12). One may have a situation in which demand for property rights and the technology to define and enforce them exist, but the arrangement is unsustainable because of distributive issues. Side payments may be required to satisfy those interested in maintaining the status quo. The exact forms the property rights take are affected by this factor. If the distributional cost hurdle is too high, individualised property rights may not emerge. Political or regulatory property rights will emerge instead.

Property-rights creation initiatives should always pay attention to the economic sustainability of the solution advanced or desired. As long as the solutions are not supported by the various economic thresholds they are unlikely to be effective. It is not enough to design and pass legislation to change rules. To become functional such rules need the support of an entire institutional apparatus. In too many cases the reform plans are made without paying the slightest attention to that apparatus and the relevant economic variables.

Property-rights technology – the pivot of the property-rights system

The rules and incentives that give substance to property-rights systems depend on institutional and technological means of defining, monitoring and enforcing them. Understanding the means by which the various economic thresholds are dealt with

in practice during the process of creating property rights is crucial
for policymakers. Although the importance of property-rights
technologies has been studied in the literature (Anderson and
Hill, 1975, 2001; Anderson and Leal, 1991; Libecap, 1989), the
full significance of the problem for attempts to create property-
rights systems in international development programmes has not
been sufficiently explored. The logic is inescapable: because the
economic (or feasibility) threshold is critical for property-rights
creation, the techniques needed or available to overcome it should
be central to the effort. As a leading scholar in the field has pointed
out, what is broadly defined as 'property-rights technologies'
necessarily occupies a key role in our strategy of creating property
rights (Yandle, 2001: 2). Understanding the nature and operation
of rules and incentives is a foundational element of a development strategy, but the applicability and viability of these insights
in creating institutional systems of property rights depend on the
technology used.

Property-rights technologies vary from simple technical
devices to complex arrangements. For example, Anderson and
Hill (1975) show how the introduction of barbed wire in the
American West allowed people to divide and enclose grazing
land at lower cost. The process starts with a demand threshold.
There was growing demand for the capability to enclose land and
exclude competing grazing animals. Creative people observed
the opportunity for profit. 'Inventions occur. Ergo, barbed
wire is born.' But this is just a part of the story. For land to be
enclosed with the help of barbed wire an environment is needed
in which rights can be defined, defended and divested so that
rights-holders have the incentive to search for ways to capture
potential profits by installing the new technology. In other

AN INTELLECTUAL TOOLBOX FOR THE CREATION OF PROPERTY RIGHTS

words, a critical element is omitted from the model if one does not take into account the entire institutional context. As Yandle (ibid.) puts it, 'the legal institutions that condition and affect the definition and enforcement of property rights need to be explicitly considered. For the barbed-wire story to hold, the cattlemen occupying western land must first be able to exercise the right to enclose the land'. Thus one could see a very interesting interplay of institutional and technological factors at work (Libecap, 1989: 60–64).

A contemporary example of how new technologies affect the definition of property rights involves the use of Global Positioning System (GPS) technology. Until recently, in order to document property boundaries topographic maps and traditional surveys were employed. Today, however, relatively low-cost Geographical Information Systems (GIS), including hand-held GPS devices, allow local people to create extremely accurate boundaries for property. In areas with difficult terrain, where there are few surveyors, or where financial resources are scarce, this technological shift allows people to identify, monitor and enforce property lines with great precision. A potential benefit of the technology is that resource-related conflicts may lessen as a result of increased accuracy.[1]

A different way of formulating the problem of property-rights creation technology is to start by considering that creating property rights is an (un)bundling process. As Yandle (2001: 3–8) explains, if landownership is seen as a bundle of potential rights, it is easy to see that 'lacking demand, some specialized rights might not be unbundled and traded in the market, just as some function

---

1   For information on this process, see Watermeier (2006).

within a firm awaiting growth in demand for a specialized service might remain integrated'. An unbundling depends on the existing property-rights technology available (including the 'institutional technology'). Thus the notion of unbundling may be a good vehicle for clarification of the idea of property-rights technology. The following simple list of actions illustrates the functions this technology fulfils: identify and measure the resource; defend the defined rights to the resource; enable rights to be transferred or divested; identify, assess and pre-empt threats and harm; provide information, feedback and recorded agreement, etc.

The concept of property-rights technology is an important component of the intellectual toolbox of reformers. At the same time one should not forget that it is an umbrella concept whose main function is practice-oriented. Considering it in a rigid fashion may miss the entire point. Instead, one should use it as a way of focusing attention on critical elements of the process of property-rights creation and, more precisely, on how this process implies the existence of functional instruments and techniques aimed at solving the numerous practical and operational problems intrinsic to it. Becoming aware of the crucial role of these instruments is a condition of a constructive policy approach. Instead of seeing property-rights creation as a mere fiat exercise in which 'laws' and 'rules' are promulgated in the hope that they will lead to the desired results, the notion of property-rights technology focuses our attention on the precise technical and institutional arrangements required to make those rules stick.

AN INTELLECTUAL TOOLBOX FOR THE CREATION OF PROPERTY RIGHTS

The crucial empirical content, relevant rules and the danger of 'slogan words'

The successful reform of property-rights institutions and the linkages between them requires an understanding of existing rules, norms and behaviour, and how these are likely to interact with new rules that are introduced. A key precondition for creating effective property rights is developing a grasp of how to ensure rules within a complex system support and reinforce each other. Accordingly, elected officials of national, state and local governments and social scientists may start by asking what rules should be changed to generate specific institutional dynamics or to solve a particular kind of problem.

Identifying the rules and understanding the operational context and implications of those rules is not easy. Authors such as Ostrom (1990, 2005) emphasise the danger of 'slogan words'. One needs to move beyond them in order to identify and describe in concrete terms how rules shape and affect the situation of concern. The task of developing a coherent understanding of how rules fit together to shape observable behaviour and outcomes is more often than not derailed – not so much by the complexity of the cases but by our own cognitive biases and confusions.

The main danger is that slogan words, such as 'privatisation', 'centralisation' or 'decentralisation', are used as substitutes for careful analysis. Instead of falling into the trap of accepting formulaic solutions, one should ask: 'What are the specific rules that we are talking about when we talk about a privatization or decentralization policy? What changes in the incentives of participants will occur if we propose a particular set of new rules versus other potential sets?' (Ostrom, 2005: 182). Indeed, the history of international development is riddled with fiascos that are the result of

97

the belief that something called 'privatisation', once announced and implemented, will miraculously solve a host of economic and social problems.

The danger is to think and approach policy in very general and abstract terms. Even if slogan words are avoided, it is not enough to think in terms of rules and consequences. By definition rules imply a degree of generality. In working with them one could easily fall into the trap of quick-fix and universal solutions inspired by the formula 'rule X should automatically lead to behaviour Y'. For practical purposes this approach is no different from using a 'slogan word'. The solution is to recognise and understand the variety and the contextual parameters determining the application of rules and the emerging consequences. This suggests that one should have more intellectual humility, 'a substantial wariness related to the capacity of humans to design optimal systems without a substantial trial-and-error process so as to learn what works in a particular environment' (ibid.: 184).

Taking the issues that are raised in this toolbox into regular account as policy changes are proposed should help to develop an appreciation that institutional creation is a complex, evolutionary process; hence, institutional change will be similarly complex. Efforts to create secure property rights should therefore begin with as clear and complete an understanding as possible of the various legal rules (formal/informal, local/national/regional/international) that exist in a given place at a given time. Only with such an understanding will policymakers and practitioners be able to identify where on the continuum between top-down legislative fiat and bottom-up evolution any given change should be positioned.

In addition to the legal environment, reformers/practitioners

AN INTELLECTUAL TOOLBOX FOR THE CREATION OF PROPERTY RIGHTS

must attend to the economic and sociological implications of a change to particular property rules. They should also identify other legal rules (banking, local government, conveyancing, labour, etc.) that interact with property rules to have a more accurate sense of the likely effectiveness of change. Add to this complexity the need to understand and appreciate prevailing social norms, to identify the existence or lack of property-rights technologies, both of which affect the cost of change, and one is faced with the daunting challenge of creating a realistic 'map' that will better guide policymaking in pursuit of more secure rights to property. Again, this is not to say that positive action is impossible; it is instead to caution against easy, one-size-fits-all solutions and to vigorously advocate a flexible and nuanced approach to the vital task of securing property rights for more people in the developing world.

REFERENCES

Anderson, T. L. and P. J. Hill (1975), 'The evolution of property rights: a study of the American West', *Journal of Law & Economics*, 18(1): 163–79.

Barry, N. (1998), *The Invisible Hand in Economics and Politics*, London: Institute of Economic Affairs.

Barzel, Y. (1997), *Economic Analysis of Property Rights* (2nd edn), Cambridge: Cambridge University Press.

Demsetz, H. (1967), 'Toward a theory of property rights', *American Economic Review*, 57(2): 350.

Ensminger, J. E. (1997), 'Changing property rights: reconciling formal and informal rights to land in Africa', in J. N. Drobak and J. V. C. Nye (eds), *The Frontiers of the New Institutional Economics*, New York: Academic Press.

Hayek, F. A. (1973), *Law, Legislation, and Liberty*, vol. 1, Chicago, IL: University of Chicago Press.

Kagwanja, J. (2006), 'Land tenure, land reform, and the management of land and natural resources in Africa', in *Land Rights for African Development*, Washington, DC: Consultative Group on International Agricultural Research.

Libecap, G. (1989), 'Contracting for property rights', New York: Cambridge University Press.

Ostrom, E. (1990), *Governing the Commons: The Evolution of Institutions for Collective Action*, Cambridge: Cambridge University Press.

Ostrom, E. (2005), *Understanding Institutional Diversity*.
    Princeton, NJ: Princeton University Press.
USAID (2007), 'Policy reform lessons learned: a review of
    economic growth related policy reform activities in
    developing countries', Washington, DC: USAID.
Watermeier, N. (2006), 'Creating and using geo-referenced field
    boundaries', Ohio Geospatial Program for Agriculture and
    Natural Resources, available at:
    http://geospatial.osu.edu/resources/GeorefBoundaries.pdf.
Yandle, B. (2001), 'Legal foundations for evolving property
    rights technologies', in T. L. Anderson and P. J. Hill (eds),
    The Technology of Property Rights, Lanham, MD: Rowman
    and Littlefield.

[15]

Institutions I

Rule of law, property and contract

A free society is fertile and creative in the sense that its freedom generates alertness to possibilities that may be of use to society; a restriction on the freedom of a society numbs such alertness and blinds society to possibilities of social improvement.

(Kirzner 1979: 239)

Institutions and alertness

The purpose of the following two chapters is to examine the institutional conditions conducive to entrepreneurship. They address the question: what does the theory of entrepreneurship imply will foster the creation, discovery and exploitation of entrepreneurial opportunities? In dealing with this issue, I draw upon the analysis in the previous chapter on the psychological determinants of entrepreneurial alertness. This chapter considers the comparative effectiveness of alternative institutions for evoking a strong sense of personal agency and stimulating entrepreneurial discovery. The starting point is to consider how different conceptions of the entrepreneurial function, its locus and character will affect such comparative analyses.

The chapter then moves on to examine the ideal of freedom as the preeminent constitutional principle for encouraging entrepreneurship. It considers how the principle of freedom is embodied in the rule of law, rights to property and the concept of contract. It puts forward conjectures on what features of constitutional, legal and regulatory rules would generate strong beliefs in personal competence and internal control and would therefore best promote entrepreneurship.

The next chapter investigates other institutions that are conducive to entrepreneurship. It examines the role of money and the impact of political and legal decentralisation on the human propensity to be alert to opportunity. Chapter 5 also considers the specific character of the freedom of entrepreneurial choice and how it is embedded in concrete economic liberties conducive to entrepreneurship. In addition, it reviews empirical studies on the relationship between economic freedom and national economic performance.

58   *Institutions I*

What are institutions?

Institutions supply the structures within which people interact with each other. 'They establish the cooperative and competitive relationships which constitute a society and more specifically an economic order' (North 1981: 201). Institutions are humanly generated constraints on people's behaviour, and they thereby exclude exogenously given constraints imposed by natural phenomena. Of course, although institutions are the result of human action, they are not necessarily the product of human design. That is, these constraints on people's activities need not be deliberately established by some human agency. They can evolve spontaneously (Menger 1996; North 1990). No one need ever have consciously intended to bring these institutions about. Furthermore, institutions can be formal in that they are written down and codified, or they can be informal in the sense that we adhere to them without knowing it and without ever formulating them explicitly.

According to North (1981), the institutional framework comprises three classes of institutional rules: constitutional rules, operating rules and normative behavioural codes. Constitutional rules determine the general character of the political order. They represent the 'superstructure' that regulates the ongoing process of making ordinary laws (i.e. operating rules). Operating rules – for example, various statute laws and regulations, specific common law decisions – specify terms of exchange within the framework of the constitutional rules. Normative behavioural rules are codes of moral behaviour that legitimate the constitutional and operating rules.

This and the next chapter focus upon constitutional rules and, to a lesser degree, operating rules. The emphasis on constitutional rules in the following discussion is not meant to imply that the term 'institutions' should only be applied to constitutional rules. Indeed, Chapter 6 considers shared behavioural norms, which are also institutional rules, as they relate to alternative cultural conceptions of the self.

Constitutional rules are the fundamental and general principles that define the underlying structure of people's rights, including property rights. They specify, allocate and limit the different powers of the state. They also define the general attributes which ordinary (i.e. sub-constitutional) laws and rules must possess in order to be implemented and enforced by government (Hayek 1979: 122). Thus, the general principles of the constitution control the content of lower-order constraints or operating rules generated by the legislature, the judiciary, the executive and the administrative bureaucracy. 'The idea of a constitution, therefore, involves not only the idea of a hierarchy of authority or power but also that of a hierarchy of rules or laws' (Hayek 1960: 178). A constitution might also include rules for modifying constitutional rules.

As stated at the outset, the aim of this chapter is to investigate 'the institutional conditions conducive to entrepreneurship'. The choice of this phrase rather than the term 'institutional *prerequisites*' is quite deliberate, the reason being that it is very difficult to identify the necessary and sufficient conditions for entrepreneurship. Certainly, some environments are more supportive than others to the flourishing of entrepreneurial initiative. But it seems that entrepreneurship can emerge in the most hostile of climates. 'Markets are like weeds, they spring up all over and are impossible to stamp out completely. Wherever there is a gap, alert economic actors will attempt to grasp the opportunity available for personal gain' (Boettke 1993: 65).

This chapter assumes that the relationship between economic institutions and outcomes (including the degree of entrepreneurship) best fits a 'multiple-peaked' vision of economic phenomena rather than a 'single-peaked' view of the world, according to which there is only one distinct set of institutional conditions that is optimally suited to a well-functioning market economy. '[T]he institutional basis for a market economy is not uniquely determined. Formally, there is no single mapping between the market and the set of non-market institutions required to sustain it' (Rodrik 2000: 13). Two societies with similar institutions might produce quite different levels of entrepreneurial activity in any given time period. Alternatively, two capitalist economies with very different institutional arrangements can generate similar degrees of entrepreneurship.

Indeed, entrepreneurship is not restricted to economies formally organised on the decentralised model of classical capitalism. In his discussion of the comparative study of long-period change, Easterbrook (1965: 69–77) claims that a profit-oriented, market-economy entrepreneur is only one particular type of entrepreneurship which is identified with a specific (and, in his opinion, historically unusual) set of institutional and ideological conditions. Schumpeter (1947: 150) too, who considered entrepreneurship exclusively within a capitalist framework, conceded that the entrepreneurial function itself 'is not absent from other forms of society; but capitalist entrepreneurship is a sufficiently distinct phenomenon to be singled out'. In the former Soviet Union, for example, entrepreneurs (in the guise of special intermediaries called *tolkachi*) sprung up within the interstices of the official planned economy, buying and selling commodities on behalf of state enterprises and thereby coordinating production and exchange activity within the overall plan itself (Grossman 1981; Hewett 1988).

In addition, we must even take care to define more precisely what we mean by conditions conducive to entrepreneurship. In particular, we must distinguish between demand-side and supply-side conditions.[1] The former relate to the structure of economic circumstances and incentives in the market environment that gives rise to entrepreneurial opportunities (e.g. market ignorance and resulting price discrepancies). In contrast, supply-side conditions relate to the factors which promote or constrain the generation and application of entrepreneurial alertness. Elsewhere a co-author and I have argued that economists should pay more attention to the supply of entrepreneurship (Hamilton and Harper 1994), and accordingly I focus upon supply-side conditions in this chapter.

60   *Institutions I*

These two sets of conditions, though interrelated, are not the same. For instance, it is conceivable that in a stationary market environment in which there is no change (i.e. no exogenous disturbances, no disappointment of people's plans over time), there are no entrepreneurial opportunities, even though the individuals in that society are potentially entrepreneurial and would be alert to opportunities if only they existed. On the other hand, it is possible that people's plans to buy and sell could be massively discordant – so that there is an abundance of entrepreneurial opportunities – but these opportunities go unnoticed because people do not have the wit to recognise that they exist, with the result that there is no entrepreneurial activity. Both of these scenarios lead to no entrepreneurship, but the reasons for this inactivity are quite different.

The implications of the function, character and unit of alertness

A further difficulty that arises in connection with examining institutional conditions for entrepreneurship is that certain institutional arrangements may favour one type of entrepreneurship over another. For example, one set of institutional conditions may foster arbitrage but discourage long-term innovation. In such situations, it may be difficult to say whether, on balance, that particular institutional framework is or is not conducive to entrepreneurship. It should be noted that this position differs from Kirzner's (1985: 68–69). Kirzner says that what is conducive for low-level entrepreneurship will also be conducive for high-level entrepreneurship, what fosters short-run arbitrage will also promote long-run innovation. The hypothesis is that numerous incremental acts of entrepreneurship – entrepreneurial discoveries of local and mundane bits of unorganised knowledge – constitute a foundation for the emergence of path-breaking Schumpeterian entrepreneurship.

Similarly, it is important to emphasise the key characteristics of entrepreneurial alertness if we are to try to understand the impact of different institutional frameworks on it. The reader will recall from Chapter 2 that entrepreneurship is *not* a factor of production, not even a special kind of productive factor. Entrepreneurial alertness is non-deployable and tacit, it is costless, people who have it cannot be identified *ex ante*, and it cannot be treated in terms of demand and supply curves.

The non-deployable and tacit nature of entrepreneurial alertness, in particular, has profound consequences for institutional analysis. First and foremost is the fact that the potential stock of entrepreneurial alertness in a society cannot be usefully treated as some 'available' quantity of a resource that is to be allocated and used by an economic system. Rather entrepreneurial alertness is *embedded* in the decisions of individuals so that their actions simply reflect their entrepreneurial hunches (Kirzner 1983b: 64–66). Entrepreneurial alertness 'somehow emerges into view at the precise moment when decisions have to be made' (p. 66).

This property of entrepreneurship in turn implies that the potential stock of entrepreneurial alertness in a society cannot be measured objectively. Thus, it is not possible to derive quantitative relationships between measures of a society's stock of entrepreneurial alertness and institutional variables (such as its degree of economic freedom), although it is possible to enquire analytically into how the institutional framework may affect the alertness in which decisions are implanted.

Another characteristic of entrepreneurship that has a major impact upon institutional analysis is that alertness is costless in the sense that no resource inputs are involved in making entrepreneurial discoveries. As mentioned in Chapter 2, alertness does not involve opportunity costs because entrepreneurial discoveries are made spontaneously in the sense that they are acquired entirely without being planned. Entrepreneurs discover profit opportunities, hitherto overlooked, without a deliberate search for information.

One implication of this feature of entrepreneurship is that operating rules (e.g. public policies, such as subsidies or R&D tax write-offs) which aim to reduce the so-called costs of entrepreneurship or search costs do not necessarily increase the supply of pure entrepreneurship because the latter is costless. The costs of entrepreneurship itself cannot be reduced by public policy or any other means.

In addition, it should be noted that price discrepancies and the resultant opportunities for entrepreneurship cannot be wholly explained in terms of high positive transaction and information costs. For even in a market with zero transaction costs, mutually beneficial exchanges between buyers and sellers might still fail to take place (and hence scope for entrepreneurial alertness may still arise). To have access (even access at zero cost) to information about trading opportunities is by no means sufficient to ensure that these opportunities will ever be discovered and exploited. (Free) *access* to information does not correspond to instantaneous *perception* and *awareness* of the usefulness of that information (Kirzner 1973: 227). The implication is that if one institutional framework has lower transaction costs than another, it may not necessarily generate more entrepreneurial activity. If the members of a society were so blinkered that they failed to exhibit one iota of alertness, there would be no discovery of even the most blatant profit opportunities, even under ideal conditions of zero transaction costs.

How the entrepreneurial function is conceived can also influence how we assess an institution's comparative effectiveness in evoking entrepreneurship. For example, if entrepreneurship is considered to be an element inherent in *all* decision-making (including that by consumers, producers, labourers, etc.), then an institutional framework should be assessed for its relative capacity to foster all types of economic agents to exercise their entrepreneurial faculties. However, if we identify entrepreneurship with the aptitudes of only a small fraction of the population (i.e. 'pure' entrepreneurs), then we must assess the degree to which an institutional framework generates individuals who are representative of the entrepreneurial type and the extent to which it excites their alertness. Different operating rules (e.g. immigration policies) will affect the size of the pool of potential entrepreneurs available to a society.

Having explored the major implications of the characteristics of alertness for institutional analysis, we can now move on to consider how institutional conditions affect people's agency beliefs and the degree of their alertness.

Rule-of-law constitutions

The institutional framework affects the entrepreneurial alertness in which decisions are embedded and determines the incentives for discovering and exploiting profit opportunities. This section focuses upon those higher-level institutional factors that are conducive to producing people with heightened entrepreneurial alertness. According to the argument developed here, the institutional environment that is most likely to produce entrepreneurs is one that calls for and encourages strong agency beliefs. As discussed in Chapter 3, personal agency beliefs reflect a person's sense of causal potency. They comprise a set of beliefs about the contingency of events on actions (i.e. locus of control beliefs) and about one's personal competence to undertake the relevant actions (i.e. self-efficacy beliefs). It was argued that alertness is an increasing function of the strength of agency beliefs. That is, people with a strong sense of internal control and personal efficacy tend to be more alert to opportunities. This chapter extends this analysis by considering the effects of the institutional frame-work on people's agency beliefs and thereby their entrepreneurial alertness and behaviour. The implication is that personal agency beliefs and entrepreneurship are endogenous; they can be influenced by political, economic and social variables.

As mentioned earlier, the constitutional framework comprises general principles and ideals that people in the community have committed them-selves to and that they respect. These principles determine the underlying rules, which specify the political, legal and economic systems of a society and therefore the basic rights of its members.

Although these general principles are contained in the constitutional framework, this does not mean that they are necessarily articulated in any constitutional documents. Indeed, these principles are often only vaguely perceived. '[C]onstitutions are based on, or presuppose, an underlying agree-ment on more fundamental principles – principles which may never have been explicitly expressed, yet which make possible and precede the consent and the written fundamental laws' (Hayek 1960: 181). For example, a social consensus about the dimensions of the private sphere of the individual might underpin a rule-of-law constitution that frames entrepreneurial and market activities.

Following Kirzner (1992: 51–54), this work regards freedom as the most important political, legal and economic ideal and constitutional principle that is conducive to entrepreneurship. Indeed, freedom can be considered to be the source of and necessary condition for all other entrepreneurial values, and it is to this general principle that the discussion now turns.

The principle of freedom

This chapter argues that entrepreneurship is most likely to flourish under constitutional arrangements that promote a maximum realisation of the principle of freedom. The central hypothesis is that an environment of freedom, and especially economic freedom, is more likely than other environments to generate strong agency beliefs and acute entrepreneurial alertness. A condition of economic liberty gives all participants the possibility of acting according to their own economic plans and decisions, so that they may direct their energies towards goals that they themselves have chosen rather than towards necessities imposed by powerful others. In an environment of economic freedom, people are more likely to be able to use their skills and knowledge as successfully as possible in the pursuit of their economic ends. Indeed, entrepreneurship in the modern market economy could not exist without a constitutional framework that grants individuals and groups of individuals a large amount of economic freedom. (The next chapter examines the nature of freedom of *entrepreneurial* choice in more detail.)

On the other hand, entrepreneurship is likely to be stifled in conditions where many people are irrevocably subject to the arbitrary will and aggressions of others. People are much less likely to develop a strong sense of agency and hence heightened alertness to economic opportunities if they are constantly coerced into acting or not acting in specific ways by somebody else who has the power to manipulate their environment.

The term freedom has not yet been defined. We must take heed of Leoni's warning that 'we cannot use the word freedom and be rightly understood without first defining clearly the meaning we attach to that word' (1972: 42). This work adopts his definition of freedom as absence of constraint exercised by other people, including the authorities, over the private life and business of each person (p. 78). The terms freedom and liberty will be used interchangeably.

Of course, freedom does not imply the total absence of constraint. There are cases in which at least some people may have to be constrained in order to preserve freedom and to protect individuals from coercion by others, such as murderers or robbers. This also suggests that any analysis of freedom must take into account people's subjective perceptions of the degree of freedom that they enjoy. 'There is no such thing as "freedom" independent of the people who speak of it' (Leoni 1972: 42). At least to the extent that their own interpretation of freedom and of constraint differs from that prevalent within the society to which they belong, some individuals must experience some constraint over their behaviour, even within a 'free' society.

64   *Institutions I*

Although freedom is a negative concept – because it describes the absence
of something, namely coercion by other people – freedom becomes positive
through what people make of it. Freedom can become a shared part of
economic, political and ethical life, an ideal that continually brings people
together and that provides infinite opportunities for them to cooperate and to
adapt themselves to one another, thereby unifying a society (de Tocqueville
1990b: 103–104). Entrepreneurs in particular may make their most valuable
contribution to society by exercising freedoms that are seldom used by others.
Freedom does not guarantee people any particular opportunity or capacity to
get what they want but it allows people to decide for themselves how best to
make use of their particular circumstances for their own purposes.

Freedom is a sociological concept that refers to the social relations
between one person and other people. It is also, and possibly chiefly, a legal
construct because it implies a skein of legal consequences. The law is the
most important institution for attempting to protect individual freedom.
'The law is an order of human freedom' (Karl Binding, as quoted in Hayek
1973: 158). Liberty exists according to the law of a society and is defined by
it. There can be no liberty without law. 'The law, in the most general sense
of the word, is the science of liberty' (Beudant 1891: 5).

Unless specifically indicated otherwise, the emphasis in this work is upon
economic freedom. The key elements of economic freedom include freedom of
entrepreneurial choice, freedom to enter and compete in markets, adherence
to the rule of law, the protection of property rights, freedom of exchange and
freedom of contract. Economic freedom is to be distinguished from political
freedom which encompasses such ingredients as the freedom of opposition
parties to organise and compete and the participation of citizens in the electoral process.

The rule of law

The previous discussion claimed that entrepreneurship in the market is
promoted by a constitutional framework that maximises everyone's freedom
from coercion, especially in the economic sphere. Here it will be argued that
such a framework is most likely to operate according to the rule of law.
Indeed, the rule of law is an essential element of constitutional government.
'Fully articulated, the rule of law amounts to a sophisticated doctrine of
constitutionalism' (Allan 1998: 369). This section defines what is meant by
the rule of law, and it seeks to explain how it affects entrepreneurship.

The rule of law is the legal embodiment of freedom and the basic conception of the law of liberty (Hayek 1944: 61; 1960: 148). The concept is open
to various interpretations. The first, most common understanding of the
term distinguishes the rule or reign of law from rule by arbitrary forms of
government. It emphasises the rule of impersonal law as opposed to
powerful persons. According to the rule of law, political power can only be
wielded within legal constraints so that government is placed under the law.

It limits the functions of government to those that can be carried out by means of general rules.

The second distinct, but related, interpretation regards the rule of law as a 'meta-legal' principle which serves to guide law-makers. In this sense, it is not strictly speaking a rule of the law but a rule *about* the law. It is an imperative about the general attributes that good laws should possess:

> The rule of law is therefore not a rule of the law, but a rule concerning what the law ought to be, a meta-legal doctrine or a political ideal. It will be effective only in so far as the legislator feels bound by it. In a democracy this means that it will not prevail unless it forms part of the moral tradition of the community, a common ideal shared and unquestioningly accepted by the majority.
>
> (Hayek 1960: 206)

Thus, the rule of law requires that all laws conform to specific principles though it does not specify what the *content* of legal rules ought to be. According to Hayek, these principles include the certainty, the generality and the equality of the law.[2] Taken together, these requirements amount to the ideal of the *universality* of the law.

The rule of law is the prerequisite for the concrete rights of the individual, including those economic freedoms that are most important for entrepreneurship. 'The rule of law can be compared to a tree which, from the invisible strong roots of freedom, lets the fruits of liberty branch out and grow and shine in splendor' (Dietze 1976: 117). In the absence of the rule of law, public authorities are prone to issue a flood of arbitrary and inconsistent decrees that can dampen people's sense of agency and therefore their alertness to opportunities:

> All too frequently, the unsystematic proliferation of rules breeds sullen conformity and dissimulation of an individual's true thoughts and motives, a condition that is the opposite of the open competition of ideas and critical assessment of new ideas and experiments; therefore, it is not conducive to effective coordination and innovation, and hence to prosperity and freedom.
>
> (Kasper and Streit 1998: 138)

It is worth emphasising that a legal system cannot sustain the rule of law if there are no shared beliefs about justice. In a democracy, the enforceability of rule-of-law constitutions requires that laws be consistent with cultural values and ethical norms that are widely held by members of the community. The legitimacy of government is based on an expectation that it will enforce widely shared beliefs about what is just. (For a general discussion of the values, norms and attitudes necessary for or conducive to the rule of law, see Voigt 1993: 505–506.)

66   *Institutions I*

More specifically, as Weingast (1995; 1997) argues, the enforceability of constitutions based on the rule of law depends upon the existence of a social consensus about the appropriate limits of state action. In this context, a social consensus does not mean that everyone shares identical values. Rather, there must be a consensus among citizens about which potential actions by the state represent a violation of constitutional constraints as well as a consensus about what they will do to defend the constitution whenever the state tries to transgress its legitimate boundaries. Only then are the constitutional limits on political officials *self-enforcing* in the sense that those in power have the incentive to comply with the restrictions on their behaviour (Hardin 1989; Ordeshook 1992). Only then is the people's threat of retaliation in the event of a fundamental transgression credible. 'The ultimate sanction on a government is the withdrawal of support by a sufficient portion of its citizens so that the government cannot survive' (Weingast 1995: 26).[3] (The discussion of political decentralisation in Chapter 5 deals with the issue of self-enforcing limits in further detail.)

Because it is difficult for citizens to coordinate their views on the legitimate role of the state, the emergence of a consensus is by no means automatic or inevitable. Failure to resolve this coordination problem hinders the enforcement of a rule-of-law constitution. In the absence of a consensus and organised opposition, the state will be able to get away with infringing the rights of all or some citizens, sometimes playing off one group against another. If governments continually succeed in violating constitutional constraints with impunity, citizens are most likely to come to perceive the constitution as a 'book of hopes' with no connection to the real world, as a 'set of *desiderata* largely irrelevant for actual government behavior' (Voigt 1998: 206). Such has been the experience of many societies in Latin America.

In addition, the rule of law requires a civil society in which citizens are, by and large, law abiding and in which informal enforcement mechanisms (such as social ostracism) supplement coercive sanctions administered by the courts. The importance of this becomes all too clear when one considers the limits to the government's ability to enforce the law through compulsion. Kasper and Streit (1998: 139) quote one estimate, admittedly highly speculative, that at any given moment government can enforce by coercion at most 3 to 7 per cent of all formal legal norms.

Let us now return to a more detailed examination of the nature of the rule of law and flesh out its implications for the supply of entrepreneurial alertness. Each of the three attributes of good laws – certainty, generality and equality – will be considered below.

The certainty of the law

It is desirable to explain what certainty of the law actually means. Leoni (1972: 95) defines certainty of the law as 'the possibility open to individuals of making long-run plans on the basis of a series of rules spontaneously adopted by people in common and eventually ascertained by judges through centuries and generations'. Certainty of the law means that the law is not subjected to sudden and unpredictable changes. Its incidence is predictable. This conception of legal certainty does not mean, and may even be incompatible with, the notion of a series of precisely worded written rules laid down by legislatures. Indeed, many rules implicit in the body of the law may never be articulated explicitly.

The certainty of the law is probably the most important principle for entrepreneurship and other economic activities. 'There is probably no single factor which has contributed more to the prosperity of the West than the relative certainty of the law which has prevailed here' (Hayek 1960: 208). The conventional wisdom is that the legal framework must be sufficiently certain to enable entrepreneurs to make their plans. Entrepreneurs must be able to find out, with reasonable confidence, whether specific actions are either demanded or proscribed by the law. They must be able to foresee with a fair degree of certainty whether their planned conduct is within or outside the law. When the decisions of courts are consistent and predictable, many commercial disputes do not result in litigation because the outcome is already clear once the relevant facts of the case are identified.

It should be noted that the certainty of the law does not mean the absence of change, but it does mean that entrepreneurs can make their plans on the basis of present legal rules without finding that the rules have been overturned overnight by legislative U-turns. In short, entrepreneurs can expect that today's legal rules will be tomorrow's rules. A consequence of such certainty of the law is that an inefficient but stable legal *rule* does not necessarily imply inefficient economic *behaviour*, provided that entrepreneurs and other participants can bargain around the rule. Consider a legal system in which judges decide cases according to precedent (i.e. by applying rulings from similar cases in the past). As Rizzo (1985) explains, this type of legal order can promote the entrepreneurial processes that generate coordination of economic action because it enforces a stable framework of legal rules against which private economic actors can bargain, assuming low transaction costs of exchange.[4] The market prices of goods and services can be in constant flux, but provided that the institutions governing market exchanges are relatively stable, entrepreneurs will by and large be able to adapt to new circumstances and bring about greater consistency in market transactions in different parts of the market. 'The seas may be choppy, but so long as the buoys are anchored firmly navigation can proceed safely' (Wagner 1998: 316). Incessant and unpredictable changes in laws render entrepreneurs unable to use legal rules to orient themselves in making their plans. As discussed later, retrospective (*ex post facto*) laws in particular flagrantly contravene the principle of legal certainty.

In order to exploit perceived profit opportunities, innovators in particular must often plan many years into the future. Innovative entrepreneurs need to foresee that the result of actions decided upon today will be free from legal interference by the authorities tomorrow. The greater the certainty of the law, the more confident they can be of the legal effects of their innovative behaviour, and the more likely they are to discover and to exploit opportunities which involve coordinating transactions entered into at different times.

However, the relationship between the certainty of the law and entrepreneurship is not quite so clear cut. For instance, single-period arbitragers can benefit from accelerated and unpredictable law-making processes which give rise to temporary profit opportunities. This is particularly the case with those entrepreneurs who specialise in the more or less instantaneous discovery and exploitation of tax loopholes created by legislative changes. Speculators too may benefit. Speculative entrepreneurs may seek to profit from legal uncertainty – the uncertainty that current statutes may be replaced at any stage by subsequent laws – especially if they believe themselves to have superior hunches about potential legal developments.

There is thus an element of apparent indeterminacy in the effects of legal certainty upon entrepreneurship. Although this difficulty is still to be resolved satisfactorily, some preliminary conjectures can be put forward now in the interests of furthering the debate.

In the first instance, it seems that expedient changes in legal rules affect what were earlier referred to as 'demand-side' institutional conditions. They relate to the structure of economic circumstances and incentives in the market environment. More formally, these legal changes constitute exogenous disturbances in Kirzner's model of the economic system. They disrupt people's previously coordinated plans and generate fresh opportunities for pure gain. As such, they create scope for entrepreneurial activity.

However, the mere existence of these opportunities is not in itself sufficient to generate entrepreneurial activity – especially if we take into account the possibility that no one may become aware of these opportunities. Some profit opportunities arising from changes in legal rules may never be discovered.

In addition, the entrepreneurial discovery process that is set in motion by successive ad hoc regulatory and legislative changes may be 'wholly superfluous', in the sense that they create entirely new profit opportunities that would not have existed in the absence of these changes (Kirzner 1985: 145). At the same time, these changes also reduce or wipe out opportunities for social improvement that might otherwise have been present in a market governed by general legal rules.

Another point is that the changes in the law that give rise to arbitrage tend not to be holistic changes. They usually involve minor tinkering within a legal *superstructure*, which, to use Lachmann's (1971) terminology, is an external institution which constitutes the outer framework of society. The broad characteristics of this 'external' legal order tend to remain relatively stable over time.

Indeed, the emergence of entrepreneurial *alertness* depends upon certainty of the legal superstructure (i.e. constitutional order). Even when they identify tax loopholes, arbitragers rely upon the fact that legal norms will continue to allow them to exploit the opportunities they discover and to retain the profits they capture. They do not expect their profits to be arbitrarily confiscated by the state. 'Some institutions must be flexible enough to adjust to change, while others, by contrast, must be sufficiently resistant to change to make the outcome of intertemporal [market] transactions predictable' (Lachmann 1979: 77).

The generality and equality of the law

The second and third principles of good laws implied by the ideal of the rule of law are the generality and the equality of the law. These two principles require that all legal rules apply equally to everybody, including those who are entrusted with political power, and that rules are of such general nature that they can be applied without arbitrary discretion. General and equal laws abstract from the specific circumstances of time and place, and they apply, in a non-discriminatory manner, whenever certain abstractly defined conditions are met (Hayek 1955: 35). This is clearly an ideal. In this sense, good laws are like universal scientific hypotheses: they are general rules rather than specific schemes relating to the state of the world at particular times and places. Indeed, generality is the most significant feature of the abstract character of law.

The generality and equality of the law are important for entrepreneurship especially given that it is not possible to preselect entrepreneurial individuals. General abstract rules are applicable to an unforeseeable range of entrepreneurs and innovative cases. These rules do not make any references to particular persons. Similarly, a fundamental characteristic of entrepreneurship in modern market economies is that entrepreneurs are not known in advance. They are generally those who are alert to possible opportunities. As a result, many unknown entrepreneurs may take part in attempts to solve any particular market problem.

Because it is not possible to identify entrepreneurs *ex ante* (at least for any particular market opportunities prior to their discovery), it is essential that the institutional framework provide each person with the maximum freedom of enterprise compatible with equal freedom for all other people. The equality of the law is aimed at equally improving the chances of as yet unknown entrepreneurs.

General and equal laws provide the most effective protection against encroachment of the state on individual liberty. The ideal of the rule of law requires that the state act under the same law and therefore be limited in the same manner as any private person. It thereby restricts the coercive activities of government:

> It is not to be denied that even general, abstract rules, equally applicable to all, may possibly constitute severe restrictions on liberty. But

when we reflect on it, we see how very unlikely this is. The chief safeguard is that the rules must apply to those who lay them down and
those who apply them – that is, to the government as well as the
governed – and that nobody has the power to grant exceptions. If all
that is prohibited and enjoined is prohibited and enjoined for all
without exception ... and if even authority has no special powers except
that of enforcing the law, little that anybody may reasonably wish to do
is likely to be prohibited.

(Hayek 1960: 154–155)

The generality of the law reinforces its certainty. General laws are more
predictable~than specific, ad hoc commands issued by a public authority. By
specifying beforehand the circumstances in which action must satisfy certain
conditions and providing the framework within which entrepreneurs can
form their plans, general rules make the legal consequences of
entrepreneurial action more predictable.

The requirement of general and equal laws for all persons is conducive to
freedom, a strong sense of personal agency – particularly internal LOC
beliefs – and hence entrepreneurship. Under the rule of law, entrepreneurs
know that their sphere of personal agency (i.e. the area of legally guaranteed
freedom) includes all actions not explicitly prohibited by general legal rules.
Because general laws specify beforehand the conditions and the manner in
which people can expect to be coerced, entrepreneurs can determine with
reasonable confidence the boundaries of the law within which they can exercise their own will and causal powers. They also know that these boundaries
apply equally to everybody. In this way, general laws allow entrepreneurs to
make the best use of their own unique competences and localised knowledge
in their seizing of profit opportunities.

In a society governed by the rule of law, entrepreneurs know that their
actions do not depend on gaining the permission of any government
authority (provided they keep within the legal delimitation of their private
sphere of agency). In addition, entrepreneurs know they will not be subject
to sudden administrative orders directing them personally to undertake
specific actions. It is true that general rules might eliminate some options
otherwise open to entrepreneurs. But the point is that they do not constrain
the choice sets of entrepreneurs to such an extent that their preferred course
of action will and must be that which most benefits some external authority
(Hayek 1960: 133, 153). Entrepreneurs do still have genuine choices to
make. The contracts they conclude are entered into voluntarily, as acts of
entrepreneurial autonomy.

General, abstract laws are long-term rules and are only ever *forward
looking* in their effect. General rules guide entrepreneurial action; they are
data that entrepreneurs can use as a basis for their planning activities. In
contrast, retroactive legislation cannot affect entrepreneurial action, since
entrepreneurs have already taken and implemented their decisions prior to

the promulgation of such laws. Retrospective legal rules add to entrepreneurial uncertainty since they undermine the standing of laws that are prospective in their effect; the likelihood of retrospective legislation, by definition, places existing and subsequent forward-looking legal rules under the threat of retrospective changes (Fuller 1964: 38–39).

The retrospective enforcement of changes in the law significantly inhibits entrepreneurial freedom and autonomy, and it diminishes entrepreneurs' sense of personal agency. In the first instance, their LOC beliefs become less internal because the outcome of market transactions is seen to be vulnerable to the whims of those in power. In particular, entrepreneurs come to perceive that the legal consequences of their transactions are less contingent upon their knowledge of existing law and their understanding of just conduct. In addition, their sense of self-efficacy is likely to fade because entrepreneurs feel they never know the legal rules that they are expected to observe. They are unable to plan their actions by relying upon the application of pre-existing law. The dampening of personal agency caused by the abuse of retrospective legislation thereby inhibits alertness to market opportunities.

The requirement of general and equal laws also implies the absence of privilege and arbitrary discrimination. General legal rules do not single out particular entrepreneurs or groups of entrepreneurs.[5] Nor do they benefit or harm identifiable business people in a predictable manner. (The principle of legal generality thus forbids so-called 'acts or bills of attainder', which is legislation that prescribes punishment for named or easily identifiable persons, whose conduct might have infuriated those in power.) Under a rule-of-law constitution, entrepreneurs are free to trade and compete as legal equals. Every entrepreneur and economic actor has the same legal status, namely, the status of a person under the law. No entrepreneur is held to be above the law.

Thorough adherence to the rule of law would deprive legislators, governments and administrative agencies of the authority and power to discriminate among economic actors by conferring economic privileges. 'It is the state itself which is to be enjoined to override the rules of the prevailing [constitutional, competitive market] order in favour of one group and at the expense of other citizens' (Böhm 1989: 64). Whenever authorities grant special privileges to one group of entrepreneurs, they are also of course simultaneously discriminating against other entrepreneurs and market participants. The rule of law and the principles of legal generality and equality also extend to the administration of justice, so that judges too are barred from making arbitrary and discriminatory decisions. Judges are bound to decide disputes strictly in accordance with an existing body of established law.

In contrast, modern law is teeming with ad hoc, discriminatory legal commands (or operating rules) that violate the principles of generality and equality, thereby constraining personal agency and stifling entrepreneurship.

Tariffs, tax write-offs, subsidies, price supports, restrictions of entry into professions or businesses, and legislative backing for forming statutory monopolies or cartels – each of these interferences by the state benefits one group of entrepreneurs at the expense of others and is inconsistent with the rule of law. The rampant privilege seeking and privilege granting that characterises the 'rent-seeking' society undermines the legal order of the market economy. It represents a 'refeudalisation of society' (Böhm 1980: 258, quoted in Vanberg 1998: 177).

Codified law is particularly hostile towards entrepreneurship when it is used merely as a means of subjecting path-breaking innovators to the arbitrary will of regulators who have been captured by existing industry players. In such situations, the legislative process may be motivated not by the desire to benefit consumers but by the politically expedient wish to benefit what Baumol (1993) calls 'runners up' – unsuccessful entrepreneurs whose enterprises are being systematically displaced by their more successful counterparts who perceive market conditions more accurately. Lobbying for governmental protection of one sort or another has the appeal that incumbents in the industry are able to insulate themselves from the pressure of competitive entry and yet escape any charge of wrongdoing by elevating misconduct to the legislative and political plane. The opportunity to invoke spurious 'national interest' and 'social justice' arguments makes this strategy even more attractive to them.

In a system replete with economic privileges and discriminatory restrictions on economic activities, 'rent extraction' might also be rife (McChesney 1987; 1991). This occurs when politicians extract wealth from particular individuals or groups by credibly threatening to impose onerous constraints on them. A notable feature of this type of rent seeking is that, when it is successful, there is no obvious trace of government intervention in the form of legislation or regulation, no clear evidence of arbitrary coercion being exercised to appropriate other people's property.

The maintenance of the rule of law requires various substantive institutions and procedural safeguards that can protect economic and political freedom from arbitrary impositions by government. One of the most fundamental institutions is a constitutional *separation of powers* between the different organs of the state – namely, a division of powers and functions between legislature, executive and judiciary. In addition, the rule of law stipulates that the law must be enforced, and violations adjudicated, by an *independent judiciary* that adheres to pre-existing rules of due process (i.e. the principles of *procedural fairness*). The separation of powers implies a *prohibition against acts (or 'bills') of attainder*, which are legislative adjudications of the guilt of particular persons, because they involve an intrusion by the legislature into the judicial sphere. Other procedural rules often used to support the rule of law include judicial review, the prohibition against *ex post facto* laws, trial by jury, the privilege of the writ of habeas corpus, the principle of 'no expropriation without just compensation' and the principle of proportionality (see Allan (1998) for a brief review). The maintenance of the rule of law also requires a political structure, such as 'market-preserving federalism', that produces self-enforcing limits on the actions of political actors (see Chapter 5).

The next sections discuss the twin pillars of the institutions of private property and contract and examine their impact on personal agency beliefs and entrepreneurial alertness. These two sets of institutions are derived from the rule of law and are an essential part of the legal bedrock that is required to support entrepreneurial processes in a market economy. 'Without these institutional prerequisites – primarily, private property rights and freedom and enforceability of contract – the market cannot operate' (Kirzner 2000: 83).

The institution of private property

A high-level entrepreneurial environment requires more than just an anonymous price system comprising faceless traders. The communication of information on markets and the governance of entrepreneurial transactions also require a diverse set of supporting institutions:

> [P]rices and markets function as part of a social system, not in isolation. A social system generates many kinds of signals and rules besides prices. ... Nonprice constraints are as much a part of a decentralized economy as are the prices they help to generate. These constraints are *reference frameworks* and *orientation points*, in terms of which actors form expectations. Prices are formed on markets composed of contracts, rules, and customs, which are part of the constraints and basis for observed behaviour. ... [Nonprice] constraints are often necessary accompaniments to markets. For example, *it is strictly impossible to imagine a 'price system' devoid of contracts and property rights.*
> (O'Driscoll and Rizzo 1996: 106; emphasis added)

Although prior ownership of property is not a prerequisite to entrepreneurial alertness, entrepreneurs would not be able to formulate or carry out their plans unless they were reasonably sure that the people with whom they trade have exclusive control over the relevant resources. In order to reallocate resources in the pursuit of profit, entrepreneurs must often purchase exclusive rights to assets in one period with the intention of selling them for a higher price in a subsequent period. Before the act of purchase, the entrepreneur will need to establish who owns those assets. Having purchased those assets, the entrepreneur will want to be certain of his or her exclusive control over them until the date of their sale. And when selling those assets, the entrepreneur will need to be confident of the claim of the buyer to the resources that are being offered in exchange for those assets. Thus, to be in a position to carry out their plans of action, entrepreneurs must rely upon a secure system of property rights.

Principles embodied in the concept of private property

The institution of private property is an essential condition for safeguarding individuals against coercion and protecting liberty. 'While property in some form is possible without liberty, the contrary is inconceivable' (Pipes 1999: xiii). As the term implies, private property rights are held in a private capacity by individuals, a group of people or a firm. They are to be distinguished from public rights, which are exercised by those who control the state or one of its political organs. As discussed later, the distinction between these two types of rights and the relative prevalence of these rights have important implications for the nature of the economic system and the scope and character of entrepreneurship.

The institution of private property embodies two main principles. The first is that people have an assured private sphere of things which they can control and which we call their property ('the right to control and benefit from resources'). One's private sphere consists of those things in one's environment with which others cannot interfere. The second principle is that these things can be transferred from the sphere of one person to that of another only by mutual consent ('the right to dispose of resources') (Hayek 1955: 31–32). Although they guarantee a certain area of freedom, these principles do not constitute absolute property rights. Under very exceptional, narrowly defined circumstances, such as war or imminent peril to life, the state and private individuals may be permitted to infringe the property rights of others in exchange for some form of just compensation (see Epstein 1995: 113–116).

The institution of private property (and the principles it embodies) has an important psychological dimension that enhances our feelings of self-efficacy, internal control and personal agency, and it thereby promotes entrepreneurial alertness. Private property rules offer people the possibility of self-determination or autonomy. 'For it is by using one's own property according to one's own values and goals, without the necessity for consultation with one's neighbour, or any collective authority, that one can most nearly approximate the status of an autonomous agent' (Gray 1989: 142). Ownership of property causes objects that we possess to be become part of our protected private sphere. By controlling, exploiting and transferring property, we can express our subjective sense of agency in the external material world of physical and intangible assets and can carry out, with varying degrees of success, the tasks necessary to sustain ourselves. When our right to own and control property is curtailed or taken away from us, we experience a dilution of our sense of personal agency.

The psychological aspect of the institution of private property (especially as it relates to consumer goods) is evident in early stages of child development, in both individualist and group-oriented cultures (Gesell and Ilg 1949; Spiro 1975). Empirical studies of children have found that psychological attachment to property (i.e. feelings of ownership) is closely associated with the development of personal identity and a perception of the contingency of events upon one's own behaviour: 'The first notions of possession revolve around what *I* control and what responds to *my* actions' (Furby 1980: 35). (For a brief literature review, see Pipes 1999: 71–76.) In addition, Furby's studies found that, across different ages and cultural groups, a sense of personal competence and efficacy was fundamental to one's understanding of, and motivation for, possession and property.

The second principle embodied in private property rules (referred to above) implies that people have the freedom to transfer the things they own to others. It thus presupposes that property is *alienable*. The alienability of property means that people are able to separate themselves from the things that they produce, so that they do not have to consume their own output. Thus, they are willing to sever the connection between the production of a good and the consumption of its services in order to obtain gains from trade. What people produce with their own labour is objectified and depersonalised, so that they are willing to make it available for use by others and to claim title to goods that they did not produce themselves (Casson 1990: 138–139).[6] The alienability of property is essential for fostering markets and for facilitating the entrepreneurial processes to coordinate market transactions.

Economic versus legal structure of property rights

The conception of property rights most relevant to entrepreneurship is economic rather than legal. The economic notion is broader than the legal conception of property rights as defined in the laws of various societies. In essence, an economic property right gives an entrepreneur the effective decision-making authority or actual power to choose the uses of an economic good, to draw the fruits from its use and to transfer the good to other people. This right is of crucial importance if entrepreneurs are to be free to exploit opportunities for reallocating specific capital goods from low-valued uses to new, hitherto unimagined, higher-valued uses. The economic conception of rights is the one most akin to the notion of internal LOC, competence and personal agency. Because economic property rights give an entrepreneur the freedom to capture profit from trading an asset and to contract over the terms with other participants, they strengthen the entrepreneur's perceptions of the contingency of potential economic rewards upon their actions, thereby increasing their internal LOC and alertness.

Economic rights may be, but are not necessarily, supported by registered legal title or formal laws enforced by the state. These rights constitute *de facto* ownership of assets and may or may not correspond to legal definitions of property (i.e. *de jure* ownership). 'While property in the legal sense of the word has something to do, and particularly historically had to do, with the property in the economic sense of the word, the legal structure of property does not reflect necessarily its economic counterpart' (Bajt 1968: 1). Indeed, economic rights can be maintained by means of physical force and the threat of social sanctions, such as ostracism. In contrast, legal property rights are defined as what the legal authority or system formally recognises and enforces as a person's property. In the legal sense, private property rights 'designate the legal institution in which the main economic rights in a resource are bundled in the hands of a single title holder' (Mackaay 1997: 4). For many types of transactions, legal rights can reduce the costs of contracting, especially with strangers, because they facilitate third-party enforcement primarily effected through the courts.

Although legal rights are neither necessary nor sufficient for the existence of economic rights, the delineation of legal rights can in general enhance economic rights, people's perceptions of personal agency and hence entrepreneurial processes. '[M]arkets without clearly defined rules tend to be limited and constrained as vehicles for economic development' (Boettke 2001: 242). This is vividly illustrated by de Soto. Although people in Third World and former communist nations may have large holdings of assets, the rights to which are governed by social conventions, they lack well-defined, universally recognised and readily alienable property rights. They also lack a formal process for legally registering their property: 'They have houses but not titles; crops but not deeds; businesses but not statutes of incorporation' (de Soto 2000: 7). According to de Soto, more than half the city-dwellers of Peru and the Philippines live in housing to which there is no clear legal title and in which rights of occupancy are supported only by informal custom (p. 33). In de Soto's view, the absence of formal legal property rights means that people cannot use their houses as collateral for loans in order to raise finance for their new entrepreneurial ventures. In the underground economy, people by and large can borrow only from those they know.[7]

Without well-developed legal property rights, entrepreneurs often encounter prohibitively high costs in contracting with strangers. Such a high level of transaction costs eliminates opportunities for mutually beneficial exchange of assets, and it therefore limits the extent of the market and the ability to realise many of the largest gains from specialisation and trade. 'A legal failure that prevents enterprising people from negotiating with strangers defeats the division of labor and fastens would-be entrepreneurs to smaller circles of specialization and low productivity' (de Soto 2000: 71). In the absence of precise and uniform legal rights to property, the investment required to exploit long-term profit opportunities is restricted, and entrepreneurship cannot develop much beyond 'kiosk capitalism'. If nations do not have the institutions that make private property rights in capital goods secure over the long run, they lose most of the gains from longer-term, capital-intensive, 'roundabout' processes of production. ('Round-aboutness' refers to a deepening in the capital structure.)

Economic decentralisation and private versus public (state) property rights

The scope for entrepreneurship and its character also depend upon the relative importance of different types of property rights in an economic system. As mentioned earlier, the private–public continuum is one of the most important dimensions over which property rights can vary. Capitalist economies depend upon private property rights, whereas socialist and communist systems stress public property rights.

Only within a decentralised system of private property are productive resources voluntarily exchanged in real markets against money, thereby enabling entrepreneurs and other market participants to attach meaningful prices to them. 'The existence of markets for productive assets is the most important feature of a market exchange system based on private property, capitalism' (Eggertsson 1990: 37). Market prices for productive resources reflect the interplay of the subjective valuations of all the individuals participating in buying and selling. The existence, in different parts of the market, of multiple money prices for the same bundle of private ownership rights over an asset represents a simple arbitrage opportunity. Indeed, entrepreneurial profit presupposes the institution of private property and associated market prices. The institutions of private property and money are essential for guiding entrepreneurs in their judgements of the potential profitability of alternative ventures (i.e. the process of monetary 'economic calculation').

In contrast, a socialist system of economic organisation is based on constitutionally established public or state ownership of the means of production, which implies the absence (or constitutional abolition) of private property rights, markets and market prices for productive resources. In its pure form, the state is the exclusive owner of all productive assets and the allocation of these assets is orchestrated by the one central planning authority only. It is only the imagination and alertness of a single mind – namely, that of the central planner – that shapes the pattern of decisions made within the single attempted plan. However, without markets for productive resources, the socialist-planning agency cannot allocate resources rationally. Because it lacks indices of the relative importance of those resources (i.e. market prices for factors of production), it is unable to reallocate scarce resources to higher-valued uses as economic conditions change. 'Every step that leads away from private ownership of the means of production and the use of money is a step away from rational economic activity' (Mises 1981: 102). In the absence of market price signals for capital goods, the central authority has no basis for reckoning the results of its planned actions. The agency has no basis for determining the full implications of one set of decisions for other decisions in its overall plan (Kirzner 2000: 146). Consequently, even if the central agency's objective were to satisfy as much as possible the wants of consumers in the socialised economy, its plan would necessarily fail.

The legal structure of property rights under socialism offers no scope for the decentralised entrepreneurial acts of discovery, motivated by the lure of pure profit, that involve trading bundles of ownership entitlements. Agents in the socialised economy are legally precluded from holding and trading property and from keeping the entrepreneurial gains from such activity:

> Government officials whose status, by definition, precludes their being able personally to profit from their commercial discoveries, cannot be depended upon to achieve through planning, or through bureaucratically setting nonmarket 'prices' to stimulate effective market activities, those discoveries the generation of which constitutes the real contribution of free markets.
>
> (Kirzner 2000: 70)

To the extent that decentralised state agents in a nominally socialist regime do engage in monetary exchanges or do exercise *de facto* (i.e. economic) private control rights over public property, then the regime is not truly socialist. For instance, in the former Soviet Union, private property rights in the economic sense were never abolished but were implicitly allocated to specific individuals, such as incumbent managers of factories. The situation is well described by Boettke:

> The Soviet system not only relied on the decentralized decisions of thousands of economic actors to coordinate plans that were supposed to be pre-reconciled by the organs of central administration, but it also remained at heart a commodity production economy. ... In other words, the Soviet economy was not a centrally planned economy radically different from any other economic system witnessed in history. It was over-regulated, abused and distorted, but it was, nevertheless, a market economy.
>
> (Boettke 1993: 69)

That different forms of property rights and entitlements will always coexist in real-world economies must also be appreciated.[8] Even in the modern market economies of Western Europe and North America, individual, private property is not the only system of rights at hand. '[M]ost of the important and difficult economic decisions taken by citizens of advanced industrial societies involve attempts to cooperate in the management of resources in which they hold some form of *common* property rights' (Seabright 1998: 594; emphasis added). In particular, *local* common property rights are by no means extraordinary. (Local common property rights in a resource are characterised, among other things, by *partial* excludability and *incomplete* contracts – the members of the group can control access to the scarce resource by excluding outsiders but they cannot exclude other members from consuming the resource, and entitlements of each are not precisely defined.) The joint-stock company, for example, is a type of common property in whose ownership separate, tradeable shares (i.e. private property rights) have been created and then sold to private, individual owners (Seabright 1998: 594).

The moral dimension of private property rights

The discussion so far has left open the question of what exactly people are *morally* entitled to claim as their property. What is considered fair or just title to the control of a resource will often be reflected in the system of legal rules. Property rights do not evolve in a moral vacuum. The definition and enforcement of property rights requires a socially recognised notion of ownership and shared ethical principles. 'The core of the institution of ownership is a matter of unquestioned and largely unconscious social and economic practices that must be rooted in non-legal developments' (Rapaczynski 1996: 88). According to John Stuart Mill, the institution of private property is founded on the notion that producers have a moral right to what they themselves have produced. Typically, in the literature this is taken to mean that people have a just title to what is produced by the resources they themselves own, including their own labour.

Kirzner rejects this identification of production solely with what derives from the ownership of factors of production. He consequently rejects the 'factor ownership' theory of property to which it gives rise (including Locke's labour theory) and its ethical implications. The reason is that this conception of production and its associated theory of property exclude the exercise of pure entrepreneurship in production (which involves no resource ownership) and the entitlement of entrepreneurs to what they have discovered. To rectify the situation, Kirzner advances an entrepreneurial view of 'what people have produced':

> In this view, a producer is entitled to what he has produced not because he has contributed anything to its physical fabrication, but because *he perceived and grasped the opportunity* for its fabrication by utilizing the resources available in the market. This is clearly an example of finding and keeping.
>
> (Kirzner 1979: 196; original emphasis)

> The finders-keepers rule asserts that an unowned object becomes the justly-owned private property of the first person who, discovering its availability and its potential value, takes possession of it.
>
> (Kirzner 1989: 98)

80   *Institutions I*

In sum, entrepreneurs have a right to own what they have discovered with their own alertness. A widely shared moral conviction that recognises the justice of this 'finders-keepers' rule as well as the injustice of confiscating what someone else has discovered reinforces a strong sense of personal agency in entrepreneurial endeavours. The discussion below on the freedom of contract examines the finders-keepers principle more closely.

Are property rights an institutional prerequisite for the emergence and existence of markets?

There are two opposing views about the underlying conditions that precede the emergence of the entrepreneurially driven market economy. The first approach, to which Kirzner subscribes, holds that the requisite ethical norms and social institutions (e.g. property and contract rights) must *pre-exist* in a society before markets and market entrepreneurship can emerge. The rival view is that the institutional conditions conducive to market entrepreneurship can be generated spontaneously as a by-product of the market process itself.

According to Kirzner, property rights are largely rooted in an extra-market ethical framework, so that there is an overriding moral basis for the assignment and evolution of property rights. Like Platteau (1994a; 1994b), Kirzner argues that a generalised morality, emphasising honesty and fair dealing, is a precondition to the creation and expansion of the market order: '[Market] forces can only be relied upon *provided a widely shared ethic already exists* which firmly recognizes the "rightness" of the property rights system and the corresponding "wrongness" of theft and fraud' (Kirzner 2000: 85; emphasis added). These ethical principles consist of explicit or implicit rules of conduct that inform people's evaluation and expectations of others' actions (p. 84). Consequently, the formation and delineation of property rights are not exclusively or principally driven by utilitarian calculations which weigh costs and benefits, though they might be partly shaped by economic conditions. 'No understanding of the market can afford to ignore the fundamental insight that its institutional foundations are to be sought directly, not in economic considerations but in ethical ones' (p. 84).

Furthermore, Kirzner argues that the institution of private property and its moral underpinnings have evolved over time in a manner quite different from the spontaneously benevolent, coordinative processes of competitive markets. He sees a clear demarcation between the sub-constitutional issue of how market processes operate within a given institutional–legal framework ('the outer limits of the market') and the constitutional issue of how the rules of the game that facilitate competitive market processes themselves come into being. The market economy cannot spontaneously generate the ethical system or the institution of private property rights that must exist in the society *before* a market economy can successfully emerge. Indeed, 'we cannot rely upon *any* spontaneous social forces to foster those institutions' (Kirzner 2000: 83; original emphasis).

The competing perspective is that the formation of market-supporting institutions, such as the property rights system, is a spontaneous process that is subject to evolutionary *economic* forces. Adherents of this view include Hume (1969), Hayek (1979; 1988) and Demsetz (1967). Through repeated experiences of market transactions in an incipient market economy, individuals come to adopt consciously or unconsciously moral beliefs, property rules and other customary practices that sustain social order in modern societies. Thus, markets arise coextensively with the legal–institutional framework in a society:

> Property rights, like most other goods, are produced in response to market demand. Although the state may satisfy a portion of this demand, market responses often come first and provide more effective solutions. Indeed, the legal responses are often only effective against a background of self-enforcing market mechanisms.
>
> (Rapaczynski 1996: 102)

In contrast to Kirzner who depicts entrepreneurs as accepting the status quo structure of property rights, Anderson and Hill (1988) describe how profit-motivated entrepreneurs respond to new situations with significant contractual innovations that recombine existing property rights and establish new ones. Entrepreneurs often create new forms of property rights when they seek to introduce innovations for which there are as yet no known rights or effective 'fences'. (A fence is defined as a technique for securing exclusive control over an asset. It includes physical barriers, such as encryption devices, but also institutional arrangements, such as rules of an industry association.) According to this view, entrepreneurs are always on the lookout for new means of making *de facto* rights more valuable, and they play a central role in extending the property rights system to new objects.

> Given that they control their [novel] product at the outset, they can design new fences, using whatever devices and techniques are available to them as part of the existing property rights order and making contractual arrangements. The fences must secure them sufficient control to bring the product to market and make a profit from it.
>
> (Mackaay 1997: 17)

It is important to note that the economic assets to which property rights refer are not *unidimensional* (Barzel 1997). These assets typically have multiple attributes, and there are often separate rights to different attributes of any given asset. Consequently, the experimental rights or fences that entrepreneurs might introduce in the pursuit of profit opportunities do not necessarily cover novel products as such but may be aimed at securing control over new attributes of *existing* assets that have only just been discovered.[9] According to the condition of presumptive control, the owners of existing assets are presumed to hold any future, but as yet unknown, rights to newly discovered attributes of those assets when those rights come into being (Demsetz 1998: 146). Thus, the development of property rights systems is a dynamic and open-ended process.

Freedom of contract

The freedom of contract is an essential component of economic liberty and is pivotal to entrepreneurial processes in a modern market economy. Contractual freedom means that entrepreneurs and other market participants are free to pursue their own interests through making binding promises, however prudent or imprudent, in the course of economic transactions. It gives entrepreneurs and other market participants the freedom to place themselves under a legal, and perhaps moral, obligation regarding their future conduct (thereby voluntarily reducing the possibilities open to them in the short run) for the purpose of expanding their range of choices in the market later on. It goes without saying that the freedom of contract guarantees neither entrepreneurial success nor any preconceived outcome.

Freedom of contract and entrepreneurs' personal agency beliefs

Like the institution of private property, the freedom of contract evokes feelings of internal LOC and reinforces people's propensity to be alert to opportunity. The concept of contract is one of the most important means that the law offers people to control their own destiny: 'The whole network of rights created by contracts is as important a part of our own protected sphere, as much the basis of our plans, as any property of our own' (Hayek 1960: 141). By voluntarily adhering to the rules of contract law, a person can broaden the scope of their protected domain. 'Inasmuch as he validly contracts, his claims on others become, as it were, an extended "property right" (just as their claims on him become part of their extended property rights)' (Rizzo 1985: 869).

If defining and specifying property rights is the central economic function of the law of property, then providing for the *transferability* of those rights to higher-valued uses is the main economic function of the law of contracts. In order to be able to advance their plans, entrepreneurs must be able to enter binding commitments with the holders of property rights over resources that have the potential for improved coordination. That other people's property can be hired or sold to other market participants in the achievement of entrepreneurs' aims is largely due to the *enforceability* of contracts.

By enforcing long-term promises, the judicial system enables entrepreneurs and other market participants to make credible commitments to cooperate with each other. In other words, contract law provides the legal scaffolding that helps contracting parties to invest in the physical and human capital that is specific to particular entrepreneurial transactions and relationships. Such investments have the potential to enhance the gains from trade since the cost of supply from highly specialised capital (e.g. customised plant and equipment) is presumably lower than that from fungible (i.e. multipurpose) capital items. But because specialised capital goods cannot, in the event of a breakdown of exchange relations between the entrepreneur and the other party, be redeployed to alternative uses or users without a significant loss of productive value (perhaps because there is no lease or resale market), the party making such investments is tightly locked into the transaction and is exposed to the threat of *ex post* hold-up by the other contractual partner (Williamson 1979; 1985). In the absence of legal safeguards upon which they can rely, parties who anticipate such opportunistic behaviour may be unwilling to sink resources into relationship-specific investments. 'Many substantive contract doctrines, ranging from the traditional common law's pre-existing duty rule to the modern duty of good faith, are designed to provide precisely this protection' (Katz 1998: 427).

Freedom of contract and the rule of law

The freedom of contract is derived from the rule of law.[10]

> Freedom of contract ... means that the validity and enforcibility [*sic*] of a contract must depend *only* on those general, equal, and known rules by which all other legal rights are determined, and not on the approval of its particular content by an agency of the government.
>
> (Hayek 1960: 230; emphasis added)

Adherence to the rule of law means that the substantive content of entrepreneurial contracts (including the agreed terms of trade) is not subject to supervision by the courts or any other public authority. The role of the courts is to enforce binding agreements; it is not to police the adequacy of consideration being exchanged to support a contract. Freedom of contract requires that the courts respect, in the absence of coercion, the contracting parties' subjective valuations of what is given or pledged in exchange for a promise. It is for participants themselves, and not the courts, to decide whether their contracts are profitable or unprofitable, wise or foolhardy, fair or unfair.

The ideal of the rule of law also implies that the general principles of contract law must be sufficiently universal and abstract to govern both discrete (i.e. one-off) and relational contracts. In a complex market economy, entrepreneurship consists of more than numerous one-shot, arbitrage transactions effected by discrete or spot contracts. Indeed, entrepreneurs often enter into relational contracts which entail not only an exchange arrived at by way of a bargain, but also an ongoing relationship between the trading partners that is supported by the contract. Innovative entrepreneurs, especially, use these contracts to govern the ongoing conduct of what Eisenberg calls *'thick relationships'* – 'relationships characterized by an involvement which is both personally intensive and broad in scope' (1998: 447). These contracts – which include business partnerships and employment contracts – are unavoidably incomplete, and they omit variables and contingencies that are relevant to the subsequent evolution of entrepreneurs' relationships with other participants. As a result, entrepreneurs and their contract partners might come to require general legal principles that enable them to cope with specific unforeseen events in reasonably predictable ways. The obligation to perform contracts in good faith is just such a principle, and it is as applicable to discrete contracts as to relational contracts. In any case, since most contracts have both discrete and relational aspects, the existence of both general-purpose contract law and special relational contract law can create uncertainty among market participants as to which set of legal rules will apply for any particular contract (Eisenberg 1998).

The rule of law also implies that there are serious risks in empowering courts to modify the terms of contracts because of changed circumstances. In New Zealand, for instance, the Employment Court's interpretation of the Employment Contracts Act 1991 (since repealed) led to the development of a body of case law which limited contractual freedom with respect to terms relating to redundancy and dismissal (New Zealand Business Roundtable and New Zealand Employers Federation 1992). The Court's decisions imposed obligations on employers, which were contrary to the express intentions of both parties at the time of entering the employment contract.

Similarly, if courts were given the power to adjust price terms of contracts in the event of changed market conditions, then they could, in the interests of evening out the burden, impose a price that reduces the loss otherwise borne by one party at the expense of the profit of the other.[11] This follows from the zero-sum quality of price adjustment within bilateral contracts. This judicial interference in economic affairs would frustrate the ability of entrepreneurs to predict, on the basis of general rules, the legal consequences of entering into contracts. This legal indeterminacy might reduce entrepreneurs' sense of control over events, diminish their sense of agency and may therefore reduce their alertness to market opportunities. If legally mandated adjustment of the contract price (a rare instance of which occurred in *Alcoa v. Essex Group, Inc.*, 499 F Supp. 53 (Pa 1980)) were the norm rather than the exception, the courts would curtail the freedom of entrepreneurs and their contractual partners to choose the price adjustment rule that is most appropriate for them (Goldberg 1998: 293).

Entrepreneurship, contractual mistakes and non-disclosure

Preserving incentives for speedy entrepreneurial discovery requires general, equal and certain rules of contract that allow entrepreneurs to take advantage of market ignorance. In considering this principle, it is useful to consider cases involving unilateral mistake and non-disclosure, which arise when one party, say the purchaser, simply remains silent and lets the unsuspecting seller contract on the basis of a mistaken belief concerning relevant material facts. For example, suppose that a team of entrepreneurs has a strong hunch that a block of land might contain valuable subsurface mineral deposits and suppose further that the entrepreneurs know that the current owner is completely unaware of its mineral-bearing potential at the time of contract formation. (Assume, for the sake of argument, no duress, fraud, misrepresentation or breach of fiduciary duty on the part of the entrepreneurs or cognitive incapacity on the part of the seller.) The entrepreneurs contract for the purchase of the land at a low price that reflects only its existing agricultural uses and, upon finding their earlier hunch to be correct, they subsequently sell the property at a much steeper price signalling its higher-valued use as a mineral reserve. (For relevant common law cases, see Kronman 1978: 19.)

At the normative level of philosophical and ethical evaluation, permitting the entrepreneurs to capture the arbitrage profit arising from the other contracting party's genuine error does not deprive that party of the freedom necessary to make his or her promises entirely voluntary and binding – at least not if the relevant concept of voluntary consent is grounded in Kirzner's theory of distributive justice. As mentioned earlier, Kirzner's finders-keepers ethic insists that entrepreneurs have full title to the 'discovered gain' that they unearth as a result of superior alertness. The gap between the prices that entrepreneurs pay and receive for resources represents pure arbitrage profit and is a gain that is spontaneously discovered solely by them without deliberate search:

> The additional value now seen by all to have resided in the resource was in fact found by the innovative entrepreneur. *If we follow a finders-keepers rule we can no longer countenance any simple revocation of the resource sale.* Simply to revoke the sale will be to assign to the seller a gain which someone else, not he, discovered. Precisely because the seller had no inkling of the 'true' higher value residing in his unit of resource he must recognize that the gain to be derived from the discovery of the higher value, justly belongs to another under a finders-keepers rule.
>
> (Kirzner 1989: 108; emphasis added)

At the level of positive economics, a rule requiring disclosure of the other party's error during contract formation would eliminate the profit of the entrepreneurial team. If the entrepreneurs were to disclose the known mistake, the current owner would then seek a higher price reflecting the surprisingly favourable new knowledge about the attributes of the resource. Alternatively, if the entrepreneurs failed to disclose the mistake, they would not be able to enforce their contract rights. Their non-disclosure would give the mistaken party grounds for avoiding any contractual obligations to the entrepreneurs. By defaulting on the transaction, the current owner would be able to appropriate the entrepreneurs' information. Thus, a disclosure rule would undermine the incentive for entrepreneurial discovery of socially valuable knowledge. There would be little, if any, incentive for entrepreneurs to discover higher-valued uses for productive resources, and the entrepreneurial process of economic coordination would become very sluggish.

> Ignorance, by checking the response of some, may be a necessary condition for any response by others. ... A general profit opportunity, which is both known to everyone, and equally capable of being exploited by everyone, is, in an important sense, a profit opportunity for no one in particular.
>
> (Richardson 1960: 57)

This account contrasts markedly with Kronman's (1978) analysis of advantage taking in the context of contractual mistake and non-disclosure. Kronman distinguishes between two kinds of information, 'information which is the result of deliberate search and information which has been casually [i.e. accidentally] acquired' (p. 2). The main economic difference between the two is that the former entails costs that are only incurred in the hope of acquiring the information in question, whereas no costs are expressly incurred for the sole purpose of acquiring the latter type of information. He argues that, on economic efficiency grounds, a party to a contract should be legally entitled to withhold information that he or she knows the other party lacks (and to profit from the other's party error) *provided* this special information results from *deliberate and costly search*. Kronman argues that a legal rule permitting non-disclosure of deliberately acquired information (which is essentially a property right in such information) is required to provide an incentive to invest in the production of such knowledge at a socially desirable level. By implication, a party should be required to disclose casually acquired information because so doing would not affect how much of this sort of information he or she will produce in the future. In effect, Kronman's analysis falls into the same trap as equilibrium economics: it fails to consider a third type of knowledge – namely, entrepreneurial knowledge, which results from neither deliberate search nor pure luck. As it stands, Kronman's rule would most likely impose a duty to disclose upon alert entrepreneurs because their superior 'knowledge' results, not from deliberate search, but from costless, spontaneous discovery of hitherto unnoticed opportunities. His rule would deny entrepreneurs a private advantage which they might otherwise obtain from their hunches, and it would therefore undermine incentives to be alert to opportunities in the future.

Contract enforcement

It should be noted that the freedom of contract in the legal sense does not just comprise the freedom of individuals to use available types of contracts for their own purposes. It also refers to the types of contracts that the legal authority will enforce. For example, in modern Western societies, the state does not try to enforce all classes of contract, such as contracts for criminal purposes, gambling contracts, price-fixing agreements and liability insurance policies against fines. In the case of contracts to sell voting rights and human organs, the state intervenes to such an extent that it prohibits the market exchange of these entitlements under all circumstances, even between a willing seller and a willing buyer. In the terminology of Calabresi and Melamed (1972), *rules of inalienability* protect the entitlement, even against the owner's temptation to sell it. By barring contracts to trade these legal entitlements, inalienability rules may be thought of as attenuating the grant of the entitlement itself.

The focus so far has been on the role of the judiciary in enforcing contracts, but there are other mechanisms besides the courts for governing contractual relations. State-supplied or judge-made contract laws often serve as a comprehensive set of default rules around which entrepreneurs and their trading partners can contract. The public legal system for enforcing contracts is far from perfect, and judicial enforcement of contracts (i.e. 'court ordering') is costly. Contracts can be enforced unilaterally, bilaterally or trilaterally. (However, these mechanisms generally still presuppose that the state will uphold the freedom of contract and set the legal baseline of entitlements in the event of possible judicial enforcement.) *Unilateral or internal governance* of contracts occurs when two contracting parties belong to the same hierarchical firm (e.g. a business start-up) established by the entrepreneur and are both subject to the authority of the latter when contractual difficulties emerge. Unilateral governance also includes the use of the household, extended family network or clan to govern economic transactions in the absence of *de jure* property rights. When both sides of a transaction to supply an input are contained within a single organisational entity, the entrepreneur can exercise greater control over whatever quantity adjustments are needed as economic conditions change.

Entrepreneurs and other participants may also depend upon *bilateral governance* structures. They may resolve their contractual disputes directly themselves through 'private ordering' and might only turn to judicial enforcement of their contracts as a last resort. Entrepreneurs' reliance upon self-enforcement mechanisms to ensure fulfilment of bilateral contracts rather than external enforcement organisations, such as the courts and police, preserves their autonomy and it may enhance their feelings of internal control over how unanticipated events will be handled. The freedom to engage in private ordering may thus strengthen entrepreneurs' sense of agency and their alertness to opportunity.

88   *Institutions I*

Indeed, many, if not most, contractual disputes that could be litigated under current law are resolved by private means, such as 'tit-for-tat' strategies, the threat of terminating the business relationship altogether, or self-help. The reason why private ordering is so common is that in 'many instances the participants can devise more satisfactory solutions to their disputes than can professionals constrained to apply general rules on the basis of limited knowledge of the dispute' (Galanter 1981: 4).

In addition, entrepreneurial contracts are also facilitated by the development of private *trilateral governance* structures to which traders have the right of recourse in the event of contractual disputes, thereby reducing transaction costs. A good example is the range of third-party arbitration tribunals that exists for resolving disputes under private commercial law. In the USA alone, merchant entrepreneurs and managers in more than fifty industries, including diamonds and cotton, have opted out of the public legal system and, through their trade associations, they have collectively developed systems of private commercial law (Bernstein 1992; 2001). These systems each comprise a network of contract default rules that are specific to the particular industry. Merchant arbitration tribunals operated by trade associations interpret and enforce these rules as codified by industry trade rules. The private commercial law systems still operate within the ambit of the public legal system in that the awards of merchant tribunals are legally enforceable by the courts. (To this extent at least, entrepreneurs operate within a state-provided superstructure of the law of contracts within which there is a plurality of *decentralised* private systems of contract laws.) However, a party rarely needs to seek judicial enforcement of a tribunal's decision because formal and social sanctions are so effective. The next chapter examines more closely decentralised processes for the production and enforcement of legal rules and their consequences for entrepreneurship.

This concludes the discussion of the institution of private property and freedom of contract. The next chapter takes a different tack. It focuses upon the phenomenon of money and the political decentralisation of economic regulatory authority, and it examines the impact of these institutional factors upon the development of personal agency beliefs and entrepreneurial alertness. It also considers the substantive economic liberties, conducive to entrepreneurship, that are provided by an institutional framework based on the rule of law, the institution of private property and freedom of contract.

References

Allan, T.R.S. (1998) 'Rule of Law', in P. Newman (ed.), *The New Palgrave Dictionary of Economics and the Law*, Volume Three, 369–381, New York: Stockton Press.

Bajt, A. (1968) 'Property in Capital and in the Means of Production in Socialist Economies', *Journal of Law and Economics* 11(April), 1–4.

Barzel, Y. (1997) *Economic Analysis of Property Rights*, Second Edition, Cambridge: Cambridge University Press.

Baumol, W.J. (1993) *Entrepreneurship, Management, and the Structure of Payoffs*, Cambridge, MA: MIT Press.

Bernstein, L. (1992) 'Opting Out of the Legal System: Extralegal Contractual Relations in the Diamond Industry', *Journal of Legal Studies* 21(1), 115–157.

Beudant, L. Charles A. (1891) *Le Droit Individuel et l'Etat: Introduction à l'Etude du Droit*, 2e éd., Paris.

Boettke, P.J. (1993) *Why Perestroika Failed: The Politics and Economics of Socialist Tranformation*, London: Routledge.

Boettke, P.J. (2001) *Calculation and Coordination: Essays on Socialism and Transitional Political Economy*, New York and London: Routledge.

Böhm, F. (1989) 'The Rule of Law in a Market Economy', in A. Peacock and H. Willgerodt (eds), *Germany's Social Market Economy: Origins and Evolution*, London: Macmillan, 46–67.

Casson, M.C. (1990) *Enterprise and Competitiveness: A Systems View of International Business*, Oxford: Clarendon Press.

Demsetz, H. (1998) 'Property Rights', in P. Newman (ed.), *The New Palgrave Dictionary of Economics and the Law*, Volume Three, 144–155, New York: Stockton Press.

Dietze, G. (1976) 'Hayek on the Rule of Law', in F. Machlup (ed.), *Essays on Hayek*, New York: New York University Press, 107–146.

Easterbrook, W.T. (1965) 'The Climate of Enterprise', in H.G.J. Aitken (ed.), *Exploration in Enterprise*, Cambridge, MA: Harvard University Press, 65–79.

Eggertsson, T. (1990) *Economic Behavior and Institutions*, Cambridge: Cambridge University Press.

Epstein, R.A. (1995) *Simple Rules for a Complex World*, Cambridge, MA: Harvard University Press.

Fuller, L.L. (1964) *The Morality of Law*, New Haven, CT: Yale University Press.

Furby, L. (1980) 'The Origins and Early Development of Possessive Behavior', *Political Psychology* 2(1), 30–42.

Galanter, M. (1981) 'Justice in Many Rooms: Courts, Private Ordering, and Indigenous Law', *Journal of Legal Pluralism* 19, 1–47.

Gesell, A.L. and Ilg, F.L. (1949) *Child Development: An Introduction to the Study of Human Growth*, New York: Harper.

Goldberg, V.P. (1998) 'Relational Contract', in P. Newman (ed.), *The New Palgrave Dictionary of Economics and the Law*, Volume Three, 289–293, New York: Stockton Press.

Gray, J. (1989) 'Hayek on the Market Economy and the Limits of State Action', in D. Helm (ed.), *The Economic Borders of the State*, Oxford: Oxford University Press, 127–143.

Grossman, G. (1981) 'The "Second Economy" of the USSR', in M. Bornstein (ed.), *The Soviet Economy: Continuity and Change*, Boulder, CO: Westview Press.

Hamilton, R.T. and Harper, D.A. (1994) 'The Entrepreneur in Theory and Practice', *Journal of Economic Studies* 21(6), 3–18.

Hardin, R. (1989) 'Why a Constitution?', in B. Grofman and D. Wittman (eds), *The Federalist Papers and the New Institutionalism*, New York: Agathon Press, 100–120.

Hayek, F.A. (1944) *The Road to Serfdom*, Chicago: University of Chicago Press.

Hayek, F.A. (1955), *The Political Ideal of the Rule of Law*, Cairo: National Bank of Egypt.

Hayek, F.A. (1960), *The Constitution of Liberty*, London: Routledge & Kegan Paul.

Hayek, F.A. (1973) *Law, Legislation and Liberty. A New Statement of the Liberal Principles of Justice and Political Economy*, Volume One, *Rules and Order*, London: Routledge & Kegan Paul.

Hayek, F.A. (1979) *Law, Legislation and Liberty. A New Statement of the Liberal Principles of Justice and Political Economy*, Volume Three, *The Political Order of a Free People*, London: Routledge & Kegan Paul.

Hume, D. (1969) *A Treatise of Human Nature*, London: Penguin. First Published 1739 and 1740.

Kasper, W. and Streit, M.E. (1998) *Institutional Economics: Social Order and Public Policy*, Cheltenham: Edward Elgar.

Katz, A.W. (1998) 'Contract Formation and Interpretation', in P. Newman (ed.), *The New Palgrave Dictionary of Economics and the Law*, Volume One, 425–432, New York: Stockton Press.

Kirzner, I.M. (1973) *Competition and Entrepreneurship*, Chicago: University of Chicago Press.

Kirzner, I.M. (1979) *Perception, Opportunity, and Profit*, Chicago: University of Chicago Press.

Kirzner, I.M. (1983) 'The Primacy of Entrepreneurial Discovery', in *The Entrepreneur in Society*, CIS Policy Forums, St Leonards, New South Wales: Centre for Independent Studies, 57–79. Reprinted in I.M. Kirzner (1985) *Discovery and the Capitalist Process*, Chicago: Chicago University Press, 15–39.

Kirzner, I.M. (1985) *Discovery and the Capitalist Process*, Chicago: Chicago University Press.

Kirzner, I.M. (1989) *Discovery, Capitalism and Distributive Justice*, Oxford: Basil Blackwell.

Kirzner, I.M. (1992) *The Meaning of Market Process: Essays in the Development of Modern Austrian Economics*, London and New York: Routledge.

Kirzner, I.M. (2000) *The Driving Force of the Market: Essays in Austrian Economics*, London and New York: Routledge.

Kronman, A.T. (1978) 'Mistake, Disclosure, Information, and the Law of Contracts', *Journal of Legal Studies* 7(1), 1–34.

Lachmann, L.M. (1971) *The Legacy of Max Weber*, Berkeley, CA: The Glendessary Press.

Lachmann, L.M. (1979) 'The Flow of Legislation and the Permanence of the Legal Order', *Order Jahrbuch für die Ordnung von Wirtschaft und Gesellschaft* 30, 69–77.

Leoni, B. (1972) *Freedom and the Law*, Los Angeles: Nash.

Mackaay, E. (1997) 'On Property Rights and Their Modification', Unpublished manuscript.

McChesney, F.S. (1987) 'Rent Extraction and Rent Creation in the Economic Theory of Regulation', *Journal of Legal Studies* 16(January), 67–100.

Menger, C. (1996) *Investigation into the Method of the Social Sciences*, Grove City, PA: Libertarian Press. First German edition 1883.

Mises, L. von (1981) *Socialism: An Economic and Sociological Analysis*, Indianapolis: Liberty Classics. First German Edition 1922.

New Zealand Business Roundtable and New Zealand Employers Federation (1992) *The Labour/Employment Court: An Analysis of the Labour/Employment Court's Approach to the Interpretation and Application of Employment Legislation*, Wellington: NZ Business Roundtable and NZ Employers Federation.

North, D.C. (1981) *Structure and Change in Economic History*, New York: W.W. Norton.

O'Driscoll, G.P., Jr and Rizzo, M.J. (1996), *The Economics of Time and Ignorance*, London and New York: Routledge.

Pipes, R. (1999) *Property and Freedom*, New York: Alfred A. Knopf.

Platteau, J.-P. (1994) 'Behind the Market Stage Where Real Societies Exist – Part I: The Role of Public and Private Order Institutions', *Journal of Development Studies* 30(3), 533–577.

Rapaczynski, A. (1996) 'The Roles of the State and the Market in Establishing Property Rights', *Journal of Economic Perspectives* 10(2), 87–103.

Richardson, G.B. (1960) *Information and Investment: A Study in the Working of the Competitive Economy*, Oxford: Oxford University Press.

Rizzo, M.J. (1985) 'Rules Versus Cost–Benefit Analysis in the Common Law', *Cato Journal* 4(3), 865–884.

Schumpeter, J.A. (1947) 'The Creative Response in Economic History', *Journal of Economic History* 7(2), 149–159.

Seabright, P. (1998) 'Local Common Property', in P. Newman (ed.), *The New Palgrave Dictionary of Economics and the Law*, Volume Two, 591–594, New York: Stockton Press.

Soto, H. de (2000) *The Mystery of Capital: Why Capitalism Triumphs in the West and Fails Everywhere Else*, New York: Basic Books.

Spiro, M.E. (1975) *Children of the Kibbutz*, Revised Edition, Cambridge, MA: Harvard University Press.

Tocqueville, A. de (1990) *Democracy in America*, Volume Two, New York: Vintage Books. First published 1840.

Vanberg, V.J. (1998) 'Feiburg School of Economics' in P. Newman (ed.), *The New Palgrave Dictionary of Economics and the Law*, Volume Two, 172–179, New York: Stockton Press.

Voigt, S. (1993) 'Values, Norms, Institutions and the Prospects for Economic Growth in Central and Eastern Europe', *Journal des Economistes et des Etudes Humaines* 4(4), 495–529.

Wagner, R.E. (1998) 'Common Law, Statute Law and Economic Efficiency' in P. Newman (ed.), *The New Palgrave Dictionary of Economics and the Law*, Volume One, 313–317, New York: Stockton Press.

Weingast, B.R. (1995) 'The Economic Role of Political Institutions: Market-Preserving Federalism and Economic Development', *Journal of Law, Economics, & Organization* 11(1), 1–31.

Williamson, O.E. (1979) 'Transaction Cost Economics: The Governance of Contractual Relations', *Journal of Law and Economics* 22(October), 233–261.

[16]

Institutions II

Money, political and legal decentralisation and economic freedom

This chapter continues the analysis of the institutional conditions for entrepreneurship. In the previous chapter, I considered the fundamental principles and rules that must be embedded in a constitutional order if it is to produce agents who are causally efficacious and alert in the economic sphere. I paid particular attention to the bedrock institutions of private property and freedom of contract. As yet, I have remained silent about the role of money or of the political order in competitive market processes.

The conventional wisdom is that the phenomenon of money presupposes the institution of private property, and like the institution of private property, money expands the extent of the market and facilitates the division of labour. Money prices are viewed as an aid to entrepreneurial decision-making ('a powerful cognitive simplifier') that, in conjunction with other kinds of knowledge, helps entrepreneurs zero in on the latent economic potential of productive resources. By signalling profit opportunities, disequilibrium money prices are a sophisticated device that spurs entrepreneurs to correct these prices and to discover new knowledge.

In contrast to previous scholarship, this chapter pays attention to how the emergence of money affects entrepreneurial alertness. It extends Kirzner's ideas on entrepreneurship by relating psychological determinants of alertness to 'monetary calculation', a particular form of cognitive operation. In particular, it focuses upon how the phenomenon of money influences people's personal agency beliefs and the complexity of the entrepreneurial knowledge problem. Among other things, money reinforces entrepreneurs' perceived self-efficacy because it gives them the means to engage in the economic calculation necessary to select, initiate and monitor capital projects and production processes.

After considering money and its surrounding institutions, the focus shifts to examining how the decentralisation of political and legal decision-making helps secure the foundations for market entrepreneurship. (Economic decentralisation has already been examined in the discussion of alternative property rights systems in Chapter 4.) It is hypothesised that political and legal systems based on decentralised control appear more likely than centralised structures to produce economic agents who have a strong

90 *Institutions II*

sense of personal agency and are alert to profit opportunities. The more decentralised are political and legal systems, the clearer are the signals of internal locus of control, since people's economic success is visibly dependent more on their own actions and less on the activities of 'powerful others', such as the state.

Having analysed the role of the political and legal order, the chapter moves on to reconsider the principle of freedom more closely. In particular, the discussion fleshes out the implications of Kirzner's notion of alertness for how we conceive entrepreneurial freedom. It also examines how the law institutionalises or embeds the principle of freedom in a framework of concrete economic liberties that are essential for entrepreneurial discovery. The last section of the chapter then surveys the empirical literature on the relationship between economic freedom and economic growth. It presents impressive empirical results that show the positive contribution that economic freedom can make to a nation's economic performance.

The phenomenon of money

Money is one of the key institutions contributing to human freedom and the development of civil society. It is one of the great social phenomena that rationalise economic life:

> It [the use of money] gives society the technical machinery of exchange, the opportunity to combine personal freedom with orderly cooperation on a grand scale, and the basis of that system of accountancy which Sombart appropriately calls 'economic rationalism'.
>
> (Mitchell 1937: 170–171)

It plays a significant role in the cultivation of entrepreneurial alertness and the ability to make judgemental decisions about the coordination of economic resources. In the absence of money, a complex economic order based on specialisation and the division of labour could not emerge. The scope for entrepreneurship would be limited to an extremely rudimentary form of production and exchange.

As discussed in Chapter 2, the scope for entrepreneurship is provided by the existence of more than one price for the 'same' good in the 'same' market. The price differential (in the form of interlocal or intertemporal price discrepancies) represents an opportunity for pure arbitrage profit arising from market participants overlooking current economic facts. The analysis of market entrepreneurship proceeded on the unstated assumption that all prices are *money* prices and that all market transactions involve exchanging goods or services for *money*. Specifying prices in cardinal numerical values presupposes that there is a specialised and universally accepted medium of exchange used in trading goods and services in which prices for market transactions can be expressed.

The analysis of market entrepreneurship has also assumed implicitly that money is 'neutral': that is, that the working of the market and the direction of market activity are exactly as they would be in the absence of money.

It should be noted that these assumptions were made for heuristic purposes only. In the real world, the introduction of a money supply into a market system affects both demand-side and supply-side conditions conducive to entrepreneurship. Because it induces changes in the degree of division of labour and specialisation in production and exchange, the division of knowledge among market participants, the extent and number of markets and goods, the duration of the period of production (degree of 'roundaboutness'), and the transaction costs of exchange, money changes the structure of economic circumstances and the totality of exchange ratios between commodities that give rise to entrepreneurial opportunities. To state it simply: the emergence of money increases the range of goods and services available on the market and the potential set of disequilibrium prices open for correction. It thereby increases the scope for entrepreneurial opportunities.[1]

The focus of this section, however, is upon how money impinges on supply-side factors that affect the generation of entrepreneurial alertness. As argued in Chapter 3, the supply of entrepreneurial alertness is a function of people's sense of agency, which in turn comprises their beliefs about their own efficacy (competency) and locus of control (contingency). This section argues that the introduction of money and a system of money prices potentially strengthens the sense of personal agency and the degree of alertness of (as yet unknown) entrepreneurs. The existence of money promotes personal agency by enhancing entrepreneurs' perceptions of self-efficacy and particularly their beliefs about their own capacity to secure the relevant knowledge, to plan rationally and to coordinate resources successfully in the pursuit of profit opportunities. In addition, a generally accepted medium of exchange bolsters entrepreneurs' perceptions of the contingency of desired economic outcomes (profit, success) upon entrepreneurial actions. It raises their expectation that economic rewards are controlled by behaviour rather than external forces. In other words, it reinforces an internal locus of control.

Money and entrepreneurs' self-efficacy beliefs

How does money affect entrepreneurs' sense of self-efficacy? This section argues that the existence of money and money prices enhances perceived self-efficacy by improving the epistemic basis of entrepreneurial action, by reducing the complexity of entrepreneurial transactions and by facilitating cognitive operations such as economic calculation and the rational planning of entrepreneurial activities. Although it comes later in history than barter, the use of money simplifies economic problems. Money changes how people think and act because it can reduce the cost of cognition and can serve as a substitute for cognition (Gifford 1999). Money is part of the institutional

92 *Institutions II*

framework that facilitates the mental division of labour and extends specialisation in cognition.

One mechanism by which money affects entrepreneurs' agency beliefs is
through its impact on their perceptions of their problem situation.
Entrepreneurs' estimates of their self-efficacy and degree of agency may
include a cognitive appraisal of the situational context in which
entrepreneurship occurs, including the nature of the goals to be achieved
and the requirements of the transactions to be carried out. Transactional
attributes include the degree of complexity and interdependence of activities, the frequency and number of sequential and coordinative steps
necessary, and the quantity and quality of resources and knowledge required
to complete the transaction successfully. The adequacy of the resources and
knowledge that the entrepreneur has access to in a domain of activity is
another contextual factor.

Money prices reinforce a sense of efficacy and agency because they
improve the epistemic and informational basis of entrepreneurial action.
Money prices reduce the amount of detail that entrepreneurs need to know
in order to make the right decisions. They make it possible for entrepreneurs
to make plans as if they had much more knowledge than they actually do.
They increase the ability of entrepreneurs to 'know' their environment, even
if that knowledge contains a heavy tacit component.

Money prices supply the knowledge base upon which entrepreneurs'
cognitive processes can operate, and they condense a tremendous amount of
contextual and historical knowledge relating to each good into a single
cardinal number (Horwitz 1998: 442). In the absence of money prices,
entrepreneurs would have to obtain and aggregate masses of *additional* data
on resource availabilities, production technologies and consumer preferences
as the basis for their activities. 'The most significant fact about this system
[the price system] is the economy of knowledge with which it operates, or
*how little the individual participants need to know in order to be able to take the
right action*' (Hayek 1948: 86; emphasis added). In exploiting the particular
price differences and profit opportunities they themselves have discovered,
entrepreneurs decide tentatively to treat many observed prices as unproblematic and reasonably reliable. In so doing, entrepreneurs make their plans
against a background of money prices, some of which they single out and
test but many of which they accept unquestioningly for the time being. 'The
economy of knowledge with which the [price] system works is due ... to a
division of entrepreneurial labor caused by the fact that each individual
"disagrees" only with a few prices while "accepting" all others' (Thomsen
1992: 60). This buffer serves to protect entrepreneurs from cognitive over-
load, a condition that would threaten their capabilities and self-efficacy
(Lavoie 1985b: 83–84).

Money prices signal, more or less faithfully, underlying economic fundamentals. 'The state of the market at any instant is the price structure, i.e. the
totality of the exchange ratios as established by the interaction of those eager

to buy and those eager to sell' (Mises 1966: 258). Money prices serve as objective proxies of the subjective valuations of individuals on both sides of the market. They are 'knowledge surrogates' that to varying degrees reduce or summarise a host of supply and preference data (Thomsen 1992: 41). Movements in money prices are interpreted as reflecting changes in relative scarcity and/or relative urgency of wants (in the absence of monetary mismanagement). Many entrepreneurs and other economic actors do not need to know the source of the change in relative scarcity of some particular commodity – be it an increase in demand and/or a decrease in supply – in order to respond to it. A market system economises on information by making the response of most agents independent of cause (Loasby 1982a: 124).

Although the price system economises on information, it must be recognised that entrepreneurs cannot treat money prices as perfect substitutes for relevant knowledge of market data. Money prices are not 'sufficient statistics' that fully convey everything that entrepreneurs need to know. As Garrison points out: 'Hayek called our attention to the *marvel* of the market economy functioning as it does on the basis of such little knowledge; he did not insist on a *miracle* in which the economy functions in the total absence of knowledge' (1982: 133; emphasis added). Prices are not the only pieces of information that potential entrepreneurs need to know in order to take the right action. Potential entrepreneurs must still be alert to a mass of *real* variables that affect money prices and the profitability of business opportunities (though, even in this connection, money prices may help entrepreneurs direct their attention to the most significant real variables). For example, most, if not all, entrepreneurs will be very keen to know why the market price of some key input into their venture has risen. They will want to know the cause of the price increase, whether the good has become scarcer because of a loss in one of its sources of supply or because new uses have been discovered for it.

But the point is still that, because of the complexity of the technical connections between capital goods and other factors in roundabout processes of production, entrepreneurs would not be able to make good use of their stocks of qualitative knowledge of market data without a system of money prices that serves as the basis for their computations of profit and loss:

> [W]ithout the ability to calculate [with meaningful numerical data or money prices], producers, *no matter how much qualitative knowledge of the economic data* they discovered or were endowed with, would never be able to use such knowledge in pursuit of their purposes.
>
> (Salerno 1993: 120)

Furthermore, even though disequilibrium money prices are imperfect and insufficient conveyors of information, they still perform an important epistemic function. They provide information to entrepreneurs that would otherwise be absent. Disequilibrium money prices signal the existence of a faulty pattern of resource use and they provide entrepreneurs with an incentive to eliminate this discoordination. '[D]isequilibrium prices provide through profits a *feedback mechanism* for their own correction that makes them a more sophisticated informational device than they may seem when concentrating only on their equilibrium role' (Thomsen 1992: 3; emphasis added). The advantage of this feedback mechanism is that entrepreneurs do not have to identify instances of imperfect coordination between market transactions per se; they simply have to identify price discrepancies for the same good.

The existence of money and money prices enhances the self-efficacy of entrepreneurs because it enables them to engage in 'economic calculation', which is an advanced cognitive operation. Money enhances the capacity of the entrepreneurial mind to deal with problems of a higher order. '[T]he very possibility of purposive action within the framework of social division of labor depends on the faculty of the human intellect to conceive cardinal numbers and manipulate them in arithmetic operations' (Salerno 1990b: 27).

Money strengthens the ability of entrepreneurs to make *rational* judgemental decisions about reallocating scarce productive resources in light of the higher-valued uses that they have discovered. '[M]onetary economic calculation is the intellectual basis of the market economy' (Mises 1966: 259). In an economy based on a complex division of labour, economic calculation is pivotal to the ability of entrepreneurs to make rational economic decisions and systematic production plans under uncertainty. 'Every single step of entrepreneurial activities is subject to scrutiny by monetary calculation' (Mises 1966: 229).

So what exactly is economic calculation? Economic calculation is an individual's numerical computation, in terms of money prices, of the consequences of his or her actions in the market (Mises 1966: 201–213). It includes the *ex ante* computation of the expected outcomes of planned actions (e.g. the expected costs and expected revenues of a project) and the retrospective computation of the results of past transactions (i.e. entrepreneurial success and failure, profit and loss).

Money is necessary for economic calculation because computation requires a common denominator (a common unit of calculation), to which exchange ratios can be reduced. 'The whole structure of the calculations of the entrepreneur and the consumer rests on the process of valuing commodities in money. Money has thus become an aid that the human mind is no longer able to dispense with in making economic calculations' (Mises 1971: 48–49).

The numbers that entrepreneurs employ in economic calculation are money prices – that is, the numerical ratios of exchange between money and other economic goods and services. '[P]rices are not measured in money; they consist in money' (Mises 1966: 217). Money prices are the mental tools of rational entrepreneurial planning and economic calculation.

The bounded rationality of entrepreneurs means that, in the absence of money prices, it would be impossible for them to monitor directly all the changes in market conditions and to determine the corresponding alterations in exchange ratios between numerous pairs of goods and services. If there were n commodities in a direct barter economy, and each commodity could be exchanged with each of the other $n - 1$ commodities, then an entrepreneur participating regularly in the market would have to monitor $\frac{1}{2}n(n - 1)$ separate exchange ratios. If, however, one of the commodities were to become a generally accepted medium of exchange and a unit of account, then the exchange matrix would be reduced dramatically to $n - 1$ exchange ratios (Brunner and Meltzer 1971: 787). By establishing money prices for every good and service, money enables market participants to compare prices easily: 'Instead of a myriad of isolated markets for each good and every other good, each good exchanges for money, and the exchange ratios between every good and every other good can easily be estimated by observing their money prices' (Rothbard 1993: 203).

Psychological research on numerical cognition supports the suggestion that money reduces the cost of obtaining, comparing and remembering exchange ratios. By supplying a common unit of calculation (i.e. a common denominator), money reduces the *problem difficulty* effect (Ashcraft 1992; Dehaene 1992). Without money, individuals would have to engage in more complex cognitive processes. The absence of a common denominator reduces the efficiency of direct memory retrieval as the predominant strategy for performing simple arithmetic in price comparisons. It also greatly increases the need to use relatively slow calculation procedures, and it affects more than just the encoding of numerical stimuli. The reaction time to perceive and quantify price differences, and the scope for error, will all be greater under barter than for comparable transactions involving exchange ratios expressed in a common unit of account.

Money prices are set by unconditional market exchanges of goods and services against money. It follows that entrepreneurs can only engage in economic calculation within an institutional framework that supports private ownership of the means of production and the exchange of goods and services against money. 'Economic calculation cannot comprehend things which are not sold and bought against money' (Mises 1966: 214).

If fallible entrepreneurs are to have the competency (efficacy) to distinguish, from among the myriad technologically feasible projects, those ventures which are profitable from those that are not, they must have recourse to calculative 'aids' of the 'human mind', such as that provided by money, in assessing the possible consequences of planned actions. Monetary calculation provides 'a guide amid the bewildering throng of economic possibilities' (Mises 1981: 101). Moreover, economic calculation does not require perfect-knowledge surrogates. In spite of the 'imperfect configuration of disequilibrium relative prices' that occurs in a world of out-of-equilibrium trading, economic calculation can still aid entrepreneurs in separating out the profitable investment projects from those that are not (Lavoie 1985a: 57).

Before embarking upon a full-scale operation, entrepreneurs are able to assess alternative methods of production by means of monetary calculations, to evaluate them symbolically and to reject or tentatively accept them on the grounds of their predicted consequences. 'Through the medium of symbols people can solve problems without having to enact all the various alternative solutions' (Bandura 1977b: 13). The cognitive capacity for economic calculation is thus embedded in symbolic ability. For example, a business plan with projections of money income and money outlay is an objective symbolic depiction of the entrepreneur's ideas. Because economic calculation enables entrepreneurs to sift their way early on through possible projects whose implementation would consume a great deal of time and effort, it quickens the pace of their learning.

Economic calculation is not only required at the *ex ante* stage of forming an entrepreneurial plan, however. It also facilitates implementation of plans and their evaluation *ex post*. '[I]n a world of partial ignorance, there is much more to effective decision-making than the selection of the correct alternative from the choice set' (Loasby 1976: 88). Because entrepreneurial decisions are made in conditions that are liable to lead to error, economic calculation is also required in assessing the success of the decisions that they have made.

Once entrepreneurs have chosen a project, they may engage in monetary calculation and profit and loss accounting so as to gauge the progress of their ventures. Feedback that conveys successful accomplishment and competence strengthens entrepreneurs' perceptions of their self-efficacy. But even negative feedback may facilitate entrepreneurial learning and the development of entrepreneurial capabilities and perceived self-efficacy. Feedback in the form of a discrepancy between actual performance and the planned decision is an important source of information in the formulation of entrepreneurs' efficacy perceptions (cf. Bandura and Cervone 1986). The frequency and immediacy of these signals help entrepreneurs to discover their errors earlier than they would otherwise in the course of carrying out their plans. In the absence of money prices, entrepreneurs would not be able to avoid errors that they can now avoid because of the condensed and detailed (albeit imperfect) information made available to them by price signals.

A whole host of abstract pecuniary concepts and practices has evolved from the use of money and economic calculation. These products of the human mind are essential tools of entrepreneurial thought and action and support what Mitchell (1937: 160) calls the 'whole countinghouse attitude toward economic activities'. For example, entrepreneurs rely upon the system of double-entry bookkeeping and the process of capital budgeting. These methods enable entrepreneurs to establish business hierarchies in which they delegate subordinate entrepreneurial tasks to their managers, thereby enabling themselves to focus on the big picture. The system of business accounting, in conjunction with market-based transfer prices for factor inputs, enables entrepreneurs to calculate the profit or loss imputed to different divisions of the enterprise and to determine their contribution to overall performance. Lewin (1998) adds the twist that business hierarchies are also *necessary* for the smooth functioning of market processes because they facilitate economic calculation by supplying a cognitive backdrop and set of procedures for the attribution of input costs.

A less obvious point is that economic calculation *always* pertains to the future. The introduction of money and monetary calculation supports 'futurity', which Lane defines as 'longer-term purposiveness, a teleological orientation that necessarily points to the future' (1991: 87). Entrepreneurs engage in economic calculation to handle changes in market conditions and to anticipate the future. They use past money prices as a starting point for forming their expectations of the future structure of market prices for particular goods and services (what Mises calls entrepreneurial 'appraisement') (Mises 1966: 331–332).[2] Entrepreneurs only take past money prices into account in economic calculation to the extent that it assists them in adjusting their actions to their current expectations of the future. But because future prices cannot be deduced from past prices, economic calculation does not supply entrepreneurs with certain knowledge of the future constellation of the market or definitive knowledge of a profit opportunity. '[I]t does not deprive action of its speculative character' (Mises 1966: 214). Even retrospective assessments of past action may rely upon speculative anticipations of future prices (e.g. the prices that will be paid on the market for assets acquired in previous transactions).

Money and entrepreneurs' locus of control beliefs

The discussion so far has focused upon the impact of money upon entrepreneurs' perceptions of self-efficacy as a determinant of alertness. The introduction of money might also have a tendency to strengthen entrepreneurs' beliefs that economic outcomes are contingent upon action rather than external forces beyond their control. That is, it might reinforce a sense of internal locus of control – the other component of personal agency beliefs that enhances alertness.

A system of direct exchange or barter is one in which all market transactions involve 'the exchange of one useful good for another, each for purposes of direct use by the party to the exchange' (Rothbard 1993: 160). There is no universally used medium of exchange; money does not exist. Goods and services are directly traded on the market against other goods and services. Each party acquires a good either for the direct satisfaction of his or her wants or for the services it renders directly to the production of other goods.

Barter is a very cumbersome and high-transaction-cost system in which every entrepreneurial transaction requires a 'double coincidence' of wants. At the very least, the entrepreneur must find two individuals, each of whom possesses a different good, and each of whom simultaneously values the good of the other more highly than his or her own. (In addition, a precondition for the existence of a profit opportunity is market ignorance: the parties are unaware of the existence of the other and do not know of the goods that the other party has and is willing to trade.)

In more complex cases of arbitrage involving the coordination of multiple direct exchanges between the entrepreneur and several other parties (i.e. multilateral clearing), the entrepreneur might anticipate a high cost in adapting his or her plans to slight changes in expected market conditions. Under barter, the success of the entrepreneur's plan is very vulnerable to surprises or exogenous shocks, such as the unexpected loss of one source of supply and the failure to complete a planned barter transaction. The cost of adjusting the plan in response to an exogenous change represents an obstacle to action that must be overcome if the entrepreneur is to continue pursuing the profit opportunity. (Of course, the cost may eliminate the profit opportunity entirely from the entrepreneur's subjective viewpoint, in which case he or she pulls the plug on the venture.) For example, if an entrepreneur employs a labourer to pick kiwifruit on the entrepreneur's orchard in exchange for a share of the orchard's kiwifruit output, and the labourer for whatever reason unexpectedly withdraws his or her services, the entrepreneur incurs the additional search cost of finding another labourer who not only wants to pick fruit but who also wants to acquire kiwifruit in exchange for services rendered.

The fragility of entrepreneurial plans involving barter transactions applies to the production and sale of even the simplest commodities. Within a barter system, the problem is substantially exacerbated in the case of indivisible goods, such as a house or boat. (The defining characteristic of an indivisible good is that it loses all, or almost all, its value when split into smaller pieces. Individual pieces have no value to other market participants.) The upshot is that under full barter entrepreneurs consider the success and profitability of even relatively simple transactions to be extremely sensitive to those external forces that can generate significant costs of adaptation. This sensitivity to external shocks dampens their perceived level of internal control, which in turn dims their alertness.

In contrast, in a fully monetised economy, the entrepreneur knows, as a result of the tacit agreement among market participants, that others will accept only one particular commodity – namely, the one that serves universally as money – as payment for the other goods and services they supply. Money represents a linking pin in all market transactions. 'Money ... is one half of all exchanges, i.e., it is the joint linking all transactions' (Boettke 1993: 116). Economic goods and services are traded in exchange for money, and money exchanges for economic goods and services. 'Every single market ... includes the money commodity as one of the two elements' (Rothbard 1993: 201). Money thereby lubricates the wheels of exchange by reducing the costs of market transactions.

In particular, the interpolation of money into market transactions removes the problems arising from a lack of coincidence of wants and the indivisibility of commodities. For example, if the entrepreneur needs to employ a new labourer for the orchard, all the entrepreneur has to do is find a labourer who is willing to supply the relevant services, and then the entrepreneur pays the agreed amount of money. It does not matter that the labourer does not want kiwifruit in exchange for services rendered. The unexpected loss of a source of supply or a prized customer has less serious consequences for the profitability of the entrepreneur's plan because the entrepreneur incurs a lower cost in searching for a replacement.

The introduction of money therefore increases the robustness and flexibility of entrepreneurial plans over a range of environments. From a different perspective, it can be said that money increases the decomposability of entrepreneurial plans. Decomposability means that a complex plan comprises subsets of transactions that are to some extent independently stable. For instance, the existence of money enables entrepreneurs to extend specialisation to every facet of the production process and to divide production into various stages, each of which might comprise relatively autonomous sequences of transactions (e.g. the production of assemblies and subassemblies in manufacturing vehicles). Unexpected disruption in one subset of planned exchanges does not completely undermine the carrying out of the entrepreneur's overall plan. 'Decomposability is of significance primarily in conditions of change – either random or systematic. ... Decomposability matters above all because it facilitates adaptation [to a change in the environment]' (Loasby 1976: 33).

The effect is that entrepreneurs perceive the profitability of their ventures to be more contingent upon action and less contingent upon unforeseeable, external changes. They see the successful execution of their plans as less subject to the vicissitudes of the market. The entrepreneur has a deeper sense of internal locus of control and of agency and is thus more alert to opportunities.

The implications of the introduction of money for economic stability have of course been considered in the wider economic literature. In contrast to Keynes (1936: viii, 293–4) who argued that a monetary economy is more subject to destabilisation than a barter system, Marshall (1920: 335, 793) noted that the use of money often stabilises markets and leads to decomposability in people's plans to buy and sell.[3]

Discretionary monetary policy and entrepreneurs' perceptions of agency

It should be noted that the origin of the phenomenon of money is independent of the power of the state. 'Money is not an invention of the state. It is not the product of a legislative act. Even the sanction of political authority is not necessary for its existence' (Menger 1994: 262).[4] A detailed analysis of the process by which money emerges is outside the scope of this chapter.[5]

100   *Institutions II*

But it suffices to emphasise that not only can money emerge spontaneously out of a barter economy through the interaction of market participants, but also money can *only* evolve organically through private market exchanges and cannot be consciously created by the state through central planning (Menger 1892; 1994). It is 'epistemologically impossible for the State to create a common medium of exchange outside the context of exchange practice' (Boettke 2001: 255). The state by itself does not have the power to transform a commodity into a generally accepted medium of exchange.[6] Although the legal order of a society can have an effect on the money character of commodities, it is only the common commercial practice of all the individuals who participate in the market that can create money. (This also implies that the institutions of property and contract must exist before money can emerge.) Furthermore, as a result of changes in economic conditions, business customs and the marketability of various assets, a commodity that once served as money may eventually be displaced over time by another more liquid commodity. 'Advanced transactions technologies, liquid spot and futures markets, and the development of financial intermediaries all contribute to the replacement of one set of exchange media by another' (Cowen and Kroszner 1994: 596–597).

Although, as a Big Player, the state or its central bank does not have the power to create a medium of exchange, it does have the power to change the value of the monetary unit and to discoordinate market processes. A Big Player is defined as 'anyone who habitually exercises *discretionary power* to influence the market while himself remaining wholly or largely immune from the discipline of profit and loss' (Koppl and Yeager 1996: 368; emphasis added). It is clear that as a Big Player, a central bank is an archetype of a 'powerful other' in Rotter's (1966) psychological sense of the term. When a central bank pursues inflationary monetary policies or intervenes to influence short-term interest rates or to defend an exchange rate, its actions distort the structure of relative prices and reduce the information content of market signals – money prices less accurately reflect underlying market fundamentals (Butos and Koppl 1999: 269).

A change in the epistemic quality of money prices brought about by discretionary monetary policies inhibits entrepreneurial alertness to market opportunities through its stifling effects on entrepreneurial self-efficacy and locus of control beliefs. Big-Player intervention in the monetary sphere reduces entrepreneurs' sense of self-efficacy because it reduces their ability to obtain useful information about market developments. 'Big Players weaken the epistemic foundations of entrepreneurial action' (Butos and Koppl 1999: 272). Discretionary policy reduces the capacity of entrepreneurs to know their environment. Entrepreneurs become less confident in the reliability of their expectations, and they feel less able to respond to changes in the data of the market.

In addition, the discretionary actions of a central bank diminish the internality of entrepreneurs' locus of control beliefs because they weaken the perceived contingency of events upon what entrepreneurs discover and do in the market.[7] Economic outcomes (profit and loss) become more dependent upon external forces, that is the actions of key central bank officials and politicians. 'Entrepreneurial success now becomes more closely tied to discovering or anticipating the behavior of the Big Player' (Butos and Koppl 1999: 270). As mentioned earlier, money is the linking pin in market transactions, the other side of all market exchanges in a monetary economy. This implies that if state intervention alters the value of the monetary unit, it also changes the pattern of exchanges in the market, the constellation of relative prices, the structure of profit opportunities and therefore the allocation of real productive resources among competing uses. When a Big Player enters the game, observed market events and the pattern of relative prices are no longer as tightly linked to shifts in the data of the market, such as changes in consumer preferences, technology and resource endowments, because they depend more and more upon political factors. '[D]iscretionary policy attenuates the link between action and the economic environment by making the underlying reality [of the market] less important. ... In short, Big Players introduce free parameters into the environment that may change in unpredictable and arbitrary ways' (Butos and Koppl 1999: 270). As a result of the declining contingency of entrepreneurial outcomes upon their actions, entrepreneurs shift their attention away from market opportunities towards political developments and the capricious actions of the monetary authority.

As long as there is a central bank and government monopoly of money, political tinkering with the money supply is likely to continue (Wagner 1989a). The state monopoly over money gives decision-makers who control or influence government an additional means for pursuing their political interests. The incumbent political party can try to buy votes through monetary manipulations that change the structure of relative prices and the distribution of income for the benefit of those whose political support is desired. Greater economic instability is thus the inevitable by-product of the rational pursuit of political gain (electoral success) in a democracy in which the state has a monetary monopoly. Cartelisation of the banking industry is also a possibility:

> Instead of being the agency for the provision of a public good, a central bank seems more reasonably seen as an agent for cartelizing a banking system that otherwise would be competitive. The member banks gain from the formation of this cartel, as the members of any cartel gain from the cartel's formation. It is the government that makes this cartel possible, and which enforces the cartel, so it too would share in the gains from the monopolization of money and credit.
>
> (Wagner 1980: 14)

One approach to constraining discretionary monetary interventions is to denationalise money and to introduce competition into the monetary sphere.

102 *Institutions II*

In addition to providing a sounder banking system and more effective administration of the money supply, a free banking system of competitive note issue is likely to enhance the alertness of entrepreneurs both within and outside the banking sector.[8] Under free banking, entrepreneurs in the market for monetary services are free from interference by monetary authorities, such as a central bank or a government deposit insurance agency. They have the freedom to issue bank notes bearing their brand name, set interest rates and introduce new types of loans and deposits, subject only to the general laws of contract. Entrepreneurs recognise that there is no official lender of last resort that will provide them with emergency loans if they make poor business decisions. Eliminating the central bank and privatising the money supply credibly signals to all potential entrepreneurs that the government is committed to a limited role in economic affairs. It takes away the ability of the government to finance its expenditures through inflation, and it thereby assures entrepreneurs that government officials will not manipulate the value of the monetary unit and distort the structure of relative prices. All in all, free banking is likely to strengthen entrepreneurs' sense of personal agency and to heighten their alertness to profit opportunities.

Political decentralisation

By itself, the rule of law, even in Hayek's thoroughgoing version, does not secure a system of personal liberty and vigorous entrepreneurship. The rule of law, and the formal requirements it imposes (certainty, generality and equality), does not guarantee an effective bulwark against the discretionary power of government. It is a mistake to present the rule of law as a *sufficient* condition for individual freedom and the unimpeded operation of spontaneous market forces, when it is possibly only a *necessary* condition (Hamowy 1971: 375). The same could be said of well-defined property rights and freedom of contract.

The fundamental problem is one of *credible political commitment* to maintaining markets and protecting economic liberties. If entrepreneurs are going to discover lucrative business opportunities and engage in the innovation that creates wealth, a political infrastructure is needed that credibly restricts the power of the state to expropriate entrepreneurial profits and other people's property.

Federalism

A sound political foundation for market processes requires political decentralisation of the authority to determine economic policy, which so far has been best achieved by a federal constitutional order. A federal system of government is one of the institutional configurations most conducive to economic freedom and development (de Tocqueville 1990a: 172). It is a way of minimising the potential for political coercion by injecting the principles of the market into the political structure (Buchanan 1995; 1995/96). The processes of entry, exit and intergovernmental competition that are essential features of federalist structures serve as a constitutional limitation on governmental power. By protecting the autonomy of private decision-makers, federalism strengthens people's beliefs in their ability to exert power over what happens in their lives, and it raises their general level of attentiveness to market opportunities. 'In a federation economic policy will have to take the form of providing a rational permanent framework within which *individual initiative will have the largest possible scope* and will be made to work as beneficently as possible' (Hayek 1948: 268; emphasis added).

So what exactly is federalism, and what form of federalism is most conducive to a strong sense of agency and heightened entrepreneurial alertness? If the overall objective is to maximise people's entrepreneurial propensity to discover opportunities in the dynamic world in which they live, then it is relatively straightforward to define the ideal of competitive federalism:

> A central government authority should be constitutionally restricted to the enforcement of *openness of the whole nexus of economic interaction*. Within this scope, the central authority must be strong, but it should not be allowed to extend beyond the limits constitutionally defined. Other political-collective activities should be carried out, if at all, by separate state-provincial units that exist side-by-side, as competitors of sorts, in the inclusive polity.
>
> (Buchanan 1995/96: 265; emphasis added)

Riker's (1994) definition of federalism captures the main elements common to most conceptions of this polycentric political order. He defines federalism as a political system that comprises a *hierarchy of governments*, each of which has its own clearly specified *sphere of authority*, and that institutionalises the *autonomy* of each government by means of *self-enforcing limitations* on political discretion.

Though necessary, these conditions are not sufficient for activating acute levels of entrepreneurial alertness and promoting wealth creation. Not all forms of federal organisation generate thriving market processes and vibrant economic development. A case in point is the *de jure* federal system in Argentina, once the world's fourth-richest country in the 1930s. Thus, extra criteria are needed for pinpointing the subset of federal systems that effectively supports competitive markets. To this end, I draw upon Weingast's (1995) concept of '*market-preserving* federalism'.

It is predicted that market-preserving federalism is the political structure that is most conducive to internal locus of control beliefs, strong self-efficacy and heightened alertness on the part of economic actors. To qualify as market preserving, according to Weingast (1995), a particular federal system must satisfy three additional requirements beyond those identified by Riker. First, the *primary authority for regulating economic activity* must reside with lower-level governments in order to curtail the national government's control over economic policy-making. Second, there must be a *unified (i.e. common) market*, unhampered by internal trade restrictions and other kinds of regional protectionism, in order to ensure free movement of goods, labour and capital among individual states or provinces. Third, the lower-level governments must be subject to *a hard budget constraint* in order to maintain fiscal discipline.

The institution of market-preserving federalism accounts for some of the most spectacular economic miracles in the economic history of the West. During the last three or four centuries, the wealthiest nations in the world have been either *de jure* or *de facto* federalist systems (Weingast 1995: 3). For instance, the economic miracle in the first half of the seventeenth century was the new Dutch Republic. In addition to sound rights to property, free trade and tolerance of religious differences that led to an influx of well-connected immigrant merchants and moneymen, the Dutch Republic was distinguished from other countries by its polycentrism: '[T]he Dutch state drew power from federalism when absolutist centralization was the norm' (Schama 1988: 223).

The Dutch were not the only people to enjoy the beneficial economic effects of market-preserving federalism. Weingast (1995) explains how this system contributed critically to the Industrial Revolution in England in the eighteenth century, the economic take-off of the USA from the ratification of the Federal Constitution in 1789 through until the Great Depression, and the success of economic reform in southern China since the late 1970s. (For an analysis of the *demise* of competitive federalism in the USA, see Higgs 1987.) Eighteenth-century England is a good example of a nation that qualifies as a *de facto* federal state, even though it was formally a unitary polity. In practice it exhibited all the characteristics of market-preserving federalism (Weingast 1995: 6). Most significantly, the national government was constrained in its power to impose regulations on the domestic economy, while local governments were an autonomous source of political authority constrained by competition among each other.

Impact of federalism on entrepreneurs' agency beliefs and alertness

So how does market-preserving federalism affect entrepreneurial alertness and the cognitive factors that switch it on? More specifically, what impact does this political structure have on people's causal beliefs about the contingency of economic outcomes upon action? What effect does it have on people's perceptions of their ability to successfully carry out entrepreneurial functions and tasks?

In general, federalism affects the 'objective' distribution of power over outcomes in the economic environment. In particular, it limits arbitrary interference by 'powerful others' in the economic affairs of private decision-makers because it separates economic policy-making responsibilities that might otherwise be bundled together in a single, all-powerful centralised government. Federalism sets an effective limit on the powers of government by dividing and balancing these powers among several rival political units, so that no one unit can transcend the delineated scope of its authority without being reined in by the others:

> The reason why a division of powers between different authorities always reduces the power that anybody can exercise is not always understood. It is not merely that the separate authorities will, through mutual jealousy, prevent one another from exceeding their authority. More important is the fact that certain kinds of coercion require the joint and co-ordinated use of different powers or the employment of several means, and, if these means are in separate hands, nobody can exercise those kinds of coercion. ... *Federal government is thus in a very definite sense limited government.*
>
> (Hayek 1960: 184–185; emphasis added)

Federalism is a self-enforcing set of institutions governing political decision-making that simultaneously restricts the power of the government and strengthens the economic freedom of private individuals and groups. '[U]nitary states are at a disadvantage relative to federal ones in establishing and maintaining credibility about keeping their governments in check' (Brenner 1994: 240). A political system of federalism is self-enforcing in that it makes it in the self-interest of political officials to limit their interference in market processes. By credibly constraining future decisions of policy-makers, a federalist system supplies the basis for the rule of law and the political foundations of economic freedom.

The three additional characteristics of market-preserving federalism referred to above – namely, a subnational locus of economic regulatory authority, a unified market region and a hard budget constraint – significantly reinforce market participants' feelings of personal control and efficacy, and they stimulate alertness to market opportunities. According to the first requirement, the federal government's scope of economic control and regulation must be much narrower than that of the several states or provinces. Indeed, domestic economic policy-making by the states is meant to be the rule and that of the national government the exception. Thus, federalism protects entrepreneurs and other economic actors from big, centralised government. The limitation on the national government's ability to regulate the domestic economy makes the government much less responsive to lobbying by established interest groups that are being displaced by the innovations of more alert entrepreneurs. It thereby limits the ability of lacklustre 'runners up' to use the political process to undermine the success of their competitors. This dimension of federalism means that both actual and potential entrepreneurs will come to expect that economic outcomes will be free of arbitrary interference, at least in the form of ad hoc national economic controls and legislation, imposed by an external central authority. Their experiences of action–outcome sequences will then become more predictable and controllable. Thus, the first additional characteristic of market-preserving federalism endows entrepreneurs with a greater sense of internal locus of control and heightens their alertness to profit opportunities.

As mentioned, the second characteristic of market-preserving federalism is a unified market together with a prohibition on trade restrictions among lower-level governments. The absence of regulatory barriers to the movement of goods, people and capital among individual states enables new entrepreneurs to set up (or to relocate) their new enterprises in regions outside established commercial centres so as to evade onerous local regulations of economic life. In the language of Hirschman (1970), entrepreneurs within a federal structure are free to exercise the 'exit' option provided by mobility whenever they judge that the quality of the local regulatory framework has deteriorated relative to that in other localities. Entrepreneurs will migrate to the state in which the bundle of regulatory laws and the supply of public goods are most consistent with their aims. They will vote with their feet.[9] If exit is to bring about improvement in the coordination of resources within a federal structure, however, there needs to be a mix of alert and inattentive market participants. If all participants were highly alert and instantaneously withdrew from one state to go to another in the event of a slight relative deterioration in the quality of the former state's institutional framework, the under-performing state would lack the necessary resources to implement improvements.

As well as the freedom to start up their ventures in new areas and to transfer their business activities across states, entrepreneurs obtain from market-preserving federalism the freedom to engage in interstate trade of goods and services. They are therefore free to exploit any interregional arbitrage opportunities that they discover in the entire unified market region. Their contractual freedom includes the freedom to transfer property rights in consumer and capital goods across state boundaries. Market-preserving federalism thus expands the extent of the market and gives entrepreneurs opportunities to capitalise on gains from further specialisation.

The prohibition on barriers to interstate commerce has important consequences for the effectiveness of ad hoc state-level industrial policies designed to favour one group of entrepreneurs at the expense of others. To be effective, industry assistance measures (such as the establishment of statutory marketing boards) that aim to limit supply and raise prices require the joint use of two or more coercive powers. But if a state lacks the power to prevent the movement of people and capital across its borders, regardless of its power to control other conditions, the state will not be able to successfully pursue coercive industrial policy: 'If goods, men, and money can move freely over the interstate frontiers, it becomes clearly impossible to affect the prices of the different products through action by the individual state' (Hayek 1948: 258).

Thus, although state governments have more scope than the federal government to regulate economic activity, their power to make economic policy is still severely limited by political competition among each other.[10] The mobility of people and capital within a common market serves as a check on the activities of state governments.

By pre-committing the federal government to respect the autonomy of lower-level governments, federalism does, however, encourage states to engage in economic experimentation. The prohibition on internal trade restrictions and the decentralisation of political decision-making set in motion a competitive discovery process among state governments that involves experimenting with different social arrangements and learning through trial and error the best method of providing public goods (Vihanto 1992; Streit 1996; Vanberg and Kerber 1994). Entrepreneurs have an important role to play in local experimentation in providing the service activities of government, such as participating in competitive bidding processes to contract out local government services. Decentralising the supply of local public goods might even allow entrepreneurs to establish private profit-seeking clubs to compete for members, each of whom pays a user charge to consume the club good (Buchanan 1965). A climate of economic experimentation, aimed at adapting institutions of governance to local conditions, fosters a sense of personal efficacy, internal locus of control and alertness of individuals.

The third additional requirement of market-preserving federalism is a hard budget constraint imposed on lower-level governments. This arrangement makes political officials accountable for their fiscal decisions. As a consequence, people see that even public decision-makers have to take responsibility for their own decisions. It affects the sequences of actions and rewards that people observe in the world around them. A hard budget constraint signals that the federal government will not bail out state governments with a cash injection if they cannot repay their debts. (For an analysis of the economic and political institutions necessary to control local defaults and central bailouts, see Inman 2001.) It makes market participants realise that they will not receive special privileges or subsidies from the federal government. People see that economic successes and failures are contingent upon action and not upon the arbitrary interference of 'powerful others', such as the federal government. Good-quality fiscal management raises people's confidence that the federal government will not overawe other decision-makers, whether public or private. Thus, a hard budget constraint imposed on subnational governments indirectly reinforces people's internal locus of control beliefs. It evokes a stronger sense of human agency and heightened alertness to commercial opportunities.

Furthermore, the fiscal discipline of market-preserving federalism might reduce the future tax burden on entrepreneurs and other market participants from what it would otherwise be in the absence of that constraint. The hard budget constraint is thus consistent with limiting the use of the government's monopoly to tax. From the point of view of entrepreneurs, the effect is that some hitherto marginally unprofitable arbitrage transactions might become profitable once the lower tax rate is taken into account.

A final point is that market-preserving federalism is bound to result in gaps in legislative control in some areas. These interstices in the statutory framework present entrepreneurs with additional degrees of freedom for hunting out opportunities and exercising their initiative. These gaps arise because states often cannot reach an adequate consensus on whether and how certain economic powers should be used, so that these powers end up not being exercised at all by either the federal government or the individual states. 'Indeed, this readiness to have no legislation at all on some subjects rather than state legislation will be the *acid test* of whether we are intellectually mature for the achievement of suprastate organization' (Hayek 1948: 266; emphasis added).

Legal decentralisation

> In fact, centralized law, like socialism, is not even plausible for a technologically advanced society. The forces that reversed the trend towards socialism and destroyed central planning are also undermining legal centrism. ... [A]s economies become more complex, efficiency demands more decentralized lawmaking, not less.
>
> (Cooter 1994: 216)

This section considers different sources of law and alternative institutions of law-making and examines their consequences for human agency and entrepreneurial alertness. It first compares the ideal type of the system of common law (i.e. judge-made law) with that of law-making processes centred on legislation. It then examines customary law as a decentralised process for producing and enforcing legal rules.

The organic common law process versus centralised law-making

A relatively decentralised law-making process, such as the common law tradition, which evolves spontaneously and gradually by judicial decisions, is more conducive to the development of a robust sense of personal agency and heightened entrepreneurial alertness than is a centralised legal system codified by the authorities and based on legislation. A decentralised process treats the law as something to be discovered rather than enacted. It is 'both incremental and purposeless. ... The process of [legal] change is as close to a continuous development as one is likely to see in human affairs' (Rizzo 1985: 872).

The impact of a common law system on personal agency beliefs (and therefore alertness) is shaped by the fact that it corresponds more closely to the ideal of the rule of law. The common law provides a system of abstract and general rules that does not impose a specific hierarchy of ends or values on society and, in this sense, it is 'policy neutral' (Rizzo 1985: 865). It enhances the prospect of a spontaneous market order in which entrepreneurs and other economic actors can effectively pursue their various purposes on the basis of their own knowledge. In other words, the abstract order of the common law promotes economic coordination, and it increases the coincidence of individual expectations and plans (Hayek 1973: 102–106). Because it offers a greater chance of many economic expectations being correct, the common law process is more likely to make the success of people's planning activities contingent upon their own actions. That is, this legal order is more likely than a centralised law-making process to generate internal LOC beliefs and alertness.

Under a common law system, entrepreneurs are better able to make and fulfil their long-run plans because the overall character of the legal order tends to be highly predictable. The long-run certainty of the common law means that entrepreneurs can enter into commercial relationships with other market participants and enjoy reasonable assurance of the governing rules of law. The power to affect the overall properties of the common law system is widely dispersed among a multitude of judges located at different times and places so that no single judge can do much to alter its overall character. One set of judges can be substituted for another without affecting the general properties of the spontaneous order of the common law. In this sense, common law judges are interchangeable personalities who lack individuality (Leoni 1972: 94). An internal LOC is encouraged as entrepreneurs can expect that the overall pattern of the common law and the legal foundations of their decision-making will not be undermined by 'powerful others'.[11]

In addition to the dispersal of power in the legal order, a key institutional source of the certainty and stability of the common law is the rule of precedent, which in the mid-nineteenth century developed into the formal doctrine of *stare decisis* ('stand by what has been decided previously'). This doctrine refers to the obligation that requires a judge to follow prior applicable precedent even when the judge, in considering the case anew, might have good reasons for reaching a different decision. In practice, the judge may be obliged to adhere to prior decisions of the same court (horizontal *stare decisis*) and/or to prior decisions of a superior court within the same jurisdiction (vertical *stare decisis*).

The doctrine of *stare decisis* contributes to an internal LOC because entrepreneurs perceive greater contingency between the legal effects of their actions in the future and legal decisions in the past. It also enhances their sense of self-efficacy because it improves their capacity to predict reasonably accurately how cases that might affect them would be determined in the courts.

The common law *doctrine of standing* is another institutional rule that strengthens the legal foundation for entrepreneurial discovery and that reinforces entrepreneurs' beliefs in strong personal agency. This traditional judicial doctrine determines who has the right to bring an action in court. In the common law, only the original parties to a contract had the right to go to court in order to enforce the contract or to sue for damages in the event of contractual non-completion. The class of potential plaintiffs granted standing was closed and highly restricted. Third parties – those who were not original parties to the contract – were denied standing to sue even when they might have gained directly from the completion of that contract (Holderness 1985).

A restrictive standing doctrine, such as those in the common law, increases entrepreneurs' sense of control over events. It enhances their capacity to adjust their individual plans in the event of unexpected economic changes. If an entrepreneur discovers a change in economic conditions that makes it no longer profitable for him or her to execute a contract that he or she has already entered into, all the entrepreneur has to do is to settle the amount of damages for the breach and negotiate new terms (such as a later date of delivery for a new product) with the person who paid his or her consideration. Restrictive standing means that the entrepreneur does not have to go about identifying and negotiating with numerous third parties who were not original parties to the contract but would benefit from the performance of the contract as written. A restricted standing doctrine thereby reduces the transaction costs that entrepreneurs incur in revising their plans in the light of new knowledge, and it increases their flexibility in coping with change.

Restrictive standing also facilitates market processes and economic coordination by increasing the transferability of property rights. It enables entrepreneurs to reallocate resources from their current uses to the higher-valued uses that they discover. In addition, a restrictive standing doctrine secures economic freedom by reducing the threat of third-party interference in the right to exercise ownership in private property.

In contrast, modern statutes, such as the Clean Air Act in the USA, have significantly expanded standing from its narrow common law basis. They thereby limit the alienability of property (including pollution rights) and entrepreneurial freedom (Jensen *et al.* 1986).

More generally, within a legal system based on legislation, people are often less free and more vulnerable to the will of others – especially legislators, politicians, their advisers, lobbyists and bureaucrats. Individuals who occupy powerful official positions can seek to produce legislation that reflects their own personal aims or the preferences of sectional interests upon whose political support they rely. Consequently, this type of legal system provides entrepreneurs with less certainty than a common law tradition, as there is a greater chance of abrupt and unpredictable changes in the legal rules governing their behaviour:

> The legal system centered on legislation, while involving the possibility
> that other people (the legislators) may interfere with our actions every
> day, also involves the possibility that they may change their way of
> interfering every day. As a result, people are prevented not only from
> freely deciding what to do, but from foreseeing the legal effects of their
> daily behavior.
>
> > (Leoni 1972: 8)

The problem is that the people and institutions that have the power to
produce legislation also have the power to repeal it. '[L]egislation cannot
guarantee its own permanence' (Sugden 1998: 489). The problem is magnified because a new legislative rule applies to the entire state or nation, not
just a localised site where a court case is decided. In addition, because no
single legislative group is able to conceive of all contingencies, precisely
formulated statutes are likely to need revising as unanticipated developments unfold. Even though political institutions might create rights
structures and practices, such as logrolling, that slow the rate of legislative
change, statute law can still be expected to provide economic decisionmakers with less stability than the common law. As a result, they are likely
to perceive a weaker degree of contingency between actions and events so
that their alertness is likely to be dampened.

Another important difference between these two processes of law-making
is that flows of knowledge in centralised legal systems are much less dense
and rich in detail than those in decentralised legal orders, and the flow is
mainly in one direction from the top to the bottom:

> In these respects a legal system centered on legislation resembles in its
> turn ... a centralized economy in which all the relevant decisions are
> made by a handful of directors, whose knowledge of the whole situation
> is fatally limited and whose respect, if any, for the people's wishes is
> subject to that limitation.
>
> > (Leoni 1972: 22)

In contrast, like a decentralised market system, the spontaneous common
law process taps into a diffuse body of detailed knowledge of the circumstances of time and place that is unavailable to any single human mind or
group of legislators. In the course of hearing cases, courts come to examine
real-world practical problems in concrete terms. By depending on litigants'
efforts in a case, the common law process draws upon richly contextual
information otherwise only accessible to the parties. In addition, courts
enjoy a significant informational advantage over a centralised group of
legislators in observing the revealed preferences of parties under current
legal rules (Parisi 2000: 3–4). For example, courts might observe that
many contracting parties are opting out of a set of default rules currently
provided by the legal system and are instead choosing alternative

provisions that they perceive to be a lower-cost means of governing their relationship.

A general hypothesis advanced in this section has been that, other things being equal, people are likely to enjoy greater freedom in a common law system than in a legal system centred on legislation.[12] Indeed, the empirical evidence on the source of law and the extent of liberty corroborates the claim that the extent of liberty under common law is greater than that under codified legal systems (Scully 1992). Furthermore, and more anecdotally, seven of the ten most economically free nations in the world in 1999 (ranked by Gwartney and Lawson's (2001) Economic Freedom of the World index) are based on common law systems. The legal systems of Hong Kong, Singapore, New Zealand, the UK, the USA, Australia and Ireland are all based on English common law. (Rounding out the top ten, Switzerland, Luxembourg and the Netherlands are all based on civil law systems.)

Common law under threat

Unfortunately, the traditional emphasis in the common law on abstract and general rules is being eroded by the expansion of administrative law and common law doctrines that favour a balancing of economic or social interests. The balancing method of legal reasoning mutes the signals of internal control that economic agents perceive, and it dulls their alertness to profit opportunities. The stimulus to this disturbing trend appears to be the emergence of the administrative and regulatory state, and the proliferation of legislation and bureaucratic discretion that comes with it. (The following explanation draws from Ackerman 1984: 9–18.) In many countries, there is now a multiplicity of different, if not conflicting, areas of laws that encroach upon almost every conceivable domain of human action. 'Specific-goal-oriented legislation, passed in an *ad hoc* piecemeal fashion, destroyed the idea of law as a seamless web' (Rizzo 1985: 882).

In addition, numerous administrative agencies, created by statute, have been granted far-reaching discretionary powers to make ad hoc decisions that affect the business and personal lives of individuals: '[T]his area of discretionary power touches upon the average person to a much greater extent than that area governed by rigid rules' (Hamowy 1971: 366). The discretion enjoyed by these agencies typically takes the form of balancing particular costs and benefits in the pursuit of specific policy goals. Moreover, in a further departure from the rule of law, these agencies are in practice subject to only limited judicial scrutiny.

The upshot is that, in response to growing pressure for consistency across the legal system, the rule-oriented approach in the common law is being displaced by cost–benefit (i.e. balancing) methods of legal reasoning that were prominent in the development of legislation. As a consequence, entrepreneurs' property and freedom are increasingly subject to the threat of interference by judicial decisions and the exercise of wide discretionary powers by officials. This has the effect of diminishing their sense of causal efficacy and their perceptual sensitivity to economic opportunities.

Customary law

Customary rules are another source of law. A customary legal system is a spontaneous and highly decentralised process of law-making that has consequences for human agency and entrepreneurial alertness that are in some respects similar to those of the common law.

Customs are norms that emerge spontaneously outside the state's machinery for producing law. They are more than just behavioural regularities; they are internalised obligations or 'felt norms' that direct behaviour of members of a group (Cooter 1993: 426). A behavioural pattern that many people do not regard as socially necessary (e.g. shaking hands upon making someone's acquaintance) does not constitute a binding custom. In addition, in order to become a customary legal rule, a behavioural practice must receive widespread recognition and acceptance from members of the relevant social group (Pospisil 1971: 63–64). Reciprocities and the recognition of mutual benefits from cooperation play an important role in the formation of customs.

There are many historical examples of customary legal systems but the most impressive is medieval commercial law or the Law Merchant (*lex mercatoria*). This law was a dynamic system of evolving legal rules that was customarily produced, privately adjudicated and privately enforced. The medieval Law Merchant illustrates how the role reversibility of merchants (who are buyers one day, sellers the next) induced them to adopt mutually desirable rules that benefited them all. Customary medieval commercial law was subsequently absorbed into the common law. Its modern-day counterpart is the 'new' Law Merchant, which includes private international commercial law and the customary rules of international trade relating to negotiation, mediation and arbitration. The new Law Merchant also includes domestic private commercial law systems, such as that in the diamond and the cotton industries in the USA, which are enforced by trade associations through the use of private reputation-based sanctions (Bernstein 1992; 2001).

Customary law percolates up from the everyday practices of business communities. Customs are created by the independent choices and ongoing interactions of members of a social group. They evolve from the *spontaneous and voluntary* behaviour of individuals in society. Because the formation of customary law requires a very high level of participation and agreement among individuals affected by the rules of conduct, it serves to strengthen people's sense of personal causation and alertness: 'Individuals are bound by a customary rule only to the extent that they concurred – actively or through voluntary acquiescence – in the formation of the emerging practice' (Parisi 2001: 22–23). In the decentralised process of making customary law, individuals are free to assess for themselves the desirability of accepting alternative behavioural practices. They can express their preferences by adopting or not adopting behaviours that accord with various rules of conduct before these practices ripen into customary obligations.

Unlike other sources of law, the process for forming customary law does not require the participation of third-party decision-makers, such as judges and legislators, who are backed by the coercive powers of the state. 'In a customary law setting, the group of lawmakers coincides with the subjects of the law' (Parisi 2000: 2). Because the formation of customary law is not under the control of any single individual or group, customary legal rules cannot be designed to satisfy the ends of policy-makers or any coercive authority. Compared with statute-making, the process of custom formation is much less vulnerable to the arbitrary pressure of special-interest groups. The very high level of participation among individuals in the formation of enforceable customs reduces the scope for powerful incumbent interests to impose constraints on unwilling minorities and innovators. Consequently, customary legal rules are likely to emphasise individual freedom and private property and to conform to the requirements of the rule of law. 'Because the source of recognition of customary law is reciprocity, private property rights and the rights of individuals are likely to constitute the most important primary rules of conduct in such legal systems' (Benson 1990: 13).

Customary law requires much less force to maintain social order. It is not imposed or enforced from above by some coercive central authority or powerful minority. The threat of boycott or total expulsion from the relevant business community (and the potential reputational loss and forgone gains from repeated-dealing arrangements) is usually sufficient to obtain a member's compliance with customary dispute-resolution processes and rulings.

In order to address potential collective action and other problems in the enforcement of customary law, proposals have recommended combining the decentralised process of making customary law with centralised law enforce-ment by the state (e.g. Cooter 1994; 1996; de Soto 1989; 2000). Accordingly, the role of the state is to provide authoritative codifications of customs and to give them the full backing of its coercive power. These proposals, however, underestimate the knowledge problems that law-makers encounter in discerning the customs of specialised business communities and in evaluating the efficiency of incentive structures that produce social norms. They also ignore the dynamics of interventionism: once customary property rules are codified in public law, there is a risk that politicians and law-makers will seek to alter those rights and to transfer them to special interests.

In light of the problems with centralised law enforcement, some free-market advocates have proposed a fully privatised model of decentralised, customary law. In such a model, there is no government involvement in the production and enforcement of law. The enforcement of legal custom depends on the private initiative of aggrieved individuals who have a direct personal stake in a dispute. The strong signal that people must take personal responsibility for their affairs encourages highly internal LOC beliefs. Benson (1990) visualises private cooperative arrangements emerging to internalise the deterrent benefits of private enforcement of customary laws. The kinds of arrangements he has in mind include informal voluntary associations, private surety organisations and firms specialising in enforcement services. In addition, Friedman (1979) suggests that free-rider problems in enforcement will not emerge if the rights of aggrieved parties to seek restitution can be sold to specialised firms that are willing to pursue alleged offenders and collect fines.

In conclusion, the decentralised, bottom-up process involved in the formation of customary law is conducive to strong feelings of personal agency and more intense alertness. In this system, entrepreneurs and other business people have the capacity to regulate their own activities through their own customary practices and to form their own mechanisms to adjudicate disputes. The obligation to comply with customary law arises voluntarily from a mutual recognition by individuals that they perceive net benefits from participating in the legal system. Furthermore, entrepreneurs in a customary legal system are free from interference by legal authorities. The emphasis in these systems upon individual freedom, private property rights and voluntary cooperation through reciprocal arrangements reinforces an internal LOC and sustained alertness to opportunities.

Freedom of entrepreneurial choice and concrete liberties

In the previous chapter, I examined the principle of freedom embodied in the rule of law. In this section, I investigate the unique character of the freedom of entrepreneurial choice and how it contrasts with the notion of freedom implicit in mainstream economics.

The standard conception of choice in economic theory identifies individual freedom with the power to achieve *given* goals. In mainstream economics, the ends between which the agent can select and the criteria of selection are given, as are the means to achieve each end. Freedom of choice in such circumstances is empty (Shackle 1969: 273). Individuals are denied the freedom to choose ends and means: they are not free to decide what to do or how to do it. Their freedom is limited to economising in the allocation of given means to achieve a set of given ends.

Moreover, in the world of mainstream economic models, the optimal course of action is determined uniquely by objective situational characteristics, such as costs, prices, consumer preferences and technology (Latsis 1972). The solution is implicit in the definition of the maximisation problem. 'Any other decision would have been unthinkable' (Kirzner 1982c: 142). This notion of freedom turns out to involve no choice at all: 'One has,

116 *Institutions II*

in this conception of choice, in effect already chosen *before* the moment of decision' (Kirzner 1979: 227).

Such a restrictive view of freedom is totally inadequate as a basis for entrepreneurship and for explaining the role of freedom in the workings of the market economy. Apart from confusing freedom with power, this view of freedom *precludes* entrepreneurship in the sense of alertness to opportunities and the discovery and creation of *new* ends–means frameworks.

The freedom of entrepreneurial choice is a 'meta-freedom' in the sense that it applies to all the other freedoms, which relate to some or other aspect of choice. Kirzner has been the first to elaborate in detail this important perspective on freedom, though it clearly derives from the Misesian conception of human action. This broader perspective grants entrepreneurs far more than just the freedom to implement the optimum solution implied in some automatically known or given problem situation:

> Freedom of choice can now be seen to encompass the *liberty to make up one's own mind as to the ranking of ends to be pursued and the means judged available for the purpose.* Once a given ends–means framework has been adopted, freedom can only mean the freedom to achieve what one has already announced that one wishes to achieve. It is this narrow view of freedom that many economists seem to have adopted. But, with the acting man seen as approaching choice without having firmly adopted any one framework of ends and means, freedom of choice is at once seen as freedom to announce (i.e., to choose) what it is one wishes to achieve.
>
> ...
>
> [T]he wider view of freedom recognizes that, when people refer to the freedom to choose, they have in mind liberty to select among a wide range of moral and value frameworks, of ethical systems, of tastes; to make their own guesses concerning present realities and future uncertainties; to determine for themselves what opportunities they are in fact confronted with.
>
> (Kirzner 1979: 226–227)

The entrepreneurial view of liberty emphasises how freedom of choice may evoke the discovery of opportunities that would be unthinkable to those to whom this freedom is denied. It stresses the open-endedness of an unimpeded market process. It also serves to warn us that the biggest perils arising from limiting freedom of entrepreneurial choice are likely to be hidden. As a general rule, individuals and groups cannot know what welfare losses have been suffered as a result of reducing entrepreneurial freedom, since no one can know what they (or the market) might have discovered in the absence of the constraint. Kirzner (1985) applies this important insight to examining the costs of regulating economic activity.

The law 'transmutes' the general principle of freedom into concrete liberties or rights. 'By means of this transmutation, the law economizes intangible freedom into tangible properties' (Dietze 1976: 115). In any particular society, the principle of freedom may or may not be applied to many kinds of human activity. Its application to property rights and contractual activity has already been discussed in the previous chapter. Table 5.1 lists some other freedoms, which are conjectured to be highly important to entrepreneurship. (Note that the inspiration for this table was Machlup (1969: 137) upon which its structure is heavily based.) These economic freedoms serve to secure a reliable sphere of unimpeded entrepreneurial action.

This list is not intended to be exhaustive. Indeed, by the very nature of liberty, it *cannot* be exhaustive. The definition of liberty and our knowledge of it are open ended. Over time, entrepreneurs and other market participants may discover and exercise liberties that have not yet been dreamed of:

> It also follows that the importance of our being free to do a particular thing has nothing to do with the question of whether we or the majority are ever likely to make use of that particular possibility. To grant no more freedom than all can exercise would be to misconceive its function completely. The freedom that will be used by only one man in a million may be more important to society and more beneficial to the majority than any freedom that we will all use.
>
> It might even be said that the less likely the opportunity to make use of freedom to do a particular thing, the more precious it will be for society as a whole. The less likely the opportunity, the more serious will it be to miss it when it arises, for the experience that it offers will be nearly unique. ... It is because we do not know how individuals will use their freedom that it is important.
>
> (Hayek 1960: 31)

Indeed, it might be that innovators come to create wealth by exercising freedoms that have hitherto been rarely exercised by other members of society. For example, an entrepreneur might be the first to see and seize the opportunity to trade with 'outsiders' from another culture. By using the freedom to have commercial dealings with strangers, the entrepreneur successfully adapts to new trading conditions and prospers relative to those who limit their opportunities to trading with 'insiders'. From an evolutionary perspective, the entrepreneur's behaviour and its imitation by less adventurous participants tend to have a positive impact upon the long-run adaptational prospects of human society (see Rizzo 1992b).

Many of the freedoms listed in Table 5.1 are conducive to the development of personal competence, internal LOC, personal agency and entrepreneurial alertness. It should also be noted that these freedoms are often connected. For example, the freedoms of choice of occupation and of consumption are so comprehensive in their scope that they *presuppose* or *include* several of the other freedoms in the list. In addition, although some of the freedoms may be independent of each other, others are *complementary* or *competing* in the sense that

Table 5.1 A catalogue of economic freedoms important to entrepreneurship

Freedom of	would mean that economic actors, including entrepreneurs, are free to:
Entrepreneurial choice	make their own discoveries, to discover and exploit perceived profit opportunities through arbitrage, speculation and innovation, 'to identify for themselves what the opportunities are which they may endeavor to grasp' (Kirzner 1992: 53)
	attempt to coordinate any transactions in any market in any place in any time period
	attempt to coordinate any kind of resources for any kind of venture in any industry or market
Achievement of rewards	'seize benefit for themselves from the opportunities they have discovered' (Kirzner 1992: 54), to make profits, to appropriate the rewards of arbitrage, speculation and innovation
Trade	import or export any kind, quantity and quality of goods and services
	discover and exploit domestic and international price differentials for the 'same' commodities
	adjust prices, quantities and qualities bid or offered in response to new market conditions
Markets	buy or sell any quantity and quality at any mutually agreed price
Contract	pursue their interests through voluntarily making binding promises, however prudent or imprudent, with any other individual, group or organisation
Competition, entry and exit	enter (or exit from) any market or industry and compete as best they can, provided that they do not interfere with the freedom of others
	displace existing organisations and industries that fail to adapt to their environment
Choice of production	adjust the bundle of inputs and methods of production in order to exploit profit opportunities arising from imperfect coordination between factor and product markets
	choose a suitable location when starting a venture
Choice of marketing	promote, advertise and distribute anything in any way
Choice of occupation	enter the occupation of their choice, to become an entrepreneur, trader or a business person rather than to work in some other kind of occupation, and not to work at all
Movement	travel according to their own choice (within and across national boundaries), to make their residence anywhere they choose and to hire employees from other countries
Ownership	own and acquire property

Table 5.1 continued

Freedom of	would mean that economic actors, including entrepreneurs, are free to:
Choice of ownership form	choose the ownership form (limited liability company etc.) most appropriate to the individual circumstances of their ventures
Coalition and association	network with other entrepreneurs and economic actors and combine with anybody for any purpose not interfering with the freedom of others
Privacy and secrecy	develop and communicate their novel ideas without the oversight of any unwelcome party
	keep their entrepreneurial hunches and knowledge secret
Expression and speech	speak privately and publicly, to express their novel ideas in any tangible form (such as a business plan or prototype) and to print and publish on any subject whatsoever
Non-conformance	be different in behaviour, habits and business practices
Experimentation	try something new, to commission R&D in any field (including marketing research), to test their ideas, to make mistakes and fail, and to bear the consequences of their own errors
Search	investigate and acquire information on any subject by any method, except with use of violence, theft or fraud
Choice of consumption	purchase any goods or services that they choose to satisfy their current wants
Revision	change their plans and decisions made in the course of exercising any of the freedoms in this list (e.g. to revise their choices of occupation or of marketing)

Source: Table is significantly adapted and expanded from Machlup (1969: 137)

more of one may allow either more or less of another. Thus, a greater degree of liberty in one sphere of human activity may make it either easier or harder to achieve freedom in another sphere (Machlup 1969: 128, 138).

Empirical studies on economic freedom and economic performance

A key argument of this work is that economic freedom is conducive to entrepreneurship and competitive market processes. But what empirical evidence, if any, is there that economic freedom spurs entrepreneurial alertness? Unfortunately, there are as yet no empirical studies that directly investigate the impact of economic freedom on people's cognitions and entrepreneurial alertness. However, if we accept that entrepreneurship is the main driver of economic growth and development, then we might be able to gain insights indirectly from empirical research on the relationship between economic freedom and economic performance.

Potential pitfalls

Unfortunately, empirical analysis in this area is bedevilled by problems that frustrate attempts to test hypotheses about the interplay between economic freedom and growth. The first significant problem has been the absence of a precise operational definition of economic freedom and a lack of a clear spec-ification of the crucial components of economic liberty. This makes it difficult to classify particular countries according to the degree of govern-ment intervention in the economy. Economic freedom is a subtle and elusive concept. It represents a highly complex, multi-dimensional aspect of a country's institutions.

The second set of problems is concerned with how to measure economic freedom and in particular how to quantify and weigh the components of economic liberty. Because economic freedom is not one dimensional, no single statistic can fully reflect its many features. Thus, economic freedom cannot be captured merely by measuring the size of the state in a nation – typically measured as total government expenditures as a percentage of GDP. Instead, it is necessary to compare alternative forms of government involvement in the economy, and to assess how they change the economic incentives that individuals face and how they might violate economic freedom.[13]

Moreover, the level of economic freedom in nations can at best only be ranked in ordinal terms; it is not amenable to cardinal (absolute) measure-ment in terms of some unit or other. In other words, it might be possible to order countries by their degree of economic freedom but it is not possible to say by how much freedom differs between one nation and the next nation in the ranking.

There is also a lack of readily available data on the relevant components of economic freedom for a broad cross-section of countries and over a suffi-ciently long time span. Many dimensions of economic freedom are inherently difficult to quantify objectively across a large number of coun-tries. For example, regulatory interventions are often complex, and their application is often subtle and idiosyncratic to a country, which makes it extremely difficult to quantify the effects of regulation objectively. Because data on many attributes of economic freedom are not available, it is often necessary to use various proxies for these attributes. 'These proxies may mirror the underlying element of liberty with some distortion' (Hanke and Walters 1997: 122).

The next problem is how to combine various components of economic freedom into a single summary measure for each nation. The problem is how to weight the components in order to construct aggregate indices of economic freedom. Different weighting techniques might yield different relative rankings of countries by their degree of economic freedom (Caudill *et al.* 2000; Scully and Slottje 1991). Similarly, the robustness of the statistical relationship between economic freedom and the growth rate of real per capita GDP depends crucially upon how freedom is measured (De Haan and Sierman 1998).

Another problem arises in connection with the protracted and variable time lags involved. How long will it take for the changes in public policy that impinge on economic freedom to affect the growth rate of output? 'The advantages that freedom brings are shown only by the lapse of time, and it is always easy to mistake the cause in which they originate' (de Tocqueville 1990b: 96). The time lag occurs because credibility in public policy is not immediate but must be secured over time, and the time period required depends upon historical factors and current political conditions (such as previous political instability and the strength of political opposition to policy initiatives already implemented). These time lags will weaken the empirical relationship between growth and changes in economic freedom in the short run. Thus, we need data for relatively long periods of time in order to test for a potential relationship between economic growth and economic freedom (both level and change).

Empirical findings

Having explored the potential pitfalls in this area, we can now consider the various studies that have been conducted into the relationship between economic freedom and economic growth.

In the early studies, democracy was used as a proxy for individual freedom. Statistical evidence that democracy is conducive to economic growth is inconclusive at best. In their survey of political regimes and economic growth, Przeworski and Limongi (1993: 64) concluded that 'the simple answer to the question with which we began is that we do not know whether democracy fosters or hinders economic growth'. Their hunch is that 'political institutions do matter for growth, but thinking in terms of regimes does not seem to capture the relevant differences' (p. 51).[14] Barro (1996) analysed the interplay of political institutions and economic outcomes in a panel of about 100 countries from 1960 to 1990. After adjusting for various factors, including the initial level of GDP, he found that democracy has, overall, a weakly negative impact on economic growth. However, there was some suggestion that more democracy has a weak positive effect on growth for countries that start with low levels of political freedom.

Gastil and Wright were the first to try to develop direct systematic measures of *economic* freedom across countries (Wright 1982; Gastil 1984; Gastil and Wright 1988). Their overall measure of economic liberty is an aggregation of four separate sub-indices of economic freedom: the right to private property, the freedom of association, the freedom of internal and external travel, and the freedom of information. Building on Gastil and Wright's earlier work, Scully and Slottje (1991) developed broader measures of economic freedom that include fifteen attributes of economic liberty. They found a statistically significant and positive correlation between the level of economic liberty in a nation for the year 1980 and the average growth rate of real per capita GDP (RGDP) for the period 1950–1985. They reported that their results show that:

> [C]ountries that rank low with respect to their relative degree of economic freedom also have relatively low levels of economic growth and overall RGDP as a consumption share. The consistency of the results-across all the rank indexes suggests *compelling evidence for a basic hypothesis that economic freedom is essential for economic development.*
>
> (Scully and Slottje 1991: 137–138; emphasis added)

Subsequent empirical investigations seek to develop much more comprehensive measures of economic freedom. The three major studies are conducted by the Economic Freedom Network (Gwartney and Lawson 2001), Freedom House (Messick and Kimura 1996) and the Heritage Foundation (O'Driscoll *et al.* 2001). The content and explanatory power of the economic freedom indices developed in these three studies have already been the subject of an extensive critical survey and need not be examined in detail here (see Hanke and Walters 1997).

For several reasons, the Economic Freedom Network's index (hereafter, the EFW index) is probably the best measure for grappling with issues concerning the institutional conditions for economic prosperity. It is the only economic freedom index that covers a substantial time period (1970–1999), which means that it is the only index that can be used to investigate the effect of changes in economic freedom on changes in levels of national income over the long run. In addition, the EFW index is based on transparent procedures that can be replicated by other researchers. The regular EFW index tries to avoid subjective assessments of variables and is derived almost exclusively from regularly published international data sources. It relies primarily on objective quantifiable variables that are used to develop finely calibrated ratings for each component for a large number of countries. Furthermore, the latest version of the EFW index employs an objective method for determining the weights that are used in constructing summary ratings of economic freedom – namely, principal component analysis (Gwartney and Lawson 2001: 7). This technique combines various attributes of economic liberty into a single summary measure that best reflects the original data. Moreover, in contrast to Freedom House's emphasis on democratic institutions and civil liberties as an essential dimension of economic freedom, the EFW index is a measure of economic freedom that deliberately excludes elements of political freedom.

In Gwartney and Lawson (2001), the regular EFW index comprises twenty-one components that are grouped into seven major categories: size of government, the structure of the economy and use of markets, monetary policy and price stability, freedom to use alternative currencies, legal structure and property rights, freedom to trade with foreigners, and freedom of exchange in capital and financial markets. 'Reliance on markets, sound money, legal protection of property rights, free trade, and market allocation of capital are important elements of economic freedom captured by the index' (Gwartney and Lawson 2001: 5).

Employing the EFW index, Gwartney and Lawson track changes in economic freedom of 123 countries during the last thirty years (1970–1999), where data are available. Higher ratings are given to countries with institutions and policies more consistent with economic freedom. In 1999, Hong Kong received the highest rating of 9.4 (out of 10), followed by Singapore (9.3), New Zealand (8.9), the UK (8.8) and the USA (8.7). In the sample, the five least-free economies are Myanmar (1.9), Algeria (2.6), the Democratic Republic of Congo (3.0), Guinea-Bissau (3.3) and Sierra Leone (3.5).

In their analysis of economic freedom and growth, Gwartney and Lawson first grouped all the countries into quintiles according to their 1999 EFW index. The EFW index for quintile groups was then related to national income (the level of per capita GDP, measured in 1998 purchasing power parity US dollars) and the rate of economic growth in the 1990s. While not rigorous, the results of this simple tabulation are consistent with those of Scully and Slottje (1991): more economic freedom is strongly correlated with higher levels of income and higher rates of economic growth. The top quintile of the most economically free nations has an average per capita real GDP of $19,846 and an average growth rate of per capita real GDP of 2.27 per cent over the period. Nations with lower levels of economic freedom tend to have lower incomes and rates of economic growth. The bottom, least-free quintile of countries had an average per capita real GDP of $2,210 and an average growth rate of minus 1.45 per cent.

The analyses of economic freedom and growth by Scully and Slottje (1991) and Gwartney and Lawson (2001) suffer from the same shortcoming: they both rely upon snapshots of the *level* of economic freedom in one year only. Such measures do not tell us anything about how long economic freedom in a nation has been at that level or whether it has been increasing or decreasing over time.

For a more rigorous econometric examination of the contribution of changes in economic freedom over time to the process of economic growth, we must turn to the study by Gwartney *et al.* (1999). They examined the determinants of the average annual growth rate in per capita real GDP during the period 1980–1995. Their sample comprised eighty-two countries and is fairly representative of the world's economies, except that a lack of data required them to omit the former Eastern bloc and other centrally planned economies, such as Cuba. Economic freedom was measured by an early, more restricted version of the EFW index.[15] Because they expected that changes in economic freedom would exert a lagged effect on growth, their models included as independent variables both the *level* of the EFW index in 1975 and the *change* in the index over the four subsequent five-year intervals.

The results of the study are striking and provide further evidence that an institutional framework that supports economic freedom is a key determinant of economic growth. The first finding is that there is a *strongly positive and robust correlation between changes in economic freedom (as measured by the EFW index) and economic growth*, and that this relationship holds even after taking into account the impact of other variables, such as investment in physical and human capital. 'Our analysis indicates that differences in economic freedom along with differences in investment in physical capital explain about 40 per cent of the variation in cross-country growth rates during the last two decades' (Gwartney *et al.* 1999: 652).

Of course finding a statistically significant correlation between economic freedom and growth is not proof that economic freedom causes growth. The correlation could arise because countries that grow faster tend to become freer. Though this alternative hypothesis seems reasonable, Gwartney *et al.* found no empirical support for this idea. Thus, the second important result of their study is that causation proceeds in one direction only: increases in economic freedom in a nation generate a faster rate of economic growth, but higher growth does not cause an increase in economic freedom in future years.

Another notable result of their regression analysis relates to the relative explanatory power of economic and political freedom. They found that economic freedom is a substantially more powerful determinant of economic growth than is political freedom (defined as the degree to which citizens are able to organise, participate and compete in the political process). More specifically, the components of the EFW index are much more strongly correlated with economic growth than are the components of political freedom, as measured by combining Freedom House's ratings of political and civil liberties for 1995–1996 (Karatnycky 1996). Political freedom explains little of the variation in growth rates across countries.

> This indicates that adoption of policies consistent with economic freedom – greater reliance on markets, freedom of exchange, openness of the economy, and monetary stability – is more important as a source of economic growth than the nature of the political regime.
> (Gwartney *et al.* 1999: 658)

In conclusion, the overall picture that emerges from empirical research is that greater economic freedom is a major determinant of higher rates of economic growth. The main ingredients of economic freedom are 'personal choice, protection of private property, and freedom of exchange' (Gwartney and Lawson 2001: 4). Societies which bind themselves to the principles of the rule of law, security of property rights, market coordination of resources, free trade and sound money grow faster than societies in which economic freedom is curtailed. Because many of the components of economic freedom are the result of public policy and explicit political decisions, it follows that the choice of institutional framework has immense consequences for economic prosperity and the wealth of nations. These empirical studies shed light on the positive effect on economic growth and development of institutions and policies that promote economic freedom. If we assume that entrepreneurial discovery is the basic microeconomic mechanism that generates growth within a particular institutional framework (Steele 1998: 52), these results thereby provide indirect evidence of the positive effect of market-oriented institutions on people's alertness to economic opportunities.

Conclusion

The last two chapters have examined how the institutional framework moulds and determines people's agency beliefs and the degree of their entrepreneurial alertness. Economic freedom is considered to be the most important institutional principle for promoting entrepreneurship. The central hypothesis is that the more freedom people enjoy, the more likely they are to hold strong beliefs in their self-efficacy and to have an internal LOC, and the more acute will be their alertness to profit opportunities.

It has been argued that the extent of freedom individuals enjoy depends, among other things, on the constitutional rules that operate within a society. A maximum of freedom is most likely to be provided in a society based on the rule of law, a spontaneous and decentralised legal order that corresponds to this rule, laws that transmute economic freedom into tangible liberties, a system of private property rights and contracts, a depoliticised monetary system that facilitates economic calculation and political decentralisation of economic regulatory authority (so-called market-preserving federalism). It follows that entrepreneurship will prosper most in a society embodying these institutions. It is most likely to flourish within a framework that maximises everyone's freedom from coercion, compatible with equal freedom for all people.

Speculations in these chapters have been limited to the issue regarding the dependence of entrepreneurship and market processes on individual liberty. The analysis has not, as Kirzner (1992: 53–54) rightly points out, investigated the dependence of a liberal social order on entrepreneurial alertness to opportunities for enhancing market coordination.

Furthermore, the institutional analysis in this and the previous chapter is expressed in terms that are most applicable to industrial and post-industrial

126   *Institutions II*

societies of the West and to relatively individualist cultural settings. Chapter 8 will address the question of whether the institutions identified as supportive of entrepreneurship are generally applicable across different cultural contexts. It argues that much of what is contained in these pages is directly relevant and capable of being adapted to the modern industrial societies of East and Southeast Asia and other group-oriented cultures.

References

Ackerman, B.A. (1984) *Reconstructing American Law*, Cambridge, MA: Harvard University Press.

Ashcraft, M.H. (1992) 'Cognitive Arithmetic: A Review of Data and Theory', *Cognition* 44(1–2), 75–106.

Bandura, A. (1977) *Social Learning Theory*, Englewood Cliffs, NJ: Prentice Hall.

Bandura, A. (1986) *Social Foundations of Thought and Action: A Social Cognitive Theory*, Englewood Cliffs, NJ: Prentice Hall.

Bandura, A. and Cervone, D. (1986) 'Differential Engagement of Self-Reactive Influences in Cognitive Motivation', *Organizational Behavior and Human Decision Processes* 38(1), 92–113.

Barro, R.J. (1996) 'Democracy and Growth', *Journal of Economic Growth* 1(1), 1–27.

Boettke, P.J. (1993) *Why Perestroika Failed: The Politics and Economics of Socialist Transformation*, London: Routledge.

Boettke, P.J. (2001) *Calculation and Coordination: Essays on Socialism and Transitional Political Economy*, New York and London: Routledge.

Brenner, R. (1994) *Labyrinths of Prosperity: Economic Follies, Democratic Remedies*, Ann Arbor, MI: University of Michigan Press.

Brunner, K. and Meltzer, A.H. (1971) 'The Uses of Money: Money in the Theory of an Exchange Economy', *American Economic Review* 61(5), 784–805.

Buchanan, J.M. (1965) 'An Economic Theory of Clubs', *Economica* (New Series), 32(125), 1–14.

Buchanan, J.M. (1995) 'Federalism as an Ideal Political Order and an Objective for Constitutional Reform', *Politics – The Journal of Federalism* 25(2), 19–27.

Butos, W.N. and Koppl, R. (1999) 'Hayek and Kirzner at the Keynesian Beauty Contest', *Journal des Economistes et des Etudes Humaines* 9(2–3), 257–275.

Caudill, S.B., Zanella, F.C. and Mixon, F.G., Jr (2000) 'Is Economic Freedom One Dimensional? A Factor Analysis of Some Common Measures of Economic Freedom', *Journal of Economic Development* 25(1), 17–39.

Cooter, R.D. (1993) 'Against Legal Centrium', *California Law Review* 81, 417–429.

Cooter, R.D. (1994) 'Structural Adjudication and the New Law Merchant: A Model of Decentralized Law', *International Review of Law and Economics* 14, 215–251.

Cowen, T. and Kroszner, R.S. (1994) 'The New Monetary Economics', in P.J. Boettke (ed.), *The Elgar Companion to Austrian Economics*, Aldershot: Edward Elgar, 593–598.

De Haan, J. and Sierman, C.L.J. (1998) 'Further Evidence on the Relationship between Economic Freedom and Economic Growth', *Public Choice* 95 (3–4), 363–380.

Dehaene, S. (1992) 'Varieties of Numerical Abilities', *Cognition* 44(1–2), 1–42.

Dietze, G. (1976) 'Hayek on the Rule of Law', in F. Machlup (ed.), *Essays on Hayek*, New York: New York University Press, 107–146.

Friedman, D. (1979) 'Private Creation and Enforcement of Law: A Historical Case', *Journal of Legal Studies* 8, 399–415.

Gastil, R.D. (1984) *Freedom in the World: Political Rights and Civil Liberties, 1983–1984*, Westport, CN: Greenwood Press.

Gifford, A., Jr (1999) 'Being and Time: On the Nature and the Evolution of Institutions', *Journal of Bioeconomics* 1(2), 127–149.

Gwartney, J.D., Lawson, R.A. and Holcombe, R.G. (1999) 'Economic Freedom and the Environment for Economic Growth', *Journal of Instititional and Theoretical Economics* 155(4), 643–663.

Gwartney, J.D., Skipton, C. and Lawson, R.A. (2001) 'A More Comprehensive Index of Economic Freedom for 58 Countries', in J.D. Gwartney and R.A. Lawson, *Economic Freedom of the World: Annual Report 2001*, Chapter 2, 23–69, Vancouver, BC: Fraser Institute.

Hamowy, R. (1971) 'Freedom and the Rule of Law in F.A. Hayek', *Il Politico* 36(2), 349–377.

Hanke, S.H. and Walters, J.K, (1997) 'Economic Freedom, Prosperity, and Equality: A Survey', *Cato Journal* 17(2), 117–146.

Hayek, F.A. (1948) *Individualism and the Economic Order*, Chicago: University of Chicago Press.

Hayek, F.A. (1960) *The Constitution of Liberty*, London: Routledge & Kegan Paul.

Hayek, F.A. (1973) *Law, Legislation and Liberty. A New Statement of the Liberal Principles of Justice and Political Economy*, Volume One, *Rules and Order*, London: Routledge & Kegan Paul.

Higgs, R. (1987) *Crisis and Leviathan: Critical Episode in the Growth of American Government*, New York: Oxford University Press.

Hirschman, A.O. (1970) *Exit, Voice and Loyalty: Responses to Decline in Firms, Organizations, and States*, Cambridge, MA: Harvard University Press.

Holderness, C.G. (1985) 'A Legal Foundation for Exchange', *Journal of Legal Studies* 14, 321–344.

Horwitz, S. (1998) 'Monetary Calculation and Mises's Critique of Planning', *History of Political Economy* 30(3), 427–450.

Inman, R.P. (2001) 'Transfers and Bailouts: Institutions for Enforcing Local Fiscal Discipline', *Constitutional Political Economy* 12(2), 141–160.

Jensen, M.C., Meckling, W.H. and Holderness, C.G. (1986) 'Analysis of Alternative Standing Doctrines', *International Review of Law and Economics* 6, 205–216.

Keynes, J.M. (1936) *The General Theory of Employment, Interest and Money*, New York: Harcourt Brace Jovanovich.

Kirzner, I.M. (1979) *Perception, Opportunity, and Profit*, Chicago: University of Chicago Press.

Kirzner, I.M. (1982) 'Uncertainty, Discovery, and Human Action: A Study of the Entrepreneurial Profile in the Misesian System', in I.M. Kirzner (ed.), *Method, Process, and Austrian Economics. Essays in Honor of Ludwig von Mises*, Lexington, MA: Lexington Books, 139–160.

Kirzner, I.M. (1985) *Discovery and the Capitalist Process*, Chicago: Chicago University Press.

Kirzner, I.M. (1992) *The Meaning of Market Process: Essays in the Development of Modern Austrian Economics*, London and New York: Routledge.

Koppl, R. and Yeager, L. (1996) 'Big Players and Herding in Asset Markets: The Case of the Russian Ruble', *Explorations in Economic History* 33(3), 367–383.

Lachmann, L.M. (1979) 'The Flow of Legislation and the Permanence of the Legal Order', *Order Jahrbuch für die Ordnung von Wirtschaft und Gesellschaft* 30, 67–77.

Lavoie, D. (1985a) *Rivalry and Central Planning: The Socialist Calculation Debate Reconsidered*, Cambridge, Cambridge University Press.

Lavoie, D. (1985b) *National Economic Planning: What is Left?*, Cambridge, MA: Ballinger.

Leoni, B. (1972) *Freedom and the Law*, Los Angeles: Nash.

Loasby, B.J. (1976) *Choice, Complexity and Ignorance: An Enquiry into Economics, Theory and the Practice of Decision-Making*, Cambridge: Cambridge University Press.

Loasby, B.J. (1982) 'Economics of Dispersed and Incomplete Information', in I.M. Kirzner (ed.), *Method, Process, and Austrian Economics. Essays in Honor of Ludwig von Mises*, Lexington, MA: Lexington Books, 111–130.

Machlup, F. (1969) 'Liberalism and the Choice of Freedoms', in E. Streissler (ed.), *Roads to Freedom: Essays in Honour of Friedrich A. von Hayek*, London: Routledge & Kegan Paul, 117–146.

Marshall, A. (1920) *Principles of Economics: An Introductory Volume*, Eighth Edition, London: Macmillan.

Menger, C. (1892) 'On the Origins of Money', *Economic Journal* 2, 239–255.

Menger, C. (1994) *Principles of Economics*, Grove City, PA: Libertarian Press. First German edition 1871.

Messick, R.E. and Kimura, K. (1996) *World Survey of Economic Freedom 1995–1996: A Freedom House Study*, New Brunswick, NJ: Transaction Books.

Mises, L. von (1966) *Human Action: A Treatise on Economics*. Third Revised Edition (Paperback), San Francisco: Fox & Wilkes.

Mises, L. von (1971) *The Theory of Money and Credit*, New Enlarged Edition, Irvington-on-Hudson, NY: Foundation for Economic Education. First German Edition 1912.

Mises, L. von (1981) *Socialism: An Economic and Sociological Analysis*, Indianapolis: Liberty Classics. First German Edition 1922.

Mitchell, W.C. (1937) *The Backward Art of Spending Money and Other Essays*, New York and London: McGraw-Hill.

Parisi, F. (2001) 'The Formation of Customary Law', George Mason University School of Law, Law and Economics Working Paper Series, 01–06.

Pospisil, L.J. (1971) *Anthropology of Law: A Comparative Theory*, New York: Harper & Row.

Przeworski, A. and Limongi, F. (1993) 'Political Regimes and Economic Growth', *Journal of Economic Perspectives* 7(3), 51–69.

Rizzo, M.J. (1985) 'Rules Versus Cost–Benefit Analysis in the Common Law', *Cato Journal* 4(3), 865–884.

Rothbard, M.N. (1993) *Man, Economy, and State*, Auburn, AL: Ludwig von Mises Institute. First published 1962.

Salerno, J.T. (1990) 'Ludwig von Mises as Social Rationalist', *Review of Austrian Economics* 4, 26–54.

Salerno, J.T. (1993) 'Mises and Hayek Dehomogenized', *Review of Austrian Economics* 6(2), 113–146.

Schama, S. (1988) *The Embarrassment of Riches: An Interpretation of Dutch Culture in the Golden Age*, Berkeley, CA: University of California Press.

Scully, G.W. (1992) *Constitutional Environments and Economic Growth*, Princeton, NJ: Princeton University Press.

Scully, G.W. and Slottje, D.J. (1991) 'Ranking Economic Liberty across Countries', *Public Choice* 69(2), 121–152.

Soto, H. de (1989) *The Other Path: The Invisible Revolution in the Third World*, New York: Harper & Row.

Steele, C.N. (1998) 'Entrepreneurship and the Economics of Growth', *Advances in Austrian Economics* 5, 51–84.

Streit, M.E. (1996) 'Competition among Systems as a Defence of Liberty', in H. Hamilton (ed.), *Libertarians and Liberalism: Essays in Honour of Gerard Radnitzky*, Aldershot: Avebury, 236–252.

Thomsen, E.F. (1992) *Prices and Knowledge: A Market-Process Perspective*, London: Routledge.

Tocqueville, A. de (1990) *Democracy in America*, Volume One, New York: Vintage Books. First published 1835.

Vanberg, V.J. and Kerber, W. (1994) 'Institutional Competition among Jurisdictions: An Evolutionary Approach', *Constitutional Political Economy* 5(2), 192–219.

Vihanto, M. (1992) 'Competition Between Local Governments as a Discovery Procedure', *Journal of Institutional and Theoretical Economics* 148(3), 411–436.

Wagner, R.E. (1980) 'Boom and Bust: The Political Economy of Economic Disorder', *Journal of Libertarian Studies* 4(1), 1–37.

Weingast, B.R. (1995) 'The Economic Role of Political Institutions: Market-Preserving Federalism and Economic Development', *Journal of Law, Economics, & Organization* 11(1), 1–31.

Wright, L.M. (1982) 'A Comparative Survey of Economic Freedoms', in R.D. Gastil and C.R. Bertz, *Freedom in the World: Political Rights and Civil Liberties 1982*, Westport, CT: Greenwood Press, 51–90.

[17]

Constit Polit Econ (2007) 18:127–143
DOI 10.1007/s10602-007-9017-1

ORIGINAL ARTICLE

Saving government failure theory from itself: recasting political economy from an Austrian perspective

Peter J. Boettke · Christopher J. Coyne ·
Peter T. Leeson

Published online: 29 March 2007
© Springer Science+Business Media, LLC 2007

Abstract The economic approach to politics revolutionized the way scholars in economics and political science approached the study of political decision-making by introducing the possibility of government failure. However, the persistent and consistent application of neoclassical models of economics also seemed to suggest that once the full costs were accounted for, this failure was an illusion. This paper counters these arguments, typically associated with George Stigler, Gary Becker and Donald Wittman, by focusing on the underlying economic theory. We develop an alternative model of political economy grounded in the Austrian conception of the dynamic market process.

Keywords Entrepreneurship · Government failure · Market failure · Market process · Public choice

JEL Classification B52 · B53 · H11

1 Introduction

The development of the economic theory of politics by Anthony Downs, Duncan Black, James Buchanan, Gordon Tullock, and Mancur Olson revolutionized the way scholars in economics and political science thought about non-market decision-making. The traditional theory of public economics (the economic role of the state) was best summarized by Baumol's (1952) *Welfare Economics and the Theory of the*

P. J. Boettke
Department of Economics, George Mason University, Fairfax, USA

C. J. Coyne (✉)
Department of Economics, Hampden-Sydney College, Hampden-Sydney, VA 23493, USA
e-mail: ccoyne@hsc.edu

P. T. Leeson
Department of Economics, West Virginia University, Morgantown, USA

 Springer

State. According to this theory, market failures, such as positive or negative externalities, would be identified and government officials would create the appropriate tax and subsidy scheme to bring social marginal cost and private marginal cost into alignment. In short, government was the corrective to market failures identified by the economist.

Keynesian macroeconomics argued along similar lines. As aggregate demand failure was identified, appropriate fiscal policy would be followed to ensure that aggregate demand would meet aggregate supply at the full employment level of output. Again, government circa 1950 economics was seen as the corrective to the shortcomings of the private market economy.

Prior to the "public choice revolution," economists viewed deliberations over public policy as if public-spirited autocrats were carrying out the process. Neither political nor material considerations would impede the selection of policies, which served the public interest. Later developments in microeconomics, such as property rights economics, would challenge market failure theory while leaving intact the conception of the state as a benevolent dictatorship. The policy debate became one where the economist would expose the unintended consequences of government intervention assuming that the intent of the policy was to advance the public interest. But the incentives that political actors faced in making policy choices were left unexamined.

The economic theory of politics challenged the literature on economic policy by demonstrating that if we allow for behavioral symmetry between market and political actors, government failure is a distinct possibility. Behavioral symmetry merely asserted that if we are going to assume self-interest on the part of market participants, we must also assume self-interest on the part of political participants. Similarly, if we are going to assume that participants in the market are cognitively limited, then we should assume cognitive limitations in politics as well. Allowing for motivational and cognitive symmetry in both the political and market spheres meant that "market failures" could not be taken as *prima facie* evidence for government intervention, as was previously believed. Self-interested, informationally-constrained rulers may be unwilling or unable to remedy market imperfections. Indeed, if political actors are modeled realistically instead of romantically, giving power to the state for this purpose may actually result in a worse outcome than before the intervention. Assuming behavioral symmetry opened the possibility that the cure could be worse than the illness.

The tale of the Roman Emperor, often invoked by Gordon Tullock, summarizes the problem of pre-public choice political economy. According to this tale a Roman Emperor is asked to judge a singing contest between two contestants. Upon hearing the first contestant sing, the Emperor awards the prize to the second singer under the assumption that she clearly cannot be any worse than the first. But the Emperor's assumption is quite possibly off the mark; the second singer could in fact be much worse. This parable highlights the proposition that imperfect markets do not necessarily justify government intervention. The consequences of this methodological demand for behavioral symmetry were damaging to the government-as-corrective conclusion of the previous generation of public economists, and augmented the unintended consequences critique of government intervention.

The first generation of the economic theory of politics in political science and economics tended to focus on the perversities in democratic decision-making. Voters can be divided into groups of those who are rationally abstinent, rationally ignorant, and specially interested. Politicians are seen as seeking campaign contributions and

 Springer

votes. Voters are demanders of policy and politicians are suppliers. In the interaction between voters and politicians, the tendency is for politicians (in their effort to secure contributions and votes) to introduce public policies, which concentrate benefits on the well-organized and well-informed specially interested voters in the short run, and disperse the costs among the unorganized and ill-informed voters in the long run. Voter preferences would enter one end of the political process and go through a series of political manipulations, producing public policies at odds with those voter preferences at the other[1] (See Fig. 1).

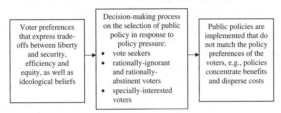

Fig. 1 First generation of the economic theory of politics

Olson first used these arguments to explain the logic of collective action (1965, 1982) and then the rise and decline of nations, focusing in particular on the demo-sclerosis produced when the narrow interests of well-organized groups out-competed the encompassing interests of society. Buchanan and Tullock (1962) used these arguments to demonstrate the decline of the constitutional order in modern society and the rise of a rent-seeking society in its place. Modern democratic politics were run by interests, not principle, to the detriment of the classical liberal state of the Founding Fathers. A solution was to be found in the constitutional craftsmanship of the political economist who took as his task to find the binding rules that constrain interest group logic so that a free and prosperous society could be established (see Buchanan, 1975, 1979).

As the constitutional political economy project associated with the Virginia School emerged in the 1960–1980 period, the economic approach to politics also developed in alternative directions in the hands of Chicago economists such as George Stigler and Gary Becker, and Rochester political scientists, such as William Riker. This Chicago-Rochester strain of work tended to focus on the equilibrium properties of political affairs (see, e.g., Stigler, 1988; Riker, 1962). Under the right conditions this work leads to a different vision of Fig. 1, one where voter preferences are accurately reflected in policy choices (See Fig. 2).

Fig. 2 Chicago-Rochester theory of politics

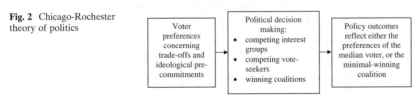

---

[1] This is a different criticism from, though not inconsistent with, the pure economic critique of public policy in terms of unintended undesirable consequences.

Ironically, the economic approach to politics, after challenging the conception of politics as benign, ends up in the Chicago–Rochester variant with a picture of the political system (under conditions of open competition) that is ruthlessly efficient in a manner analogous to the perfectly competitive market. Consumers in the market and voters in politics will get what they desire constrained by technological and political feasibility, and some approximation of a willingness to pay criterion.[2]

There is, however, something strange with this picture that we hope to correct. The problem as we see it is as follows:

(1) Economic theory informs us that $20 bills (unexploited opportunities) cannot persistently lay on sidewalks without being picked up;
(2) The very same economic theory that informs us about the non-persistence of inefficiencies is also what we use to identify inefficiencies (gains from trade that are currently unexploited);
(3) When we examine policy reality in light of that economic theory we see inefficient policies all the time, e.g., protectionist legislation.

How do we square propositions (1)–(3) without abandoning economic theory? We see the choice as pushing in one of two directions. On the one hand we could argue that (2) and (3) are illusions that economists must pierce through. The $20 bill is not there because it would actually cost $25 to reach down and pick it up. In other words, if a lower cost alternative were available it would be employed; and since it is not, the policy reality must reflect the political economy reality efficiently. No unexploited opportunity for mutually beneficial action remains in the political process.

On the other hand, if we reject this approach, as we do but Stigler (1992) does not, then we have to explain why these $20 bills are lying on the sidewalk and actors are not picking them up. This paper takes this alternative approach as a starting point. In doing so we rely on a theory of *structural ignorance* to go hand in hand with theories of rational ignorance to describe the political environment in which actors make choices (see, e.g., Kirzner, 1985). In short, the knowledge required to alert participants in the process to the existence of $20 bills to be picked up is the result of a specific institutional context.

Although in the private property market economy this knowledge of unexploited opportunities is revealed through the lure of pure entrepreneurial profits, in the political process *this* knowledge is not produced.[3] This does not mean that no knowledge is produced in the political process. On the contrary, clearly the political process produces some knowledge relevant to *political actors*. But this knowledge

---

[2] The move from preference induced equilibrium to structure induced equilibrium associated with Shepsle and Weingast (1981), while an important analytical step, does not solve the problem we are concerned with in this paper. The problem is that the analysis in Shepsle and Weingast leads to the position that given the constraints of the institutional structure agents find themselves acting within, they are still pursuing the optimal course of action.

[3] "What the official knows, he knows, and what he knows he does *not* know, one may imagine him diligently undertaking to find out, through appropriate cost–benefit-calculated search. But one can hardly imagine him discovering, except by the sheerest accident, those opportunities for increasing efficiency of which he is completely unaware. The official is not subject to the entrepreneurial profit incentive, which...appears continually and successfully to inspire discovery of hitherto undreamed of possibilities for eliminating unnecessary expenditures. Nothing with the regulatory process seems to be able to simulate even remotely well the discovery process that is so integral to the unregulated market" (Kirzner, 1985: 141).

leads to superfluous discoveries from the point of view of economic efficiency. In other words, knowledge generated in the political context may enable individuals to survive in the competitive environment of politics, but it does not lead them to exploit the opportunities for gains from economically beneficial trades and eradicate economic inefficiencies. The knowledge necessary to alert actors to these possibilities for entrepreneurial profit simply does not exist because the entrepreneurial context is absent. Instead, actors are alert to alternative possibilities that generate an entirely different pattern of consequences than what would appear in the unregulated market economy. Our argument is not that the cost of acquiring relevant knowledge is too high; it is that knowledge generated is always context specific, and in the political context this knowledge of entrepreneurial profit opportunities is necessarily absent.[4]

Thus, in addition to the distinction between economic (cost–benefit) and technological efficiency (input–output), we introduce the notion of political efficiency (winning coalitions). And just as technologically feasible projects must be sorted for their economic efficiency through the process of rational economic calculation (see Boettke, 1998), the set of politically efficient states must be examined in light of economics to judge whether political choices are economically beneficial or not. The persistence of economically inefficient policy is not an illusion because it is possible for politically efficient policies to be economically inefficient. Whereas within a market system technologically possible projects are subjected to the economic test of profit and loss, the economic test of profit and loss is not employed in assessing political choices.

This critical distinction between economic and political efficiency is blurred in equilibrium states where all profit opportunities are exhausted. We therefore propose a recasting of political economy that makes this distinction readily apparent. We argue that the necessary recasting is best informed by the Austrian theory of the entrepreneurial market process and the Virginia School of political economy with its focus on rent-seeking and constitutional craftsmanship.

The current theoretical orientation in political economy was explicitly built on the value theory of neoclassical economics and the core concept of maximizing behavior and market equilibrium. Compared to the normative theorizing and psychological explanations of 1950s political science this was a major step forward; but it did not come without a cost. The value paradigm in economics tends to turn a blind eye to the exchange activity that drives an economic system (see Kohn, 2004). We see the Virginia School as the lever by which we can recast political economy while maintaining the strengths of the economic approach to politics precisely because James Buchanan and Gordon Tullock always saw their effort in the context of the exchange behavior that is exhibited in political life.

2 Policy as efficient

The critical responses to the theory of market failure came in four kinds of arguments. The first variety was to deny that the so-called market failures could in fact be

---

[4] The reason why this idea has been under explored in the economics literature is because of the difficulty of operationalizing contextual knowledge, as opposed to the ease of operationalizing information as a commodity. On the distinction between knowledge and information in economics see Boettke (2002).

identified using sound economic theory. Rothbard (1962: 765–890) held perhaps the most uncompromising position in this regard. However correct this position may be judged in retrospect, we will not emphasize it here because it did not impact the evolution of economic argumentation in the subsequent professional discussion.

The second variety insists that while the concept of "market failure" may have some logical coherence in positive theory, the transition from positive to normative theory is problematic for a number of reasons—not the least of which is that the ideal belies a nirvana fallacy and the invoking of an unexamined alternative commits a "grass is always greener" fallacy. Demsetz (1969), for example, in his now-famous piece entitled, "Information and Efficiency: Another Viewpoint," points out that Kenneth Arrow, in following a nirvana view, commits the "grass is always greener fallacy" by invoking an unexamined alternative—in this case a government corrective—to a so-called market failure. "To say that private enterprise is inefficient," Demsetz argues, "because indivisibilities and imperfect knowledge are part of life, or because people are susceptible to the human weaknesses subsumed in the term moral hazards, or because marketing commodity-options is not costless, or because persons are risk-averse, is to say little more than that the competitive equilibrium would be different if these were not the facts of life" (1969: 19).

According to Demsetz, perfect competition and Pareto optimality are not useful for the main task before political economists, which is not irrelevant comparisons to an ideal world populated by non-humans, but instead "the design of institutional arrangements that provide incentives to encourage experimentation (including the development of new products, new knowledge, new reputations, and new ways of organizing activities) without overly insulating these experiments from the ultimate test of survival" (1969: 19).

Ronald Coase similarly condemned the traditional market failure approach. "It is my belief," Coase wrote, "that the failure of economists to reach correct conclusions about the treatment of harmful effects cannot be ascribed simply to a few slips in analysis. It stems from basic defects in the current approach to problems of welfare economics." (1960: 153). Of course, the defects Coase is referring to are those resulting from the standard welfare economics assumption that correcting identified deficiencies is costless. Coase advocates an "opportunity-cost" approach to examining alternative policy solutions to economic problems. In doing so, he insists "we have to take into account the costs involved in operating the various social arrangements (whether it be the working of a market or of a government department) as well as the costs involved in moving to a new system" (1960: 156). Failure to do so leads to erroneous conclusions regarding the efficacy of state correction.

An important point to stress is that this Coase–Demsetz style of argument, while damaging to the Samuelson-Bator-Arrow presentation of market failure, led to the Panglossian fallacy that we will deal with later. Consider, for example, the argument concerning monopoly that emerges from a consistent application of the Alchian-Demsetz style of reasoning. The standard monopoly diagram yields a deadweight loss—gains from trade are unexploited because of monopoly power. But the question asked by the property rights economists was: why wouldn't the monopolist perfectly price discriminate and capture the surplus, eliminating the deadweight loss? The standard reply to this query was that the monopolist cannot perfectly price discriminate because the monitoring costs of preventing resale among consumers are too high. But these monitoring costs, the property rights economists concluded, are transaction costs. If these costs are seen as transaction costs, they should be included

 Springer

in the marginal cost curve. Once we shift to the new representation of the marginal cost curve to reflect all relevant costs incurred in making additional transactions, the monopoly-competitive distinction disappears and price will equal marginal cost.[5]

The only time monopolies generates negative welfare effects is if a deadweight loss is due not to transaction costs, but to political barriers to entry that prevent individuals from realizing the gains from exchange (Demsetz, 1982). Either the system is ideal, or it is blocked by legal restrictions from achieving the ideal. In other words, markets do not fail to produce optimal results, but government restrictions may prevent markets from working effectively, for instance when government grants monopoly privileges to certain firms.

The third type of argument that emerged in the 1960s and 1970s against the standard welfare economics of market failure theory is what could be called the dynamic adjustment model of markets.[6] From this perspective, most closely associated with Hayek (1969) and Kirzner (1973), markets process information effectively and are continually adjusting to changing circumstances. In this world, inefficiencies at any one point in time are admitted but recognized to be the source of entrepreneurial action and subsequent market correction. Today's inefficiency is tomorrow's profit opportunity. The imperfections identified in the nirvana approach are actually the factors that drive markets in the discovery of new ways to meet consumer demand, new and better products, and new and cheaper production techniques. For instance, Klein and Foldvary (2005) have recently published a collection of articles examining how changing technologies explode previous arguments for market failure by finding ways to fence externalities, erode market power, and improve the structure of incentives and the flow and quality of information.

The fourth kind of argument raised against traditional market failure theory was the public choice critique of government. The welfare economics of Pigou through

---

[5] The analysis conforms to what Reder (1982) refers to as the Chicago "tight prior," where the equilibrium conditions of: (i) the market price being equal to marginal cost of production, or (ii) that the market price of any input is equal to the value of its marginal product, or (iii) that the marginal cost of producing any product is the least cost method of production, are imposed on the world to make sense of it. The construction of the thought experiment being conducted requires that theory dominates any evidence to the contrary, and that the way to make sense of the evidence is to fit it to the theory. Scientific explanation in economics, in this framework, results from describing any social phenomena in a manner consistent with these equilibrium conditions.

[6] In *Capitalism and Freedom* (1962), Friedman did not emphasize dynamic adjustments nor did he emphasize public choice issues, but in dealing with the charge of market failure due to monopoly he argues that an unregulated monopoly will outperform a regulated monopoly in satisfying consumer demand. The argument he provides is mainly focused on the insulation from survival tests that regulation provides. In addressing other public policy errors, e.g., in the area of fiscal and monetary policy, Friedman's argument in the early 1960s was one of intellectual error—analytical error and error in historical interpretation. The Great Depression, for example, was not a product of the inherent instability of the capitalist order but a consequence of policy errors on the part of the government authorities. In the late 1960s, Friedman also developed an argument that this policy task was too cumbersome to leave to discretion. Given the long and variable lag between the recognition of a problem in the economic system, the devising of an appropriate response, the implementation of the response, and the impact of the policy change on the economy, it could very well be that the original problem would have already been corrected by market adjustments. Discretionary policy, rather than a cure, could in fact destabilize the situation. Finally, by the publication of *Free to Choose* (1980), Friedman had started to rely on public choice explanations of interest group manipulations to explain the disjoint between demands for government as a corrective and the reality of government as a disturbance to the economic order. Friedman is exempt from the criticism of the Chicago style of political economy we will offer.

🖄 Springer

Samuelson assumed government provided a costless solution to market failures. But upon examination, the theory of government failure had to be set up alongside the theory of market failure. Public choice did not challenge the standard theory of market failure as we saw in the first three responses. It is not that Buchanan and Tullock did not follow these arguments (in fact, in different writings they contributed to them). But for the sake of argument they were content to admit that markets fail while questioning government policy as a reliable corrective. When government actions are critically examined for the incentives generated and the information utilized in assessing policy trade-offs, they argued, government failure would exacerbate whatever problems might have been identified as market failures.

By the 1980s the public choice critique was absorbed into the mainstream of economic teachings. The link between the original Demsetz critique of the nirvana fallacy and the Hayek–Kirzner discovery notion of the market was all but forgotten in the preoccupation with equilibrium analysis. In fact, the Demsetzian critique of Arrow was swept aside in the 1970s and 1980s by the ascendancy of powerful arguments from Joseph Stiglitz, who developed a new theory of market failure that emphasized the informational inefficiencies of market economies. Instead of spurring on an equal ascendancy of the market process and discovery answer to imperfect information, the Coase–Demsetz "whatever is, is efficient" aspect of comparative institutional analysis was pursued in political economy.[7]

In the hands of economists less consistent than Chicago economists, the Coase–Demsetz demand that we examine alternative arrangements considering the cost of transition perfectly complemented the public choice critique of government laid out by Buchanan and Tullock. But this is only because the full implications of the Coase–Demsetz line of argument were arbitrarily cut short. Their argument complemented the Buchanan–Tullock argument only if the former was not fully teased out to its logical conclusion. In the hands of George Stigler and Gary Becker, however, cutting short the full implications of the Coase–Demsetz line of reasoning was not going to happen.

Stigler (1982, 1992) pursued the Coase–Demsetz reasoning to its logical end. Whatever current arrangement is in practice must by definition be the most effective, or a lower cost alternative would be in use instead. In competitive equilibrium this would be as true for the production of legislation as it is for the production of widgets. The economist could abandon his role as a scientist and instead address the preferences of the populace, but in so doing he ought to admit that he is now "preaching" and not engaged in "science" (1982). Subsidies, protectionism, regulation, legal decisions, etc. are all rational responses to political realities by various actors. The traditional theory of government failure suffered from the "grass is always greener fallacy" in the same way that the traditional theory of market failure did.

Unless the costs of transitioning to a new arrangement are accounted for, the analysis is incomplete. And when those costs are accounted for, many so-called government failures disappear, as the costs of transition to the new arrangement would exceed the benefits that would follow from the new institutional setting

---

[7] The "survivorship" principle was invoked to provide any *status quo* with the efficiency presumption. Contrast that with Buchanan's position on the *status quo*, where the current arrangement of affairs is given no normative weight except that it is, and must form, the starting point for any theory of reform through political negotiation and compensation. For a discussion of Buchanan's position see Boettke (2001).

(Stigler, 1992). In other words, while it may appear that a $20 bill is lying on the sidewalk in the policy world, it would cost $21 or more to pick it up. The survival of sugar subsidies in the competitive environment of politics demonstrates that no lower cost alternative has been forthcoming. The survivorship principle is the ultimate bottom line in social affairs. Stigler's view of the political operation of democracy emerges from an application of the Coase theorem to this realm of human interaction, and an insistence that scientific economics be grounded in maximizing behavior and equilibrium theorizing.

Becker (1983) developed a sophisticated treatment of this question in his model of pressure groups under conditions of open democratic access. What Becker demonstrates is that under these conditions, pressure groups serve to efficiently deliver public policy to the median voter. Egregious government failure does not emerge in situations where pressure groups simulate the conditions of competitive markets. Instead, just as in the competitive market, competitive politics will yield the best delivery of goods and services available given technological constraints and voter preferences. Politics is about transfers, but politicians have every incentive to conduct these transfers as efficiently as possible and thus political allocations under democracy are analogous to resource allocations in competitive markets. Maximizing and equilibrium entail zero profit conditions—all the gains from trade have been pursued to exhaustion—and this is true for democratic politics just as it is for competitive markets.

Wittman (1995) has taken this argument even further, arguing that democratic failure is an outright myth. Voters get what they want under democracy, just as consumers get what they want under perfectly competitive markets. Voters have very effective disciplinary devices in place to penalize politicians who do not conform to their will.[8] Consider the basic Ferejohn principal/agent model of politics (Ferejohn, 1986). The agent is the politician, the principal are the voters and the voter decides to hire or fire the politician. The voter will pick an aggregate proxy for a job well done, e.g., per capita GDP. If in the current term per capita GDP goes up, the voter will rehire the politician. But if per capita GDP goes down, the voter will fire the politician come election time. This simple exercise is enough to discipline the agent to act in the interest of the principal. And since there is a fiercely competitive market in politicians seeking election, the market for politicians serves as effectively as the market for managerial labor to discipline deviant behavior.[9]

---

[8] Wittman distances himself from the Stigler–Becker claims of efficiency and makes a bolder claim to democratic efficiency. It is not that democratic politics is "efficient" when we include the transaction costs associated with policy change. Instead, Wittman argues that democracy is efficient in the sense that voters cast informed votes and politicians are effectively disciplined so that wealth maximizing policies are introduced and sustained. His argumentative strategy is to demonstrate that any argument for government failure requires an empirical assumption (e.g., the existence of extreme voter stupidity; the lack of competition in the political sphere; high negotiating costs which prevent political bargains from being struck). Market-oriented economists reject similar types of assumptions all the time in examining market-failure, and so Wittman insists they should be rejected in the political setting as well.

[9] But note that in the standard analysis of the principal/agent the market for corporate control also plays a major role in disciplining market participants. The stock price of a firm reflects the expected profitability of the firm, and if market participants believe that earnings of a firm do not represent the capabilities of that firm, a take over will clean out the ineffective management and replace it with a more effective management. Profit and loss accounting serve the vital function of providing necessary knowledge to market participants. But what is the equivalent in the realm of politics?

Wittman's argument can be seen as flipping the symmetry argument employed in the first generation of the economic theory of politics back on itself. As he puts it: "nearly all of the arguments claiming that economic markets are efficient apply equally well to democratic political markets; and, conversely, that economic models of political-market failure are no more valid than the analogous arguments for economic-market failure" (1995: 2). The claim that emerges in Wittman is that political allocations under democracy are wealth maximizing. The intellectual energies of political economists, Wittman argues, should shift from efforts to identify government failures to a focus on optimal organizational design, or how various organizational mutations in governmental institutions (such as political parties, candidate information, and governing structures) serve to ameliorate potential problems in the political marketplace.

How do we respond to the Stigler–Wittman challenge to the economic approach to politics? It is our contention that we must go back to the earlier passages quoted from Demsetz and pursue the economics contained in his parenthetical clause about dynamic adjustments, discovery, the inapplicability of competitive equilibrium and Pareto optimality as it relates to questions of public policy. In doing so, we can recast political economy in a manner that retains the critique of government, and does not devolve into the Panglossian fallacy for either the market economy or the democratic polity.

3 Overturning the Chicago/Rochester/Virginia alliance

The Stigler–Wittman critique of government failure has not gone unchallenged in the political economy literature. Representatives of the Virginia School of political economy, however, have been far more vocal in this regard than any Chicago political economists or Rochester rational choice political scientists. The reason for the paucity of response from Chicago and Rochester is due to their intellectual commitment to maximizing behavior and equilibrium theorizing. As mentioned above, these intellectual approaches are committed to the value paradigm versus the exchange paradigm (see Kohn, 2004).

The Virginia School, however, has always been grounded in the exchange paradigm rather than the maximization approach (see Buchanan, 1964). Economic analysis is not about Crusoe's allocation decisions as an isolated actor battling the scarcity of his environment. Nor is market analysis about competitive conditions and a system of simultaneous equations that provide a unique price and quantity vector that will clear all markets. Buchanan's conception of the market *process* is summarized as follows:

> A market is not competitive by assumption or by construction. A market *becomes* competitive, and competitive rules *come to be* established as institutions emerge to place limits on individual behavior patterns. It is this *becoming* process, brought about by the continuous pressure of human behavior in exchange, that is the central part of our discipline, if we have one, not the dry rot of postulated perfection. A solution to a general-equilibrium set of equations is not predetermined by exogenously determined rules. A general solution, if there is one, *emerges* as a result of a whole network of evolving exchanges, bargains, trades, side payments, agreements, contracts which, finally

at some point, ceases to renew itself. At each stage of this evolution toward a solution there are *gains* to be made, there are exchanges possible, and this being true, the direction of movement is modified (1964: 29, italics in original).

The "equilibrium always" vision of economic activity is focused on that state of affairs where action has ceased, and thus it tends to blind us to the processes by which such a state could ever be achieved. In fact, in the Walrasian conception of the market all plans had to be *pre-reconciled* before exchanges could be transacted, lest 'false' prices would lead economic actors astray. But in the exchange paradigm the focus is on the *reconciliation process* between economic actors and the institutions within which their efforts to truck, barter and exchange take place.

Both the value and exchange paradigms are grounded in the neoclassical framework of the pure logic of choice. The crucial distinction in the approaches can be found in the (a) cognitive capabilities assumed for actors, and (b) the institutional infrastructure required to achieve a coordination of plans in a manner which tends toward wealth maximization. In the value paradigm, the cognitive capability of actors is usually heroic and does the vast majority of the heavy lifting in the analytical explanation about how order emerges in society. In the exchange paradigm, however, the actors are imbued with very limited and sometimes even crippling cognitive capacity, and the institutional environment (and the structure of incentives it possesses and the learning of existing opportunities and new possibilities for mutual gain it engenders) does the intellectual heavy lifting. As can be seen in the Buchanan quote, the market order is seen as an emergent process unfolding through time as the gains from trade are continually identified and pursued.

Rational choice, as if the choosers were human, substitutes for lightening calculators of pleasure and pain, and institutional settings in which property and contracts (and their enforcement) are examined in detail for their incentive effects and learning properties substitutes for the institutionally antiseptic theory of general competitive equilibrium. This is why the Virginia School serves as the lever we rely on in our narrative about the recasting of political economy. But the reader should be clear that the sort of economic theory we have just described is most closely associated with the Austrian school of economics as evidenced in the writings of Carl Menger, Ludwig von Mises, F.A. Hayek and Israel Kirzner. Of course, the non-Ricardian British economists, such as Richard Whately can be invoked as well, but the exchange paradigm was explicitly developed in the work of Mises (1949) and Hayek (1948, 1976).

Our effort is to save the Virginia School from the pull of Chicago by presenting the Austrian school as the appropriate foundational theory of economic interaction. Once we recognize the different underlying economic framework, the critique of the Stigler–Wittman conjecture that democratic policy is efficient in the same way the market competition is, sharpens. Critiques inspired by the publication of Wittman's study have been offered by Boudreaux (1996), Buchanan (1996), Rowley (1997), Rowley and Vachris (1994, 2003), Sutter (2002), and Wagner (1996). At one level the debate can be boiled down to a metaphysical faith in, or rejection of, the proposition that whatever is, is efficient. But each of these authors also offers good reasons to believe that a critique of this proposition can be offered without resorting to metaphysical squabbling.

If we do not imbue actors with cognitive capacities beyond that of humans, and we examine not only the incentive structure, but also the learning properties of alternative institutional arrangements, then we can identify crucial differences in the

 Springer

behavior of markets within an environment of private property and freedom of contract, and the democratic political process of voting and policy deliberation. The political process generates incentives and learning that are entirely different than what is exhibited in the competitive market process. The bundled nature of political goods creates problems that are solved in market exchange by unbundling; the political process tends to concentrate benefits and disperse costs, whereas the marketplace tends to concentrate costs and disperse benefits; decisions in the market to either buy or abstain from buying are a direct signal to sellers, whereas in the political process voters do not have the same extent of feedback opportunities with respect to public policy offerings because they vote only periodically for representatives and their vote is rarely decisive.

Relying again on the description of how markets prod us toward continually realizing the gains from trade, the institutional environment of politics does not present us with the continuous feedback opportunities we experience in markets for mutual adjustment, nor does the political process require us to continually learn about the best opportunities available. The nature of the choice problem in politics is simply different than the one we are confronted with in markets. As Fernandez and Rodrik (1991) point out, this goes a long way to explaining why there is a status quo bias in politics that does not exist in markets. Policies once rejected never get reconsidered, and policies once accepted are rarely challenged due to uncertainty over the distribution of the gains from policy change. In the market process, errors are continually identified and acted upon, if not by the individual entrepreneur who made the initial error, then by his entrepreneurial counterpart who is continually looking for a way to realize profits (Leeson, Coyne, & Boettke, 2006).

Once political economy is recast along these lines, then the distorting impact of public ignorance, voting behavior, ideology, and the distributional battle of pressure groups on the *economic system* can move to the center stage of political economic analysis. Policies may in fact be adopted for very sensible political reasons and reflect political efficiency, but they can simultaneously deviate significantly from efficiency-enhancing economic policies that would be adopted if politics were able to operate on economic criteria.

The Wittman contention that democratic policy-making is wealth maximizing is a consequence of confusing political and economic processes. Survivorship of perverse policy does not indicate, as Stigler thought, that we are wrong to identify it as perverse. The coin of the realm in politics is different than that in economics. And thus the knowledge feedback that would be discovered in that process to identify a politically efficient policy choice but an economically inefficient one is not in operation. The context for efficient decision-making has shifted. The market context within which entrepreneurs are prodded to discover errors and act in a manner less erroneous than before in the hope of securing entrepreneurial profit is non-existent in the context of politics. "There is no entrepreneurial process at work," writes Israel Kirzner, "and there is no proxy for entrepreneurial profit and loss that easily might indicate where errors have been made and how they should be corrected...No systematic process seems at work through which [politicians] might come to discover what they have not known" (Kirzner, 1985: 140).

Structural ignorance is a different concept than rational ignorance, in that it stresses the link between useable knowledge and specific institutional contexts. Sanford Ikeda (2003) has discussed the difference between "neoclassical" and "Austrian" political economy perspectives in relation to the connection between

 Springer

intentions and outcomes in policy space. Neoclassical political economy infers intentions from outcomes, while Austrian political economy does not presume that such an inference is possible. Instead, Austrian political economy focuses on the unintended and undesirable consequences from the point of view of the proponents of government action.

But Ikeda's analysis incorrectly characterizes all public choice analysis as grounded in the perfect knowledge assumption and equilibrium analysis. As such, while Ikeda is completely aware of the issue of structural ignorance, he does not address the issue of structural ignorance in politics in the same way that we do.[10] In his rendering of neoclassical political economy, policies emerge that are the intended outcome of favored interest groups, but leave deadweight losses in their wake that nobody has an incentive to remove.

The distinction we have drawn between political efficiency and economic efficiency explains this state of affairs. The economic inefficiencies are not dissipated because the knowledge necessary to act in a manner to eliminate the deadweight losses is not generated within the political context. Richard Wagner makes this point when he states: "The incentive to acquire knowledge and the judgment to identify something as knowledge in the first place depend upon the institutional setting within which people act" (1989: 56). To illustrate this point Wagner invokes the classic story of a business error—the Edsel—and he asks his readers "what if the Edsel had been a government product...Would production have been halted as quickly?" (1989: 54). The profit and loss calculations made in the market direct production and force market participants to adjust their plans quickly and ruthlessly. In the democratic process, however, the incentives/knowledge for error detection and correction, and the guiding function of this knowledge for necessary adjustments, are not necessarily grounded in the economics of profit seeking and cost minimizing.

As we have seen, Wittman insists that politics is as competitive as the most efficient markets. But what Wittman does not address is the different knowledge that is generated within the contexts of private property markets and democratic politics. Mitchell and Simmons may provide the most succinct statement of the basic point we are trying to make when they state that since, "government officials are not permitted to sell their official service or goods...they never learn the precise values citizens place on activities and goods" (1994: 68). Without a market, the *economic value* of political goods and services is impossible to ascertain. In the context of the market economy, comparative costs and relative prices continually provide guidance to market participants on the least cost methods of production, the most urgent consumer demands and the opportunities for mutually beneficial exchange. "Political actors have no such guidance, and without it efficient choices become, as Ludwig von Mises and Frederich A. von Hayek argued, impossible" (Mitchell & Simmons

---

[10] Ikeda instead focuses on government failure resulting from an examination of means-ends and the demonstration that policy often results in outcomes which are undesirable from the point of view of the policy advocate. While we do not dispute the unintended and undesirable consequences of government action, we also do not want to push aside the cleavage between the policy preferences of the voting populace and the policy consequences that result because of clash of group interests in political decision making. In short, there are indeed deadweight losses that are not removed because the political process not only fails to provide the incentive for their removal, but also because the political process has no way to provide participants with the *economic* knowledge required to eliminate the inefficiency.

1994: 68). Neither the production nor provision of public goods can be carried out in an economically efficient manner.[11]

The analogy between the market economy and democratic politics is broken. It is not just that each institutional setting has its own structure of incentives, but both also have unique epistemic properties.[12] To insist that markets are not identical to politics is not to violate the symmetry assumption, as Wittman suggests. We can assume identical behavioral postulates, but we must recognize that context matters. The unique structural context of choice provides a structure of incentives that actors face, and a flow of information that actors utilize, in making their choices. All we are insisting on is the recognition that political calculations are wholly different from the economic calculations made by entrepreneurs in the market place. And if this is so, then there are at any given point in time opportunities for improvement with regard to economic policy that are not being pursued because the signals that alert economic actors to potential gains from trade are not being generated within the context of politics.

To give one example, politicians are concerned with minimal winning coalitions, but businessmen do not need majorities to operate a successful business. The number of votes matters more than the intensity of any one vote because each vote is equally weighted. In the market process, though, the entrepreneur is concerned with the intensity of buyer preferences because it determines the willingness to pay. Economic actors need to know *how much* buyers want this or that particular good or service; political actors need to know *how many* voters desire this or that particular policy. The two questions are categorically different from one another.

Other factors leading to the break down of the analogy between politics and markets are scattered throughout the writings of economists in the Austrian tradition.[13] These factors all raise serious doubts about the veracity of Wittman's insistence of a tight argument from analogy with respect to the disciplinary mechanisms that ensure the adoption of wealth maximizing policies. Boettke and Leeson (2004) provide a survey of this literature from Bohm-Bawerk to Mises and Hayek to Schumpeter, and highlight the issues of public ignorance, ideology, interest groups, dynamics of interventionism, and unintended consequences. Boettke and Lopez (2002) introduce and collect a series of essays devoted to exploring the areas of commonality between Austrian and Virginia political economy. Wohlgemuth (1999) has argued that democratic politics is not organized as an ongoing market process.

---

[11] Wagner (1997) develops this argument further in the context of discussing the contributions of the Italian economist Maffeo Pantaleoni.

[12] Hayek (1937) challenged economists to augment their incentive based arguments with an analysis of the learning properties of different social environments. Human ignorance, limited cognitive capacity, and how alternative institutional environments work to ameliorate the problems generated due to these issues becomes of the main theme of Hayek's work from that article forward throughout his long career. Hayek, rather than offering either a ruthless efficiency or a natural rights based defense of the liberal order, offers a humility based one: "Liberty is essential in order to leave room for the unforeseeable and unpredictable; we want it because we have learned to expect from it the opportunity of realizing many of our aims. It is because every individual knows so little and, in particular, because we rarely know which of us knows best that we trust the independence and competitive efforts of many to induce the emergence of what we shall want when we see it" (1960: 29).

[13] Rothbard (1962, 1977) made the case for a categorical rejection of any similarity between the two realms insisting that markets are the arena of *voluntary* exchange whereas politics is the domain of *power* and *coercion*.

This is because competitive politics more resembles a natural monopoly where exclusive control over the means of legitimate coercion is granted to the state for the production and provision of political goods. Voters are in a different situation than buyers, and politicians are confronted with an array of choices categorically different than the ones an entrepreneur must face.

4 Conclusion

We have argued that a recasting of the economic theory of politics along Austrian or entrepreneurial market process lines can retain the argumentative structure of public choice theory while not succumbing to the logical straightjacket of the Panglossian fallacy. The key idea is to base the economic foundation of political analysis in a theory of exchange as opposed to a theory of value maximization. Once exchange, and the institutions within which exchange takes place, moves to the forefront of the intellectual enterprise, the idea that context matters follows naturally. Behavioral symmetry does not result in symmetry in performance provided we do not assume pure benevolence and pure omniscience. Incentives prod individuals to behave in one way rather than another. We are attentive to that which is in our interest to be attentive to in whatever setting we find ourselves. Cognitively limited actors must learn not only to be attentive, but also what it means to be attentive within specified contexts.

We have argued that much of the confusion over the "efficiency" of democracy is due to semantic confusions. Democracy may very well tend to generate politically efficient decisions, but in the context of democratic politics, the knowledge required to ensure economically efficient policy choices is absent. Political actors are *structurally ignorant* of the knowledge of comparative costs and the relative prices that would guide the production and provision of public goods and services in an economically efficient direction. Instead, deadweight losses abound. Even if we could remove the problem of rational ignorance and guarantee competitive politics, the structural ignorance problem would remain as a result of the different context of choice in politics and the market.

Whereas market failures, if allowed to exist, spur entrepreneurial discovery so that wealth-enhancing exchanges are continuously being brokered, the existence of economically inefficient (wealth destroying) policies does not automatically yield political "profits" for politicians to grab. Instead, it is conceivable, and in fact likely, that such policies will garner a minimal winning coalition under democracy even though they will fail to deliver on their promises, and distort the pattern of resource allocation.

Acknowledgments We would like to thank Steve Horwitz, Sandy Ikeda, Roger Koppl, Edward Lopez, Mario Rizzo and Daniel Sutter for useful comments and suggestions. An earlier version of this paper was presented at the Workshop in Applied Political Economy at San Jose State University and the Department of Economics Seminar Series at West Virginia University. We thank the participants for useful comments and suggestions. This paper was originally prepared for the Wirth Institute for Austrian and Central European Studies conference on The Austrian School of Economics, University of Alberta, Edmonton, Alberta, Canada, October 7–8, 2005. The financial support of the Mercatus Center is acknowledged.

 Springer

References

Baumol, W. (1952). *Welfare economics and the theory of the state*. London Schoolof Economics and Political Science: Longmans, Green.

Becker, G. (1983). A theory of competition among pressure groups for political influence. *Quarterly Journal of Economics, 98*(3), 371–400.

Boettke, P. J. (1998). Economic calculation: The Austrian contribution to political economy. *Advances in Austrian Economics, 5*, 131–158.

Boettke, P. J. (2001). Putting the political back into political economy. In J. Biddle, J. Davis, & S. Medema (Eds.), *Economics broadly considered: Essays in honor of Warren Samuels* (pp. 203–216). New York: Routledge.

Boettke, P. J. (2002). Information and knowledge: Austrian economics in search of its uniqueness. *The Review of Austrian Economics, 15*(4), 263–274.

Boettke, P. J., & Leeson, P. T. (2004). An 'Austrian' perspective on public choice. In C. Rowley & F. Schneider (Eds.), *The encyclopedia of public choice*, (Vol. 2, pp.27–32). Boston: Kluwer Academic Publishers.

Boettke, P. J., & Lopez, E. (2002). Austrian economics and public choice. *Review of Austrian Economics, 15*(2/3), 111–119.

Boudreaux, D. J. (1996) Was your high school civics teacher right after all? Donald Wittman's the myth of democratic failure. *The Independent Review, 1*(1), 111–128.

Buchanan, J. M. (1964, 1979). What should economists do? In: *What should economists do?* Indianapolis, IN: Liberty Fund.

Buchanan, J. M. (1975). *The limits of liberty: Between anarchy and leviathan*. Chicago: University of Chicago Press.

Buchanan, J. M. (1979). *Freedom in constitutional contract*. College Station TX: Texas A & M Press.

Buchanan, J. M. (1996). The best of all possible worlds? New efforts to prove that political institutions works as well as markets, *Times Literary Supplement*, January 26, 4843, p. 13.

Buchanan, J. M., & Tullock, G. (1962). *The calculus of consent*. Ann Arbor: University of Michigan Press.

Coase, R. (1960). The problem of social cost. *Journal of Law and Economics, 3*, 1–44.

Demsetz, H. (1969). Information and efficiency: Another viewpoint. *Journal of Law and Economics, 12*(1), 1–22.

Demsetz, H. (1982). Barriers to entry. *American Economic Review, 72*(1), 47–57.

Ferejohn, J. (1986). Incumbent performance and electoral control. *Public Choice, 50*, 5–26.

Fernandez, R., & Rodrig, D. (1991). Resistance to reform: Status Quo Bias in the presence of individual-specific uncertainty. *American Economic Review, 81*(5), 1146–1155.

Friedman, M. (1962). *Capitalism and freedom*. Chicago: Chicago University Press.

Friedman, M., & Friedman R. (1980). *Free to choose*. New York: Harcourt Brace Jovanovich.

Hayek F. A. (1937). Economics and knowledge. *Economica N.S., 4*, 33–54.

Hayek, F. A. (1948). *Individualism and economic order*. Chicago: University of Chicago Press.

Hayek, F. A. (1960). *The constitution of liberty*. Chicago: University of Chicago Press.

Hayek, F. A. (1969). Competition as a discovery procedure. In *New studies in philosophy, politics, economics and the history of ideas*. Chicago: University of Chicago Press.

Hayek, F. A. (1976). *Law, Legislation and Liberty*, Vol. 2. Chicago: University of Chicago Press.

Ikeda, S. (2003). How compatible are public choice and austrian political economy. *Review of Austrian Economics, 16*(1), 63–75.

Kirzner, I. (1973). *Competition and entrepreneurship*. Chicago: The University of Chicago Press.

Kirzner, I. (1985). *Capitalism and the discovery process*. Chicago: University of Chicago Press.

Klein, D. B., & Foldvary, F. (2005). *The half-life of policy rationales: How new technology affects old policy issues*. New York: New York University Press.

Kohn, M. (2004). Value and exchange. *CATO Journal, 24*(3), 303–339.

Leeson, P. T., Coyne C. J., & Boettke P. J. (2006). Does the market self-correct? *Review of Political Economy, 18*(1), 79–90.

von Mises, L. (1949, 1966). *Human action*. Chicago: Henry Regnery.

Mitchell, W. C., & Simmons, R. T. (1994). *Beyond politics: markets, welfare and the failure of bureaucracy*. Colorado: Westview Press.

Olson, M. (1965). *The logic of collective action*. Cambridge: Harvard University Press.

Olson, M. (1982). *The rise and decline of nations*. Connecticut: Yale University Press.

Reder, M. (1982). Chicago economics: Permanence and change. *Journal of Economic Literature, 20*(March), 1–38.

 Springer

Riker, W. (1962). *The theory of political coalitions*. Connecticut: Yale University Press.

Rothbard, M. N. (1962). *Man, economy and state*, (2 vols). Princeton NJ: D.Van Nostrand.

Rothbard, M. N. (1977). *Power and market*. Menlo Park CA: Institute for Humane Studies.

Rowley, C. (1997). Donald Wittman's the myth of democratic failure. *Public Choice, 92*(1–2), 15–26.

Rowley, C. K., & Vachris V. A. (1994). Why democracy does not necessarily produce efficient results. *Journal of Public Finance and Public Choice/Economia Delle Scelte Pubbliche, 12*, 95–111.

Rowley C., & Vachris V. A. (2003). Efficiency of democracy? In C. Rowley & F. Schneider (Eds.), *The encyclopedia of public choice*, Vol. 2 (pp. 189–195). Dordrecht: Kluwer Academic Publishers.

Shepsle, K. A., & Weingast, B. R. (1981). Structure-induced equilibrium and legislative choice. *Public Choice, 37*, 503–519.

Stigler, G. (1982). *The economist as preacher and other essays*. Chicago: University of Chicago Press.

Stigler G. (Ed.) (1988). *Chicago Studies in political economy*. Chicago: University of Chicago Press.

Stigler, G. (1992). Law or economics? *Journal of Law & Economics, 35*(2), 455–468.

Sutter, D. (2002). The democratic efficiency debate and definitions of political equilibrium. *The Review of Austrian Economics, 15*(2/3), 199–209.

Wagner, R. (1989). *To promote the general welfare*. San Francisco, CA: Pacific Research Institute.

Wagner, R. (1996). Review of Donald Wittman's the myth of democratic failure. *Constitutional Political Economy, 7*, 153–160.

Wagner, R. (1997). Parasitical political pricing, economic calculation, and the size of government: Variations on a theme by Maffeo Pantaleoni. *Journal of Public Finance and Public Choice, 15*, 135–146.

Wittman, D. A. (1995). *The myth of democratic failure: Why political institutions are efficient*. Chicago: University of Chicago Press.

Wohlgemuth M. (1999). Entry barriers in politics, or: Why politics, like natural monopoly, is not organized as an ongoing market process. *Review of Austrian Economics, 12*(2), 175–200.

Part V
Market Chosen Law

[18]

MARKET CHOSEN LAW

Edward Stringham[*]

Central planning and state control are often cast aside as inferior replacements to far more efficient and humane voluntary market transactions. Still there is one area that most believe must be run collectively through the state. The realm of law is often the foundation of government, and the suggestion that central control be abandoned shocks most people as something impossible. Philosophers, from Hobbes to Rand, believe that for all encounters there must exist one authority to create and enforce laws. They are baffled by what would happen if two parties had a conflict without an overarching judicial system. They assume that only the public sector can prevent and resolve disputes, but they have failed to notice the many private arrangements already in existence to deal with such dilemmas.

There are numerous non-government institutions that protect individuals on both local and global levels. Examining these arrangements can give insight on how private law can function, thereby eliminating any need to speculate on how future firms might operate. The market allows consumers to choose different types and degrees of services and this could be true in the realm of law. Choice does not mean chaos and does not mean that people will be forced to deal with laws that they have not chosen. Most legal problems probably can be attributed to public law enforcement, so we do not need to assume that private law would be perplexed with the same dilemmas. A private legal system could allow individuals to agree ahead of time to follow certain rules. Judges would not need to compare individuals' utilities; they would solely make judgments in accordance with consumers' agreed-upon wants.

Government police and courts are inefficient and inhumane. There is no reason that consumers be forced to deal with a central monopoly when there are other alternatives. The legal realm is no different from any other industry; the market will allow consumers to buy services provided by entrepreneurs that are far superior than anything statists can imagine. Private law al-

[*]Edward Stringham is a graduate student in economics, and a Fellow at the James Buchanan Center for Political Economy at George Mason University.

The author is grateful to Walter Block for his guidance and comments. The author bears full responsibility for any errors in this paper.

ready provides many solutions but is ultimately restricted by the leviathan state. If the state stopped intervening, the consumer would finally be sovereign and the market would finally be able to flourish.

HOW WOULD THE MARKET LOOK?

If government law enforcement is to be rejected, then its alternatives must be examined. Even though we are not fortunate enough to be able to observe a fully functional modern-day private system we must realize that there are many ways of administering law other than those practices of the massive state apparatus. During the height of communism in the Soviet empire, there was no reason to assume that central planning was the only possibility. The idea of non-government law may strike many as outrageous, but others have not failed to notice that there already exists a considerable degree of private law. While they do not have the exact appearance as the governmental police and courts, many private institutions provide protective services.

When discussing whether or not government law enforcement should be abandoned, we need not look into a crystal ball to view how private judicial systems will operate. We already have existing examples that provide answers today. John Hasnas wrote, "So, what would a free market in legal services be like? As Sherlock Holmes would regularly say to the good doctor, 'You see, Watson, but you do not observe.' Examples of non-state law are all around us."[1] Hasnas pointed out many examples of market arrangements to provide order, which are quite common. They operate on both local and global levels and while presently the state prevents a completely private system from operating, the presence of market arrangements shows that private police and courts are possible.

The market for legal services is not different intrinsically from any other. Businesses will continually create better and more efficient products, which without competition would have seemed inconceivable.[2] Currently there are severe limits on incen-

---

[1] John Hasnas, "The Myth of the Rule of Law," *Wisconsin Law Review* (1995): 227.

[2] Consider the case of radio and television. At one time, statists claimed that private broadcasts would be impossible. Despite this, private radio and television have proven themselves to be successes. Companies have discovered revenue solutions which would have been inconceivable at the outset. To solve its supposed non-excludability nature, companies found ways to finance the broadcast using advertisements, and those companies not interested in broadcasting advertisements found ways to scramble broadcasts, enabling exclusion of non-payers. It

tives for private investment in this area, but this does not mean that the realm is inherently closed. If government ceased imposing its law on everyone, most likely the nature of law enforcement would be vastly different from today's nature. How exactly would a system of competing law agencies function? Hasnas addressed the question as he wrote,

> I am always tempted to give the honest and accurate response to this challenge, which is that to ask the question is to miss the point. If human beings had the wisdom and knowledge-generating capacity to be able to describe how a free market would work, that would be the strongest argument for central planning.[3]

He pointed out that markets allow a multitude of suppliers to attempt to solve dilemmas, which no one person or monopoly could ever be able to. Trying to predict the exact structure of the market is an impossible task to undertake, and it is foolish to think that one person can anticipate all solutions offered by entrepreneurs and businesses.

CONTEMPORARY SOLUTIONS
OFFERED ON A LOCAL LEVEL

How would it ever be possible for people to live peacefully without being controlled by the government? This question has been the subject of many discourses. Of why there must be a state authority, John Locke wrote:

> First, There wants an established, settled, known law, received and allowed by common consent to be the standard of right and wrong, and the common measure to decide all controversies between them. For though the law of nature be plain and intelligible to all rational creatures; yet men, being biased by their own interest, as well as ignorant for want of study of it, are not apt to allow of it as a law binding to them in the application of it to their particular cases.

> Secondly, In the state of Nature there wants a known and indifferent judge, with authority to determine all differences according to established law. For everyone in that state, being both judge and executioner of the law

---

is unlikely that bureaucrats would have discovered these solutions, but profit-motivated businesses did. At the time television was invented, no one could have anticipated that market, but this is no grounds for banning private operation. There are strong parallels to law enforcement.

[3] Hasnas, "The Myth of the Rule of Law," p. 226.

> of nature, men being partial to themselves, passion and
> revenge is very apt to carry them too far.[4]

Locke believed that in the absence of government, since people are biased in their own favor, they are unfit judges over themselves. Accordingly, the state must act as the arbiter; otherwise violence would ensue. While he may be correct that often times third party judges are needed, there is no reason to assume that only state officials can perform this role.

There are many cases of private law enforcement, one of the most common can be seen at institutions of higher learning. Although private security officers and dean's offices differ greatly from their bureaucratic counterparts, they nevertheless perform the job supposedly only government police and courts are capable. Many other entities also produce a safe atmosphere in a similar manner: shopping malls, amusement parks, resorts, and private housing developments are cases in point. Just because they are not as ostentatious as the state does not mean that they are not providing protection. These institutions show that not only is the notion of private security possible, but that it is widespread.

A college is a self contained community that offers a whole array of services including security. While education is its main service, to attract students it needs to provide a pleasant and safe environment. The Vice President of Business Affairs & Treasurer at the College of the Holy Cross, writes, "We employ a small police force, handle a variety of legal matters and operate small judicial and governance bodies— a small claims court and a town government rolled into one."[5] Along with education, the college provides other services, many of them so-called public goods. Colleges do not charge students separate fees for security, but it is included in the price of tuition. The school operates to keep students safe from each other and from outsiders, fostering a safe atmosphere where students can live peacefully, with little facilitation of government police.

Private universities are interested in providing as good a service as possible; they engage in profit-maximizing behavior.[6] It is in their best interest to provide as pleasant an atmosphere as possible, at the same time minimizing costs. The goal is not mere-

---

[4] John Locke, "The Second Treatise of Civil Government," in *The Portable Enlightenment Reader*, Isaac Kramnick, ed. (New York: Penguin Books, 1995), p. 403.

[5] William R. Durgin, "Holy Cross as a Business," *Holy Cross Crossroads* 31, no.5, p. 32.

[6] This analysis does not apply to public universities that cannot go bankrupt if they do a poor job.

ly to get tough on crime, but rather to cultivate a pleasant atmosphere to satisfy the customers and to attract even more. The system must not be too harsh, nor too lackadaisical, because in both cases it would deter students. If a school were too strict for students' tastes, applications and attendance would decline, and at the opposite extreme, if a school were too chaotic and dangerous, demand would also decline.

Private universities have also created entire "private judicial systems." Although it might seem elementary to even examine them, it is important to do so, because most people do not appreciate the parallels between universities' services and those of the government. It is fairly typical at a college for students to live in dormitories, along with Resident Advisor student employees who deal with minor problems and student concerns. These Resident Advisors operate under the supervision of non-student Complex Directors, who live in the dormitories to oversee the buildings and deal with larger problems. Problems beyond the scope of the Complex Directors are attended to by many Assistant and Associate Deans. For even larger or more difficult issues, the Dean of Students acts as the ultimate judge.

While these college employees do not have portraits painted of themselves displayed on the walls and do not wear long robes, they all perform essentially the service that government officials claim to do. While the latter system is highly complicated and bureaucratic, involving local, state, and federal judges as well as appellate and supreme courts, the university system can still be compared to it. For example, when a case is not solved by the Resident Advisor, Complex Director, Assistant, nor Associate Dean "Courts," the case is sent to the Dean of Students—the "Supreme Court." On campus, he renders the ultimate decision binding on all students, who have explicitly agreed beforehand to be adhere to this procedure when they chose to attend this college.

The entire process of resolving dilemmas at the university is done in a timely and efficient manner, because universities are competing for students. A university does not want to make the process too protracted or unpleasant, because it would ultimately lead to a lowering of quality of the total service provided by the school. Despite the alleged impossibility of a functional private judicial system, it is apparent that at the local level of a university campus, such private systems do exist. Thus, such communities internalize production of security and hardly rely on local public police at all.

CONTEMPORARY SOLUTIONS
OFFERED ON A GLOBAL LEVEL

While advocates of the state might grant that private services are possible on a local level, they still believe that on a
larger scale all communities must operate under the jurisdiction
of a single government. They cannot fathom anything but conflict
if all parties were not forced to be under the jurisdiction of one
overarching state. As seventeenth-century philosopher Thomas
Hobbes wrote:

> Therefore, before the names of just and unjust can have
> place, there must be some coercive power to compel men
> equally to the performance of their covenants, by the ter-
> ror of some punishment greater than the benefit they ex-
> pect by the breach of their covenant, and to make good
> that propriety which by mutual contract men acquire, in
> recompense of the universal right they abandon; and
> such power there is none before the erection of the com-
> monwealth.[7]

He believed that without a Leviathan that held authority over
all people, there would be no possible way for them to interact
with one another. The belief is that chaos would ensue if all individuals were not under control of a single authority.

What would happen if people were not all under the authority of a monopolist law enforcer? The most typical objection is
that two parties, not under jurisdiction of the same government,
would unavoidably come to an impasse. As Ayn Rand wrote:

> Suppose Mr. Smith, a customer of Government A, sus-
> pects his next-door neighbor, Mr. Jones, a customer of
> Government B, has robbed him; a squad of Police A
> proceeds to Mr. Jones's house and is met at the door by a
> squad of Police B, who declare that they do not accept
> the validity of Mr. Smith's complaint and do not recog-
> nize the authority of Government A. What happens
> then? You take it from there.[8]

Although this would not pose a problem within a university
campus between contractually bound students, there are many
cases that parties who do not live in the same vicinity come in
contact with one another. What would happen if a student of

[7] Thomas Hobbes, *Leviathan: With Selected Variants From The Latin Edition of 1668*,
Edwin Curly, ed. (Indianapolis, Ind.: Hackett Publishing, 1994), p. 89.

[8] Ayn Rand, *Capitalism: The Unknown Ideal* (New York: New American Library,
1967), p. 335.

University A has a dispute with a student of University B? How exactly would those problems between these parties be solved? While it is tempting to try to try to solve these hypothetical dilemmas,[9] perhaps instead these questions should be reformulated in a different but equivalent manner, which will give insight to how these questions can be solved.

For example, what happens when a baseball team from the United States plays one in Canada? What rules would they follow and would both teams play by different rules? What would happen if there were a dispute about the rules? If the Canadian players are not under jurisdiction of the United States government and the United States players do not recognize the authority of any government but their own, who would solve the disputes? Since parties are biased in their own suits, would not the players be unable to reach a common agreement? Would these two parties be able to find a solution to their dilemmas, or would absolute chaos ensue?

Although it might seem absurd to even raise let alone answer these questions, it should be evident that they are equivalent to the arguments in favor of a monopolist law enforcer. Baseball teams, even if they are from different political jurisdictions, decide ahead of time to play by the same rules. While not all players are citizens of the same government, they allow the same baseball league officials to umpire games. The rules of the game are agreed upon by all participants, and in the case of disputes, the league officials, who have been privately contracted, resolve the issue. If, for some reason, specific league officials are not performing their tasks well, they can be replaced by the league. If the league as a whole is not performing its tasks well, players and fans are free to discontinue their business with the league and patronize another.

It should be noted that there is no compulsion in present baseball institutional arrangements. All parties have made their transactions on the market voluntarily. The league, the umpires, and the players, are all operating under the constraints of the market. If any one of them perform poorly, they will earn less revenue in the future. The league officials act in an unbiased manner, because that is what they are paid to do. If there were

---

[9] To read speculative hypotheses about ways future private companies could solve these disputes, see Murray Rothbard, *Power and Market: Government and the Economy*, 2nd ed. (Kansas City: Sheed Andrews and McMeel, 1977), pp. 6-7; also David Friedman, *The Machinery of Freedom: Guide to a Radical Capitalism*, 2nd ed. (La Salle, Ill.: Open Court, 1989), chap. 29.

any chicanery, individual employees and the entire league would lose out. There obviously is no problem with settlement of disputes in the realm of athletics, so it is questionable why one would assume that there would be difficulties were this applied elsewhere.

Some might argue that baseball is a low-stakes matter, and that a sports contest is a completely different matter than one with potential infractions against person or property. When there are property rights at stake, sports rules would not be applicable. Even if this were true, it would still imply that there must be a monopolist enforcer.

Once again, it is helpful to reformulate the original criticisms against a market for law enforcement, this time for international business. Take the case, for example, when a producer in the United States sells goods to a purchaser in a country such as Singapore. What happens if there is a dispute?[10] Would they both adhere to different trade customs? Who makes and enforces the rules? If the company from Singapore is not within the jurisdiction of the United States government and the company from the United States is not under the jurisdiction of the government of Singapore, who would solve the disputes? Since parties are biased in their own suits, wouldn't they both deny allegations and be unable to reach a settlement? In the case of global trade, where there is no monopolist enforcer, would there be chaos?

These questions may seem absurd, but they are all analogous to the original criticisms against polycentric law enforcement. There is no single world government that has jurisdiction over all traders, yet somehow—astonishingly—companies are able to do business. Even though anarchy exists between nations, firms are able to engage in commerce peacefully. Since there is no coercively imposed and enforced legal system, obviously something else must provide order; else, no one would deal internationally. Many bodies of privately created law have been adopted voluntarily in order to facilitate business.

While there are potentially many different answers to these dilemmas, none of them involve a monopolist government. The common practice is for firms to contract ahead of time, agreeing to follow certain rules and to be bound by a specific arbitrator in the case of dispute. The laws of the sea were developed completely outside the jurisdiction of any government. Benson stated, "Law

---

[10] Suppose that the purchaser does not pay the producer, or that the producers ships faulty products but denies the allegation.

Merchant effectively shatters the myth that government must define and enforce 'the rules of the game.'"[11] It was not governments, but rather businesses acting in their own self interest who developed customary laws.

By agreeing to follow arbitration companies, businesses can eliminate the need to utilize government courts. These private courts exist both at international and national levels. The American Arbitration Association describes itself as itself as "dedicated to the resolution of disputes through the use of mediation, arbitration, negotiation, elections and other voluntary dispute resolution methodologies." Parties use alternative dispute resolution for a more efficient way of resolving problems. Instead of using the bureaucratic methods, these companies can use faster and simpler procedures.

How does a system of enforcing rules work if there is no army threatening force as does the state? While most people assume that violence is the only possible way to enforce laws, this is far from the practice used in business. Firms can choose to do business only with other companies who are members of certain commerce organizations, which indicate that they are reputable and will follow appropriate business procedures. For companies that have not established connections with commerce associations, there is yet another option. Before trades take place, both companies can deposit sums of money with a specific arbitrator who has the discretion to bestow the money to a party if the arbitrator finds the other party at fault. There is no world government, and yet firms find ways to resolve disputes. Such arrangements do work, and there is no unsolvable problem due to the lack of an overarching state.

INTEGRATION OF LOCAL AND NON-LOCAL SERVICES

It has been shown that local privately produced order is common, as is true for the global variety. Government police on both a local and international level are not necessarily needed. Could a completely private system work on a universal scale? One concern is that while it is possible for community residents to contract with one another, it is unfeasible for everyone to enter into restrictive covenants with all others on earth. When individuals do not have the resources and the wherewithal to investigate business partners as large corporations do, there would need to be some type of solution that could work for them on a large scale.

---

[11] Bruce Benson, *The Enterprise of Law: Justice Without the State* (San Francisco: Pacific Research Institute for Public Policy, 1990), p. 30.

Happily, once again, we do not have to speculate about how this could be accomplished. The institution of private credit cards shows that markets can offer a wide degree of differing services, linking people from all over the world in a commercial network. There is no state monopoly in the credit card market and—shockingly—it works quite well.

When a customer wishes to make a purchase with a credit card, what would happen if the store owner was affiliated with a local bank, and the customer with a bank located across the continent? Would Mr. Smith's bank not recognize the validity of Mr. Jones's bank, and would there be absolute chaos? To alleviate these dilemmas, could private banks find solutions or would there need to be a state monopoly? Merely to pose matters in this format is to reveal the ludicrousness of the question. The answer is clear: there is no coercive monopoly needed. Markets already enable many individuals and their respective banks to interact. It is common for customers to subscribe to local services, yet these banks make arrangements with non-local systems that enable customers to use their charge cards almost universally.

To return to private universities, let us look at credit cards often offered through college alumni associations. Even though the credit card is specifically designed for the college, this does not mean it is only compatible with others who have the same card. This card is designed to be able to work all across the globe. It might be difficult for each college to fully integrate a credit card into a global credit network, but a college association need not handle all of the specific credit issues itself. Associations that wish to offer credit cards can offer them through large banks (such as Citibank or MBNA), with the banks handling the details of the transactions. The university organization is able to choose the bank with which their card will be contracted.

Even though banks provide credit cards for smaller organizations, this does not solve the compatibility problem, because there could still be a dilemma if Mr. Smith uses Citibank and Mr. Jones uses MBNA. Does this situation call for a socialist monopoly, or is there a way for these companies to sort things out? Although each bank operates independently, it can choose to operate under the larger umbrellas of a Mastercard or Visa. These organizations compete with one another, as well as with others such as American Express, Discover, Diner's Club, and many others to offer wide acceptability and reliable service.

No firm or individual is forced to pay taxes for a state monopoly in this realm, and these companies have discovered a way to make their cards acceptable in all civilized countries. If a customer wants to reap the benefits of Mastercard, he can choose to do so, but he is not forced to do so. Customers can pick Mastercard, a competitor, or they can eschew credit cards entirely. The individual who does not use credit cards does not hurt others; he simply cannot conduct business with certain firms. The market allows people to voluntarily conform to standards, but it does not compel anyone to do so.

Although it would be difficult for all businesses to investigate each individual customer's credit history, the credit card market solves this seemingly overwhelming task with ease. A business does not need to know a thing about a customer's financial situation or history, except for the single fact that the customer uses a reputable credit card.[12] The retailer relies on the credit card companies to deal with the customer's credit, and is guaranteed payment by the credit lender. A business can simply state that it accepts Mastercard and Visa only, and if a customer cannot supply a qualifying type of payment, then no transaction will take place. It is that simple.

How does the consumer transactions market relate to privately produced safety? It is similar because it is one possible way for businesses to make sure that their clientele meets certain qualifications. On university campuses, one often needs to present identification to security or insert identification card into electronic card readers to be able to access certain areas. For example, any college-age appearing student might be allowed on a campus, but only those who live in a certain dormitory have electronic access to enter that particular building. Similarly, each floor could have its own separate access system.[13] An institution can make these cautionary measures as strict or as lackadaisical as it sees fit.

It is beyond our knowledge of how entrepreneurs could create superior systems of security, but it is not difficult to envision the simple expansion of university-style security practices, coupled with credit card practices. Just as colleges may allow only resi-

---

[12] Bryan Caplan described a situation when consumers use credit cards as collateral. He wrote, "Consider video rentals—before we can get a rental card, we must authorize the renter to use our credit card if we do not return the video or pay our fees. Our credit card company in effect guarantees our trustworthiness; and if we break our agreement, it pays the video rental firm." Bryan Caplan, "The Economics of Non-State Legal Systems," (working paper, Princeton University, (1993).

[13] Another similar example, although not as complex as the electronic card readers in place on college campuses, is when patrons enter a bar and are required to present identification that they are of a certain age.

dent students into the dormitories and just as businesses may choose to commercially interact only with customers who satisfy certain criteria, one could imagine people choosing to interact only with others who meet specific qualifications. Student interaction falls under the jurisdiction of the Dean of Students, debates between the Boston Red Sox and the Toronto Blue Jays are handled by the Baseball Commissioner, and business transactions with credit cards holders are administered by Mastercard or Visa. Critiques of private law have already been anticipated by higher education, baseball, and the banking industries.

It seems to be a common instinct to attempt to criticize any alternatives to government control of law, but the fact of the matter is that there already exist many solutions not involving government. The classical Randian criticism, involving the hypothetical Mr. Smith and Mr. Jones not under the jurisdiction of a monopolist governments, is really not that difficult to refute. Locally, as well as the internationally, private industries are already able to solve these dilemmas. The classic criticism is somewhat senseless, because no one on earth is now under the jurisdiction of a single world government. Unless we are to implement such an institution, we are being logically inconsistent. There are billions of cases where individuals encounter others not under the jurisdiction of the same government, and somehow there is not this chaos that statists envision. Markets can and will be able to provide security solutions without any need for government.

DIFFERENT SERVICES FOR DIFFERENT PREFERENCES

Just as consumers choose different types of credit cards, it could be possible for consumers to choose different legal arrangements. We have grown accustomed to certain structures and arrangements, but new ways of establishing and maintaining order might be discovered. Just as not all consumers choose identical services in other industries, nor would they be forced to do so in this case. Different tastes could be satisfied with specialized services. The amount of protection could be chosen, as could the very nature of the protection. It is possible that people would choose very different legal systems from one another. It is common nature to attempt to create a blueprint of how a society would look by asking the questions: What would be the nature of the laws? How strict would they be? What would the punishments be like? Would there restitution, prisons, or death penalties? What standards of proof would the legal systems?[14] While all of these questions are grappling ones to answer if one is trying to centrally plan a monopoly, under a system with competing agencies and competing systems, these questions can be answered easily. Certain law enforcement procedures will be adopted, depending on consumer wants.

For internal disputes between contractually bound individuals, some could decide with one another to follow strict rules and others looser guidelines. It could be possible for one covenant to provide that certain crimes will warrant capital punishment. For example, a condominium association could state that any members of the private community who trespassed onto another member's property would receive the death penalty. When discussing whether or not it is humane for the government to administer such punishment, the opposing views are probably as irreconcilable as can be, but when the matter concerns parties who want to create and follow such a rule, the issue is not as problematic. Is it immoral or inefficient for individuals to voluntarily decide to abide by strict rules? This would be an issue decided only by those who would be voluntarily bound by these rules.

Another commune might state ahead of time to all joining members that there would be no private rights in that commune. The moral question concerning what degree internal aggressors would (or would not) be punished would be decided by the members of the covenant. Would it be immoral for individuals to voluntarily decide to live with few or no rules within a community? This would also be an issue for the members to decide.

Property owners could contract a legal system to define exactly what constituted an aggression within that property.[15]

---

[14] Instead of solely relying on witnesses' accounts as evidence, some property owners might want to set up complex surveillance systems that electronically monitor the whereabouts of all individuals on the property. This is the case at buildings that require key cards for access, enabling management to see which people open which doors and when they do so. Now it is true that some people might not prefer to patronize such an environment, but these people would not have to do so. There are many people who choose not to work at companies with security access cards, but there are others who do. Some people might desire their everyday lives recorded so there can be no doubt whether or not they are innocent of a crime. There might be a lot of incentive to choose to have one's activities recorded. Surely, businesses motivated by profits would have a lot of incentive to find solutions.

[15] For a similar discussion, see Friedman *The Machinery of Freedom*, pp. 117–18. The difference between his analysis and the one contained here is that he is addressing inter-group disputes while this only addresses intra-group disputes. On pp. 196–97, Friedman brings up questions of whether flashlight rays and laser beam rays should be considered invasions of property, but he spoke about people who were not contractually bound to the same rules. It could be possible for private covenants to in-

Theoretically, the answer could easily be decided by each property owner. It is very difficult to define the limits of legal behavior for all people, but as Hasnas theorized, "In a free market, the law would not come in a one-size fits all."[16] People have different tastes from one another and different social norms. While certain behavior, such as murder, is almost always defined as a violation of conduct, with other behavior it is not so clear cut.

When does the aggression of an altercation begin, during the first exchange of words, during the first physical movement, or during the first moment of contact between the parties? It may seem difficult to answer that question, but with a system of market-chosen rules, the customers would be in a position to make that determination. The classic statement of parents, "While you are under my roof, you follow my rules," could be applied by each respective property owner. For example, one eating-and-drinking establishment could state to arriving customers that acting impolite would be not be tolerated, and that the management would take action against anyone who used inappropriate language. In contrast, another such establishment could state that fighting was allowed inside the bar, and thus all altercations would have been voluntarily agreed to upon entrance of that bar. These different establishments could have completely different ways of dealing disputes.

While norms differ greatly between different groups of people, the government court system assigns a set of uniform guidelines for everyone to obey. This would not have to be the case with competing legal systems. People who have all agreed to abide by certain rules could handle disputes among themselves very differently from other groups. Hasnas writes:

> Given the current thinking about racial and sexual identity, it seems that many disputes among members of the same minority group or among women would be brought to "niche" dispute resolution companies composed predominantly of members of the relevant group, who would use their specialized knowledge of group "culture" to devise superior rules and procedures for intra-group dispute resolution.[17]

In their midst, people who have agreed with each other could follow any rules type they desire. These practices would not

---

ternalize most of those externalities to eliminate confusions. Certain private condominium associations could allow members to have bright lamps, while others could prohibit lamps altogether.

[16] Hasnas, "The Myth of the Rule of Law," p.228.

[17] Hasnas, "The Myth of the Rule of Law," p.229.

apply to all people, but only those who have chosen to interact in such a way.

As another example, the issue of what constitutes a violation of rights is especially controversial when it comes to defining sexual harassment. Once again this issue could be decided by the property owners of each establishment. It seems that there could be different guidelines for what constitutes acceptable behavior in a nunnery versus a singles bar. If disputes arose, instead of relying on the uniform laws set forth by the legislators, each group could deal with the problems differently. It seems likely that, if private establishments informed parties of the rules ahead of time, considerably fewer disputes would arise. The issue of harassment in the workplace is a perfect example where employers and employees are having a difficult time operating together with the laws set forth by the United States government. To avoid any such confusion to begin with, certain companies could state that relatively high degrees of sexual harassment would be allowed, while other companies could state that any non-work related comments would be intolerable. This way, the employees could decide which atmosphere was most desirable, and the market would lead to an efficient solution where all parties were satisfied.[18]

Certain people, who wanted more employee protection or more consumer protection, could work for companies or shop at stores that had a high degree of protection or even paternalism if desired. They would be in essence contracting legal systems that were more protective. Anyone wishing to do business in such a manner would be required by the business owners to adhere to their restrictions but no one would be forced to. Such a system would be a way for people to voluntarily choose personal regulations through the market. These regulations, unlike the bureaucratic regulations, would necessarily pass the market litmus test, with burdensome self regulations leading to a decrease in business among the concerned parties. Businesses could compete to provide the best internal atmosphere for its members, creating an atmosphere where people would tend to be satisfied. By being able to frequent businesses that had different sets of internal of rules, consumers would in essence be able to have a variety of legal choice.

---

[18] The only problem with this would be that the neo-puritans would not be able to impose their religious beliefs, through the use of law, onto all people.

VARIETY OF LEGAL CHOICE DOES NOT MEAN CHAOS

It seems possible that there could exist many different types of legal systems, but some might wonder if it would lead to disorder if there was not one set of universal laws. When people who followed different sets of rules encountered one another, would there be confusion or an impasse? Would people operating under completely different rules constantly come in contact with one another and constantly have disagreements? Government advocates, such as Ayn Rand, with their hypothetical scenarios concerning two people who cannot come to agreement on a single arbitrator, create horrid pictures of a non-monopolistic system, but it must be reiterated that they are only hypothetical.

The major detail that is always left out of the scenario is on what property the two parties meet. The scenario assumes that strangers with no connection with each other and who have not agreed ahead of time what rules they are going to follow. If two astronauts are floating around in outer space and they come into contact with another, there could be the chance that the two do not abide by similar court systems, but in the real world, almost all encounters occur on property, which could enable the property owners to state the rules.[19] The property owners can lay down the law, stating that all patrons will necessarily follow their rules and procedures. This is similar to how stores operate with credit cards, with retailers stating that all customers must pay using certain credit cards, otherwise no transaction will take place. All encounters on a university campus could be under the jurisdiction of that institution, and all encounters in a shopping mall could be under its respective jurisdiction.

If each property owner were to set its own rules, would there be difficulty when people from different areas visited the property? Would it be impossible for each individual business to deal with so much "immigration" into its establishment? There could be many different ways to deal with these issues, such as joining larger trade associations, but there already is evidence that this is not a problem. Llewellyn Rockwell wrote about the entertainment park Disney World, saying, "It has even shown us how the immigration problem can be handled. Disney World attracts 30

---

[19] Block described how private road owners could create their own traffic guidelines. "In a free market, each road owner will decide upon the rules his customers are to follow, just as nowadays rules for proper behavior in some locations are, to a great extent, determined by the owner of the property in question." Walter Block, "A Free Market in Roads," *The Libertarian Reader*, Tibor Machan, ed. (Totowa, N.J.: Rowman and Littlefield, 1982), p. 169.

million visitors per year without disruption."[20] Even though visitors travel from all over the world, this private park does not experience problems with foreigners.

Profit-motivated parks create a security system that is accommodating for all of their guests. They need to act courteously to their customers, so it is no surprise that they would not follow the same procedures as government police. In a *Boston Globe* article, a patron of Disney quoted a Disney security supervisor as saying, "There is no Constitution at Disneyland. . . . We have our own laws."[21] Since Disney does not follow the exact same procedures as government police, does not mean that they will operate in an unjust way. A Disney spokesman stated, "Guest service and how we treat our guest continues to be our highest priority. . . . Our security people are friendly and helpful, but they are also very serious about the job they perform."[22] It is clear that even though private establishments such as Disney deal with many concerns, they do so in a manner that pleases their patrons. If visitors or employees of a private park are unhappy with the way they are being treated, they can choose to discontinue their personal business. Since many people choose to continue to do business with private firms such as Disney, it demonstrates that they are operating in a satisfying manner.

At parks such as Disney, there is no problem with unsolvable disputes between people from different parts of the globe whose governments have no connections with one another.[23] In the case of encounters on Disney property, the park has its own system to create order. While the thinkers of the scenario applicable to astronauts did not have outer space in mind, they probably did have in mind the common everyday encounters of strangers on the street. The fault in the logic is that they are thinking about lands that are currently owned and policed by the government.[24]

---

[20] Llewellyn Rockwell, "Slouching Towards Statism," *The Free Market* 15, no. 1: 5.

[21] Anne Mulkern, "Accusers say Disney Security Isn't for Kids," *Boston Globe* (November 7, 1996): A10.

[22] Mulkern, "Accusers say Disney Security Isn't for Kids."

[23] Another example is a vacation cruise where there is absolutely no government. The ship is run by business people, and there are no government police anywhere on board. It is doubtful that there is any legal recourse for any of the vacationers, yet crime and disputes between vacationers do not seem to be a problem.

[24] The approach given here also differs from other advocates of private law. Certain theorists attempt to map out how multiple policing agencies would operate in one geographic region. Under their scenarios, each neighbor on a street could subscribe to a different protection agency. One can question why they assume that there would be multiple policing agencies in a given geographic location. At Disney World, there is only one security agency, as is true for most privately policed areas. It is a mistake to presuppose that the

This being the case, there is the tragedy of the commons, where no one has any incentive or ability to exclude nefarious individuals from the streets.

In a sense, public roads are similar to the outer space example because nobody knows what criminal elements one will encounter on the poorly policed city streets. As soon as the issue concerns private property, the owners have incentives to make sure that their property is safe.[25] When discussing private police on government land, the issue can seem perplexing, but why must one assume that all land must be perpetually owned by the state? Lawless confusion is a problem that should be attributed to incapable governments, not to private establishments.

The issue of whether a plural existence of legal orders would lead to confusion, chaos, or inefficiency can once again be contrasted with the credit card industry. Different credit card firms offer different terms to their members, but this does not mean that the cards are incompatible. Each bank might have agreements with its members that are completely different from the others and still the customers are able to conduct business with one another. It is true that people often choose to conform to standards for the sake of simplicity but this is done voluntarily. The "one size fits all" solution is not required in the realm of consumer credit cards, nor is it necessarily required in the realm of law enforcement.

INTERPERSONAL UTILITY COMPARISONS

Critics of this analysis might make the claim that if consumers are allowed to purchase the services they desire, the enforcement of their laws will necessarily fall onto people and decrease others' utility. If private law sacrifices individuals' utility for the benefit of others, then the entity which supports or enforces

---

structure of private law would fit into the mainstream economists' model of perfect competition. It is equivalent to believing that the free market would consist of many different hagglers bartering in an open market place, when in fact the free market can consist of large corporations. Large regions such as North America would likely have more than one law enforcement agency, but this does not mean different neighbors in the same gated community would hire competing firms. In some places, different agencies may very well operate side by side, but this is not something that we should assume.

[25] Block wrote about how on public streets it is common for men to verbally harass women, while on private property, such behavior can be prevented if desired. He wrote, "In the public sector, it is in no business person's financial interest to end the harassment. . . . But in the realm of private enterprise, every entrepreneur who hopes to employ or sell to women (or to men who object to this maltreatment of women) has a strong pecuniary incentive to end it." Walter Block, *Defending the Undefendable*, 2nd ed. (San Francisco: Fox and Wilkes, 1991), pp. 27–28.

that private law would be just as guilty as violating rights as is the government. While most people might agree that the notion of interpersonal comparisons is not ideal, they still believe that it is a necessary evil that all theorists, including judges, economists, and the government, must estimate. Critics might claim, "Is it not true that when an undoubtedly guilty criminal is required to pay reparations his utility is being lowered?" They say that when defining aggression and deciding reparations, any arbitrator, even private, must rely on interpersonal comparisons of utility. While this attempts to justify the aggregationist methodology, the argument is faulty. Not only is the idea of comparing utility unreasonable, it is also unnecessary. A system of private arbitration can attempt to solve this problem, without any need to aggregate and/or compare utility.

Self described "utilitarians" such as David Friedman say that there is no way to avoid interpersonal comparisons of utility. Friedman believes that it is necessary to at least estimate and compare individuals' utility. He wrote:

> Consider a court awarding damages. If we really know nothing at all about other people's utility, how can a court decide how much someone owes me for breaking my arm? For all the judge knows, I enjoyed having my arm broken. Assuming that I disliked it, he has no way of knowing whether my disutility for a broken arm is measured by a penny or a billion dollars.[26]

Friedman and others say that one might as well base an entire legal framework around interpersonal comparisons of utility, because all proposed legal systems must necessarily make such comparisons.

Even if a court definitively finds an offender guilty, the punishment for the aggressor is not objectively clear. Regardless of whether the system is based on restitution or retribution, the judge must decide the extent of the damages owed by examining the harm suffered by the victim. Barnett wrote, "The subjectivity of punishment and reward suggests a potential problem with a restitutive theory that must be considered: Individuals attach their own value to the rights they possess, and the value of these rights cannot be measured objectively."[27] If the judge finds a mugger guilty of robbing money, should the criminal be required to

---

[26]Friedman, *The Machinery of Freedom*, p. 179.
[27] Randy Barnett, "Pursuing Justice in a Free Society: Part One—Power vs. Liberty," *Criminal Justice Ethics* (Summer/Fall 1985):.66.

pay back solely the money, or be required to pay additional damages to compensate for pain and suffering? It is impossible to
know exactly how much pain was inflicted on the victim, so if
the judge is to award reparations, without relying on interpersonal comparisons of utility, what criterion can he use?

Even some of the most severe critics of such comparisons sometimes concede that interpersonal comparisons of utility are necessary in cases such as damage awards. If the utilitarian asked,
"Without interpersonal comparisons of utility, what would the
exact level of damages be?" Block, an adamant critic of utilitarianism, acquiesced when he wrote:

> If he [the non-utilitarian] is honest, he would have to
> concede that there is indeed an element of arbitrariness
> involved in any such juridical finding, and further, that
> it would be justified to make it, despite this undeniable
> fact. There seems to be no possible better alternative.
> Complex choices cannot always be made in tiny water-
> tight compartments, no matter how highly desirable.
>
> However, just because reality impinges with its
> rough edges does not mean we have to embrace it when
> there are alternatives. Damage awards do indeed violate
> economic strictures against interpersonal comparisons
> of utility.[28]

For Block, too, there seems to be no way to avoid making such
comparisons, however unscientific they may be. It might seem
that the aggregationist utilitarianism must be embraced, but this
is not the case.

Insofar as legal systems are chosen on the market voluntarily
by all parties involved, one need never rely on invalid interpersonal comparisons of utility. Private firms operating on the market can eliminate such a problem. To see how, let us borrow a
page from the Health Maintenance Organization (HMO). HMOs
decide which medical procedures are worth while and which
are not.[29] In efforts to control costs, it does not allow all patients
to receive unlimited supplies of medical treatment. While individual decisions must be made by doctors and administrators, it

---

[28] Walter Block, "O.J.'s Defense: A Reductio Ad Absurdum of the Economics of
Ronald Coase and Richard Posner," *European Journal of Law and Economics* 3 (1996):
277.

[29] Does Mr. X value his extra examination more, or does Mr. Y value his elective
procedure more? Can the HMO see into each of its patients' minds? What if Mr. X
really wants the examination? Is the HMO making invalid interpersonal comparisons of utility when it does not allow Mr. X to receive his examination, but it does
allow Mr. Y to receive his procedure?

is clear that all patients agreed ahead of time to follow the decisions of the organization. If patients thought the practices unreasonable, they would purchase another type of health insurance. It can be said that **all** patients' utility increases *ex ante* when they decide to join such an organization.

This analysis of health maintenance organizations applies to arbitrators; they need not rely on interpersonal comparisons of utility. It is true that individual judges must decide guilt and decide damages, but as long all parties involved chose the arbitrator, they agreed to follow the judge's decision ahead of time. This, as before, is a case where **both** parties' utility increases *ex ante*. Any party whose utility would certainly be unjustly sacrificed by an arbitration company would choose a different type of arbitration service, just as a patient would choose something rather than the unsatisfactory HMO. As long as an arbitration service is chosen voluntarily, the judges are merely enforcing the rules that the consumers have chosen. When a judge awards damages, he is doing so in a manner that had attracted the consumers in the first place. It therefore is not a matter of judges forced to make interpersonal comparisons of utility; rather, it is a matter of judges enforcing the rules according to the chosen contracts, and awarding damages in way that was agreed upon by all parties.

There are many ways in which an arbitration system could administer such decisions. At one extreme, there could be a complex set of written rules explaining the procedures for every imaginable case. With such a code, the judges would merely attempt to find the relevant guideline among the written rules for each specific case. This system could focus on the letter of the law, but would require an inordinate amount of guidelines to be created. For example, there could be tables of exactly how much thieves would have to pay for their crimes, depending on the circumstances. While theoretically it might be possible that this could be done, it is likely unfeasible to be able to address every single concern ahead of time. This being the case, arbitrators would need to instead rely on an alternative manner of judging disputes, rather than looking up each case in a complex rule book.

At the opposite extreme, there could be absolutely no rule book whatsoever, with each case decided by the will or even the whims of a certain judge. While this might appear undesirable, this is not necessarily the case. The judge could be a wise person, chosen because all parties have a great respect for his opinion. He could rely on his own moral judgment, which could be based on any number of sources, such as religious code or libertarian code or some other sense of justice. The judge would not need to have any set of rules to go by, but people could still trust his decisions.

While I have mentioned two extremes, consumers possibly could choose something in between the two, or possibly something that does not remotely resemble either.[30] An example that does falls somewhere in between these two extremes is the college Dean of Students, who has certain guidelines to follow, but also relies on personal judgment. When students decide to attend a college, they agree to abide by all of the rules and decisions of the Dean of Students. As a specific example, students today who choose a Jesuit college agree to abide by all of the decisions of the local person in charge of that order. If this Jesuit renders decisions undesirable by the students, they can transfer. The mere fact that a school has been in existence for many years, shows that the operation has been found satisfactory by the bulk of its consumers.[31]

The issue then is not whether in each individual case a party's utility is judged or lowered by the decisions made; the real issue is whether the parties agreed to abide by the rule of the arbiter. If the answer is affirmative, then it is evident that the total services provided by the arbitrators have *ex ante* increased the utility of all of the consumers. By electing to abide by certain rules, consumers have demonstrated the legal code they desire. This is analogous to consumers choosing the sort of health care or financial organization they wish.

This analysis applies to those with preexisting contractual legal arrangements. But what of disputes between strangers, such as a mugging on the street? Hasnas warned that one must not

---

[30] We have grown accustomed to third parties judging affairs, but once again there is no reason to assume that all communities would desire such a structure. In some communities, there might be no need for any judges at all. For examples, most families do not rely on outside judges to work out family issues. Often, a third party cannot know enough about private business of a family to make a good decision, so in many cases it may not make sense to leave an issue to a relative stranger.

[31] What would happen if an arbitrator made bad decisions? This is analogous to asking what would happen if a bank showed bad judgment and decided not to repay any of its depositors. This rarely happens with banks, because they can only stay in business if they do not operate in such a manner. A bank that did not repay its creditors would not be in business for long, nor would an arbitrator who made unpredictable and undesirable decisions. Although some might think that banks do not default because of federal regulations and deposit "insurance," this is certainly not the case with overseas banks, which need to rely on established reputation or other means of insurance. It is possible that arbitrators would deal with similar constraints placed upon them by the market, which would offer consumers insurance and security. Consider again credit cards. If a consumer is charged erroneously, he does not get stuck paying for the fraud; instead, the banks often choose to assume responsibility.

Stringham – Market Chosen Law   75

simply try to speculate on how private firms would perform the same tasks performed by government today. He wrote:

> Static thinking occurs when we imagine changing one feature of a dynamic system without appreciating how doing so will alter the character of all other features of the system. For example, I would be engaging in static thinking were I to ask how, if the state did not provide the law and courts, the free market could provide them in their present form. . . . Once this static thinking is rejected, it becomes apparent that if the state did not provide the law and the courts, they simply would not exist in their present form.[32]

Although there are many problems that need to be dealt with under public law enforcement, it is likely that private law would not be prone to the same obstacles. There are common police procedures to haul suspects into custody, but there is no reason to assume that even remotely similar practices would be used in a private system.[33] It is possible that private police would never need to drag anyone into court who has not made prior agreements with that specific legal institution. Addressing the issue of which court would have jurisdiction in a dispute between complete strangers, there is little reason to presuppose that this would even be a problem. Likely this is merely a public land problem, which would not occur in a private system.

Strangers do not come into conflict with one another on the golf course at a country club, because only members are only allowed to enter. On college campuses and in amusement parks such as Disney, all people on the premises have agreed to abide by the property owner's rules. Just as easily, were this legal, store and restaurant owners, as well as street and road owners,[34] would create private rules to govern all patrons. In the case of public roads, no one is able to exclude anyone or to arrange contractual rules, so it is unsurprising that people have become accustomed to the chaos spawned by the state. If private road owners were able to create rules only allowing those who had agreed to abide by them to set foot on the property, then they could eliminate most of the problems between strangers, and they would already have rules in place concerning how any remaining problems would be handled.

---

[32] Hasnas, "The Myth of the Rule of Law," p. 228.

[33] Probably the best advice to give to private security for them to act in a just manner would be to not act anything like government police.

[34] See Block, "A Free Market in Roads," for the feasibility of this.

Individuals and businesses could choose to interact with only those who agree to certain rules. Whenever people agreed to certain rules, doing so would demonstrate that they have increased their utility. Not all people would be forced to conduct business in such a manner, just as not all people are forced to belong to health maintenance organizations or to use credit cards. With HMOs and credit cards, non-customers are unable to do business with certain physicians and certain firms. It could be similar with law as well. Those who do not agree to abide by certain rules would not be able to do business with certain individuals and certain firms. When there is trade, or even absence of trade, it is done out of the volition of all parties involved.

When trade takes place, such as the agreement to follow certain rules or arbitrators, the utility of all parties involved increases. While it is true that judges would have to render decisions that could even seem arbitrary, they would be doing so in a way that was contracted for by the consumers. Thus when a judge awards damages in a case,[35] he does not need to rely on invalid interpersonal comparisons of utility; he renders his decision in a way that passes the market litmus test. Interpersonal comparisons of utility are invalid and cannot be justified. The only way to avoid such nonscientific calculations is for the government to discontinue intervening into the market and to allow the voluntary adoption of a system of private law.

CONCLUSION

There are numerous cases where parties choose to enter into private legal arrangements. On a local level, universities, condominium associations, and shopping malls all provide rules and security to create a safe atmosphere. On a global level, trading and arbitration companies provide guidelines and dispute settlements for businesses not under any single governing authority. If on both a local and non-local level there are numerous cases where government is not utilized, then a government monopoly in this field is hardly the necessity that is claimed by its apologists. Private companies already provide both local and non-

---

[35] There actually is no reason to assume that aggressors need to be forced to pay for their damages. With the example of credit card companies, they do not seek damages from those who default on their loans. Instead they create incentives, such as good credit ratings and continued business, for borrowers to want repay their loans. Credit card companies cease to conduct business with bad clients, but they do necessarily pursue damages against them. This example may be distorted by current court costs, but the model can be effective nonetheless.

local protection for their customers, arguments to the contrary not withstanding.

Despite the existence of private law in modern society, the government nonetheless frequently intervenes. By forcibly imposing a uniform system on all people, the state prevents individual agents from purchasing the type and degree of services they desire. The unhampered market would allow people to procure a vast array of differing legal systems. This is not to say that competition would lead to chaos; quite the contrary, firms could offer a high degree of compatibility with rival legal systems, or they could offer high degrees of specialized services for their members. In all cases, customers would know what they were dealing with.

If customers agree to be bound by certain rules and procedures, this could eliminate the need for any interpersonal comparisons of utility, with the adjudication simply being made in accordance with the desires of all parties. Once we realize that a market in law would likely provide vastly different outcomes than anything we have at present, we do not need to spend time speculating on how private law enforcement agencies will solve problems that perplex today's governments. It is likely that many of the problems are only the products of the disorder caused by government law. It should be clear that government law enforcement is not perfect, not even desirable, and certainly not necessary. A market would allow private institutions to provide people with safety and security on an efficient and voluntary basis.

[19]

NORTH-HOLLAND

The Quarterly Review of Economics and Finance
43 (2003) 321–344

The QUARTERLY REVIEW
of ECONOMICS
And FINANCE

The extralegal development of securities trading in seventeenth-century Amsterdam

Edward Stringham

*Department of Economics, San Jose State University, San Jose,
CA 95192-0914, USA*

Received 13 March 2001; received in revised form 18 December 2001; accepted 18 December 2001

Abstract

It is often argued that government rule enforcement is necessary for the development of a stock market (Glaeser, Johnson, & Shleifer, 2001). Work by Boot, Stuart, and Thakor (1993), Klein and Leffler (1981), and Telser (1980), however, suggests that repeated interaction and reputation can create incentives for contracts to be self-enforcing. This paper investigates these claims by examining the first stock market, the Amsterdam Bourse. At a time when many financial contracts were unenforceable in government courts the market developed surprisingly advanced trading instruments. Descriptions by seventeenth-century stockbroker, De la Vega [*Confusion de Confusiones*], indicate that a reputation mechanism enabled extralegal trading of relatively sophisticated contracts including short sales, forward contracts, and options.
© 2002 Board of Trustees of the University of Illinois. All rights reserved.

JEL classification: L14, N23, G28

Keywords: Extralegal; Enforcement; Reputation

1. Introduction

From stock markets in former socialist countries to new electronic trading networks in the West, there is much debate over the proper amount of oversight of financial exchanges (Frye, 2000; Macey & O'Hara, 1999). A market without rules would hardly be conducive to trade (Brennan & Buchanan, 1985) so it is often concluded that government rules and regulations are necessary for a stock market to function (Glaeser, Johnson, & Shleifer, 2001). What happens

---

E-mail address: estringh@gmu.edu (E. Stringham).

1062-9769/02/$ – see front matter © 2002 Board of Trustees of the University of Illinois. All rights reserved.
PII: S 1062-9769(02)00153-9

when a legal system is not equipped to deal with complicated financial transactions? Boot, Stuart, and Thakor (1993), Klein and Leffler (1981), and Telser (1980), give us theories of how contracts can take place even without external enforcement. Among other things they illustrate that repeated interaction and reputation can align incentives such that it pays to abide by one's contracts. This paper uses evidence from the first stock market to investigate the degree to which financial markets are able to function without state enforced rules.

In the seventeenth century, the Amsterdam Bourse developed surprisingly advanced trading instruments at a time when government courts were unaccustomed and unable to deal with what today would be considered common financial transactions. Much of the dealings that took place were actually prohibited by law, although the law was ineffective and not strictly enforced. This relatively free atmosphere allowed the traders to experiment and devise new trading instruments, even though they were officially proscribed. The development of the instruments on the Amsterdam Bourse was not due to government directive but self-interest of traders who found it profitable to engage in new financial dealings. In contrast to the position that financial markets depend on government rules and regulations, the historical record lends credence to the theories that contracts can be self-enforcing and that market participants can police themselves.

The paper has the following structure: Section 2 discusses theories of exchange without external enforcement. Section 3 outlines the beginnings the Amsterdam Bourse, the companies traded, and the regulatory climate. Section 4 uses evidence from seventeenth-century stockbroker Joseph Penso de la Vega who gave a first hand account of the types of trading that occurred on the Bourse. Section 5 analyzes the reputation mechanism in use. Evidence shows that even though the law prohibited the trading of various derivatives the market was able to develop to a surprising degree of sophistication.

2. Exchange without external enforcement

In an article discussing emerging financial markets Glaeser et al. (2001, p. 853) ask "Who should enforce laws or contracts: judges or regulators?" They argue the theory that unregulated financial markets can be efficient "crucially relies, among other assumptions, on the possibility of effective judicial enforcement of complicated contracts" (2001, p. 854) and conclude that when the legal system is lacking, government regulation is needed. It is a common notion that without government enforcement parties have incentives to cheat and welfare-enhancing trades will not take place.

Tullock (1985, 1999), however, points out that the prisoners' dilemma is not as ubiquitous as we might believe; with continuous dealings parties will not want to jeopardize the benefits of long-term relationships and will choose to cooperate. Still it is questioned how far this can be extended. For example Tullock (1972) states:

> It is clear, however, that there are many situations in which we could not depend upon this very simple variant of the discipline of continuous dealings . . . Transactions in which large payments will be made in the future would be *impossible* if we depended solely on the discipline of continuous dealings. (1972, p. 69, emphasis added)

E. Stringham / The Quarterly Review of Economics and Finance 43 (2003) 321–344   323

Likewise, Olson (1996) believes that some trades can take place without external enforcement but not complicated financial transactions. He declared:

> Though the low-income societies obtain most of the gains from self-enforcing trades, they do not realize many of the largest gains from specialization and trade. They do not have the institutions that enforce contracts impartially, and so they lose most of the gains from those transactions (like those in the capital market) that *require* impartial third-party enforcement. (1996, p. 22, emphasis added)

In recent years much work has been done on markets that can function without a legal system but if theorists such as Tullock, Olson, and Glaeser et al. correct the results cannot be generalized to financial markets. Cattle ranchers (Ellickson, 1991), Kwakiutl Indians (Johnsen, 1986), diamond dealers (Bernstein, 1992), and medieval merchants (Benson, 1989, 1990; Greif, 1989, 1993; Greif, Milgrom, & Weingast, 1994; Milgrom, Douglass, & Weingast, 1990) may be able to conduct business without legal recourse but is it the case that complicated financial transactions that involve large payments through time necessarily depend on external enforcement? Upon looking at the historical record it becomes evident that the answer is no. In seventeenth-century Amsterdam there were many complicated financial transactions involving large payments through time despite the fact that the legal system was not enforcing these contracts.[1]

This is akin to the findings of Quinn (1997) and Neal and Quinn (2001) who analyze seventeenth-century goldsmith-bankers in London. These bankers faced a comparable predicament: they had little redress if others failed to redeem their bills of exchange. But to allay this problem they used repeated dealings and an informal network to convey information about others' reliability. Even when there are complicated contracts that involve large payments over time reputation encourages contractual performance.

It is interesting to note that this dilemma was addressed by an economist at least as early as Smith's (1766) *Lectures on Jurisprudence*. Smith described how time bargains were unenforceable yet still took place. He stated:

> This practice of buying stocks by time is prohibited by government, and accordingly, tho' they should not deliver up the stocks they have engaged for, the law gives no redress. There is no natural reason why 1,000£ in the stocks should not be delivered or the delivery of it enforced, as well as 1,000£ worth of goods. But after the South Sea scheme this was thought upon as an expedient to prevent such practices, tho' it proved ineffectual. In the same manner all laws against gaming never hinder it, and tho' there is no redress for a sum above 5£, yet all the great sums that are lost are punctually paid. Persons who game must keep their credit, else no body will deal with them. It is quite the same for stockjobbing. They who do not keep their credit will be turned out, and in the language of Change Alley be called lame duck. (1766/1982, p. 538)

He went on to argue that:

> Of all the nations in Europe, the Dutch, the most commercial, are the most faithful to their word ... This is not at all to be imputed to national character, as some pretend ... It is far more reduceable to self interest, that general principle which regulates the actions of every

man, and which leads men to act in a certain manner from views of advantage, and is as deeply implanted in an Englishman as a Dutchman. A dealer is afraid of losing his character, and is scrupulous in observing every engagement. When a person makes 20 contracts in a day, he cannot gain so much by endeavouring to impose on his neighbours, as the very appearance of a cheat would make him lose. (1766/1982, p. 538)

Smith described how people must be in good standing else others will not deal with them. Rather than relying on Glaeser et al. (2001, p. 855) preferred solution of "a highly motivated regulator to enforce the rules," we see the invisible hand guiding traders to abide by their contracts.

With external enforcement lacking, one of the most important mechanisms used is reputation (Klein, 1997). A known cheat will have difficulty finding business, so even when contracts are unenforceable, fear of having a bad reputation can create incentives to abide by one's word. By putting one's reputation on the line with each transaction, it is like posting a bond for each trade (Bernstein, 1996). Rather than taking a one time gain from cheating, traders are better off by cooperating, thereby developing a good reputation, which signals one's trustworthiness.

Good standing can be established through a number of means. One way is if traders are members of the same close-knit ethnic community (Landa, 1981, 1994). This mechanism, however, does not hold as one moves away from trade within close circles. Greif (1989, 1993) and Clay (1997a, 1997b) show how trade can be extended across long distances between merchants who seldom interact. As long as information about the reliability of prospective trading partners can be shared, much of the incentives for cheating are eliminated. If traders wish to deal with others in the future they will work to be known as a reliable partner. This multilateral reputation mechanism (Greif, 1993; Greif et al., 1994) facilitates trade between those who have no previous experience with each other and those who do not plan to interact with each other in the future. In both cases it is not in the interest of a trader to cheat since others will be informed. As will be discussed, this paper finds that in seventeenth-century Amsterdam a multilateral reputation mechanism enabled stockbrokers to engage in advanced contracts even though they were not backed by law. The Amsterdam stockbrokers, without a legal system to rely on, conducted trade on the discipline of continuous dealings and reputation alone.

3. The beginnings of the stock market

It was shortly after the establishment of the Dutch East India Company in 1602 when equities began trading on a regular basis.[2] Trading took place at the Amsterdam Bourse, an open aired venue, which was created as a commodity exchange in 1530 and rebuilt in 1608.[3] Commodity exchanges themselves were a relatively recent invention, existing in only a handful of cities.[4] Rather than being a bazaar where goods were traded intermittently, exchanges had the advantage of being a regularly meeting market, which enabled traders to become more specialized and engage in more complicated transactions (Braudel, 1979, p. 92). Kellenbenz reports:

As early as the middle of the sixteenth century, people in Amsterdam speculated in grain and, somewhat later, in herring, spices, whale-oil, and even tulips. The Amsterdam Bourse in particular was the place where this kind of business was carried on. This institution as an open-air market in Warmoestreet, later moved for a while to the 'New Bridge,' which crosses the Damrak, then flourished in the 'church square' near the Oude Kerk until the Amsterdam merchants built their own exchange building in 1611. (1957, p. 133)[5]

They created contracts for the future delivery of commodities that were "sometimes even years in advance" (Dehing and Hart, 1997, p. 53).[6] The Bourse was large enough to hold 500 people and was the site of trading of over 300 commodities (Bloom, 1937, p. 179; Dehing and Hart, 1997, p. 53).[7] Upon issuance of shares in the East India Company in 1602 it was only natural for equities to be traded there as well, with the stockbrokers occupying a section at the edge of the Bourse (Bloom, 1937, pp. 179–180). According to Bloom (1937, p. 181), "Marranos from the Spanish Netherlands brought with them a knowledge of exchange technique in the realm of produce which in Amsterdam they employed in money and securities."

Garber (2000, p. 23) remarks that by the 1630s "the Netherlands was a highly commercialized country with well-developed and innovative financial markets and a large population of sophisticated traders." Amsterdam did have a brokers guild, whose members swore not to trade on their own account, but large numbers of unlicensed brokers conducted business in their midst (De la Vega, 1688, pp. 184–186).[8] The count of all licensed brokers was 300–500 and the number of unlicensed ones was probably twice that (Dehing & Hart, 1997, p. 53; Bloom, 1937, p. 183).[9] In the mid-eighteenth century there were 100 stockbrokers (Bloom, 1937, p. 183), which likely is just over the amount in latter half of the seventeenth century.[10]

3.1. Equities traded

The primary company that was traded on the Amsterdam Bourse was the Dutch East India Company (VOC), which was the biggest joint stock venture to date (Dehing & Hart, 1997, p. 54).[11] This large scale and widely held endeavor was open to Dutchmen and foreigners alike and allowed numerous investors to reap the benefits of foreign trade without requiring them to risk their entire fortune. The company issued shares by region[12] with the Amsterdam Chamber raising over half of the funds from 1,130 investors[13] (Israel, 1989, p. 70; 1995, pp. 321–326) (Table 1).

The initial share price was 3,000 guilders,[14] a substantial sum of money for the average person, but it appears that it was possible to subscribe to less than one full share (De la Vega, 1688, p. 149). In all there would have been just over 2,100 shares, roughly half of

Table 1
Investors in the Amsterdam chamber of the East India Company in 1602

	All investors		Chief investors	
	Number	Guilders invested	Number	Guilders invested
North Netherlanders	785	2,023,715	40	635,100
South Netherlanders	302	1,418,700	38	871,160
Germans	38	137,900	3	60,000
English	3	6,900	0	0
Portuguese Jews	2	4,800	0	0

Source: Israel (1995, p.346).

which were for the Amsterdam Chamber. For its first 10 years the company paid no dividends and reinvested profits, until the 11th and 12th year where combined dividends amounted to 3,000 guilders (De la Vega, 1668, p. 149).

As Dehing and Hart (1997, p. 54) point out, "Initially, it was set up for a limited number of years, like most early modern trade enterprises," but this was to change. Barbour explains:

> It was on the Amsterdam Bourse in this period that the share completed its evolution from subscription of money to any amount in a trading venture, recoverable only when the enterprise or company should be terminated and the joint stock wound up, to a unit of investment value in a permanent undertaking which implied no active participation in the business thus financed, and which the investor could sell or dispose of at will. (1950, p. 79)

By 1609 the company made the shares enduring, requiring investors to sell their shares if they wished to cash out so they could not withdraw their capital from the company (Neal, 1990a, p. 195).[15] Neal reports how shares were transferred from person to person:

> Transfer and ledger books were maintained at each of the six chambers of the company . . . The transfer books were available 4 or 5 days a week and recorded the ledger entries for both the seller and the buyer, the amount of stock transferred, and the names of two witnesses and the clerk. A very small transfer fee was charged per share. Delays did occur due to the sloppiness of the clerks in recording entries and the necessity of checking to make sure the seller had at least the number of shares being sold to his or her credit in the main ledger. Dissatisfaction with the speed of transfers meant that most trading in VOC shares were done on the basis of forward, or *termijn*, contracts. These were settled at regular *rescontre* dates established every 3 months. (1997, p. 62)[16]

Shares that were repeatedly traded back and forth did not need to be officially transferred each time so stockbrokers figured out how to keep track of their dealings with each other. They created settlement days, "at which all bargains could be either adjusted or continued to the next settlement" (Dickson, 1967, p. 491).

Popularity of the stock market rose with the good fortune of the East India Company, which was significant (Fig. 1). Over the course of 120 years dividends on the original capital of the VOC ended up averaging 22.5% annually making it an attractive investment (Neal, 1990b, p. 17).[17] By 1688 the company had over 20,000 employees and over 300 ships traveling between the East Indies and Europe (Israel, 1989, p. 258; 1995, p. 942).[18]

The other principal company traded at the Amsterdam Bourse was the West India Company, founded in 1621 (Israel, 1995, pp. 326–327). Like its counterpart, the Company of the West raised over six million guilders, almost half in the Amsterdam Chamber (Israel, 1989, p. 159). In contrast, this company had difficulties earning profits, which was reflected in its market value (Fig. 2). In 1672 West India shares were almost worthless and the company had to be restructured (De la Vega, 1688, p. 174; Israel, 1989, p. 294). At the time De la Vega wrote *Confusion de Confusiones* the restructured shares were trading at 110 with the company's dividends over a 14-year period amounting to only 26% (De la Vega, 1688, p. 174). While there were other companies in the Netherlands (Israel, 1989, pp. 109–112) none were as long lasting or large as the East and West India Companies, which constituted most of the stock market (Dehing & Hart, 1997, p. 54; De la Vega, 1688, p. 173).[19]

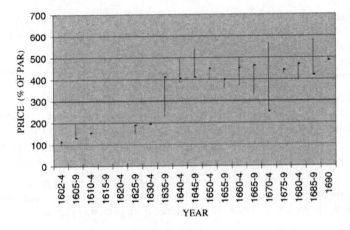

Source: Data are from Garber, 2000:77; Israel, 1989:86, 186;
Israel, 1995: 848; Kellenbenz. 1957: 134.

Fig. 1. Share prices of the East India Company in Amsterdam, 1602–1690.

3.2. Regulatory climate

In some ways the stock market was not heavily regulated and left to its own devices (Neal, 1997, p. 63; Schama, 1987, p. 348)[20] officially, however, the government was not laissez faire. The state permitted the most straightforward sales but was not tolerant of everything that went

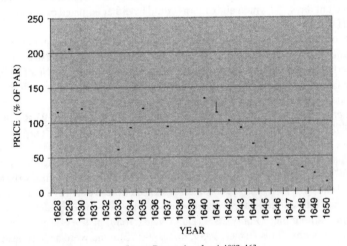

Source: Data are from Israel, 1989: 163.

Fig. 2. Share prices of West India Company in Amsterdam, 1628–1650.

on at the Bourse. Government viewed the market and its various forms of speculation with suspicion. Officials had long sought to limit speculation, as De Vries and Van Der Woude explain:

> Speculation in prices, with associated hoarding, was a constant source of concern to medieval municipal authorities, and it gave rise to mountains of legislation intended to guarantee supplies, prevent hoarding, and restrict the role of middlemen and nonmarket transactions. The Netherlands, under both Habsburg and Republican governments, had its share of ordinances. (1997, p. 150)

Within the first decade of equity trading brokers engaged in short sales and forward contracts, but these types of trades were frowned upon by officials. De Vries and Van Der Woude note:

> As early as 1609, futures trading emerged in the shares of the VOC... The following year the States General prohibited short-selling and other *windhandel*, a prohibition that would be repeated many times in later decades. But speculation in the prices of VOC and other joint-stock company shares continued. (1997, p. 151)

Modern economics has shown the benefits of short selling but at the time they thought that these sales were solely used to manipulate and suppress the stock prices, so the government attempted to prohibit these markets.[21] According to Garber (2000, p. 30) there were numerous pamphlets released in the Netherlands that were "motivated by a moralistic attach against speculation by the authorities."

It was believed that outlawing speculation would eliminate much of the price volatility and price declines. One event that caused a stir was when, in 1608, the price of the stock fell from 200 to 130, which they attributed to a large number of shorts (Kellenbenz, 1957, p. 134). The government claimed outlawing short selling would prevent further such episodes. Wilson (1941, p. 14) states, "In February 1610, selling '*in blanco*' was prohibited, and it was stipulated that shares which were sold must be transferred to the purchaser a month after the sale at the latest." The law pronounced that only those who owned the stock could engage in sales. Kellenbenz recounts:

> [O]n the 27th of February 1610, the first edict was published prohibiting activities of this sort, especially 'windhandel,' that is, the dealing in shares were not in possession of the seller. The sale of shares of the Company by *bona fide* owners for future delivery was allowed. In 1621, after the outbreak of war with Spain, a second edict against the 'wind trade' had to be issued, and further prohibitions followed; but apparently the abuses could not be eliminated. (1957, pp. 134–135)

In the following decades official prohibitions continued with additional ordinances passed in 1621, 1623, 1624, 1630, 1636, and 1677 (Dehing & Hart, 1997, p. 55; Garber, 1994, p. 78).[22] But despite these bans the speculative market still persisted.

Pronouncing something illegal and actually prohibiting it are separate matters. De Vries and Van Der Woude (1997, p. 150) point out, "the reality of the entrepôt repeatedly undermined the feasibility of traditional municipal market regulation, certainly in the major commercial centers." Decades after the first prohibition on selling stocks short the market still continued.

E. Stringham / The Quarterly Review of Economics and Finance 43 (2003) 321–344 329

Wilson writes:

> By 1630, then, most of the elements of a speculative market in shares were already present on the Amsterdam Bourse. Speculators commonly sold shares which they did not possess at the time of sale, and surpluses were settled up on *rescontre* (settling day). This only became a regular feature in the second half of the seventeenth century. (1941, p. 14)

Speculation of various forms had become so widespread the government was nearly powerless in preventing such transactions. Schama (1987, p. 350) notes, "it was virtually impossible to stifle impromptu speculation. If it was driven from the Bourse, the chances were that it would develop spontaneously elsewhere." The historical accounts given by others such as Braudel (1979, p. 101) and Barbour (1950, p. 74) also point to the ineffectiveness of these regulations at eliminating these speculative markets;[23] they were "unenforceable prohibitions" (De Vries & Van Der Woude, 1997, p. 151). Barbour states:

> Repeated efforts of the States General to put a stop to the sale of actions by persons who owned none, to buyers who were not always able to pay for them, failed repeatedly. Only in 1689 was the policy of repression abandoned, when Amsterdam undertook to regulate and to tax the traffic in actions. By this date speculative trading had reached a strikingly modern stage of expertness. (1950, pp. 77–78)

Through the end of the seventeenth century it was evident that these prohibitions were ineffective.

For whatever reason the authorities did not stringently punish violators and hence they did not stamp out the speculative markets. Simply not enforcing contracts is less of an impediment than actually punishing those who engage in unsanctioned trading. In other societies there were restrictions placed on the market but the difference lies in whether the laws were actively enforced.[24] There are a few explanations why Dutch authorities were not ironhanded in their prohibitions. According to Hart, Jonker, and Zanden (1997, p. 3) the States General was not extremely powerful and operated in a "highly fragmented institutional structure." As Clay (1997a, p. 503), points out, "In economic models, the courts often operate costlessly; in reality, however, they involve real costs." Not only is it costly for the general public to use courts, the sense in which the quote refers, but it is also costly for officials. Governments have limited budgets and are not able to effortlessly put into effect every regulation they declare (Benson, 1990, pp. 96–101). In seventeenth-century Holland, rulers had many other things to worry about ranging from enforcing prohibitions against French brandy (Israel, 1989, p. 290) to the recurring wars against England (Israel, 1995, 713, 766, 785, 975). From the standpoint of the financial traders the key was that the government did not actively interfere; *de facto* it was pretty much hands off.

4. The account given by Stockbroker Joseph Penso de la Vega

To investigate the degree to which the market functioned let us examine a primary source. *Confusion de Confusiones* was published in 1688 by Joseph Penso de la Vega who was a stockbroker and writer.[25] The work was composed in Spanish in the form of a dialogue between three

characters, with one character, the shareholder, who "is usually the vehicle for the pronouncement of the author's judgments" (Kellenbenz, 1957, p. 133).[26] The narrative, although informal,
provides an interesting account of a quite developed financial market.[27] English translator Her-
mann Kellenbenz (1957) has declared, "If one is able to look through or around the literary
peculiarities of the volume, he will find in it a reasonably realistic description of the whole
stock market."[28] De la Vega describes the trading that took place in shares in the East and the
West India Companies; short sales, forward contracts, option contracts, and other transactions
all existed despite the fact that much of them had been officially outlawed since they began
appearing throughout that century.

4.1. Short sales

First let us look at De la Vega's account of short sales and their prohibition. In the text, he
refers to the ordinances that prohibited short sales: "Frederick Henry, too, a shining star in the
house of Orange-Nassau, promulgated (with wise motives) an ordinance for these provinces,
according to which he who sold shares for future delivery without putting them on a time
account should be exposed to a danger (because he sold something he does not own) that the
buyer will not take the pieces at the time fixed upon." (152) Although the first laws prohibiting
short sales had been passed before the time of Stadholder Frederick Henry, the chief executive
of the Netherlands from 1625 to 1647, the traders referred to the ordinances of Frederick Henry
since many were passed while he was in office.

Short sales were *de jure* illegal so one might assume that no such short sales took place,
but based on *Confusion de Confusiones* it is clear that the ordinances did not stamp short sales
out. De la Vega describes how people did engage in short sales but would be tempted to not
follow through on their deal when the price took an unfavorable turn. De la Vega (153) wrote,
"There are many persons who refer to the decree [which proclaims the unenforceability of short
sales] only when compelled to do so, I mean only if unforeseen losses occur to them in their
operations." When someone did not have the money to cover their position they might "appeal
to Frederick" (De la Vega, p. 153)[29] and declare that their deal was not valid, but if everyone did
this no one would agree to deal with short sellers. We can see that this was not the case as De la
Vega (153) noted, "When a loss occurs, the losers are expected to pay at least what they have
available at the moment, and it might be expected that, when the wound is fresh, there would
be no new injury ... Other people gradually fulfill their obligations after having sold their last
valuables and thus meet with punctuality the reverses of misfortune." Despite the ability of
short sellers to call upon the law to get out of their predicaments this was not prevalent and we
see that short sellers did attempt to deliver or pay what they owed.[30]

4.2. Forward contracts

Beyond short sales other transactions with unclear legal status took place at the Amsterdam
Bourse. We can see evidence of forward contracts, which were negotiated with settlement dates
many months in advance. De la Vega described them:

> The third kind of transaction takes place *at later dates* still. Here the shares must be deliv-
> ered and be paid for on the twentieth and twenty-fifth of the month which is specified in

the contract, unless one makes use of the mysterious prolongations of which I disapprove because they damage the credit and endanger the reputation [of the party who asks for the prolongation]. For these time bargains the brokers use printed *contract forms* with the customary stipulations and conditions of the business. On these forms spaces are left only for the names, dates, and prices. When two copies have been filled out and signed, the contracts are exchanged by the two parties; [later], and after the establishment of the profit or loss in the business by the rescounters, they are re-exchanged by the signatories. (181–182)

Since they were for long periods of time, forward contracts required traders' counterparts to still be around with what the owed when the time came due.

One might assume that the law was the reason why traders followed through with contracts, but from *Confusion de Confusiones* we can see otherwise since time bargains were prohibited. De la Vega wrote:

As to the unactionable feature of any speculative transaction to be settled by the payment of the differences, you are right in remarking that with *cash transactions* the regulation lacks pertinence. It is, however, valid in the case of *time bargains* unless the seller has the shares transferred to the time account of the purchaser within a fortnight. Then the buyer is obliged to take up the shares, or declare himself insolvent.

Though the opinion prevails generally that this regulation does not apply in the case of the seller but only in that of the buyer, this is an error introduced by bad practice. The lawyers assert that the seller as well as the buyer is allowed to raise the objection [envisaged by Frederick Henry's edict].

The public also presumes that, if the seller of stocks buys them back (from someone who had purchased them earlier), the law does not apply. That is undoubtedly an error also. (For instance), the edict does not apply when I buy shares at [540], sell it at [520], and declare before witnesses that the stock so sold will serve to settle the account of shares previously purchased. By this action I have declared myself debtor for the difference of 20% [of the face value] which I have lost. Therefore, I am not permitted to appeal to the regulation, since I have already assumed the debt; I must pay the difference or become insolvent. But if I have bought a share at [540] from one and without subsequent declaration I sell him another share at [520], [the seller in neither case really owning the stock,] I need neither declare myself bankrupt in order to free myself [from the obligation] nor disappear in order to shake loose; [I can merely appeal to the edict]. (182–183)

Shares needed to be settled or transferred within 2 weeks of the initial transaction, otherwise a contract would violate the law. Luckily for the traders, however, the regulations were not strictly enforced and they went on making forward contracts with each other despite their doubtful legal status.

4.3. Options

Equity trading had begun only earlier that century so it may be surprising to the modern reader that seventeenth-century traders developed an options market. De la Vega (182) described some of the details options contracts, "For the *option business* there exists another sort of *contract form*, from which it is evident when and where the premium was paid and of what kind are the signatories obligations." In this area too options contracts had an uncertain legal standing. The regulations only added confusion since it was unsure how they applied. De la Vega wrote:

> As to whether the regulation is applicable to *option contracts*, the opinions of experts diverge widely. I have not found any decision that might serve as a precedent, though there are many cases at law from which one [should be able to] draw a correct picture. All legal experts hold that the regulation is applicable to both the seller and the buyer [of the contract]. In practice, however, the judges have often decided differently, always freeing the buyer from the liability while often holding the seller [to the contract] .... With regard to the put premium, however, there are also great differences of opinion, for, while the scholars assume that no [legally valid] claims can be made because of the regulation, there are contrary decisions by the courts, so that law and legal opinion, the regulation and the reasons for the decisions are contradictory. The theory remains uncertain, and one cannot tell which way the adjudication tends. (183)

It was unclear whether the law declared that buyers were not liable or if it said that both buyers and sellers were not liable to follow through with their contracts. Either way, with whole classes of contracts unenforceable, it seems that the options market had to develop without the aid of the law.

The regulation stated that one could not trade stock not owned, but some claimed that it did not apply as long as the stocks were purchased eventually. This interpretation essentially paid no heed to the regulation. De la Vega explained:

> However, if the payer of a put premium possesses the stocks on the day of the negotiation of the contract so that he could offer to make delivery to me and to have them transferred to my account [within] a fortnight after the offer, it is unlikely that in such a situation, embarrassing though it might be to me, the regulation can be appealed to. According to the opinion of some people, it is sufficient if the payer of the premium possesses the shares on the day when he declares [himself ready to make] the delivery and not already on the day when he entered into the premium contract, in order to make all objections on grounds of the regulation ineffective. (183–184)

Regardless of the how the officials intended the regulations to apply they were not strictly enforced and options trading persisted.

4.4. Hypothecation

Not only was there confusion over the legality of options, there was also confusion over the law concerning other practices, such as the hypothecation of shares as collateral for a loan. After buying shares there were three choices: the sale of shares, the transference of the shares into one's own name at the Bank, or hypothecation. The last option entailed pledging one's shares to obtain a loan at 80% of their value. This, in De la Vega's (152) words, "is done even by the wealthiest traders without harm to their credit." De la Vega (182) described the contract, "The *forms for hypothecating* are different also. Stamped paper is used for them, upon which

E. Stringham / The Quarterly Review of Economics and Finance 43 (2003) 321–344   333

regulations concerning the *dividends* and other details are set down, so that there can be no doubt and no disagreement regarding the arrangements." Even though they signed clear contracts, in this area too it was unclear what was legal. De la Vega wrote:

> The same uncertainty of adjudication exists with respect to the hypothecation of stocks. While it is generally assumed that, if the shares fall below the value used as the basis of the loan, the mortgagee is obliged to pay in the difference or declare himself insolvent, a few very speculative minds have argued (uncertain doubtless because of the paucity of facts to sustain their position) that if the shares have not been transferred to the time account which I as money lender maintain, within a fortnight after the start of hypothecation arrangement, and if the shares remain in the account [of the borrower] until the date of payment [of the loan], I can raise objections [under the regulation] in order to garner a profit as well as to save myself from a possible loss. (184)

If the value of the shares fell enough, the party in possession of the shares would not be able to sell them for as much as the monetary value of the loan so as soon as this happened De la Vega said the consensus was that borrower must pay the difference. De la Vega pointed out that others maintained that such loans were in violation of the regulations unless the money borrower had transferred the equities into the moneylender's account. The latter position could not have been universally held, otherwise, there would not have been any of these loans.

4.5. Securitization

By the late 1600s the price of each share of the East India Company had reached quite a high value. Where, in modern times, we would see the company announcing a stock split or stock dividend at the time such practices had not yet been introduced. Traders began to offer derivatives of standard shares to allow those with less wealth to participate. De Vries and Van Der Woude explain:

> [S]hare speculation must have been encouraged by the difficulty of actually buying shares. Although the original subscription in 1602 allowed investors to place any amount of money, later trading usually took the form of single 'shares' ... [which by 1650 cost] a small fortune. Much of the interest in futures trading came from persons whose modest means precluded the actual purchase of shares. A further encouragement to futures trading was the [East India Company's] practice of making legal transfer of share ownership only when the books were opened for the payment of dividends—twice per year at most. In time the *Beurs* established *rescounter* dates, quarterly deadlines for the settlement of mutually contingent financial contracts (monthly in the case of *ducat-actions*). (1997, p. 151)

With average daily wages around 0.9 guilders (Hart, 1997, p. 33) and the price of shares at over 15,000 guilders it would have taken a laborer's entire life earnings to purchase one full share.[31] Trader innovations opened the market to a whole new range of people who otherwise would have been precluded.

This was described by De la Vega:

> Some clerks have discovered that the speculation in ordinary shares (which are called *large* or *paid-up shares*) was too hazardous for their slight resources. They began, therefore, a less

334   E. Stringham / The Quarterly Review of Economics and Finance 43 (2003) 321–344

daring game in which they dealt in small shares. For while with whole shares one could win or lose 30 gulden of Bank money for every point that the price rose or fell, with the small shares one risked only a ducaton [3 gulden] for each point. The new speculation, called trading in *ducaton shares*, began in 1683. (185)

Ducaton shares, named for a coin in the Netherlands, were equivalent to one-tenth of a large share, and it appears that that people could trade in even smaller units as well (De la Vega, p. 188). De la Vega gave an analogy for the process of securitization:

> When a mirror is broken, each piece of crystal remains a mirror, the only difference being that the small mirrors reflect one's countenance in miniature and the large ones in larger size... Stocks shares are similar to mirrors... persons broke this mirror [the large 'East' shares] and cut the crystal into pieces by agreeing to regard each 500 pounds of the large shares as 5,000 small ones. (187)

Trading in these shares was more affordable than in large shares so they allowed more people to access the market (Dehing & Hart, 1997, p. 55). De la Vega (186) declared, "This branch of trade has been increasing during the last 5 years to such an extent (and mainly with a certain group which is as boisterous as it is quick-witted) that it is engaged in by both sexes, old men, women, and children." Apparently trading in ducaton shares became quite popular according to De la Vega (188) who wrote, "Even children who hardly know the world and at best own a little pocket money agree that each point by which the large shares rise or fall will mean a certain amount of their pocket money for their small shares... If one were to lead a stranger through the streets of Amsterdam and ask him where he was, he would answer, 'Among speculators,' for there is no corner [in the city] where one does not talk shares."

The trade of ducaton shares was an unofficial business, but they worked out a somewhat elaborate system of monthly or semimonthly settlements. Ducaton shares did not actually change hands (Kellenbenz, 1957, p. 141) but would be kept in the ledger of a cashier who was paid by the parties to keep the records and inform them on settlement date what they should pay or receive. The following passage from *Confusion de Confusiones* gives details:

> For a simple mode of clearing the transactions, the aid of a man who is called the General Cashier was secured. This man put down all contracts in a book, although previously only oral agreements had existed. For every contract that was put down, the General Cashier got a *placa* [the Spanish word for the small coin called a *stuiver* by the Dutch] from each party. Before the transactions were booked definitively, the cashier communicated with the two parties. One rarely agrees in this business to a transaction with a longer time to run than 1 month, because the resources of the people concerned are not sufficient. On the first day of each month when the clock of the Exchange shows one-thirty p.m., the cashier is told the price of the shares by two impartial stock-exchange men and, in accordance with these statements, he specifies the value of the small shares. This comedy is called 'raising the stick,' because formerly a stick was raised by the cashier, until this custom was given up because of the noise that was made each time. The fixing of the price is followed by the settlement of the transactions (in so far as they have not been settled in the middle of the month). Payment is made in cash, and is more punctual than with the large shares, so that even the most experienced businessmen take part in this trade in small shares, for, tempted

E. Stringham / The Quarterly Review of Economics and Finance 43 (2003) 321–344   335

by punctuality, they overlook the dubious reputation of the business and endorse it [by their actions]. (185–186)

It is often presumed that the third party necessary to enforce a contract must be the government but here we see the speculators hiring a private third party. The cashier would find out the price of the large share from two members of the Amsterdam Bourse and then declare the settlement price of the small shares.

In this area as well, ducaton contracts were not ultimately enforced by the courts of law. By the time the government courts addressed the trading in ducaton shares it was only to declare them illegal. De la Vega (208) described, "In the ducaton speculation the damage was still more disturbing. (Speculation was [in ducaton shares] was declared by court to be a game or a bet, and thus the transactions in them were denied the character of true business.) Therefore, it was not even necessary to appeal to Frederick Henry's decree to refuse payment." Again if the market in ducaton shares was to exist at all it clearly was not due to the support of government courts.

5. Analysis

From the examples given above we can see that official regulations were outlawing whole markets, not assisting them. For such extralegal markets to function there must have existed some other mechanism to ensure that traders followed their contracts. Rather than relying on law, there are various other ways of inducing contractual performance; sanctions against cheating can be physical, religious, social, or economic (Clay, 1997a, p. 513). There is no evidence that brokers used physical force, so it must be some combination of the other three. In passing Neal remarks:

> The number of stock traders in the Amsterdam Beurs in 1688 was sufficiently limited enough for them to prefer to deal only with other members of a close-knit group already dealing with them. In this way, any breach of contract in stock-trading could be compensated by an offsetting breach of contract in some other transaction unrelated to the stock market, but very much part of the group's activities. The group that emerged by the end of the seventeenth century in the Amsterdam Beurs was comprised of members of the Sephardic Jewish community. (1997, p. 63)

While this may be correct to a degree it seems likely that social and religious sanctions were not the only, or most important, factors. There were 300 licensed brokers in 1612, a number which increased to 500 over the next century, but of those only two were Jewish at century's beginning, 8 in 1612, 30 in 1645, and 50 through century's end (Bloom, 1937, pp. 182–183). It may be the case that a disproportionate amount of unlicensed brokers were Jewish and focused on the stock market (Israel, 1990), but it does not appear that the Bourse was an extremely homogenous group, socially or religiously.[32] In *Confusion de Confusiones* there are no apparent references to religious or social sanctions and the only reference to Judaism's influence is that on Saturdays less people attend the market (Bloom, 1937, pp. 179, 191). We can see that a substantial part, perhaps even most, of the exchange was not between the Sephardis so it appears that religious and social sanctions were not the most important factor.[33] This is more in line with the findings of Neal and Quinn (2001, p. 10) who describe seventeenth-century bankers where, "Kinship or religious ties were often insufficient to cover the wide network of commerce that had then developed."

This leaves us with economic enforcement. Economic incentives for cooperation can be created if people wish to have enduring relationships. This can be at the individual level or within a group. With bilateral interaction consisting of repeated, one-on-one, long-term relationships, when someone cheats he risks that specific relationship. With interaction within a group, if someone cheats not only does he risk that specific relationship, he runs the risk of not finding any other trading partners (Clay, 1997a, p. 511). Though the Amsterdam brokers had no formal rules and could not exclude cheats, they could share information about trustworthiness and it would be in their interest to boycott those who were unreliable (Caplan & Stringham, in press).[34] Even when two brokers had no personal experience with each other or did not plan to trade with each other again, they would think twice about cheating because they knew that information about their behavior could be shared. This reputational network would create incentives for brokers to follow through with their contracts.

There are many passages from *Confusion de Confusiones* that illustrate the importance of reputation. De la Vega (172) wrote, "The Exchange business is comparable to a game. Some of the players behave like princes and combine strength with tenderness and amiability with intelligence, but there are some participants who lose their reputation and others who lack devotion to their business even before play begins." We would expect the untrustworthy brokers to not be very successful. Sure enough De la Vega (201) mentioned the disreputable, "Since the status, the insignificant capital, the low reputation, and the limited trustworthiness of such people are well known, they do not dare attempt to carry on any considerable business."

Though brokers with bad reputations were precluded from most dealing, the stock market was not a closed club. The text indicates the Bourse was composed of various sorts. De la Vega (185) remarked, "There exists an infinite number of these free brokers. This occupation is [in many cases] the only recourse for impoverished [businessmen], and the best place of refuge for many ruined careers." While many brokers live opulently, "Nevertheless there are numerous people in the business simply for the reason of providing decently for their families." (190) Although the Bourse was open to newcomers, participants did have to work to build their reputation before they could make substantial trades. For example, in one dialogue a novice believed his limited capital would preclude him and that "there would be nobody to give me credit," but he is told he can start with options until he "gains in reputation for his generosity as well as his foresight" (150–151).

At the Amsterdam Bourse each broker had to work to get business. Capitalists and merchants were able to make the trades themselves so they would only choose to go to the broker and pay his fee (De la Vega, p. 179) if they were getting value out such an arrangement. When confronted with this situation we would expect the brokers to act judiciously, which is confirmed by De la Vega (176) who wrote, "so great is the loyalty of some brokers to their principals, whom they usually call their masters, and so great is their industry, their activity, their zeal, and their vigilance that the customers get their money's worth."[35] The brokers would need to act in a virtuous manner if they were to expect patronage.

For this reason it was in the traders' interest to keep their promises and abide by their word. The following passage from *Confusion de Confusiones* illustrates this well:

> [To be sure, there is widespread honesty and expedition on the Exchange. For example,] the business in stocks and the bustle of the sales which are made when unforeseen news arrives is wonderful to behold. Nobody changes the decisions which he makes in his momentary passion, and his words are held sacred even in the case of a price difference of 50%; and, although tremendous business is done by the merchants without the mediation of brokers who could serve as witnesses, no confusion occurs and no quarrels take place . . . Such honesty, co-operation, and accuracy are admirable and surprising. (172)

Deals stuck at the spur of the moment were presumably without formal contracts, yet they did not break down.[36] In such an anarchic market it is not feasible for brokers' contracts to be continually reviewed and adjudicated in the courts, yet in absence of legal oversight we see that bargains are kept.[37] Because of the discipline of continuous dealings, 'such honesty, cooperation and accuracy' is not surprising.

In the 1600s, the first century when equities were traded, we can see that there was a considerable degree of financial innovation. We also see that most of the financial instruments were officially outlawed by the state. Brokers discovered new trading instruments and abided by their contracts not because of legal compulsion but because of market incentives. The regulations were not advancing the market, they were trammeling it, though the market developed in spite of the law. Contrary to the idea that the government is needed for financial innovation and contractual performance, the case of the Amsterdam Bourse provides evidence that securities markets can function successfully with little assistance from the state.

Notes

1. It seems that even if we go along with Tullock and Olson's distinction between regular transactions and complicated financial transactions, the results of the analysis do not greatly differ.
2. Although it is usually considered to be the first stock market, Braudel (1979, p. 100) argues that this is not precisely true: "It is not quite accurate to call [Amsterdam] the first stock market, as people often do. State loan stocks had been negotiable at a very early date in Venice, in Florence before 1328, and in Genoa, where there was an active market in the *luoghi* and *paghe* of Casa di San Giorgio, not to mention the *Kuxen* shares in the German mines which were quoted as early as the fifteenth century at the Leipzig fairs, the Spanish *juros*, the French *rentes sur l'Hotel de Ville* (municipal stocks) (1522) or the stock market in the Hanseatic towns from the fifteenth century. The statutes of Verona in 1318 confirm the existence of the settlement or forward market . . . In 1428, the jurist Bartolomeo de Bosco protested against the sale of forward *loca* in Genoa. All evidence points to the Mediterranean as the cradle of the stock market. But what was new in Amsterdam was the volume, the fluidity of the market and publicity it received, and the speculative freedom of transactions."
3. Trading also took place on the Dam, the square across from the Palace, before the Bourse would open its doors (De la Vega, 1688, p. 176).

4. Previously merchants had gathered in large numbers at fairs, which met only on occasion. Braudel (1979, p. 100) writes, "An Exchange was, relatively speaking, like the top section of a fair, but one in permanent session. Because the important businessmen as well as a host of intermediaries met here, business of every sort could be transacted: operations in commodities, currency exchange, shareholding, maritime insurance where the risk was spread among several guarantors; and it was a money market, a finance market and a stock market. It was natural that such activities should tend to become organized independently. In Amsterdam there was already by the beginning of the seventeenth century a separate Corn Exchange."

5. Schama (1987, p. 348) writes, "Even by the first years following the creation of the East India Company in 1602 (although of course the Bourse traded in all manner of stock), it had become plain that the old informal dealings in open-air markets on the Warmoesstraat and near the Oude Kerk would no longer suffice. The new Bourse was built on the Rokin in 1608." The building itself was modeled after the Bourse of Antwerp, which had been constructed in 1531. De Clerck (1998, p. 1) writes, "the Antwerp exchange, a large square with a courtyard surrounded by covered walkways, was the first building designed solely for the purpose of trade." Before the 1531 building the Bourse of Antwerp dates back to 1460 (Braudel, 1979, p. 99). Amsterdam had taken many of its cues from Antwerp, which it surpassed as the most popular area for trade in Europe in the late sixteenth century (Barbour, 1950, p. 20; De Vries & Van Der Woude, 1997, p. 366; Wilson, 1941, p. 13).

6. De Vries and Van Der Woude (1997, p. 150) explain, "Because of the *de facto* character of the new commercial practices, documentation is incomplete. But already in the 1550s, Amsterdam merchants practiced an early form of futures trading, when they wrote contracts for future delivery of Baltic grain and North Sea herring before the grain had been harvested or the herring had been caught. The enlargement of the range of goods traded in the Republic and the establishment of continuous markets at the Amsterdam Beurs created an environment in which speculative practices could spread and mature. In the seventeenth century, futures contracts came to be written for a large range of products, including pepper, coffee, cacao, saltpeter, brandywine, whale oil, and whale bone. Moreover, purchasers of these contracts increasingly had no intention of taking delivery, just as sellers did not possess and did not intend to acquire the promised goods."

7. For lists of commodities, and their prices, traded on the Bourse in 1585–1914 see Posthumus (1964).

8. Bloom (1937, p. 183) reports, "Sometimes, the brokers guild put obstacles in the way of the unsworn brokers. For instance, a certain Jew, Jacob Piemontel, citizen of Amsterdam, complains to the burgomasters that he is now (August 1675) hindered in his business by the authorities of the brokers guild, in spite of the fact that he only charges a commission of 5 cents on each 100 guilders. . . . He requested that he be left unimpended in his activity. His petition was supported by 38 Gentile signatures." De la Vega (1688, p. 186) stated, "If the free brokers were to be sued, they would have to pay a fine for impairing the income [of the sworn brokers]; but such action is taken only in cases of personal revenge, otherwise clemency and indulgence toward these brokers prevail, instead of the sworn brokers attending to their own interests."

9. The estimates are for the early 1720s and range from 700 to 1000.

10. Bloom (1937, p. 183) reports that in 1760, "Of the total number of brokers, sworn and unsworn, there were between 250 and 300 bill brokers, 80 wine and brandy brokers, 100 stock brokers and 100 insurance brokers." This fits with the allusions of De la Vega (1688, p. 164) who stated, "Formerly 20 speculators ruled the exchange... Today there are as many speculators as merchants." De la Vega (1688, p. 150) classifies frequenters of the exchange into three categories: wealthy capitalists who buy and hold, merchants who invest in a share or two at a time, and speculators who seek to profit on price movements. Although he does not specify the number of merchants we can gather the number at the exchange was significantly greater than 40.

11. Joint-stock ventures with transferable shares date back to classical Rome but these were not long lasting endeavors so no stock market existed (Neal, 1997, p. 61). The first modern joint stock company was the Muscovy Company, which was chartered in England in 1553 (Kindleberger, 1984, p. 196).

12. There were six chambers which, "kept their capital, and commercial operations, separate from each other, while observing general guidelines, and policies, set by a federal board of directors" (Israel, 1995, p. 321). The board of directors consisted of 17 members who were appointed by chambers in proportion to their size; shareholders at this time had no voting power (Neal, 1997, p. 60).

13. For perspective the estimated population of Amsterdam in 1600 was 60,000 (Israel, 1995, p. 328).

14. A guilder, also referred to as a florin, contained about 10 g of fine silver (Dehing & Hart, 1997, p. 41).

15. Kellenbenz (1957, p. 134) explains the creation of East India Company shares: "Trade and speculation in shares first appeared there when in 1602, the six local 'chambers' for East Indian trade were united into a general Dutch East India Company. According to the official pronouncement, every inhabitant of the United Provinces had an opportunity to participate in the Company. At the beginning the rights deriving from the initial payments were called 'paerten,' 'partieen,' or 'partijen,' the word being taken over from the practice of 'participation' in the shipping business. It was not until 1606 that the word 'actie' (i.e., share) seems to have come into use. The possibility of trading these 'participations' was assured by the fact that each owner of shares could, by payment of a fee, transfer holdings, in whole or in part, to another person."

16. The development of regular settlement dates was later adopted by the English in the 1740s (Dickson, 1967, p. 491, 507–510).

17. Inflation in the century was negligible (Dehing & Hart, 1997, p. 41) and ordinary loans received interest of 2.5–3% (De la Vega, 1688, p. 164). For more on interest rates and banking in seventeenth-century Netherlands see Neal (2000), Dickson (1967, p. 474), and Dehing and Hart (1997, p. 53).

18. The trade included spices, tea, coffee, silk, and cotton (Israel, 1989, p. 336–8).

19. The shares traded at the Amsterdam Bourse were for the Amsterdam Chamber. Shares were nontransferable between chambers and though all received equal dividends "because speculation does not exist at the other places in these Provinces" shares for the other chambers traded at a discount of 5–30% (De la Vega, 1688, p. 165).

340   E. Stringham / The Quarterly Review of Economics and Finance 43 (2003) 321–344

20. Schama (1987, p. 348) writes, "Confined within its handsome Flemish-mannerist colon-naded court, the Bourse was more or less left to its own regulation. Rules were not so much devised by the city for the exchange, as barriers set between it and the rest of the town's commerce."

21. Banner (1998) gives a history of Anglo attitudes towards the stock market and regulation from the seventeenth to the nineteenth century.

22. Garber, (2000, p. 34) states, "The authorities continually regarded futures trading as immoral gambling."

23. In commodities markets there were these problems as well. Barbour (1950, p. 75), writes, "In 1698 the States General denounced by plakkaat a practice evidently not uncommon: the sale of large quantities of grain by persons who had none, or at least not the quantities of which they affected to dispose. Sales at time and transactions in options were forbidden, but continued notwithstanding."

24. The fall of the Antwerp Bourse can be attributed to draconian political measures which included expelling the Jewish population (Bloom, 1937, p. 181) and banning ships traveling directly to the city (Israel, 1989, p. 30).

25. De la Vega, a Sephardi of Portuguese origin, was born around 1650 and grew up mostly in Amsterdam. He was a businessman and an author who wrote mainly in Spanish and occasionally in Hebrew and Portuguese (Amzalak, 1944, p. 33; Boer and Israel, 1991, pp. 443, 451; Penslar, 1997, pp. 33–34).

26. Even though the book was written in Amsterdam it was not translated into Dutch until the twentieth century (Kellenbenz, 1957, p. 146) which was also when it was translated into to German and English. The Spanish original (1688/1977), has parts that were not translated into English, but the translation does contain most of the material pertaining to the stock market. All quotes in this paper are from the 1996 English version.

27. Few if any descriptions of the Amsterdam stock exchange existed at the time, as the German translator for *Confusion de Confusiones* Otto Pringsheim noted, "a few pamphlets treating the speculation in shares were published in 1642 and 1687. The author does not know of them at all, or makes no mention of them because he thinks them too irrelevant." (as quoted in Kellenbenz, 1957, p. 168). Bloom (1937, p. 191) remarked, "It is worthy to note that although de la Vega knew Dutch when he wrote the book his book [was] in Spanish, appealing to a circle of Jewish readers beyond the boundaries of Holland. De la Vega may have had the English Sephardim in mind. Many Amsterdam Jews had by this time established themselves in England. Two of De la Vega's brothers lived in London."

28. The book, however, is not without its shortcomings; since De la Vega did not have the good fortune of being trained in modern economics or finance it is no surprise that much of the inferences he draws are faulty. For example, some of his reasoning of why people participate in the market seems to posit a sort of irrationality on the part of participants. Also, he spends a lot of time describing various schemes where people attempt to trick others into thinking the price of the stock will fall or rise, which although possible, would require a large degree of gullibility. Due to an absence of a high degree of sophistication in economics and finance during that era, it is understandable there are flaws, but for its time it is a quite advanced book.

29. Such appeals were not literally appealing to Frederick Henry since he had died 40 years before *Confusion de Confusiones* was written.
30. As will be discussed next some contracts were for the delivery of shares while others simply required parties to pay the difference. With the latter one would "win or lose 30 gulden of Bank money for every point that the price rose or fell" (De la Vega, p. 185) but need not need actually transfer the share. I would like to thank an anonymous referee for this clarification.
31. Many contracts did not actually require the purchase of a share but even ones that involved paying the difference could require payment of 300 guilders, a year's salary for some, for each 10 points the stock moved in the wrong direction. I would like to thank an anonymous referee for pointing this out.
32. Although the Sephardis' native tongue was Portuguese or Spanish, Dutch was the language, "which most of the speculators or others concerned with the stock market must have used." (Kellenbenz, 1957, p. 146) De la Vega (1688, p. 166) mentioned that a mixture of languages was evident on the stock exchange, including words from Latin, Dutch and French.
33. After mentioning a handful of ethnic groups Neal (1997, p. 64) states, "It is likely that trading in the stock markets was done largely among individuals in these separate groups rather than between these groups." In the eighteenth century one-quarter of the shareholders were Jewish (Bloom, 1937, p. 190) so it may be the case that Jewish investors used Jewish stockbrokers but of the other three-quarters it seems unlikely that native Dutchmen had close religious or ethnic ties with their brokers. By 1688 the population of Amsterdam had grown to 200,000 which included residents of various religions originating from places such as Germany, Portugal, and Scandinavia (Israel, 1995, pp. 621–627). This seems too large to depend on close-knit ties or religious bonds for cooperation.
34. In Amsterdam, the brokers guild did not seem very important and it was not until the eighteenth century when printed rules appeared (Bloom, 1937, p. 188). The London stock market, which began in the late seventeenth century taking many cues from Amsterdam (Schubert, 1988, p. 300; Neal, 1987, p. 98) did not have an exclusive stock exchange until 1801 (Mirowski, 1981; Michie, 1999; Stringham, 2002). For a review of formal self-regulating organizations see Mahoney (1997) and Frye (2000).
35. Johnsen's (1994, p. 103) description of present stock market is similar, "On Wall Street, where news travels notoriously fast and a person's reputation is his stock in trade, a soft dollar broker who clearly cheats one client, say, by front-running, might well be terminated by a large number of his other clients."
36. In addition to the examples of people going along with their contracts, De la Vega described that of when people made legitimate errors the other party would not hold them liable. De la Vega (171) wrote, "It is an inviolable practice on the Exchange (which once was a mere usance) that that the party making a mistake is not obliged to suffer for it, if a transaction, not done at the price of the day, contains an error of 10% [of the par value]."
37. As Telser (1987, p. 187) wrote, "Since it is costly to rely on the intervention of third parties such as courts to enforce agreements and to assess damages of violations, the

parties to an agreement devise the terms to make it self-enforcing, if this can be done cheaply enough."

Acknowledgments

I would like to thank George Berger, Peter Boettke, James Buchanan, Bryan Caplan, Bruce Johnsen, Leonard Liggio, Gordon Tullock, two anonymous referees, and seminar participants at the Center for the Study of Public Choice, George Mason Law School, New York University, and the Southern Economics Association Meetings for helpful comments and suggestions. Financial support provided by the Olofsson Weaver Fellowship is greatly appreciated. The usual disclaimer applies.

References

Amzalak, M. (1944). Joseph Da Veiga and Stock Exchange Operation in the seventeenth century. In E. Levine (Ed.), *Essays in honour of the Very Rev. Dr. J. H. Hertz* (pp. 33–49). London: E. Goldston.

Banner, S. (1998). *Anglo-American securities regulation: Cultural and political roots, 1680–1860*. Cambridge: Cambridge University Press.

Barbour, V. (1950/1976). *Capitalism in Amsterdam in the seventeenth century*. Ann Arbor: University of Michigan Press.

Benson, B. (1989). The spontaneous evolution of commercial law. *Southern Economic Journal, 55*, 644–661.

Benson, B. (1990). *The enterprise of law*. San Francisco: Pacific Research Institute for Public Policy.

Bernstein, L. (1992). Opting out of the legal system: Extralegal contractual relations in the Diamond Industry. *Journal of Legal Studies, 21*, 115–157.

Bernstein, L. (1996). Merchant law in a merchant court: Rethinking the code's search for immanent business norms. *University of Pennsylvania Law Review, 144*, 1765–1821.

Bloom, H. I. (1937/1969). The economic activities of the Jews of Amsterdam in the seventeenth and eighteenth centuries. Port Washington, NY: Kennikat Press.

Boer, H. D., & Israel, J. (1991). William III and the glorious revolution in the eyes of Amsterdam Sephardi writers: The reactions of Miguel de Barrios, Joseph Penso de la Vega, and Manuel de Leão. In J. Israel (Ed.), *The Anglo-Dutch Moment* (pp. 439–461). Cambridge: Cambridge University Press.

Boot, A., Stuart, G., & Thakor, A. (1993). Reputation and discretion in financial contracting. *American Economic Review, 83*, 1165–1183.

Braudel, F. (1979/1982). *Civilization and capitalism 15th–18th century: The wheels of commerce* (Vol. II) (trans.). Sian Reynolds, New York: Harper & Row.

Brennan, G., & Buchanan, J. (1985). *The reason of rules*. Cambridge: Cambridge University Press.

Caplan, B., & Stringham, E. (2002). Networks, law, and the paradox of cooperation. *Review of Austrian Economics*, in press.

Clay, K. (1997a). Trade, institutions, and credit. *Explorations in Economic History, 34*, 495–521.

Clay, K. (1997). Trade without law: Private-order institutions in Mexican California. *Journal of Law, Economics and Organization, 13*, 202–231.

De Clerck, G. (1998). Antwerp stock exchange closes. *Belgium Today, 3*, 1.

Dehing, P., & Hart, M. T. (1997). Linking the fortunes: Currency and banking, 1550–1800. In M. T. Hart, J. Jonker, & J. L. van Zanden (Eds.), *A financial history of the Netherlands* (pp. 37–63). Cambridge: Cambridge University Press.

De la Vega, J. P. (1688/1977). *Confusion de Confusiones* (reprint). Valencia, Spain: Saetabis.

De la Vega, J. P. (1688/1996). In H. Kellenbenz (Ed.), *Confusion de Confusiones* (trans.). Martin Fridson, New York: Wiley.

De Vries, J., & Van Der Woude, A. (1997). *The first modern economy: Success, failure, and perseverance of the Dutch economy, 1500–1815.* Cambridge: Cambridge University Press.

Dickson, P. G. M. (1967/1993). *The financial revolution in England: A study in the development of public credit, 1688–1756.* Aldershot, Hampshire, UK: Gregg Revivals.

Ellickson, R. (1991). *Order without law: How neighbors settle disputes.* Boston: Harvard University Press.

Frye, T. (2000). *Brokers and bureaucrats: Building market institutions in Russia.* Ann Arbor: University of Michigan Press.

Garber, P. (1994). Tulipmania. In R. Flood & P. Garber (Eds.), *Speculative bubbles, speculative attacks, and policy switching* (pp. 55–82). Cambridge, MA: MIT Press.

Garber, P. (2000). *Famous first bubbles.* Cambridge, MA: MIT Press.

Glaeser, E., Johnson, S., & Shleifer, A. (2001). Coase versus the coasians. *Quarterly Journal of Economics, 116,* 853–899.

Greif, A. (1989). Reputation and coalitions in medieval trade: Evidence on the Maghribi traders. *Journal of Economic History, 49,* 857–882.

Greif, A. (1993). Contract enforceability and economic institutions in early trade: The Maghribi traders' coalition. *American Economic Review, 83,* 525–548.

Greif, A., Milgrom, P., & Weingast, B. R. (1994). Coordination, commitment, and enforcement: The case of the Merchant Guild. *The Journal of Political Economy, 102,* 745–776.

Hart, M. T. (1997). The merits of a financial revolution: Public finance, 1550–1700. In M. T. Hart, J. Jonker, & J. L. van Zanden (Eds.), *A financial history of the Netherlands* (pp. 11–36). Cambridge: Cambridge University Press.

Hart, M. T., Joost, J., & van Zanden, J. L. (1997). *A financial history of the Netherlands.* Cambridge: Cambridge University Press.

Israel, J. (1989/1991). *Dutch primacy in world trade, 1585–1740.* Oxford: Oxford University Press.

Israel, J. (1990). The Amsterdam Stock Exchange and the English Revolution of 1688. *Tijdschrift voor Geschiedenis, 103,* 412–440.

Israel, J. (1995). *The Dutch Republic: Its rise, greatness, and fall, 1477–1806.* Oxford: Oxford University Press.

Johnsen, D. B. (1986). The formation and protection of property rights among the southern Kwakiutl Indians. *Journal of Legal Studies, 15,* 41–67.

Johnsen, D. B. (1994). Property rights to investment research: The agency costs of soft dollar brokerage. *Yale Journal on Regulation, 11,* 75–113.

Kellenbenz, H. (1957/1996). Introduction to Confusion de Confusiones. In M. Fridson (Ed.), *Confusion de Confusiones* (pp. 125–146). New York: Wiley.

Kindleberger, C. (1984). *A financial history of Western Europe.* London: George Allen & Unwin.

Klein, D. (1997). *Reputation.* Ann Arbor: University of Michigan Press.

Klein, B., & Leffler, K. (1981). The role of market forces in assuring contractual performance. *Journal of Political Economy, 89,* 615–641.

Landa, J. (1981). A theory of ethnically homogenous middleman group: An institutional alternative to contract law. *Journal of Legal Studies, 10,* 349–362.

Landa, J. (1994). *Trust, ethnicity, and identity.* Ann Arbor: University of Michigan Press.

Macey, J., & O'Hara, M. (1999). Regulating exchanges and alternative trading systems: A law and economics perspective. *Journal of Legal Studies, 28,* 17–53.

Mahoney, P. (1997). The exchange as regulator. *Virginia Law Review, 83,* 1453–1500.

Michie, R. (1999). *The London Stock Exchange: A history.* Oxford: Oxford University Press.

Milgrom, P., Douglass, N., & Weingast, B. (1990). The role of institutions in the revival of trade: The law merchant, private judges, and the champagne fairs. *Economics and Politics, 2,* 1–23.

Mirowski, P. (1981). The rise (and retreat) of a market English joint stock shares in the eighteenth century. *Journal of Economic History, 41,* 559–577.

Neal, L. (1987). The integration and efficiency of the London and Amsterdam stock markets in the eighteenth century. *Journal of Economic History, 47,* 97–115.

Neal, L. (1990a). The Dutch and English East India Companies. In J. Tracy (Ed.), *The rise of merchant empires* (pp. 195–223). Cambridge: Cambridge University Press.

Neal, L. (1990b). *The rise of financial capitalism: International capital markets in the age of reason.* Cambridge: Cambridge University Press.

Neal, L. (1997). On the historical development of stock markets. In H. Brezinski & M. Fritsch (Eds.), *The emergence and evolution of stock markets.* Cheltenham, UK: Edward Elgar Publishing.

Neal, L. (2000). How it all began: The monetary and financial architecture of Europe during the first global capital markets, 1648–1815. *Financial History Review, 7,* 117–140.

Neal, L., & Quinn, S. (2001). Networks of information, markets, and institutions in the rise of London as a financial center in the seventeenth century. *Financial History Review, 8,* 7–26.

Olson, M. (1996). Big bills left on the sidewalk: Why some nations are rich, and others poor, and others poor. *Journal of Economic Perspectives, 10,* 3–24.

Penslar, D. (1997). The origins of Jewish political economy. *Jewish Social Studies, 3,* 26–60.

Posthumus, N. (1964). *Inquiry into the history of prices in Holland.* Leidin: E.J. Brill.

Quinn, S. (1997). Goldsmith-banking: Mutual acceptance and interbanker clearing in restoration London. *Explorations in Economic History, 34,* 411–432.

Schama, S. (1987). *The embarrassment of riches: An interpretation of Dutch culture in the Golden Age.* New York: Alfred Knopf.

Schubert, E. (1988). Innovations, debts, and bubbles: International integration of financial markets in Western Europe, 1688–1720. *Journal of Economic History, 48,* 299–306 (The Tasks of Economic History).

Smith, A. (1766/1982). *Lectures on jurisprudence.* Indianapolis: Liberty Classics.

Stringham, E. (2002). The emergence of the London Stock Exchange as a self policing club. *Journal of Private Enterprise, 17,* 1–20.

Telser, L. G. (1980). A theory of self-enforcing agreements. *Journal of Business, 53,* 27–44.

Telser, L. G. (1987). *A theory of efficient cooperation and competition.* Cambridge: Cambridge University Press.

Tullock, G. (1972). The edge of the jungle. In G. Tullock (Ed.), *Explorations in the theory of Anarchy* (pp. 65–75). Blacksburg, VA: Center for the Study of Public Choice.

Tullock, G. (1985). Adam Smith and the prisoners' dilemma. *Quarterly Journal of Economics, 100*(Suppl.), 1073–1081.

Tullock, G. (1999). Non-prisoner's dilemma. *Journal of Economic Behavior & Organization, 39,* 455–458.

Wilson, C. (1941). *Anglo-Dutch commerce in the eighteenth century.* Cambridge: Cambridge University Press.

[20]

The Journal of Private Enterprise 17(2), 2002, 1-19

The Emergence of the London Stock Exchange as a Self-Policing Club

Edward Stringham[*]

George Mason University

Abstract

In the early stock market in London there were substantial risks of non-payment and fraud. (Mortimer, 1801) According to Hobbesian theory, we would expect stock markets to develop only after government has implemented rules and regulations to eliminate these problems. The historical account, however, provides evidence that solutions to these problems did not come from the state. This article outlines the emergence of the London Stock Exchange, which was created by eighteenth century brokers who transformed coffeehouses into private clubs that created and enforced rules. Rather than relying on public regulation to enforce contracts and reduce fraud, brokers consciously found a way to solve their dilemmas by forming a self-policing club.

JEL Codes: L51, N23, D2, G28
Keywords: Financial history; Stock markets; Self-governance; Self-regulation

I. Introduction

It is commonly held that government is needed to enforce contracts in financial markets. According to Hobbesian theory, without external enforcement, the incentives to cheat would prevail and welfare-enhancing trades would not take place (Glaeser et al., 2001; Buchanan, 1975; Tullock 1972, 1974).

---

[*] The author wishes to thank Peter Boettke, Tyler Cowen, Paul Mahoney, Andrew Sellgren, and seminar participants at George Mason University and the Association of Private Enterprise Meetings for helpful comments. The usual disclaimer applies.

2   *E. Stringham / The Journal of Private Enterprise 17(2), 2002, 1-19*

While it is certainly true that rules can improve contractual performance, a major option that is often ignored is the possibility of privately-generated rules. Upon examining the historical record we can see that, by and large, rules governing financial trading developed independently from the state. The focus of this paper is the evolution of the London Stock Exchange (Silber, 1981; Carlton, 1984; Fischel and Grossman, 1984; Macey and Kanda, 1990; Chambers and Carter, 1990; Mahoney, 1997; Banner, 1998; Macey and O'Hara, 1999).[1] Rather than having public origins, the London Stock Exchange emerged when eighteenth-century brokers transformed coffeehouses into private clubs to form a system of self-regulation.

Beyond merely providing buyers and sellers a location to meet, one of the most important functions of a stock exchange is fostering an orderly atmosphere where traders follow a common set of rules. Exchange members must constantly seek ways to attract business and one way to improve business is by providing assurances against fraud (Banner, 1998, p.132). By cooperating and forming a club for the joint provision and consumption of rule enforcement, stockbrokers enhance the value of their enterprise (Buchanan, 1965). This stands against the idea that stock exchanges would fail to organize properly without direction from the state (Frye, 2000).

There are many advantages of market regulation over government regulation. First and foremost, when the private sector has the ability to experiment, brokers can try different regulations to see which ones are most successful. It is choice that allows groups of freely associating individuals to discover new ways of governing their conduct. As Hayek wrote, "the value of freedom consists mainly in the opportunity it provides for the growth of the undesigned, and the beneficial functioning of a free society rests largely on the existence of such freely grown institutions" (Hayek, 1978, p.61). If private

---

[1] For book-length histories of the London Stock Exchange see Wincott (1946), Morgan and Thomas (1969), Jenkins (1973), and Michie (1999).

E. Stringham / The Journal of Private Enterprise 17(2), 2002, 1-19 3

clubs, such as stock exchanges, have the choice to pick their self-regulations they can attempt to discover what ones are beneficial. This contrasts with the position that rules need to imposed from the top down from the state. Hayek explained it well:

> There is an advantage in obedience to such rules not being coerced, not only because coercion as such is bad, but because it is, in fact, often desirable that rules should be observed only in most instances... It is this flexibility of voluntary rules which in the field of morals makes gradual evolution and spontaneous growth possible, which allows further experience to lead to modifications and improvements. Such an evolution is only possible with rules which are neither coercive or deliberately imposed—... Unlike any deliberately imposed coercive rules, which can be changed only discontinuously and for all at the same time, rules of this kind allow for gradual and experimental change. The existence of individuals and groups simultaneously observing partially different rules provide the opportunity for selection of the more effective ones (Hayek, 1978, p.62–63).

If brokers have the ability to choose they can continuously adopt new ways of self-policing.[2] While it may be the case the regulation of a stock market is necessary there is no reason to conclude that it must be done by the state.

---

[2] This is not to say at every given instant people will break their bargains, insisting that the old rules no longer apply; they will, however, have to capability of adopting new arrangements and procedures for future contracts (Benson 1990, 1993; Stringham, 1999).

4 E. Stringham / The Journal of Private Enterprise 17(2), 2002, 1-19

The Emergence of Stock Exchanges

Stock exchanges were not suddenly invented. No governor declared the establishment of the London Stock Exchange; rather it evolved over time (Smith, 1929, p.206; Wincott, 1946, p.1). Joint stock companies had first come into being in the sixteenth century and it was not for some time before there were enough tradable stocks to warrant the specialized occupation of stockbrokers (Kindleberger, 1984, p.196).[3] At first ownership of stocks was not widespread, and sales were conducted on a small scale directly between buyers and sellers, with trades typically consisting of one owner divesting his shares to another owner or someone else on the restricted list of eligible buyers (Jenkins, 1973). Liberalization of the banking sector at the end of the seventeenth century increased the ability for companies to borrow funds, which led to an increase in the quantity of joint stock companies from fifteen to a hundred and fifty in a matter of six years (Jenkins, 1973). The earliest evidence of stockbrokers in England appears in the late seventeenth century, and in 1692 the trade was important enough for the weekly periodical *Collection for Improvement of Husbandry and Trade* to begin publishing stock prices for eight companies (Houghton, 1727; Neal, 1987, p.99).

Initially brokers dealt in stocks as a side business, but eventually people began specializing in stockbrokerage (Jenkins, 1973).[4] They traded at the Royal Exchange, which housed other merchants such as grocers, druggists, and clothiers (Wincott, 1947, p.7). As the number of stockbrokers grew it became evident they were not entirely welcome at the Royal Exchange, and in 1696 the government passed an act

---

[3] The Amsterdam Bourse of the seventeenth century is considered the first stock market (Allen and Gale, 1994, p.13). This paper focuses on the growth of stock trading in London, which eventually became the more developed market.

[4] Jenkins points out, "they were by no means necessarily stock-brokers. They could deal in anything they liked—stockes, gold, haberdashy, fish, bread, carpentry, spectacles, even bows and arrows" (1973, p.19–20).

"To Restrain the Number and the Practice of Brokers and Stockjobbers."[5] This act was to regulate and license brokers but they were able to avoid it merely by leaving the Royal Exchange and setting up business elsewhere in the city (Reed, 1975, p.5; Morgan and Thomas, 1969, p22–24). With the exception of dealings in foreign issues, most brokers left the Royal Exchange in 1698.[6]

The Use of Coffeehouses

Since there was no area designated as a stock exchange, trading took place in informal quarters, largely in the various coffeehouses between Cornhill and Lombard streets (Jenkins 1973; Wincott, 1946). Eighteenth century writer Thomas Mortimer wrote the "usual rendezvous of Stock-jobbers" was "Jonathan's Coffee-house, in Exchange-Alley" (Mortimer, 1801). The coffeehouses accommodated various brokers, some of whom even had offices there (Jenkins, 1973, p.40). One broker put out the following advertisement in 1695 in *Collection for Improvement of Husbandry and Trade*, "John Castaing at Jonathan's Coffee House on Exchange, buys and sells all Blank an Benefit Tickets; and all other Stocks and Shares" (reprinted in Mirowski, 1981, p.564). Brokers would go to the same coffeehouses every day to conduct their business.[7] One who

---

[5] Lest it be thought that the atmosphere was completely laissez faire, there were quite a few restrictions on the market (Banner, 1998), but from a modern economics viewpoint we can tell that most of them were not advancing the market.

[6] Some trading took place on the streets and alleys, but as of 1700, London city officials did not allow such congregating in an effort to keep the streets clear (Morgan and Thomas, 1969; Wincott, 1947).

[7] The English coffeehouses were different from most modern American coffee shops, serving bottled beer, wines, spirits, sandwiches, biscuits, and cheese in addition to coffee (Jenkins, 1973, p.41; Morgan and Thomas, 1969, p.67). Various coffeehouses provided their customers with a meeting place that appealed to different types of people: writers and critics went to Will's, philosophers went to the Grecian, White's Chocolate House

had been successful in his dealings was described by his peers as "the leader and oracle of Jonathan's Coffee House" (Morgan and Thomas, 1969, p.46).

Since this was what might be considered a more complicated market, and it was common to make bargains that were settled quarterly, there were many things that could go wrong (Mortimer, 1801; Dickson, 1967). One problem was deliberate fraud. John Houghton wrote in his periodical in 1692, "Without a doubt, if those trades were better known, 'twoud be a great advantage to the kingdom; only I must caution beginners to be very wary, for there are many cunning artists among them" (Houghton, 1727, p.5). Another problem was unintentional default. Since many weeks could pass before trade came to completion, brokers ran the risk of if their trading counterparts not being able to pay on settlement day. Mortimer stated, "problems arise if the person making the trade does not have the ability (cash) to settle, for in many cases a broker and his customer had no money" (Mortimer, 1801, p.53–54).

The first response to this problem is we see defaulters being shunned and banned from the Jonathan's. If a broker did not follow through with his bargains, he was labeled a lame duck. In 1761 Thomas Mortimer's described a lame duck as "A name given in 'Change Alley to those who refuse to fulfil their engagements…There are some at almost every rescounter. The punishment for nonpayment is banishment from Jonathan's but they can still act as brokers at the offices" (reprinted in Morgan and Thomas, 1969, p.61). They did not physically punish bad brokers but merely turned them away from the coffeehouse; being expelled from meant a significant loss of business for a broker (Jenkins, 1973).

Despite being banished defaulters would later come back to the coffeehouses, which would pose a problem for those who were unaware they were dealing with someone with a bad track record. As a solution they decided to write the names of

---

attracted gamblers, and Lloyd's Coffee House, which later became Lloyd's of London, specialized in shipping and marine insurance (Jenkins, 1973, p.41; Raynes, 1948, p.110).

E. Stringham / The Journal of Private Enterprise 17(2), 2002, 1-19   7

defaulters on a blackboard as a warning to others not to deal with them (Morgan and Thomas, 1969) This form of boycott acted as form of non-coercive enforcement against those who were unreliable (Caplan and Stringham, 2001).[8]

Forming an Exclusive Club

While shunning functioned to a degree, eventually some brokers decided that coffeehouses open to the public left more to be desired. Brokers felt the need to become more exclusive to avoid having to deal with, in the words of one historian, "riff-raff" (Jenkins, 1973). During this time period different groups experimented with different settings to trade stocks or other securities. In 1765 the Bank of England built a Rotunda where trading took place, but this did not prove to be successful. An 1824 book described the trading there as of a "less respectable description" (reprinted in Mitchie, 1999, p.44) Brokers were noisy and were generally considered with disrepute. These settings were too chaotic to conduct business, so a better solution was needed (Jenkins, 1973; Morgan and Thomas, 1969).[9]

It is not surprising that hoards of traders, including dishonest ones, would attempt to conduct business in the same few places. With the potential gains high, cheaters could theoretically dissipate the rest of the traders' profits. Eventually one group of brokers devised a strategy to eliminate some of the disarray. In 1761 Thomas Mortimer wrote, "The gentlemen at this very period of time…have taken it into their heads that some of the fraternity are not so good as themselves…and have entered into an association to exclude them from J-----'s coffee-house" (reprinted in Smith, 1929, p.215). In 1762 one hundred and fifty brokers formed a club and contracted with Jonathan's

---

[8] Caplan and Stringham (2001) discusses boycotts as an enforcement mechanism.

[9] We can imagine if such an arrangement was successful, trading might take place in establishments such as the London Stock Rotunda and the New York Stock Rotunda.

8   E. Stringham / The Journal of Private Enterprise 17(2), 2002, 1-19

Coffeehouse to use it exclusively. Each member would pay eight pounds per year to rent out the Coffeehouse (Morgan and Thomas, 1969). By transforming Jonathan's into a private club they would be able to exclude nonmembers and expel those who were unruly. Historians refer to the founders of the club as the 'more substantial' (Morgan and Thomas, 1969, p.68) and the 'better sort' (Jenkins, 1973, p.45) of brokers. If only reputable brokers were allowed in the club, there would be a lot less potential for bad dealings.

Unfortunately for the new venture an ejected broker brought suit against the newly formed club, and the government interfered with their plans by declaring that Jonathan's Coffeehouse did not have the right to exclude outsiders (Morgan and Thomas, 1969; Jenkins, 1973). This put a damper on using coffeehouses as a private exchanges, so as an alternative strategy in 1773 brokers organized to purchase a building for their own use. This new building was known as New Jonathan's and was open to anyone so long as they paid the daily admission fee, which covered expenses such as rent (Wincott, 1946). In 1773 the *Gentlemen's Magazine* reported, "New Jonathan's came to the resolution that instead of its being called New Jonathan's, it should be called The Stock Exchange, which is to be wrote over the door" (reprinted in Jenkins, 1973, p.45). Although it was known as the Stock Exchange, it must be noted that it is different from modern notions of a Stock Exchange. In 1801 Thomas Mortimer stated, "Brokers assemble at a very large coffeehouse, called the Stock-Exchange" (Mortimer, 1801, p.150). This coffeehouse/stock exchange had no formal membership and was run by two committees, one representing the coffeehouse owners and another representing the customers (Morgan and Thomas, 1969; Jenkins, 1973).

Still there was no formal membership, and anyone could enter upon paying the daily entrance fee. The fee might have been enough to keep out some vagrants, but after a few years it became evident that it did not suffice. The price of admission was low enough that untrustworthy brokers were still present, causing problems for both investors and brokers (Wincott, 1946). Brokers wanted to have an even more exclusive club,

E. *Stringham* / *The Journal of Private Enterprise 17(2), 2002, 1-19*   9

and in 1801 they decided to require that entrants be subscribed members (Morgan and Thomas, 1969). They posted the following:

> The Proprietors of the Stock Exchange, at the solicitation of a very considerable number of the Gentlemen frequenting it, and with the unanimous concurrence of the Committee appointed for General Purposes, who were requested to assist them in forming such regulations as may be deemed necessary, have resolved unanimously, that after 27 February next this House shall finally be shut as a Stock Exchange, and opened as a Subscription Room on Tuesday 3 March at ten guineas per Annum ending 1 March in each succeeding year. All person desirous of becoming subscribers are requested to signify the same in writing to E. Whitfor, Secretary to the joint committees on or before 31 inst. In order to their being balloted for by the said committees (reprinted in Mitchie, 1999, p.35).

Brokers were required to follow a set of rules in order to be a member of the Subscription Room. They stated in 1801 that it "being desirous that the Stock Subscription Room should acquire and preserve the most respectable character and considering that for such purpose it is indisputably necessary to prevent the practice of every disorderly action" they would levy fines on rule breakers "to be paid to the Secretary of the Committee for general Purposes and by them applied to charitable uses" (reprinted in Morgan and Thomas, 1969, p.69).[10] This new enforcement mechanism would inhibit misconduct by keeping club members under control.

---

[10] It is interesting to note that the fines were donated to charity rather than used a means of enriching those levying the fines. For an

10   *E. Stringham / The Journal of Private Enterprise 17(2), 2002, 1-19*

As with all new ventures there were some wrinkles in this new Stock Subscription Room, and it would take some reorganization before problems were ironed it. Many of the frequenters did not want to see the changes and were generally uncooperative. One member was fined but refused to pay, contending that he should not have to go along with the new rules (Morgan and Thomas, 1969).[11] In the following months the Stock Subscription Room disintegrated, leaving those who desired a stricter more exclusive club with no choice but to go off and start a new exchange. With much preparations and an offer to old exchange brokers to become members, they raised funds by issuing four hundred shares at £50 each, of which each person could own up to four shares, and constructed the new building over the next year (Morgan and Thomas, 1969; Reed, 1975).

Challenges and Competition

The new Stock Exchange at Capel Court could now enact rules that had been unanimously agreed upon by it members, but not surprisingly the excluded brokers were unhappy with their position.[12] In 1810 some petitioned the government to undermine the Stock Exchange by forcing it open to the public. The proposed bill stated:

> There is at this time no open Public Market for the sale and purchase of the Public Stocks, Funds, Government and other securities; and that they place wherein the chief part of this business hath been hitherto and is now transacted, is a private room from which the

account of the rise of criminal law as a means of enriching the government, see Benson (1990, 1994).

[11] Interestingly one David Ricardo was a member at this time, but he eventually resigned (Jenkins, 1973 p.51).

[12] Around this time the Bank of England considered building a new public exchange – it decided against it (Morgan and Thomas, 1969).

E. Stringham / The Journal of Private Enterprise 17(2), 2002, 1-19   11

> public is excluded; and it would be of great
> convenience and advantage to His Majesty's
> subjects if a public open market were
> established in a suitable situation for the
> purchase and sale of the said Stocks, Funds and
> Securities (reprinted in Morgan and Thomas,
> 1969, p.72).

If the government interfered with this private arrangement, the untrustworthy brokers could have achieved forced access into the new location.

Fortunately for the Exchange the government did not demand public access as it had in the case with Jonathan's Coffeehouse. A member declared that the 1810 bill was "under the specious pretext of creating an open Stock Market within the City of London," but that it truly was, "to shelter convicted defaulters and afford new facilities to the criminal designs of notorious and unprincipled gamblers." With its establishment the Stock Exchange would be "open to honourable men and closed shut for ever to notorious cheats" (reprinted in Morgan and Thomas, 1969, p.72). The London Stock Exchange was now able to enact and enforce rules internal to its members; anyone who was not a member was barred from the premises (Johnstone, 1814).

The fact that membership is costly and exchanges can expel brokers has led some to call this exclusivity an example of cartel behavior (Demsetx, 1969; Welles, 1975). Could it be that such cooperation between brokers was simply a form of collusion (Cowen, 1992; Cowen and Sutter, 1999)?[13] While the ability to enforce rules does allow brokers to punish non-cooperators, it does not enable them to enforce any rule they wish. As Mahoney points out:

> An exchange's attempts to charge a monopoly
> price for its members' services will harm only

---

[13] Cowen and Sutter (1999) claim that cooperation between competitors is a recipe for collusion.

the members if the exchange faces sufficient
competition from other markets. Other
exchanges will capture trading volume by
offering lower transaction costs and investors
will be no worse off by virtue of a foolish
attempt to charge a monopoly price in a
competitive market. If stock markets face
sufficient competition, then, restrictive rules will
survive only to the extent they are efficient
(Mahoney, 1997, p.1447).[14]

Rules that enhance the value of the product, such as
assurances against fraud, will be self-enforcing, and as long as
there are no legal barriers to entry, rules that are collusive will
break down (Telser 1980; Caplan and Stringham, 2001).[15] If
Exchange rules were simply collusive, customers would gladly
seek brokers who did not follow the rules and charged less for
the same service. This competition would make the cartel
dissolve. On the other hand, if the rules were actually providing
assurances against fraud, there would be little incentive for
customers to actively seek out brokers who did not abide by
Exchange rules.[16]

At the time, the London Stock Exchange members faced
competition from a number of sources, making the market
quite contestable. Those who wished to operate outside of the

---

[14] Mahoney (1997, p.1482) adds, "Restrictive exchange rules may
appear more benign when viewed as a means of preventing free
riding and appropriation by non-members."

[15] Collusive rules will face pressure both from outside competition
and from within the exchange. As Mahoney (1997, p.1491) writes,
"The fact that different exchange members have different
preferences regarding restrictive rules reduces the danger of a stable
brokers' cartel."

[16] This is not to say that customers would only use brokers who were
members of the Exchange. Brokers who established enough trusting
relationships would be in less need of Exchange rules, and bargain
hunters who were willing to take their chances with a bucket shop
could do so.

E. Stringham / The Journal of Private Enterprise 17(2), 2002, 1-19   13

Stock Exchange's rules could conduct business at private offices, the Royal Exchange, the Bank of England, other regional exchanges, or in foreign exchanges such as the Amsterdam Bourse (Mortimer 1801; Kregel, 1995; Morgan and Thomas, 1969; Michie, 1985; Neal, 1987; Stringham, 2001). This competition kept a check on the Stock Exchange that prevented it from enacting rules that are highly inefficient. In some cases rules were too onerous but were struck down because of the threat of losing business to nonmembers (Morgan and Thomas, 1969). These outsiders were considered an "annoyance," which is hardly surprising since they were in direct competition. To attract business the London Stock Exchange advertised in the press, publicizing that nonmembers were not "under the control of the Committee" (reprinted in Morgan and Thomas, 1969, p.141) serving as an indication that members of the London Stock Exchange were more dependable.

For many years the London Stock Exchange had no formal constitution, and it was not until 1812 that they issued their first rulebook (Mirowski, 1981; Morgan and Thomas, 1969). The need to attract business not legal rules made the exchange act in a judicious manner (Boot et al., 1993).[17] It was in the interest of the exchange to have a good reputation otherwise it would lose business. In 1877 even the government declared that the Stock Exchange's rules "had been salutary to the interests of the public" and that the Exchange acted "uprightly, honestly, and with a desire to do justice." It concluded by saying that their private rules were "capable of affording relief and exercising restraint far more prompt and often satisfactory than any within the read of the courts of law" (reprinted in Wincott, 1946, p.27). The club has an incentive to make sure the

---

[17] Boot et al. (1993, p.1178) write, "Since a discretionary guarantee of a highly reputed guarantor can be more valuable than an enforceable guarantee of a less reputable guarantor, prices of discretionary guarantees need not be less than those for enforceable guarantees." On the importance of incentives rather than legal rules, see Hasnas (1995a, 1995b) and Klein (1997).

exchange is operating properly and so will enact and enforce rules as efficiently as they know how. A disinterested court or regulator on the other hand would have little incentive and even less knowledge to be able to enforce the rules of a stock exchange (Stringham, 1999).

Conclusion

Although there may good reason to worry that in a complicated stock market there are greater chances of fraud, it seems clear that there was no missing market in this realm. Rather than relying on public regulation to enforce contracts, brokers consciously found a way to solve this dilemma by creating and enforcing a system of private rules. Since it was their goal to promote trade, the interest of the members was aligned with the interest of its customers. It was their ability to experiment and their need to attract business that allowed for the discovery of better ways of organizing and self-regulating.

Under laissez faire, firms and clubs, such the London Stock Exchange, can choose to organize in any way they wish, and those that find successful ways of operating will flourish.[18] Since the London Stock Exchange did not have a legal monopoly it needed to make sure that its existence was beneficial. Dennis Carlton writes, "It is useful to view exchanges as competing (or potentially competing) with each other. As in other markets, competition is a substitute for regulation. The more competition there is, the more likely it is that exchanges themselves will promulgate rules and regulations that benefit and protect consumers in much the same ways as competition in other markets protects consumers" (Carlton, 1984, p.259) When exchanges are free to organize without government regulation, it allows for the discovery process of the market to operate. In their quest for more profits brokers will have the incentive to discover better ways of self-policing. The evolution of the London Stock

---

[18] Other stock exchanges such as those in America evolved with quite different structures (Michie, 1986).

E. Stringham / The Journal of Private Enterprise 17(2), 2002, 1-19   15

Exchange provides evidence that beneficial regulations can be created through the market.

References

Allen, Franklin, and Douglas Gale. 1994. *Financial Innovation and Risk Sharing*, Cambridge, MA: MIT Press.

Banner, Stuart. 1998. *Anglo-American Securities Regulation: Cultural and Political Roots, 1690-1860*. Cambridge: Cambridge University Press.

Benson, Bruce. 1994. "Are Public Goods Really Common Pools?" *Economic Inquiry*, 32: 249–71.

Benson, Bruce. 1990. *The Enterprise of Law*. San Francisco: Pacific Research Institute for Public Policy.

Benson, Bruce. 1993. "The Impetus for Recognizing Private Property and Adopting Ethical Behavior in a Market Economy: Natural Law, Government Law, or Evolving Self-Interest." *The Review of Austrian Economics*, 6(2): 43–80.

Banner, Stuart. 1998. "The Origin of the New York Stock Exchange, 1791-1860." *Journal of Legal Studies*, 27: 113–40.

Boot, A., S. Greenbaum, and A. Thakor. 1993. "Reputation and Discretion in Financial Contracting." *The American Economic Review*, 83(5): 1165–83.

Buchanan, James. 1965. "An Economic Theory of Clubs." *Economica*, 32: 1–14.

Buchanan, James. 1975. *The Limits of Liberty*, Chicago: University of Chicago Press.

Caplan, Bryan, and Edward Stringham. 2001. "Networks, Law, and the Paradox of Cooperation." *Review of Austrian Economics*, forthcoming.

Cowen, Tyler. 1992. "Law as a Public Good: The Economics of Anarchy." *Economics and Philosophy*, 8: 249–67.

Cowen, Tyler, and Daniel Sutter. 1999. "The Costs of Cooperation." *The Review of Austrian Economics*, 12: 161–73.

Carlton, Dennis. 1984. "Futures Markets: Their Purpose, Their History, Their Growth, Their Successes and Failures." *The Journal of Futures Markets*, 4(3): 237–71.

Chambers, Scott, and Colin Carter. 1990. "US Futures Exchanges as Nonprofit Entities." *The Journal of Futures Markets*, 10(1):79–88.

Demsetz, H. 1969. "Perfect Competition, Regulation, and the Stock Market." In *Economic Policy and the Regulation of Corporate Securities*, ed. H. Manne, 1–22. Washington: American Enterprise Institute.

Dickson, PGM. 1993. *The Financial Revolution in England: A Study in the Development of Public Credit 1688–1756*. Aldershot, Hampshire, England: Gregg Revivals. (Orig. pub. 1967.)

Fischel, Daniel, and Sanford Grossman. 1984. "Customer Protection in Futures and Securities Markets." *The Journal of Futures Markets*, 4(3): 273–95.

Frye, Timothy. 2000. *Brokers and Bureaucrats: Building Market Institutions in Russia*. Ann Arbor: University of Michigan Press.

Glaeser, Edward, Simon Johnson, and Andrei Shleifer. 2001. "Coase versus the Coasians." *Quarterly Journal of Economics*, 116: 853–99.

Hayek, F.A. 1978. *Constitution of Liberty*, Chicago: University of Chicago. (Orig. pub. 1960.)

Hasnas, John. 1995a. "Back to the Future: From Critical Legal Studies Forward to Legal Realism, or How Not to Miss the Point of the Indeterminacy Argument." *Duke Law Journal*, 45: 84–132.

Hasnas, John. 1995b. "The Myth of the Rule of Law" *Wisconsin Law Review*, 1995: 199–233.

Houghton, John. 1727. *Husbandry and trade improv'd,* Vol 1. London: Woodman and Lyon.

Jenkins, Alan. 1973. *The Stock Exchange Story.* London: Heinemann.

Johnstone, Andrew. 1814. *The Caluminous Aspersions Contained in the Report of the Sub-committee of the Stock-Exchange,* 3d ed. London: W. Lewis.

Kindleberger Charles P. 1984. *A Financial History of Western Europe.* London: George Allen & Unwin.

Klein, Daniel. 1997. *Reputation.* Ann Arbor: University of Michigan Press.

Kregel, J.A. 1995. "Neoclassical Price Theory, Institutions and the Evolution of Securities Market Organisation." *The Economic Journal,* 105: 459–70.

Macey, Jonathan, and Hideki Kanda. 1990. "The Stock Exchange as a Firm: The Emergence of Close Substitutes for the New York and Tokyo Stock Exchanges." *Cornell Law Review,* 75: 1007.

Macey, Jonathan, and Maureen O'Hara. 1999. "Regulating Exchanges and Alternative Trading Systems: A Law and Economics Perspective." *Journal of Legal Studies,* 28: 17.

Mahoney, Paul. 1997. "The Exchange as Regulator." *Virginia Law Review,* 83: 1453–1500.

Michie, Ranald. 1985. "The London Stock Exchange and the British Securities Market, 1850–1914." *Economic History Review* Second Series, 38(1): 61– 82.

Michie, Ranald. 1986. "The London and New York Stock Exchanges, 1850–1914." *Journal of Economic History,* 46(1): 171–87.

Michie, Ranald. 1999. *The London Stock Exchange: A History,* Oxford: Oxford University Press.

Mirowski, Philip. 1981. "The Rise (and Retreat) of a Market; English Joint Stock Shares in the Eighteenth Century." *Journal of Economic History*, 41(3): 559–77.

Morgan, E.V., and W.A. Thomas. 1969. *The London Stock Exchange.* NY: St. Martin's Press. (Orig. pub. 1962.)

Mortimer, Thomas. 1801. *Every man his own broker; or, A guide to the Stock Exchange.* 13th ed., considerably improved, republished. London: W. J. & J. Richardson.

Neal, Larry. 1987. "The Integration and Efficiency of the London and Amsterdam Stock Markets in the Eighteenth Century." *Journal of Economic History*, 47(1): 97–115.

Raynes, Harold. 1948. *A History of British Insurance.* London: Pitman & Sons.

Reed, M.C. 1975. *A History of James Capel & Co.* London: James Capel & Co.

Rothbard, Murray. 1970. *Power and Market.* Kansas City: Sheed, Andrews, and McMeel.

Silber, William. 1981. "Innovation, Competition, and New Contract Design in Futures Markets." *The Journal of Futures Markets*, 1(2): 123–55.

Smith, C.F. 1929. "The Early History of the London Stock Exchange." *The American Economic Review*, 19(2): 206–16.

Stringham, Edward. 1999. "Market Chosen Law." *Journal of Libertarian Studies*, 14(1): 53–77.

Stringham, Edward. 2001. "The Extralegal Development of Financial Trading in Seventeenth–Century Amsterdam." Paper presented at the Southern Economics Association Meetings, Tampa, FL.

Telser, Lester. 1980. "A Theory of Self-Enforcing Agreements." *Journal of Business,* 53: 27–44.

Tullock, Gordon, ed. 1972. *Explorations in the Theory of Anarchy.* Blacksburg, VA: Center for the Study of Public Choice.

Tullock, Gordon, ed. 1974. *Further Explorations in the Theory of Anarchy.* Blacksburg, VA: Center for the Study of Public Choice.

Welles, C. 1975. *The Last Days of the Club.* New York: E.P. Dutton.

Wincott, Harold. 1946. *The Stock Exchange.* London: Sampson Low, Marston & Co

[21]

COMPETITION BETWEEN NATIONAL LEGAL SYSTEMS: A CONTRIBUTION OF ECONOMIC ANALYSIS TO COMPARATIVE LAW

> When governments become sufficiently plentiful, and when the scope of laws matches the domain of their costs and benefits (that is, when costs and benefits are all felt within the jurisdiction enacting the laws), competitive forces should be as effective with governments as they are with private markets.[1]

A. Introduction

Three main tasks can be identified for comparative law. The first is to investigate differences between legal systems and, in particular, to distinguish between "real" differences, where the outcomes of the application of principles diverge between legal systems, and "superficial" differences, where similar outcomes are masked by the conceptual structures of the relevant systems. The second is to trace developments in the relationships between legal systems and thus to explore tendencies of convergence or divergence (in terms of "real" differences), noting that in some areas convergence may be required under international legal instruments. The third task is to explain and to evaluate such developments: why do systems converge or diverge? Is convergence desirable or undesirable?

The convergence issue has been the subject of an intense debate among comparative lawyers.[2] As regards the positive dimension, the majority view appears to be that, except in relation to the domain of moral or religious norms (e.g. family law), and at least as between jurisdictions at an equivalent stage of social and economic development, there has been a tendency for legal principles from different jurisdictions to converge.[3] Others believe that such convergence is superficial: apparent consensus on principles has been unable to overcome real differences emanating from divergent legal cultures.[4] So also on the normative dimension. The orthodox line is that to facilitate dealings with the law, particularly in the context of international trade, harmonisation is—with the exception of the moral and religious domain—desirable.[5] Conversely, the dissidents hold that the genuine transplantation of concepts from one legal

---

1. F. Easterbrook, "Federalism and European Business Law" (1994) 14 Int.Rev. Law and Economics 125, 127–128.
2. Cf. B. De Witte, "The Convergence Debate" (1996) 3 Maastricht J. European and Comparative Law 105.
3. W. Van Gerven, "Bridging the Unbridgeable: Community and National Tort Laws after *Francovich* and *Brasserie*" (1996) 45 I.C.L.Q. 507; and, more generally, K. Zweigert and H. Kötz, *An Introduction to Comparative Law* (2nd edn, 1987), pp.23–27.
4. Notably P. Legrand, "European Legal Systems Are not Converging" (1996) 45 I.C.L.Q. 52.
5. E.g. O. Lando, "Why Harmonize the Contracts Law of Europe", in P. Sarcevic (Ed.), *International Contracts and Conflicts of Law* (1990), chap.1; B. S. Markesinis, "Learning from Europe and Learning in Europe", in B. S. Markesinis (Ed.), *The Gradual Convergence:*

406   *International and Comparative Law Quarterly*   [VOL. 48

tradition to another is impossible[6] or at least produces unintended and unwanted consequences.[7]

This article aims to contribute to the debate with the aid of economic analysis. Implicit in the positive convergence assertion is the hypothesis that there is a link between the social and economic order and the evolution of legal principles.[8] Now, while the disciplines of history, anthropology and sociology have been invoked to study this link,[9] economic theory has been largely ignored. A serious attempt to remedy the deficiency has been made recently by Ugo Mattei.[10] His important pioneering work includes some major insights, but so far has not generated an overarching theoretical framework to explain the relationships between different legal systems. I focus on, and develop, one of Mattei's key propositions,[11] that competition between the suppliers of legal rules will significantly affect the evolution of law (Section B). In order to use this basic concept to predict and evaluate the relationship between national legal orders, I argue that it is necessary to distinguish situations in which legal rules can be envisaged as a homogeneous product and therefore convergences between jurisdictions are likely spontaneously to occur (Section C) from those in which it has heterogeneous qualities and convergence is less likely (Section D).

The normative issue is of immense importance to the current debate on harmonisation or subsidiarity in European law, but the contribution of comparativists to the debate has tended to be superficial because the costs and benefits of harmonisation are not investigated with any rigour and little or no notice has been taken of the rich economics literature on the question. In Section E, I address the issue, challenging the orthodox view of comparative lawyers, that convergence of national laws (at least in the business sphere) is invariably desirable and that, if necessary, it should be promoted by mandatory harmonisation.

B. *Competitive Markets for the Supply of Law*

If suppliers of a product or service have to compete with one another, consumers can choose according to the quality and price of what is offered. On certain

Foreign Ideas, Foreign Influences and English Law on the Eve of the 21st Century (1994), chap.1.

6. P. Legrand, "The Impossibility of 'Legal Transplants'" (1997) 4 Maastricht J. European and Comparative Law 111; "Against a European Civil Code" (1997) 60 M.L.R. 44.

7. G. Teubner, "Legal Irritants: Good Faith in British Law or How Unifying Law Ends Up in New Divergences" (1998) 61 M.L.R. 11.

8. For a detailed examination of the hypothesis, see A. Watson *The Evolution of Law* (1985). He argues that though the initial impetus for convergence might arise from social and economic forces, the phenomenon is largely attributable to lawyers who find it convenient to imitate legal principles developed in other jurisdictions.

9. Zweigert and Kötz, *op. cit. supra* n.3, at pp.8–12.

10. U. Mattei, *Comparative Law and Economics* (1997), which contains a number of previously published papers on the subject. See also U. Mattei and F. Cafaggi, "Comparative Law and Economics", in P. Newman (Ed.), *The New Palgrave Dictionary of Economics and the Law* (1998), Vol.1, pp.346–351.

11. U. Mattei and F. Pulitini, "A Competitive Model of Legal Rules", in A. Breton *et al.* (Eds), *The Competitive State: Villa Colombella Papers on Competitive Politics* (1991), pp.207–219.

assumptions, that should mean that consumer preferences are met at lowest cost. The corollary is that monopolist suppliers will not necessarily meet consumer preferences and they lack the incentive to constrain costs.

These simple propositions can be applied to the supply of law within a single jurisdiction. Although the lawmaker in a nation-State would seem to have a monopoly over the supply of law as it affects citizens within the territory, nevertheless we can identify elements of competition which may constrain how the power is exercised.[12] First, and most obviously, if the lawmaker is a democratically elected legislature, there is competition *ex ante* to acquire that power. The election manifestos of the political parties contain legislative proposals and citizens express their preferences between such proposals by their voting behaviour.[13] The phenomenon can be likened to that in which a monopolistic franchise power to supply a public service is allocated by a system of competitive bidding, the competition serving (in theory) to ensure efficient price and quality.[14] Second, while constitutions normally determine the hierarchy of lawmaking powers of the legislature, executive and judiciary, there may be *de jure* or *de facto* some degree of competition between them. This may occur also between different court systems with overlapping jurisdictions[15] or between self-regulatory agencies exercising delegated lawmaking powers.[16]

More significantly for the purposes of this article, interactions with other jurisdictions may create external competition for the supply of law.[17] Theorists do not seem as yet to have developed a general model for the functioning of such competition,[18] but we may readily speculate on how this is likely to occur. If domestic industries competing in international markets find that their national legal system imposes on them higher costs than those incurred by their foreign competitors operating under a different jurisdiction, they will apply pressure on their lawmakers to reduce the costs. That demand will be strengthened by the threat of migration to the more favourable jurisdiction, assuming that there are no barriers to the freedom of establishment and to the movement of capital. As regards supply, lawmakers are likely to respond positively to the demand from domestic industries because pressure by the latter can have a decisive influence on

---

12. A. Breton, *Competitive Governments* (1996).

13. The analogy with ordinary product markets should not, of course, be exaggerated because, *inter alia*: (except for referenda) voters must express preferences for a package of proposals rather than for single proposals; there is no way of indicating the intensity of their preferences; and "contracts" between prospective legislators and voters are not legally enforceable. See A. Ogus, *Regulation: Legal Form and Economic Theory* (1994), pp.59–61.

14. H. Demsetz, "Why Regulate Utilities?" (1968) 11 J. Law and Economics 55.

15. The famous struggle between the English Chancery Court and its common law rivals had a very significant impact on the evolution of legal principles: T. Plucknett, *Concise History of the Common Law* (5th edn, 1956), pp.159–163, 589–595, 644–645.

16. A. Ogus, "Rethinking Self-Regulation" (1995) 15 Oxford J. Legal Studies 97.

17. Mattei, *op. cit. supra* n.10, at chap.4; S. Woolcock, "Competition Among Rules in the Single European Market", in W. Bratton, J. McCahery, S. Picciotto and C. Scott (Eds), *International Regulatory Competition and Coordination: Perspectives on Economic Regulation in Europe and the United States* (1996), chap.10.

18. For a model applicable to regulatory competition within the EU, see J.-M. Sun and J. Pelkmans, "Regulatory Competition in the Single Market" (1995) 33 J. Common Market Studies 67.

politicians' behaviour.[19] Lawmakers will also be motivated, particularly in small countries heavily dependent on international trade,[20] to attract firms from other jurisdictions and multinational corporations since that should entail increased investment, demand for labour and tax revenue.[21] Of course there will be many variables operating on decisions as to location, but it is reasonable to envisage that at the margins the nature of the legal regime and its costs may have a substantial impact.[22] If so, market actors perform an arbitrage function in respect of different legal regimes.[23]

As an alternative to physical migration, and to the extent that this is allowed by the private international law of their home jurisdiction, firms may be able to select the jurisdiction whose principles are to apply to their transactions or business.[24] The decision should reflect not only the perceived advantages of the national legal regime but also the legal expertise available in the jurisdiction and its potential for reducing transaction costs.[25] Although the chosen jurisdiction will not acquire the benefits associated with physical migration, it may derive revenue from taxes or charges arising from the legal connection[26] and there will be a marked increase in the income of its lawyers.[27]

The strength of these competitive pressures will, of course, crucially depend on the costs,[28] as well as the legal freedom, of mobility and choice of law. But we can observe a number of twentieth-century developments that have facilitated the process: the growth of international trade, multinational corporations and joint ventures; the globalisation of markets and the elimination of barriers to trade;

---

19. Woolcock, *op. cit. supra* n.17, at p.306. For the role of private interest groups in influencing legislation, see C. K. Rowley, R. D. Tollison and G. Tullock (Eds), *The Political Economy of Rent-Seeking* (1988) and, for a summary of the literature, Ogus, *op. cit. supra* n.13, at chap.4.

20. D. W. Leebron, "Lying Down with Procrustes: An Analysis of Harmonization Claims", in J. N. Bhagwati and R. E. Hudec (Eds), *Fair Trade and Harmonization*, Vol.1: *Economic Analysis* (1996), chap.2.

21. Law more favourable to individuals may also increase tourism to the relevant jurisdiction: J. G. Brown, "Competitive Federalism and Legislative Incentives to Recognize Same-Sex Marriage in the USA", in Bratton *et al.*, *op. cit. supra* n.17 at pp.271–274.

22. Woolcock, *op. cit. supra* n.17, at pp.305–306.

23. S. Picciotti, "The Regulatory Criss-Cross: Interaction Between Jurisdictions and the Construction of Global Regulatory Networks", in Bratton *et al.*, *op. cit. supra* n.17, at p.110; Sun and Pelkmans, *op. cit. supra* n.18, at pp.83–84.

24. L. E. Ribstein, "Choosing Law by Contract" (1993) 18 J. Corporation Law 247.

25. "There seems little doubt that English commercial law is highly regarded by foreigners, who regularly select English law to govern their contracts and agree to submit their disputes to the English courts even where the transaction has no particular connection with this country. That is no doubt an acknowledgment of the pragmatism of English law and its sensitivity to legitimate business needs and a tribute to the expertise of our judges and the efficiency of our systems for the resolution of commercial disputes": R. Goode, *Commercial Law in the Next Millennium* (1998), p.94. See also on Delaware as a chosen jurisdiction for corporate law R. Romano, "Law as a Product: Some Pieces of the Incorporation Puzzle" (1985) 1 J. Law, Economics and Organization 225.

26. 16% of the total tax revenue of Delaware is derived from incorporation fees: R. Romano, *The Genius of American Corporate Law* (1993), pp.8–9.

27. J. Macey and G. Miller, "Toward an Interest-Group Theory of Delaware Corporate Law" (1987) 65 Texas L.Rev. 469.

28. Including information costs: Sun and Pelkmans, *op. cit. supra* n.18, at p.84.

and, within private international law, the relaxation of control by the *lex fori*, as exemplified by the principle of free choice of law for contracts and extension of the recognition and enforcement of foreign law in domestic courts.

If, and to the extent that, competition between national legal systems emerges, we can predict that this will impact on the content of law. In response to the demand from market actors, national lawmakers will compare their own legal products with those available in competing jurisdictions; if the latter better meet the preferences of the actors, they will be motivated to adapt their products. In short, free movement in goods and services may be matched by free movement in legal rules.[29]

Hitherto such movement has been envisaged in terms of one national lawmaker importing, or imitating, rules from another jurisdiction. Exporting is another possibility. Governments may promote the foreign adoption of their own laws by providing assistance in the preparation of legislation and the training of lawyers.[30] Their motivation to do so may not be just a question of prestige, a traditional comparative lawyer's explanation for legal transplants.[31] It may reflect the anticipated benefit to national lawyers from the transplant and, perhaps more significantly, to market actors wishing to trade with, or establish joint ventures in, the foreign jurisdiction.

The above reasoning would seem to lead to the prediction that, as a result of competition, there will be some convergence of national laws, by the reforming State either accepting a "transplant" from another or emulating its legal principles. Meeting the demand of market actors by this kind of action is cheap in terms of information and administrative costs.[32] In fact, the situation is more complex as there are other variables relevant to the analysis.

First—and this is classic comparative law methodology[33]—we need to recognise that conceptual differences between national legal principles may mask functional similarities. Market actors may be indifferent to divergent legal formulations provided they lead to outcomes which match their preferences. It matters not whether a tort claim for pure economic loss will be rejected because there is "no duty of care" (English law) or because it is "*dommage indirecte*" (French law).[34] The result is the same:[35] the differences are "superficial" rather than "real".

---

29. J. M. Smits, "A European Private Law as a Mixed Legal System: Towards a Ius Commune through the Free Movement of Legal Rules" (1998) 5 Maastricht J. European and Comp.L. 328.

30. J. M. Smits, "Systems Mixing and in Transition: Import and Export of Legal Models: The Dutch Experience", in E. H. Hondius (Ed.), *Netherlands Reports to the Fifteenth International Congress of Comparative Law* (1998). For an account of how Dutch law has thereby been exported to countries in the former Soviet Union, see *idem*, pp.54–68.

31. Cf. R. Sacco, "Legal Formats: A Dynamic Approach to Comparative Law" (1991) 39 A.J.Comp.L. 343.

32. A. Watson, *Legal Transplants: an Approach to Comparative Law* (1974); I. Ayres, "Supply-Side Inefficiencies and Competitive Federalism: Lessons from Patents, Yachting and Bluebooks", in Bratton *et al.*, *op. cit. supra* n.17, at pp.241–242.

33. Zweigert and Kötz, *op. cit. supra* n.3, at pp.31–33.

34. E. K. Banakas (Ed.), *Civil Liability for Pure Economic Loss* (1996).

35. In a contractual setting, even a difference in outcome may of little significance, if the parties can consensually prescribe their preferred outcome: R. Coase, "The Problem of Social Cost" (1960) 3 J. Law and Economics 1.

Second, and as a corollary to this, the information and administrative cost advantages of convergence may prove to be illusory when account is taken of the institutional structure and legal culture of different jurisdictions.[36] The cost of accommodating a concept foreign to the domestic legal culture, such as the trust for French property law,[37] or good faith for English contract law,[38] may be too high.

Third, and most importantly, we need to explore in greater depth the nature of the demand for change in legal rules. It is wrong to assume that all market actors have the same preferences or that, even if they do, their demand will always prevail over that of other parties (including lawyers) who also are affected by the relevant law.

To clarify these issues, and in consequence to sharpen the predictions, I draw a distinction between homogeneous and heterogeneous legal products.

C. Competition Relating to Homogeneous Legal Products

Homogeneous legal products are those as to which there is unlikely to be a significant variation in preferences as between market actors in different jurisdictions. The best examples are to be found in "facilitative law", that area of law which provides mechanisms for ensuring mutually desired outcomes: contracts, corporations, other forms of legal organisations and dealings with property. The assumed preference is for the minimisation of legal costs[39] consistent with ensuring the outcomes desired by those involved in the transactions. Since, in relation to these areas of law, reforms lowering legal costs will generate gains to the actors but no losers (except those who gain from more costly law, notably lawyers), competition between jurisdictions, where effective, should drive national legal principles towards cost-minimising formulations. Systematic empirical validation of the hypothesis may be lacking but it is not difficult to identify developments which support it.

Take first corporate law. The readiness of continental European jurisdictions, in the mid-nineteenth century, to imitate the English introduction of limited liability may reasonably be attributed to competitive pressures.[40] More recently, studies of the large number of American firms reincorporating in Delaware clearly indicate that the minimisation of legal costs there was a major motivation and that other States have attempted to stem the tide by changes to their own corporate laws.[41]

---

36. "Traditional or cultural factors may be construed as real-world transaction costs and/or patterns of path dependency that resist the evolution towards efficiency": Mattei, *op. cit. supra* n.10, at p.121.

37. D. B. Walters, "Analogues of the Trust and Its Constituents in French Law from the Standpoint of Scots and English Law", in W. A. Wilson (Ed.), *Trusts and Trust-Like Devices* (1981), pp.117–136.

38. M. Bridge, "Does Anglo-Canadian Contract Law Need a Doctrine of Good Faith?" (1984) 9 Can. Business L.J. 385.

39. These include the costs of enforcing legal rights.

40. D. C. Perrott, "Changes in Attitude to Limited Liability—the European Experience", in T. Orhnial (Ed.), *Limited Liability and the Corporation* (1982), chap.5.

41. Romano, *op. cit. supra* n.25; W. J. Carney, "Federalism and Corporate Law: A Non-Delaware View of the Results of Competition", in Bratton *et al.*, *op. cit. supra*, n.17, at chap.5.

Next, two examples from contract law. In the 1970s English courts became aware that other jurisdictions had taken the lead in restricting the doctrine of State immunity, which prevented State organs from being sued even when acting in a commercial capacity. As a consequence of international competition, the judges felt compelled to adapt English law.[42] Reform may consist of the removal of procedural requirements the benefits accruing from which are exceeded by their costs. French contract law contains a traditional requirement that defaulting promisors should be given a formal notice (*mise en demeure*) of their default and that damages for delayed performance should run only from the date of such notice.[43] Characterised by one author as "*formalisme primitif*" and attributed to the moral value of "*patience*",[44] the requirement imposes unnecessary costs on commercial actors and unsurprisingly has been much attenuated by *jurisprudence*.[45]

We have already seen that, for institutional and cultural reasons, the costs of imitating foreign legal principles may be unduly high. In such circumstances, the foreign model may be accommodated only to the extent that it is recognised under the rules of private international law. In comparison with civil law equivalents, the Anglo-Saxon trust has proved to be a particularly cost-efficient device for certain financial transactions.[46] While jurisdictions of mixed civilian and common law heritage (e.g. Louisiana and Quebec) have assimilated the device, pure civilian systems have adopted the limited private international law approach.[47] Nevertheless, Mattei has felt able to conclude that the "[t]rust has obtained an easy and well-deserved victory in the competition in the market of legal doctrines".[48]

The above analysis suggests that competition between jurisdictions should lead to some convergence of legal principles relating to homogeneous products. But we must be careful to acknowledge the possibility that powerful interest groups may impede such developments.[49] Mobility between legal systems and freedom in the choice of law may undercut the rent-seeking potential which national law confers on interest groups.[50] Therefore they may seek to create barriers to competition by influencing the law reform processes.

Firms established in jurisdictions with more costly legal structures, and which have already invested resources in complying with such regimes, will not wish to

---

42. *Trendtex Trading Corporation* v. *Central Bank of Nigeria* [1977] Q.B. 529: see Goode, *op. cit. supra* n.25, at p.92.

43. Code Civil, Arts.1139 and 1146.

44. J. Carbonnier, *Droit Civil*, Vol.4 (17th edn, 1993), No.77.

45. *Ibid.* An English law equivalent is the softening of the requirement for consideration to support modifications to contractual obligations: J. Adams and R. Brownsword, "Contract, Consideration and the Critical Path" (1990) 53 M.L.R. 536.

46. F. Sonneveld and H. L. van Mens, *The Trust: Bridge or Abyss Between Common and Civil Law Jurisdictions?* (1992).

47. See, especially, the Hague Convention on the Law Applicable to Trusts and their Recognition, 1985.

48. U. Mattei, "Efficiency in Legal Transplants: An Essay in Comparative Law and Economics" (1994) 14 Int.Rev. Law and Economics 3, 10.

49. L. E. Ribstein and B. H. Kobayashi, "An Economic Analysis of Uniform State Laws" (1996) J. Legal Studies 131, 142–144.

50. Easterbrook, *op. cit. supra* n.1, at p.128.

lose the competitive advantage which they thereby acquire over newcomers. They can therefore be expected to resist cost-reducing reforms to the law.[51]

Lawyers constitute perhaps the most influential pressure group in relation to law reform.[52] Their impact on competition will, however, vary according to their function. Those engaged in long-term contracts with firms will, provided they are faithful to the interests of their clients, have the same motivations (whether to advance[53] or resist the competitive process) as those that employ them. To ascertain the interests of lawyers as a more general class of potential income-earners requires a careful investigation of their profit-making possibilities.[54] On the one hand, they can benefit from the increased demand for their services arising from firms migrating to their jurisdiction, or adopting it under choice of law principles. That would suggest a strategy both of facilitating the competitive process and of supporting cost-reducing law reform. On the other hand, once firms are established in the jurisdiction, lawyers benefit from constraints on competition and, if such constraints exist, from rendering the law more complex and costly.[55]

Barriers to competition can be erected, or maintained, by adherence to restrictive choice of law rules. For example, the European adherence to the rule that the law governing a company's existence and internal affairs should be that of its "real seat" (thus inhibiting freedom of choice) has been attributed to the fear of French authorities that chartering business would be lost to competing jurisdictions.[56] Lawyers may also gain by opposing the international harmonisation or mutual recognition of rules. In 1981 the Law Society of England and Wales opposed the Vienna Convention on Contracts for the International Sale of Goods on the ground, *inter alia*, that it would result in a diminished role for English law within the international trade arena.[57] The profit motivation for such opposition to cost-reducing reform proposals is often disguised by atavistic or parochial references to local legal culture.[58]

D. *Competition Relating to Heterogeneous Legal Products*

Large areas of law are not "facilitative" in the sense described above. Rather, they are "interventionist" in that they protect defined interests and/or supersede

---

51. *OECD Report on Regulatory Reform* (1997), Vol.II, chap.4.

52. See, generally, P. H. Rubin and M. J. Bailey, "The Role of Lawyers in Changing the Law" (1994) 23 J. Legal Studies 807.

53. For evidence as to how lawyers engaged by transnational corporations have been able to exploit differences in national regulatory regimes and hence perform an arbitrage function, see Picciotto, *op. cit. supra* n.23, at pp.104–109.

54. Macey and Miller, *op. cit. supra* n.27; Carney, *op. cit. supra* n.41.

55. M. J. White, "Legal Complexity and Lawyers' Benefit from Litigation" (1992) 12 Int.Rev. Law and Economics 381.

56. W. Carney, "The Political Economy of Competition for Corporate Charters" (1997) 26 J. Legal Studies 303, 315–318. Note, too, that in so far as judges are responsible for developing choice of law rules, they can be expected to favour formulations which benefit domestic lawyers: M. E. Solimine, "An Economic and Empirical Analysis of Choice of Law" (1989) 24 Georgia L.Rev. 49, 73.

57. R. G. Lee, "UN Convention on Sale of Goods: OK for the UK?" [1993] J. Business L. 131, 132.

58. Mattei, *op. cit. supra* n.48 at p.16.

voluntary transactions. This covers tort and regulatory law, but also those aspects of contract, property and corporate law which confer protection on parties assumed to be disadvantaged by processes of free bargaining, for example consumers, employees, tenants and (in some contexts) shareholders.

Such "interventionist" law creates winners (the beneficiaries of protection) and losers (the subject of legal obligations). If there is competition between national legal systems, what will happen? Both the potential winners and the potential losers will attempt to exert pressure on lawmakers for more favourable law. Success will be a function of the costs of obtaining information regarding differences between legal regimes, the costs of migration, the benefits to the chosen jurisdiction of attracting (or retaining) legal subjects and the relative power of actors to influence legal developments. In these terms we may expect potential losers (normally enterprises) to be more successful than potential winners (normally individuals) since they have lower costs of information as to legal differences, lower migration costs (individuals typically have cultural and family reasons for remaining within a jurisdiction); they can confer larger benefits on the chosen jurisdiction; and they can more easily organise into coherent and powerful pressure groups.[59]

The *apparent* predictable outcome is then, as with "facilitative" law and subject to the same caveats, a convergence of legal principles. But here, since this will be to meet the preference of those subjected to interventionist obligations, the consequence will be that the level of protection provided by the law will be reduced. This is the famous "race to the bottom" prediction.[60]

However, the alleged winner–loser dichotomy must be explored with greater care: if costs are incurred by losers under an interventionist law, who ultimately bears them? The answer is not simply shareholders of the firms subject to the regime, but also their employees and consumers of their products or services (the exact distribution of the burden will vary from case to case according to the degree of price elasticity in the relevant capital, labour and product markets[61]). Once the apparently clear dichotomy between winners and losers disappears and the diversity of interests involved becomes more complex, predictions of how lawmakers will be influenced become more difficult, given that the strength of the interested groups, including lawyers, will vary according to the political and constitutional structures in each country.

Let us, however, proceed on the (perhaps heroic) assumption that national lawmakers can be adequately informed on, and will faithfully attempt to meet, the aggregated preferences of their citizens. We can then recognise that interventionist law is a heterogeneous product: preferences may vary between countries, regions and localities as to the different combinations of the levels of legal intervention and of the price which must be paid for them. If this is the case, there

---

59. M. Olson, *The Logic of Collective Action* (1965).
60. W. Cary, "Federalism and Corporate Law: Reflections on Delaware" (1974) 88 Yale L.J. 663; P. P. Swire, "The Race to Laxity and the Race to Undesirability: Explaining Failures in Competition Among Jurisdictions in Environmental Law" (1996) 14 Yale J. Regulation 67.
61. S. Rea, "Regulating Occupational Health and Safety", in D. Dewees (Ed.), *The Regulation of Quality: Products, Services, Workplaces and the Environment* (1983), pp.127–128.

is no necessary expectation that competition between national legal systems will lead to convergence, since much will depend on national preferences regarding the level of protection.[62] And this would seem to be borne out by the wide divergencies of "interventionist" law, even within the European Union.[63] For example, French law has offered a high level of protection for road accident victims, compared with English law;[64] and German law has had more extensive regimes for consumer protection than those applicable in most European jurisdictions.[65]

The above reasoning presupposes that the costs as well as the benefits of legal protection are internalised to citizens within the boundaries of the national jurisdiction. The predictions alter if there are significant transboundary effects, that is, international externalities. We may use the paradigm example of pollution, but the arguments would apply *mutatis mutandis* to product liability and other instances of such externalities.

If the costs of pollution abatement are predominantly incurred in State A, but the benefits accrue mainly in State B, we may anticipate that competition between national legal systems will have the following consequences.[66] First, it will be in the interests of citizens in State A to press for a lowering of the relevant level of environmental protection, since they will gain and citizens in State B will lose. This will be accompanied by perverse incentives for firms in State A to export more of their pollution to State B than would otherwise be justified: for example, by locating discharges close to the frontier with State B, or by building higher chimney stacks. Second, firms in State B, competing with the polluting State A firms, will apply pressure on State B lawmakers to reduce pollution standards in that jurisdiction. Third, State A will be reluctant to facilitate private transboundary legal actions by pollution victims in State B, unless there are perceived to be reciprocal benefits arising from such a development.

These considerations may suggest that, where there are significant international externalities, there will be some convergence of national laws towards a lowering of protection.[67] Empirical support for the prediction is nevertheless weak: studies tend to show that "races to the bottom" are rare.[68] There would seem to be two principal explanations for this.[69] In the first place, we must

62. R. Van den Bergh, "The Subsidiarity Principle in European Community Law: Some Insights from Law and Economics" (1995) 2 Maastricht J. European and Comp.L. 337.

63. R. Van den Bergh, "Subsidiarity as an Economic Demarcation Principle and the Emergence of European Private Law" (1998) 5 Maastricht J. European and Comp.L. 129.

64. A. Tunc, "It Is Wise not to Take the Civil Codes too Seriously", in P. Wallington and R. Merkin (Eds), *Essays in Memory of Professor F. H. Lawson* (1986), chap.7.

65. A. von Mehren, "A General View of Contract", *International Encyclopedia of Comparative Law*, Vol.7, chap.1 (1977), paras.79–80.

66. W. E. Oates and R. M. Schwab, "Economic Competition Among Jurisdictions: Efficiency Enhancing or Distortion Inducing?" (1988) 35 J. Public Economics 333.

67. R. B. Stewart, "Pyramids of Sacrifice? Problems of Federalism in Mandating State Implementation of National Environmental Policy" (1977) 86 Yale L.J. 1196.

68. K. Gatsios and P. Holmes, "Regulatory Competition", in Newman, *op. cit. supra* n.10, at Vol.3, pp.271, 274.

69. For a fuller discussion, see R. L. Revesz, "Rehabilitating Interstate Competition: Rethinking the 'Race-to-the-Bottom' Rationale for Federal Environmental Regulation" (1992) 67 N.Y.U.L.R. 1210.

recognise that lawmakers will find it difficult and costly to target less stringent regimes on activities which generate significant transborder effects but little or no domestic effects. Second, there may be some benefits to firms in being established in jurisdictions with stricter regimes: the higher standards may generate technological improvements to processes which confer competitive advantages on the firms complying with them.[70]

The general conclusion to be drawn from this section is that competition between national systems will not necessarily lead to a convergence of "interventionist" law, since preferences as to the content of that law may vary significantly. The existence of transboundary externalities may alter this prediction, but empirical support for the "race to the bottom" thesis is relatively weak.

E. The Normative Dimension

As we have seen in the preceding sections, the normal processes of trade and the existence of competition between jurisdictions should lead to the convergence of principles in some areas of law. The main question to be addressed in this section is the desirability of more proactive harmonisation, whether this be by a mandatory unification measure, as imposed by European directives and international treaties, or by voluntary codes, exemplified by the output of UNIDROIT and the Lando Commission,[71] which serve as model laws that States are free to adopt or which may influence courts in the development of judicial doctrine.[72]

Comparative lawyers have been committed advocates for, and active participants in, both harmonisation processes, particularly the second.[73] Indeed it seems obvious that substantial benefits may be acquired thereby: those engaged in international transactions will incur reduced costs in acquiring information as to the governing legal principles and, if necessary, in enforcing rights and obligations. But the ready appreciation of these advantages often blinds commentators to the costs which unifying law may generate.[74]

Let us take first homogeneous legal products. As we have seen, competition between jurisdictions should spontaneously induce some convergence towards least-cost legal principles. The very process of evolution from a pattern of diverse laws enables jurisdictions to experiment with different legal arrangements.[75] Spontaneous convergence has the additional, and perhaps even more significant, advantage over imposed or more formal harmonisation that the evolution

---

70. Woolcock, *op. cit. supra* n.17, at p.318; J. Bhagwati and T. N. Srinivasan, "Trade and the Environment: Does Environmental Diversity Detract from the Case for Free Trade?", in Bhagwati and Hudec, *op. cit. supra* n.20, at pp.171–172.

71. O. Lando and H. Beale (Eds), *Principles of European Contract Law* (1995).

72. See further on types of harmonisation Ribstein and Kobayashi, *op. cit. supra* n.49 and Smits, *op. cit. supra* n.29.

73. Lando, *op. cit. supra* n.5; J. Baselow, "Un Droit Commun des Contrats pour le Marché Commun" (1998) 50 Rev.Int. Droit Comp. 7.

74. Van den Bergh, *op. cit. supra* n.62. See also Ribstein and Kobayashi, *op. cit. supra* n.49.

75. Woolcock, *op. cit. supra* n.17, at p.299; Ribstein and Kobayashi, *op. cit. supra* n.49, at pp.140–141. Both this, and the last, proposition are derivable from the Hayekian theory of law: F. A. Hayek, *Law, Legislation and Liberty* (1979); and see A. Ogus, "Law and Spontaneous Order: Hayek's Contribution to Legal Theory" (1989) 16 J. Law and Society 393.

towards common solutions should occur only where it is economically appropriate; that is, where the benefits of convergence exceed its costs.[76] Now, while the reduction in information and other costs of harmonising legal principles may be substantial, such benefits may be outweighed by the costs of formulating uniform principles, reaching agreement on, and subsequently adapting national legal systems to, them. And, as regards the latter, we should note that private law is more problematic than regulatory law, since it is generally deeply entrenched in national legal culture.[77]

Of course, as we have seen, private interest groups, particularly practising lawyers, may be able to obstruct the processes of competition between jurisdictions, thus impeding evolution towards economically justifiable common principles. Should that occur, the case for mandatory harmonisation is strengthened. At the same time, we should recognise that comparative lawyers have themselves an interest in the harmonisation process: it generates a demand for their services and confers on them significant non-financial utility, such as that derived from increased prestige and agreeable meetings in attractive locations! We may therefore expect comparative lawyers to promote harmonisation even when it is not objectively justifiable.

The arguments against harmonisation of heterogeneous legal products are, in general, even stronger. Here, as we have seen, citizens in different jurisdictions may have different preferences regarding the level of protection to be imposed and the price to be paid for it. Obviously, such preferences may be overreached, with attendant welfare losses, if the uniform legal principles are imposed on purely domestic arrangements. Even when harmonisation is confined to activities with an international dimension, selection of the uniform principle may involve the supplanting of one jurisdiction's preferences by those of another, an outcome which might be avoided through a principle of mutual recognition or by appropriate choice of law rules.[78] Arguments for the harmonisation of *minimum* standards of protection[79] stand on a different footing since this may proceed on the assumption of homogeneity of preferences: it is reasonable to infer that the citizens of all affected jurisdictions would agree on the relevant threshold.

There remain two oft-cited justifications for uniformity of legal principles: transboundary externalities and fair competition. We have seen that the ability of firms to export to other countries the harmful effects of their activities, while capturing the benefits of those activities for themselves and others in their jurisdiction, *may* lead to the promulgation of lax standards. This would appear to be the paradigm case for mandatory harmonisation,[80] and yet we should not rush to that conclusion without recognising that it is a costly exercise and that alternative, cheaper solutions may be available.[81]

---

76. Leebron, *op. cit. supra* n.20, at p.54.

77. Van den Bergh, *op. cit. supra* n.63, at pp.146–147.

78. Leebron, *op. cit. supra* n.20.

79. This is now the policy favoured by the European Commission towards harmonisation of regulatory standards: see J. Pelkmans, "The New Approach to Technical Harmonization and Standardization" (1987) 25 J. Common Market Studies 249.

80. Leebron, *op. cit. supra* n.20, at pp.55–57.

81. R. L. Revesz, "Rehabilitating Interstate Competition: Rethinking the 'Race-to-the-Bottom' Rationale for Federal Environmental Regulation" (1992) 67 N.Y.U.L.R. 1210; R.

The ideal alternative solution would be to offer to those affected in the receiving jurisdiction the level of protection which would meet their preferences if they had to pay the increased costs of complying with that standard. In the case of product liability this may be feasible. A tort claim made by victims in their own jurisdiction would be governed by the law of that jurisdiction,[82] and the cost of meeting such potential claims would be reflected in the prices charged by importers and retailers. The same would apply if the import and sale of the product were governed by regulatory standards imposed by the receiving jurisdiction. With transboundary pollution this solution would not be viable, since there is no direct way of internalising to the pollution victims the costs of higher environmental protection. It would be necessary for the application of the receiving jurisdiction's environmental law to the polluter—itself a problematic task—to be combined with a system of subsidies to offset the necessary abatement costs incurred by pollution exporters and financed, at least in part, by a tax on those resident in the affected State.[83]

Finally, there is the familiar assertion that diversity of interventionist legal principles can create non-tariff barriers to international trade and thus impede fair competition. I cannot in this article adequately address the broad and complex range of economic and non-economic issues which this justification raises.[84] I will limit myself to some general observations, suggesting that caution should be exercised in invoking this set of arguments.

In the first place, there is the traditional economic reasoning, dating from Adam Smith:[85] while laxer interventionist laws in one jurisdiction may confer a competitive advantage on firms subject to those laws, the consequence should be lower prices of the products and services available in the international market with welfare gains to those in the States of the industries whose prices have been undercut. The resources hitherto used for the latter can then largely be shifted to other, more productive uses. Subject to short-term frictional losses, the aggregate welfare consequences for both jurisdictions are likely to be beneficial. In other words, the problem—if any—is distributional rather than economic:[86] for the more general good, some losses will be incurred by the industries previously complying with the stricter laws.[87]

Second, if the argument is for harmonisation at a higher level of protection than that provided in some jurisdictions, why should the preferences of their citizens

Van den Bergh, M. Faure and J. Lefevere, "The Subsidiarity Principle in European Environmental Law: An Economic Analysis", in E. Eide and R. Van den Bergh (Eds), *Law and Economics of the Environment* (1996), pp.121–166.

82. P. Kelly and R. Atree (Eds), *European Product Liability Law* (1992), chap.17.

83. Bhagwati and Srinivasan, *op. cit. supra* n.70.

84. See especially Oates and Schwab, *op. cit. supra* n.66; D. Salvatore (Ed.), *Protectionism and World Welfare* (1993): Bhagwati and Hudec, *op. cit. supra* n.20; M. Trebilcock and R. Howse, "Trade Liberalization and Regulatory Diversity: Reconciling Competitive Policies" (1998) 6 European J. Law and Economics 5.

85. *The Wealth of Nations* (Ed. W. R. Scott, 1921), Book IV.

86. Judged by the Kaldor–Hicks measure of economic efficiency: cf. Ogus, *op. cit. supra* n.13, at pp.24–25.

87. Leebron, *op. cit. supra* n.20.

for lower standards at a lower cost be overreached?[88] One answer is that there may be legitimate doubts as to whether the law in fact reflects those preferences, but it is far from clear that foreign observers are in a good position to decide whether or not there is political failure of this sort. Another possible answer is that the standards may be so low as to infringe widely held perceptions of human rights. Rights may, in this instance, justifiably "trump" efficiency;[89] or the matter may, rather, be characterised as a negative externality, foreigners deriving disutility from observing the plight of victims in the offending State. In either case there is still the difficulty of determining the legitimate boundaries of human rights or the disutility function of foreigners.[90]

F. Conclusions

In this article I have explored some of the ways in which economic analysis can contribute to an understanding of some key aspects of the relationships between national legal regimes and thus provide an important methodology for comparative law. The predictive part of the analysis suggests that competition between jurisdictions will generate a tendency for national legal principles to converge in those areas of law designed primarily to facilitate trade. In contrast there is, in general, no reason to expect this phenomenon to apply to interventionist areas of law because national preferences regarding the level of protection are likely to differ. In relation to both areas of law, the case for institutionally led harmonisation is weaker than comparative lawyers tend to assume.

ANTHONY OGUS*

88. A. K. Klevorick, "Reflections on the Race to the Bottom", in Bhagwati and Hudec, *op. cit. supra* n.20, chap.12.
89. R. Dworkin, *Taking Rights Seriously* (1977), chap.4.
90. Trebilcock and Howse, *op. cit. supra* n.84, at pp.14–15.
* Professor of Law, University of Manchester; Research Professor, University of Maastricht. The article is a revised version of a paper presented at the 15th Annual Conference of the European Association of Law and Economics, Utrecht, Sept. 1998. I gratefully acknowledge the helpful comments of Fabrizio Cafaggi and other participants at the conference.

[22]

Trading with Bandits

Peter T. Leeson *West Virginia University*

Abstract

Is it possible to trade with bandits? When government is absent, the superior strength of some agents makes it cheaper for them to violently steal what they desire from weaker agents than to use trade to obtain what they want. Such was the case with middlemen who interacted with producers in late precolonial west central Africa. In the face of this threat, producers employed two mechanisms to make exchange with middlemen possible. On the one hand, they used credit to alter middlemen's cost-benefit structure of engaging in plunder versus trade. On the other hand, producers demanded tribute from traveling traders as a risk premium. By transforming traveling traders' incentive from banditry to peaceful trade and reducing producers' costs associated with interacting with middlemen, these mechanisms enhanced both parties' ability to capture the gains from exchange.

> How wonderful is commerce. (David Livingstone [1963, p. 32], nineteenth-century British explorer of the remote interior of west central Africa)

1. Introduction

No sane economist would argue that it is possible to trade with bandits. We have all learned that the market alone is insufficient to prevent the strong from plundering the weak. Indeed, the threat of violence is perhaps the oldest, most well accepted justification for government. Even Adam Smith ([1776] 1965, p. 670) believed this was true: "It is only under the shelter of the civil magistrate that the owner of . . . property . . . can sleep a single night in security. He is at all times surrounded by unknown enemies, whom, though he never provoked, he can never appease, and from whose injustice he can be protected only by the powerful arm of the civil magistrate continually held up to chastise it."

The market, however, might be better at negotiating threats of violence than

I am grateful to Robert Bates, Peter Boettke, Tyler Cowen, Chris Coyne, Andrei Shleifer, Melissa Thomas, Richard Wagner, the editors, and an anonymous referee for indispensable comments and suggestions. I also benefited from the comments of seminar participants at Harvard University, where I presented an earlier draft of this paper. The financial assistance of the Oloffson Weaver Fellowship is gratefully acknowledged.

[*Journal of Law and Economics*, vol. 50 (May 2007)]

we once thought. Could economists have underestimated the market's power and beauty in this regard?

A growing body of research considers how agents can overcome dishonesty where state enforcement is absent (see, for instance, Clay 1997; Greif 1989, 1993; Kranton 1996; Landa 1994; Leeson 2006; Milgrom, North, and Weingast 1990; Zerbe and Anderson 2001). These studies, however, exclusively consider commitment problems that involve the potential for what might be called "peaceful theft" in that recourse to physical violence is not used to take advantage of the wronged party. For peaceful theft, a separation of payment and provision, not a difference in actual strength, accounts for an individual's ability to defraud his or her exchange partner.

Equally important when government is absent is what might be called "violent theft." Here the perpetrator is a bandit who uses physical force to overwhelm his or her victim. His or her superior strength gives him or her the ability to defraud others.

Introducing bandits into standard models of peaceful theft can cause them to break down. These models rely in various ways on the folk theorem to work. The shadow of the future in conjunction with the threat of multilateral punishment can create cooperation if agents are patient enough. But when some agents are sufficiently stronger than others, multilateral punishment may no longer secure cooperation. Weaker agents can eternally boycott stronger agents who behave violently, but boycott does not prevent stronger agents from simply taking what they want from weaker ones.

This need not always be the case. If the stronger agent is stationary but the weaker agent is mobile, boycott is effective. This is the case, for instance, in the medieval situation described by Greif, Milgrom, and Weingast (1994). However, in situations where individuals have disparate strengths and stronger agents are mobile while weaker ones are not, multilateral punishment cannot work. Weaker agents may refuse to interact with stronger individuals who behaved violently toward them in the past, but if they cannot run and the stronger agents can, their refusal will not prevent them from being plundered again. Something other than the threat of lost revenue from repeated exchange is needed to create cooperation.

Unlike peaceful theft, the topic of violent theft has received relatively little attention. Existing models that consider the potential for violent theft assume that both parties can transform their resources into useful goods or coercive power (see, for example, Bush and Mayer 1974; Umbeck 1981; Hirshleifer 1988, 1995, 2001; Skaperdas 1992, 2003; Anderson and McChesney 1994; Anderson and Hill 2004; Skaperdas and Syropoulos 1997; Neary 1997; Grossman 1998; Grossman and Kim 2002; Bates, Greif, and Singh 2002).[1] While this assumption is reasonable in many cases, it is not in many others. For instance, if one player

---

[1] For a superb discussion of the emergence of property rights and their defense in the absence of formal enforcement, see also Anderson and McChesney (2002).

has a monopoly on the technology of greatest violence, the other may be severely limited in his or her ability to invest in strength for the purpose of defense or aggression. In these models, introducing severe limitations on the ability of certain agents to invest in additional strength leads to a situation in which those who are not so constrained plunder those who are. Permanently weak agents cannot avoid violent theft in equilibrium (see, for instance, Hausken 2004).

With both multilateral punishment and investment in greater strength eliminated as means for coping with the threat of violent theft, it would seem that there is no way for permanently weak individuals to exchange with stronger ones. Despite this, I contend that trade between permanently weak and permanently strong individuals is possible without government. Weaker individuals' inability to rely on mechanisms described by the folk theorem and to invest in force for defense or aggression does not prevent them from making exchange with bandits self-enforcing in the face of threats of violent theft.

To examine my hypothesis, I consider the case of late precolonial Africa.[2] European settlers on the west coast of Africa employed middlemen to collect the goods they needed for export from producers in the remote interior of Central Africa.[3] In addition to this, some Africans operated as middlemen on their own account—connecting European exporters and others with producers in the interior. Caravans of traveling middlemen were frequently stronger than the communities of producers with whom they interacted. They were thus tempted to overwhelm these communities with force and steal the goods they desired rather than trading for them.[4]

I argue that communities of producers used two mechanisms to transform middlemen's equilibrium strategy from banditry to peaceful trade. First, I discuss producers' use of credit as a means of enhancing the efficiency of producer-middleman exchange relations. Second, I look at producers' demands for tribute from middlemen as a kind of risk premium promoting producers' ability to interact with traveling traders. These mechanisms are new in that, until now, they have not been used to explain how agents make exchange self-enforcing in the face of threats of violent theft.[5]

Because multilateral punishment cannot create cooperation where one class is permanently weak, unlike most models of self-enforcing exchange, mine does not rely on reputation or repeated play to achieve cooperation. Similarly, since

[2] For a classic treatment of West African trade in the colonial period through the early 1950s, see Bauer (1954).
[3] As Serpa Pinto (1881, p. 22) summarized it, "[T]rade in Africa was divisible into two branches, viz. the purchasing of goods from the whites and selling them the produce of the country, and purchasing such produce from the blacks and selling to them the aforesaid goods." This trade was conducted by traveling middlemen.
[4] The problem I consider here is somewhat analogous to a violent version of the traditional holdup problem discussed by Williamson (1975, 1985), Klein, Crawford, and Alchian (1978), and Hart and Moore (1988), among others.
[5] For an excellent and pioneering discussion on institutions of credible commitment in the context of violent conflict, see Schelling (1960).

one class of players is unable to substantially affect its strength through investment, the emphasis of my analysis shifts from individuals' optimal investments in coercive capital (the focus in existing models that deal with violence) to the strategies employed by permanently weaker individuals to alter the incentive of stronger agents for trade versus banditry.[6]

To examine these strategies, I utilize primary-source materials regarding interaction between middlemen and producers in west central Africa in the latter half of the nineteenth century. These sources are composed from the in-depth reports of about 20 European travelers to the area during this period. Many of these travelers were themselves traders, while others were explorers interested in learning more about the state of African trade for their home countries and spreading the word of Christianity.

2. The Context of Producer-Middleman Relations in Late Precolonial Africa

In examining late precolonial interaction between middlemen and producers in west central Africa, this paper deals primarily with the inhabitants around the Upper Zambezi and Kasai, Portuguese-speaking settlers along the Angolan coast, and the middlemen they employed.[7] Middlemen typically traveled in caravans and were constantly on the move.[8] These caravans consisted of other free middlemen, security charged with protecting the caravan on the road, and often a great number of slaves who carried the items for sale. Caravans ranged in size from tens to thousands, although on the basis of the evidence available in travelers' reports, the modal caravan consisted of about 70 or 80 people (Miller 1988, p. 191; Cameron 1877, p. 251; Soremekun 1977, p. 87; Capello and Ivens 1969, 1:17–18; Dias de Carvalho 1890, pp. 186, 192, 193, 700; Harding 1905, p. 214; Johnston 1893, p. 34). Common imports carried by traveling traders to the interior included tobacco, gin, beads, shells, and brass, which were used as body ornaments, cloth, and firearms. As the sole suppliers of firearms to interior communities, middlemen controlled the weaponry reaching producers of goods and thus typically had the upper hand when it came to implements used in fighting.[9]

---

[6] Olson (1993) and McGuire and Olson (1996) consider the case in which the stronger party finds it in his or her interest to establish permanent hegemony over the weaker individuals. If his or her interest is stable and encompassing, and the ruler is sufficiently patient, he or she can make more this way than by sporadically pillaging weaker parties. This paper considers the use of informal mechanisms that create a cheaper means for stronger agents to credibly commit not to plunder weaker ones than establishing government over them.

[7] Interaction between middlemen and producers in the interior of west central Africa appears to have begun around 1790 (Botelho de Vasconcellos [1844] 1873).

[8] Capello and Ivens (1969, 1:103), for example, described the middlemen of Bihe as "eminently devoted to traveling."

[9] There is no evidence to suggest that middlemen were cartelized or in any way coordinated their actions to prevent arms from reaching producers. Nevertheless, they appear to have infrequently supplied firearms to producers.

Producers consisted of village chiefs, or headmen, and their citizens in the remote interior. These individuals rarely traveled far beyond the bounds of their communities where the resources used in production could be found.[10] Their immobility was strengthened by the costliness of spending significant time away from home, especially in light of the fact that, as producers, traveling for, say, the purposes of trade was not to their comparative advantage. In this way, specialization contributed to their immobility. Since I consider exchange in the postslave export era, commodities supplied by these individuals consisted mostly of ivory, beeswax, and wild rubber. Despite the fact that slave trading was prohibited in Angola in 1836, however, slaves continued to be a source of profit to traveling traders who obtained slaves both for illegal sale to coastal traders[11] and for sale to other African communities.

In the nineteenth century, most of interior west central Africa consisted of disparate communities ruled by chiefs who decided over disagreements among their citizens, including those that dealt with credit and exchange. The relationship of ruler to ruled in these societies was considerably less formal than a modern Western notion of government would imply.[12] Furthermore, the presence of numerous sovereigns created a vacuum of authority for interactions involving the members of different communities. In this sense, it is reasonable to speak of these societies as quasi stateless in that mechanisms of enforcement between communities and, to a lesser extent, within communities were overwhelmingly informal. As two European travelers characterized a portion of the interior they visited, for example, "[I]t is only in extraordinary cases that one can suspect that such a thing as a law exists" (Capello and Ivens 1969, 2:242; see also 1:183).[13]

On the European side, crown-established governors ruled Portuguese settlements on the coast and oversaw trade posts they set up slightly further inland. Of course, the laws of these settlements did not formally bind Africans in the interior. Nor did the customs of interior African communities formally bind the inhabitants of these settlements. The presence of multiple states in west central Africa—both those of indigenous communities and those of European settlements—created ungoverned interstices for interactions between these people.

[10] While some indigenous precolonial agents inside the remote interior of west central Africa migrated within the areas composing this region, very few migrated outside of it, and these were not producers. According to Capello and Ivens, "The natives of T'Chiboco," for instance, "seldom travel beyond their own country, and it is a rare sight to behold a caravan of Ma-quioco journeying westward for the purposes of trade" (1969, 1:225; see also Serpa Pinto 1881, p. 255; Harding 1905, p. 307).

[11] According to Crawford (1914, p. 28), for instance, the governor at Benguela allowed illicit slave trading to go on under his watch.

[12] As Livingstone (1963, p. 410) observed, for instance, "So far as I can at present understand, there are no such things as nations or kingdoms in the interior of Africa." See also Capello and Ivens (1969, 2:49, 2:242).

[13] Even where colonial outposts had been established, formal authority was not really effective. For instance, as Arnot commented, "Though Bailundu and Bihe are within the province of Benguella, Portuguese authority has not very much influence there" (1889, p. 111; see also Harding 1905, p. 306; Johnston 1893, p. 59).

2.1. The Threat of Violent Theft

To profit, middlemen needed to obtain the goods of producers in the interior of Central Africa and bring them to outlying communities and coastal exporters. These goods could be obtained in one of two ways, peaceful trade or violent theft. In connecting stationary producers with people outside the narrow bounds of their communities, middlemen had the capacity to enable producers to realize significant gains from exchange they would have been otherwise unable to capture.[14] The fact that they tended to be stronger than the communities of producers with whom they interacted, however, created a situation in which middlemen were tempted to use force rather than trade to realize their ends (see, for instance, Harding 1905, pp. 93, 108, 124, 138; Cameron 1877, pp. 226, 253, 292, 331, 472; Johnston 1893, pp. 40–41; Gibbons 1904, 1:67; Livingstone 1874, 2:29; 1857, pp. 180, 297; 1960, p. 277; 1963, 1:12). As Cameron (1877, p. 393) observed, for example, left unchecked, caravans "profited by rapine and robbery in passing through countries where people did not possess guns."[15] Thus, a potentially highly beneficial situation for producers could easily turn into a massively harmful one.

Like all behavior, the decision to engage in banditry over trade is guided by the relative marginal cost and marginal benefit of these alternative modes of action. Sufficiently superior strength lowers the marginal cost of plunder below that of trade as a means of obtaining desired goods. Where an individual is strong enough to take what he or she wants with little or no resistance, it is cheaper to steal than to pay for the desired objects. His or her payoff-maximizing strategy is therefore to violently overwhelm weaker agents.

Two primary features of middlemen accounted for the fact that they were often the stronger force in interactions with interior producers. First, as noted above, middlemen were the source of modern weaponry for producers. Producers by themselves had no access to guns except by way of those sold or given to them by traveling traders. By controlling the quantity and quality of firearms reaching interior communities, middlemen could effectively secure their strength superiority, giving them a decisive advantage should they decide to attack these communities. This advantage was heightened by the fact that usually "in the interior . . . the villages are open and unprotected," making producers easy targets for better armed middlemen (Serpa Pinto 1881, 1:177). Clearly, this advantage was not always sufficient to ensure victory in an attack. If a caravan was sufficiently small and the community it attempted to plunder was sufficiently

---

[14] As two travelers to the interior put it, "Commerce, by obliging them [traveling traders] to make repeated journeys, carries with it, as a necessary consequence, the establishment of relations and the making of contracts with distant peoples" (Capello and Ivens 1969, 2:18).

[15] Caravan leaders often made this bad situation worse by encouraging their groups to steal from the villages to which they traveled. Leaders were usually responsible for providing their group's provisions on the road, and provisions became very costly when caravans were large (see, for instance, Serpa Pinto 1881, 1:165). Theft was thus sometimes promoted as a cost-cutting measure. As Cameron (1877, p. 259) observed, for example, "At Kwakasongo there is an Arab settlement of some size. . . . [T]hey send out their caravans. . . . These fellows get no pay, but are allowed to loot the country all round in search of subsistence and slaves."

large, better weaponry was meaningless. Of course, overcoming this potential obstacle to banditry was not all that difficult. Middlemen simply needed to be selective about the communities they targeted for attack.

Second, middlemen were highly mobile, and producers were highly stationary. This meant two things for middlemen's success in plundering expeditions. On the one hand, middlemen could always return to the coast or their home bases near the coast and gather additional members if greater numbers were needed to succeed in violently stealing from interior communities of producers. Perhaps even more important, however, the relative immobility of producers meant that middlemen could escape from conflict with their booty by fleeing to the coast without much worry that they would be overtaken later by bands of producers who would need to locate, track down,[16] and recover what had been stolen.[17]

2.2. Modeling the Threat of Violent Theft

Modeling the threat of the violent theft that producers confronted is straightforward. Consider an economy of complete and perfect information with one community of producers and one caravan of middlemen. Because it is stationary and sufficiently weaker than the caravan of middlemen, the community of producers does not have a choice about whether or not it will interact with middlemen. If the caravan approaches the community of producers, it cannot avoid interaction. Multilateral punishment, which requires the ability to terminate future interaction in the event of noncooperative behavior, is therefore not an effective strategy for preventing banditry here. While the community of producers does not control whether or not it will interact with the caravan that approaches it, it does control a different variable of the game—how much it produces.

Producers move first and decide whether to produce for trade or for subsistence. Producing for trade means producing a relatively large quantity of goods that producers may either consume or use for immediate trade with the caravan if it approaches them. Producing for subsistence means producing a small quantity of goods just larger than necessary for producers' personal consumption. Production for trade therefore involves a surplus stock of goods that affords producers additional consumption and additional trade, while production for subsistence involves a stock just large enough to sustain the population and permits only a minimal level of trade.

The caravan of middlemen moves second and chooses to do one of the following: stay home, that is, not travel to the community of producers at all; travel

---

[16] According to Crawford (1914, pp. 22–23), agents in west central Africa at this time also frequently changed their names. This, of course, would have contributed to the difficulty of tracking down violent middlemen. However, it remains unclear how pervasive this practice was.

[17] A third reason for middlemen's strength superiority could also be added. Namely, the fact that they were mobile and producers were stationary meant that middlemen had the ability to initiate surprise attacks on communities of producers. This may help to explain Serpa Pinto's (1881, 1:178) comment, "It is a noteworthy circumstance connected with wars in this part of the Africa, that the attacking party is ever the victor."

to the community of producers and trade; or travel to the community of producers and plunder. Following the discussion in Section 2, the caravan's attempt to plunder is always successful and met without resistance such that the community loses all it has produced when it is plundered.

If producers produce for trade and middlemen stay home, producers receive H_p and middlemen receive H_m—what each can earn without interacting with the other. If middlemen trade, both producers and middlemen earn a higher payoff from exchanging, E_p and E_m, respectively, where E_m is middlemen's payoff net of traveling expenses. If middlemen plunder, they receive an even higher payoff yet, which when travel expenses are deducted gives them P. Producers, on the other hand, receive their lowest payoff in this case, $-H_p$.

The situation is similar if producers produce for subsistence, but the payoffs change because a smaller stock of goods is available for producers to consume, for middlemen to violently take if they choose to plunder, and for producers to trade with middlemen if middlemen decide to exchange. Only middlemen's payoff from staying home, which is unaffected by the stock of goods producers keep on hand, does not change when producers produce for subsistence. Thus, if producers produce for subsistence and middlemen stay home, middlemen continue to earn H_m. Producers, however, earn less. Because the inconvenience of producing just enough to sustain the community is costly, producers receive a payoff of only h_p, where h_p is equal to H_p minus the value they place on the forgone stock in consumptive uses. If middlemen plunder, producers receive $-h_p$, which is their smallest payoff when they produce for subsistence but which is larger than what they receive when middlemen plunder and they produce for trade $(-H_p)$. Middlemen in this case earn p, which is more than they earn by trading but, because there is so little to steal, is smaller than the payoff of staying home (H_m). Finally, if middlemen trade, producers earn e_p, which is smaller than what they earn from trade when they produce for trade (because there is a smaller stock available for trading) but which is still their highest payoff when they produce for subsistence. Middlemen in this event earn e_m, their smallest payoff, which includes the cost of travel. To summarize, for producers, $E_p > H_p > e_p > h_p$, and for middlemen, $P > E_m > H_m > p > e_m$, where $E_p + E_m > P - H_p$, which is to say that the higher level of trade is socially efficient. This game is depicted in Figure 1.

The unique subgame perfect Nash equilibrium of this game involves producers producing for subsistence and traveling traders staying home. If they produce more, producers increase middlemen's payoff from banditry by making more available to steal. This entices middlemen to plunder, which generates losses for producers. To avoid these losses, producers produce only what is needed to sustain themselves. As a result, there is little available for theft, which creates a situation for middlemen in which staying home yields a higher return than plundering. In equilibrium, producers earn h_p and middlemen earn more, H_m. Producers pay for their strength inferiority by incurring the cost associated with reducing stocks to a level that prevents middlemen from engaging in banditry.

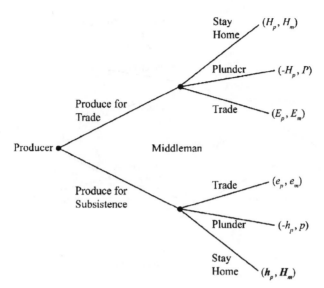

Figure 1. The threat of violent theft

In discouraging middlemen from interacting with them, producers also forgo significant potential gains from trade. The threat of being plundered, however, did not prevent trade between middlemen and producers in the late precolonial period. Indeed, legitimate exports supplied by remote interior producers leaving Angola alone amounted to close to $4 million per year by the end of the nineteenth century (Vellut 1979, p. 101). How did producers overcome the threat of violent theft posed by trading with bandits?

3. A Clever Use of Credit: You Can't Steal What's Not There, but You Can Trade with It

To capture the gains from trade with middlemen, producers required a strategy that would keep middlemen's payoff from plunder below the payoff from staying home, as in the case in which they produced for subsistence, but raise middlemen's payoff from trade above the payoff from staying home, as in the case in which they produced for trade. Credit made these two seemingly incompatible goals possible. Although middlemen could not steal goods that did not yet exist, credit enabled producers to trade with goods that did not yet exist. By keeping current stocks low but exchanging with middlemen on credit, producers could produce for subsistence, thus deterring plunder but still enabling trade, which would allow both sides to reap the benefits from exchange.

To see explicitly how the use of such credit arrangements enhanced producer-middleman exchange, consider the game in Figure 2. This game is like that from

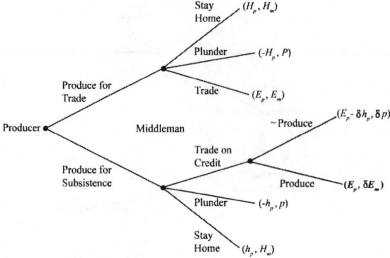

Figure 2. A clever use of credit

Figure 1, only now when producers produce for subsistence, let middlemen's trade strategy be trade on credit rather than simultaneous exchange. This modification makes the analysis dynamic. When trade on credit is chosen, each round is composed of two subperiods: one in which middlemen provide credit and another in which, if producers have produced, exchange takes place, and if they have not, they are plundered to clear off as much of the debt as possible.[18]

The payoffs on the Produce for Trade branch of the tree remain the same as before. Likewise, the payoffs from {Produce for Subsistence, Stay Home} and {Produce for Subsistence, Plunder} remain the same. However, because it now involves trading on credit, which increases the volume of exchange that is possible, the payoff of trade under subsistence production rises.

Since credit is provided in the first subperiod, middlemen receive what they are owed in the second subperiod only if production has actually occurred. If middlemen provide credit and producers subsequently produce, producers receive the same payoff as when they produce for trade and middlemen trade under the Produce for Trade branch of the tree, E_p. Middlemen, on the other hand, earn δE_m, where δ is the caravan's discount factor and $\delta \in (0, 1)$. The reason for discounting middlemen's payoff is straightforward. Because trade in this case is conducted on credit in the first subperiod, middlemen only receive all or part of the gains from exchange via repayment in the second subperiod.

---

[18] For instance, when the traveling trader "Hassani of Dugumbe got [a] chief into debt" and the chief could not repay, Hassani "robbed him of ten men and ten goats to clear off the debt" (Livingstone 1874, 2:35).

If after receiving credit in the first subperiod, when the caravan arrives to receive payment in the second subperiod, producers have not produced, middlemen punish them by plundering what is available. If this happens, producers receive $E_p - \delta h_p$—what they received on credit in subperiod 1, less the discounted value of what is taken from them in subperiod 2. Middlemen, on the other hand, receive δp—the discounted value of what they are able to take as compensation in subperiod 2.

What course of action the caravan of middlemen now finds most profitable depends on its discount rate and the credibility of producers' promises to produce in subperiod 2. Where $\delta > H_m/E_m$ and producers can credibly commit to produce, trade is more profitable for the caravan than staying home. Where δ does not satisfy this inequality or producers cannot credibly commit to produce, the caravan finds staying home more profitable. Since $E_p > E_p - \delta h_p$ for any $\delta \in (0, 1)$ and $E_p > h_p > -H_p$, producers can credibly commit to produce for re-payment in subperiod 2. Given this, for middlemen whose discount rates satisfy $\delta > H_m/E_m$, trading on credit is the payoff-maximizing strategy. For middlemen whose discount rates do not satisfy this inequality, staying home is payoff max-imizing. In equilibrium, the caravan travels to the community of producers only if it is going to trade (on credit) and stays home if the caravan poses a threat of violence. Plunder is therefore avoided, and producers and middlemen who are sufficiently patient realize the gains from exchange.

The use of credit for this purpose in producer-middleman exchange was ubiquitous. As the traveling trader Henrique Augusto Dias de Carvalho put it, "[T]he trader sees himself forced to give credits, and this is indispensable for anyone who takes the risk of trading in such a region, if he wants to do it with any success" (1890, p. 700; translation from Oppen 1994). Producers' efforts to keep stocks of "thievable" goods low was considerably eased by the fact that many of the goods desired by middlemen—for instance, ivory, rubber, and wax—required harvesting before they were available in exportable form. These goods remained in the ground, so to speak, until collected by producers. To keep stocks perpetually low, producers protracted the process of debt repayment (see, for instance, Cameron 1877, p. 47; Livingstone 1874, 1:305; Dias de Carvalho 1890, p. 699). Consider, for example, the observation of a European traveler to the Upper Zambezi and Kasai, Paul Pogge:

The native would be little inclined to gather the products of his country, were he not given the payment in advance. . . . [*Ambaquista* middlemen—A.v.O.] can buy some products in the interior, these being brought to them by the natives and paid [imme-diately]. . . . In general, however, they cannot purchase very many commodities in this way but instead give the native credit. Where rubber occurs in the forest, and where the elephant occurs, the Baptist [*Ambaquista*] gives payment in advance to the elephant hunter for so and so many tusks, and to the one who wants to bring rubber or beeswax payment for so and so many pounds of rubber or wax. *These people then have to wait for months and years until their debtors satisfy them* (Oppen 1994, pp. 397–98; emphasis added [translation of Pogge 1880, p. 16]; see also Buchner 1883, p. 82).

The goods that producers desired that middlemen extend to them on credit—for instance, alcohol, cloth, and tobacco—were typically the kind of goods that producers consumed shortly after receiving them. Middlemen were therefore not able to extend goods to producers on credit and then retake them by force when they returned to a village to receive an installment of debt repayment. Obviously, however, producers could not reduce their stocks of goods to zero. They needed to keep some provisions on hand to survive. In addition, some goods desired by traveling traders—for instance, slaves—could not be made unavailable in the way that others could. There was consequently always something available for stronger middlemen to steal if they so desired. Nevertheless, by significantly reducing their holdings, producers could concomitantly reduce the benefits of violent theft to middlemen bent on banditry. Furthermore, it was unnecessary for producers to reduce their stock of goods to zero to have the desired effect. As long as stocks were kept low enough that the value of the goods available for plunder was lower than the payoff from trading on credit, middlemen would trade with producers rather than plunder them.

The pattern of historical references to producer-middleman credit agreements closely tracks the declining importance of slaves and rising importance of ivory, rubber, and wax from the 1840s and 1850s onward following the abolition of Angolan slave trading in 1836 and then slavery itself in 1858. In the first half of the nineteenth century, credit agreements are rarely mentioned.[19] In the second half of the century, however, they are common. This reflects the fact that, for reasons discussed above, the credit mechanism was not especially effective in preventing plunder by middlemen seeking slaves but was highly effective in preventing plunder by middlemen seeking other goods.

While my model considers the bilateral case, in actuality multiple caravans of middlemen interacted with multiple communities of producers.[20] The presence of multiple communities of producers and caravans introduced the possibility of one caravan plundering the goods harvested by producers to repay another caravan as part of a previous credit agreement. For two reasons, however, it seems unlikely that caravans could effectively pursue this strategy. First, for such theft to be effective, caravans would require specific knowledge of when the goods produced to repay other caravans were available for stealing before they had been collected.

Second, caravans had strong incentives to ensure that other crews of middlemen would not plunder the goods owed to them. The use of credit created a stake for middlemen in the well-being of producers. By indebting themselves to

---

[19] Where credit is mentioned, producers rather than middlemen were the creditors. See, for instance, Baptista (1873).

[20] For instance, Buchner refers to Mwant Yav's "business relations with a number of traders from the coastal areas" (Oppen 1994, p. 360 [translation of Buchner 1883, p. 62]).

middlemen, producers transformed their status in the eyes of these traders from targets of violence to productive assets. To produce the goods necessary to repay their debts, producers needed to be alive and well. It was therefore in the interest of middlemen to ensure the health and safety of those to whom they made loans. To protect their valued investments, middlemen had an incentive to abstain from using violence against producers who owed them goods and to deter other middlemen from using violence against these producers. One way they accomplished this was by punishing middlemen who wronged them. For instance, as Arnot (1889, p. 179) records in one case, "[T]hree Garganze caravans had been plundered and many men killed—one at Bihe, another in the Lovale country, the third in the Lunda country, but all at the instigation of Bihe chiefs and traders, who thought that they had been unjustly dealt with in certain business transactions they had with Msidi."

It is not clear whether certain caravans were able to establish monopoly control over some areas. Securing an effective monopoly would require a significant, lasting strength disparity between caravans such that potential competitors could be forcibly excluded from trade with particular villages. Such a disparity may have existed in some instances, but clearly did not in many others. A monopoly caravan would create quite unfavorable terms of trade for producers. In principle, monopoly middlemen could get away with paying producers just slightly more than their payoff of producing for subsistence and not trading on credit (producers' equilibrium payoff from Figure 1). Where competition was absent then, it would be reasonable to expect poor bargaining power among producers and near-subsistence wages. However, the historical record indicates that for some producers quite the opposite prevailed. As one traveler complained about the villagers he encountered, for example, "[T]he people being satiated with cloth, owing to their constant intercourse with the coast, would sell us nothing, or asked higher prices than we could afford" (Cameron 1877, p. 390).

4. Tribute as a Risk Premium

In communities where wealth was predominantly held in the form of humans (slaves) and livestock, producers were constrained in their ability to reduce the size of their thievable stocks. As long as stocks were not so large as to make banditry more profitable than trading on credit regardless of a caravan's discount rate, sufficiently patient caravans continued to find trading on credit the most profitable course of action. To see this, consider a community that, because it holds much of its wealth in the form of humans and livestock, cannot reduce its stock of goods as low as other communities that do not hold most of their wealth in these forms. The benefit of plundering this community is therefore higher, Ψ, where $\Psi > H_m$. Despite this, if $\Psi < E_m$, there exists some caravan that will continue to find the payoff from trading on credit (δE_m) to be greater than the payoff from plundering (Ψ). Specifically, where $H_m < \Psi < E_m$, caravans with discount rates that satisfy $\delta > \Psi/E_m$ will trade on credit.

However, caravans with discount rates where $\delta < \Psi/E_m$ will not. In fact, because $\Psi > H_m$, some caravans that would rather stay home than trade on credit with producers who can reduce their stock of thievable goods sufficiently would rather plunder producers who cannot do this than stay home. For these middlemen, banditry is the most profitable course of action in this case. Thus, while producers who could reduce their stocks sufficiently were safe from plunder and could trade with bandits, those who held their wealth in the form of humans and livestock could not. Sufficiently patient middlemen would trade with them on credit, but impatient ones would plunder them.

To overcome this problem, communities of vulnerable producers demanded tribute from traveling traders who approached them for exchange. Typically, village headmen[21] were the gatekeepers to producers and required middlemen to meet their tribute demands before trade relations could be consummated.[22] As the prominent middleman Antonio Francisco Ferreira da Silva Porto recorded, for example, tribute payment "'*was necessary to open the door!*' We tried to find the solution to this enigma and found out that it was necessary to give some pannos [yards of cloth—A.v.O.] to obtain permission for the people of the caravan and of the country to buy and sell provisions and other commodities, without which nothing could be done" (Silva Porto 1885, p. 580 [translation from Oppen 1994, p. 390]; see also Crawford 1914, p. 118; Harding 1905, p. 148).

The way tribute worked is straightforward. Let caravans of middlemen be heterogeneous in discount rates such that ρ is the proportion of caravans with discount rates that satisfy $\delta > \Psi/E_m$ and $1 - \rho$ is the proportion of caravans with discount rates that do not satisfy this inequality. Obviously, if a caravan of middlemen was excessively impatient and so intended to plunder a community, demanding tribute was worthless. The stronger caravan would simply overwhelm the community, refuse tribute payment, and go about violently stealing what it

[21] Tribute was sometimes kept and consumed by the chief, or headman, who received it. This did not, however, inhibit tribute's usefulness as compensation for the cost imposed on villagers by violent middlemen. Occasionally, local rulers would declare a monopoly right to trade with middlemen who approached them. In this event, tribute functioned as a premium offsetting the ruler's risk of trading with the outsider. In addition, tribute consumed by local leaders indirectly reached villagers in the form of public investments undertaken by the ruler, for which tribute was his pay. For instance, resolving community disputes (via arbitration) was a common duty of rulers, as was generally maintaining community order. Likewise, rulers could be charged with providing food in the event the community encountered hard times—a form of social insurance. Tribute collected and consumed by a chief functioned as payment for performing such public services, indirectly compensating community members for the risk posed by impatient middlemen.

[22] As noted previously, some chiefs, or headmen, had coercive power. When this power was greater than that of a visitor, he could use this to coerce tribute payment. More often than not, however, for reasons described above, it seems that this was not the case. Instead the power of chiefs was in (1) preventing access to their community. This was the case, for instance, if a river separated a chief's community and those desiring to visit it and the canoe was on the chief's side of the river (see, for instance, Cameron 1877, p. 266). The power of the chiefs was also in (2) refusing to furnish guides or assistants to visitors who did not know the area or how to safely get to the next village or who required additional protection when traveling between villages, and so on.

desired. For those caravans that were not too impatient, however, demanding tribute was effective.

These middlemen found peaceful exchange more profitable than plunder and were therefore willing to pay for the opportunity to trade. Where producers cannot reduce their stocks sufficiently and the resulting benefit from plunder is Ψ, their expected payoff of producing for subsistence and trading on credit is given by $\rho(E_p) + (1 - \rho)(-h_p)$, which is greater than producers' expected payoff of producing for subsistence and not trading on credit for any $\rho > 0$. Sufficiently patient middlemen earn $\delta E_m > \Psi$ when producers agree to trade on credit and Ψ when they do not. This being the case, producers could demand tribute T from sufficiently patient middlemen in order to exchange with them on credit, where $T \leq \delta E_m - \Psi$, and these middlemen would pay this (in addition to those others cited here, see, for instance, Arnot 1889, pp. 71, 80, 102, 135, 136, 137, 151, 159, 204; 1893, p. 26; Harding 1905, pp. 81, 95–96, 142, 148, 290; Serpa Pinto 1881, 1:67–68, 1:90, 1:175, 1:228–29; Graca 1890; Johnston 1893, p. 111; Capello and Ivens 1969, 1:87, 1:116–17, 1:137–38; Livingstone 1963, 1:9, 1:33, 1:98; Cameron 1877, p. 77).[23] Thus, "it is not surprising that tribute is paid to the [every] village headman where one sets up the camp" (Silva Porto 1885, p. 577; translation from Oppen 1994).

Tribute demands acted as a risk premium charged by communities of vulnerable producers. They helped to protect producers against the risk of interacting with traveling traders who, as a general class, consisted of some patient and some impatient members. In particular, tribute acted as a tax on patient middlemen that was used to subsidize the banditry of violent impatient middlemen. By taxing middlemen who expressed a desire to exchange, producers were able to extract compensation from patient middlemen (who traded with them) to cover losses imposed by impatient ones (who plundered them).[24] This helps to explain François Coillard's (1897, p. 611) remark about the Luvale chief—Chief Kakenge—when he noted the "homage or rather a tax he exacts from black Portuguese traders who enter his country."

Often, although not always, tribute took two forms: goods that producers consumed immediately or shortly after receiving them, for instance, an ox that would be slaughtered and eaten right away, alcohol, or tobacco; or European novelties (for example, a watch) that were not sought by middlemen to bring

[23] It should also be noted that as the proportion of impatient caravans in the population increases, the credibility of producers' threat to not trade on credit with those who refuse to pay tribute increases as well. As $\rho \to 0$, the gains producers forgo by adhering to this strategy fall.

[24] Where the total population of middlemen is θ, producers generate $\rho\theta T$ in revenue from demanding tribute, which is used to help offset losses in the amount $(1 - \rho)\theta(-h_p)$. To completely offset the losses imposed by impatient middlemen, $T = -[(1 - \rho)(-h_p)]/\rho$. As already noted, however, the amount producers could demand in tribute was bound at the upper limit by $\delta E_m - \Psi$. Whether or not full compensation was possible therefore depended on how much greater the payoff of trade was over the payoff of plunder for patient middlemen (which in turn depends on how patient patient middlemen are), the proportion of impatient middlemen in the population, and the value of the stock lost in the event of plunder (which, of course, depends on the extent to which producers are able to reduce their stocks).

to coastal European traders for export. The reason for this is clear—to avoid tribute payments contributing to vulnerable communities' stocks of thievable goods. If tribute was either consumed quickly or consisted of goods middlemen were not looking for, producers did not need to fear losing it to banditry by a violent caravan.[25]

Key to its usefulness as a risk premium, tribute also needed to constitute a net gain to recipient producers. This ruled out the possibility of present recip-rocation, as was practiced in gift exchange arrangements between some villages.[26] Thus, although communities of producers often offered traveling traders food or temporary shelter after receiving tribute, these "gifts" were worth substantially less than those they demanded (Miller 1970, p. 193), which left a large effective premium in place. Noting this value discrepancy, Livingstone, for instance, com-plained, "[T]he Negroes do not seem to have the smallest idea of presents being reciprocal" (1963, p. 253; see also, Harding 1905, pp. 192, 290).

5. Conclusion

My analysis leads to three conclusions. First, individuals can in fact trade with bandits. Conventional wisdom underestimates the market's power to solve the problem of violent theft. Even in the extreme case where weak individuals cannot use multilateral punishment or invest in additional strength to fend off stronger ones, the absence of state policing need not bring exchange activities to a halt. While the potential for violent theft poses a significant threat to the ability of individuals to realize the gains from trade, the benefits of preventing this threat from becoming a reality compel agents to develop informal solutions to the problem of banditry. By altering the cost-benefit structure of trade versus vio-lence, these solutions have in common the fact that they transform stronger agents' incentive from plunder to peaceful exchange.

Second, although credit is often the cause of commitment problems involving peaceful theft, it serves as a solution to the problem of violent theft where one party to an interaction is stronger and more mobile than the other. By minimizing stocks of desired goods and trading on credit, vulnerable parties simultaneously reduce the benefit of violent theft by stronger individuals who are tempted to take advantage of their superior strength and increase the benefit of exchange.

Third, to the extent that some stronger individuals are prone to use force to

---

[25] The fact that thievable goods were sometimes demanded as tribute is attributable to two possible factors. On the one hand, this may reflect that some communities of producers assigned a relatively low probability to being plundered by a caravan of violent middlemen. On the other hand, even though the tribute a community received—say, a slave—would ultimately be stolen by a violent caravan, in the time between when the community received it and the time it was stolen, the employment of the slave yielded some benefit to the community. If the slave were needed enough, this benefit could outweigh the benefit of a nonthievable tribute, even though its employment would not be permanent. In this case, the slave would be preferred as tribute to say, an ox, even though the former was at risk for theft while the latter was not.

[26] For an excellent analysis of the gift exchange system see Landa (1994).

obtain the goods they desire and others are inclined to trade (owing to a difference in discount rates), agents who are part of a weaker group may be able to protect themselves against the risk of interacting with members of a stronger group by demanding a premium from them in order to exchange. Although permanently weak agents cannot refuse to interact with stronger individuals who want what they have, weak individuals can refuse to exchange on credit with stronger individuals because the goods in question do not yet exist. Members of the stronger group who are inclined to trade rather than plunder will therefore pay this premium when it is required for them to enable exchange. This premium helps to offset the losses experienced by members of the weaker group when they interact with members of the stronger group who are prone to use force to obtain what they desire. By compensating vulnerable agents for the risk of interacting with unknown members of the stronger group, this premium makes exchange possible despite the risk inherent for permanently weaker agents.

References

Anderson, Terry, and Peter J. Hill. 2004. *The Not So Wild, Wild West.* Stanford, Calif.: Stanford University Press.

Anderson, Terry, and Fred McChesney. 1994. Trade or Raid? An Economic Model of Indian-White Relations. *Journal of Law and Economics* 37:39–74.

———. 2002. *Property Rights: Cooperation, Conflict and Law.* Princeton, N.J.: Princeton University Press.

Arnot, Frederick S. 1889. *Garenganze; or, Seven Years' Pioneer Mission Work in Central Africa.* London: James E. Hawkins.

———. 1893. *Bihe and Garenganze; or Four Years' Further Work and Travel in Central Africa.* London: James E. Hawkins.

Baptista, Pedro Joao. 1873. Journey of the "Pombeiros." Pp. 165–244 in *Lacerda's Journey to Cazembe, and Journey of Pombeiros, etc.,* edited by Richard F. Burton. London: John Murray.

Bates, Robert, Avner Greif, and Smita Singh. 2002. Organizing Violence. *Journal of Conflict Resolution* 46:599–628.

Bauer, Peter T. 1954. *West African Trade.* Cambridge: Cambridge University Press.

Botelho de Vasconcellos, Alexandre Jose. [1844] 1873. *Annaes maritimos e coloniais.* Pp. 24–25 in *Lacerda's Journey to Cazembe, and Journey of Pombeiros, etc.,* edited by Richard F. Burton. London: John Murray.

Buchner, Max. 1883. Das Reich des Mwata Yamvo und seine Nachbarlander. *Deutsche Geographische Blatter* 1:56–67.

Bush, Winston, and Lawrence Mayer. 1974. Some Implications of Anarchy for the Distribution of Property Rights. *Journal of Economic Theory* 8:401–12.

Cameron, Verney Lovett. 1877. *Across Africa.* New York: Harper & Brothers Publishers.

Capello, Hermengildo, and Roberto Ivens. 1969. *From Benguella to the Territory of Yacca,* translated by Alfred Elwes. 2 vols. New York: Negro Universities Press.

Clay, Karen. 1997. Trade without Law: Private Order Institutions in Mexican California. *Journal of Law, Economics, and Organization* 13:202–31.

Coillard, François. 1897. *On the Threshold of Central Africa,* translated by Catherine Mackintosh. London: Hodder & Stoughton.

Crawford, David. 1914. *Thinking Black: Twenty-two Years without a Break in the Long Grass of Central Africa.* London: Morgan & Scott.

Dias de Carvalho, Henrique Augusto. 1890. *Ethnographia e historia tradicional dos povos da Lunda.* Vol. 5 of *Expedicao portugueza ao Muatianvua.* Lisboa: Imprensa Nacional.

Gibbons, Alfred St. Hill. 1904. *Africa from South to North through Marotseland.* 2 vols. London: John Lane.

Graca, Joaquim. 1890. Expedicao ao Muatayanvua. Diario de Joaquim Rodrigues Graca. *Boletim da Sociedade de Geographia de Lisboa* 9a ser., 8:365–468.

Greif, Avner. 1989. Reputation and Coalitions in Medieval Trade: Evidence on the Maghribi Traders. *Journal of Economic History* 49:857–82.

———. 1993. Contract Enforceability and Economic Institutions in Early Trade: The Maghribi Traders' Coalition. *American Economic Review* 83:525–48.

Greif, Avner, Paul Milgrom, and Barry Weingast. 1994. Coordination, Commitment, and Enforcement: The Case of the Merchant Guild. *Journal of Political Economy* 102:745–76.

Grossman, Herschel. 1998. Producers and Predators. *Pacific Economic Review* 3:169–87.

Grossman, Herschel, and Minseong Kim. 2002. Predation, Efficiency and Inequality. *Journal of Institutional and Theoretical Economics* 127:393–407.

Harding, Colin. 1905. *In Remotest Barotseland.* London: Hurst & Blackett.

Hart, Oliver, and John Moore. 1988. Incomplete Contracts and Renegotiation. *Econometrica* 56:755–85.

Hausken, Kjell. 2004. Mutual Raiding of Production and the Emergence of Exchange. *Economic Inquiry* 42:572–86.

Hirshleifer, Jack. 1988. The Analytics of Continuing Conflict. *Synthese* 76:201–33.

———. 1995. Anarchy and Its Breakdown. *Journal of Political Economy* 103:26–52.

———. 2001. *The Dark Side of the Force.* New York: Cambridge University Press.

Johnston, James. 1893. *Reality versus Romance in South Central Africa.* London: Hodder & Stoughton.

Klein, Benjamin, Robert Crawford, and Armen Alchian. 1978. Vertical Integration, Appropriable Rents, and the Competitive Contracting Process. *Journal of Law and Economics* 21:297–326.

Kranton, Rachel. 1996. Reciprocal Exchange: A Self-Sustaining System. *American Economic Review* 86:830–51.

Landa, Janet. 1994. *Trust, Ethnicity, and Identity.* Ann Arbor: University of Michigan Press.

Leeson, Peter T. 2006. Cooperation and Conflict: Evidence on Self-Enforcing Arrangements and Heterogeneous Groups. *American Journal of Economics and Sociology.* 64: 891–907.

Livingstone, David. 1857. *Missionary Travels and Researches in South Africa.* London: John Murray.

———. 1874. *The Last Journals of David Livingstone in Central Africa,* edited by Horace Waller. 2 vols. London: John Murray.

———. 1960. *Livingstone's Private Journals, 1851–1853,* edited by Isaac Schapera. London: Chatto & Windus.

———. 1963. *Livingstone's African Journal, 1853–1856,* edited by Isaac Schapera. 2 vols. London: Chatto & Windus.

McGuire, Martin, and Mancur Olson. 1996. The Economics of Autocracy and Majority Rule: The Invisible Hand and the Use of Force. *Journal of Economic Literature* 34:72–96.

Milgrom, Paul, Douglass North, and Barry Weingast. 1990. The Role of Institutions in the Revival of Trade: The Medieval Law Merchant, Private Judges, and the Champagne Fairs. *Economics and Politics* 1:1–23.

Miller, Joseph. 1970. Cokwe Trade and Conquest in the Nineteenth Century. Pp. 175–201 in *Pre-Colonial African Trade*, edited by Richard Gray and David Birmingham. London: Oxford University Press.

———. 1988. *Way of Death.* Madison: University of Wisconsin Press.

Neary, Hugh. 1997. Equilibrium Structure in an Economic Model of Conflict. *Economic Inquiry* 35:480–94.

Olson, Mancur. 1993. Dictatorship, Democracy, and Development. *American Political Science Review* 87:567–76.

Oppen, Achim von. 1994. *Terms of Trade and Terms of Trust.* Hamburg: Lit Verlag.

Pogge, Paul. 1880. *Im Reich des Muata-Jamvo.* Berlin: Reimer.

Schelling, Thomas. 1960. *The Strategy of Conflict.* Cambridge, Mass.: Harvard University Press.

Serpa Pinto, Alexandre de. 1881. *How I Crossed Africa,* translated by Alfred Alwes. 2 vols. Philadelphia: J. B. Lippencott & Co.

Silva Porto, Antonio Francisco Ferreira da. 1885. Novas jornadas de Silva Porto nos sertoes africanos. *Boletim da Sociedade de Geographia e da Historia de Lisboa* 5a ser., 1:3–36, 3:145–72, 9:569–86, 10:603–42.

Skaperdas, Stergios. 1992. Cooperation, Conflict, and Power in the Absence of Property Rights. *American Economic Review* 82:720–39.

———. 2003. Restraining the Genuine *Homo Economicus*: Why the Economy Cannot Be Divorced from Its Governance. *Economics and Politics* 15:135–62.

Skaperdas, Stergios, and Constantinos Syropoulos. 1997. The Distribution of Income in the Presence of Appropriative Activities. *Economica* 64:101–17.

Smith, Adam. [1776] 1965. *An Inquiry into the Nature and Causes of the Wealth of Nations,* edited by Edwin Cannan. New York: Modern Library.

Soremekun, Fola. 1977. Trade and Dependency in Central Angola: The Ovimbundu in the Nineteenth Century. Pp. 82–95 in *The Roots of Rural Poverty in Central and Southern Africa,* edited by Robin Palmer and Neil Parsons. London: Heinemann.

Umbeck, John. 1981. Might Makes Rights: A Theory of the Formation and Initial Distribution of Property Rights. *Economic Inquiry* 19:38–59.

Vellut, Jean-Luc. 1979. Diversification de l'economie de cueillette miel et cire dans les societes de la foret Claire d'Afrique centrale (c. 1750–1950). *African Economic History* 7:93–112.

Williamson, Oliver. 1975. *Markets and Hierarchies: Analysis and Antitrust Implications.* New York: Free Press.

———. 1985. *The Economic Institutions of Capitalism.* New York: Free Press.

Zerbe, Richard O., and Leigh Anderson. 2001. Culture and Fairness in the Development of Institutions in the California Gold Fields. *Journal of Economic History* 10:114–43.

[23]

An-*arrgh*-chy: The Law and Economics of Pirate Organization

Peter T. Leeson

George Mason University

This article investigates the internal governance institutions of violent criminal enterprise by examining the law, economics, and organization of pirates. To effectively organize their banditry, pirates required mechanisms to prevent internal predation, minimize crew conflict, and maximize piratical profit. Pirates devised two institutions for this purpose. First, I analyze the system of piratical checks and balances crews used to constrain captain predation. Second, I examine how pirates used democratic constitutions to minimize conflict and create piratical law and order. Pirate governance created sufficient order and cooperation to make pirates one of the most sophisticated and successful criminal organizations in history.

> Nature, we see, teaches the most Illiterate the necessary Prudence for their Preservation . . . these Men whom we term, and not without Reason, the Scandal of human Nature, who were abandoned to all Vice, and lived by Rapine; when they judged it for their Interest . . . were strictly just . . . among themselves. (Captain Charles Johnson 1726–28, 527)

I am especially grateful to Steven Levitt and two anonymous referees for thorough and insightful comments on an earlier draft of this paper. I also thank Pete Boettke, Tyler Cowen, Chris Coyne, Josh Hill, Bill Reece, Andrei Shleifer, Russell S. Sobel, Werner Troesken, and William Trumbull for helpful comments and suggestions. The financial support of the Kendrick Fund and the Kaplan Fund is also gratefully acknowledged.

[*Journal of Political Economy*, 2007, vol. 115, no. 6]

I. Introduction

Pirates are known for raucousness, recklessness, and chaotic rapine. Pirate reality, however, is quite another picture. Real-life pirates were highly organized criminals. Unlike the swashbuckling psychopaths of fiction, historical pirates displayed sophisticated organization and coordination.

Pirates could not use government to enforce or otherwise support cooperative arrangements between them. Despite this, they successfully cooperated with hundreds of other rogues. Amidst ubiquitous potential for conflict, they rarely fought, stole from, or deceived one another. In fact, piratical harmony was as common as harmony among their lawful contemporaries who relied on government for social cooperation. How did "these men whom we term . . . the Scandal of human Nature, who were abandoned to all Vice, and lived by Rapine" (Johnson [1726–28] 1999, 527)[1] accomplish this impressive level of order?

Becker (1968) was the first to apply the logic of rational-choice decision making to criminals. Following him, a number of others extended this logic to decision making in the context of organized outlaws. Fiorentini and Peltzman (1995) provide the best and most comprehensive collection of essays that consider the economics of criminal organization. In addition, a large literature discusses the economic impact of organized crime, activities of criminal organizations, optimal strategies for preventing organized crime, and reasons for its emergence (see also, e.g., Anderson 1979; Reuter 1983, 1987; Jennings 1984; Arlacchi 1986; Jankowski 1991; Dick 1995; Konrad and Skaperdas 1998; Garoupa 2000; Skaperdas 2001; Chang, Lu, and Chen 2005).

Unlike these topics, the internal governance institutions of violent criminal organizations have received relatively little attention.[2] The difficulty of "getting inside" criminal organizations is largely responsible for this. Levitt and Venkatesh's important work on street gangs (Levitt and Venkatesh 2000; Venkatesh and Levitt 2000) is an exception to this rule, as are Gambetta's (1993) and Reuter's (1983) superb studies of the Mafia. However, Levitt and Venkatesh focus on the financial organization of gangs rather than on their governance structures. Gambetta's and Reuter's studies are primarily concerned with the Mafia's provision of protection to outsiders and the organization of the illegal markets it serves.

---

[1] All page references to Johnson refer to the 1999 reprint. Page references to other early sources also refer to reprint editions if available.

[2] Anderson (1979), Reuter (1983), and Gambetta (1993) are the closest exceptions in this regard. Their excellent work considers some internal governance aspects of the Mafia but tends to focus primarily on the Mafia's relationship to protection and other markets. Important research by Polo (1995) examines governance institutions of criminal organizations, but does so theoretically.

This article investigates the internal governance institutions of violent criminal enterprise by examining the law, economics, and organization of pirates.[3] These "most treacherous rogues" terrorized the Caribbean, Atlantic Ocean, and Indian Ocean during the seventeenth and eighteenth centuries. Pirates formed a loose confederation of maritime bandits outside the law of any government.

To effectively organize their banditry, pirates required mechanisms to prevent internal predation, minimize crew conflict, and maximize piratical profit. I argue that pirates devised two institutions for this purpose. First, I analyze the system of piratical checks and balances that crews used to constrain captain predation. Second, I examine how pirates used democratic constitutions to minimize conflict and create piratical law and order. Pirates adopted both of these institutions before seventeenth- and eighteenth-century governments.

Their governance institutions were self-enforcing by necessity. Appealing to the formal enforcement mechanisms of the state is not an option for criminal organizations, including pirates. Although the maritime nature of piratical expeditions makes certain aspects of their internal organization and governance specific to pirates, my analysis highlights important problems that any form of organized criminal enterprise faces, as well as the institutional solutions such organizations employ to overcome these problems.

The literature that addresses the economics of organized crime focuses on the criminal organization as a supplier of some service, usually protection, to other actors inside and outside the criminal world. Schelling (1971), for instance, who was among the first to conduct this research, identifies the provision of enforcement services to other agents and, in line with this function, a monopoly on coercion as the distinguishing features of organized crime.

While this definition is perhaps appropriate for the Mafia, it neglects equally important organized criminal activities that do not provide useful services to others and do not involve a monopoly on coercion. An army of thieves, for instance, that coordinates its activities, requires internal mechanisms of governance, and combines in a long-term arrangement for concerted plunder is as much a criminal organization as the Mafia.

Pirates were clearly organized criminals and yet were not primarily in the business of providing services to anyone other than their members.[4] Nor did they have a monopoly on force. Because of this, unlike

---

[3] This article is also closely connected to the literature that examines the private emergence of law and governance institutions. See, e.g., Friedman (1979), Benson (1988, 1989, 1990), Anderson and McChesney (2002), Anderson and Hill (2004), Anderson, Benson, and Flanagan (2006), and Leeson (2007a, 2007b, forthcoming).

[4] However, pirates did trade with European colonists.

most discussions of criminal organization, mine takes a broader view of organized crime. This view encompasses any long-term arrangement between multiple criminals that requires coordination and involves agreements that, owing to their illicit status, cannot be enforced by the state.[5] The emphasis of my analysis therefore shifts from the organization of criminal markets (the focus of existing research on the economics of organized crime) to the internal predation problem that criminal organizations face and the institutions that emerge in response to it.

To examine these features for pirates, I draw on a series of historical documents that provide a firsthand glimpse into their organization. The first of these is Captain Charles Johnson's *General History of the Pyrates* (1726–28), which contains reports on a number of history's most infamous pirates related by a pirate contemporary.[6] I also draw on Alexander Exquemelin's (1678) invaluable account of the seventeenth-century buccaneers. Exquemelin was a surgeon who sailed with the buccaneers and provides a detailed, firsthand account of their raids, system of rules, and social organization. The buccaneer William Dampier (1697–1707) also published a journal relating to his maritime exploits, which I make use of as well.

Buccaneers differ from "pure" pirates in that they frequently plundered ships with government sanction. However, many other times they plundered without official permission, as full-blown pirates. These protopirates, many of whom turned to pure piracy when governments stopped issuing licenses for plunder, influenced and anticipated the organization of pure pirates in the late seventeenth and early eighteenth centuries. Buccaneer records are therefore important for understanding the institutions and organization of seventeenth- and eighteenth-century pirates.

In addition to these sources, correspondence from colonial governors relating to piracy and records from the trials of various pirates, such as testimony from individuals taken prisoner by pirate ships and the tes-

---

[5] My definition of a criminal organization is therefore similar to Polo's as "one that cannot rely on the external enforcement of the judicial institutions and whose behaviour and possibilities are not constrained by the law" (1995, 87).

[6] "Captain Johnson" is a pen name used by the author of *A General History of the Pyrates*. His true identity remains unknown. In 1932, John R. Moore claimed that Johnson was in fact Daniel Defoe. In the late 1980s, however, this view was overturned (see Furbank and Owens 1988), and today many pirate historians do not believe that Defoe is the author of this important book (see, e.g., Rediker 2004; Cordingly 2006; Woodard 2007; for the opposing view, see Rogozinski 2000). Whatever Johnson's true identity, it is agreed that he "had extensive first-hand knowledge of piracy" (Konstam 2007, 12). While it is widely acknowledged that Johnson's work contains some errors and apocryphal accounts (such as the community of Libertalia), "Johnson is widely regarded as a highly reliable source for factual information" on pirates (Rediker 2004, 180) and remains a definitive source historians rely on in constructing their accounts of seventeenth- and eighteenth-century piracy. As eminent pirate historian David Cordingly puts it, this book "is the prime source for the lives of many pirates of what is often called the Golden Age of Piracy" (2006, xx).

timony of pirates themselves, form an important part of the historical record this article relies on.[7] Finally, a few pirate captives, such as William Snelgrave (1734), whose captors ultimately released them, published longer works describing their harrowing captivity by pirate crews.[8] I also draw on these accounts, which provide important firsthand records describing piratical governance and organization.[9]

II.   A "Nest of Rogues"

Seventeenth- and eighteenth-century pirates occupied the waterways that formed major trading routes.[10] These included the waters surrounding the Bahamas that stood between ships traveling from Central America to Spain; the waters connecting Europe and the North American seacoast; those between Cuba and Haiti, which separated ships traveling from Europe and the west coast of Africa to Jamaica; and the waters around Madagascar traveled by ships sailing to and from India (Cordingly 2006, 88). These areas encompass major portions of the Atlantic and Indian Oceans, Caribbean Sea, and Gulf of Mexico. The trade routes connecting the Caribbean, North America's Atlantic seacoast, and Madagascar consequently formed a loop called the "pirate round" that many pirates traveled in search of prey.

The "golden age" of piracy, when pirates were at their strongest, extended from 1690 to 1730 (Konstam 2002, 94).[11] The years from 1716 to 1722 mark the height of the golden age. "This was at a Time that the Pyrates had obtained such an Acquisition of Strength, that they were in no Concern about preserving themselves from the Justice of Laws" (Johnson 1726–28, 87). The pirates of this era include many well-known

---

[7] Jameson (1923) has edited an excellent collection of such records. Unless otherwise noted, all depositions and examinations quoted here are contained in his collection.

[8] Importantly, drawing on the historical episode of pirates helps overcome the problem of "getting inside" criminal organizations, noted above. Records from individuals who had direct experiences with pirates, as well as those that shed light on piratical governance mechanisms from pirates themselves, allow me to view pirates' criminal organization "from the inside."

[9] Additionally, this article relies on and is greatly indebted to a voluminous modern literature covering all aspects of piracy, including those considered here, written by contemporary historians. Some of the best discussions belong to Gosse (1946), Pringle (1953), Rankin (1969), Rediker (1981, 1987), Cordingly (1996, 2006), Rogozinski (2000), and Konstam (2002).

[10] The "nest of rogues" terminology in this section's heading comes from Governor William Spotswood, who, in a letter to the British Lords of the Admiralty, complained of the growing pirate problem in New Providence (July 3, 1716 [1882, 2:168]).

[11] The dates given by historians to mark the golden age of piracy vary. Cordingly (2006) provides a slightly larger range, from about 1650 to 1725. Still others, such as Rankin (1969), date the great age of piracy as encompassing the years between 1630 and 1720. The further back in this range one goes, the more one is dealing with buccaneers as opposed to pure pirates.

sea robbers, such as Blackbeard, whose real name was Edward Teach, Bartholomew Roberts, and others.

Pirates were a diverse lot.[12] A sample of 700 pirates active in the Caribbean between 1715 and 1725, for example, reveals that 35 percent were English, 25 percent were American, 20 percent were West Indian, 10 percent were Scottish, 8 percent were Welsh, and 2 percent were Swedish, Dutch, French, and Spanish (Konstam 2002, 9). Others came from Portugal, Scandinavia, Greece, and East India (Marx 1996*b*, 103).

Pirate crews were also racially diverse. Based on data available from 23 pirate crews active between 1682 and 1726, the racial composition of ships varied between 13 and 98 percent black. If this sample is representative, 25–30 percent of the average pirate crew was of African descent (Kinkor 2001, 200–201).

The pirate population is difficult to precisely measure but by all accounts was considerable.[13] According to the reports of contemporaries and estimates of pirate historians, in any one year between 1716 and 1722 the loop that formed the pirate round contained between 1,000 and 2,000 sea bandits (see, e.g., Johnson 1726–28, 132; Pringle 1953, 185; Rediker 1987, 256; Marx 1996*b*, 102, 111; Konstam 2002, 6).[14] The buccaneering community of the seventeenth century must have been even larger than this since, as I discuss below, some firsthand observers report single expeditions of 2,000 men (Exquemelin [1678] 2000, 171).

Contrary to most people's images of pirate crews, they were quite large. On the basis of figures from 37 pirate ships between 1716 and 1726, it appears that the average crew had about 80 members (Rediker 1987, 256; see also Deposition of Simon Calderon 1682, Public Record Office, Colonial Office Papers 1:50, no. 139). A number of

---

[12] Pirates also exhibited some diversity in social standing. Although most pirates were uneducated and came from the lower classes of society, a few, such as Dr. John Hincher, were well educated and came from higher stations in life (Cordingly 2006).

[13] Pure pirates should be distinguished from buccaneers, privateers, and corsairs. Pure pirates were total outlaws and attacked merchant ships indiscriminately for their own gain. Privateers and corsairs, in contrast, were both state-sanctioned sea robbers. Governments licensed the former to attack enemy ships in times of war. Governments licensed the latter to attack the ships of other nations on the basis of religion. "Buccaneering was a peculiar blend of piracy and privateering in which the two elements were often indistinguishable" (Marx 1996*a*, 38). Oftentimes, buccaneers plundered with official sanction, making them more like privateers than pirates. Many other times, however, they did not. In these cases they were acting as pure pirates.

[14] These numbers are especially large when one puts them in historical perspective. The Royal Navy, e.g., averaged only 13,000 men in any one year between 1716 and 1726, making the pirate population in a good year more than 15 percent of the navy population (Rediker 1987, 256). In 1680, the total population of the American colonies was less than 152,000 (Hughes and Cain 1994, 20). In fact, as late as 1790, when the first U.S. census was taken, only 24 places in the country had populations greater than 2,500 (Hughes and Cain 1994, 28).

pirate crews were closer to 120, and crews of 150–200 were not uncommon (see, e.g., Snelgrave [1734] 1971, 199; Examination of John
Brown, May 6, 1717, Suffolk Court Files, no. 11945, paper 5; Deposition of Theophilus Turner, June 8, 1699, Public Record Office,
Colonial Office Papers 5:714, no. 70 VI; Examination of John Dann,
August 3, 1696, London, Public Record Office, Colonial Office Papers 323:2, no. 25; Deposition of Adam Baldridge, May 5, 1699, Public
Record Office, Colonial Office Papers 5:1042, no. 30 II; Johnson
1726–28, 442; Cordingly 2006, 165).

Several pirate crews were bigger than this. For example, Blackbeard's
crew aboard the *Queen Anne's Revenge* was 300 men strong (Public Record
Office, Colonial Office Papers 152/12, no. 67, iii; quoted in Cordingly
2006, 165–66; see also Marx 1996*b*, 112). Even a sixth-rate Royal Navy
ship in the early eighteenth century carried more crew members than
the average pirate vessel (about 150). But compared to the average 200-
ton merchant ship, which carried only 13–17 men, pirate ships were
extremely large (Rediker 1987, 107). Furthermore, some pirate crews
were too large to fit in one ship. In this case they formed pirate squad-
rons. Captain Bartholomew Roberts, for example, commanded a squad-
ron of four ships that carried 508 men (Cordingly 2006, 111).

In addition to this, multiple pirate ships sometimes joined for concerted plundering expeditions. The most impressive fleets of sea bandits
belong to the buccaneers. Alexander Exquemelin, for example, records
that Captain Morgan commanded a fleet of 37 ships and 2,000 men
sufficient to attack coastal communities on the Spanish Main (1678,
171). Elsewhere, he refers to a group of buccaneers who "had a force
of at least twenty vessels in quest of plunder" (69; see also 85, 105, 93).
Similarly, William Dampier ([1697–1707] 2005, 62) records a pirating
expedition that boasted 10 ships and 960 men.[15] Though their fleets
were not as massive, eighteenth-century pirates also "cheerfully joined
their Brethren in Iniquity" to engage in multicrew pirating expeditions
(Snelgrave 1734, 198).

III.   Merchant Ship Organization

A.   *Efficient Autocracy*

Although some pirates came from the Royal Navy, most sailors who
entered piracy came from the merchant marine. Merchant ships were

---

[15] In the South China Sea, Cheng I commanded a pirate confederacy that boasted an
astonishing 150,000 members (Konstam 2002, 174). Chinese pirates sometimes sailed
together in fleets of several hundred ships.

organized hierarchically.[16] On top was the captain, below him were his officers, and far below these were ordinary seamen. This hierarchy empowered captains with autocratic authority over their crews. The captain's authority gave him control over all aspects of life aboard his ship, including provision of victuals, wage payment, labor assignment, and, of course, crew member discipline.

Merchant ship autocracy reflected an efficient institutional response to the specific economic situation these ships confronted and, in particular, the ownership structure of merchant vessels. Merchant ships were owned by groups of typically a dozen or more landed merchants who purchased shares in various trading vessels and financed their voyages.[17] In addition to supplying the capital required for ships' construction and continued maintenance, owners outfitted their vessels, supplied them with provisions, advanced sailor wages, and, most important, solicited customers (who were other landed merchants) and negotiated terms of delivery and freight.

Merchant ship owners were absentee owners of their vessels; they did not sail on their ships.[18] They were landlubbers. Most merchant ship owners did not desire to take their chances with brutal life at sea, and in any event could earn more by specializing in their area of expertise—investment and commercial organization—hiring seamen to sail their ships instead.[19]

Because they were absentee owners, merchant ship owners confronted a principal-agent problem with respect to the crews they hired. Once a ship left port it could be gone for months.[20] At sea, the owners' ship was beyond their watchful eyes or reach. Thus, ship owners could not directly monitor their sailors.

This situation invited various kinds of sailor opportunism. Opportun-

---

[16] Navy ships were also organized hierarchically. Their captains were commissioned by the Admiralty (typically on the recommendation of superior commissioned officers) and had command over crew activities, power to physically punish sailors (or to direct/authorize lower-ranking officers to do so), etc. Captains of larger naval ships did not, however, have control over victuals, which were instead controlled by a warrant officer called the "purser." The purser's logs, which documented victuals distributed, were often approved by the captain.

[17] Ownership groups were sizable because of the need to diversify the risk of merchant shipping. Each merchant purchased a small share in many ships rather than being the sole owner of one.

[18] Because most merchant ships were owned by groups of investors, even in cases in which a merchant captained his vessel himself, there remained absentee owners, his co-investors.

[19] Absentee ownership was further assured by the fact that the members of merchant vessel ownership groups engaged in many more commercial activities besides their concern in a particular merchant ship. These other commercial activities often required merchants to be on land to tend to their affairs rather than at sea.

[20] Although merchant ships engaged in coastal trade were at sea for shorter periods, merchant ships engaged in long-distance trade could be gone for periods of nine months or more.

ism included negligence in caring for the ship, carelessness that damaged cargo, liberality with provisions, embezzlement of freight or advances required to finance the vessel's voyage, and outright theft of the vessel itself.

To prevent this, ship owners appointed captains to their vessels to monitor crews in their stead. Centralizing power in a captain's hands to direct sailors' tasks, control the distribution of victuals and payment, and discipline and punish crew members allowed merchant ship owners to minimize sailor opportunism. As noted above, merchant ships tended to be quite small. Consequently, captains could cheaply monitor sailors' behavior to prevent activities (or inactivities) that were costly to ship owners and secure sailors' full effort.[21]

Admiralty law facilitated captains' ability to do this by granting them authority to control their crews' behavior through corporal punishment. The law empowered captains to beat crew members with the infamous (and ominous) cat-o-nine-tails, imprison them, and administer other forms of harsh physical "correction" to sailors who disobeyed orders, shirked in their duties, and so forth. It also permitted captains to dock sailors' wages for damaging or stealing cargo and insubordination.

To align owner-captain interests, owners used two devices. First, they hired captains who held small shares in the vessels they were commanding or, barring this, gave small shares to their captains who did not. Merchant ship captains continued to draw regular fixed wages like the other sailors on their vessels.[22] But unlike regular sailors, captains became partial residual claimants of the ships they controlled, aligning their interests with those of the absentee owners.[23] Second, whenever

---

[21] In addition to using autocratic captains to cope with this principal-agent problem, merchant ships also held back a portion (or sometimes all) of sailors' wages until a voyage was complete.

[22] A few merchant ships engaged in part-time fishing used a share system of payment similar to the one privateers, whalers, and pirates used. However, the overwhelming majority of merchant ships used a fixed wage system. In vessels engaged in coastal shipping, sailors were paid lump-sum wages. In vessels engaged in long-distance shipping, sailors were paid monthly wages.

[23] The owner-sailor principal-agent problem could not have been overcome by converting every crew member's fixed wage to a profit-sharing scheme. Even under profit sharing, sailors would still have an incentive to consume cargo, liberal provisions, etc., and then blame the loss on the uncertainties of the sea, such as pirates or wrecks. Although this opportunism would reduce each sailor's share of the voyage's net proceeds, since the cost of such behavior is borne partially by the absentee owners, sailors have an incentive to act opportunistically. Further, converting sailor wages to shares would not have deterred the crew from the most costly kind of opportunism—absconding with the ship and its freight. Because the benefit of such theft would exceed the crew's fraction of a successful voyage's proceeds, which are shared with the absentee owners under a profit-sharing scheme, without an authority to monitor and control their behavior, crews would still have an incentive to steal the ships they sailed on. This is why both privateers and whaling ships, e.g., which used a pirate-like profit-sharing system but also had absentee owners, still required and used autocratic captains. On the efficiency of the fixed wage system for

possible, absentee owners appointed captains with familial connections to one of the members of their group (Davis 1962, 128). This ensured that captains did not behave opportunistically at the absentee owners' expense since, if they did, they were more likely to face punishment.[24]

The reason merchant ship owners required *autocratic* captains to effectively serve their interests is straightforward. A captain who did not have total authority over his crew could not successfully monitor and control sailors' behavior. Reducing the captain's power over victuals, payments, labor assignment, or discipline, and vesting it in some other sailor's hands instead, would have concomitantly reduced the captain's power to make sailors behave in the absentee owners' interest.

Similarly, if merchant ship owners did not appoint their captains as the permanent commanders of their voyages, but instead permitted a ship's sailors to popularly depose the captain and elect another member of the crew to this office at their will, the captain's capacity as acting manager of the ship's absentee owners would cease to exist. To see this, simply imagine what kind of captain merchant sailors would elect if given the power to democratically select him. Sailors' interests were best served by a lax, liberal captain who let them do as they pleased—exactly the opposite sort of captain that best served the owners' interests. Merchant ship autocracy was therefore essential to overcoming the owner-crew principal-agent problem and thus to merchant ship profitability.

Merchant ship autocracy worked quite well in this respect. Although some sailors still managed to steal from the ships they sailed on, disobey command, and, as I discuss below, in several cases mutiny and abscond with the owners' ship, these were relatively unimportant exceptions to the general rule whereby merchant sailors, under the authority of autocratic captains, served their absentee owners' interests.

B.　The Problem of Captain Predation

Although merchant ship autocracy largely overcame the principal-agent problem that absentee owners confronted with respect to their crews, in doing so it created potential for a different kind of problem: captain predation. The trouble was that a captain endowed with the authority required to manage his crew on the ship owners' behalf could also easily turn this authority against his seamen for personal benefit. As British

---

the merchant marine and efficiency of the share system for privateers and whalers, which also applies to pirates, see Gifford (1993).

[24] A third device owners used for this purpose, though of declining importance over time, was that of the supercargo—an agent hired by the ship's owners who sailed on the ship and managed commercial aspects of the voyage, such as buying and selling cargo at port, and sometimes deciding what ports the ship should stop at, when the captain could not be trusted in these capacities (Davis 1962).

LAW AND ECONOMICS OF PIRATE ORGANIZATION   1059

marine commander William Betagh characterized the problem, "unlimited power, bad views, ill nature and ill principles all concurring" "in a
ship's commander," "he is past all restraint" (1728, 41).

Betagh's opinion of some captains' "ill nature" notwithstanding, merchant captains were not necessarily bad men. But they were rational
economic actors and thus responded to the incentives their institutional
environment created. Endowed with autocratic authority over their
crews, some merchant captains used the power their employers and
Admiralty law gave them to prey on their sailors. As a result of merchant
ships' autocratic organization, captains "had absolute authority over the
mates, the carpenters and boatswain, and the seamen." They had the
power to "make life tolerable or unbearable as they wished" (Davis 1962,
131–32). Unfortunately for seamen, more than a few captains opted for
the latter.

As Marcus Rediker points out, according to several pirates, merchant
captain mistreatment of ordinary seamen was largely responsible for
driving sailors from this profession into the arms of sea bandits. The
pirate John Archer's last words before being put to death testify to this.
As he lamented, "I could wish that Masters of Vessels would not use
their Men with so much Severity, as many of them do, which exposes
us to great Temptations" (Johnson 1726–28, 351). In 1726 the pirate
William Fly pleaded similarly while awaiting his death sentence: "Our
Captain and his Mate used us Barbarously. We poor Men can't have
Justice done us. There is nothing said to our Commanders, let them
never so much abuse us, and use us like Dogs" (quoted in Rediker 1981,
218).

Captain predation took a number of forms, each the result of abusing
the autocratic power captains had at their disposal. Predatory captains
cut sailors' victual rations to keep costs down or to leave more for them
and their fellow officers to consume. As one sailor testified, for example,
although the members of his crew "were att short allowance and wanted
bread," the officers "were allowed . . . their full allowance of provisions
and liquors as if there had been no want of scarcity of any thing on
board" (*Babb v. Chalkley* 1701, High Court of Admiralty Papers, 24/127;
quoted in Rediker 1987, 247). Predatory captains also fraudulently
docked sailors' wages or paid sailors in debased colonial currency (Morris 1965, 237; Rediker 1987). They might also voyage to a location where
the crew had not contracted to sail (Gifford 1993, 144).

To keep their hungry and uncomfortable men in check, abusive captains could and did use all manner of objects aboard their ships as
weapons to punish insolent crew members. They hit sailors in the head
with tackle or other hard objects on board, crushing their faces, and
used other barbaric tactics to discipline seamen (*Jones v. Newcomin* 1735,
High Court of Admiralty Papers, 24/138; quoted in Rediker 1987, 216).

As merchant ship captain Nathaniel Uring described how he dealt with a "seditious Fellow" on his ship, for instance, "I gave him two or three such Strokes with a Stick I had prepared for that purpose . . . the Blood running about his Ears, he pray'd for God's sake that I not kill him" ([1726] 1928, 176–77).

Besides preventing dissension, captains also used their kingly power to settle personal scores with crew members. Admiralty law considered interfering with captain punishment mutinous and thus prohibited crew members from doing so (Morris 1965, 264–65). Since captains effectively defined when punishment was legitimate, they were free to abuse seamen at will. As one seaman warned a newcomer, "There is no justice or injustice on board ship, my lad. There are only two things: duty and mutiny—mind that. All that you are ordered to do is duty. All that you refuse to do is mutiny" (quoted in Rediker 1987, 211).[25]

While the historical record contains plenty of charges of captain predation, it is important to avoid overstating the extent of this abuse.[26] Although merchant captains had ample latitude to prey on their crews, this was not without limit. Several factors, economic and legal, constrained captain predation to some extent.[27]

But none was able to prevent it entirely. English law, for example, created several legal protections that were supposed to insulate sailors from captain predation. To a certain extent these protections were successful. Merchant seamen could and did take predatory captains to court for their actions, many times successfully.

However, as is often the case with the law, many other times it failed. Part of the difficulty here stemmed from the well-known uncertainties of the sea and the fact that, once they were afloat in the briny deep, there were rarely impartial spectators to be had to verify a sailor's word against a captain's. Did a captain dock a sailor's pay because the sailor damaged freight, as he was entitled to under the law? Or was the captain simply self-dealing? Had a captain exceeded the powers of corporal

[25] This quotation is from a late eighteenth-century sailor but captures the situation in the earlier part of the century as well.

[26] It is also important to note that captain predation notwithstanding, a merchant sailor's life was not a singularly cruel and oppressed one. As Earle (1998) points out, e.g., sailor society on merchant ships was in many ways a microcosm of landed life in seventeenth- and eighteenth-century England. Rodger (1996, 2006) makes a similar point regarding life aboard naval vessels. My discussion here is not intended to suggest that life was exclusively or exceptionally poor aboard merchant (or navy) ships. My argument is only to point out that the necessarily autocratic organization of merchant ships created scope for merchant captain predation, which a number of captains seized on.

[27] A check on the extent of captain predation not discussed here was captains' ability to complete their voyages. If a predatory captain, for instance, maimed or otherwise severely injured too many crew members through overzealous discipline, he might not have enough healthy crew members to complete the voyage. This surely constrained captain abuse to some extent, though it did not provide an incentive to reduce abuse to zero nor to refrain from other kinds of predatory behavior discussed above.

punishment afforded him under the law? Or was his discipline justified? In many cases it was difficult to say.

Further, the law itself regarding these matters could be unclear. Some sailors successfully sued their captains for merely pinching provisions. In other cases far more abusive captain conduct was supported by the law. In one case, for example, a captain beat his sailor with a one-and-a-half inch rope for cursing. The court found he "had Lawful provocation to Correct the Complainant and had not Exceeded the bounds of Humanity" and dismissed the sailor's claim (*Broughton v. Atkins*, Massachusetts Vice-Admiralty Records, box II, fol. 25, 1727; quoted in Morris 1965, 264).

Reputation could also be effective in constraining captain predation. Although the sailor population in the mid-eighteenth century approached 80,000 (Gifford 1993, 147), there were fewer than 10,000 captains. The relatively small population of captains facilitated information sharing about captain behavior. Since merchant ships had to voluntarily attract sailors, this helped to dampen the predatory inclinations of some merchant captains.

Nevertheless, some captain-sailor relations were anonymous and non-repeated. For example, when in 1722 merchant ship captains Isham Randolph, Constantine Cane, and William Halladay petitioned the colonial governor of Virginia for greater authority to discipline their sailors (who they complained were insolent for want of "fear of correction"), they wrote that "it is frequently the misfortune of Masters of Ships at their fitting out in England, to be obliged to ship men for forreign Voyages of whose disposition and character they have no knowledge" (quoted in Morris 1965, 271). Their letter suggests that the market for merchant sailors was, at least in some cases, largely anonymous. This implies not only that captains did not know the identity of sailors they employed, but also that sailors in some cases did not know the captains who employed them.

A number of sailors were the "fair weather" sort, drifting between employment at land and at sea, as job and pay prospects permitted. Others went to sea in between their regular work and thus had only sporadic interaction with a few members of the maritime community separated by lengthy periods. These features of the merchant sailor labor market made information sharing more difficult and rendered reputation a less effective constraint on captain abuse.

In assessing reputation's ability to check merchant captains' predatory inclinations, it is also important to remember that seventeenth- and eighteenth-century merchant shipping took place in the context of European mercantilism. Although some of England's mercantilist policies, such as bounties for shipbuilding, contributed to competition between merchant ships, others, such as the colonial law that forbade merchant ship captains from hiring away sailors who had already agreed to sail for another captain and the law that restricted foreign merchant captains from competing with English ones, retarded merchant ship competition and thus reputation's ability to check captain predation.

Another potential check on captain predation was the threat of mutiny. However, like other forms of revolution, mutiny was a risky and costly method of checking an authority's abuse. Crew members faced a collective action problem that often prevented them from overthrowing predatory captains.

Even on a merchant ship where every crew member agreed that the captain should be removed, sailors confronted the standard collective action problems of small-scale revolution. If crew members could coordinate their hatred and jointly revolt against a captain, in many cases they might have succeeded. However, since merchant ship crews were quite small, it was important to have all the sailors, or at least a significant majority, willing to fight. A successful mutiny might require not only the commitment of the common seamen but the commitment of the captain's officers as well. Acquiring certainty on the part of each sailor that if he rebelled against his captain, his fellow sailors would as well, was problematic. If one or several crew members "chickened out" at the last minute, the revolting sailor(s) might be defeated and, worse yet, face captain retribution.

Captain retribution involved using any of the powers at the captain's disposal to punish the mutineers. This ranged from imprisonment to extreme corporal punishment, further cutting the mutineers' rations or pay, or assigning them the most dangerous tasks on the ship (see, e.g., Uring 1726). Unless each sailor was assured that his fellow seamen had the courage and wherewithal to follow through on revolt, he was unwilling to rebel against his predatory captain.

This is not to say that merchant sailors never mutinied. Indeed, they did, but quite rarely. In the half century between 1700 and 1750, there were fewer than 60 documented mutinies on English and American merchant ships, about 1.18 per year (Rediker 1987, 227–28). It is possible that many more mutinies went undocumented. But even if we quadruple this number, which seems quite unreasonable, the number of merchant ship mutinies is tiny compared to the number of merchant ship voyages over this period. Further, this includes all attempted mutinies, not only the successful ones, which were even more rare. According to Rediker, only half of those documented between 1700 and 1750 were successful (228).[28] Thus, it appears that the collective action

---

[28] Notably, however, several pirate crews had their genesis in successful mutiny. According to Rediker (1987, 228), one-third of successful mutinous crews (i.e., those that succeeded in taking control of the ship) in the first half of the eighteenth century entered piracy.

problem mutiny posed for merchant sailors was quite severe. Maritime revolution, then, was not a reliable method of reining in predatory merchant ship captains.

Why didn't those on the receiving end of captain predation—the common seamen—simply pool their resources, purchase their own merchant ship, and sail it themselves? Several factors appear to have prevented this possibility. Although a merchant ship officer might, after several years, save enough to purchase a small share in a merchant vessel, "Only if a seaman could raise the money to buy, not a tiny fraction but a substantial share—a half or more—would such a financial gesture by itself be sufficient to attract co-owners" (Davis 1962, 127).

Merchant shipping was not as simple as carrying goods from point A to point B. It crucially depended on connections with landed merchants, both at home and abroad, who were willing to take the risk of doing business with a particular group of ship owners, trade with these owners on credit, and so on. Landed merchants had established reputations along these lines, making it possible for them to secure investors and customers.

Salty sea folk, in contrast, did not. The common seventeenth- or eighteenth-century seaman occupied one of the lowest stations in the economic foodchain. He was "from the lowest ranks of society . . . from young men who were dissatisfied with, or could obtain no employment in, the lowest of shore occupations" (Davis 1962, 114). He had neither business experience nor connections. Needless to say, merchants were not lining up to put their valuable cargo under the care of sailor-owned and operated ships.

Even if several seamen had sufficient faith in one another's abilities to make a go of the seafaring portion of merchant shipping and, furthermore, were willing to risk dumping several years' savings into buying a ship owned together with other sailors, they would have had no reason to think that any of their co-owners commanded the business knowledge or connections required to make such a venture profitable. Nor would they have been able to attract the capital required to withstand even one unsuccessful voyage that resulted from shipwreck, pirate attack, or any of the other uncertainties of merchant shipping.[29] Just as specialization required merchants to devote their time to organizing the commercial aspects of merchant voyages, leaving the sailing to the sailors, so too did specialization require seamen to focus on the sailing aspects

---

[29] In addition to this, there is considerable doubt that many common seamen, even after years of toil, were in a position to own any part of a merchant vessel. One of the few, preserved, near-complete bills of merchant vessel sale before England required ship registration in 1786 corroborates this. Among the 338 owners of 53 ships it lists, only 28 noncaptain mariners, or about 8 percent of the total, owned any share of a merchant vessel (Davis 1962, 100).

of merchant voyages, leaving the commercial organization to the merchants.

IV. Pirate Ship Organization

Like merchant ship organization, the particular economic situation pirate ships confronted crucially shaped their organization. Most notably, pirates did not confront the owner-crew principal-agent problem that merchant ships did. The reason for this is simple enough: pirates did not acquire their ships legitimately. They stole them.[30]

Pirate ships therefore had no absentee owners. On a pirate ship, the principals were the agents. As one historian described it, in this sense a pirate ship was like a "sea-going stock company" (Pringle 1953, 106). As a result, pirates did not require captains to align the crew's interests with those of the ship's absentee owners. This feature of piracy largely explains the stark contrast between merchant and pirate ship organization.

However, the absence of the owner-crew principal-agent problem on pirate ships does not mean that pirates did not need captains. They certainly did. Many important piratical decisions, such as how to engage a potential target, how to pursue when "chasing" a target or being chased by authorities, and how to react if attacked, required snap decision making. There was no time for disagreement or debate in such cases, and conflicting voices would have made it impossible to undertake the most essential tasks. Furthermore, pirate ships, like all ships, needed some method of maintaining order, distributing victuals and payments, and administering discipline to unruly crew members.

The office of captain overcame such difficulties by vesting autocratic control over these matters in the hands of an authority. In this sense, although pirate ships differed from merchant ships in requiring captains to solve an owner-sailor principal-agent problem, pirate ships were similar to merchant ships in requiring some kind of authority for their undertaking's success. Although a pirate ship's activity—violent plunder—was wholly different from a merchant ship's, both kinds of vessels shared the need to create internal order to achieve their ends.

The need for captains posed a dilemma for pirates. On the one hand, a captain who wielded unquestioned authority in certain decisions was critical for success. On the other hand, what was to prevent a captain with this power from behaving toward his pirate crew in the same manner that predatory merchant ship captains behaved toward their crews?

Since pirates did not have absentee owners but instead jointly owned

---

[30] There is at least one eighteenth-century pirate, however, Stede Bonnet, who actually purchased the first ship he went on the account with.

the stolen ships they sailed on, although they required captains, unlike merchant ships, they did not require autocratic captains. Thus, in sharp contrast to the situation on merchant ships, pirates could and did democratically elect their captains without problem. Since the pirates sailing a particular ship were both the principals and the agents, democracy did not threaten to lead to captains who served the agents at the principals' expense. On the contrary, pirate democracy ensured that pirates got precisely the kind of captain they desired. Because pirates could popularly depose any captain who did not suit them and elect another in his place, pirate captains' ability to prey on crew members was greatly constrained compared to that of merchant ship captains.

Similarly, because pirates were both principals and agents of their ships, they could divide authority on their vessels to further check captains' ability to abuse crew members without loss. Unlike merchant ships, which could not afford a separation of power since this would have diminished the ability of the absentee owners' acting agent (the captain) to make the crew act in the owners' interests, pirate ships could and did adopt a system of democratic checks and balances.

A. Piratical Checks and Balances

Because of the threat of captain predation, pirates "were adamant in wanting to limit the captain's power to abuse and cheat them" (Rogozinski 2000, 174). To do this they instituted a democratic system of divided power, or piratical checks and balances, aboard their ships. As the pirate Walter Kennedy testified at his trial, "Most of them having suffered formerly from the ill-treatment of Officers, provided thus carefully against any such Evil now they had the choice in themselves . . . for the due Execution thereof they constituted other Officers besides the Captain; so very industrious were they to avoid putting too much Power into the hands of one Man" (Hayward [1735] 1874, 1:42).

The primary "other officer" pirates "constituted" for this purpose was the quartermaster. The way this office worked is straightforward. Captains retained absolute authority in times of battle, enabling pirates to realize the benefits of autocratic control required for success in conflict. However, pirate crews transferred power to allocate provisions, select and distribute loot (there was rarely room aboard pirate ships to take all they seized from a prize), and adjudicate crew member conflicts/administer discipline to the quartermaster, whom they democratically elected:

> For the Punishment of small Offences . . . there is a principal
> Officer among the Pyrates, called the Quarter-Master, of the
> Men's own choosing, who claims all Authority this Way, (ex-

cepting in Time of Battle:) If they disobey his Command, are quarrelsome and mutinous with one another, misuse Prisoners, plunder beyond his Order, and in particular, if they be negligent of their Arms, which he musters at Discretion, he punishes at his own dare without incurring the Lash from all the Ship's Company: In short, this Officer is Trustee for the whole, is the first on board any Prize, separating for the Company's Use, what he pleases, and returning what he thinks fit to the Owners, excepting Gold and Silver, which they have voted not returnable. (Johnson 1726–28, 213).

William Snelgrave, who observed the pirates' system of checks and balances firsthand, characterized the relationship between captain and quartermaster similarly: "the Captain of a Pirate Ship, is chiefly chosen to fight the Vessels they may meet with. Besides him, they chuse another principle Officer, whom they call Quarter-master, who has the general Inspection of all Affairs, and often controuls the Captain's Orders" (1734, 199–200). This separation of power removed captains' control over activities they traditionally used to prey on crew members, while empowering them sufficiently to direct plundering expeditions.

The institutional separation of powers aboard pirate ships predated its adoption by seventeenth- and eighteenth-century governments. France, for example, did not experience such a separation until 1789. Nor did the United States. The first specter of separated powers in Spain did not appear until 1812. In contrast, pirates had divided, democratic "government" aboard their ships at least a century before this. Arguably, piratical checks and balances predated even England's adoption of similar institutions. England did not experience a separation of powers until the Glorious Revolution of 1688. However, the buccaneers, who used a similar, if not as thoroughgoing, system of democratically divided power as their pure pirate successors, had in place at least partial democratic checks and balances in the early 1680s (Rogozinski 2000).

Piratical checks and balances proved quite successful. According to Johnson, owing to the institution of the quartermaster, aboard pirate ships "the Captain can undertake nothing which the Quarter-Master does not approve. We may say, the Quarter-Master is an humble Imitation of the Roman Tribune of the People; he speaks for, and looks after the Interest of the Crew" (1726–28, 423). As noted previously, the only exception to this was "in Chase, or in Battle" when crews desired autocratic authority and thus, "by their own Laws," "the Captain's Power is uncontroulable" (139, 214).[31]

---

[31] Of course, even pirates' democratic system of checks and balances could not prevent all instances of captain predation. For instance, since he controlled battle-related decisions, a pirate captain could still put a crew member he disliked in harm's way.

Austrian Law and Economics II

In addition to this separation of powers, pirates imposed a further check to balance captains' authority. They converted the office to a democratically elected one, "the Rank of Captain being obtained by the Suffrage of the Majority" (Johnson 1726–28, 214). The combination of separated powers and democratic elections for captains ensured that pirates "only permit him to be Captain, on Condition, that they may be Captain over him" (213).

Crews could vote captains out of office for any number of reasons. Predation was one, but so was cowardice, poor judgment, and any other behavior a crew did not feel was in its best interest. In this way pirates could be sure that captainship "falls on one superior for Knowledge and Boldness, Pistol Proof, (as they call it)" (Johnson 1726–28, 214).

The historical record contains numerous examples of pirate crews deposing unwanted captains by majority vote or otherwise removing them from power through popular consensus. Captain Charles Vane's pirate crew, for example, popularly deposed him for cowardice: "the Captain's Behavior was obliged to stand the Test of a Vote, and a Resolution passed against his Honour and Dignity . . . deposing him from the Command" (Johnson 1726–28, 139). Similarly, Captain Christopher Moody's pirate crew grew dissatisfied with his behavior and "at last forced him, with twelve others" who supported him "into an open Boat . . . and . . . they were never heard of afterwards" (Snelgrave 1734, 198).[32]

Crews sometimes elected quartermasters who displayed particular valor or keen decision making to replace less capable or honorable captains. For example, when one pirate crew "went to Voting for a new Captain . . . the Quarter-Master, who had behaved so well in the last Affair . . . was chosen" (Johnson 1726–28, 479). This helped create competition among pirate officers that tended to check their abuses and encouraged them to serve the interests of their crews.[33]

Pirates took seriously the limitations they imposed on captains' authority through their system of checks and balances. A speech made by one of the pirates aboard Captain Bartholomew Roberts' ship testifies to this. As he told his crew, "should a Captain be so sawcy as to exceed Prescription at any time, why down with him! it will be a Caution after he is dead to his Successors, of what fatal Consequence any sort of assuming may be" (Johnson 1726–28, 194–95). This pirate was exag-

---

[32] In some cases, crews also physically punished their captains for behavior they deemed inconsistent with their interests. For example, Oliver La Bouche was deprived of his captain position and flogged for attempting to desert his crew (de Bucquoy 1744, 103; translated and quoted in Rogozinski 2000, 177). Occasionally, crews also deserted predatory captains (Council of the Leeward Islands, May 18, 1699, Public Record Office, Colonial Office Papers, 152:3, no. 21).

[33] This competition likely explains the rarity of cases of captain-quartermaster collusion against crews.

gerating—but only slightly. Crews quickly and readily deposed old captains and elected new ones when the former overstepped the limited power crews gave them.

The seriousness with which pirates sought to limit their captains' power is reflected in other ways as well. For instance, in contrast to merchant vessels, on pirate ships, captains were unable to secure special privileges for themselves at their crews' expense. Their lodging, provisions, and even pay were nearly the same as that of ordinary crew members. As Johnson described it, aboard pirate ships "every Man, as the Humour takes him . . . [may] intrude [the captain's] Apartment, swear at him, seize a part of his Victuals and Drink, if they like it, without his offering to find Fault or contest it" (1726–28, 213–14). In other cases, "the Captain himself not being allowed a Bed" had to sleep with the rest of the crew in far less comfortable conditions (Snelgrave 1734, 217). Or, as one pirate fellow-traveler marveled, "even their Captain, or any other Officer, is allowed no more than another Man; nay, the Captain cannot [even] keep his own Cabin to himself" (Downing [1737] 1924, 99; quoted in Rogozinski 2000, 175).

One pirate captive records an event in which the captains of a pirate fleet borrowed fancy clothes that were part of the loot their crews acquired in taking a recent prize. These captains hoped that their stolen finery would attract local women on the nearby shore. Although the captains intended only to borrow the clothes, the crews became outraged at their captains whom they saw as transgressing the limits of their narrowly circumscribed power. As the observer described it, "The Pirate Captains having taken these Cloaths without leave from the Quartermaster, it gave great Offence to all the Crew; who alledg'd, 'If they suffered such things, the Captains would for the future assume a Power, to take whatever they liked for themselves'" (Snelgrave 1734, 257).[34]

One can also get an idea of the effectiveness of piratical checks and balances by considering the remarks of one contemporary that point to the rarity of pirate captain predation. Perplexed by an anomalous pirate captain who abused his crew, he puzzled, "The captain is very severe to his people, by reason of his commission, and caries a very different form from what other Pirates use to do . . . often calling for his pistols and threatening any that durst speak to the contrary of what he desireth, to knock out their brains" (quoted in Rogozinski 2000, 139;

---

[34] This decentralization of authority and elimination of captain privilege aboard pirate ships were radical departures from conditions in the legitimate maritime world. Observers were therefore shocked at the incredible absence of hierarchy aboard pirate ships. Commenting on their democratic form of governance, e.g., the Dutch governor of Mauritius marveled, "Every man had as much say as the captain" (quoted in Ritchie 1986, 124).

see also Deposition of Benjamin Franks, October 20, 1697, Public Record Office, Colonial Office Papers, 323:2, no. 124).[35]

This success helps explain why, counterintuitively, "the People [pirates overtook] were generally glad of an opportunity of entring with them" (Snelgrave 1734, 203). Indeed, pirates frequently "strengthen'd themselves with a great many fresh Hands, who most of them enter'd voluntarily" (Johnson 1726–28, 170; see also 228; Deposition of Jeremiah Tay, July 6, 1694, Suffolk Court Files, no. 3033, paper 6; Colonial Office Papers, May 31, 1718, fol. 18).[36]

B.   Pirate Constitutions

Pirates' system of checks and balances effectively prevented captains from preying on their crews. However, a significant problem remained. In vesting many of the powers captains typically held in quartermasters instead, what was to prevent quartermasters from abusing their authority to privately benefit at crews' expense?

As discussed above, quartermasters had numerous roles aboard pirate ships. They were in charge of the distribution of booty and provisions, conflict resolution, and crew member punishment. This gave them ample latitude to prey on crews. I have already discussed one check on quartermaster predation, which also checked captain predation—democratic elections. As with their captains, pirate crews elected quartermasters and could depose them if they overstepped their authority.

But what precisely did this include? Were, for instance, quartermasters free to divide booty and provisions as they saw fit? Could they punish crew members at their discretion? Furthermore, according to what "laws" were they supposed to adjudicate disputes between those on board?

After all, not only were pirates afraid of captain predation; they opposed any situation that threatened to jeopardize their ability to cooperate for organized banditry, including the institution of the quartermaster. To solve this problem, pirate crews forged written constitutions that specified their laws and punishments for breaking these laws and more specifically limited the actions that quartermasters might take in carrying out their duties.

Pirate constitutions originated with "articles of agreement" followed

---

[35] The captain referred to here is William Kidd, a privateer-turned-pirate, who was ultimately executed for his crimes. Notably, Kidd's privateer ship was financed by absentee owners.

[36] Many individuals ostensibly forced to join pirate crews in fact joined voluntarily. Officially, they asked to be "forced" and occasionally put up a show to their comrades to this effect so that in the event their pirate crew was ever captured, they could claim that they were compelled as a defense (Pringle 1953; see also Rankin 1969).

on buccaneer ships in the seventeenth century. The buccaneers called their articles a *chasse-partie*. These articles specified the division of booty among the officers and crew along with other terms of the buccaneers' organization. All sea bandits followed the basic rule of "no prey, no pay." Unless a pirating expedition was successful, no man received any payment.

Exquemelin (1678, 71–72) describes the *chasse-partie* that governed his crew's expedition in detail:

> The buccaneers resolve by common vote where they shall cruise. They also draw up an agreement or chasse partie, in which is specified what the captain shall have for himself and for the use of his vessel. Usually they agree on the following terms. Providing they capture a prize, first of all these amounts would be deducted from the whole capital. The hunter's pay would generally be 200 pieces of eight. The carpenter, for his work in repairing and fitting out the ship, would be paid 100 or 150 pieces of eight. The surgeon would receive 200 or 250 for his medical supplies, according to the size of the ship.
>
> Then came the agreed awards for the wounded, who might have lost a limb or suffered injuries. They would be compensated as follows: for the loss of a right arm, 600 pieces of eight or six slaves; for a left arm 500 pieces of eight or five slaves. The loss of a right leg also brought 500 pieces of eight or five slaves in compensation; a left leg 400 or four slaves; an eye, 100 or one slave, and the same award was made for the loss of a finger. If a man lost the use of an arm, he would get as much as if it had been cut off, and a severe internal injury which meant the victim had to have a pipe inserted in his body would receive 500 pieces of eight or five slaves in recompense.
>
> These amounts having first been withdrawn from the capital, the rest of the prize would be divided into as many portions as men on the ship. The captain draws four or five men's portions for the use of the ship, perhaps even more, and two portions for himself. The rest of the men share uniformly, and the boys get half a man's share.
>
> . . . When a ship is robbed, nobody must plunder and keep his loot to himself. Everything taken—money, jewels, precious stones and goods—must be shared among them all, without any man enjoying a penny more than his fair share. To prevent deceit, before the booty is distributed everyone has to swear an oath on the Bible that he has not kept for himself so much as the value of a sixpence, whether in silk, linen, wool, gold, silver, jewels, clothes or shot, from all the capture. And should

any man be found to have made a false oath, he would be
banished from the rovers, never more be allowed in their
company.

Over time, the buccaneers institutionalized their articles of agreement
and social organization. The result was a system of customary law and
metarules called the "Custom of the Coast," or the "Jamaica Discipline."

Eighteenth-century pirates built on this institutional framework in
developing their own constitutions. Pirates created them "for the better
Conservation of their Society, and doing Justice to one another" (Johnson 1726–28, 210). The basic elements of pirate constitutions displayed
remarkable similarity across crews (Rediker 1987, 261). In describing
the articles on Captain Roberts' ship, for instance, Johnson refers to
"the Laws of this Company . . . principle Customs, and Government,
of this roguish Commonwealth; which are pretty near the same with all
Pyrates" (1726–28, 213).

Frequent intercrew interactions led to information sharing that facilitated constitutional commonality.[37] More than 70 percent of Anglo-
American pirates active between 1716 and 1726, for example, can be
connected back to one of three pirate captains: Benjamin Hornigold,
George Lowther, or Edward Low (Rediker 1987, 267). Thus, a significant
proportion of all pirates during this period were associated with one
another in some way, via traveling on the same ship, in concert with
other ships, and so forth.

Articles of agreement required unanimous consent. Consequently,
pirates democratically formed them in advance of launching pirating
expeditions. "All [pirates] swore to 'em," sometimes on a Bible or, for
one pirate crew, "upon a Hatchet for want of a Bible." The crew forged
its articles alongside the election of a captain, quartermaster, and occasionally other smaller officers. Pirates sought agreement on their articles ex ante "to prevent Disputes and Ranglings afterwards" (Johnson
1726–28, 342). In the event a pirate disagreed with their conditions, he
was free to search elsewhere for more satisfactory terms.[38]

---

[37] A letter from colonial governor Alexander Spotswood to the Board of Trade highlights
the effectiveness of pirates' information-sharing network. Spotswood, who having "been
markt as the principle object of their vengeance, for cutting off their arch pirate Thatch
[a.k.a. Blackbeard]" complained of finding a place to escape to "where neither Master
nor Sailors know me, & so may possibly escape the knowledge of ye pirates" (Colonial
Office Papers, June 16, 1724, 5/1319: fols. 190–92; quoted in Rediker 1987, 254, 134).

[38] Pirate ships often required crew members to agree to stay on until a certain sum was
earned or an expedition completed. However, if a ship became too crowded or some
other compelling reason came along for a crew to split, it did so. In this case, new articles
were drawn up and pirates had the option to sign on with the new crew or stay with the
old. There do not appear to be any cases of pirate constitutions being altered or amended
midcruise. The status of forced men on pirate ships seems to have varied. Some appear
to have been compelled to sign the ship's articles. Others were not compelled to do so
but did not have a vote in the company's affairs until they signed (Rediker 2004, 79–81).

When multiple pirate ships joined together for an expedition, they created similar articles establishing the terms of their partnership. Upon encountering one another at Grand Cayman, for example, Captain George Lowther and Edward Low's pirate crews forged such an agreement. Lowther "offering himself as an Ally; *Low* accepted of the Terms, and so the Treaty was presently sign'd without Plenipo's or any other Formalities" (1726–28, 319).

Likewise, crews that objected to the proposed articles or some other element of an intended multiship expedition were free to depart peaceably. In one such case, for example, "a Spirit of Discord" emerged between three pirate crews sailing in consort "upon which . . . [they] immediately parted, each steering a different Course" (Johnson 1726–28, 175).

Charles Johnson's records contain several examples of pirate constitutions, through which, as one court remarked, these rogues were "wickedly united, and articled together" (Johnson 1726–28, 253). Consider, for instance, the articles aboard Captain Roberts' pirate ship, as relayed by Captain Johnson (211–12):

I. Every Man has a Vote in the Affairs of Moment; has equal Title to the fresh Provisions, or strong Liquors, at any Time seized, and may use them at Pleasure, unless a Scarcity make it necessary, for the Good of all, to vote a Retrenchment.

II. Every Man to be called fairly in Turn, by List, on board of Prizes, because, (over and above their proper Share) they were on these Occasions allowed a Shift of Cloaths: But if they defrauded the Company to the Value of a Dollar, in Plate, Jewels, or Money, Marooning was their Punishment. If the Robbery was only betwixt one another, they contented themselves with slitting the Ears and Nose of him that was Guilty, and set him on Shore, not in an uninhabited Place, but somewhere, where he was sure to encounter Hardships.

III. No person to Game at Cards or Dice for Money.

IV. The Lights and Candles to be put out at eight a-Clock at Night: If any of the Crew, after that Hour, still remained enclined for Drinking, they were to do it on the open Deck.

V. To keep their Piece, Pistols, and Cutlash clean, and fit for Service.

VI. No Boy or Woman to be allowed amongst them. If any Man were found seducing any of the latter Sex, and carry'd her to Sea, disguised, he was to suffer Death.

VII. To Desert the Ship, or their Quarters in Battle, was punished with Death or Marooning.

VIII. No striking one another on board, but every Man's Quarrels to be ended on Shore, at Sword and Pistol.

IX. No Man to talk of breaking up their Way of Living, till each shared a 1000 l. If in order to this, any Man should lose a Limb, or become a Cripple in their Service, he was to have 800 Dollars, out of the publick Stock, and for lesser Hurts, proportionately.

X. The Captain and Quarter-Master to receive two Shares of a Prize; the Master, Boatswain, and Gunner, one Share and a half, and other Officers one and a Quarter [everyone else to receive one share].

XI. The Musicians to have Rest on the Sabbath Day, but the other six Days and Nights, none without special Favour.

Several important features stand out from these examples of pirate articles. First, they created a democratic form of governance and explicitly laid out the terms of pirate compensation. This was to clarify the status of property rights aboard pirate ships and to prevent officers, such as the captain or quartermaster, from preying on crew members. In particular, making the terms of compensation explicit helped to circumscribe the quartermaster's authority in dividing booty.

When booty was indivisible or there was question as to its value and thus how many shares it counted for in payment, pirates sold or auctioned the troublesome items and distributed the divisible proceeds accordingly (Snelgrave 1734; Rogozinski 2000, 169). This practice prevented conflict between crew members. More important, it constrained the discretion of the quartermaster, who might otherwise be in a position to circumvent the terms of compensation when loot was indivisible or of ambiguous value.

Second, pirate articles prohibited activities that generated significant negative externalities and threatened the success of criminal organization aboard their ships. Thus, pirate articles required crew members to keep their weapons in good working order; on Roberts' ship limited drunken raucousness to allow nonparticipant pirates to get sufficient sleep, and to "give a Check to their Debauches" (Johnson 1726–28, 211); prohibited onboard fighting that might jeopardize the entire crew's ability to function; and prohibited activities, such as gambling, that were likely to lead to onboard brawls. On similar grounds, crews' articles often prohibited women (and young boys), who it was thought would invite conflict or tension among crew members aboard their ships. "This being a good political Rule to prevent disturbances amongst them, it is strictly observed" (Snelgrave 1734, 256–57; see also Johnson 1726–28, 212).

In the same way, some pirate ships forbade activities such as firing one's guns or smoking in areas of the ship that carried highly flammable goods, such as gunpowder. According to the articles aboard John Phillips' *Revenge*, for example, "That Man that shall snap his Arms, or smoak Tobacco in the Hold without a Cap to his Pipe, or carry a Candle lighted without a Lanthorn, shall suffer the same Punishment as in the former Article" (Johnson 1726–28, 342–43).

Third, pirate constitutions contained articles that provided incentives for crew member productivity and prevented shirking. One manifestation of this was their creation of social insurance for pirates injured during battle. As in the examples from Exquemelin and Roberts above, articles specified in detail what a lost arm was worth, a lost leg, and so on. They even went as far as to assign different insurance values depending on whether it was, for instance, the right or left appendage that was mutilated or lost, according to the importance pirates assigned to these body parts.

Another manifestation of these incentive provisions was the use of bonuses for crew members who displayed particular courage in battle, were the first to spot potential targets, and so forth. Because pirate crews were large, quartermasters could not easily monitor individual pirates' effort. As I discuss below, this is why pirates used profit sharing rather than fixed wages for payment.

The problem with a share system is that it can create incentives for free riding. Further, one team member's laziness directly reduces the income of the others. To deal with this, pirates, like privateers and whalers, who also used a share system, created bonuses. According to the rule aboard Exquemelin's buccaneering vessel, for instance, "Those who behaved courageously and performed any deed of extraordinary valour, or captured a ship, should be rewarded out of the common plunder" (1678, 156). Or, as Johnson records, "It must be observed, they [pirates] keep a good Look-out; for, according to their Articles, he who first espies a Sail, if she proves a Prize, is entitled the best Pair of Pistols on board, over and above his Dividend" (1726–28, 191).

Finally, pirate articles stipulated punishments for failure to adhere to their rules. As discussed above, for more minor infractions, crews typically delegated punishment power to the ship's democratically elected quartermaster. As Johnson described it, the quartermaster "acts as a Sort of civil Magistrate on board a Pyrate Ship" (1726–28, 213).[39] In the case

[39] When this failed, the quartermaster refereed a duel between the parties, which would take place on land so as not to destroy the ship. "The Quarter-Master of the Ship, when the Parties will not come to any Reconciliation, accompanies them on Shore with what Assistance he thinks proper, and turns the Disputants Back to Back, at so many paces Distance: At the Word of Command, they turn and fire immediately . . . . If both miss, they come to their Cutlashes, and then he is declared Victor who draws the first blood" (Johnson 1726–28, 212; see also 339).

of more severe infractions, crew members voted on punishments. In both cases pirate crews tended to follow the punishments for various infractions identified in their articles. By specifying punishments in their articles, crews were able to limit the scope of quartermasters' discretion in administering discipline, checking quartermasters' power for abuse.

Punishments for article violations varied from physical torture, such as "slitting the Ears and Nose of him that was Guilty," to marooning— a practice Captain Johnson described as the "barbarous Custom of putting the Offender on Shore, on some desolate or uninhabited Cape or Island, with a Gun, a few Shot, a Bottle of Water, and a Bottle of Powder, to subsist with or starve" (1726–28, 211).[40] On Captain Phillips' ship, for example, article violations were punished with "Moses's Law (that is, 40 Stripes lacking one) on the bare back" (342–43).

In this sense, "Pirates exercised greater cruelty in maintaining discipline among themselves than in their treatment of prisoners" (Rankin 1969, 37). Pirates considered theft aboard their ships especially heinous. Their articles reflected this and frequently punished theft with torture, marooning, or death. To help keep themselves honest, some crews used random searches to hunt for anyone who might be holding back loot (Exquemelin 1678, 205–6).[41] To ensure that the quartermaster did not hide booty from the crew, some pirates prohibited their valuable plunder from being kept under lock and key. As pirate Peter Hooff described the situation on Captain Sam Bellamy's *Whydah*, for instance, the "money was kept in Chests between Decks without any Guard, but none was to take any without the Quarter Masters leave" (quoted in Rediker 2004, 67; see also Marx 1996*a*, 44).

Since pirate articles tended to be short and simple, they could not cover all possible contingencies that might affect a crew. In this sense they were always incomplete. To deal with this, when a significant issue emerged, the crew gathered to act as a kind of judiciary to interpret or apply the ship's articles to situations not clearly stipulated in the articles themselves: "In Case any Doubt should arise concerning the Construction of these Laws, and it should remain a Dispute whether the Party had infringed them or no, a Jury was appointed to explain them, and bring in a Verdict upon the Case in Doubt" (Johnson 1726–28, 213). Through this "judicial review" process, pirate crews were able to further limit quartermasters' discretionary authority, restraining the potential for quartermaster abuse.

The historical record points to the effectiveness of pirate constitutions

---

[40] Marooning was sometimes coupled with ostracism in the event that the transgressor managed to survive. See, e.g., Exquemelin (1678, 72).

[41] Oath taking was commonly used among pirates as well as a method of staking one's reputation to help enforce piratical articles and custom. See, e.g., Exquemelin (1678, 68, 71–72, 100, 104, 156, 161).

in this capacity, evidenced by the rarity of accounts of quartermaster abuse. Equally important, in the infrequent event that abuse did occur, the evidence indicates that crews successfully removed abusive quartermasters from power. For example, in 1691 quartermaster Samuel Burgess cheated his crew in the division of food. In response, his crew marooned him (Rogozinski 2000, 177).

The evidence also suggests that piratical articles were successful in preventing internal conflict and creating order aboard pirate ships. Pirates, it appears, strictly adhered to their articles. According to one historian, pirates were more orderly, peaceful, and well organized among themselves than many of the colonies, merchant ships, or vessels of the Royal Navy (Pringle 1953; Rogozinski 2000). As an astonished pirate observer put it, "At sea, they perform their duties with a great deal of order, better even than on the Ships of the Dutch East India Company; the pirates take a great deal of pride in doing things right" (de Bucquoy 1744, 116; translated and quoted in Rogozinski 2000, viii).

Though it is strange to think about such order prevailing among pirates, the peculiarity fades when one recognizes that their organized criminal enterprise's success depended on it. The remark of one perceptive eighteenth-century observer indicates precisely this. As he put it, "great robbers as they are to all besides, [pirates] are precisely just among themselves; without which they could no more Subsist than a Structure without a Foundation" (Slush 1709, viii; quoted in Rediker 1987, 287).

The fact that pirate crews unanimously consented to the articles that governed them, ex ante, also plays an important role in explaining their success. Pirates recognized that "it was every one's Interest to observe them, if they were minded to keep up so abominable a Combination" (Johnson 1726–28, 210). Since pirates agreed to these rules before sailing, rules were largely self-enforcing once in place.

V. Was Pirate Organization Efficient?

In light of the sharp contrast between merchant and pirate ship organization, an important question arises concerning the efficiency of pirate institutions. After all, merchant ships were legitimate vessels and therefore had the government's formal enforcement power at their disposal. This gave them a wider range of organizational options than pirates, who were criminals and therefore did not have the government backing that afforded the same organizational choices. One possibility, then, is that pirate organization merely reflects this smaller menu of opportunities. Perhaps if pirates could have relied on government enforcement, they too would have opted for merchant ship–like institutions.

Alternatively, pirate ship organization was an efficient institutional response to the unique economic situation pirates faced, quite apart from their inability to rely on government. Although pirates faced a constraint that merchant ships did not—inability to rely on government—as discussed above, merchant ships faced a constraint that pirate ships did not—the need to solve an owner-crew principal-agent problem. Given the very different economic situations pirate and merchant ships confronted in this regard, it would not be surprising if the efficient mode of organizing these ships was different as well—this difference being driven by the economic differences between the two rather than by their different legal status.

A.   Pirate Booty

As a first cut at this issue we can look to the success of piratical expeditions. If pirates seized only small prizes, or no prizes at all, clearly their organization was not an effective one. On the other hand, if pirates succeeded in taking very valuable prizes, our confidence in pirates' organizational efficiency should grow.

The evidence suggests that if pirates' inability to organize autocratically was inhibiting piratical efficiency, it could not have been doing so greatly. Although we do not have data that would allow us to compute anything like the average pirate's wage, what evidence is available suggests that incredibly large pirate prizes were not unheard of.

Of course, this evidence must be interpreted with caution. These seizures were recorded precisely because of their spectacular size. More common were undoubtedly more modest prizes. Nevertheless, the examples we have are enough to point to the significant success of piratical plunder in some cases and the opportunity piracy offered sailors for becoming incredibly wealthy.

"At a time when Anglo-American seamen on a trading voyage to Madagascar were collecting less than twelve pounds sterling a year . . . the deep-water pirates could realize a hundred or even a thousand times more" (Marx 1996c, 141). In 1695, for example, Henry Every's pirate fleet captured a prize carrying more than £600,000 in precious metals and jewels. The resulting share-out earned each member of his crew £1,000 (Konstam 2007, 98), the equivalent of nearly 40 years' income for an able merchant seaman at the time. In the early eighteenth century, Captain John Bowen's pirate crew plundered a prize "which yielded them 500 *l. per* Man." Several years later Captain Thomas White's crew retired to Madagascar after a marauding expedition, each pirate having earned £1,200 from the cruise (Johnson 1726–28, 480, 485). In 1720, Captain Christopher Condent's crew seized a prize that earned each pirate £3,000. Similarly, in 1721, Captain John Taylor and Oliver La Bouche's pirate consort earned an astonishing £4,000 for each crew member from a single attack (Marx 1996*c*, 161, 163). Even the small pirate crew captained by John Evans in 1722 took enough booty to split "nine thousand Pounds among thirty Persons"—or £300 a pirate—in less than six months "on the account" (Johnson 1726–28, 340).

To put these earnings in perspective, compare them to the able merchant seaman's wage over the same period. Between 1689 and 1740 this varied from 25 to 55 shillings per month, a meager £15 to £33 per year (Davis 1962, 136–37).

In the absence of data for a larger number of pirate hauls, it is not possible to say whether the average seventeenth- or eighteenth-century pirate consistently earned more than the average seventeenth- or eighteenth-century merchant sailor. It is certainly possible that this was the case, however. As one pirate testified at his trial, for instance, "it is a common thing for us [pirates] when at Sea to acquire vast quantities, both of the Metal that goes before me [silver, referring to the silver oar of the Admiralty court], and of Gold" (quoted in Hayward 1735, I:45).

This pirate's remark may very well reflect his desire to impress the court more than it reflects piracy's profitability. Still, what the evidence on piratical plunder does clearly point to is the tremendous potential "upside" of piratical employment. Unlike employment as a merchant sailor, which guaranteed a low, if regular, income, a single successful pirating expedition could make a sailor wealthy enough to retire. This is no doubt largely the reason why, as one eighteenth-century colonial governor remarked, "so many are willing to joyn them [pirates] when taken" (Colonial Office Papers, May 31, 1718, fol. 18; quoted in Rediker 1987, 260).

If pirates did in fact earn substantially more than their legitimate counterparts, this raises the question of why more merchant sailors did not join the ranks of the pirates, eliminating any difference between pirate and merchant sailor wages. Bearing in mind again that we cannot know for certain whether or not the average pirate earned more than the average merchant sailor, there are two reasons sailors did not flock in greater numbers to life beneath the black flag even if this were the case.

The first was simply the risk of being caught. Piracy was a capital offense. In the eighteenth century, if a sailor was found guilty of piracy, he was hanged. Although pirates largely escaped the arm of the law in the seventeenth century, by the third decade of the eighteenth century England's renewed campaign against sea banditry was successfully capturing and hanging pirates regularly, rendering piracy an exceptionally dangerous employment.

Second, a merchant sailor who entered piracy had to be willing to plunder other ships, murder innocents, and brutally torture resisters. Although many sailors were surely drawn to the idea of piracy by the prospect of riches, in light of the brutal features of piratical employment, it is not surprising that many sailors were unwilling to become sea marauders despite the potentially superior pay.

B.   A Comparison to Privateer Organization

Pirates' plunderous success does not necessarily point to their organization's efficiency, however. Pirates may have been quite successful despite their institutions rather than because of them. Ideally, to assess pirate organization's efficiency we would want to see how marine vessels that engaged in the same economic activity as pirates, violently taking prizes—but did so legitimately and thus enjoyed government enforcement—were organized. If we could identify such vessels and they exhibited some of pirate ships' important institutional features, we could more confidently conclude that pirate organization reflected an efficient response to the economic activity pirates were engaged in, not merely the fact that they did not enjoy government support.

Fortunately, such vessels exist and indeed operated contemporaneously with seventeenth- and eighteenth-century pirate ships. These vessels are privateers. Privateers were private warships licensed by governments to harass the merchant ships of enemy nations. Privateers shared a predetermined portion of the proceeds from this activity with the commissioning government.[42] Their licenses, sometimes called "letters of marque," granted them official permission to plunder enemy merchant ships and established their legitimacy under the law.[43] Thus, the institutions and arrangements that privateers used to regulate their ships were legal agreements, enforceable by the commissioning government.

Privateers, like merchant ships, were owned by absentee merchants. Consequently, privateers did not have elected captains or a system of separated powers, as pirate ships did. Owing to the absentee ownership structure privateers shared with merchant ships, the principal-agent problem privateers confronted was similar to the one merchant ships faced. A privateer captain who could be popularly deposed or did not wield absolute authority over his crew would undermine the vessel's profitability for its owners. Given the chance, crew members would elect lax, liberal, and corrupt captains who would allow sailors to relax when they desired, have free reign with provisions, lie to the vessel's owners

---

[42] However, in England, the Prize Act of 1708 entitled privateers to the full value of prizes they took.

[43] There were two kinds of privateers. The first were "full-time" privateers, which sailed exclusively for the purpose of prize taking. The second kind were merchant ships with permission to take prizes they might happen upon and profitably seize in the course of their shipping activity (Rodger 2006, 156). My discussion is concerned with the former, since the latter were in the business of merchant shipping rather than the business of prize taking.

about what plunder they had taken so the crew could hold back a greater share for itself, and so forth. Thus, a variant on the same principal-agent problem merchant ships confronted, which required autocratic captains for its solution, also plagued privateers to a large extent, necessitating autocratic captains on these vessels as well.[44]

Despite this important difference, privateers and pirate ships shared several significant economic features. Most notably, both engaged in plunder. Because of this, privateers, like pirate ships, carried large crews, sometimes of 100 men or more. This was so that they could overcome the smaller merchant ships they preyed on. Similarly to pirate vessels, the size of privateers made it difficult for captains to monitor sailors' effort on these ships. This led privateers to use a pirate-like share system of payment instead of the fixed wages merchant ships used owing to their dramatically smaller size.[45]

Privateers' use of the share system is important because we know that since they enjoyed the full benefit of government enforcement, the absence of such enforcement could not be the reason privateers adopted this compensation scheme. This suggests that the share system's efficiency for pirates was rooted in a specific economic situation pirates confronted (large crews engaged in plunder), shared by privateers, not in an inability to rely on state enforcement.

Privateers also used constitutions similar to those on pirate ships. Woodes Rogers, for instance, records his crew's adoption of a "Constitution," as he called it, for the privateering expedition he commanded between 1708 and 1711 (Rogers [1712] 2004, 7). Several of this constitution's articles resemble those in pirate constitutions. Article 1, for example, specifies the division of plunder between crew members. Article 3 states "that if any Person on board . . . do conceal any Plunder

---

[44] Some privateer captains, such as Woodes Rogers, consulted a council of their fellow officers in making decisions. But democratic voice did not extend to the crew. It should be noted, however, that late seventeenth-century and early eighteenth-century sea raiders who blurred the distinction between pirates and privateers by sailing sometimes with a commission and many other times without typically employed piratical governance institutions.

[45] Privateers were not the only legitimate vessels that used the pirates' share system. Whaling vessels did as well. Although whaling vessels were smaller than pirate ships or privateers, they were typically larger than merchant ships, again making it more difficult to monitor sailor effort. This necessitated share payment, called a "lay," instead of fixed monthly or lump-sum wages (Davis, Gallman, and Gleiter 1998). Navy ships also relied partially on a share system to compensate sailors. Although in peacetime sailors received fixed monthly wages, in wartime they received both monthly wages and a share of their prizes' proceeds, as well as "head money" for each of the enemy sailors these prizes carried. Since naval vessels were very large, incentive-based pay helped to overcome the difficulty of monitoring individual sailors. Additionally, navy vessel pay scales (including prize shares) were steeply skewed according to rank. To elicit crew members' full effort, navy vessels thus combined incentive pay in the context of a tournament system. See, e.g., Benjamin and Thornberg (2007).

exceeding one Piece of Eight in value, 24 hours after the Capture of any Prize, he shall be severely punish'd, and lose his Shares of the Plunder." Article 6 stipulates "that a Reward of twenty Pieces of Eight shall be given to him that first sees a Prize of good Value, or exceeding 50 Tuns in Burden." Like pirate articles, which required unanimous consent, this privateering constitution, Rogers tells us, was similarly signed by every member of the crew "without any Compulsion" (23).

Since Rogers' expedition enjoyed the full protection of government enforcement, this constitution could not have been adopted because the vessels did not have state backing. Instead, such privateer constitutions must have been efficient for reasons unrelated to this. Common obstacles faced by both pirates and privateers suggest what these reasons are.

First and foremost, both pirates and privateers were in the business of sea banditry. Because the goods they dealt with and carried were always stolen, property rights to these goods could be somewhat unclear. For instance, if upon boarding a vessel a pirate or privateer came upon some valuable, was it his to keep? Or was this part of the common loot to be divided among the crew? Once the stolen booty was transferred to the pirate or privateer ship, was it fair game? After all, no one on the pirate or privateer ship could claim to legitimately own it. To clarify the status of property rights on their ships, both privateers and pirates used constitutions to make explicit crew member property rights to plunder.

Contrast this situation with the status of property rights on merchant vessels. On these ships, property rights were totally clear. The cargo they carried clearly belonged to the ships' owners (or their customers) and not the crew. Explicating the property rights over the goods merchant ships carried was therefore unnecessary, and for this reason, merchant ships did not do so.

Similarly, since both pirates and privateers used a share system to compensate crew members, the laziness of one crew member directly affected the payment of the others. To attenuate this problem and elicit full crew member effort, both privateers and pirates constitutionally codified bonuses on their ships. Contrast this situation again with the one on merchant ships, which used fixed wages. Here, each sailor's income was independent of his fellow crew members' behavior. Thus, bonuses were unnecessary.[46]

The similarities between certain aspects of pirate and privateer institutions, as well as the differences between their shared institutions and

---

[46] Ship captains sometimes received bonuses, however. "Primage and average," for example, were paid to ship captains and constituted bonuses of a sort, though these were paid by the freighter rather than by the owners.

those of merchant ships, suggests two important items. First, the institutional differences between pirate and merchant ships were driven at least in part by the different economic situations they confronted, not the difference in their ability to rely on government support. Second, at least some major features of pirate organization were efficient independent of pirates' inability to rely on government. Their efficiency derived from the particular economic situation pirate ships faced, which they shared partially with privateers.

On the other side of this, at least one important part of the economic situation pirates and privateers faced was very different: the ownership structure of their ships. In terms of this feature, privateers and merchant ships were similar, whereas pirate ships, which had no absentee owners, were very different. This explains why privateers and merchant ships both used autocratic captains, which they required to solve the owner-crew principal-agent problem they consequently faced. In contrast, since on pirate ships the principals were the agents, pirates could use a democratic system of separated power to constrain captain predation.

C. A Comparison to Explorer Organization

A crucial feature of pirate organization's efficiency was its ability, or inability, to facilitate crew cooperation. Since pirates lived and worked together in close quarters among fellow criminals for extended periods of time, their ability to cooperate for coordinated plunder was a critical determinant of their enterprise's success.

Merchant ships secured crew cooperation through the command of their autocratic captains. Indeed, as discussed above, merchant ships could not do without autocracy for this purpose. In contrast, pirate ships did not have the state backing required for autocratic organization. Although the evidence considered above suggests that pirates cooperated successfully under democratic organization, this fact raises the question of pirates' organizational efficiency.

Perhaps pirates could have secured even more cooperation had they been able to organize autocratically as merchant ships did and would have sought to secure cooperation this way if they could. Alternatively, pirates' organization may have been superior in creating crew cooperation, in which case pirates used it (at least partly) for this reason, not because autocratically organizing their ships was not an option.[47] To get

---

[47] As for the organizational features discussed above, here too it is important to emphasize that if pirate organization was in fact superior in creating crew cooperation, this would not mean that merchant ship organization was inefficient *for merchant ships*. Merchant ships faced a different economic situation than pirates, most important, the owner-crew principal-agent problem. Constrained by the need to solve this problem, merchant ships could secure crew cooperation only through autocracy. Thus, even if it came at the

at this issue we need to examine the comparative ability of autocratic and democratic ship organization to facilitate crew cooperation.

Since the difficulty of achieving crew cooperation likely varied according to the activities different kinds of vessels were engaged in, it is important to consider how autocratic versus democratic ship organization affected crew cooperation on vessels engaged in the same activity. Comparing cooperation on pirate and merchant ships, then, is not helpful. Further, since all pirate ships were organized democratically and all merchant ships were organized autocratically, we cannot gain insight into this question by looking only at pirate ships or only at merchant ships.[48]

Fortunately, a different kind of ship we have not yet considered provides an excellent case for examining this issue: explorer vessels. Explorer vessels are useful here for two reasons. First, between the sixteenth and twentieth centuries, explorer ships embarked on long, often grueling, voyages to uncharted waters. Their crews spent years together at sea under conditions in which cooperation was at a premium. Second, there is significant variation in the modes of organization explorers employed for this purpose. Some pursued more autocratic organization, as merchant ships did. Others pursued more democratic organization, as pirate ships did, and with differing success.

Unlike merchant, privateer, or pirate voyages, most explorer voyages did not seek profits. Their purpose was to discover (and sometimes claim) unknown parts of the world and then to report their findings to curious landlubbers.[49] This is significant because in contrast to the vessel types considered thus far, economic concerns did not play a significant role in determining explorer organization.

Instead, the party organizing an exploratory expedition determined the ship's institutional organization. When government chiefly financed and organized an expedition, the explorer's institutions tended to reflect the autocratic institutions of the government's navy. The resulting organization was similar to that on merchant ships. When an adventurer himself chiefly organized and raised the finances for an expedition, the ship's institutions tended to be more democratic.

---

price of less crew harmony, for merchant ships, autocratic organization was still superior to democratic organization, which would have rendered merchant shipping unprofitable for owners.

[48] The Barbary pirates, who were really corsairs, did not organize democratically. However, this article is not concerned with them.

[49] Although some explorer voyages, such as Magellan's, certainly had as their ultimate goal discovery for the purpose of profit, the exploratory expedition itself was almost always a "nonprofit" voyage. In Magellan's case the attitude seemed to be, if the exploratory voyage itself makes money, all the better. But pure exploration for the purpose of *future* gain was the voyage's primary aim, even if, e.g., the exploratory voyage itself did cover its own costs.

I consider five explorer voyages between the sixteenth and twentieth centuries. Government directly or indirectly organized three of these, which displayed autocratic organization: Ferdinand Magellan's three-year voyage around the world between 1519 and 1522, James Cook's three-year voyage in search of "the Discovery of the Southern Continent" between 1768 and 1771,[50] and Robert F. Scott's Antarctic expedition in the *Discovery* between 1901 and 1904. Private adventurers organized the remaining two explorer voyages, which displayed more democratic organization: Roald Amundsen's search for the Northwest Passage in the *Gjøa* between 1903 and 1906 and Ernest Shackleton's Antarctic expedition in the *Endurance* between 1914 and 1916.

Magellan's voyage consisted of five ships carrying 270 men in total. The Spanish government organized his expedition hierarchically, consisting of lieutenants, masters, captains for each ship, and, at the apex, Magellan himself, "captain-general" of the voyage. The Crown appointed Magellan to this position and issued a long and detailed list of regulations (74 in all) governing the terms of the exploration and how it should proceed. Chief among these were the government's strict instructions to the crew "to defer to the opinion and order of Magellan" (Guillemard 1890, 127–28) and Magellan's "power of deciding and executing short and summary justice by sea or land in case of suits or disputes arising in the fleet" (Stanley 1874, xxxi).

As one of Magellan's crew members put it, "the captain ordered that his regulations . . . be strictly observed" (Pigafetta [1525] 1994, 39). These regulations dictated the sail of the fleet's ships, the crew members' duties, and even crew members' ability to trade with and accept gifts from the exotic foreigners they encountered on their journey (72).

Although there was a division of labor on Magellan's voyage, there was no division of power. Ultimately, the captain-general's orders directed his subordinate officers, who in turn directed the crew. There was one instance of limited democracy on Magellan's journey, which occurred when Magellan unexpectedly died. The crew "made and elected two commanders" to operate in the absence of their captain-general (Pigafetta 1525, 88). However, this seems to be the only democratic moment in the voyage, which was otherwise governed autocratically.

The effectiveness of Magellan's autocratic organization was mixed. On the one hand, considerable crew member turmoil plagued his expedition, culminating in a violent mutiny of three of Magellan's five ships against the captain-general, ostensibly because he had put the crew on short rations. Magellan emerged victorious out of the violent mixup

---

[50] The other duty the Admiralty instructed Cook to accomplish was to charter King George's Island.

and punished the mutineers, some by execution, others by imprisonment. Later in the voyage, one entire ship deserted Magellan's fleet.

However, it is important to be careful in interpreting this conflict as a sign of total failure. The magnitude of the venture must be kept in mind, and, ultimately, the voyage did return to Spain. This constituted the first circumnavigation of the globe, albeit one that claimed the lives of 252 of the 270 sailors who undertook it.

The British government organized Captain James Cook's expedition. In command of *His Majestys Bark Endeavour,* Cook's captainship combined the powers of commander and ultimate disciplinarian along the lines observed in the merchant and navy marine. Indeed, Cook's regulations of his crew drew explicitly on those in operation in the navy at the time. As he instructed his crew, for example, "if by neglect [any sailor] looseth any of his Arms or woorking tools, or suffers them to be stole [by natives where the ship stops], the full Value thereof will be charge'd against his pay according to the Custom of the Navy in such cases, and he shall receive further punishment as the nature of the offence may deserve" (Cook, April 17, 1769 [2000, 40]).

This regulation was one of five "Rules to be observ'd by every person in or belonging to His Majestys Bark the Endeavor, for the better establishing a regular and uniform Trade for Provisions &c with the Inhabitants of Georges Island" (April 17, 1769, 39–40).

As on Magellan's fleet, Cook also made use of a division of labor, sometimes delegating punishment duties to his officers. But ultimately Cook dictated and enforced corporal punishment. As his journal entry dated November 30, 1768, records, for instance, "Punished Rob Anderson Seaman and Will Judge Marine with twelve lashes each, the former for leaving his duty a Shore and attempting to disert the Ship, and the latter for useing abusive language to the Officer of the Watch, and John Readon Boatswains Mate with twelve lashes for not doing his duty in punishing the above two Men" (22). Similarly, elsewhere Cook records, "Punished Rich Hutchins Seaman with 12 lashes for disobaying command," highlighting both the hierarchy of the ship's organization and Captain Cook's authority to administer punishments (April 16, 1769, 44).

Cook successfully accomplished his voyage; but his journal suggests that crew cooperation and harmony were strained. Here, Cook records instances of disgruntled sailors, insolence, theft, and even intracrew murder (see, e.g., the entries for April 13, 1769, 38; June 21, 1769, 60; June 4, 1769, 55; June 19, 1769, 58; and March 26, 1769, 35).

The Royal Society and Royal Geographic Society organized Robert Scott's early twentieth-century Antarctic exploration and appointed Scott captain of the expedition. Like Cook, Scott was a navy officer. In addition to several nonnaval mariners, a number of other navy seamen manned Scott's *Discovery*, which observed the traditional naval hierarchy. For instance, Scott imprisoned the cook and later chained him to the deck for insubordination (Huntford 1999, 146).

Like Cook's expedition, Scott's also suffered from sailor discontent. As one of his sailors remarked, Scott's autocratic method of governing the ship "is causing a lot of discontent on the mess deck," that is, among the nonofficer crew. Another noted how the crew's men had become "short tempered and low spirited" (quoted in Huntford 1999, 151). The *Discovery*'s troubles peaked when it became lodged in ice in the Ross Sea. In an embarrassing finale to the debacle, the Royal Navy had to rescue it.

Roald Amundsen's organization aboard the *Gjøa* provides an interesting contrast to Scott's. Amundsen's voyage took place only a few years after Scott's and sought to explore the Arctic. In contrast to the voyages discussed above, Amundsen organized his exploration on his own behalf. He was therefore not obliged to organize the *Gjøa* according to the navy pattern. On the contrary, he chose to organize his ship in a highly democratic, decentralized fashion, not unlike pirate organization. As Amundsen described his vessel's organization, "We have established a little republic on board *Gjøa*. . . . After my own experience, I decided as far as possible to use a system of freedom on board—let everybody have the feeling of being independent within his own sphere. In that way, there arises . . . a spontaneous and voluntary discipline, which is worth far more than compulsion . . . . The will to do work is many times greater and thereby the work itself" (quoted in Huntford 1999, 84).

As one sailor aboard the *Gjøa* commented, "No orders were given, but everyone seemed to know exactly what to do" (quoted in Huntford 1999, 84). Unlike Scott's voyage, Amundsen's proved exceedingly smooth. The crew was happy and the expedition successful.

When one of Scott's former sailors aboard the *Discovery*, Ernest Shackleton, decided to explore the Antarctic himself, he also employed a more democratic organization for his vessel, the *Endurance*. Shackleton did not allow his crew to elect any of the ship's officers; but he did appoint his second in command, Frank Wild, to act as an arbitrator for the ship's men, removing himself from this authority. Shackleton set routines for his men and generally directed their activities. However, he assigned his men to the unpleasant and more pleasant tasks on the ship in shifts, regardless of their status, rather than basing their assignments on rank.

As one of his crew members observed, "When Shackleton took over control of the ship, the ship officers had to climb down a peg or two." According to him, "The ship's officers became units with no more authority than the rest of the crowd, and their position on the floe was the same" (quoted in Morrell and Capparell 2002, 89, 134). Officers and nonofficers received identical victuals and were treated equally in all other affairs.

Shackleton's quasi-democratic organization aboard the *Endurance* created good order and cooperation among the crew. As Thomas Orde-Lees, a crew member of the *Endurance*, commented, for example, "We seem to be a wonderfully happy family but I think Sir Ernest is the real secret of our unanimity." Similarly, as another sailor recorded, "We are now six months out from England and during the whole of this time we have all pulled well together and with an almost complete lack of friction" (quoted in Morrell and Capparell 2002, 99).

The evidence from the five explorers considered here suggests that democratic or self-governing vessel organization, such as the kind pirates used, facilitated crew cooperation at least as successfully as autocratic vessel organization, and probably more so. Magellan, Cook, and Scott each seemed to face greater problems maintaining accord on their ships than Amundsen or Shackleton. Since pirates did not require autocratic organization to overcome the owner-crew principal-agent problem that merchant ships confronted, this suggests that even if pirates had government enforcement at their disposal, they would likely have opted for a democratic organization, such as the one they used. Although it is of course not possible to establish this definitively, it does not seem likely, then, that autocratic organization was in fact superior in this regard and that pirates would have used it if only they enjoyed government support.

The case of explorers also sheds light on the issue of captain predation. In contrast to merchant ships, there does not appear to have been a problem of captain predation on democratic or autocratic explorer vessels. Only on Magellan's voyage is there evidence that the crew suspected captain self-dealing, and here the charge seems to be unfounded (see, e.g., Guillemard 1890).

An important economic difference between merchant ships, on the one hand, and even autocratically organized explorer vessels, on the other, suggests itself as the likely reason for this. With the exception of Magellan, none of the explorer captains considered above stood to directly profit from cutting crew member rations, shorting crew members their pay, and so forth. These explorer captains were not residual claimants of their voyages, as merchant ship captains were.

Explorer captains gained very little if upon their vessels' return they had succeeded in defrauding the crew out of victuals or wages.[51] The expedition's costs were borne largely by external financiers who did not

[51] Although he may not benefit monetarily, a predatory captain might still have some incentive to pinch provisions to make more available to himself, however.

"invest" in the expedition for profit. Further, the explorer captains them-selves did not aim at turning a profit on the exploratory voyage itself. They therefore had little incentive to prey on their crew members.

Magellan is somewhat of an exception in this regard in that, under the terms of his agreement with the Spanish Crown, he was to receive 20 percent of any net proceeds his expedition directly generated. Thus, he could have tried to generate larger gains for himself by, for instance, illegitimately cutting crew member rations, which, as noted above, some crew members (wrongly) accused him of. However, Magellan's payoff of preying on his crew in this way paled in comparison to his payoff of making the exploration a successful one.

According to his agreement with Spain, if Magellan succeeded in discovering any new isles or countries, he was perpetually entitled to one-twentieth of all revenue they generated for Spain. Further, if his exploration succeeded in forging a route to the Spice Islands, he would be allowed to send 1,000 ducats' worth of goods on every Spanish ar-mada sent to trade with the islands. However, to reap these much greater financial rewards, Magellan had to keep his crew intact sufficiently to weather the long and onerous voyage. Since cheating crew members would have seriously threatened this already difficult task, it was not in Magellan's greater financial interest to do so.

This absence of predatory incentives for captains on explorers stands in stark contrast to the situation on merchant ships in which every voyage's purpose was to make money, and absentee owners and share-holder captains often stood to directly profit from predation. Thus, while autocratic organization opened the door for captain abuse on merchant ships, it did not seem to do so significantly on explorer ships.

VI. Conclusion

Over the last decade or so there has been a resurgence of piracy off the horn of Africa and in the Straits of Malacca (see, e.g., Gottschalk and Flanagan 2000; Burnett 2002; Langewiesche 2004). Like seven-teenth- and eighteenth-century pirates, the modern variety choose to plunder ships in waters in which government enforcement is weak, such as those around Somalia and Indonesia, and commercial vessels are abundant.

Beyond this, however, modern pirates share little in common with their predecessors. Seventeenth- and eighteenth-century pirates lived together for long periods of time at sea. Although they retired to land between expeditions, they spent much of their time together prowling the expanses of the ocean in search of prey. Because of this, their ships formed miniature "floating societies." Like all societies, pirates' floating

Austrian Law and Economics II

ones also required social rules and governance institutions if pirates were to maintain their "abominable combination."

In contrast, modern pirates spend almost no time together on their ships. Their "raids" take one of two forms. The first and most common method constitutes little more than maritime muggery. Pirate "crews" of two to six hop in small speedboats with guns; pull alongside legitimate ships, usually in territorial waters close to the coast; and threaten their prey at gunpoint to give up their watches, jewelry, and whatever money the boat may be carrying. They then return to their villages on the coast, where they live among nonpirates and resume regular employment.

These pirates do not live, sleep, and interact together on their ships for months, weeks, or even days on end. They therefore do not constitute a society and face few, if any, of the problems of social cooperation and order their forefathers did.

The second and far less common method of modern piracy is somewhat different. Crews again are small—between five and 15 men—and spend very little time together at sea. But professional land-based criminals hire these modern pirates to steal boats, which they then convert into "phantom ships" and resell. They pay these modern pirates lump sums and contract them on a case-by-case basis. Like the maritime muggers, pirates-for-hire rely predominantly on hijacking methods to steal ships, though for larger vessels they have been known to plant "insiders"—sailors who pretend to be legitimate sailors seeking employment on the ship in question—who later hijack the target from the inside.

Since modern pirates sail in very small groups and spend very little time together at sea, they do not exhibit any discernible organizational structure, as seventeenth- and eighteenth-century pirates clearly did. Unlike older pirates, privateers, merchantmen, or explorers, the "in-and-out" character of modern pirates, coupled with the fact that crews are so small, means that they do not require rules for creating order, rationing provisions, or assigning tasks. Modern pirates do not even require captains in the usual sense. There is, of course, someone who steers the motorboat and acts as a leader among the six or so pirates; but he is not a captain in the way that eighteenth-century pirate, privateer, or merchant captains were.

Even organizational problems related to the distribution of plunder are largely absent for modern pirates. The sea muggers need to divide what they steal. But nothing structured is required since, unlike seventeenth- and eighteenth-century pirates, modern sea robbers do not sail for extended periods with growing piles of booty. Their trips are evening cruises. When they end, the pirates return to their day jobs. Modern pirates-for-hire do not even confront a distribution of booty problem to this extent. The landed thieves who employ them pay them wages. Once the pirates have taken a prize, they hand it over to their employer. Sadly, then, modern pirates are far less interesting from an economic or organizational point of view than their predecessors.

The institutions of seventeenth- and eighteenth-century pirates, in contrast, provide an important glimpse into the typically invisible governance mechanisms that support cooperation inside criminal organizations. My analysis of the law, economics, and organization of pirates leads to three conclusions.

First, ordinary "foot soldiers" inside criminal organizations may face a problem of leader predation similar to the problem citizens under governments face with respect to political rulers. Importantly, organized criminals' inability to rely on state-created institutions to overcome this problem does not prevent them from developing private, self-enforcing institutions for this purpose instead. "Kings were not needed to invent the pirate system of governance" (Rogozinski 2000, 184). It is unlikely that they are needed to invent systems of governance in other criminal organizations either.

Second, the institutions that constituted the pirates' system of governance—democratic checks, the separation of power, and constitutions—are remarkably similar to those governments employ to constrain ruler predation in the "legitimate world." Government does not have a monopoly on these institutions of governance any more than it has a monopoly on the ability to generate cooperation and order. The success of pirate "an-arrgh-chy" highlights both of these facts.

In the same way that merchant ship autocracy reflected an efficient institutional response to the particular economic situation that merchant ships faced, pirate organization reflected an efficient institutional response to the particular, and rather different, economic situation that pirate ships faced. The efficiency of piratical institutions, it seems, resulted at least in part from this economic difference between pirate and merchant ships, not from the former's inability to rely on government support for autocratic organization.

Finally, organized criminals are as interested in creating order among themselves as noncriminals. They, too, have an incentive to develop solutions to obstacles that otherwise prevent them from cooperating for mutual gain. The fact that they direct their cooperation at someone else's loss does not alter this. Thus, while Captain Charles Johnson described the pirates' criminal organization as "that abominable Society" (1726–28, 114), it is important to acknowledge that, however abominable, it was nevertheless a society.

References

Anderson, Annelise Graebner. 1979. *The Business of Organized Crime: A Cosa Nostra Family.* Stanford, CA: Hoover Inst. Press.

Anderson, Terry L., Bruce L. Benson, and Thomas E. Flanagan, eds. 2006. *Self-Determination: The Other Path for Native Americans.* Stanford, CA: Stanford Univ. Press.

Anderson, Terry L., and Peter J. Hill. 2004. *The Not So Wild, Wild West: Property Rights on the Frontier.* Stanford, CA: Stanford Univ. Press.

Anderson, Terry L., and Fred S. McChesney, eds. 2002. *Property Rights: Contract, Conflict, and Law.* Princeton, NJ: Princeton Univ. Press.

Arlacchi, Pino. 1986. *Mafia Business: The Mafia Ethic and the Spirit of Capitalism.* London: Verso.

Becker, Gary S. 1968. "Crime and Punishment: An Economic Approach." *J.P.E.* 76 (March/April): 169–217.

Benjamin, Daniel K., and Christopher Thornberg. 2007. "Organization and Incentives in the Age of Sail." *Explorations Econ. Hist.* 44 (April): 317–41.

Benson, Bruce L. 1988. "Legal Evolution in Primitive Societies." *J. Inst. and Theoretical Econ.* 144 (December): 772–88.

———. 1989. "The Spontaneous Evolution of Commercial Law." *Southern Econ. J.* 55 (January): 644–61.

———. 1990. *The Enterprise of Law: Justice without the State.* San Francisco: Pacific Res. Inst. Public Policy.

Betagh, William. 1728. *A Voyage round the World . . . .* London: Combes, Lacy, and Clarke.

Bucquoy, Jacobus de. 1744. *Zestien Jaarige Reis nass de Inidien gedan door Jacob de Bucquoy.* Haarlem: Bosch.

Burnett, John S. 2002. *Dangerous Waters: Modern Piracy and Terror on the High Seas.* New York: Plume.

Chang, Juin-Jen, Huei-Chung Lu, and Mingshen Chen. 2005. "Organized Crime or Individual Crime? Endogenous Size of a Criminal Organization and the Optimal Law Enforcement." *Econ. Inquiry* 43 (July): 661–75.

Cook, James. [1768–80] 2003. *James Cook: The Journals.* Edited by Philip Edwards. New York: Penguin Classics.

Cordingly, David, ed. 1996. *Pirates: Terror on the High Seas, from the Caribbean to the South China Sea.* Atlanta: Turner Pub.

———. 2006. *Under the Black Flag: The Romance and the Reality of Life among the Pirates.* New York: Random House.

Dampier, William. [1697–1707] 2005. *The Buccaneer Explorer: William Dampier's Voyages.* Edited by Gerald Norris. Woodbridge, UK: Boydell.

Davis, Lance E., Robert E. Gallman, and Karin Gleiter. 1998. *In Pursuit of Leviathan: Technology, Institutions, Productivity, and Profits in American Whaling, 1816–1906.* Chicago: Univ. Chicago Press (for NBER).

Davis, Ralph. 1962. *The Rise of the English Shipping Industry in the Seventeenth and Eighteenth Centuries.* London: Macmillan.

Dick, Andrew R. 1995. "When Does Organized Crime Pay? A Transaction Cost Analysis." *Internat. Rev. Law and Econ.* 15 (January): 25–45.

Downing, Clement. [1737] 1924. *A History of the Indian Wars.* Edited by William Foster. London: Oxford Univ. Press.

Earle, Peter. 1998. *Sailors: English Merchant Seamen, 1650–1775.* London: Methuen.

Exquemelin, Alexander O. [1678] 2000. *The Buccaneers of America.* Translated by Alexis Brown. Mineola, NY: Dover.

Fiorentini, Gianluca, and Sam Peltzman, eds. 1995. *The Economics of Organised Crime.* Cambridge: Cambridge Univ. Press.

Friedman, David. 1979. "Private Creation and Enforcement of Law: A Historical Case." *J. Legal Studies* 8 (March): 399–415.

Furbank, Philip N., and W. R. Owens. 1988. *The Canonisation of Daniel Defoe.* New Haven, CT: Yale Univ. Press.

Gambetta, Diego. 1993. *The Sicilian Mafia: The Business of Private Protection.* Cambridge, MA: Harvard Univ. Press.

Garoupa, Nuno. 2000. "The Economics of Organized Crime and Optimal Law Enforcement." *Econ. Inquiry* 38 (April): 278–88.

Gifford, Adam, Jr. 1993. "The Economic Organization of 17th- through Mid 19th-Century Whaling and Shipping." *J. Econ. Behavior and Organization* 20 (February): 137–50.

Gosse, Philip. 1946. *The History of Piracy.* New York: Tudor.

Gottschalk, Jack A., and Brian P. Flanagan. 2000. *Jolly Roger with an Uzi: The Rise and Threat of Modern Piracy.* Annapolis, MD: U.S. Naval Inst. Press.

Guillemard, Francis H. H. 1890. *The Life of Ferdinand Magellan, and the First Circumnavigation of the Globe, 1480–1521.* London: Philip and Son.

Hayward, Arthur L., ed. [1735] 1874. *Lives of the Most Remarkable Criminals . . . . : Collected from Original Papers and Authentic Memoirs.* 2 vols. London: Reeves and Turner.

Hughes, Jonathan R. T., and Louis P. Cain. 1994. *American Economic History.* 4th ed. New York: HarperCollins.

Huntford, Roland. 1999. *The Last Place on Earth: Scott and Amundsen's Race to the South Pole.* New York: Random House.

Jameson, J. Franklin, ed. 1923. *Privateering and Piracy in the Colonial Period: Illustrative Documents.* New York: Macmillan.

Jankowski, Martin Sanchez. 1991. *Islands in the Street: Gangs and American Urban Society.* Berkeley: Univ. California Press.

Jennings, William P., Jr. 1984. "A Note on the Economics of Organized Crime." *Eastern Econ. J.* 10 (July–September): 315–21.

Johnson, Charles. [1726–28] 1999. *A General History of the Pyrates, From Their First Rise and Settlement in the Island of Providence, to the Present Time.* Edited by Manuel Schonhorn. New York: Dover.

Kinkor, Kenneth J. 2001. "Black Men under the Black Flag." In *Bandits at Sea: A Pirates Reader*, edited by C. R. Pennell. New York: New York Univ. Press.

Konrad, Kai A., and Stergios Skaperdas. 1998. "Extortion." *Economica* 65 (November): 461–77.

Konstam, Angus. 2002. *The History of Pirates.* Guilford, CT: Lyons.

———. 2007. *Scourge of the Seas: Buccaneers, Pirates and Privateers.* New York: Osprey.

Langewiesche, William. 2004. *The Outlaw Sea: A World of Freedom, Chaos, and Crime.* New York: North Point.

Leeson, Peter T. 2007a. "Efficient Anarchy." *Public Choice* 130 (January): 41–53.

———. 2007b. "Trading with Bandits." *J. Law and Econ.* 50 (May): 303–21.

———. Forthcoming. "Social Distance and Self-Enforcing Exchange." *J. Legal Studies.*

Levitt, Steven D., and Sudhir Alladi Venkatesh. 2000. "An Economic Analysis of a Drug-Selling Gang's Finances." *Q.J.E.* 115 (August): 755–89.

Marx, Jenifer G. 1996a. "The Brethren of the Coast." In *Pirates: Terror on the High Seas, from the Caribbean to the South China Sea*, edited by David Cordingly. Atlanta: Turner Pub.

———. 1996b. "The Golden Age of Piracy." In *Pirates: Terror on the High Seas, from the Caribbean to the South China Sea*, edited by David Cordingly. Atlanta: Turner Pub.

———. 1996c. "The Pirate Round." In *Pirates: Terror on the High Seas, from the Caribbean to the South China Sea*, edited by David Cordingly. Atlanta: Turner Pub.

Morrell, Margot, and Stephanie Capparell. 2002. *Shackleton's Way: Leadership Lessons from the Great Antarctic Explorer.* New York: Penguin.

Morris, Richard B. 1965. *Government and Labor in Early America.* New York: Harper and Row.

Pigafetta, Antonio. [1525] 1994. *Magellan's Voyage: A Narrative Account of the First Circumnavigation.* Translated and edited by R. A. Skelton. New York: Dover.

Polo, Michele. 1995. "Internal Cohesion and Competition among Criminal Organisations." In *The Economics of Organised Crime*, edited by Gianluca Fiorentini and Sam Peltzman. Cambridge: Cambridge Univ. Press.

Pringle, Patrick. 1953. *Jolly Roger: The Story of the Great Age of Piracy.* New York: Norton.

Rankin, Hugh F. 1969. *The Golden Age of Piracy.* Williamsburg, VA: Colonial Williamsburg.

Rediker, Marcus. 1981. "'Under the Banner of King Death': The Social World of Anglo-American Pirates, 1716 to 1726." *William and Mary Q.* 38 (April): 203–27.

———. 1987. *Between the Devil and the Deep Blue Sea: Merchant Seamen, Pirates and the Anglo-American Maritime World, 1700–1750.* Cambridge: Cambridge Univ. Press.

———. 2004. *Villains of All Nations: Atlantic Pirates in the Golden Age.* Boston: Beacon.

Reuter, Peter. 1983. *Disorganized Crime: The Economics of the Visible Hand.* Cambridge, MA: MIT Press.

———. 1987. *Racketeering in Legitimate Industries: A Study in the Economics of Intimidation.* Santa Monica, CA: Rand.

Ritchie, Robert C. 1986. *Captain Kidd and the War against the Pirates.* Cambridge, MA: Harvard Univ. Press.

Rodger, N. A. M. 1996. *The Wooden World: An Anatomy of the Georgian Navy.* New York: Norton.

———. 2006. *A Naval History of Britain.* Vol. 2. *The Command of the Ocean, 1649–1815.* New York: Norton.

Rogers, Woodes. [1712] 2004. *A Cruising Voyage round the World.* Santa Barbara, CA: Narrative Press.

Rogozinski, Jan. 2000. *Honor among Thieves: Captain Kidd, Henry Every, and the Pirate Democracy in the Indian Ocean.* Mechanicsburg, PA: Stackpole Books.

Schelling, Thomas C. 1971. "What Is the Business of Organized Crime?" *J. Public Law* 20 (1): 71–84.

Skaperdas, Stergios. 2001. "The Political Economy of Organized Crime: Providing Protection When the State Does Not." *Econ. Governance* 2 (3): 173–202.

Slush, Barnaby. 1709. *The Navy Royal: Or a Sea-Cook Turn'd Projector.* London: Bragg.

Snelgrave, William. [1734] 1971. *A New Account of Some Parts of Guinea and the Slave-Trade.* London: Cass.

Spotswood, Alexander. 1882–85. *The Official Letters of Alexander Spotswood.* 2 vols. Richmond: Virginia Hist. Soc.

Stanley, Henry Edward, trans. and ed. 1874. *The First Voyage round the World, by Magellan.* London: Hakluyt Soc.

Uring, Nathaniel. [1726] 1928. *The Voyages and Travels of Captain Nathaniel Uring.* London: Cassell.

Venkatesh, Sudhir Alladi, and Steven D. Levitt. 2000. "'Are We a Family or a Business?' History and Disjuncture in the Urban American Street Gang." *Theory and Society* 29 (August): 427–62.

Woodard, Colin. 2007. *The Republic of Pirates.* New York: Harcourt.

Part VI
Minimizing the State

[24]

politics, philosophy & economics   article

© SAGE Publications Ltd

London
Thousand Oaks, CA
and New Delhi

1470-594X
200302 2(1) 115–128
030426

Reflections on the minimal state

John Hasnas

George Mason University School of Law, USA

abstract   This article challenges the traditional argument for the state that holds that because the market is unable to supply the rule-making, adjudicative, and enforcement services that are essential to life in society, the state must, and hence is morally justified. The author argues that the market's inability to supply these basic services proves only that the state must ensure that they are supplied, not that it must supply them itself. This implies that the traditional concept of the minimal state as one that supplies only these basic services is flawed. The 'remedial state' (one that regulates the private provision of these services) is actually the minimal state.

keywords   anarchy, libertarianism, minimal state, political obligation, protective agency, public goods

Introduction

Since John Rawls revitalized political philosophy with the publication of *A Theory of Justice*[1] in 1971, there has been much scholarly debate over the ethical justification for political obligation. Scholars involved in this debate typically share the assumption that there is a legitimate moral basis for state power, but disagree about what it is. Beginning with Robert Nozick,[2] however, a subset of these scholars explicitly questioned this assumption and seriously considered whether the state can be ethically justified at all.[3] As a result, over the past quarter-century, several scholars have examined the fundamental moral justification for state power.

Like all normative arguments, the basic argument for the moral justification of the state has both a normative and an empirical premise. The normative premise

John Hasnas is Associate Professor of Law at George Mason University School of Law,
3301 North Fairfax Drive, Arlington, VA 22201, USA [email: jhasnas@gmu.edu]

is usually expressed as a conditional asserting that if the state is necessary for the delivery of certain essential services, then state provision of these services is morally justified. The empirical premise then asserts that the state is, in fact, necessary for the delivery of these services. The evaluation of this argument almost always focuses on the empirical premise. Critics try to show how the services in question can be adequately supplied by a free market; defenders counter by attempting to demonstrate how the market will fail.[4] In this article, I have no intention of entering the fray over the empirical premise. Rather, I will argue that the normative premise is false in an interesting way that may render the debate over the empirical premise moot and should cause us to revise our conception of the minimal state.

The basic concepts

Most scholars who consider the matter follow Max Weber[5] in identifying the state with an organization that asserts a monopoly on the use of force over some geographic area and raises its revenue through coercive taxation.[6] Tyler Cowen gives a somewhat looser set of indicia, treating the state as an organization characterized by 'finance through taxation, claim of sovereignty, ultimate decision-making authority, and prohibitions on competitive entry.'[7] Either of these locutions may suffice for present purposes. What appears to be essential for an organization to be considered a state is that it monopolizes the basic policing, rule-making, and adjudicative functions in an identifiable area and funds these functions through taxation.

A state that performs *only* these basic functions is usually, following Nozick,[8] referred to as the 'minimal state'. The minimal state is thought to present a crucial test case because it is assumed that for any state to be morally justified, it, at least, must be. Therefore, the basic argument for the state consists in an attempt to provide a moral justification for an organization that is empowered both to compel its customers to pay for its police, rule-making, and adjudication services and to use its coercive power to suppress all competitors.

The exemplar: the argument from Locke's *Second Treatise*

The exemplar of the argument for the state can be taken from Chapter 9 of John Locke's *Second Treatise of Government*.[9] There, Locke contends that in the state of nature, that is, in the absence of a state, human beings can have no 'established, settled, known law', no 'known and indifferent judge', and no 'power to back and support [a] sentence when right, and to give it due execution.'[10] The lack of a uniformly accepted body of law and any recognized judicial and enforcement authority means that individuals' lives and property are always at risk of invasion by others. Because only a state can supply the rule-making, adjudicative, and enforcement services that individuals require for 'the mutual preservation of their lives, liberties and estates',[11] the state is essential for human social existence, and is therefore morally justified.[12]

Translated into more modern terminology, the basic argument for the state may be rendered as follows:

1) If the market cannot supply the rules of law, impartial adjudicators, and effective enforcement agencies necessary for human beings to live a secure and peaceful life in society, then a state that supplies these services is morally justified.

2) The market cannot supply the rules of law, impartial adjudicators, and effective enforcement agencies necessary for human beings to live secure and peaceful lives in society.

3) A state that supplies rule-making, adjudicative, and enforcement services is morally justified.

An important caveat should be added. This argument is offered as an exemplar of the argument for the state's domestic power. As a state of nature argument, it proceeds by assuming that states do not exist and asking what essential goods or services human beings would be unable to obtain if that were the case. Because under the assumption that states do not exist there is no threat of foreign state aggression, arguments of this type do not address the issue of national defense. This is useful because it allows us to consider the moral justification for state power outside of the context of interstate warfare. As the discussion in the next section will make evident, this is the context in which the debate over the empirical premise has taken place in the literature. In the real world, of course, states do exist, and there is a need for protection against foreign state aggression as well as against domestic criminal activity. Whether the market can supply this type of protective service, however, will not be addressed in this article.[13]

Contemporary consideration of the empirical premise

When Locke wrote, and for centuries thereafter, the argument for the state went unquestioned. Because both premises were regarded as obviously true, political philosophy focused on *how extensive* a state was justified rather than *whether* the state was justified. More recently, however, political philosophers and economists have turned their attention to the status of the second, empirical, premise of the argument. Many of these have been willing to entertain seriously the question of whether the market can provide the basic rule-making, adjudicative, and enforcement services human beings need, and if not, why not.

The explanation most frequently given for market failure in this regard is that these basic services have, in whole or in part, the character of public goods, and thus will be underproduced by the market. Public goods are defined by the features of indivisibility and non-excludability such that 'Once produced, [they are] available to everyone at no additional cost (indivisibility), and it is not feasible or efficient to exclude individuals from the benefit of the good[s] (non-excludability).'[14] These features give individuals an incentive to enjoy the goods without contributing to their production, which prevents them from being produced in the desired amounts.

The public goods argument is most frequently advanced with regard to enforcement services. It is claimed that because private patrols or other measures designed to discourage criminal activities benefit those who do not pay for them as well as those who do, there is a strong incentive for non-payers to free-ride on the expenditures of others with the result that too little will be spent on protective services.[15] Christopher Morris provides a clear example of the argument in this context:

> Security of person is to a large degree a collective good . . . [An] important part of the service provided by public police and systems of criminal justice generally is to *deter* potential violators from harming people. And this deterrence is an indivisible non-excludable good to neighbors and visitors . . . In addition to deterrence, there may be the benefits that follow from incarceration of the thief — namely, incapacitation — benefits that are also indivisible and nonexcludable.

> Social order, at least security of persons and possessions, then, is to a considerable degree a collective good. Accordingly, to the degree that this is the case, social order may not be efficiently provided in the absence of a state.[16]

William Landes and Richard Posner make a similar argument with regard to rule-making services.[17] They contend that because the existence of definite and widely known rules of behavior provides a non-excludable benefit to all, private providers of adjudicative services lack an incentive to establish the clear precedents that give rise to rules. This is because clear precedents 'would confer an external, an uncompensated benefit, not only on future parties, but also on competing judges. If anything, judges might deliberately avoid explaining their results because the demand for their services would be reduced by rules that, by clarifying the meaning of the law, reduce the incidence of disputes'.[18]

Not all theorists agree that the rule-making, adjudicative, and enforcement services human beings need to live secure and peaceful lives with others are public goods that cannot be adequately produced in the absence of a state. Economists Murray Rothbard, David Friedman, and Bruce Benson and legal scholar Randy Barnett have each advanced extended arguments designed to show that these services can, in fact, be privately provided.[19] Although it would not be to the point to rehearse their arguments in detail, these scholars introduce both historical evidence and economic reasoning to show how private companies or organizations can supply the basic protective services individuals need in return for voluntary payments. These 'protective agencies' can take many forms, but are often analogized to health or automobile insurance companies that sell contracts for various levels of protection in return for premiums paid in advance. These scholars similarly suggest that adjudicative services can be supplied by companies such as the American Arbitration Association or JAMS/Endispute, although they also suggest that such services are likely to come bundled with protective services in much the same way automobile insurance companies handle the litigation arising from traffic accidents for their clients. In the latter case, disputes with other clients of one's protective agency would be adjudicated according to the procedures specified in one's policy. Disputes with clients of other protective agencies would be handled according to procedures that have been antecedently specified by the protective agencies to reduce the cost of inter-agency conflict. Lastly, with regard to rule-making, these scholars claim that widely understood rules of behavior would arise from free-market adjudicative services in precisely the same way that our present rules of law arose from customary law and common law processes.

Although most scholars do not believe that the arguments of Rothbard, Friedman, Benson, and Barnett demonstrate that fundamental rule-making, adjudicative, and enforcement services can be provided privately, few have responded to them directly. One who has is Tyler Cowen.[20] He argues that because the services that the posited protective agencies would provide have the characteristics of public goods, the protective agencies will inevitably band together into an abusive monopoly.

Professor Cowen concedes that private agencies can supply the protective services necessary for a secure life in society if they can avoid violent conflict when disputes arise between their clients and the clients of rival agencies. He also concedes that this can be achieved by the type of antecedent inter-agency agreements envisioned by the advocates of the market, and indeed, that such agreements can give rise to a contractual network that can internalize 'adjudication externalities'[21] and provide society with the effective equivalent of a single legal code. According to Professor Cowen, however, this is precisely the problem because 'The existence of a common arbitration network creates a vehicle for protection agency collusion.'[22] Professor Cowen suggests that the same ability to cooperate that allows protection agencies to avoid Hobbesian strife enables them to collude together to exercise monopoly power, which, given the economic incentive to reap monopoly profits, they will surely do. Thus, Professor Cowen concludes that 'Competing legal systems are either unstable or collapse into a monopoly agency or network'.[23] Further, because the services that the cartel monopolizes include the exercise of coercive power, the cartel is both extraordinarily stable and extraordinarily dangerous. It is stable because 'Neither free entry nor defection from the cartel provides the usual protection against collusion that we find in other markets'.[24] It is dangerous because its monopoly on the exercise of coercive power allows it to initiate coercion against its customers, which in turn allows the cartel to raise its revenue through the equivalent of taxation and to extend its monopoly over other segments of the economy.

Professor Cowen argues that it is the public goods characteristics of the

politics, philosophy & economics 2(1)

services the protective agencies provide that cause the agencies to collapse into an abusive monopoly:

> The protection of property rights contains both public and private good elements. The private good element allows markets to produce protection services, but the public good element implies that a monopoly firm or network will arise because of externalities in the adjudication process. The provision of protection with mixed public and private features implies that some set of institutions or economic agents will enjoy monopoly power and reap economic rents.

> The same contractual and cooperative relationships that overcome externalities problems in provision of the public element of protection also allow for successful interfirm collusion.[25]

Thus, Professor Cowen's argument implies that the libertarian anarchists have not really overcome the public goods problem.

If Professor Cowen's account is correct, it constitutes strong support for the empirical premise of the argument for the state. Advocates of the state can point out that when rule-making, adjudicative, and enforcement services are provided by a constitutionally limited state staffed by democratically elected officials, there are many safeguards against the abusive exercise of coercive power. On the other hand, the collusive monopoly of protective agencies Professor Cowen describes is bound by neither constitutional limitations on its power nor the democratic election of its officials. Therefore, if Professor Cowen is correct that a market for these basic services can avoid Hobbesian anarchy only by evolving into a collusive monopoly, it would appear that the market cannot safely deliver these services.

Advocates of the market have responded to Professor Cowen's argument by attempting to show that private protective agencies need not collapse into a collusive cartel and that market incentives provide a better check on the abuse of power than can any constitutional or democratic limitations on a state monopoly, and the debate continues.[26] However, my present purpose is not to resolve this debate, but to illustrate that most of the consideration given to the argument for the state has been devoted to the empirical premise. In the sections that follow, I will suggest that this is unfortunate because there is much to learn from a closer examination of the normative premise, and, more specifically, that such an examination has the potential to render the debate over the empirical premise moot or, alternatively, to point to a pragmatic method for resolving it.

An objection to the normative premise

Perhaps because most contemporary critics of the argument for the state attack the empirical premise, the normative premise has received scant attention. As a result, it appears not to have been remarked that in the form in which it is usually advanced, it is clearly untrue.

The normative premise asserts:

> If the market cannot supply the rules of law, impartial adjudicators, and effective enforcement agencies necessary for human beings to live a secure and peaceful life in society, then a state that supplies these services is morally justified.

However, the consequent of this conditional clearly does not follow from its antecedent. Proving that the market cannot supply the rule-making, adjudicative, and enforcement services human beings need does not prove that a state must supply these services, merely that a state must remedy the market's failure to provide them. Therefore, the antecedent of the normative premise proves, at most, that a state that remedies this market failure is morally justified, not that a state that supplies the services itself is.

If, as a matter of fact, the *only* way to remedy the market's failure to supply the necessary rule-making, adjudicative, and enforcement services is for the state to provide them itself, then the normative premise can be shown to be true. However, it is far from evident that this is the case. Assume, for example, that Landes and Posner are correct that because private adjudication services lack incentives to establish clear precedents they will fail to produce adequate rules of behavior. Although this might justify the existence of a state that subsidized the private production of precedents, it does not require and, therefore, does not justify the existence of a state that monopolizes the production of precedents itself. Consider also Professor Cowen's argument. Assume that he is entirely correct that the private provision of basic protective and adjudicative services will lead to a dangerous cartel. This would seem to justify the existence of a state with the power to prevent protective agency collusion, not one that required all citizens to purchase protective and adjudicative services exclusively from itself.

I submit that in the absence of strong evidence that the only way to remedy the market's failure to provide adequate protective, adjudicative, and rule-making services is to supply them via a tax-supported monopoly, the normative premise of the argument for the state cannot be regarded as true. For this reason, even if the empirical premise is true, the argument cannot establish its conclusion: that the minimal state, one that monopolizes the basic rule-making, adjudicative, and enforcement services, is morally justified.

Some thoughts about the minimal state

I have argued that the normative premise in the traditional argument for the state is false because it is too strong. Although its antecedent may justify state action to remedy the market's failure to provide essential rule-making, adjudicative, and enforcement services, it does not justify state provision of the services. This, of course, suggests that the following, weaker version of the premise might be true:

> If the market cannot supply the rules of law, impartial adjudicators, and effective enforcement agencies necessary for human beings to live secure and peaceful lives in society, then a state that ensures that these services are provided is morally justified.

politics, philosophy & economics 2(1)

Let us assume, for the present, that the empirical premise of the argument for the state is true: that the market cannot supply the rules of law, impartial adjudicators, and effective enforcement agencies necessary for human beings to live secure and peaceful lives in society. There would then appear to be a legitimate argument for the existence of a state of some kind, although not for what has, perhaps inaccurately, been called the minimal state.

Consider for a moment the following rather fanciful situation. Following the revolution that resulted from the revelation that Al Gore actually carried Florida in the 2000 election by 10,000 votes, a constitutional convention is called to establish a truly minimal state; that is, one that will perform only those functions necessary for citizens to live together in security and peace. The delegates to the convention include the country's most brilliant economists, who are thoroughly familiar with both the public goods and abusive monopoly arguments against the market provision of basic state services.

The constitution that emerges from this convention has several familiar features. It creates a government of enumerated powers enclosed within a system of checks and balances designed to prevent the abuse of these powers. It authorizes the election of a congress every two years from representative districts and a president every four years by the populace as a whole, although it prohibits the president from succeeding himself or herself. It also retains the pre-revolutionary foreign policy structure of government, investing the congress with the power to declare war and the president, as commander-in-chief of the country's all-volunteer armed forces, with the power to prosecute it subject to all pre-revolutionary constitutional restrictions. What makes the new constitution distinctive, however, is the number and nature of the enumerated domestic powers.

The constitution invests the new government with only two domestic powers: the power to prevent dangerous protective agency collusion and the power to subsidize the production of rule-making, adjudicative, and enforcement services. The exercise of these powers is divided among the three branches of the new government. The congress possesses no direct domestic legislative authority of any kind. It is invested with only three functions: (1) to appoint the members of the Supreme Antitrust Court and the Supreme Public Goods Court, (2) to impeach any president who exercises domestic power without express authorization from one of these courts or otherwise violates his or her constitutional obligations, and (3) to impeach any member of the Supreme Antitrust Court and the Supreme Public Goods Court who abuses his or her position. Further, the members of the two courts must be selected from among highly qualified economists who have been certified as such by the American Economic Bar Association.

The Supreme Antitrust Court constantly surveys the protective and adjudicative services market looking for any evidence of the type of dangerous collusive behavior Professor Cowen warns about. Should it detect such behavior, the court can issue cease and desist orders, impose monetary penalties, or order the break-up or dissolution of the offending companies. The Supreme Public Goods Court constantly surveys the markets for rule-making, adjudicative, and enforcement services looking for evidence of the type of public goods problems that could result in the underproduction of these services. Should it detect such problems, the court can order the disbursement of funds to subsidize the production of the services in question or other forms of necessary remedial action. Thus, if Landes and Posner's critique of the market for adjudicative services is correct, the court could authorize payments for clear precedents to correct the shortfall produced by the market.

As chief executive officer, the president is responsible for enforcing the orders of the antitrust and public goods courts in precisely the same manner as the pre-revolutionary president was responsible for enforcing the orders of the old Supreme Court. For this purpose, he or she has executive powers analogous to those possessed by the pre-revolutionary president, for example, command of FBI agents and federal marshals, the ability to call out the national guard,[27] and in case of insurrection, to declare martial law and call out the military.[28] Under the new constitution, however, the president is strictly prohibited from acting domestically unless explicitly authorized by one of the two new courts.

Consider the characteristics of the new government. It does not legislate. It does not adjudicate interpersonal disputes. It does not provide general police services, only those necessary to prevent protective agency collusion. It does, however, have sufficient power to prevent or remedy the types of market failure that are assumed to doom the private provision of these services. Further, this power is embedded within a system of constitutional checks and balances and democratic elections designed to insulate it from potential corruption by market forces.

It is unclear precisely how active the new government will be. It may have to intervene frequently to ensure that adequate rule-making, adjudicative, and enforcement services are produced and to prevent or break up malevolent efforts to corner the market for enforcement services. On the other hand, a single intervention to establish a continuous flow of necessary subsidies may be all that is required to ensure adequate services, and the deterrent effect of state scrutiny coupled with the threat of forceful intervention may discourage collusion sufficiently to make direct intervention virtually unnecessary. If the latter is the case, the new government, while remaining vigilant, may be rather inactive. What is certain, however, is that even at its most active, the new government will do considerably less than one that must directly supply citizens with rule-making, adjudicative, and enforcement services. In other words, the new government will do considerably less than the 'minimal' state.[29]

This suggests that it is a misnomer to refer to a state that does nothing more than monopolize the basic rule-making, adjudicative, and enforcement functions in an identifiable area as the minimal state. I would submit that the new government described above is a better candidate for that appellation. However, for the sake of clarity and convenience, let us refer to this new form of government as the 'remedial state'.[30]

The remedial state appears to be a state that ensures that citizens have the rule-making, adjudicative, and enforcement services they need to live secure and peaceful lives without providing them itself. Therefore, if the empirical premise of the argument for the state is true, the normative premise, which cannot establish that the minimal state is morally justified, may be strong enough to establish that the remedial state is.

One additional observation needs to be made. The argument in this section proceeded under the assumption that the empirical premise of the argument for the state is true and that the market cannot effectively supply basic rule-making, adjudicative, and enforcement services. If we set up a remedial state and this turns out to be incorrect, no real harm will be done.[31] The remedial state will simply have nothing to do. If, as the critics of the empirical premise contend, the market really can safely and effectively supply the needed services, the remedial state may give us a glimpse of that rarest will-o'-the-wisp: a state that really would wither away.

A reflection on the nature of the state

The discussion of the last section seems to lead to a conundrum. The remedial state seems to violate the semantic convention noted in the second section of this article that defines a state as an organization that monopolizes the basic rule-making, adjudicative, and enforcement functions in an identifiable area. Because the remedial state does not do this, it does not seem to qualify as a state under the accepted definition. Yet, it is based on a constitution, finances its activities through taxation, claims sovereignty over its geographical area, and exercises ultimate decision-making authority within its limited sphere of competence. The remedial state certainly looks like a state; it just does not do the things a state usually does. Applying the accepted definition, the remedial state seems to be a non-state state.

I think this apparent paradox can be rather easily explained. It stems from the fact that we derive the definition of the state historically rather than analytically. We determine the essential characteristics of the state by examining states that have actually existed rather than by conducting a *tabula rasa* search for the logically necessary features of a state. As far as I know, all actual states exercise monopolistic authority over the legislative, adjudicative, and enforcement functions and gain their funding through taxation. This is entirely unsurprising since most states throughout history were created by agents seeking power over others. But the result of this historical uniformity is that we do not think to question Locke's description of the state as the exclusive supplier of these essential services. Because all the states in our experience do, in fact, supply these services, it is natural to assume that doing so must be an essential characteristic of a state.

This perfectly understandable assumption is incorrect, however. One cannot conclude from the historical fact that all existent states claim exclusive control over the use of coercive power that such exclusive control is logically necessary for an organization to be a state. From a purely analytical standpoint, the essential features of the state are limited to those that are necessary for it to realize its purposes. However these purposes may be defined, if they can be achieved without monopolizing the legislative, judicial, and enforcement functions, there can be a state that does not exercise such a monopoly. Since, in the present context, we are discussing the minimal state, its purpose is, by hypothesis, the provision of the minimal amount of services necessary for citizens to live together in peace and security. If the remedial state can ensure that these services are provided, there is no reason why it should not be regarded as a true state, even though it does not provide the services itself. Thus, if nothing else is gained from this reconsideration of the argument for the state, it may at least teach us that we need to revise our basic definition of the state.

Conclusion and a final suggestion

Most political philosophers take it for granted that the state is morally justified. Among those who entertain the possibility that it may not be, the focus of debate is on whether the state is truly necessary or whether the market can safely supply the basic rule-making, adjudicative, and enforcement services that human beings need. I have ventured no opinion on this subject in this article, but I have argued that proving that the market cannot supply these essential services does not prove that a state must, and hence does not provide a moral justification for what is conventionally called the minimal state. I have also argued that proving that the market cannot supply these services *might* provide a moral justification for the remedial state, one that ensures that citizens receive essential rule-making, adjudicative, and enforcement services, but does not supply them itself. Lastly, I have argued that from an analytical standpoint, there is no reason why the remedial state should not be regarded as a true state. This last point carries the implication that it is a misnomer to refer to a state that is limited to the monopolistic provision of rule-making, adjudicative, and enforcement services as the minimal state. Because the remedial state does considerably less than one which legislates, maintains a judicial system, and runs a police force, it would appear to be a better candidate for designation as the minimal state.

Let me close with the suggestion that the idea of the remedial state, rather than being merely a whimsical theoretical construct, may ultimately prove to have some value. For, consider what would be required to settle the dispute over the empirical premise of the argument for the state, that is, to determine whether the state is truly necessary. Since supporters and opponents of the premise could probably argue about what will or will not happen indefinitely, the only way to resolve the point may be to put it to the test in the real world. But how can such a test ever be conducted? Those who believe that a market for rule-making, adjudicative, and enforcement services will necessarily lead to tyranny will certainly not be willing to dispense with the state's monopoly and its constitutional and democratic limitations merely to settle a point. Yet as long as the state monopolizes these functions, the proposition can never be tested.

The remedial state appears to offer a way around this impasse. Because its power is the power to prevent tyranny and because this power is itself constrained by constitutional and democratic limitations, it possesses the safeguards the opponents of the market regard as necessary. But because it permits a competitive market for rule-making, adjudicative, and enforcement services to exist, it allows the claims of the advocates of the market to be tested. If the opponents of the market turn out to be correct, the remedial state will be quite active, and may ultimately convince us that the state should monopolize the provision of the basic services. But if the advocates of the market turn out to be correct, the remedial state will do nothing, and can eventually be dissolved. If the latter is the case, the value of the remedial state will be to facilitate the transition from state to anarchy.

notes

The author wishes to thank Bruce Benson and the other participants at the Liberty Fund colloquium on Polycentric Law, Liberty, and Justice held in Tallahassee in March 2000 for stimulating his thinking on this subject. The author also wishes to thank Christopher Morris, David Schmidtz, Eric Mack, Tom Bell, Daniel Shapiro, Douglas Den Uyl, Richard Greenstein, Jan Narveson, Jack Sanders, Scott Arnold and Ann C. Tunstall for their extremely helpful comments.

1. John Rawls, *A Theory of Justice* (Cambridge: Harvard University Press, 1971).
2. Robert Nozick, *Anarchy, State, and Utopia* (New York: Basic Books, 1974).
3. A nice sampling of these scholars (along with some that defend the state) is provided by the collection of articles in John T. Sanders and Jan Narveson, *For and Against the State* (Lanham, MD: Rowman & Littlefield, 1996).
4. Not all critics of the state are market anarchists, who assert that all necessary basic services would be produced by the competitive forces of a free market. Others argue that these services can be supplied by cooperative, rather than competitive, non-coercive social mechanisms. For purposes of convenience, however, and because it is the market anarchists who usually press the arguments discussed in this article, I have expressed the argument for the state in terms of a corrective for market failure. This will not be inaccurate if the term 'market' is understood in a broad sense as encompassing both competitive and cooperative non-coercive methods of supplying the necessary services.
5. Max Weber, *Economy and Society: An Outline of Interpretive Sociology* (Berkeley: University of California Press, 1978), p. 56.
6. See, for example, Murray N. Rothbard, *For a New Liberty* (New York: Macmillan, 1973), pp. 49–50; John Hospers, 'What Libertarianism Is', in *Liberty for the 21st Century*, edited by Tibor R. Machan and Douglas B. Rasmussen (Lanham, MD: Rowman & Littlefield, 1995), p. 14; David Boaz, *Libertarianism* (New York: Free

Press, 1997), p. 187; Robert Paul Wolff, *In Defense of Anarchism* (New York: Harper & Row, 1970), p. 1; Ludwig von Mises, *Liberalism in the Classical Tradition* (New York and San Francisco: Cobden Press, 1985), p. 35.

7. Tyler Cowen, 'Law as a Public Good: The Economics of Anarchy', *Economics and Philosophy* 8 (1992): 250.

8. Nozick, *Anarchy, State, and Utopia*, p. 26.

9. John Locke, *Second Treatise of Government*, edited by C.B. Macpherson (Indianapolis, IN: Hackett Pub. Co., 1980), pp. 65–8.

10. Ibid., p. 66.

11. Ibid.

12. I am obviously glossing over the issue of consent that is at the heart of Locke's argument for the state, but is not centrally relevant to the present concern.

13. If this troubles the reader, I would be willing to assume *arguendo* that state provision of national defense is justified and can be supplied subject to the same constitutional and democratic restraints that exist in the USA today (or any stronger set of constraints that the reader feels is necessary to protect against a military takeover of government). This would recast the question under consideration as whether, *under the assumption that the state exists to provide essential protection against foreign aggression*, there is any justification for its domestic power. Locke's argument can then be seen as an exemplar of the argument designed to establish this more limited conclusion.

14. Christopher W. Morris, *An Essay on the Modern State* (New York: Cambridge University Press, 1998), pp. 59–60. This definition may be a bit strong. To qualify as a public good, a good need not be available to everyone, but merely to many who do not pay for it and who cannot be efficiently excluded from its enjoyment. I am grateful to Jack Sanders for pointing this out to me.

15. See, for example, Richard A. Epstein, *Takings: Private Property and the Power of Eminent Domain* (Cambridge, MA: Harvard University Press, 1985), p. 5; Gordon Tullock, *Private Wants, Public Means: An Economic Analysis of the Desirable Scope of Government* (Lanham, MD: University Press of America, 1970), pp. 127–8.

16. Morris, *An Essay on the Modern State*, pp. 60–1.

17. See William M. Landes and Richard A. Posner, 'Adjudication as a Private Good', *Journal of Legal Studies* 6 (1979): 235–84.

18. Ibid., p. 238.

19. See Rothbard, *For a New Liberty*; David Friedman, *The Machinery of Freedom*, second edition (La Salle, IL: Open Court, 1989); Bruce Benson, *The Enterprise of Law* (San Francisco, CA: Pacific Research Institute for Public Policy, 1990); Randy Barnett, *The Structure of Liberty* (New York: Oxford University Press, 1998).

20. See Cowen, 'Law as a Public Good'.

21. Ibid., p. 256.

22. Ibid., p. 259.

23. Ibid.

24. Ibid.

25. Ibid., p. 265.

26. See, for example, David D. Friedman, 'Law as a Private Good: A Response to Tyler

Cowen on the Economics of Anarchy', *Economics and Philosophy* 10 (1994): 319–27; Tyler Cowen, 'Rejoinder to David Friedman on the Economics of Anarchy', *Economics and Philosophy* 10 (1994): 329–32.

27. As President Eisenhower did to enforce *Brown* v. *Board of Education*, 347 U.S. 483 (1954).

28. As George Washington did in the case of the Whiskey Rebellion.

29. There would be no difference between the remedial and minimal state with regard to the provision of protection against foreign state aggression. Both would have to supply this service to the same degree.

30. I confess that this is a somewhat inelegant designation. However, Nozick has already appropriated the uncomfortably oxymoronic 'ultraminimal state' (see Nozick, *Anarchy, State, and Utopia*, p. 26), and locutions such as the 'micro-' or 'nano-minimal state' would only make things worse.

31. This is not literally true because we will have created a concentration of power that could be subverted and put to oppressive use. However, at this point, I am accepting for the sake of argument the hypothesis of the advocates of the state that constitutional and democratic restrictions are effective safeguards against the corruption of state power.

[25]

Public Choice (2008) 135: 67–78
DOI 10.1007/s11127-007-9246-x

Coordination without command: Stretching the scope of spontaneous order

Peter T. Leeson

Received: 7 September 2007 / Accepted: 5 October 2007 / Published online: 30 October 2007
© Springer Science+Business Media, LLC. 2007

Abstract How far can we stretch the scope of spontaneous order? Gordon Tullock's important work on the economics of non-human societies shows how these societies are able to coordinate without command despite features economists typically see as limiting the scope of spontaneous order. Using Tullock's insights, I search for the "human ant nest"—spontaneous institutional arrangements that create human cooperation despite the presence of these obstacles. I find two significant examples of this, both in precolonial Africa. The first demonstrates the effectiveness of spontaneous order in the face of threats of violent theft. The second shows the effectiveness of spontaneous order in the face of social heterogeneity. These cases suggest a broader scope for spontaneous order than conventional wisdom permits.

Keywords Anarchy · Spontaneous order · Gordon Tullock

1 Introduction

How far can we stretch the scope of spontaneous order? A sizeable and growing literature points to the successful operation of spontaneous institutional arrangements of cooperation within at least limited bounds. For instance, multilateral punishment in conjunction with the shadow of the future can secure honest behavior despite the absence of government, provided agents are sufficiently patient. Research by Landa (1994), Bernstein (1992), Ellickson (1991), Greif (1993), and others provides evidence of this.

However, this same literature points to serious limitations on spontaneously-ordered institutional arrangements (see, for instance, Greif 2002; Landa 1994). At least two factors constrain the scope of their application, violence and social heterogeneity.[1] Violence poses

---

[1]Some economists would point to many more limitations. However, these are the two I have encountered most commonly and are also the most sensible.

P.T. Leeson (✉)
Department of Economics, George Mason University, MSN 3G4, Fairfax, VA 22030, USA
e-mail: pleeson@gmu.edu

 Springer

68   Public Choice (2008) 135: 67–78

a problem because threats of ostracism, for example, do not prevent physically stronger individuals from using their strength superiority to overwhelm weaker ones. A weaker agent may announce his intention never to deal again with anyone who cheats him, but this does not prevent physically stronger agents from using force to take what they want from weaker ones when government is absent.

Social heterogeneity is also problematic. Although multilateral punishment, for instance, functions effectively in small homogeneous groups, it does not for social interactions involving members from different groups. Heterogeneity raises the cost of communication with outsiders, making it more difficult to convey information about individuals' histories throughout the relevant population. Further, where agents have different norms, beliefs, and practices, it is difficult to coordinate on mutual understandings of what constitutes dishonest behavior and how such behavior should be punished. This leads self-enforcing cooperation to break down.

Given these impediments to the effectiveness of spontaneous institutional arrangements, it would seem that spontaneous order has rather limited applications. The spontaneous order of the marketplace is effective, but only in the context of government-enforced property rights. Society requires hierarchical command to overcome the obstacles described above.

The idea of spontaneous order is most famously associated with Friedrich Hayek, but also plays an important role in the work of one of Public Choice's founding fathers, Gordon Tullock.[2] There is a tension in Tullock's research that deals with spontaneous order. On the one hand, he is a great admirer of the market, and like many of those influenced by his work, sees it along with Hayek as perhaps the greatest coordinating device known to man, yet one which does so without central direction.

On the other hand, Tullock is no anarchist. Like nearly all other economists, he explicitly rejects the arguments of some political economists who would substitute the coercive hierarchy of the state with the spontaneous order of purely private institutional arrangements (Tullock 1972, 1974, 2005).[3] In his view, spontaneously ordered institutional arrangements are limited along the lines discussed above.

One would get a very different sense of the scope of spontaneous order, however, if he read only Tullock's (1994) work on *The Economics of Non-Human Societies*. In this book, Tullock seeks to explain how it is that a great part of the non-human world, from the mole rat to amoeba, engages in intricate cooperative arrangements without anything that resembles central direction. In fact, Tullock's original manuscript for this book was entitled, "Coordination without Command," which I have shamelessly appropriated for my paper.

In this work, Tullock emphasizes that he "is not suggesting that human society is something which we can understand by animal societies" (1994: 3). Recognition of the fact that ant societies, for instance, facilitate widespread cooperation without the use of coercive institutions does not imply the workability of anarchy for humans. Perhaps this claim is humility on Tullock's part. More likely, however, it is recognition of the fact that although human and non-human societies share much in common at the broadest level, beyond this, they seem to share very little.

This paper uses Tullock's insights in *The Economics of Non-Human Societies* to address the scope of spontaneous order for human societies. I challenge his claim that human organization has nothing but the broadest lessons to learn from its non-human counterpart. The

---

[2] Actually, Adam Ferguson was the first to apply the concept of "spontaneous order" (though not these words) to human institutions. But it is commonplace to ignore this and attribute the idea to Hayek, which I will do as well.

[3] See, for instance, Anderson and Hill (2004), Benson (1990), Coyne (2003), Friedman (1973), Leeson (2003, 2007a, 2007b, 2006), Leeson and Stringham (2005), and Rothbard (1973).

Public Choice (2008) 135: 67–78   69

application of spontaneous order in the non-human social world may have more in common with the human social world than Tullock admits.

Tullock's work points to coordination without command in non-human societies despite the presence of features like those discussed above, which economists typically see as limiting the scope of spontaneous order. On the basis of his result, I search for the "human ant nest"—spontaneous institutional arrangements that create human cooperation in the face of these features. I find two significant examples of this, both in precolonial Africa. The first demonstrates the effectiveness of spontaneous order in the face of threats of violent theft. The second shows the effectiveness of spontaneous order in the face of social heterogeneity. These cases suggest a broader scope for spontaneous order than conventional wisdom permits.

Tullock's discussion starts by taking concepts devised to investigate human interactions, such as the division of labor, games of conflict, and the idea of coordination itself, and applying them somewhat anthropomorphically to the world of insects, animals, and cells. My method here is to reverse Tullock's path of inquiry, or perhaps more correctly, to pick up where he leaves off and in doing so come full circle. He generates conclusions about spontaneous order in non-human societies by applying concepts of human societies to non-human ones. I apply these conclusions to the case of human societies with the hope that doing so will improve our understanding of spontaneous order for mankind.

The remainder of this paper proceeds as follows. Section 2 considers the social dilemma faced by humans and non-humans alike. Section 3 examines the operation of spontaneous order in non-human societies. Section 4 searches for analogs in the societies of humans. It focuses on the operation of spontaneous orders under conditions present in non-human societies, which are believed to cause human spontaneous orders to collapse. Section 5 concludes.

2 The social dilemma

The problem of social organization is fundamentally one of transforming situations of potential conflict into situations of coordination.[4] This, in fact, is the source of the economic justification for government. In the state of nature as Hobbes famously described it and virtually all political economists since him, including Tullock, have conceived it, individuals face the dilemma depicted in Fig. 1.

Individuals may follow one of two basic strategies when dealing with others, cooperate or defect. Cooperation refers to any individual behavior consistent with the ends of the other members of society. This includes, for instance, peacefully trading, contributing to a 'public good,' and generally respecting the property rights of others. Defection refers to the opposite form of behavior. Here, an individual acts in a way that benefits him at the expense of others. Fraud, theft, free riding, and physical violence are examples of this.

When both individuals cooperate, they both receive α. If one cooperates and the other does not, the cooperative individual who is taken advantage of receives θ, while the defector receives γ. If neither individual cooperates, they both earn less than they could by cooperating and each receives only β. In this game, $\gamma > \alpha > \beta > \theta$, where $2\alpha > (\gamma + \theta) > 2\beta$, which is to say that mutual cooperation is socially efficient.

---

[4]For a related and excellent discussion of the prisoners' dilemma, its 'solutions' and the limitations on these solutions, see Munger (2006), who considers these issues in the context of terrorism.

70   Public Choice (2008) 135: 67–78

Fig. 1 The social dilemma

	Cooperate	Defect
Cooperate	α α	θ γ
Defect	γ θ	β β

The unique equilibrium of the one-shot version of this game is for both individuals to defect. Strictly speaking, the logic of the game suggests that in the state of nature individuals will never cooperate.[5] This situation—the game's pure strategy Nash equilibrium—is clearly Pareto dominated by that in which both agents behave peacefully towards one another.

If the game is infinitely repeated, or what is equivalent, terminates with some constant unknown probability, cooperation is possible. This is what traditional spontaneous institutional arrangements of self-enforcement, such as multilateral punishment, are concerned with. To see how multilateral punishment can sustain cooperation, consider an infinitely-repeated, n-player version of the game in Fig. 1. Let agents' common discount factor be δ, where $\delta \in (0, 1)$. Using the payoffs from before, players cooperate if an only if $n \sum_{t=0}^{\infty} \alpha_t \delta^t \geq \gamma$. Rewriting this expression gives $\frac{\delta n \alpha}{1-\delta} \geq \gamma$, and solving this for δ yields, $\delta \geq \frac{\gamma}{n\alpha+\gamma}$. Provided agents are patient enough to satisfy this inequality, they cooperate under the spontaneous institutional arrangement of multilateral punishment.

However, a number of conditions must be satisfied for this solution to the social dilemma to work. As the Folk Theorem suggests, if cooperation is sustainable at all there will normally be an infinite number of equilibria. These include defection as a possible outcome. In the infinitely-iterated game involving multiple players, cooperation requires: (1) sufficiently patient individuals; (2) low information-sharing costs; (3) equally strong agents; (4) shared ideas about "defection" and how it should be punished.[6]

Condition (1) is usually assumed away because it also poses a problem for government as a solution to the social dilemma. If agents have unusually high discount rates, society is doomed to conflict whether government exists or not. To see this clearly, imagine the limiting case in which we all only cared about our future five minutes from now and completely discounted our futures beyond this point. If we were strictly self-interested payoff maximizers, as this game assumes, we would all try and plunder our neighbors right now, consequences be damned, including incarceration or even the death penalty.

With the other three conditions, however, things are different. If the n members of society are socially heterogeneous, for instance they have different languages, their ability to communicate the identity of defectors and thus to punish cheaters through this mechanism can become quite difficult. This violates condition (2), preventing cooperation.

---

[5]Tullock (1999) has an excellent piece on the "non-prisoners' dilemma" in which he points out that if communication, which is prohibited in the strict model, is in fact permitted (which more closely corresponds with real world prisoners' dilemma type situations) cooperation is easy to sustain.

[6]On the role of focal points and the evolution of cooperation without government in the presence of multiple equilibria, see, Leeson et al. (2006).

Public Choice (2008) 135: 67–78 71

If some members of *n* are substantially stronger than other members, so that their aggression is met with little resistance, the threat of community boycott is worthless. The stronger agents can simply seize what they want by force. This violates condition (3) and cooperation again breaks down.

Finally, if the *n* members of society are socially diverse, they are likely to have several different notions about what it means to defect or about how they respond to defection. In this event, multilateral punishment cannot be sustained. This violates condition (4), preventing the cooperative equilibrium.

Introducing government ostensibly overcomes all of this. By providing formal enforcement for our interactions with others, centralized coercion both prevents stronger individuals from plundering us and reduces the risk of interacting with diverse strangers. We can be confident stronger agents and outsiders will not take advantage of us because if they do government will punish them and compel them to pay restitution. State enforcement means that conditions (2)–(4) need not be satisfied for individuals to capture the gains from cooperation. Thus, we get the argument that the scope of spontaneous order is necessarily limited and some authority of command is needed for social coordination.

3 Coordination without command in non-human societies

Tullock notes that the social dilemma depicted in Fig. 1 is not unique to humans. Consider, for example, an ant nest. "The individual ant that just did not do anything, except eat, would also be a free rider. Also the ant that carried out whatever from the ant's standpoint are aesthetic preferences and, let us say, produce things in the nest that it liked, which were not useful for the nest, would be another" (Tullock 1994: 30). In other words, each individual member of an ant society faces the same social dilemma as each individual member of human society. Their dominant "strategy" is to "defect" rather than "cooperate."

Unlike humans, ants and other social non-humans do not have governments to facilitate cooperation. They do not appeal to centralized command to overcome the social dilemma. Remarkably, despite this, each ant left to his own "devices" is somehow able to coordinate his activities into part of a seamless whole that promotes the existence of his ant city.

For example, ant societies use a refined division of labor whereby some ants are "employed" in the collection of food, others the discovery of new avenues of city growth, some specialize in taking care of the young, others are soldiers who guard the city from potential predators, some build and maintain roads between their city and food sources, others yet are porters who carry the food discovered by foragers back to the city. Among the ants engaged in food collection, labor is subdivided further. Some foragers specialize in the procurement of nectar, others "meat" from insects, and still others search for other kinds of food.

Within the ant nest this elaborate division of labor continues. Some "citizens" of the ant city specialize in caring for the eggs and "callows"—new born ants, not yet fully developed. This involves cleaning and feeding the young and moving the eggs around the nest throughout the day to make sure they are kept in the right temperature and humidity so that the embryonic ants they contain do not die. Food production also occurs in the nest. Some ants even "raise livestock (root aphids, if they are kept permanently in the nest), engage in fungus farming, or simply build up large supplies of foodstuffs for the off seasons of the year" (Tullock 1994: 39).

To facilitate the prosperity of their cities, ants "invest" in substantial capital. To farm fungus, for example, ants must collect leaves and grass and convert this into a form of mulch. Once this is done their fungus farms require continual attention to produce. There is

 Springer

72   Public Choice (2008) 135: 67–78

also the considerable capital tied up in their nests, which require continual care and greatly increase the efficiency of ant organization. Again, all of this goes on without any central direction from other ants, or any other living thing for that matter.

Surprisingly (or perhaps not in light of ants' incredible coordination under the division of labor), ants have created quite a high "standard of living" cooperating without the direction of authority (Tullock 1994: 32). The average wood ant, for instance, lives more than two years—a stunning achievement in light of its tiny size, which renders it effectively defenseless against predators when outside the nest.

Ant cities can grow to be quite populous. A city might have half a million adult ants, all of whom the city supports on a daily basis. Equally stunning, ant cities do not exist in isolation. They are frequently part or larger ant "nations" composed of multiple cities. When these nations grow too large one or several cities may even secede.

Of course, as Tullock points out, much of the language he uses and I use above attributes purpose to ants, which at least at this stage of our knowledge about them there is no reason to think they actually have. Ants do have small brains, but it seems unlikely they are sufficiently complex to consciously coordinate all of this behavior. Nevertheless, this tremendous coordination occurs without central or hierarchical direction of any kind; ant civilizations are spontaneous orders.

Significantly, these non-human spontaneous orders overcome the very circumstances believed to cause problems for human ones. First, ant societies are populated by members with substantial strength disparities, yet violence is rare. Within ant societies, for example, substantially physically stronger and larger ants engaged in tasks like "protection" do not use their strength superiority to "extort" other nest members only a fraction of their size who are engaged in mold farming (Tullock 1994: 25). Second, members of non-human societies can be significantly heterogeneous—often from different species—creating a variant of the problem of social heterogeneity discussed above. Despite this, multi-species interaction and coordination is commonplace (Tullock 1994: 2).

Obviously, these obstacles to the application of human spontaneous orders take on a rather different character here. Recall that in the human case, for example, spontaneous order broke down in the presence of social heterogeneity because of communication costs related to conveying the history of cheaters and an inability to coordinate on common understandings/punishment of cheating. For non-human societies, in contrast, the problem of social heterogeneity must be of a somewhat different nature. In the first place, non-humans, such as ants, presumably do not "gossip" to one another like humans or tell one another about who the "good" ants are versus the "bad" ones.

But this does not mean that communication plays no role in their cooperation. For example, Tullock describes an "antler tapping" mode of communication between ants and display of "excitement" to indicate that they have found a new source of food. Ants also leave behind distinct scents that enable them to identify one another. If different species become involved in the ant society, both of these forms of "communication" may become more difficult. Thus, in ant societies too, member heterogeneity should in principle also lead to problems coordinating without command.

Things are similar with the ant version of the threat of violence. In the human case this refers to using one's strength superiority to seize the goods of another. In the case of ants, the problem strength disparities could pose for social cooperation without command is quite similar. Although it is highly unlikely that ants "think" about taking "what they want" from others, there remains the possibility that substantially stronger ants, such as the "guards," might use their strength to appropriate the food share of the smaller members of their society, such as the fungus farmers.

 Springer

Public Choice (2008) 135: 67–78 73

Although the problems of violence and heterogeneity that are supposed to limit the scope of human spontaneous orders take on a somewhat different flavor for ant societies, it stands to reason that they pose their own "ant versions" of these problems that erect obstacles to non-human spontaneous orders. Evidently, however, these potential obstacles do not cause problems for spontaneous order in the non-human social world. Social cooperation is achieved without command despite the presence of both these allegedly insuperable obstacles to spontaneous order.

4 In search of the "human ant nest"

Tullock's discussion of spontaneous order's effectiveness in non-human societies despite the threat of violence and problem of heterogeneity presents us with cause to rethink the conventional wisdom about human spontaneous order's ineffectiveness in the face of these obstacles. If ants can surmount these problems and thus come to rely purely on spontaneous orders to coordinate social cooperation, why can't humans?

Tullock suggests a reason. Ants are genetically programmed for cooperation; presumably, humans are not.[7] In non-human social species, natural selection has genetically endowed "agents" with what amounts to a cooperative gene. This genetic inheritance enables them to overcome the social dilemma by biologically directing them to perpetually cooperate.

Humans, in contrast, are rational and therefore can use their calculative abilities to tabulate the payoffs in Fig. 1. This ability is what leads them to defect in this game. Using reason, humans discover that no matter what others do, they maximize their own payoff by shirking cooperation. Further, humans are able to determine that the payoff-maximizing strategy is defection even if spontaneous institutional arrangements, such as multilateral punishment, are present, so long as they are stronger than others or society is socially diverse.

Humans' capacity to reason, however, is a double-edged sword. While it can be the source of conflict identified in the social dilemma, it can also be used as a powerful weapon to overcome obstacles that stand in the way of our ability to cooperate and solve the social dilemma. It stands to reason that something like the "human ant nest"— spontaneous institutional arrangements that promote cooperation in the face of obstacles to these arrangements—might also exist.

Importantly, our search for the "human ant nest" is of more than mere hypothetic interest. If government truly worked as most economists seem to think it does, the state alone could be relied upon as a sufficient solution to the social dilemma in all cases. However, government may not be an effective solution to the social dilemma for at least three reasons.

First, government may be highly predatory and fail to provide the punishment required to coordinate individuals. This is the case, for example, in much of the developing world. Second, it may be prohibitively costly to use government for this purpose. If, for instance, the cost of government, G, exceeds the gains from mutual cooperation, 2α, society will not find it profitable to introduce government for this purpose, leaving individuals in the Defect–Defect equilibrium (Leeson 2007b). Third, and perhaps most importantly, the state's eye cannot be everywhere all the time. Even where the first two problems are overcome, there remains the simple fact that most of our interactions on a daily basis occur outside the state's shadow. You could, for instance, shoplift in many cases and clearly get away with

---

[7]Although, on this issue see Seabright (2005) and Field (2003), both of whom suggest that at least part of humans' "hardwiring" does pre-program us for cooperation.

74   Public Choice (2008) 135: 67–78

it. There are not policemen on every corner to prevent this even if they were cost effective and perfectly benevolent. In fact, most parts of the world for most of their history had no governments at all, at least that we would recognize as such.

These three features of "real world" governments mean that our search for the "human ant nest" has practical importance. Since even today, in many parts of the world individuals cannot rely upon government to solve the social dilemma, they must rely on spontaneously-ordered institutional arrangements for this purpose instead (Boettke and Leeson 2006). Further, if these arrangements are to have sufficient scope to support cooperation beyond small homogeneous networks of roughly equally strong people, they must somehow overcome the problems of violent theft and social heterogeneity believed to prevent spontaneous institutional arrangements from working.

4.1 Spontaneous order in the presence of violent threats

The potential for violent theft results from a strength disparity between individuals. Some individuals are substantially stronger than others, and where this gap is sufficiently large, find it cheaper to forcibly take what they want from others rather than trading for what they desire. This is in large part what has led everyone from Adam Smith to Gordon Tullock to declare the necessity of government. As Adam Smith put it, "It is only under the shelter of the civil magistrate that the owner of . . . property. . . can sleep a single night in security. He is at all times surrounded by unknown enemies, whom, though he never provoked, he can never appease, and from whose injustice he can be protected only by the powerful arm of the civil magistrate continually held up to chastise it" (1965[1776]: 670). Spontaneous order alone is insufficient to prevent the strong from plundering the weak.

As noted above, however, Tullock's work on ant nests describes a commandless society in which agents with massive strength disparities are able to cooperate for mutual benefit just fine. Is there anything like this in human affairs?

One needs to look no further than precolonial Africa to find cooperation between individuals of significantly different physical strengths despite the absence of government (Leeson 2007a). In late-19th century Angola there was a flourishing export trade consisting of slaves (before this trade was outlawed in 1836), beeswax, ivory, and wild rubber, for which there was a large foreign (European) demand. These goods were produced by indigenous Africans in the remote interior of west-central Africa.

There were two sides to this export-related trade. On the one side were middlemen and the European agents who employed them to obtain ivory and the rest from interior producers. On the other side of this trade network were the producers themselves. Middlemen were highly mobile, usually armed, and traveled in large caravans. Producers, in contrast, were stationary, typically unarmed, and lived in small villages.

From looking at the records left by producers and middlemen from this period, there is no doubt that middlemen constituted the substantially stronger force in the interactions between members of these two groups. Indeed, when they could, caravans of middlemen violently plundered interior producers—stealing instead of trading for the goods they desired. However, peaceful trade rather than violent theft characterized the preponderance of these interactions. In fact, the export trade based on producer–middlemen exchange flourished during this time. Angola was one of the largest exporters in the world.

This exchange was extensive and durable, though there was no government enforcement of property rights. Most of the interior communities of producers were stateless. Even the African "kingdoms" that had more formal rulers were hardly formal from a modern Western perspective. The Europeans (mostly Portuguese) had outposts closer to the coast, but these

Public Choice (2008) 135: 67–78   75

outposts had no official authority over indigenous communities in the interior. Furthermore, since there was no overarching formal authority to oversee the interactions of individuals from different indigenous or European communities, there existed large ungoverned interstices for the interactions between members of these different groups.

Confronted with the threat of middlemen violence, producers developed an institution to encourage middlemen cooperation instead. Producers had a strong incentive to find a solution to this obstacle to exchange since, largely stationary and cut off from global markets, by themselves they could earn very little. Interactions with middlemen presented an opportunity for greater profits, but also made them vulnerable to violent plunder.

The institution producers employed for this purpose was credit. Normally we think of credit agreements as the cause of potential opportunism. The separation of payment and provision makes the creditor vulnerable to debtor default. However, in the context of producer–middleman relations it had quite the opposite effect.

The way that credit supported cooperation without command is straightforward. In time t, producers would produce effectively nothing. They would leave wax, rubber, and ivory unharvested. When caravans of middlemen looking for goods to steal would travel to outlying interior producers and come upon a village, they would find little to forcibly take. This was problematic from middlemen's perspective, as traveling to the interior tended to be quite costly.

Producers would then offer middlemen the goods they were seeking on credit. Middlemen would pay up front and producers would harvest the goods after the middlemen departed. Middlemen would later return in time $t + 1$ to collect what they were owed. By indebting themselves to stronger middlemen, producers created an incentive for middlemen to avoid physically abusing them and to ensure that other middlemen did not use violence against them. The reason for this is simple. In order to repay what they owed, producers needed to be in alive and in good health. The financial health of the middlemen who provided producers goods on credit became linked to the physical health of producers who were their debtors.

When middlemen returned to collect on the agreement, all that was on hand to plunder was what they were owed. If they wanted more they could either contract a new round of the credit exchange or leave knowing that the next time they returned there would again be nothing to take back to their employers for export. Since visits to the interior were costly, middlemen frequently chose to renew their credit relationships. In this way, credit emerged as a spontaneous institutional arrangement that prevented violence and enabled both sides to realize the gains from trade despite the absence of government and strength superiority of some members of society.

Notably, these credit arrangements did not create the problem of ex post opportunism on the part of producers, which normally attends credit agreements. Given the strength superiority of their creditors, producers knew that if they failed to deliver, middlemen could easily punish them through their greater strength. This spontaneous order solved multiple commitment problems that emerge under the social dilemma at once and in each case substituted cooperation for conflict.

4.2 Spontaneous order in the presence of social heterogeneity

Contrary to conventional wisdom, socially distant individuals frequently cooperate on a regular basis even where state enforcement is absent (Leeson 2006, 2007c). As Fearon and Laitin (1996) point out, for example, in most of the world where a functioning legal system does not exist or is extremely weak, societies are highly diverse and cooperation is the rule

 Springer

76 Public Choice (2008) 135: 67–78

instead of the exception. This constellation of facts suggests that spontaneous institutional arrangements are in fact capable of succeeding in the presence of social heterogeneity. Unfortunately, this has escaped the attention of most economists who continue to argue that social distance poses insuperable obstacles to the operation of these arrangements.

To delve deeper into the effectiveness of spontaneous order in the face of a socially diverse population, the case of precolonial Africa is again instructive. While forms of governance different widely across the continent and time during this period, a substantial portion of the continent encompassing large numbers of people was effectively stateless. As much as 25 percent of West Africa, for example, was entirely stateless on the eve of colonization. The Tiv system of Nigeria extended to nearly a million people (Curtin 1995: 71); the Nuer system of the southern Sudan extended to over a quarter million people (Evans-Pritchard 1940); and the Bedouin Arabs throughout Northern Africa were all more or less effectively stateless too (Bohannan 1968: 172). So were areas in Northern Uganda, Karamoja, and the East African River Valley. Many more regions were "quasi-stateless" in that while more formal rulers did exist, they were so weak as to constitute near anarchy.

To benefit from widespread trade the members of diverse communities needed to venture beyond their community networks and interact with outsiders from other tribes. However, in the absence of government, this could be risky since the uncertainty of interacting with others increased as one went outside these bounds. Socially distant outsiders might be honest and thus no problem. But they also might be dishonest.

Given their physical separation and social distance, individuals could not rely upon ex post mechanisms of enforcement along the lines discussed in Sect. 2 to secure cooperation. However, this did not prevent social cooperation and exchange. On the contrary, long before Europeans appeared on the scene in Africa there were extensive domestic trade routes cutting across the continent and exchange relations involved individuals from different tribes who were often complete strangers (Cohen 1969). This directly contradicts the "problem of social heterogeneity" hypothesis as it relates to the effectiveness of spontaneous institutional arrangements.

How did these socially distant strangers overcome the uncertainty of interacting with one another for trade? Instead of using ex post punishment to ensure honest conduct, which would not work in this context for the reasons discussed in Sect. 2, they used ex ante screening that accomplished the same end. In particular, precolonial Africans used social distance-reducing signals to communicate their credibility to outsiders, which in turn enabled inter-group trade (Leeson 2005a, 2005b, 2007c).

Individuals adopted the customs and practices of outsiders they desired to interact with, such as gift giving, ritual taboos related to land, and other such behaviors. They also adopted others' religious practices or converted to their religion, and agreed to follow an outside group's internal mechanisms of governance, such as dispute settlement.

Each of these signals was costly to invest in. Converting to an outsider's religion, for instance, sometimes involved a financial payment. But even when it did not it could involve costly sacrifices of one's personal belongings as part of rituals, restrictions on behavior, such as diet, and continually investing time in religious ceremonies. Similarly, gift giving involved sacrificing a part of one's wealth, the value of which agents could only recoup over time through repeated cooperative interaction with outsiders.

Because the investment cost of these signals could be substantial and was only recoverable through repeated play over time, only those individuals who intended to "be in it for the long haul" with a group of outsiders found it profitable to invest in them. In order to remain in the group's good graces, however, outsiders had to behave cooperatively. If they did not, they could be booted from the group.

 Springer

Public Choice (2008) 135: 67–78 77

As a result, the agents who found these investments worthwhile tended to be those who planned to behave cooperatively. Cheaters, who would be kicked out of the community when they cheated, did not find investing in these signals worthwhile. Their dishonest conduct would result in their removal from the group before they had a chance to recover the value of their signal investment. In this way, social distance-reducing signals could be used to screen outsiders and ensure that only honest ones were permitted to interact with in-group members. Thus, ex ante screening accomplished what ex post punishment alone could not. Through this process, social distance-reducing signaling emerged as a spontaneous institutional arrangement that facilitated cooperation in the absence of government and in the face of socially diverse individuals.

5 Concluding remarks

Gordon Tullock's (1994), *Economics of Non-Human Societies*, is an important contribution not only to economists' understanding of the general features uniting social organization between humans and non-humans, but also to our understanding of the role of spontaneous order in human society, per se. Although Tullock does not see this work as providing lessons regarding human social organization, and certainly does not see it as contributing to an understanding of the workability of anarchy for humans, it points us to instances of human cooperation without command under circumstances in which command is normally thought to be required. In doing so, even if he did not intend it to, Tullock's work on non-human societies encourages us to rethink the scope of spontaneous order in the human world. I have argued that engaging in this enterprise is a fruitful one and have indicated a few instances where I believe the productivity of this enterprise is apparent.

Although the cases I discussed are surely insufficient to change most economists' minds (including Tullock's) about the effective scope of spontaneous order, it should provide some at least a little pause to reconsider their insistence that only command will work in the contexts described. At the very least, it should shed some additional illumination on the prospect of coordination without command in the human social context. If this is in fact the case, then Tullock's project of examining social organization among non-humans has benefited our appreciation of spontaneous order in the human context despite his claim that it could not do so.

Acknowledgements I thank the participants of a seminar on Gordon Tullock's contribution to the study of spontaneous order at George Mason University for helpful comments and suggestions. Michael Munger's comments were especially useful. I also gratefully acknowledge the financial assistance of the Fund for Spontaneous Order Studies, whose generous support made this research possible.

References

Anderson, T. L., & Hill, P. J. (2004). *The not so wild, wild west: Property rights on the frontier.* Stanford: Stanford University Press.

Benson, B. L. (1990). *The enterprise of law: Justice without the state.* San Francisco: Pacific Research Institute.

Bernstein, L. (1992). Opting out of the legal system: Extralegal contractual relations in the diamond industry. *Journal of Legal Studies, 21*(1), 115–157.

Boettke, P. J., & Leeson, P. T. (2006). Two-tiered entrepreneurship and economic development. Mimeo.

Bohannan, P. (1968). Stateless societies. In R.O. Collins (Ed.), *Problems in African history.* Englewood Cliffs: Prentice Hall.

 Springer

78 Public Choice (2008) 135: 67–78

Cohen, A. (1969). *Custom and politics in urban Africa: A study of Hausa migrants in Yoruba towns*. Berkeley: University of California Press.

Coyne, C. J. (2003). Order in the jungle: Social interaction without the state. *Independent Review, 7*(4), 557–566.

Curtin, P. D. (1995). Africa north of the forest in the early Islamic age. In P. D. Curtin, S. Feierman, L. Thompson, & J. Vansina (Eds.), *African history: From earliest times to independence*. London: Longman.

Evans-Pritchard, E. E. (1940). *The nuer: A description of the modes of livelihood and political institutions of a Neolitic people*. Oxford: Clarendon Press.

Fearon, J. D., & Laitin, D. D. (1996). Explaining interethnic cooperation. *American Political Science Review, 90*(4), 715–735.

Field, A. J. (2003). *Altruistically inclined? The behavior sciences, evolutionary theory, and the origins of reciprocity*. Ann Arbor: University of Michigan Press.

Friedman, D. D. (1973). *The machinery of freedom: A guide to radical capitalism*. New York: Arlington House.

Greif, A. (1993). Contract enforceability and economic institutions in early trade: The Maghribi traders coalition. *American Economic Review, 83*, 525–548.

Greif, A. (2002). Institutions and impersonal exchange: From communal to individual responsibility. *Journal of Institutional and Theoretical Economics, 158*(1), 168–294.

Ellickson, R. C. (1991). *Order without law: How neighbors settle disputes*. Cambridge: Harvard University Press.

Landa, J. T. (1994). *Trust, ethnicity, and identity*. Ann Arbor: University of Michigan Press.

Leeson, P. T. (2003). Contracts without government. *Journal of Private Enterprise, 18*(2), 35–54.

Leeson, P. T. (2005a). Endogenizing fractionalization. *Journal of Institutional Economics, 1*(1), 75–98.

Leeson, P. T. (2005b). Self-enforcing arrangements in African political economy. *Journal of Economic Behavior and Organization, 57*(2), 241–244.

Leeson, P. T. (2006). Cooperation and conflict: Evidence on self-enforcing arrangements and heterogeneous groups. *American Journal of Economics and Sociology, 65*(4), 891–907.

Leeson, P. T. (2007a). Trading with bandits. *Journal of Law and Economics, 50*(2), 303–321.

Leeson, P. T. (2007b). Efficient anarchy. *Public Choice, 130*(1–2), 41–53.

Leeson, P. T. (2007c, forthcoming). Social distance and self-enforcing exchange. *Journal of Legal Studies*.

Leeson, P. T., & Stringham, E. (2005). Is government inevitable? *Independent Review, 9*(4), 543–549.

Leeson, P. T., Coyne, C. J., & Boettke, P. J. (2006). Converting social conflict: Focal points and the evolution of coordination. *Review of Austrian Economics, 19*(2–3), 137–147.

Munger, M. (2006). Preference modification vs. incentive manipulation as tools of terrorist recruitment: The role of culture. *Public Choice, 128*(1), 131–146.

Rothbard, M. N. (1973). *For a new liberty: The libertarian manifesto*. New York: Macmillan.

Seabright, P. (2005). *The company of strangers: A natural history of economic life*. Princeton: Princeton University Press.

Smith, A. (1965[1776]). *An inquiry into the nature and causes of the wealth of nations*. New York: The Modern Library. E. Cannan (Ed.).

Tullock, G. (Ed.). (1972). *Explorations in the theory of anarchy*. Blacksburg: Center for the Study of Public Choice.

Tullock, G. (Ed.). (1974). *Further explorations in the theory of anarchy*. Blacksburg: Center for the Study of Public Choice.

Tullock, G. (1994). *The economics of non-human societies*. Tucson: Pallas Press.

Tullock, G. (1999). Non-prisoners dilemma. *Journal of Economic Behavior and Organization, 39*(4), 455–458.

Tullock, G. (2005). Anarchy. In E. Stringham (Ed.), *Anarchy, state and public choice*. Northampton: Edward Elgar Publishing.

 Springer

[26]

Public Choice (2006) 130:41–53
DOI 10.1007/s11127-006-9071-7

ORIGINAL ARTICLE

Efficient anarchy

Peter T. Leeson

Received: 23 February 2005 / Accepted: 20 June 2006
© Springer Science + Business Media B.V. 2006

Abstract Can anarchy be efficient? This paper argues that for reasons of efficiency, rational, wealth-maximizing agents may actually choose statelessness over government in some cases. Where markets are sufficiently thin or where government is prohibitively costly, anarchy is the efficient mode of social organization. If total social wealth under conditions of relatively lower levels of trade is not substantially smaller than it is under conditions of relatively higher levels of trade, the cost of government may exceed the social benefits it provides. Likewise, if the cost of a state is sufficiently large, even substantial differences in social wealth under these two scenarios may prove too small to justify the formation of government from a cost-benefit perspective. The framework I provide explains the persistence of anarchy in two major areas where we tend to observe it: among primitive societies and at the global level. (*JEL* P48)

Keywords Anarchy · Social efficiency · Institutions · Nuer · International trade

1. Introduction

Can anarchy be efficient? Conventional wisdom emphatically answers no. By providing centralized[1] enforcement, government enables individuals to realize gains from exchange they could not capture if the state were absent. Rationally self-interested agents therefore choose to form government. This rationale for the state is at least as old as Hobbes but remains alive and well in modern social science. Economics is no exception. As Nobel Prize winner Doug North put it: "Throughout history, individuals given a choice between a state – no matter how exploitative it might be – and anarchy, have decided for the former" (1981: 24). Political economists have accepted the efficiency of government in organizing society

P. T. Leeson
Department of Economics, West Virginia University, Morgantown, WV 26506-6025
e-mail: ptleeson@mail.wvu.edu

[1] Throughout this paper I use the term "centralized" synonymously with the term "state." Centralized institutions (enforcement, rules, etc.) stand in contrast to those I call "private," which refer to non-state institutions (enforcement, rules, etc.).

42 | Public Choice (2006) 130:41–53

without question.[2] Is it possible that in some cases anarchy is actually optimal from the standpoint of social wealth?

The ubiquity of government today causes us to forget that numerous societies were stateless for most of their histories and that many remained so well into the 20th century. Some of these groups encompassed significant numbers of people. Consider, for instance, African groups such as the Tiv, which included over one million individuals, the Nuer whose population has been estimated at 400,000, or the Lugbara with over 300,000 members. More striking yet is the fact that, globally, the world has and continues to operate in the context of "international anarchy." The continued presence of numerous sovereigns creates massive ungoverned interstices for many of the interactions between the inhabitants of these different nations.

The observed absence of government in these environments requires explanation. If Hobbes and the generations of economists who have followed him are correct, anarchy is inefficient and government should have quickly replaced vacuums of centralized authority. But why then did statelessness among numerous societies last so long? For that matter, what accounts for the continued existence of international anarchy? In short, how do we explain the persistence of significant arenas of anarchy over time?[3]

North (1990) suggests that inefficient forms of social organization may persist because of path dependence. Since in *most* instances where we observe the absence of effective state enforcement (for example, in many transitioning economies) this arrangement is inefficient, it is tempting to conclude that in *all* instances where we observe this arrangement that this is so. It would therefore be very easy to mistakenly dismiss all instances of anarchy's persistence by reference to path dependence. In contrast, this paper will explore why it may actually be rational in some cases for wealth-maximizing individuals to choose *not* to form any government at all.

There are two general explanations for government's presence – social contract theory and predatory theory. The former suggests that agents choose to form government because it is socially efficient. Individuals recognize that by introducing the state they can move from a situation of conflict (or lesser cooperation) to one of greater cooperation (see Buchanan, 1975; Buchanan & Brennan, 1980; North, 1981; North & Thomas, 1973). The predatory theory of government on the other hand suggests that the state emerges out of the self-interested behavior of some agent (or group of agents) with a comparative advantage in using force (see Olson, 1993; McGuire & Olson, 1996).[4]

This paper employs the social contract theory of government (or in this case, absence of government) described above. I do not take this theory to be an accurate description of the actual emergence of governments nor do I believe that governments consist of benevolent, social welfare-maximizing agents and do not suffer from the standard problems of public choice.[5] Nevertheless, I adopt the contract theory of government because it offers the strongest

---

[2] David Friedman (1973), Murray Rothbard (1977), Bruce Benson (1999b), and Randy Holcombe (2004) are rare exceptions in this regard.

[3] While no one has addressed this question, a small but growing literature deals broadly with the economics of anarchy. See for instance, Dixit (2003, 2004) Hirshleifer (1994), Bates et al. (2002). Dixit's (2003) analysis is probably the most closely related to mine in that it considers the limits of self-governance and when centralized governance becomes efficient.

[4] Levi (1988) points out that consent and predatory theories of the state are not mutually exclusive, since in either event a ruler requires the consent of at least some people to govern. While I accept this important insight, it is nevertheless possible to conceptually distinguish between these theories on the grounds outlined above.

[5] It is important to emphasize that assuming away predatory behavior on the part of government for my analysis is purely for the purposes of addressing the 'hardest case' for anarchy – when government only aims

Public Choice (2006) 130:41–53 43

justification for the state and thus allows me to demonstrate that, even in this case, there are important conditions under which anarchy is the socially efficient arrangement.

Section 2 of this paper considers the determinants of anarchy's efficiency. It looks at what factors impact the cost of having government and what factors impact the benefit government provides by moving society from a lower trade equilibrium to a higher trade one.[6] Section 3 applies this framework to observed instances of anarchy. In particular it uses this framework to shed light on why we tend to see statelessness in primitive societies and on the global scale. Section 4 concludes by discussing transitions from anarchy to government.

2. When is anarchy efficient?

As previous work has shown, in the absence of government, private institutional arrangements emerge to prevent conflict and encourage cooperation (Benson, 1989; Anderson & Hill, 2004; Leeson, 2004, 2006; Greif, 1989, 1993, 2002; Ellickson, 1991, Clay, 1997; Landa, 1994; Milgrom et al., 1990; Greif et al., 1994). These arrangements, such as the use of multilateral punishment among small groups via ostracism or boycott, the emergence of conflict inhibiting social norms, and the use of arbitration organizations for international trade, operate primarily through mechanisms of reputation.

For the most part, however, reputation mechanisms successfully secure exchange without state enforcement among small, close-knit communities.[7] Their ability to enable agents to realize the gains from trade is therefore limited (see for instance, Dixit, 2004; Greif, 1993, 2002; Zerbe & Anderson, 2001). As the traditional rationale for government suggests, by reducing the state of uncertainty that surrounds interacting with agents outside of one's social network, government can improve social wealth by enabling additional exchange.

In a simple two-person model of exchange, let H be the sum of the payoffs to each individual of trade when government is present and let L be the sum of the individual payoffs of the relatively lower level of trade when government is absent where, $H > L > 0$. Individuals may coordinate either on the high trade equilibrium by introducing government, or the low trade equilibrium. For government to be efficient and rationally self-interested agents to prefer its presence, the cost of government, G, must be smaller than the benefits it provides. The benefit of government is the difference between social wealth in the two states of the world described above – that in which government exists and agents are in the higher trade equilibrium, and that which it does not and agents are in the lower trade equilibrium. Government is therefore an efficient solution to the social dilemma if and only if $G < H - L$.

---

at enhancing social wealth. As a factual matter, both theory and evidence strongly suggest that political agents are self-interested and engage in predatory behaviors. In other words, although it is not considered here, the cost of government includes the potential for large "public choice costs," stemming from predatory political activities. For an excellent discussion of the public choice costs of government in its capacity as definer and enforcer of property rights see Anderson and McChesney (2003). Also, see de Soto (1989) who examines the outcomes of predatory governments on trade and social welfare. Finally, for a discussion of public choice costs of government in the context of international law see Benson (1999a).

[6] The paper employs cost/benefit considerations to explain/predict statelessness. Libecap's (2003) excellent work uses a similar approach to explain/predict when individuals contract for property rights where the state is absent. Following up on this, Haddock's (2003) important work considers the use of force to establish such rights where contracting for them is prohibitively expensive.

[7] Klein's (1992) work on credit ratings suggests that reputation can be effective in large groups. Also on the effectiveness of reputation in large groups see Leeson (2004). However, the applicability of reputation mechanisms among large populations is overwhelmingly rejected in the literature that discusses its application. See for instance, Dixit (2004), Greif (1993, 2002) and Zerbe and Anderson (2001) among others.

44 Public Choice (2006) 130:41–53

Where $G > H - L$, anarchy is efficient. Whether G is actually greater than $H - L$ obviously depends upon two things. First, the size of G, and second the size of the gap between social wealth when agents are in the higher trade equilibrium vs. when they are in the lower trade equilibrium.

2.1. The cost of government

The cost of government can be broken into three primary components: (1) first, there is a simple organizational cost of creating a state – the cost of organizing collective action. Concretely, the organizational costs of government include (a) the decision-making costs of arriving at the specific set of rules the state is to enforce and (b) the external costs of collective decisionmaking, which result from the fact that the group may sometimes make choices that are contrary to the interests of the individual (Buchanan & Tullock 1962). The organizational cost of government thus depends upon, in addition to other possible factors, the form of government or decision-making process that is followed in determining what set of rules the state is to enforce.

(2) The second cost of government is the cost of enforcing decided upon rules. These costs are expenditures associated with creating and maintaining police and military forces, and a court system. Enforcement costs are increasing in population size, as it is more expensive to police 1000 people, for instance, than it is to police 10. Besides population size, the enforcement costs of government are also increasing in population heterogeneity. Ethnically, religiously, linguistically, and otherwise fractionalized populations are more prone to disagreement, mistrust, and violent conflict than those that are less fractionalized (see for instance, Alesina et al., 2003; Alesina & Spolaore, 2003; Alesina & La Ferrara, 2002). The state's enforcement entities – for instance the police and courts – are therefore deployed more frequently for the purposes of preventing and settling disputes among socially disparate populations than among more homogeneous ones. Finally, the form of government may influence enforcement costs as well.

(3) The third cost of government is the cost of providing public goods other than those necessary to enforce decided upon rules (such as police and courts, which falls under the enforcement costs of government in (2)), but which contribute to the ability of individuals to engage in higher levels of trade.[8] Roads, for instance, which permit interactions between larger numbers of individuals, are an example of this. The public goods cost of government is largely determined by the same factors as enforcement costs. Public goods costs are increasing in the size of the population because it is more expensive to supply an adequate system of transportation for a large population, for instance, than a small one. Similarly, *ceteris paribus*, public goods costs will be higher among socially heterogeneous populations than more homogeneous ones (Alesina, Baqir & Easterly, 1999). Where agents have more diverse characteristics they have more diverse needs, requiring multiple forms of the same public goods (for instance roadways coming from, and going to, different places), which raises the cost of providing such services.

---

[8] These goods need not be non-excludable and non-rivalrous, per the classic definition of public goods. Roads, for example, are both excludable and rivalrous, and yet government is traditionally viewed as the appropriate provider of transportation systems. An important strand of work points out that many if not most of the public goods traditionally thought of as within the purview of state provision (including roads) can actually be provided for privately and have been historically. See for instance, Bieto et al. (2002), which contains a number of examples of this. Here, however, I am taking the more traditional view held by most economists, which assumes that government will provide these goods.

🖄 Springer

Public Choice (2006) 130:41–53   45

2.2. The benefit of government

The factors above determine G's size. The efficiency of anarchy, however, depends upon the cost of government relative to the benefit that government provides by moving society to the higher trade equilibrium. What then affects the size of $H - L$?

The difference between social wealth when individuals engage in higher trade vs. when they engage in lower trade is determined by the potential for gains from exchange. The size of these gains is in turn a function of the range of exchange opportunities that are available to them. Five main factors affect this range:

(1) Individuals' endowments – *Ceteris paribus*, where agents begin with more disparate endowments the gains from trading will be larger and vice versa.
(2) The size of the potential trading population – A larger population of potential exchange partners means a larger number of opportunities to gain from trading. A smaller population means fewer potential gains from exchange.
(3) Individuals' productive abilities – *Ceteris paribus*, where individuals' productive abilities are more disparate there are larger gains from them exchanging. Where productive abilities are more similar the opposite is true.
(4) Individuals' preferences – *Ceteris paribus*, more diverse agent preferences create more opportunities for exchange. Less diverse preferences mean fewer opportunities from exchange.
(5) The presence or absence of private institutional arrangements that facilitate exchange – Where private institutions, like arbitration, reputation mechanisms, or community norms compelling cooperation are present, agents are able to realize additional gains from exchange. Thus social wealth in the lower trade equilibrium will be higher than it would have been without these institutions (though because of the limitations discussed above, still lower than if government existed). The presence of private institutional arrangements facilitating exchange thus shrinks the gap between social wealth in the higher and lower trade equilibrium. The absence of such institutions increases this gap.

These five factors together determine the thickness of the market. Thick markets have many (i.e., widespread) opportunities for exchange and thus generate high gains from trade. Thin markets, in contrast, have very few opportunities for exchange and thus generate minimal gains from trade.

It should be clear that when markets are sufficiently thin the relative difference in social wealth between a situation in which agents engage in higher trade and a situation in which they engage in lower trade is negligible. This corresponds to the case when $H - L$ is very small. Alternatively, when markets are very thick this difference will be large.

Having established what affects the cost of government and what affects the benefits government provides by moving society from a lower trade equilibrium to a higher trade one, it is now possible to distinguish two types of efficient anarchy: (1) "big G anarchy," in which despite the presence of a substantial gap between social wealth in the higher vs. lower trade equilibrium, government is too costly to justify its emergence, and (2) "small $H - L$ anarchy," in which even though government may be inexpensive to create, the difference between social wealth in the higher and lower trade equilibrium is so small as to make the state inefficient on cost-benefit grounds. At least theoretically then, these are situations in which statelessness is socially optimal. A society of rationally self-interested agents operating in either environment would thus (rationally) choose anarchy over government.

This framework therefore predicts anarchy in two distinct sets of circumstances: one in which the costliness of the state prevents government from emerging (big G anarchy) and

 Springer

46   Public Choice (2006) 130:41–53

one in which the absence of trading opportunities makes the benefit of introducing the state prohibitively small (small $H - L$ anarchy). I explore the evidence supporting this prediction below.

3. Two archetypes of actual anarchy

3.1. Small $H - L$ anarchy

The first archetype of statelessness – small $H - L$ anarchy – is characteristic of statelessness observed in small, primitive societies.[9] The historical presence of long-standing, primitive anarchic societies spans the entire globe. Consider, for example, societies such as the Eskimo tribes of the North American Arctic (Hoebel, 1954), Pygmies in Zaire (Turnbull, 1961), Indian tribes like the Yoruk of North America (Benson, 1989), the Ifugao of the Philippines (Barton, 1967), the Massims of East Papuo-Melanesia (Landa, 1994), Indian tribes of South America like the Kuikuru (Dole 1966), the Kabyle Berbers of Algeria, the Land Dyaks of Sarawak and the tribal Santals of India (Barclay, 1990), none of which had governments. In several cases primitive anarchic societies remained as such well into the 20th century. The Kapauku society of West New Guinea, for instance, was stateless until about 1960 (Pospisil, 1963).

In his classic anthropological work, E. E. Evans-Pritchard (1980 [1940]) described the Nuer society of the southern Sudan circa the 1930s. The Nuer people were not alone in pre-colonial Africa in rejecting government. Inside Africa, the Barabaig, Dinka, Jie, Karamojong, Turkana, Tiv, Lugbara, Konkomba, Plateau Tonga and others all long stood as stateless or near-anarchic orders as well.[10] The Nuer, however, is among the best studied of these groups and in many ways typifies general features found among other primitive anarchic societies. For this reason I consider the Nuer exclusively here, though it should be kept in mind that the lessons of this analysis apply generally to other primitive anarchic societies with similar characteristics, as I will try and highlight below.

Primitive societies like the Nuer represent instances in which rationally self-interested individuals choose anarchy over government because the difference between social wealth in the higher trade and lower trade equilibrium is extremely small. Since the formation of even the leanest government involves some fixed cost and this cost is not insignificant, a very small $H - L$ is enough make anarchy the efficient pattern of social organization.

The small gap between payoffs from higher and lower trade in primitive societies is a function of five main factors, which tend to make potential markets inside of them extremely thin:

(1) These societies are typically rather small, meaning there are relatively few opportunities for exchange even if government is introduced. This tends to make lower levels of trade enabled by private institutional arrangements not much less profitable than higher levels of trade that presumably would be made possible if government were established.[11] The size of the relevant trading population is largely determined by the size of the population over

---

[9] This is not to say, however, that anarchy is only efficient and therefore only arises in situations where H and L are themselves small. $H - L$ can also be small when H and L are both large. For instance, as discussed below, modern international has a large L because of highly effective private institutions. Thus, adding government will not add substantially to trade, making $H - L$ small despite the fact that H and L are themselves large.

[10] For reference to these and other stateless societies-in Africa see Bohannan (1968) and Barclay (1990).

[11] I say presumably here because it is not at all clear that government would actually enable a higher level of trade in these societies. There are many examples of tribal societies that have had governments imposed

Public Choice (2006) 130:41–53   47

which government is introduced. Thus to understand why the relevant potential trading population for the Nuer was very small, we need to first understand why government among the Nuer, if it were introduced, would have been introduced at a low level – i.e., over a small population.

The Nuer were actually one the largest primitive stateless societies.[12] The most liberal estimate of the Nuer population is around 400,000 individuals (Barclay, 1990). However, Evans-Pritchard, who studied the Nuer most closely, estimated the Nuer population at only half this size. This figure is inclusive of all Nuer group members. This inclusive population was divided into 11 tribes: the Bul, Leek, western Jikany, Nyuong, Dok, Jagei, Gaawar, Thiang, Lak, Lou, and eastern Jiknay. Each tribe was in turn subdivided into numerous sections based on lineage, and these sections were further subdivided into numerous village communities. Nuer communities tended to be extremely close-knit, as they were composed of individuals connected by lineage.

The largest Nuer organizational unit in which private rules and arbitration procedures were respected by other individuals was the tribe. Beyond the bounds of each tribe there was no recognition of such rules or procedures. The largest conceivable level at which government might have been introduced among the Nuer would therefore have been the tribal level. Even this, though, is questionable. Evans-Pritchard, for instance, indicates that in many cases the largest effective organizational unit of the Nuer was actually much smaller, perhaps somewhere between the village and tribal levels. This suggests that were government introduced, it would have been over an even smaller population. In any event, the relevant population of the Nuer, which as already noted was considerably larger than many other anarchic primitive societies, was not very large. The presence of private institutions such as the "leopard-skin chief" who arbitrated disagreements among tribe members enabled some degree of exchange between individuals at this level. While introducing government at the tribal level might increase this exchange somewhat, the small population involved coupled with private institutions like the leopard-skin chief suggests that this increase would be minimal.

(2) Individuals in primitive societies typically have very similar productive abilities. Most are either pastoral or horticultural. The Nuer, who were of the pastoral variety, were overwhelmingly a cattle-herding people. Though they were sometimes forced to raise crops (for instance, when rinderpest destroyed their livestock), a combination of the natural environment they found themselves in and Nuer culture created a situation in which there was very little differentiation in agents' productive capacities.

Evans-Pritchard described the fundamental environmental features of Nuerland as follows: "(1) It is dead flat. (2) It has clay soils. (3) It is very thinly and sporadically wooded. (4) It is covered with high grasses in the rains. (5) It is subject to heavy rainfall. (6) It is traversed by large rivers that flood annually. (7) When the rains cease and the rivers fall it is subject to severe draught" (1980: 55). While these conditions allowed for occasional horticulture, hunting and fishing, they overwhelmingly dictated the productive activity of cattle herding that the Nuer were so fond of. Production was thus almost exclusively directed at raising cattle for meat and milk.

Nuer culture, which was from top to bottom organized around the importance of cattle, reinforced herding as the virtually exclusive productive activity of the Nuer people. As

---

on them by colonizers, and then following the withdrawal of the colonial government, have economically crashed. In these societies, trade was more expansive under statelessness than it was following the imposition of government. Leeson (2005) examines such cases in precolonial/postcolonial Africa.

[12] To my knowledge, only the Tiv and the Lugbara were larger.

48   Public Choice (2006) 130:41–53

Evans-Pritchard put it: nearly all of Nuer "social behavior directly concerns their cattle" (1980: 18). This fact was manifest in practices and institutions among the Nuer from the giving of names (which were based on the names of family cattle), their networks of kinship ties (which were based upon cattle ownership), to rituals and religious activities. This intensely focused interest on cattle that was fundamental to Nuer culture strengthened the singularly directed aims of Nuer productive activities in herding.[13] Neither this feature of Nuer life nor the fact that the Nuer environment was not suitable for much other than cattle herding is to deny that innately occurring comparative advantage among individuals in say the production of milk vs. the production of meat allowed for some specialization. However, for the reasons discussed above, the degree of this specialization was severely limited. This in turn limited the gains that could be had from higher levels of exchange, which introducing government might bring.

(3) Not always, but frequently, the agents who populate primitive societies have homogeneous preferences. In the case of the Nuer, as mentioned above, this preference was nearly uni-dimensional and aimed at the ownership of cattle. This lack of diversity tended to diminish the increase in exchange opportunities that introducing government might bring. As Evans-Pritchard observed, the "Nuer have nothing to trade except their cattle and have no inclination to dispose of these; all they greatly desire are more cattle . . . This narrow focus of interest causes them to be inattentive to the products of other people, for which, indeed, they feel no need and often enough show contempt" (1980: 88).[14]

(4) Individuals in primitive societies often have very similar endowments. Because they are frequently egalitarian, these societies create a situation in which across current members and even generations, individuals have the same level and forms of wealth. For the Nuer, while disparities in wealth levels were permitted, the form of individual endowments was nearly identical for all individuals in that wealth was construed almost exclusively in the form of cattle, which was singularly desired.

(5) Because of their small, close-knit nature, primitive societies are often able to effectively use private institutional arrangements based on norms and reputation to facilitate cooperation. Within the same communities, for instance, the Nuer shared common norms regarding the settlement of disputes, which typically involved cattle. Disagreeing members would see the leopard-skin chief who, sometimes in conjunction with community elders, would recommend how the dispute should be settled. This form of private arbitration enabled community interaction despite the absence of government.

Similarly, within the same tribe, the institution of the feud, which involved specific steps for dealing with more serious transgressions, was respected by the Nuer and provided a strong incentive for individuals to refrain from theft and violence.[15] The strong presence of these private mechanisms of governance raised the relative payoff to indi-

---

[13] The Nuer focus on cattle was both a cause and consequence of the cultural characteristics described.

[14] To satisfy basic dietary requirements to sustain life, the Nuer were forced to spend some time in agricultural activity directed at producing carbohydrate-rich foods. In their case this was grain. However, as discussed above, for reasons of climate and preferences, the time they spent doing so was minimal. Evans-Pritchard described the situation as follows: "(1) that Nuer cultivate only enough grain for it to be one element in their food-supply and not enough to live on it alone; (2) that with their present climate and technology considerable increase in horticulture would be unprofitable; and (3) that the dominance of the pastoral value over horticultural interests is in accord with oecological relations which favour cattle husbandry at the expense of horticulture" (1980: 81).

[15] For an excellent analysis of the feud and leopard-skin chief as institutions of self-enforcement see Bates (1983).

🕿 Springer

Public Choice (2006) 130:41–53

49

viduals in the lower trade equilibrium, which served to shrink the gap between social wealth in this and the higher trade equilibrium and with it the benefit of introducing a state.

3.2. Big G anarchy

Anarchy may also be efficient if the cost of government is extremely large. In this case even a substantial gap between social wealth in the higher vs. lower trade equilibrium may not be large enough to make the state efficient from a cost-benefit perspective. In this environment, rationally self-interested agents will again be led to prefer anarchy over government. Big G anarchy is thus the second archetype of statelessness I consider.

Instances of big G anarchy are less prevalent than instances of small $H - L$ anarchy simply because the cases in which G is likely to be massive are also the cases in which government is being extended over a massive population, which means that the potential increase in gains from trading are also massive. It is therefore hard for the cost of government to be larger than the difference between social wealth in the lower vs. higher trade equilibrium.

Nevertheless, one particular instance of big G anarchy is hard to miss: international anarchy. In recent decades there has been some growth of supranational organizations aimed at increasing the degree of centralized enforcement in the international sphere. Such organizations include, for instance, the World Court and the United Nations. These organizations, however, have not fundamentally affected the anarchic nature of the international sphere in that none of them give final, ultimate authority to the governing body to offer binding decisions on the parties involved. In short, they do not override national sovereignty but instead rely fundamentally upon the willingness and voluntary consent of the various sovereigns involved. If a sovereign chooses not to appear before such a court or does not abide by the court's decision, there exists no centralized authority to compel it do otherwise.

It might be assumed that the difference between social wealth in the higher and lower trade equilibrium in the international sphere would be very substantial, given the considerable population of the world. Even if this is the case, however, the organizational and enforcement costs of a global government extending over 6.5 billion people are prohibitively expensive. Consider, for instance, the substantial increase in organizational costs that would result from most voters being far removed from their public representatives (at least at the highest level). Organizational costs would also rise considerably because of the vast increase in the heterogeneity of the relevant population. If it is difficult to arrive at a decision regarding where a new police station is to be located within a community of 20,000 suburbanites, imagine the difficulty of coming to a much larger decision when over a billion people are involved from Beirut to Mexico City. Increased heterogeneity among the relevant population will lead to substantial increases in enforcement and public goods costs for similar reasons. Indeed, as the recent research of Alesina and Spolaore (2003) shows, the attendant increase in such costs associated with extending government over larger and more socially diverse populations is a primary constraint on the effective size of nations. At the size necessary to effectively govern the entire globe, any economies of scale in having a centralized state that normally exist on the national level are overwhelmed by the diseconomies of an encompassing world state.

Although it relates to the difference between $H - L$ instead of the size of G, it must be noted that the strong presence of private institutions that facilitate exchange in the international arena also contributes to the efficiency of anarchy in this sphere. Modern-day international trade is based largely on the set of private institutions that governed such exchange

 Springer

50   Public Choice (2006) 130:41–53

when it first emerged on a significant scale in 12th century Medieval Europe. This set of private institutions is called the *lex mercatoria*, or law merchant.[16]

The law merchant is a complex polycentric system of customary law that arose from the desire of traders in the late 11th century to engage in cross-cultural exchange. In the absence of state enforcement, this custom-based system relied on private arbitration for resolving disputes. Between the early 12th and late 16th centuries virtually all European trade operated this way with great success.[17] This system enabled large numbers of merchants to expand trade significantly and realize substantial additional gains from international exchange (Milgrom et al., 1990).

Contemporary international trade continues to make wide use of private arbitration as a means of settling disputes. Today at least 90 percent of all international trade contracts contain arbitration clauses (Volckart & Mangles, 1999; Casella, 1996). Among the most notable arbitration organizations that exist for this purpose are the International Chamber of Commerce (ICC), the London Court of International Arbitration (LCIA), the Arbitration Association of the Stockholm Chamber of Commerce, and the American Arbitration Association's International Center for Dispute Resolution (ICDR). In 2001 nearly 1,500 parties from over 115 nations across the globe utilized the services of the ICC alone (ICC Bulletin, 2001). The amounts in dispute varied from $50.000 to more than $1 billion with over 60 percent of all disputes involving sums of money between $1 million and $1 billion (ICC Bulletin, 2002). Similarly, the ICDR arbitrated a caseload in 2001 worth more than $10 billion involving parties from 63 countries across the globe (ICDR, 2002).

These arbitration associations rely heavily upon evolved customary law that dictates how exchange disagreements are to be settled and "arbitral awards are most generally promptly and willingly executed by business people" (David, 1985: 357). Indeed, virtually "[e]very research into the practice of international arbitration shows that by far the great majority of arbitration awards is fulfilled without the need for enforcement" (Böckstiegal, 1984: 49). In a study published in 1981, for instance, a survey of international oil traders indicated that over 88 percent of all contracts entered were carried out without dispute. Of the remaining 12 percent, respondents indicated that 76 percent of disputes were arbitrated successfully by private adjudication (Trakman, 1983: 53). The world's largest international arbitration association, the ICC, estimates that 90 percent of all its arbitral decisions are complied with voluntarily (Craig et al., 2000: 404).

The presence of private institutional arrangements like private arbitration and reliance upon customary law in the international sphere enables a substantial amount of trade despite the absence of government. Consider for a moment the staggering level of international trade. In 2003, world exports of merchandise and commercial services alone exceeded $9 trillion (WTO, 2004). Thus, although without centralized enforcement, agents may be situated in the lower trade equilibrium, this level of trade is not very low at all and quite possibly not significantly lower than it would be if an agency of centralized enforcement were introduced. In conjunction with the fact that the cost of such an agency would be extremely high, this strongly suggests that anarchy is the most efficient way of organizing the international arena. While some attempts have been made to introduce bodies of centralized enforcement on the

---

[16] For a discussion of the law merchant, both modern and medieval see: Mattli (2001); Volckart and Mangles (1999); Casella (1996); Benson (1989).

[17] As Benson notes, "In fact, the commercial revolution of the eleventh through fifteenth centuries that ultimately led to the Renaissance and industrial revolution could not have occurred without... this system" (1990: 31).

Public Choice (2006) 130:41–53 51

global level, it should therefore not be particularly surprising that global anarchy continues to persist.

4. Concluding remarks: From anarchy to government

The efficiency of anarchy in some primitive stateless societies and on the international level does not mean that statelessness is always or will remain efficient in these areas. If, for example, the members of primitive societies like the Nuer decided to widen their preferences, diversify their productive activities further, be more inclusive of other groups or, what is equivalent, take an interest in interacting with a wider, more diverse population, the thickness of potential markets would grow and with it so too would the gap between social wealth in the higher and lower trade equilibrium. If this gap grows large enough, the introduction of a state may become efficient and thus prove desirable.

Clearly, a significant factor contributing to this process – enlarging the number and range of individuals agents will interact with – is partially endogenous to the presence of government. The establishment of a state may make agents feel more secure in interacting with outsiders and thus increase market thickness, which increases the benefit of having a state in the first place. This does not mean, however, that introducing government in small $H - L$ anarchies would necessarily make government efficient. In addition to the other factors affecting the distance between social wealth in the higher and lower trade equilibrium that are not endogenous to government, agents would need to desire to interact with those outside their relatively small communities.[18] In the case of the Nuer, for instance, it does not seem that this was so.

In other cases, however, it was clearly the case. As Greif (2002) points out, Genoese traders initially employed primarily private institutions to facilitate trade with one another. At some point, however, they desired to interact beyond these bounds and believed that centralized arrangements were necessary to achieve this. Thus they shifted from reliance upon private institutions of enforcement to state enforcement.

Acknowledgements I am grateful to Peter Boettke, Tyler Cowen, Chris Coyne and an anonymous referee for indispensable comments and suggestions. The financial assistance of the Oloffson Weaver Fellowship is also gratefully acknowledged. I conducted this research in my time as a Visiting Fellow in the Political Economy and Government program at Harvard University.

References

Alesina, A., Baqir, R., & Easterly, W. (1999). Public goods and ethnic divisions. *Quarterly Journal of Economics*, 1234–1284.
Alesina, A., Devleeschauwer, A., Easterly, W., Kurlat, S., & Wacziarg, R. (2003). Fractionalization. *Journal of Economic Growth*, 155–194.

---

[18] In addition to this, if the benefits that introducing government creates are not immediate (or at least not completely so), agents will need to be sufficiently forward looking for the state to be profitable to adopt. If agents are sufficiently impatient, or if a significant portion of the benefits from introducing government will only come near the end of (or only after the end of) current inhabitants' lives, government will remain prohibitively costly to merit its introduction. In societies where life spans are not very long, this may present a problem. Short-lived agents will find government too costly to adopt, and their resulting failure to adopt government will in turn contribute to the short life span of the next generation, which will confront the same dilemma.

52 Public Choice (2006) 130:41–53

Alesina, A., & La Ferrara, E. (2002). Who trusts others? *Journal of Public Economics*, 207–234.

Alesina, A., & Spolaore, E. (2003). *The size of nations*. MA: MIT Press.

Anderson, T., & Hill, P. (2004). *The not so wild, wild west: property rights on the frontier*. Stanford: Stanford University Press.

Anderson, T., & McChesney, F. (2003). *Property rights: cooperation, conflict and law*. Princeton: Princeton University Press.

Barclay, H. (1990). *People without government: an anthropology of anarchy*. London: Kahn and Averill.

Barton, R.F. (1967). Procedure among the Ifugao. In: Bohannan, P. (ed.), *Law and Warfare*. NY: The Natural History Press.

Bates, R., Greif, A., & Singh, S. (2002). Organizing violence. *Journal of Conflict Resolution*, 599–628.

Bates, R. (1983). *Essays on the political economy of Central Africa*. Cambridge: Cambridge University Press.

Beito, D., Gordon, P., & Tabbarok, A. (2002). *The voluntary city: choice, community and civil society*. Ann Arbor: University of Michigan Press.

Benson, B. (1989). The spontaneous evolution of commercial law. *Southern Economic Journal*, 644–661.

Benson, B. (1989). Enforcement of private property rights in primitive societies: law without government. *Journal of Libertarian Studies*, 1–26.

Benson, B. (1990). *The enterprise of law*. San Francisco, CA: Pacific Research Institute for Public Policy.

Benson, B. (1999a). To arbitrate or litigate: that is the question. *European Journal of Law and Economics*, 91–151.

Benson, B. (1999b). An economic theory of the evolution of governance and the emergence of the state. *Review of Austrian Economics*, 131–160.

Böckstiegal, K.-H. (1984). *Arbitration and state enterprises: a survey of the national and international state of law and practice*. Deventer, Netherlands: Kluwer Law and Taxation Publishers.

Bohannan, P. (1968). Stateless societies. In: Collins, R. (ed.), *Problems in African history*. Englewood Cliffs, NJ: Prentice-Hall.

Buchanan, J. (1975). *The limits of liberty: between anarchy and leviathan*. Chicago: University of Chicago Press.

Buchanan, J., & Brennan, G. (1980). *The power to tax*. New York: Cambridge University Press.

Buchanan, J., & Tullock, G. (1962). *The calculus of consent: logical foundations of constitutional democracy*. Ann Arbor: University of Michigan Press.

Casella, A. (1996). On market integration and the development of institutions: the case of international commercial arbitration. *European Economic Review*, 155–186.

Clay, K. (1997). Trade without law: private-order institutions in Mexican California. *Journal of Law, Economics, and Organization*, 202–231.

Craig, W.L., Park, W., & Paulsson, I. (2000). *International chamber of commerce arbitration*. New York: Oceana Publications.

David, R. (1985). *Arbitration in international trade*. Deventer, The Netherlands: Kluwer Law and Taxation Publishers.

De Soto, H. (1989). *The other path: the invisible revolution in the Third World*. NY: Harper and Row.

Dixit, A. (2004). *Lawlessness and economics: Alternative modes of governance*. Princeton: Princeton University Press.

Dixit, A. (2003). Trade expansion and contract enforcement. *Journal of Political Economy*, 1293–1317.

Dole, G. (1966). Anarchy without chaos: Alternatives to political authority among the Kuikuru. In Swartz, M. Turner, V., & Tuden, A. (eds.), *Political Anthropology*. Chicago: Aldine.

Ellickson, R. (1991). *Order without law: how neighbors settle disputes*. Cambridge, MA: Harvard University Press.

Evans-Pritchard, E.E. (1940). *The nuer*. Oxford: Oxford University Press.

Friedman, D. (1973). *The machinery of freedom*. Chicago: Open Court Publishing.

Greif, A. (1989). Reputation and coalitions in medieval trade: evidence on the Maghribi traders. *Journal of Economic History*, 857–882.

Greif, A. (1993). Contract enforceability and economic institutions in early trade: The Maghribi traders' Coalition. *American Economic Review*, 525–548.

Greif, A. (2002). Institutions and impersonal exchange: from communal to individual responsibility. *Journal of Institutional and Theoretical Economics*, 168–204.

Greif, A., Milgrom, P., & Weingast, B. (1994). Coordination, Commitment and enforcement: the case of the merchant guild. *Journal of Political Economy*, 745–776.

Haddock, D. (2003). Force, threat, negotiation: the private enforcement of rights. In: Anderson, T., & McChesney, F. (eds.), *Property rights: cooperation, conflict, and law*. Princeton: Princeton University Press.

Hirshleifer, J. (1994). The dark side of the force. *Economic Inquiry*, 1–10.

Hoebel, E.A. (1954). *The law of primitive man*. MA: Harvard University Press.

Public Choice (2006) 130:41–53

53

Holcombe, R. (2004). Government: unnecessary but inevitable. *Independent Review*, 325–342.

ICC (2002). *International court of arbitration bulletin*. Spring 13(1).

ICC (2001). *International court of arbitration bulletin*. Spring 12(1).

ICDR (2002). *Press release*.

Klein, D. (1992). Promise keeping in the great society: a model of credit information sharing. *Economics and Politics*, 117–136.

Landa, J. (1994). *Trust, ethnicity, and identity*. Ann Arbor: University of Michigan Press.

Leeson, P.T. (2004). Cooperation and conflict: evidence on self-enforcing arrangements and heterogeneous groups. *American Journal of Economics and Sociology*, forthcoming.

Leeson, P.T. (2005). Endogenizing fractionalization. *Journal of Institutional Economics*, 75–98.

Leeson, P.T. (2006). Trading with bandits. *Journal of Law and Economics*, forthcoming.

Levi, M. (1988). *Of rule and revenue*. Berkeley: University of California Press.

Libecap, G. (2003). Contracting for property rights. In: Anderson, T., & McChesney, F (eds.), *Property rights: cooperation, conflict, and law*. Princeton: Princeton University Press.

Mattli, W. (2001). Private justice in a global economy: from litigation to arbitration. *International Organization*, 919–947.

McGuire, M., & Olson, M. (1996). The economics of autocracy and majority rule: the invisible hand and the use of force. *Journal of Economic Literature*, 72–96.

Milgrom, P., North, D., & Weingast, B. (1990). The role of institutions in the revival of trade: the medieval law merchant, private judges, and the champagne fairs. *Economics and Politics*, 1–23.

North, D. (1981). *Structure and change in economic history*. New York: WW & Norton Co.

North, D. (1990). *Institutions, institutional change, and economic performance*. New York: Cambridge University Press.

North, D., & Thomas, R. (1973). *The rise of the western world: a new economic history*. New York: Cambridge University Press.

Olson, M. (1993). Dictatorship, democracy, and development. *American Political Science Review*, 567–576.

Pospisil, L. (1963). *The Kapauku Papuans of West New Guinea*. New York: Holt, Rinehart, and Winston.

Rothbard, M. (1977). *Power and market: government and the economy*. New York: Columbia University Press.

Trakman, L.E. (1983). *The law merchant: the evolution of commercial law*. Littleton, CO: Fred B. Rothman & Co.

Turnbull, C. (1961). *The forest people*. NY: Simon and Schuster.

Volckart, O., & Mangles, A. (1999). Are the roots of the modern lex mercatoria really medieval? *Southern Economic Journal*, 427–450.

World Trade Organization (2004). *Recent trends in international trade policy developments*. Geneva: World Trade Organization.

Zerbe, R., & Anderson, L. (2001). Culture and fairness in the development of institutions in the California gold fields. *Journal of Economic History*, 114–143.

 Springer

[27]

How Important is State Enforcement for Trade?

Peter T. Leeson, *George Mason University*

According to conventional wisdom, state-provided contract enforcement is critical to an expansive, growing trade. This paper estimates state enforcement's impact on international trade for one hundred and fifty-seven countries over the last half a century. I find that state enforcement increases trade between nations by about fifteen to thirty-eight percent. This effect is significant though modest compared to intuition about the importance of government enforcement, the long-run growth of trade, and the estimated effect of trade's other determinants. Thus, while state enforcement appears to enhance trade, it does so less impressively than its status as essential for flourishing trade tends to suggest. (*JEL* F10, F53, F55)

Commerce . . . can seldom flourish . . . [where] the faith of contracts is not supported by the law, and . . . [where] the state is not supposed to be regularly employed in enforcing the payment of debts from all those who are able to pay.
—Adam Smith (1976 [1776], p. 910).

I thank Pete Boettke, Chris Coyne, Tyler Cowen, John Donohue, Michael Makowsky, Andrew Rose, Jesse Shapiro, Andrei Shleifer, Russell Sobel, Thomas Stratmann, Bob Subrick, and an anonymous referee for helpful comments and suggestions. Special thanks are also owed to the ICC, LCIA, and ICDR for generously providing me with arbitration data.

Send correspondence to: Peter T. Leeson, Department of Economics, George Mason University, MSN 3G4, Fairfax, VA 22030, USA; E-mail: pleeson@gmu.edu.

American Law and Economics Review
doi:10.1093/aler/ahn003
Advance Access publication April 10, 2008

62   American Law and Economics Review V10 N1 2008 (61–89)

1. Introduction

Is state-provided contract enforcement important for trade? Most economists certainly think so. Many would go as far as to say that a high volume of growing trade *requires* state enforcement. The rationale underlying this conventional wisdom is highly sensible. Formal enforcement pulls individuals out of anarchy. In doing so, it gives anonymous and distantly located strangers security to contract major transactions without fear of fraud.[1] The importance of state enforcement seems so sensible as to nearly place it beyond the realm of propositions deserving empirical investigation. This likely explains why no one has econometrically examined the effect of state-provided contract enforcement on trade. But do we really know that state enforcement is so important for trade?

The international arena provides an excellent ground to investigate this question. With the exception of a multinational treaty known as the New York Convention, international commerce is conducted in the absence of formal contract enforcement. Private international arbitration associations govern commercial disputes between international traders.[2] No supranational authority exists for this purpose.[3] In fact, there is not even a formal, universal body of international commercial law such an authority could use to adjudicate transnational commercial agreements if one existed (see, for instance, Oye, 1986, p. 1; Plantey, 199, p. 69). Despite the lack of formal global governance, international trade is large and growing rapidly. Today, it accounts for some twenty-five percent of global economic activity. Since 1960, the real value of global exports has increased thirteen-fold; and

---

1. A burgeoning literature finds that self-enforcing mechanisms such as reputation can support *low* volumes of trade between relatively small populations but concludes that such arrangements cannot support growing, high volumes exchange among large, diverse populations. See for instance, Greif (2002). Against this view, see leeson (forthcoming).

2. Casella (1996) considers arbitration's connection to the growth in international trade, while Mattli (2001) examines various forms of arbitration in response to differing needs of international traders.

3. The United Nations International Court of Justice settles disputes (for instance, regarding the interpretation of treaties) between states, not private individuals. Likewise, the European Court of Justice, which applies only to members of the European Union, is designed to adjudicate disputes between member countries concerning "European Community law." The United Nations International Criminal Court applies to private individuals but deals only with international criminal matters—not commercial ones.

in 2003, world exports of merchandise and commercial services exceeded $9.5 trillion (World Bank, 2004).

In 1958, members of the global community introduced a multinational treaty called the United Nations New York Convention on the Recognition and Enforcement of Foreign Arbitral Awards, creating state enforcement for private commercial agreements in the international arena. International arbitration and the New York Convention (NYC) are connected in the following way. Private parties to international commercial contracts agree to have their disputes settled by arbitration associations. Since these associations are private, they cannot formally compel losers to comply with their decisions. However, under the terms of the NYC, winners can have their arbitral decisions enforced by losers' governments if these governments are members of the convention.

A simple example illustrates how the NYC provides state enforcement for international traders. Suppose a Bulgarian importer contracts with an Argentinian exporter for a shipment of grade A quality leather. When the shipment arrives, the Bulgarian finds that the leather is only of B quality, though his trade partner insists it is A. Before 1958 these traders would have privately settled their dispute through an international arbitration association. If the arbitrator decided the Argentinian did not fulfill his end of the contract and ordered him to pay, the Bulgarian had no means of compelling payment should the Argentinian refuse. However, the introduction of the NYC in 1958 changed this. Traders still use private arbitration to settle disagreements. But now, under the NYC, if the Argentinian refuses to pay, the Bulgarian can call on the Argentinian government, which has signed the NYC, to enforce his arbitral award.

The NYC provides a straightforward way to empirically evaluate the impact of state enforcement on trade. I use a gravity model to examine the bilateral trade flows of one hundred and fifty-seven countries over the last half a century. If state enforcement increases trade, I expect members of the NYC to have higher trade than non-members. As it turns out, they do—but less dramatically than the wisdom that state enforcement is essential for trade to flourish suggests. I find that state enforcement increases trade between nations by about fifteen to thirty-eight percent. This effect is significant, but modest compared to intuition about the importance of government enforcement, the long-run growth of trade, and the estimated effect of trade's other determinants.

This paper is most closely connected with important work by Anderson and Marcoullier (2002), which considers how the quality of countries' domestic institutions, and in particular of their courts, impacts international commercial contract enforcement. These authors do not mention the NYC. But in suggesting the importance of domestic court quality for private international contract enforcement, their analysis implicitly assumes that domestic courts are indeed capable of enforcing international commercial agreements. My paper complements this research by examining the explicit institutional mechanism through which this is made possible: the NYC.

2. International Arbitration and the NYC

Private international arbitration is the dominant means of settling disputes arising from international transactions (see, for instance, Schultsz and van den Berg, 1982; Mentschikoff, 1961; Craig et al., 2000; Salacuse, 1991). [4] An estimated ninety percent of all international commercial contracts include arbitration clauses (see, for instance, Volckart and Mangels, 1999; Casella, 1996). As one leading international practitioner put it, " in today's world the dispute resolution mechanism will invariably be arbitration" (Aksen, 1990, p. 287).

International traders use arbitration to settle disputes for several reasons. First, they are interested in avoiding the home court of the other party. Parties fear being subjected to unknown laws, having a decision rendered in an unknown language via unknown procedure, being subjected to law or procedure they disagree with, or they fear that a state court will favor their adversary if he is a citizen of that nation. [5] Second, there is an important question as to which state court, if either, has jurisdiction in the matter of a dispute. Competing claims to jurisdiction are problematic. [6] But equally

---

4. For classic treatments of international arbitration within the legal literature, see, David (1985) and Trakman (1983).

5. Issues of conflicting law may be especially problematic when one of the parties involved comes from a common law legal system and the other from a civil law system.

6. As Rusk (1984, p. 19) has pointed out, even in some cases where jurisdiction seems clear, "some countries are strongly committed to the idea that such disputes should be settled within the jurisdiction of their own national court". Private international law contains conflict of law principles meant to deal with questions of jurisdiction. However, it consists merely of differing national laws regarding declarations of jurisdiction in certain

troublesome is the unwillingness of either state court to decide a dispute when neither feels equipped to adjudicate an international matter. Third, the decisions of state courts regarding matters of international commerce are difficult to enforce (Dezalay and Garth, 1996, p. 6). In some cases, state courts do not recognize foreign judgments. Even when they do, it is difficult to seize the assets of the loser if he is not from the country where the court's decision is made.[7]

International arbitration overcomes these problems by "delocalizing" dispute resolution.[8] Under arbitration, parties may choose the variables concerning the adjudication of their disputes. These variables include the site of dispute resolution and the law that will govern their dispute, which ranges from any national law to the evolved customs called the *lex mercatoria* (law merchant) that through common practice and usage have come to govern international commerce.[9] Parties may also select the number of arbitrators who will decide their dispute, the identity of these arbitrators, or the process by which they are appointed. If parties do not agree on one or more of these

---

cases, which may come into conflict with the competing claim of another nation to have right of jurisdiction in that case. The Hague Conference on Private International Law and more recently UNCITRAL have contributed to the harmonization of conflict rules in an effort to mitigate this problem.

7. Two other benefits of international arbitration are its speed, enabled by an extremely limited capacity to appeal, and the privacy it affords. Arbitration institutions pride themselves on keeping both disputes brought to their attention, as well as the decisions in such disputes, private. Indeed, this is part of the problem in obtaining specific data regarding international arbitration. A concern for privacy in the process of dispute resolution is especially important to firms that keep closely guarded trade secrets they do not wish to be made public.

8. This useful terminology comes from Cutler (2003).

9. For discussions of the modern law merchant within the legal literature, see, among others, Berman and Kaufman (1978), Cremades and Plehn (1983–1984), Carbonneau (1984), and Schmitthoff (1961). Leeson (2006), Benson (1989), and Volckart and Mangles (1999) consider the historical roots of modern international arbitration in the medieval *lex mercatoria*. For a game-theoretic treatment of how international traders secured cooperation in the context of the medieval law merchant, see, Milgrom, North, and Weingast (1990). On the role that merchant guilds played in the expansion of international trade within the medieval law merchant system, see, Greif, Milgrom, and Weingast (1994). Bernstein (1992, 2001), and Benson (1995) examine the use domestic arbitration within the United States. Dixit (2003) considers the general role of arbitration in providing improved information, though he is not concerned with international arbitration. Also, for an analysis of the market's ability to provide the optimal level of adjudication, see Landes and Posner (1979).

66   American Law and Economics Review V10 N1 2008 (61–89)

variables, they may stipulate that a neutral third party—the arbitrators of their case, for instance—decide these items for them.[10]

There are hundreds of international arbitration forums globally (Graving, 1989, p. 328). The largest of these include the International Chamber of Commerce's (ICC) International Court of Arbitration, the London Court of International Arbitration (LCIA), the American Arbitration Association's International Center for Dispute Resolution (ICDR), and the Arbitration Institute of the Stockholm Chamber of Commerce. The biggest and most significant of these is the ICC.[11]

The community of international arbitration users is large and diverse. Between 1923 and 1976, three thousand requests for international arbitration were submitted to the ICC—an average of about fifty-seven cases per year over the period. Between 1976 and 1998, the ICC received its ten thousandth case—an average of over three hundred and eighteen cases per year over the period (Craig et al., 2000, p. 2). In 2000, the ICC arbitrated a caseload involving nearly fifteen hundred parties from close to one hundred and twenty countries worldwide (ICC Bulletin, 2002).[12] The sums at stake between these parties are substantial. Table Identifies the amounts in dispute in international arbitration through the ICC from 1988–1998 and 2001.

The sums in contention typically rise throughout the arbitration process, so this table tends to understate the value of these disputes. Furthermore, the cases that come before international arbitration forums without specified

---

10. In recent years, both UNCITRAL and UNIDROIT have contributed to the harmonization of international commercial law and arbitration practices by encouraging inter state cooperation toward this end, drafting model laws regarding international commerce that states may adopt, drafting model arbitration clauses that may be used by parties to arbitration, drafting arbitration rules that may be used in *ad hoc* arbitration procedures, and other such efforts.

11. In addition to institutional arbitration conducted by such forums, parties to international trade may also use *ad hoc* arbitration, which is based on the same general principles as institutional arbitration, but is generally more open ended with respect to procedure. *Ad hoc* arbitration is organized and administered by individuals independent of any institutional arbitration forum. Because of its nature, data regarding *ad hoc* arbitration and specific information regarding the details of its operation and outcomes are unavailable.

12. Although I do not discuss it here, governments and government entities may also resolve disputes via international arbitration. These cases, however, comprise only a very small percentage of international arbitration users. In 2000, for instance, only 5% of all parties to international arbitration through the ICC, and 12% of its cases, involved state or parastatal entities (ICC Bulletin, 2001).

Table 1. Amounts in Dispute Through the ICC

	1988–1991 (%)	1992–1995 (%)	1996–1998 (%)	2001 (%)
<$50K	4.9	4.5	3.1	1.1
$50K–$200K	13.1	11.1	12.1	9.8
$200K–$1M	25.3	24.0	23.1	22.0
$1M–$10M	33.1	36.7	34.6	31.4
>$10M	11.3	14.7	16.0	22.6
Amount not indicated	12.3	9.1	11.0	13.1

Notes: Average per period. Source: Craig et al., 2000; ICC Bulletin, 2002.

amounts are often the largest, some in excess of $1 billion.[13] Although the typical case brought before international arbitration involves a substantial sum of money, the value of trade arbitrated relative to the total value of international trade is very small since only a small percentage of trades results in disagreement.

The NYC makes private international arbitral awards enforceable in state courts and for this reason is considered the "cornerstone of current international commercial arbitration" (van den Berg, 1981, p. 1). Between 1959 and 2003, one hundred and thirty-four nations signed this treaty. Its terms are simple and stipulate that signing nations agree to recognize and enforce international arbitral decisions brought to them for enforcement by parties to international arbitration.[14] If the losing party to arbitration does not comply with the arbitrators' decision, the winning party may have this decision enforced by the loser's state court if the loser's state has signed the NYC. The NYC provides the formal teeth to the otherwise private, informal process of commercial contract dispute resolution in the international sphere.

---

13. This pattern holds for the other major international arbitration institutions as well. For instance, the ICDR, a much smaller international arbitration forum than the ICC or the LCIA, arbitrated a caseload worth more than $10 billion involving parties from 63 countries across the globe (ICDR, 2002). See also, LCIA (1998, 1999, 2000, 2001, 2002).

14. The NYC allows nations to sign subject to two reservation conditions: (1) The reciprocity condition—states are not required to enforce arbitral awards rendered in nations that are not also signatories of the treaty (Article 1(3)). Sixty-eight nations have signed subject to this condition. (2) The commercial reservation—states are not required to enforce arbitral awards related to noncommercial matters, with the commerciality of a matter being defined by the state's national law (Article 1(3)). Forty-three nations have signed subject to this condition.

The ICC estimates that ninety percent of its arbitral awards are complied with voluntarily (Craig et al., 2000, p. 404). This provides an indirect estimate ($\approx 10\%$) of the number of cases that seek enforcement under the NYC, but cannot be taken as a measure of the (un)importance of state enforcement for trade. The overwhelming extent of voluntary compliance reported by the ICC may simply be evidence that formal enforcement provided by the NYC is working precisely as it was designed to. Traders' knowledge that refusal to comply with an arbitral award will result in state enforcement under the NYC compels them to voluntarily comply at the arbitration stage. In other words, as a result of the NYC, voluntary compliance always occurs in the "shadow of the state." Establishing the importance of state enforcement therefore requires an approach that econometrically isolates the impact of formal enforcement on trade.

3. Empirical Strategy

To investigate the importance of state enforcement for trade, I use the most conventional and widely accepted empirical approach (and data, as I discuss below) for determining the impact of various factors on international trade. I follow Rose (2004a) who employs a gravity model of bilateral trade, which explains trade using the distance between countries and their joint income. I want to control for as many factors affecting trade as possible, both "natural" and "man-made," so I augment the basic gravity equation with additional variables. These variables include: culture (e.g., if a pair of countries share the same language), geography (e.g., whether either country is landlocked), history (e.g., whether one colonized the other, whether both were colonized by the same country, etc.), and membership in trade agreements (e.g., if the two countries are members of the same regional trade agreement, if one or both are members of the WTO, or one country was a GSP beneficiary of another country and vice versa), which might be important in accounting for the volume and pattern of exchange. Appendix B describes my variables comprehensively.

I estimate the augmented gravity equation:

$$\log(X_{ijt}) = \alpha + \beta_1 \, BothinNYC_{ijt} + \beta_2 \, OneinNYC_{ijt} + \gamma \mathbf{Z}_{ijt} + \varepsilon_{ijt} \quad (1)$$

where X_{ijt} is the average value of real bilateral trade between i and j at time t, β_1, and β_2 are my parameters of interest, and ε_{ijt} is a random error term. $BothinNYC_{ijt}$ is a binary variable that is 1 if both i and j are members of the NYC at time t, and 0 otherwise. $OneinNYC_{ijt}$ is a binary variable that is 1 if either i or j is a member of the NYC at time t, and 0 otherwise. β_1 measures the effect of the NYC on trade when both trading partners are members of the convention and β_2 measures the effect of the NYC on trade when one country is a member and the other is not. I search for the effect of state enforcement using variation across countries, since not all countries are members of the NYC, and across time, since membership grows over the sample. If state enforcement is highly important for trade, β_1 and β_2 should be positive and large relative to the nuisance coefficients γ on the variables I use to condition the gravity model. These variables are given by the vector of controls Z_{ijt}.

I use ordinary least-squares (OLS) with standard errors that are robust to clustering by country-pairs to estimate the gravity model. I also use year-specific fixed effects to account for factors that are constant across countries but vary across time, such as oil shocks, the global business cycle, etc.[15] Anderson and van Wincoop (2003) suggest that it is important to include country fixed effects to account for multilateral trade resistance between countries, which, if left unaccounted for, may bias gravity model estimates. Thus, in addition to year fixed effects, I also add country fixed effects to account for multilateral trade resistance between countries and to capture any other unobservable features of countries that might affect trade. I use a single set of country fixed effects for this purpose instead of separate importer and exporter effects. In doing this, I follow Rose and van Wincoop (2001) and Rose (2004a) who employ the gravity model for purposes similar to my own.[16] Finally, since multilateral resistance may vary over time for each country, I also try estimating a specification that includes time-varying country fixed effects. My full panel covers 50 time periods for more than 150 countries. Comprehensive time-varying fixed effects would thus require about 8000 new dummy variables. To avoid the computational difficulties of this, I define only five time periods for this specification: 1950–1959, 1960–1969, 1970–1979, 1980–1989, and 1990–1999. Sections 7 and 8 perform sensitivity analyses for my benchmark regression. These

---

15. The Hausman test rejects the use of random effects. $\chi^2 = 6607.82$.

16. For a discussion of the appropriateness of a single set of country fixed effects vs. separate importer and exporter fixed effects, see, Rose (2004b).

examine the potential for a lagged effect of NYC membership, address the issue of intrafirm trade, investigate whether the NYC's impact on trade may be development-dependent, and include a number of other robustness checks.

4. Data

Data for my regressand (the natural logarithm of trade) are from Rose (2004a) who uses the IMF's "Direction of Trade" data set. My sample covers bilateral merchandise trade for one hundred and fifty-seven countries over fifty years between 1950 and 1999. A list of these countries is presented in Appendix A. Using these data, Rose creates an average value of bilateral trade between a country pair by averaging the four available measures (exports from country 1 to country 2, imports into country 2 from country 1, etc.). These values are deflated by the American CPI for all urban consumers (1982–1984 = 100).

My data for real GDP and GDP per capita (in constant US dollars) are from the Penn World Table v. 6.1 and cover the years from 1950 through 1999. Data for my variable of interest—membership in the NYC—are from the Stockholm Chamber of Commerce (2004), which reports the list of 109 member countries from the convention's first effective year in 1959 through 1999. Six countries joined the NYC in its first year: Egypt, France, Israel, Morocco, Syria, and Thailand. By 1965, twenty-nine sample countries had signed the NYC, including Finland, Germany, France, India, Japan, the Netherlands, Norway, Russia, and Switzerland. Over the next decade, fifteen additional countries joined, including some "big players," such as the United Kingdom (in 1970) and the United States (in 1975), bringing the total number of nations covered by the NYC to 44. By 1985, fifty-nine nations were members of the convention; and between 1986 and 1995, thirty-eight new countries joined (including Canada)—the largest number of new additions in the NYC's history. In 1999, the total number of countries that had ratified the convention stood at one hundred and nine. A complete list of NYC signatories and the years they joined is presented in Appendix A.

Data for my remaining regressors are from Rose (2004a) who draws on a number of standard sources to construct these variables. Data from the CIA *World Factbook* are used to create controls relating to land area, landlocked and island status, shared border, language, and colonization. Data regarding whether a pair of countries was part of a currency union are from Glick and Rose (2002). Data used to create an indicator of regional trade agreements

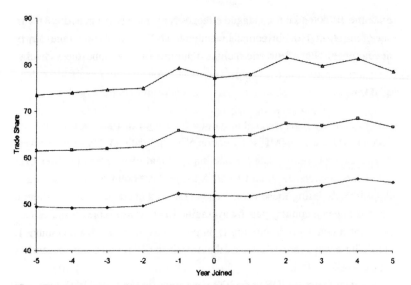

Figure 1. Trade Share within ±5 Years of Joining the New York Convention.
Notes: Middle line: simple average of 50 NYC members' trade shares
([exports+imports]/GDP) in the 10 years surrounding the dates they joined. Top
line: confidence interval of +2 SD. Bottom line: confidence interval of –2 SD. The
vertical line separates the five years before NYC ratification from the five years
after NYC ratification. Trade share data cover 1960–1998 (i.e., NYC members that
joined between 1965 and 1993).

come from the WTO and include: ASEAN, EEC/EC/EU; US-Israel FTA;
NAFTA; CARICOM; PATCRA; ANZ-CERTA; CACM, SPARTECA, and
Mercosur. Finally, data from the WTO website and the UN's publication,
the *Operation and Effects of the Generalized System of Preferences* (1974,
1979, 1984), are used to construct variables for membership in GATT/WTO
and the GSP, respectively.

5. The NYC and Trade at a Glance

A casual look at the data suggests that state enforcement has had a
positive, but small, impact on trade. Figure 1 presents a graphical 'event
study' that examines the trade share ([exports + imports]/GDP) of fifty
countries that joined the NYC five years before and after they joined the
convention. I use trade share data from *World Development Indicators* (2004)
for the years 1960 through 1998, and look only at those countries for which
trade share data are available for all ten years surrounding the date of NYC

72   American Law and Economics Review V10 N1 2008 (61–89)

ratification. The middle line depicts the average trade share in each year for these countries. The horizontal lines above and below show a confidence interval of ± 2 SD. The vertical line at the center of the graph separates the five years before countries joined the NYC from the five years after they joined. Average trade shares in the half-decade after countries join the NYC are slightly higher than in the half-decade before they join. Figure 1 suggests that state enforcement has enhanced trade, but very modestly.

6. Benchmark Results

Table 2 presents the results of my regressions that attempt to econometrically isolate state enforcement's impact on trade. My benchmark specification is the augmented gravity model estimated using ordinary least-squares with country and year fixed effects and robust standard errors over the entire sample. Column 1 reports these findings. My results for the variables that Rose (2004a) uses are similar to those he finds and those found elsewhere in the literature. Economically larger and richer countries trade more, while those that are further apart trade less. Additionally, countries that are members of the same regional trade agreement trade more, as do countries that have a common language, share a border, share a currency, or share colonial history. Also, like Rose, I find that membership in the Generalized System of Preferences (GSP) has a large positive effect on trade and that membership in the WTO/GATT has an economically weak impact.

What about the NYC? In my benchmark specification, the NYC increases trade $(e^{0.325} - 1 \approx)$ 38 percent when both countries are members and 15 percent when only one is. The lower bound of the 95 percent confidence interval for these estimates suggests that the NYC increases trade 28% and 8%, respectively. To put this in perspective, the NYC has roughly the same impact on trade as sharing a common language. This effect is significant, but modest compared to intuition about the importance of state courts, the long-term growth of trade, and the effect of many of the other variables impacting trade. Membership in a regional trade agreement, for example, increases trade 164 percent. Similarly, sharing a currency increases trade nearly 200 percent. My estimations evidently can deliver positive, economically large effects on trade. But state enforcement is not one of them.

When I incorporate time-varying country fixed effects in column 2, the NYC's impact on trade becomes small and negative. One explanation for this is that NYC membership is endogenous. In an effort to jump-start their

Table 2. The Effect of the New York Convention on Trade

	1 Country and Year Fixed Effects	2 Time-Varying Country Fixed Effects
Both in NYC	0.33	−0.26
	(0.04)	(0.03)
One in NYC	0.14	−0.14
	(0.03)	(0.03)
Both in GATT/WTO	0.13	−0.11
	(0.05)	(0.05)
One in GATT/WTO	0.03	−0.12
	(0.05)	(0.05)
GSP	0.68	0.67
	(0.03)	(0.04)
Log distance	−1.28	−1.28
	(0.02)	(0.02)
Log product real GDP	0.28	0.76
	(0.06)	(0.01)
Log product real GDP p/c	0.92	0.32
	(0.06)	(0.02)
Regional FTA	0.97	1.01
	(0.14)	(0.15)
Currency union	1.09	0.97
	(0.14)	(0.13)
Common language	0.32	0.33
	(0.05)	(0.05)
Land border	0.36	0.39
	(0.12)	(0.12)
Number landlocked	0.22	−0.67
	(0.45)	(0.04)
Number islands	0.96	−0.04
	(0.31)	(0.05)
Log product land area	0.32	0.03
	(0.04)	(0.01)
Common colonizer	0.65	0.67
	(0.07)	(0.07)
Currently colonized	0.69	0.45
	(0.34)	(0.33)
Ever colony	1.27	1.32
	(0.12)	(0.12)
Common country	−0.54	−0.21
	(0.40)	(0.38)
Observations	175,508	175,508
R^2	0.73	0.74
RMSE	1.69	1.66

Notes: Regressand: log real trade. OLS with country and year effects (column 1) and time-varying country effects (column 2) (intercepts not reported). Robust standard errors (clustering by country-pairs) in parentheses.

trade, countries that are experiencing trade difficulties are more likely to join the NYC than countries that are not. Baier and Bergstrand (2004), for instance, argue that membership in free-trade agreements is endogenous. This may also apply to the NYC.

In principle, it is possible to correct for endogeneity using instrumental variables. Like Rose (2004a), however, in practice I find it difficult to find variables that are reasonably well correlated with NYC membership but are not also highly correlated with trade. I have experimented with the same instrumental variables as did Rose—measures of democracy and freedom, as well as some of my own, including legal origin and distance from Paris (where the ICC is located)—but confront the same problem that he did: poorness of fit in the first stage. My instrumental variables are not well correlated with NYC membership.

Fortunately, I can still address the question of how potential endogeneity may be influencing my results by examining how economic and trade considerations may impact countries' decisions to join the NYC. To do this, I consider the relationship between whether or not a country joins the NYC during a 5-year period and its (log) GDP per capita, GDP per capita growth, (log) trade share, and trade share growth during this period. Table 3 presents the results of these estimations.

The most striking feature of table 3 is the third column, which reports the relationship between nations' (log) trade shares during a 5-year period and whether or not they joined the NYC during this period. In six of the eight time periods considered here, the relationship between trade share and NYC membership is negative; and in every case where this relationship is significant, it is negative. Consistent with the "jump-start hypothesis" mentioned above, this implies that countries struggling with trade are more likely to join the NYC than countries that are not. Since it is not possible to correct for endogeneity, it is important to bear this in mind when interpreting my results.

7. Sensitivity Analysis

Countries that are at different stages of development may experience differential benefits from having state enforcement for international commercial contracts. For instance, contractual violations might be less frequent in exchange relationships involving individuals from more developed coun-

Table 3. The Determinants of New York Convention Membership

	Log GDP p/c	GDP p/c Growth	Log Trade Share	Trade Share Growth	Observations	R^2
Join 1959–1964	0.05	−0.02	−0.08	0.03	4100	0.03
	(0.01)	(0.08)	(0.01)	(0.03)		
Join 1965–1969	0.02	−0.00	−0.01	0.00	4100	0.01
	(0.00)	(0.04)	(0.00)	(0.02)		
Join 1970–1974	0.03	0.02	−0.06	0.03	4100	0.03
	(0.00)	(0.05)	(0.01)	(0.02)		
Join 1975–1979	0.06	−0.02	−0.05	0.01	4100	0.06
	(0.00)	(0.04)	(0.01)	(0.01)		
Join 1980–1984	0.02	0.11	0.01	0.02	4100	0.01
	(0.00)	(0.05)	(0.01)	(0.03)		
Join 1985–1989	−0.01	0.08	−0.02	−0.00	4100	0.00
	(0.00)	(0.07)	(0.01)	(0.02)		
Join 1990–1994	−0.02	−0.00	−0.00	0.01	4100	0.01
	(0.00)	(0.06)	(0.01)	(0.03)		
Join 1995–1999	−0.01	−0.01	0.00	−0.03	4100	0.01
	(0.00)	(0.07)	(0.01)	(0.02)		

Notes: Regressand: A binary variable that is unity if a country joins the New York Convention in a 5-year period and zero otherwise. OLS with year effects (intercepts not reported). Robust standard errors in parentheses.

tries, where institutions are of better quality and people may exhibit a higher level of commercial honesty. In this case, we should expect the benefit of formally provided contract enforcement to be greater for poorer countries. On the other hand, richer countries may benefit more from the NYC since domestic courts, which ultimately do the enforcing under the NYC, tend to be of higher quality in these places. To determine if there are development-dependent effects of state enforcement, I break my sample into four income groupings.

The results of these regressions, presented in table 4, support the latter in tuition. Trading pairs with at least one high- or middle-income country experience about the same or slightly more gains from state enforcement than the sample as a whole, while trading pairs with at least one low-income or least-developed country experience slightly smaller gains than the sample as a whole. In the same table, I examine how the effect of state enforcement may be geographically dependent. Trading pairs with at least one country from South Asia do the worst, while those with at least one country from Latin America and the Caribbean do the best. Overall, however, the results in table 4 support the modest trade-enhancing effect of state enforcement identified in the benchmark regression.

Table 4. New York Convention Impact by Income and Region

	Both in NYC	One in NYC
Full sample	0.33	0.14
	(0.04)	(0.03)
High income	0.32	0.14
	(0.04)	(0.03)
Middle income	0.37	0.22
	—	—
Low income	0.29	0.09
	(0.06)	(0.05)
Least developed	0.20	0.09
	—	—
South Asia	−0.27	−0.37
	(0.11)	(0.09)
East Asia	0.21	0.08
	(0.12)	(0.09)
Sub-Saharan Africa	0.32	0.08
	(0.07)	(0.05)
Middle-East or North Africa	0.28	0.23
	(0.12)	(0.09)
Latin America or Caribbean	0.34	0.15
	(0.06)	(0.05)

Notes: Regressand: log real trade. OLS with country and year effects (intercepts not reported). Robust standard errors (clustering by country pairs) in parentheses. Regressors included but with unreported coefficients: both in WTO; one in WTO; GSP; log distance; log product real GDP; log product real GDP per capita; regional FTA; currency union; common language; land border; number landlocked; number islands; log product land area; common colonizer; currently colonized; ever colony; common country.

Anderson and Marcoullier (2002) consider a measure of countries' domestic court quality for 1996 using survey data from the World Economic Report's "Executive Opinion Survey." Interacting this measure with NYC membership would help us to shed light on how the NYC's effect might depend on the signatory's court quality. On the one hand, higher domestic court quality might enhance the importance of the NYC since, as table 4 suggests, well-functioning domestic courts are important to receive the full benefit of the NYC. On the other hand, domestic courts and international arbitration might be substitutes. If this is the case, when the quality of domestic courts rises, the importance of international arbitration, and thus of the NYC, which makes international arbitral awards enforceable in state courts, should fall.

The survey data Anderson and Marcoullier (2002) consider are available for only a fraction of the years covered by my panel, and even then, in

Table 5. Interaction

Both in NYC	−0.78
	(0.47)
One in NYC	−1.92
	(0.40)
Both in NYC × log product GDP p/c	0.07
	(0.03)
One in NYC × log product GDP p/c	0.13
	(0.02)

Notes: Regressand: log real trade. OLS with county and year effects (intercepts not reported). Robust standard errors (clustering by country pairs) in parentheses. Regressors included but with unreported coefficients: both in WTO; one in WTO; GSP; log distance; log product real GDP; log product real GDP per capita; regional FTA; currency union; common language; land border; number landlocked; number islands; log product land area; common colonizer; currently colonized; ever colony; common country.

most years, for only a small number of the countries my panel considers. However, since institutional quality and income are highly correlated, it is possible to examine the question of how domestic court quality influences the importance of the NYC for my entire panel, albeit somewhat more indirectly, by interacting NYC membership with the (log) product of trading partners' real GDP per capita.

Table 5 presents these results. The coefficients on both interaction terms are small but positive and significant, confirming the results in table 4. Richer trading pairs, which tend to have higher quality courts, receive a bigger boost from NYC membership than poorer trading pairs, which have lower quality courts. Equally important is the fact that the impact of the NYC on trade remains modest. When the interaction terms are added, the coefficient on joint NYC membership drops to −0.78 and on singular NYC membership drops to −1.92. Since the sample mean of log product real GDP per capita is 16.81, this implies that the net average effect of state enforcement is $(0.07 \times 16.81) - 0.78 \approx 0.40$ and $(0.13 \times 16.81) - 1.92 \approx 0.27$, respectively.

Perhaps nations realize greater benefits of state enforcement, but only some years after joining the NYC. If there is such a lag in the effect of joining the NYC, countries that joined earlier should exhibit a larger positive impact of NYC membership than those that joined later. Table 6 examines this possibility. I create four new "dummy" variables equal to one if either country in a trading pair joined the NYC 5, 10, 15 or 20 years ago.

The coefficient on joint NYC membership remains approximately of the same size as in the benchmark specification, though the coefficient on

78 American Law and Economics Review V10 N1 2008 (61–89)

Table 6. Dynamic Analysis

	OLS	Prais–Winsten	Prais–Winsten	Random effects	Random effects	Random effects	Lagged dependent variable
Residual autocorrelation coefficient	—	0.78	0.78	—	0.59	0.59	—
Both in NYC	0.31 (0.04)	0.16 (0.03)	0.15 (0.03)	0.34 (0.02)	0.33 (0.02)	0.33 (0.02)	0.07
One in NYC	0.04 (0.03)	0.07 (0.02)	0.06 (0.02)	0.14 (0.01)	0.16 (0.01)	0.14 (0.02)	0.04
Join 5 years ago	0.25 (0.02)	—	0.14 (0.01)	0.12 (0.01)	—	0.11 (0.01)	—
Join 10 years ago	0.13 (0.02)	—	0.14 (0.01)	0.05 (0.01)	—	0.05 (0.01)	—
Join 15 years ago	0.14 (0.02)	—	0.12 (0.01)	0.07 (0.02)	—	0.05 (0.02)	—
Join 20 years ago	0.15 (0.02)	—	0.11 (0.01)	0.01 (0.02)	—	-0.02 (0.02)	—

Notes: Regressand: log real trade. OLS, Prais–Winsten, and random effects estimator with country and year effects (intercepts not reported). Standard errors (robust for OLS and Prais–Winsten, clustering by country pairs) in parentheses. Regressors included but with unreported coefficients: both in WTO; one in WTO; GSP; log distance; log product real GDP; log product real GDP per capita; regional FTA; currency union; common language; land border; number landlocked; number islands; log product land area; common colonizer; currently colonized; ever colony; common country.

single NYC membership falls substantially. The coefficients on the joined 5, 10, 15, or 20 years ago dummies are positive and significant but small, suggesting there is no substantial delayed benefit of NYC membership. In the next column I use a Prais–Winsten estimator, which delivers similar, albeit somewhat smaller, coefficients. As a robustness check, in columns 4–6 I also use a country-pair random effects estimator, which again produces similar results. As the final robustness test for the potential for a delayed effect of state enforcement, the last column of table 6 performs an OLS estimate including a lagged dependent variable. Here, the impact of state enforcement becomes economically negligible.

8. More Technical Concerns

One potential concern is the extent to which my findings are influenced by "intrafirm trade"—trade between affiliates of large multinationals located in different countries. If a large proportion of bilateral trade is between arms of the same firm in different nations, the NYC's effect on trade will be understated. The reason for this is straightforward: intrafirm trade does not face the same kinds of contract enforcement concerns that interfirm trade does.

The creation of the NYC in 1958 and its reputation as "the cornerstone of modern international trade" among scholars of international trade law strongly suggests that a substantial portion of international trade is of the interfirm variety. So does the fact that an estimated 90 percent of all international commercial contracts contain arbitration clauses to provide for the possibility of dispute. Still, it is possible that intrafirm trade is an important consideration in evaluating the impact of state enforcement on trade.

Ideally, I would like to "net out" intrafirm trade from yearly bilateral trade flows before estimating the gravity model. Unfortunately, data on intrafirm trade is available for only a few countries (the United States, Japan, Canada and Sweden) in sporadic years.[17] Nevertheless, since the rise of multinationals and intrafirm trade is a relatively recent phenomenon of globalization, I can address this issue by looking only at bilateral trade before intrafirm exchange started to become prominent in international trade. The

---

17. See, for example, Bonturi and Fukasaku (1993). See also, Zeile (1997) and Rangan (2001).

80   American Law and Economics Review V10 N1 2008 (61–89)

Table 7. New York Convention Impact on Pre-Intrafirm Trade

	Both in NYC	One in NYC
Full sample	0.33	0.14
	(0.04)	(0.03)
Pre-1965	0.07	−0.01
	(0.09)	(0.04)
Pre-1970	−0.04	−0.01
	(0.07)	(0.04)
Pre-1975	0.05	0.05
	(0.06)	(0.04)
Pre-1980	0.17	0.08
	(0.05)	(0.03)
Pre-1985	0.24	0.10
	(0.05)	(0.03)

Notes: Regressand: log real trade. OLS with country and year effects (intercepts not reported). Robust standard errors (clustering by country pairs) in parentheses. Regressors included but with unreported coefficients: both in WTO; one in WTO; GSP; log distance; log product real GDP; log product real GDP per capita; regional FTA; currency union; common language; land border; number landlocked; number islands; log product land area; common colonizer; currently colonized; ever colony; common country.

cutoff I establish for this purpose is 1970. This date provides a conservative cutoff point since this is around the time that intrafirm trade began growing in USA, and USA led the growth of multinational firms globally.

If intrafirm trade is biasing my coefficients of interest downwards, when I re-estimate looking only at years before 1970, the NYC variables should exhibit a substantially larger effect on trade than they do when my panel covers all years. Table 7 reports the results of this estimation. My coefficients of interest are substantially *smaller* pre-1970 than they are for the entire period between 1950 and 1999. The NYC's impact on trade is negligible ($\approx 4\%$), negative, and statistically insignificant. I check the sensitivity of this result to several other cutoff dates, both before and after 1970, and continue to find that state enforcement's impact is smaller than it is for the entire period.

Following the NYC, a few, much smaller, multinational agreements were also created to provide state enforcement for international arbitral awards. These include the EU Convention, created in 2003; the Panama Convention, created in 1975; the Brussels/Lugano Convention, created in 1968; and the UN Convention on the Carriage of Goods by Sea, created in 1978. Nearly every member of each of these conventions is also a member of, and thus covered by, the NYC—the "grand-daddy" of multinational treaties concerning the recognition and enforcement of international arbitral awards. One member of the Panama Convention—Nicaragua—is not a member of the New York Convention, and five members of the UN Convention on the Carriage of Goods by Sea are not members of the NYC—Democratic Republic of Congo, Gambia, Malawi, Pakistan, and Sierra Leone.

Since NYC membership varies over time, it is possible that the effect of state enforcement is understated if in some years of the sample some countries are not yet members of the NYC but are members of one of these other treaties with the same purpose as the NYC.[18] This seems unlikely for two reasons. First, each of these conventions covers only a small group of countries, while the NYC covers more than one hundred. Furthermore, most were already members of the NYC at the time they joined these other treaties. Still, since in principle this could affect my estimates, I compare state enforcement's effect on trade considering only the NYC with state enforcement's impact on trade considering membership in *any* agreement with the purpose of creating formal enforcement for international arbitral awards. To do this, I create a new binary variable that is equal to unity if a country is a member of *any* agreement with this purpose and zero otherwise. I again construct separate variables for when both countries in a trading pair are members of such a treaty and when only one is.[19]

Table 8 presents the results of this regression. The coefficients on my variables of interest are similar to those in the benchmark regression. State enforcement, measured as membership in any treaty with the end of providing formal enforcement for international arbitral awards, increases trade ($e^{0.29} - 1 \approx$) 34 percent when both countries are members and 15 percent when only one is. The additional NYC-inspired treaties evidently do not bias my coefficients of interest when only the NYC is used to measure state enforcement.

---

18. The EU Convention poses no potential problem for my estimates since it was not created until 4 years after my sample ends.

19. To construct these variables, I use data on Panama Convention membership available at: http://www.sela.org and Brussels/Lugano Convention membership available at: http://www.fco.gov.uk/Files/kfile/statusbrussels,0.pdf.

Table 8. The Impact of Any Treaty of State Enforcement on Trade

Both in any treaty	0.29
	(0.04)
One in any treaty	0.14
	(0.03)
Both in GATT/WTO	0.13
	(0.05)
One in GATT/WTO	0.03
	(0.05)
GSP	0.70
	(0.03)
Log distance	−1.29
	(0.02)
Log product real GDP	0.25
	(0.06)
Log product real GDP p/c	0.95
	(0.06)
Regional FTA	0.96
	(0.13)
Currency union	1.09
	(0.14)
Common language	0.32
	(0.05)
Land border	0.36
	(0.12)
Number landlocked	0.22
	(0.45)
Number islands	0.96
	(0.31)
Log product land area	0.32
	(0.05)
Common colonizer	0.65
	(0.07)
Currently colonized	0.70
	(0.34)
Ever colony	1.27
	(0.12)
Common country	−0.54
	(0.40)
Observations	175,508
R^2	0.73
RMSE	1.69

Notes: Regressand: log real trade. OLS with country and year effects (intercepts not reported). Robust standard errors (clustering by country-pairs) in parentheses.

9. Concluding Remarks

The evidence suggests that the source of state contract enforcement in international trade has enhanced this trade—though not in the impressive way one would expect from a function considered essential for trade to flourish. The modest impact of formal enforcement in conjunction with international trade's considerable success strongly suggests that, in addition to formal enforcement, some private mechanisms of enforcement are also at work supporting international trade. Important research by Gould (1994), Rauch (2001), Casella and Rauch (2002), and Rauch and Trindade (2002), for example, demonstrates the significance of coethnic networks in creating private enforcement for international commercial agreements. Another private mechanism likely lessening the importance of state enforcement for trade is the use of *ex ante* arrangements, such as letters of credit, and other forms of third-party intermediation that mitigate the need for *ex post* enforcement.

Dixit's (2003) important theoretical work provides some additional conceptual underpinning for this paper's finding. His research suggests not only how formal enforcement may fail to add to trade in some cases, but how it might actually *reduce* trade by "crowding out" private enforcement mechanisms like those discussed above.

Ironically, another potential factor that may be contributing to the NYC's modest effect is the inability to formally enforce the terms of the NYC itself. Like all multinational treaties, for the NYC as well, there is no formal supranational agency of authority to compel states that have joined it to abide by its terms. This leaves the enforcement of the NYC to informal mechanisms, such as reputation, and the interstate equivalent of international arbitration through such organizations as the UN. Unfortunately, data on the frequency with which NYC member states default on the terms of their agreement, which could shed light on this issue, are not available.

Finally, as Helpman, Melitz, and Rubinstein (forthcoming) point out, traditional gravity estimations ignore countries that do not trade with each other and in doing so may generate biased estimates. To determine how accounting for such bias might affect state enforcement's impact on trade, future research should consider the NYC's effect in the context of the new model Helpman, Melitz, and Rubinstein have designed to address this problem.

84   American Law and Economics Review V10 N1 2008 (61–89)

Appendix A. Trading Countries in Sample

Albania	Congo, Dem. Rep. of	Iceland	Mozambique (1998)
Algeria (1989)	Congo, Rep. of	India (1960)	Namibia
Angola	Costa Rica (1987)	Indonesia (1981)	Nepal (1998)
Antigua and Barbuda (1989)	Cote d'Ivoire (1991)	Iran	Netherlands (1964)
Argentina (1989)	Croatia (1993)	Ireland (1981)	New Zealand (1983)
Armenia (1997)	Cyprus (1980)	Israel (1959)	Nicaragua
Australia (1975)	Czech Republic (1993)	Italy (1969)	Niger (1964)
Austria (1961)	Denmark (1972)	Jamaica	Nigeria (1970)
Azerbaijan	Dominica (1988)	Japan (1961)	Norway (1961)
Bahrain (1988)	Dominican Republic	Jordan (1979)	Oman (1999)
Bangladesh (1992)	Ecuador (1962)	Kazakhstan (1995)	Pakistan
Barbados (1993)	Egypt (1959)	Kenya (1989)	Panama (1984)
Belarus (1960)	El Salvador (1998)	Kuwait (1978)	Papua N. Guinea
Belgium (1975)	Equatorial Guinea	Kyrgyz Republic (1996)	Paraguay (1997)
Belize	Estonia (1993)	Lao People's Dem. Rep. (1998)	Peru (1988)
Benin (1974)	Ethiopia	Latvia (1992)	Philippines (1967)
Bermuda	Fiji	Lebanon (1998)	Poland (1961)
Bhutan	Finland (1962)	Lesotho (1989)	Portugal (1994)
Bolivia (1995)	France (1959)	Liberia	Qatar
Botswana (1971)	Gabon	Libya	Romania (1961)
Brazil	Gambia	Lithuania (1995)	Russia (1960)
Bulgaria (1961)	Georgia (1994)	Luxembourg (1983)	Rwanda
Burkina Faso (1987)	Germany (1961)	Macedonia (1994)	Samoa
Burundi	Ghana (1968)	Madagascar (1962)	Sao Tome & Principe
Cambodia (1960)	Greece (1962)	Malawi	Saudi Arabia (1994)
Cameroon (1988)	Grenada	Malaysia (1985)	Senegal (1994)
Canada (1986)	Guatemala (1984)	Mali (1994)	Seychelles
Cape Verde	Guinea (1991)	Malta	Sierra Leone
Central African Rep. (1962)	Guinea-Bissau	Mauritania (1997)	Singapore (1986)
Chad	Guyana	Mauritius (1996)	Slovakia (1993)
Chile (1975)	Haiti (1983)	Mexico (1971)	Slovenia (1992)
China (1987)	Honduras	Moldova (1998)	South Africa (1976)
Colombia (1979)	Hong Kong	Mongolia (1994)	Spain (1977)
Comoros	Hungary (1962)	Morocco (1959)	Sri Lanka (1962)
St. Kitts & Nevis	Syria (1959)	Turkey (1992)	Vietnam (1995)
St. Lucia	Tajikistan	Uganda (1992)	Yemen, Rep. of

(continued overleaf)

Appendix A. (*Continued*)

St. Vincent & Gren.	Tanzania (1964)	Ukraine (1960)	Zambia
Sudan	Thailand (1959)	United Kingdom (1975)	Zimbabwe (1994)
Swaziland	Togo	United States (1970)	
Sweden (1972)	Trinidad and Tobago (1966)	Uruguay (1983)	
Switzerland (1965)	Tunisia (1967)	Venezuela (1995)	

Notes: Countries with years beside them are members of the New York Convention. The year refers to when they joined.

Appendix B. Variable Descriptions

Independent variable	Description
Both in NYC	A binary variable that is unity if a country pair belongs to the New York Convention at time *t* and zero otherwise. Source: Stockholm Chamber of Commerce (2004).
One in NYC	A binary variable that is unity if either country in a country pair, but not the other, belongs to the New York Convention in time *t* and zero otherwise. Source: Stockholm Chamber of Commerce (2004).
Both in GATT/WTO	A binary variable that is unity if a county pair are GATT/WTO members at time *t* and zero otherwise. Source: Rose (2004a).
One in GATT/WTO	A binary variable that is unity if either country in a country pair, but not the other, is a GATT/WTO member at time *t* and zero otherwise. Source: Rose (2004a).
GSP	A binary variable that is unity if either country in a country pair was a GSP beneficiary of the other at time *t* and zero otherwise. Source: Rose (2004a).
Log distance	The log of the distance between a pair of countries. Source: Rose (2004a).
Log product real GDP	The log of the product of the real GDP of each country in a country pair in time *t*. Source: Penn World Table v. 6.1 (2002).
Log product real GDP p/c	The log of the product of real GDP per capita of each country in a country pair in time *t*. Source: Penn World Table v. 6.1 (2002).
Regional FTA	A binary variable that is unity if a country pair belongs to the same regional trade agreement at time *t* and zero otherwise. Source: Rose (2004a).
Currency union	A binary variable that is unity if a country pair uses the same currency at time *t* and zero otherwise. Source: Rose (2004a).

(*continued overleaf*)

Appendix B. *(Continued)*

Common language	A binary variable that is unity if a country pair has the same language and zero otherwise. Source: Rose (2004a).
Land border	A binary variable that is unity if a country pair shares a land border and zero otherwise. Source: Rose (2004a).
Number landlocked	The number of landlocked countries in the country pair (0, 1, or 2). Source: Rose (2004a).
Number islands	The number of island nations in the country pair (0, 1, or 2). Source: Rose (2004a).
Log product land area	The log product of the land areas of two countries in a country pair (in square kilometers). Source: Rose (2004a).
Common colonizer	A binary variable that is unity if a country pair were ever colonies post-1945 with the same colonizer and zero otherwise. Source: Rose (2004a).
Currently colonized	A binary variable that is unity if one country in a country pair is a colony of the other at time *t* and zero otherwise. Source: Rose (2004a).
Ever colony	A binary variable that is unity if one country in a country pair ever colonized the other and zero otherwise. Source: Rose (2004a).
Common country	A binary variable that is unity if a country pair remained part of the same nation during the sample and zero otherwise. Source: Rose (2004a).

References

Aksen, Gerald. 1990. "Arbitration and Other Means of Dispute Settlement," in David Goldsweig, Roger Cummings, eds., *International Joint Ventures: A Practical Approach to Working with Foreign Investors in the U.S. and Abroad.* Chicago:American Bar Association.

Anderson, James, and Douglas Marcoullier. 2002. "Insecurity and the Pattern of Trade: An Empirical Investigation," 84 *Review of Economics and Statistics* 342–52.

Anderson, James, and Eric van Wincoop. 2003. "Gravity with Gravitas: A Solution to the Border Puzzle," 93 *American Economic Review* 170–92.

Baier, Scott L., and Jeffrey H. Bergstrand. 2004. "Economic Determinants of Free Trade Agreements," 64 *Journal of International Economics* 29–63.

Benson, Bruce L. 1989. "The Spontaneous Evolution of Commercial Law," 55 *Southern Economic Journal* 644–61.

Benson, Bruce L. 1995. "An Exploration of the Impact of Modern Arbitration Statutes on the Development of Arbitration in the United States," 11 *Journal of Law, Economics and Organization* 479–501.

Berman, Harold, and Colin Kaufman. 1978. "The Law of International Commercial Transactions," 19 *Harvard International Law Journal* 221–77.

Austrian Law and Economics II

Bernstein, Lisa. 1992. "Opting Out of the Legal System: Extralegal Contractual Relations in the Diamond Industry," 21 *Journal of Legal Studies* 115–57.

Bernstein, Lisa. 2001. "Private Commercial Law in the Cotton Industry: Creating Cooperation Through Rules, Norms, and Institutions," 99 *Michigan Law Review* 1724–1790.

Bonturi, Marcos, and Kiichiro Fukasaku. 1993. "Globalisation and Intra-Firm Trade: An Empirical Note," OECD Economic Studies No. 20.

Carbonneau, Thomas. 1984. "Arbitral Adjudication: A Comparative Assessment of its Remedial and Substantive Status in Transnational Commerce," 19 *Texas International Law Journal* 33–114.

Casella, Alessandra. 1996. "On Market Integration and the Development of Institutions: The Case of International Commercial Arbitration," 40 *European Economic Review* 155–86.

Casella, Alessandra, and James Rauch. 2002. "Anonymous Market and Group Ties in International Trade," 58 *Journal of International Economics* 19–47.

Craig, W. L., William Park, and Ian Paulsson. 2000. *International Chamber of Commerce Arbitration*. New York: Oceana Publications.

Cremades, Bernardo, and Steven Plehn. 1983–1984. "The New Lex Mercatoria and the Harmonization of the Laws of International Commercial Transactions," 3 *Boston University International Law Journal* 317–48.

Cutler, A. Claire. 2003. *Private Power and Global Authority: Transnational Merchant Law in the Global Political Economy* Cambridge: Cambridge University Press.

David, Rene. 1985. *Arbitration in International Trade*. Dordrecht, The Netherlands: Kluwer.

Dezalay, Yves, and Bryant Garth. 1996. *Dealing in Virtue: International Commercial Arbitration and the Construction of a Transnational Legal Order*. Chicago, IL: University of Chicago Press.

Dixit, Avinash K. 2003. *Lawlessness and Economics: Alternative Modes of Governance*. Princeton, NJ: Princeton University Press.

The Economist (7/18-24/1992).

Gould, David. 1994. "Immigrant Links to the Home Country: Empirical Implications for U.S. Bilateral Trade Flows," 76 *Review of Economics and Statistics* 302–16.

Graving, Richard. 1989. "The International Commercial Arbitration Institutions: How Good a Job are they Doing?," 4 *American University Journal of International Law and Policy* 319–76.

Greif, Avner. 1993. "Contract Enforceability and Economic Institutions in Early Trade: The Maghribi Traders' Coalition," 83 *American Economic Review* 525–48.

Greif, Avner. 2002. "Institutions and Impersonal Exchange: From Communal to Individual Responsibility," 158 *Journal of Institutional and Theoretical Economics* 168–204.

Greif, Avner, Paul R. Milgrom, and Barry R. Weingast. 1994. "Coordination, Commitment, and Enforcement: The Case of the Merchant Guild," 102 *Journal of Political Economy* 745–76.

Heston, Alan, Robert Summers, Bettina Aten. 2002. *Penn World Table Version 6.1*. Philadelphia, PA: Center for International Comparisons at the University of Pennsylvania.

Helpman, Elhanan, Marc Melitz, and Yona Rubinstein. Forthcoming. "Estimating Trade Flows: Trading Partners and Trading Volumes," *Quarterly Journal of Economics*.

Hwang, Michael, and Andrew Chan. 2001. "Enforcement and Setting Aside of International Arbitral Awards—The Perspective of Common Law Countries," in A. J. van den Berg ed., *International Arbitration and National Courts: The Never Ending Story*. The Hague, The Netherlands: Kluwer Law International.

ICC. 2002. 13 *International Court of Arbitration Bulletin*, Spring.

ICC. 2001. 12 *International Court of Arbitration Bulletin*, Spring.

ICDR. 2002. *Press Release*.

Landes, William W., and Richard A. Posner. 1979. "Adjudication as a Private Good," 8 *Journal of Legal Studies* 235–84.

LCIA. 1998. *LCIA Newsletter*.

LCIA. 1999. *LCIA Newsletter*.

LCIA. 2000. *LCIA Newsletter*.

LCIA. 2001. "Director-General's Review 2001."

LCIA. 2002. "Director-General's Review 2002."

Leeson, Peter T. 2006. "Cooperation and Conflict: Evidence on Self-Enforcing Arrangements and Heterogeneous Groups," 65 *American Journal of Economics and Sociology* 891–907.

Leeson, Peter T. Forthcoming. "Social Distance and Self-Enforcing Exchange," *Journal of Legal Studies*.

Mattli, Walter. 2001. "Private Justice in a Global Economy: From Litigation to Arbitration," 55 *International Organization* 919–47.

Mentschikoff, Soia. 1961. "Commercial Arbitration," 61 *Columbia Law Review* 846–69.

Milgrom, Paul R., Douglass C. North, and Barry R. Weingast. 1990. "The Role of Institutions in the Revival of Trade: The Medieval Law Merchant, Private Judges, and the Champagne Fairs," 2 *Economics and Politics* 1–23.

Oye, Kenneth. 1986. "Explaining Cooperation Under Anarchy: Hypotheses and Strategies," in Kenneth Oye, ed., *Cooperation Under Anarchy*. Princeton, NJ: Princeton University Press.

Oye, Kenneth. 1983. "Belief Systems, Bargaining, and Breakdown: International Political Economy," PhD dissertation, Harvard University.

Plantey, Alain. 1993. "International Arbitration in a Changing World," *International Arbitration in a Changing World* in A. J. van den Berg ed., Deventer, The Netherlands: Kluwer Law and Taxation Publishers.

Rangan, Subramanian. 2001. "Explaining Tranquility in the Midst of Turbulence: U.S. Multinationals' Intrafirm Trade, 1966–1997," Working Paper 336, Bureau of Labor Statistics.

Rauch, James E. 2001. "Business and Social Networks in International Trade," 39 *Journal of Economic Literature* 1177–1203.

Rauch, James E., and Vitor Trindade. 2002. "Ethnic Chinese Networks in International Trade," 84 *Review of Economics and Statistics* 116–30.

Rose, Andrew K. 2004a. "Do We Really Know that the WTO Increases Trade?," 94 *American Economic Review* 98–114.

Rose, Andrew K. 2004b. "Response to Subramanian and Wei," Unpublished paper.

Rusk, Dean. 1984. "The Role and Problems of Arbitration with Respect to Political Disputes," in Thomas Carbonneau, ed., *Resolving Transnational Disputes Through International Arbitration*. Charlottesville, VA: University of Virginia Press.

Salacuse, Jeswald. 1991. *Making Global Deals: Negotiating in the International Marketplace*. Boston, MA: Houghton Mifflin.

Schmitthoff, Clive M. 1961. "International Business Law: A New Law Merchant," 129 *Current Law and Social Problems* 129–53.

Schultsz, Jan, Albert van den Berg. 1982. *The Art of Arbitration* Dordrecht, The Netherlands: Kluwer.

Trakman, Leon E. 1983. *The Law Merchant: The Evolution of Commercial Law* Littleton, CO: Fred B. Rothman & Co.

United Nations. 1946. *International Court of Justice Statute*.

United Nations. 1958. *New York Convention on the Recognition and Enforcement of Foreign Arbitral Awards*.

van den Berg, Albert Jan. 1981. *The New York Arbitration Convention of 1958* Deventer, The Netherlands: Kluwer Law and Taxation Publishers.

Volckart, Oliver, and Antje Mangels. 1999. "Are the Roots of the Modern Lex Mercatoria Really Medieval?," 65 *Southern Economic Journal* 427–50.

World Bank. 2004. *World Development Indicators*, CD-ROM.

Zeile, William J. 1997. "U.S. Intrafirm Trade in Goods," 72 *Survey of Current Business* 23–38.

[28]

Is Voluntary Government Possible?
A Critique of Constitutional Economics

by

WALTER BLOCK AND THOMAS J. DILORENZO*

"A 'social contract' theory of government ... can be used to place
a stamp of approval on all, or most, of the actions of the *existing*
government (for example, Rousseau). Thus, the theory of the divine right of kings began as a check on government, as an order to
the King to stay within divinely-commanded laws; it was transformed, by the State, into a divine stamp of approval for anything
the King might decide to do." (Murray Rothbard)

According to public choice theory, the market and the state are both devices
through which cooperation is organized and made possible. This theme of voluntary government is most prevalent in the subset of public choice known as constitutional economics. We believe that the analogy between politics and markets
made by constitutional economists is theoretically weak and clouds rather than
enhances our understanding of political economy. Politics has very little in common with non-coercive, voluntary exchange in the marketplace. (JEL: D 72)

1. Introduction

Public choice theory attempts to model politics as just another market. Political
"exchange" is said to be analogous to market exchange, although certain differences are acknowledged. Consequently, the widely-acknowledged benefits of free
markets are said to be the result of certain (not all) political "exchanges." "The
market and the State are both devices through which co-operation is organized and
made possible [where] ... two or more individuals find it mutually advantageous
to join forces to accomplish certain purposes," BUCHANAN AND TULLOCK [1962,
19] wrote in their landmark study, *The Calculus of Consent*. The public choice ap-

---

* We wish to thank Randy Holcombe, Ralph Raico, and participants in sessions at the
1998 Southern Economic Association meetings and the 1999 Austrian Scholars' Conference
at Auburn University for their comments. Gordon Tullock's critical comments were especially helpful. Two anonymous referees also provided insightful comments for which we
are grateful.

proach to the analysis of political decision making, wrote BUCHANAN AND TULLOCK [1962, 23f.], incorporates political activity as a particular form of exchange; and, as in the market relation, mutual gains to all parties are ideally expected to result from the collective action ... the political process ... may be interpreted as a positive sum game."

The theme of voluntary government is most prevalent in the subdiscipline of public choice known as constitutional economics, which has its roots in *The Calculus of Consent* and in much of Buchanan's post-1962 research agenda (Tullock's career took a somewhat different path after that early collaboration). We believe that the analogy between politics and markets that is made by constitutional economists is theoretically weak, often factually mistaken, and clouds rather than enhances our understanding of political economy. Government is an inherently coercive institution that has little in common with the non-coercive, voluntary exchange of the marketplace.

2. State and Market

In *The Calculus of Consent*, the first modern work on constitutional economics, Buchanan and Tullock espouse the so-called public goods theory of the state whereby members of society voluntarily agree to coerce themselves to pay taxes for the provision of public goods. In a Robinson Crusoe economy, they assert, both men (Crusoe and Friday) will recognize the advantages to be secured from constructing a fortress (BUCHANAN AND TULLOCK [1962, 19]). Yet, one fortress is sufficient for the protection of both. Hence, they will find it mutually advantageous to enter into a political "exchange" and devote resources to the construction of the common good. It is in this sense that politics is said to be "voluntary" and "efficient."

But is it not in human nature to avoid taxing oneself if one can tax someone else instead? And is not this kind of exploitive behavior the very essence of democratic government, since voting rules never require unanimity? All governmental decisions in a democracy are necessarily exploitive of someone.

Political action is typically a means by which one group of people is able to coerce another group to pay for its own free rides. Indeed, in those cases where there is unanimity of agreement within a community on some issue, that issue would not need to be addressed by government at all but would remain in the domain of the private sector. Citizens coalesce every day to voluntarily organize the provision of myriad community benefits – from neighborhood childrens' sports leagues to multi-million member nonprofit, charitable organizations – without resorting to governmental coercion. If agreement is truly unanimous, and the parties to the agreement have the right to secede from it, then there is no need to involve the state at all.[1] Only when there are dissenters, is the state invoked to override and

---

[1] An anonymous referee suggests that it is difficult to conceive that such institutions as mandatory elementary schooling, mandatory old-age insurance, and public street cleaning

crush the dissent, as the history of tax revolts proves (ADAMS [1993], [1998]; BEITO [1989]).

Buchanan and Tullock realize that a voting rule of unanimity – which is required for the neoclassical definition of efficiency – is never attainable, so they explore the features of "relative unanimity." But relative unanimity is simply not a substitute for the real thing. It cannot be concluded that coerced minorities (however, small in number) benefit from being coerced. By their revealed preferences, the minorities have shown that they would, in fact, be harmed. The only way in which so-called relative unanimity can be labeled as economically efficient is if one presumes that it is possible to make interpersonal utility comparisons, which it is not.

The state is an institution whereby a controlling group uses its powers to exploit non-controlling groups.[2] One cannot realistically expect the controlling group to promote something called "the public interest" when it can promote the interests of the members of the controlling group instead (KALT [1981]). Even when governments appear to be altruistic – at least with regard to another group in society – they are practicing such "altruism" by taxing one group and giving that group's wealth away to yet another group (usually in return for the subsidized group's political support).

2.1 "Conceptual" Unanimity

Buchanan and Tullock posit in *The Calculus of Consent*, as does Buchanan in numerous subsequent publications, that government can be viewed as "efficient" and "voluntary" in the "constitutional stage of decision making." That is, just as self-interested behavior in the free market can "further the general interests of everyone in the community" (the invisible hand theorem), an "acceptable theory of collective choice can perhaps do something similar in pointing the way toward those rules for collective choice-making, the constitution, under which the activities of political tradesmen can be similarly reconciled with the interests of all members of the social group" (BUCHANAN AND TULLOCK [1962, 23]). There may not be unanimous agreement over each individual policy choice, but those individual choices can nevertheless be deemed "voluntary" and not coercive, according to Buchanan

---

are a means by which one group of people coerces another group to pay for its free rides. This point is well taken as long as one only (or primarily) considers monetary values. But if we include subjective or psychic benefits, it is not too hard to conceive. After all, there must be some reason why one group (the majority) would coerce another group to pay for something the second group does not wish to pay for. It may be to save themselves money or there may be ideological reasons, such as with the public school movement. All we can deduce is that there is some reason why the first group works to coerce the second group.

[2] Some public choice theorists have argued that no real exploitation occurs in a democracy since the losers in one contest may become winners in another. This is the view of Dennis C. MUELLER [1989], a former president of the Public Choice Society. We find this view that, as long as governmental exploitation is pervasive, it really does not exist – to be bizarre.

and other "contractarians," if one assumes that when the rules of the political game (i.e., the constitution) were chosen there *was* unanimity.

Evidence of actual unanimity is not necessary, only "conceptual unanimity" is. As BUCHANAN [1977, 127] stated in a more recent publication, "[t]o the contractarian that law is legitimate, and just, which might have emerged from a genuine social contract in which he might have participated. That law is illegitimate, and unjust, which finds no such contractual basis." This statement is more or less the keystone of what Viktor VANBERG [1998] has referred to as Buchanan's "enterprise of developing a theoretical approach to the state as a voluntary institution" (i.e., constitutional economics).

According to this viewpoint, the constitution may or may not be a written document. It may merely consist of the existing features of society that theorists can assume everyone (implicitly) agrees to. Politics is admittedly a series of predatory zero-sum games, but in reality such games are really positive-sum because "each and every participant has implicitly accepted the 'contract' embodied in the rules of the game ... " (BUCHANAN AND TULLOCK [1962, 254]).

Moreover, there need not be any actual political convention at which voting rules are agreed upon by the citizens; their mere existence gives them their legitimacy. And these rules may be in a constant change of flux, even though members of society do not hold any formal constitutional conventions to change the rules. "The 'social contract' is best conceived as subject to continual revision and change, and the consent that is given must be thought of as being continuous" (BUCHANAN AND TULLOCK [1962, 260]). Why it "must" be thought of as such is never explained, only asserted.

In a later publication BUCHANAN [1975, 96] claims the existence of an "existing and ongoing implicit social contract, embodied and described in the institutions of the *status quo*." This impossible-to-verify "implicit" contract should cement in place the legitimacy of the *status quo*, according to Buchanan, even "when an original contract may never have been made, when current members of the community sense no moral or ethical obligation to adhere to the terms that are defined in the *status quo*, and ... when such a contract ... may have been violated many times over ... The *status quo* defines that which exists. Hence, regardless of its history, it must be evaluated as if it were legitimate contractually" (BUCHANAN [1975, 84 f.]).

It is worth noting that David HUME [1965, 263] long ago dismissed this notion of tacit "contractual" consent with his example of the conscripted sailor who, by refraining from committing suicide by jumping overboard, does not thereby "consent" to the ship captain's alleged "authority" over him.[3] Hume understood that the greatest of governmental tyrannies could be rationalized by cleverly-crafted theories of "tacit" consent – even if the authors of those theories would themselves be appalled by the governmental actions for which their theories provided intellectual support.

---

[3] This was brought to our attention by Leland YEAGER [1985, 270].

We must also point out that, despite Buchanan's assertions that constitutional political economy has its roots in the political theory of the American founding fathers, the most renowned founding father, George Washington, explicitly rebuked this kind of thinking. In his September 19, 1796 Farewell Address, President Washington warned of the tyranny that would result from any changes in the Constitution that were not the result of a formal convention. "If in the opinion of the People, the distribution or modification of the Constitutional powers be in any particular wrong, let it be corrected by an amendment in the way which the Constitution designates. But let there be no change by usurpation; for though this, in one instance, may be the instrument of good, it is the customary weapon by which free governments are destroyed" (ALLEN [1980, 521]).

There is also a logical difficulty here. Constitutional economists try to derive a theory of human and property rights from their constitutional framework and they seek to do so on a consensual basis. But how can people give their consent to a contract before it is clear that they have any rights to do so? Where do these rights come from? How can a person agree to be bound by a constitution if it is this very document which can alone establish his rights? If rights are established only by constitutions, then before their advent individuals have no rights. But if they have no rights, what "right" do they have to participate in the construction of a constitution?

3. The Myth of the Consensual Origins of the State

Constitutional economics fails to adequately confront the voluminous philosophical, historical, sociological, and economic literature which points to the fact that the origins of the state have always been based on conquest and exploitation, not consent. Buchanan and Tullock and other constitutional economists frequently argue that their theories are normative and, consequently, that their policy prescriptions should be beyond criticism. But in *The Calculus of Consent* and elsewhere the normative theories are used to rationalize actual policy interventions, and in doing so the authors frequently mix normative and positive analyses, including many real-world examples. As such, constitutional economics can become more or less a stamp of approval for virtually any and all government interventions. We reject this line of thought and believe that it is entirely appropriate to criticize such theories from an historical perspective, as we do in the remainder of this section.

Many historians have noted that the origins of the Roman Empire, like other empires in antiquity, were in war and conquest. In the sixteenth century philosophers began investigating this question, and most of them came to agree with Jean Bodin, who wrote in *Six Books of the Commonwealth,* that "[r]eason and common sense alike point to the conclusion that the origin and foundation of commonwealths was in force and violence" (OPPENHEIMER [1997, 1]). A contemporary of Bodin's, Blaise PASCAL [1932, 81], concurred that "[m]ight is the sovereign of the world," and that "[m]en will doubtless fight till the stronger party overcomes the weaker, and a dominant party is established."

In *A Treatise on Human Nature* David HUME [1978, 556] argued that "this certain, that if we recount to the first origin of every nation, we shall find, that there scarce is any race of kings, or form of a commonwealth, that is not primarily founded on usurpation and rebellion ... " HUME [1987, 473] reiterated this theme in his essay, "Of the Original Contract," in which he stated that "[a]lmost all the governments, which exist at present, or of which there remains any record in history, have been founded originally, either in usurpation or conquest, or both, without any pretense of a fair consent, or voluntary subjection of the people." Hume further explained that citizens typically were lulled into accepting the state and reconciling themselves to its authority.

Anne-Robert-Jacques TURGOT [1973, 69], a precursor of the modern Austrian School of Economics, wrote in 1750 that "[t]he first [governments] were necessarily the product of war, and thus implied government by one man alone. We need not believe that men ever voluntarily gave themselves *one master.*" Another Frenchman, the historian Augustin Thierry, asserted that every government has been "created by the mixture of several races: the race of the invaders ... and the race of those invaded" (OPPENHEIMER [1997, xiii]). And Friederich Nietzsche believed that "the State originates in the cruelest way through conquest" (OPPENHEIMER [1997, xiii]).

The German sociologist Ludwig GUMPLOWICZ [1963, 199], whom Franz Oppenheimer called the "pathfinder" of the conquest theory of the state, explained in great detail why he believed that "[e]very political organization ... begins at the moment when one horde permanently subjugates another."

In the late eighteenth century the British philosopher Josiah Tucker pointed out that the Lockean philosophical system, which had inspired the recently-concluded American revolution and which argued that governments derive their just powers only from the consent of the governed, constituted a test that no government could ever pass. The Lockean system, TUCKER [1967, 101] argued, was "an universal Demolisher of all Civil Governments, but not the builder of any." Tucker supported his position by pointing out that the newly-created American government, which was supposedly based on Lockean "natural rights," in fact ignored these principles by not allowing any citizens, not even the residents of a single state, the right to live in a "state of nature" without any government at all.

Edmund BURKE [1968, 53] wrote in 1756 that "all empires have been cemented in blood" and that "the greatest part of the governments on earth must be concluded tyrannies, impostures, violations of the natural rights of mankind, and worse than the most disorderly anarchies."

Franz OPPENHEIMER [1997] carried this tradition forward by using the inductive method of history and the deductive method of economic theory (the kind of theory favored by the Austrian School) to show that the origins of the state lie in conquest, subjugation, and exploitation.

Albert Jay NOCK's [1983, 40] description of the origins of the state also seems much more accurate than the theories of constitutional economists. According to Nock, "the State invariably had its origin in conquest and confiscation. No primitive State known to history originated in any other manner ... no primitive State could possibly have had any other origin ... the sole invariable characteristic of the State is the economic exploitation of one class by another."

BUCHANAN AND TULLOCK [1962, 12] simply assume this historical tradition away with the statement that "we ... reject any theory or conception of the collectivity which embodies the exploitation of a ruled by a ruling class ... Any conception of State activity that divides the social group into the ruling class and the oppressed class, and that regards the political process as simply a means through which this class dominance is established and then preserved, must be rejected as irrelevant for the discussion which follows."

No reason is offered for this. It is merely asserted that the phenomenon of one class of citizens using the powers of the state to exploit and plunder another class – a feature of governments throughout human history – "must be rejected." In doing so, Buchanan and Tullock ignore not only Marxist class analysis but all other non-Marxist theories of class domination without offering any explanation for their rejection.

One political theorist who understood and explained virtually every political phenomenon that has been studied by modern public choice scholars is John C. Calhoun, whom many historians consider to have been the last of the American founding fathers in terms of his educational background and political philosophy (LENCE [1992]). Calhoun spent four decades (1811–1850) as a US congressman, senator, secretary of war, and vice president. Once democratic government is established, Calhoun wrote in his "Disquisition on Government," the community will inevitably be "divided into two great parties, a major and a minor, between which there will be incessant struggles on the one side to retain, and on the other to obtain the majority – and, thereby, the control of the government and the advantages it confers" (LENCE [1992, 16]).

This "deeply seated tendency" that is common in all democracies is sure to divide every political community into "two great hostile parties" which are not Marxian class interests but "the payers of the taxes and the recipients of their proceeds" (LENCE [1992, 17]). The "necessary result" of democratic government is "to divide the community into two great classes; one consisting of those who, in reality, pay the taxes, and, of course, bear exclusively the burden of supporting the government; and the other, of those who are the recipients of their proceeds," or of "taxpayers and tax-consumers" (LENCE [1992, 19]).

While Buchanan and Tullock assert that even an unwritten or "conceptual" constitution is sufficient for what they believe to be voluntary government, Calhoun issued a dire warning against such thinking more than a century earlier. He thought that even a written constitution that ostensibly prohibited the plundering of one class by another is unworkable, and history seems to have proven him correct. Over time, the majority would "endeavor to elude" any constitutional restrictions on its powers and would simply ignore the arguments of the strict construc-tionists. Appeals to reason, truth, justice, or the obligations imposed by the consti-tution would be sneered at by the ruling class as "folly" with the result being a "subversion of the constitution" (LENCE [1992, 27]).

Calhoun was an intellectual descendant of the early nineteenth-century French "Industrialist" school of political economy, which originated the study of class conflict not in the Marxian sense but in the sense of one group of citizens being exploited by another group via the auspices of the state. Among the members of this school were Augustin Thierry, Charles Comte, Charles Dunoyer, Destutt de Tracy, Benjamin Constant, and Jean-Baptiste Say (RAICO [1998], EUSZENT AND MARTIN [1984]). The French Industrialists anticipated the modern economic con-cept of rent (or rather, loot) seeking, for they distinguished between "producers" (businessmen, working people) and "exploiters" who used politics to live off the labor of others.

BUCHANAN AND TULLOCK [1962, 22] claim to reject all such analyses as "irrel-evant" to their discussion, yet at one point they refer to "preventing the undue ex-ploitation of one group by another through the political process."

More recently, SOWELL [1998, 5] focused on the cultural effects of governmental conquest down through the ages. But his work also sheds light on the essential nature of the state and its origins. In cataloguing the history of conquests from the Roman empire through the twentieth century, Sowell observes that "spontaneous atrocities and deliberate, systematic terror have long marked the path of the conqueror."

Another contemporary author who has catalogued the exploitive essence of the state is Fred MCCHESNEY [1997] who argues persuasively that much of contem-porary government is essentially an extortion and protection racket whereby poli-ticians threaten (with proposed laws and regulations) to confiscate the wealth of various individuals or groups unless they receive political payoffs and bribes in the form of campaign contributions and other benefits.

Government, in MCCHESNEY's [1997, 2] opinion, seems hardly different from a legalized Mafia. "Payments to politicians often are made, not for particular favors but to avoid ... political disfavor, that is, as a part of a system of political extortion ... Because the state, quite legally, can (and does) take money and other forms of wealth from its citizens, politicians can extort from private parties payments not to expropriate private wealth." Among the tools of political extortion are threats to impose price controls, to close off business opportunities, increase a business's costs through regulation or taxation, deny occupational licenses, or even to nation-alize an industry.

4. A Blank Check for Interventionism

Applying the constitutionalist perspective, Buchanan has even argued that a thief really favors strict law enforcement and the punishment of thieves. The thief does not want his own property to be stolen any more than anyone else does. Thus, it can be said that a thief consents to his own punishment. But, as a rule and as a

Vol. 156/4 (2000)   *Is Voluntary Government Possible?*   575

practical matter, professional criminals do not frequently run to the police for help or lobby for harsher punishment of criminals. Murderers are not enthusiastic supporters of the death penalty, nor are thieves supporters of the Middle Eastern custom of cutting off the hands of those who are caught stealing.

Myriad other government interventions have been rationalized and endorsed by contractarians based on the idea that there must be "conceptual" unanimity, even for policies that appear to benefit only a small number of citizens while imposing enormous costs on everyone else. Sometimes elaborate mathematical models are presented to argue that laws that appear to everyone to benefit only narrow special interests really do benefit everyone after all.

One especially clear example is an article by BUCHANAN AND LEE [1992] which addressed a growing body of historical research showing that the original antitrust laws – including the 1890 Sherman Act – were designed to benefit special interests (i.e., uncompetitive businesses that could not compete with the trusts). They argue that the Sherman Act was not necessarily a special-interest law, despite the evidence of special-interest influence in the economic history literature. It is conceivable, they theorize, that the "common interest" of a "coalition of cartels" was served by the antitrust laws.

The essence of their argument is that each private cartel wants protection from competition, but if such protection becomes too widespread then individual cartels may lose out. They do not want to pay monopoly prices for the things they purchase any more than anyone else does. A "coalition of cartels" may voluntarily attempt to police output restrictions, but it is cheaper to let government do it. This is what antitrust laws can do – at least conceptually.

BUCHANAN AND LEE [1992, 223] do not assert that anything like this ever actually happened, but that there just may possibly be a situation whereby "the coalition [of cartels] can be thought of as implicitly supporting [antitrust legislation] by accepting it, and accommodating to it. It is in this sense that we argue that it is useful to conceive of our coalition of cartels, and of its support for antitrust legislation and enforcement."

No cartel actually lobbies for the law; they all just silently accept whatever legislation other politically-active special-interest groups provide for them, in this case the Sherman Antitrust Act. This is essentially a conscripted sailor theory of antitrust. Because businesses did not wantonly violate the antitrust laws (and face criminal penalties) or openly revolt against them too vigorously (and face regulatory retribution, tax audits, or prison), Buchanan and Lee assume that American businesses can be modeled as having "conceptually" supported antitrust laws.

But there is no need to invent such fictions. There is an historical record to study, and research indicates that the Sherman Act benefited smaller, less competitive businesses and gave the Republican Party, which dominated Congress at the time, political cover for the McKinley tariff, which was sponsored by Senator John Sherman himself and passed just three months after the Sherman Act was passed in June of 1890 (DILORENZO [1985], DILORENZO AND BOUDREAUX [1995], HAZLETT [1992]).

In *The Calculus of Consent* Buchanan and Tullock assert that the non-poor can be construed as really being in favor of a welfare state, even if they voice opposition to it publicly. The reason they are for it is that it supposedly provides a form of "income insurance" that is available to them should they become unemployed. Again, as long as everyone is coerced, no one is really being coerced.

Despite their affinity for framing their analysis in constitutional terms, however, Buchanan and Tullock fail to offer an explanation of why government-enforced income transfers for the purpose of establishing a welfare state were outlawed by the US Constitution, at least until the constitutional order was overthrown by the American Civil War. James Madison, the acknowledged "father" of the Constitution, repeatedly denied that such income transfers were constitutional.

The American welfare state did not appear in any significant size until the 1930s, and even then there was fierce opposition to it. Indeed, much of the New Deal was ruled unconstitutional by the US Supreme Court, although later courts, influenced more by politics than by reverence for the Constitution, eventually gave the welfare state their stamp of approval. Still, nothing close to actual unanimous consent with regard to the welfare state has ever existed. There were tax revolts during the Great Depression (BEITO [1989]) and John T. FlYNN [1998] catalogued myriad other opponents of the new welfare state during that period.

If one observes the plight of the typical welfare recipient living in squalor in a government housing project in one of America's cities, where law enforcement is weak if not non-existent, the schools are dysfunctional, and job opportunities are scarce, it is just not believable that this is what any rational person would consider to be a desirable system of "income insurance" worth purchasing.

There is much evidence, moreover, that welfarism has encouraged illegitimacy, family breakup, and a weakening of intergenerational linkages (MURRAY [1984], [1993]; AN, HAVEMAN, AND WOLFE [1993]; SCHULTZ [1994]). Families used to be the major source of "income insurance" in times of economic trouble or old age, but the welfare state has imposed serious damage on the institution of the family. As a recent article in the *American Economic Review* concludes, the family has traditionally served as "an informal self-insurance, or 'family-security' setup," but this "setup" has been severely damaged by government old-age insurance, which induces many people to rely on government, rather than families, to provide such security (EHRLICH AND ZHONG [1998, 151]).

There is a name for genuine (as opposed to "conceptual") income insurance: savings. But the welfare state and the high level of taxation to finance it deters savings by increasing the rate of time preference.[4] Furthermore, by draining hundreds of billions of dollars annually from the pockets of productive people, the welfare state makes it more likely that more citizens will be in need of charity at some point in their lives.

---

[4] As Hans-Hermann HOPPE [1993, 121] has stated, the introduction of government as "an agency that can effectively claim ownership over resources it has neither homesteaded, produced, nor contractually acquired, also raises the social rate of time preference of homesteaders, producers, and contractors, and hence creates involuntary impoverishment . . . "

Contractarian theories provide theoretical cover for what Buchanan has labeled "apparent" coercion and "apparent" redistribution of income from government policy. One may try to interpret away acts of coercion and theft by calling them "apparent," but they remain acts of coercion and theft. We agree with Leland YEAGER [1985, 271] that the very word "conceptual," as used by contractarian theorists, "indicates that a 'conceptual' agreement is not an actual one, that a 'conceptually' true proposition is not actually true. It is no mere joke to say that 'conceptually' is an adverb stuck into contractarians' sentences to immunize them from challenge on the grounds of their not being true."

5. Constitutional Economics versus Constitutional History

Despite its repetition of the word "constitution," *The Calculus of Consent* and much of the literature on constitutional economics frequently ignores the actual history of the ratification of the US Constitution. Granted, Buchanan and Tullock claim that theirs is primarily a normative theory. But their book is full of policy discussions, propositions, and specific proposals for welfare programs, ways of dealing with externality problems, financing government fire departments, etc. (BUCHANAN AND TULLOCK [1962]). They invoke historical facts to support their theory and claim that their work is in the same philosophical spirit as that of the American founders who, after all, were involved in creating a practical political document when they wrote the Constitution. For these reasons, we believe it is fair and appropriate to discuss the actual history of the US Constitution as a source of criticism of constitutional economics.

The Constitution was anything but unanimously supported; women did not have the right to vote at the time, nor did non-property owners (not to mention millions of slaves). It was adopted with a majority vote of only nine of the thirteen states through statewide political conventions. The Articles of Confederation, which were replaced by the Constitution, did require the support of all thirteen states.

When the Constitution was ratified about three-fourths of the adult males failed to vote in the elections to send delegates to the state ratification elections – either because they were disinterested or because they were disenfranchised by property qualifications. Thus, the delegates to the state ratification conventions were elected by a vote that included only about one sixth of adult males (BEARD [1986, 325]). Many of the states that did vote to adopt the Constitution barely did so, and no state voted unanimously in its favor. Virginia, which was the wealthiest and most influential state at the time, passed it by a margin of 89 to 79 votes; New York voted to ratify by a vote of 30 to 27; Rhode Island's margin was a mere two votes, 34 to 32; and North Carolina initially rejected the Constitution by a 184 to 84 margin, voting a year later to ratify once the new constitution was an accomplished fact (McDONALD [1958]).

These four states explicitly reserved the right to withdraw from the Union should the new government threaten their liberties. Patrick Henry was so alarmed by the preponderance of military men among the state convention delegates who favored the Constitution that he warned his fellow Virginians of the possibility of "armed hordes [of soldiers] marching under the banner of the new government to subvert Virginia's liberties" (McDONALD [1958, 262]). At the Virginia ratifying convention Henry exhibited "stamina, argument, and rhetoric unmatched on either side" of the debate, wrote Herbert J. STORING [1985, 293], the chronicler of the anti-federalist movement.

Henry's main objections were that by centralizing too much power in the central government, the Constitution effectively destroyed genuine federalism; the document represented a quest for "glory and riches" through empire, rather than liberty; there would be no real checks and balances on governmental responsibility, putting citizens at the mercy of "the virtue of the rulers;" the federal power to tax would effectively neutralize the states and impose unspeakable burdens on the people; the Constitution was unduly militaristic, "pretending external dangers and internal turbulence where none exists;" and the absence of a Bill of Rights would inevitably lead to tyranny (STORING [1985, 294f.]).

George Mason, the author of the Virginia Bill of Rights, which was the model for the Constitution's Bill of Rights, was another vigorous opponent of the Constitution who campaigned tirelessly against it.

The so-called anti-federalists were a large and influential group. They feared that the particular form the Constitution had taken would encourage a dangerous centralization of governmental power (dangerous to liberty, that is).

The notion that there was anything near unanimous consent over the adoption of the Constitution is a myth. Albert Jay NOCK [1983, 90] even argued quite convincingly that the framers of the Constitution "executed a [non-violent] *coup d'Etat,* simply tossing the Articles of Confederation into the waste-basket, and drafting a constitution *de novo,* with the audacious provision that it should go into effect when ratified by nine units [i.e., states] instead of by all thirteen."

6. The Failures of Market Failure Theory

In *The Calculus of Consent* Buchanan and Tullock develop their "interdependence cost" model in the context of a discussion of various examples of externality or spillover effects. It is these "market failure" examples that provide their conceptual rationale for the state based on "cost minimization" arguments.

One example is the organization of a "village fire department" which the authors assume to possess public goods characteristics. Conceptually, the fire department can exist through "purely voluntary co-operative action" under the auspices of a "voluntary" government (BUCHANAN AND TULLOCK [1962, 49]). But, if it were truly voluntary, there would be no need to label it as "government." There are, in fact, myriad volunteer fire departments that are not funded by taxes. Nor is it necessarily true that "individual protection against fire may not be profitable," as BUCHANAN AND TULLOCK [1962, 44] assert. It seems to us that it would be impossible for a homeowner to purchase homeowners' insurance without fire protection. This would surely provide a powerful incentive for individuals to voluntarily purchase fire protection – in addition to the incentive provided by not wanting to die in a house fire.

Nor is a Department of Swamp Drainage necessary. Buchanan and Tullock use swamp drainage as another example of a public good because of its mosquito-abatement effects. But private land developers have ample incentives to drain swamps before developing their land. And if some swamps remain undrained, so what? Because benefits and costs are subjective, and because interpersonal utility comparisons are impossible, coerced swamp drainage cannot possibly be Pareto-optimal. In a free market some swamps will remain undrained because it is simply not worth it to drain them.

Higher education is another questionable example of the supposed need for state intervention on the grounds of spillover effects. BUCHANAN AND TULLOCK [1962, 54] argue that because of the inability of students to "mortgage" their future earning power they are unable to borrow the appropriate capital in private financial markets to sufficiently finance higher education. "[C]ollective or state action may be taken which will remove or reduce the private externalities involved here."

But the reason for this supposed market failure is government intervention, not the free market. Promising to work for an employer, or to work to earn money to pay off one's "educational mortgage," is essentially a form of indentured servitude, the method that, historically, allowed hordes of immigrants to come to the US. But the 1866 passage of the Thirteenth Amendment to the Constitution outlawed this practice. Thus, the problem is not that such contracts do not arise on the free market; the problem is that they are prohibited by government. The "restrictions on full freedom of contract" that Buchanan and Tullock allude to are not free-market phenomena.

Municipal zoning is also said to be an appropriate intervention where the costs of dealing with spillover effects coercively, through government, are lower than doing so privately through restrictive covenants or corporate ownership. Buchanan and Tullock cite the example of the large bargaining costs involved in the case of a developer seeking to purchase a large number of individual housing units in a city when individual holdouts may have the ability to stop development altogether.

To advocate government zoning laws in this instance is again to embrace the notion of interpersonal utility comparisons. The explicit assumption is that the increased utility of the developer is necessarily higher than the diminished utility of the "holdouts" whom the state forces to sell out. Such comparisons are an impossibility.

A third example of market failure offered by Buchanan and Tullock is the necessity for government-imposed traffic control (lights, etc.). Surely, virtually everyone would agree that this is a proper role for government. But it cannot be denied that in a world of private road ownership there would be no need for *gov-*

ernment traffic lights; the private owners would have a strong incentive to provide them because of the liability costs to them of not doing so. Furthermore, it should also be acknowledged that in many American cities the phrase "traffic control" is an oxymoron, as traffic has become more and more chaotic – and dangerous. Government "controls" traffic about as well as it operates the post office or the department of motor vehicles (BLOCK [1983]).

Buchanan and Tullock chose these examples of externality and public goods problems in the early 1960s and, to be fair, we must acknowledge that it is possible that they would choose different examples today. New forms of contracts with lower transaction costs may well have been invented in the intervening years. Nevertheless, fire departments, swamp drainage, zoning, higher education, and traffic lights are still widely cited throughout the literature on externalities and market failure and are therefore worthy of comment.

7. Conclusions

The fatal flaw in the voluntary theory of the state advanced by constitutional economists is that no state ever has been, or ever could be, voluntary. If one really wants to explore the elements and ramifications of a voluntary society, we suggest closer scrutiny of the libertarian philosophy that no person or group of people may legitimately aggress upon the person or property of anyone else; and that every person has a right to private property, including one's own body and the natural resources which they transform by their labor (ROTHBARD [1978], [1998]). The application of this doctrine is a promising means of understanding what is meant by a voluntary society.

Recent applied work by Fred FOLDVARY [1994] on the market provision of social services; Robert ELLICKSON [1991] on the private, voluntary resolution of disputes over externality problems; Robert AXELROD's [1984] work on the evolution of cooperation; Bruce BENSON's [1998] analysis of private criminal justice systems; and free-market environmentalism are just a few among many promising efforts in this regard (ANDERSON AND LEAL [1991]). Exploring actual institutions based on voluntarism, as opposed to relabeling the inherently coercive institution of government as conceptually, but not actually, voluntary, is a much more promising avenue of research.

Our disagreement with constitutional economics is more than a definitional one. Buchanan and Tullock label a wide range of seemingly voluntary collective choice institutions as "government" and, admittedly, a reasonable case can be made that, say, a village fire department might make a good example of voluntary government, at least on a relatively small scale. But the distinguishing characteristic is that in a truly voluntary setting the parties to an agreement have a right to secede from the agreement. If they do not wish to be taxed to pay for fire protection, they are free to live outside the agreement and forego the services or seek them elsewhere. This is not the case with tax-financed services. For example, joining a swimming club is a genuinely voluntary act, whereas paying taxes to support a municipal swimming pool necessarily involves some degree of coercion. The phrase "voluntary government" is simply a contradiction in terms.

References

ADAMS, C. [1993], *For Good and Evil: The Impact of Taxes on the Course of Civilization*, Madison Books: New York.

– – [1998], *Those Dirty Rotten Taxes: The Tax Revolts that Built America*, The Free Press: New York.

ALLEN, W. B. (ed.) [1980], *George Washington: A Collection*, Liberty Fund: Indianapolis, IN.

AN, C., R. C. HAVEMAN, AND B. WOLFE [1993], "Teen Out-of-Wedlock Births and Welfare Receipt," *Review of Economics and Statistics*, 75, 195–208.

ANDERSON, T., AND D. LEAL [1991], *Free Market Environmentalism*, Pacific Institute for Public Policy Research: San Francisco, CA.

AXELROD, R. [1984], *The Evolution of Cooperation*, Harvard University Press: Cambridge, MA.

BEARD, C. [1986], *An Economic Interpretation of the Constitution of the United States*, Free Press: New York.

BENSON, B. [1998], *To Serve and Protect: Privatization and Community in Criminal Justice*, New York University Press: New York.

BEITO, D. T. [1989], *Taxpayers in Revolt: Tax Resistance During the Great Depression*, University of North Carolina Press: Chapel Hill, NC.

BLOCK, W. [1983], "Public Goods and Externalities: The Case of Roads," *Journal of Libertarian Studies*, 7, 1–34.

BUCHANAN, J. M. [1975], *The Limits of Liberty*, University of Chicago Press: Chicago, IL.

– – [1977], *Freedom in Constitutional Contract*, Texas A&M Press: College Station, TX.

– – AND D. LEE [1992], "Private Interest Support for Efficiency Enhancing Antitrust Policies, *Economic Inquiry*, 30, 218–224.

– – AND G. TULLOCK [1962], *The Calculus of Consent: Logical Foundations of Constitutional Democracy*, University of Michigan Press: Ann Arbor, MI.

BURKE, E. [1968], "A Vindication of Natural Society," in: E. Burke (ed.), *Selected Writings and Speeches*, Peter Smith: Gloucester, MA.

DiLORENZO, T. J. [1985], "The Origins of Antitrust: An Interest-Group Perspective," *International Review of Law and Economics*, 5, 73–90.

– – AND D. C. BOUDREAUX [1993], "The Protectionist Roots of Antitrust," *Review of Austrian Economics*, 6, 81–96.

ELLICKSON, R. C. [1991], *Order Without Law*, Harvard University Press: Cambridge, MA.

EHRLICH, I., AND J.-G. ZHONG [1998], "Social Security and the Real Economy," *American Economic Review*, 88, 151–157.

EUSZENT, P. J., AND T. L. MARTIN [1984], "Classical Roots of the Emergent Theory of Rent Seeking: The Contribution of Jean-Baptiste Say," *History of Political Economy*, 16, 225–262.

FOLDVARY, F. [1994], *Public Goods and Private Communities: The Market Provision of Social Services*, Edgar Elgar: Brookfield, VT.

FLYNN, J. T. [1998], *The Roosevelt Myth*, Fox and Wilkes: San Francisco, CA.

GUMPLOWICZ, L. [1963], *Outlines of Sociology*, Paine-Whitman: New York.

HAZLETT, T. [1992], "The Legislative History of the Sherman Act Revisited," *Economic Inquiry*, 30, 263-276.

HOPPE, H.-H. [1993], *The Economics and Ethics of Private Property: Studies in Political Economy and Philosophy*, Kluwer: Boston, MA.

HUME, D. [1965], "Of the Original Contract," in: A. MacIntyre and D. Hume (eds.), *Hume's Ethical Writings*, Collier Books: New York.

– – [1978], *A Treatise on Human Nature*, Oxford University Press: Oxford.

– – [1987], *Essays: Moral, Political, and Literary*, Liberty Fund: Indianapolis, IN.

KALT, J. [1981], "Public Goods and the Theory of Government," *Cato Journal*, 1, 565-584.

LENCE, R. M. [1992], *Union and Liberty: The Political Philosophy of John C. Calhoun*, Liberty Fund: Indianapolis, IN.

McCHESNEY, F. [1997], *Money for Nothing*, Harvard University Press: Cambridge, MA.

McDONALD, F. [1958], *We the People: The Economic Origins of the Constitution*, University of Chicago Press: Chicago, IL.

MUELLER, D. [1989], *Public Choice II: A Revised Edition of Public Choice*, Cambridge University Press: New York.

MURRAY, C. [1984], *Losing Ground*, Basic Books: New York.

– – [1993], "Welfare and Family: The US Experience," *Journal of Labor Economics*, 2, 224–262.

NOCK, A. J. [1983], *Our Enemy, the State*, Hallberg Publishing Co.: Delean, WI.

OPPENHEIMER, F. [1997], *The State*, Fox & Wilkes: San Francisco, CA.

PASCAL, B. [1932], *Pascal's Pense'es*, J. M. Dent & Sons: London.

RAICO, R. [1998], "Classical Liberal Rots of the Marxist Doctrine of Classes," pp. 189–220 in: Y. Maltsev (ed.), *Requiem for Marx*, Ludwig von Mises Institute: Auburn, AL.

ROTHBARD, M. [1978], *For a New Liberty*, Fox & Wilkes: San Francisco, CA.

– – [1997], *The Logic of Action II*, Edward Elgar: Cheltenham.

– – [1998], *The Ethics of Liberty*, New York University Press: New York.

SCHULTZ, P. [1994], "Marital Status and Fertility in the United States," *Journal of Human Resources*, 29, 637–669.

SOWELL, T. [1998], *Conquests and Cultures: An International History*, Basic Books: New York.

STORING, H. J. [1985], *The Anti-Federalist: Writings by Opponents of the Constitution*, University of Chicago Press: Chicago, IL.

TUCKER, J. [1967], *A Treatise Concerning Civil Government*, Augustus Kelley: New York.

TURGOT, A.-R.-J. [1973], "On Universal History," pp. 41–118, in: R. L. Meek (ed.), *Turgot on Progress, Sociology, and Economics*, Cambridge University Press: Cambridge.

VANBERG, V. [1998], "The Impossibility of Rational Regulation? Regulation, Free-Market Liberalism, and Constitutional Liberalism," Paper presented at the Annual Meeting of the Mont Pelerin Society, Washington, DC, August 31.

YEAGER, L. [1985], "Rights, Contract, and Utility in Policy Espousal," *Cato Journal*, 5, 269–289.

Thomas J. DiLorenzo
Department of Economics
Loyola College in Maryland
Baltimore, MD 21210
U.S.A.

Walter Block
Department of Economics and Finance
University of Central Arkansas
Conway, AR 72035
U.S.A.

Government: Unnecessary but Inevitable

———— ✦ ————

RANDALL G. HOLCOMBE

L udwig von Mises, Friedrich Hayek, and Milton Friedman, perhaps the best-
known twentieth-century academic defenders of liberty, envisioned a role for
limited government in protecting liberty.[1] Friedman's (1962) defense of freedom includes proposals for a negative income tax and school vouchers; Hayek (1960)
advocates limited government to enforce the rule of law despite his concern about
excessive government;[2] and Ludwig von Mises, who also warns of the dangers of big
government,[3] states, "the task of the state consists solely and exclusively in guaran-
teeing the protection of life, health, liberty, and private property against violent
attacks" (1979, 52). In contrast, by the end of the twentieth century, many libertarians, guided by the work of Murray Rothbard and others, viewed orderly anarchy as a
desirable and potentially achievable state of affairs and—some would argue—the only
state of affairs consistent with a libertarian philosophy.[4] My purpose in this article is to
examine that proposition critically and to defend and extend the classical liberal idea
of limited government. My conclusions align more with those theorists, such as

---

Randall G. Holcombe is DeVoe Moore Professor of Economics at Florida State University.

1. I refer only to academic defenders of liberty because other libertarians need not be so rigorous in their
analysis of alternatives to the status quo. H. L. Mencken, for example, could offer trenchant critiques of
government without having to offer an alternative. Ayn Rand, a novelist, did not need to offer alternatives
but did offer them, and she also belongs to the limited-government camp. The Libertarian Party in the
United States runs candidates for political office, a few of whom are elected. Although some people view
libertarianism as consistent with only the elimination of all government, many people who call themselves
libertarians see a role for limited government.

2. Hayek argues for limited government despite his reservations (for example, in Hayek 1944) about the
expansion of government.

3. See, for example, Mises 1998, 715–16, for a discussion of the role of government. Elsewhere, Mises
(1945) expresses his reservations about government.

4. Rothbard 1973 explains how private arrangements effectively can replace all of government's functions,
and Rothbard 1982 gives an ethical argument for the complete elimination of government.

The Independent Review, v. VIII, n. 3, Winter 2004, ISSN 1086-1653, Copyright © 2004, pp. 325–342.

Hayek and Mises, who see a need for limited government than with those who see the libertarian ideal as an orderly anarchy.

The debate over limited government versus orderly anarchy typically turns on the effectiveness of government versus private means to achieve certain ends. Government's defenders argue that markets cannot provide certain goods and services as efficiently as government can—in some cases, markets may be completely unable to provide certain desired goods—whereas the advocates of orderly anarchy argue that private contractual arrangements can provide every good and service more effectively and can do so without the coercion inherent in government activity. I maintain, however, that the effectiveness of government versus that of private arrangements to produce goods and services is irrelevant to the issue of the desirability of government in a libertarian society. Governments are not created to produce goods and services for citizens. Rather, they are created and imposed on people by force, most often for the purpose of transferring resources from the control of those outside government to the control of those within it.

Without government—or even with a weak government—predatory groups will impose themselves on people by force and create a government to extract income and wealth from these subjects. If people create their own government preemptively, they can design a government that may be less predatory than the one that outside aggressors otherwise would impose on them.[5]

Anarchy as an Alternative to Government

One strand of the libertarian anarchist argument is the claim that everything the government does, the market can do better, and therefore the government should be eliminated completely.[6] A second strand is the proposition that government is uneth-

---

5. Robert Higgs has written, "Without government to defend us from external aggression, preserve domestic order, define and enforce property rights, few of us could achieve much" (1987, 1). He recently reevaluated his position, however, and now declares, "When I was younger and even more ignorant that I am today, I believed that government . . . performs an essential function—namely, the protection of individuals from the aggressions of others. . . . Growing older, however, has given me an opportunity to reexamine the bases of my belief in the indispensability of the protective services of government. . . . As I have done so, I have become increasingly skeptical, and I now am more inclined to disbelieve the idea than to believe it" (2002, 309). In this more recent article, Higgs does not deal with the argument that private protective services work under the umbrella of the state and that without the state to check their power they might evolve into organizations more predatory than a constitutionally limited state. In my view, Higgs's earlier position retains merit.

6. In Holcombe forthcoming, I discuss some of this literature. See, for example, the critiques by de Jasay (1989), Foldvary (1994), and Holcombe (1997) of the public-goods rationale for government, and by Berman (1983), Foldvary (1984), D. Friedman (1989), Benson (1989, 1990, 1998), Stringham (1998–99), and Tinsley (1998–99) on how law can exist without the state, how property rights can be defined, and how externalities can be internalized through private arrangements. Rothbard (1973) and D. Friedman (1989) more generally describe how the private sector can handle better all activities the state currently undertakes. Another justification for the state is the social contract theory that goes back at least to Hobbes ([1651] 1950) and appears in the work of Rawls (1971) and Buchanan (1975). De Jasay (1985, 1997) and Yeager (1985) present extensive critiques of the social contract theory, and Axelrod (1984), Foldvary (1984), de Jasay (1989), Rothbard (1973), D. Friedman (1989), Benson (2001), and many others have shown how private arrangements can overcome the prisoners' dilemma problem. In Holcombe 2002b, I note that the actual activities of government do not correspond with the social contractarian framework.

ical because of its use of force.[7] Murray Rothbard has been the leading proponent of both arguments, and his 1973 book *For a New Liberty* is his most direct defense of orderly anarchy. Rothbard illustrates how the private sector can undertake more effectively all government activities, including national defense. All of Rothbard's arguments are persuasive, but his national-defense argument is worth reviewing here because it has direct relevance to my thesis.

Rothbard argues first that national defense is needed only because the governments of some countries have differences with the governments of others. Wars occur between governments, not between the subjects of those governments. Without a government to provoke outsiders, outside governments would have no motivation to attack, so a group of people living in anarchy would face a minimal risk of invasion from a foreign government. An auxiliary line of reasoning is that if a government does try to use military force to take over an area with no government, such a takeover would be very difficult because the aggressor would have to conquer each individual in the anarchistic area. If those people have a government, a foreign country has only to induce the other country's head of state to surrender in order to take over that other country, but in taking over a country without a government an aggressor faces the much more daunting task of getting everyone to surrender, going from house to house and from business to business, a formidable and perhaps impossible undertaking.[8]

Jeffrey Rogers Hummel offers an interesting extension of Rothbard's arguments regarding defense. Hummel (1990) argues that national defense against foreign aggression is a subset of the problem of protecting people from any state, domestic or foreign, and Hummel (2001) notes that if people can design institutions to protect themselves from domestic government, those same institutions should suffice to protect them from foreign governments. In this line of reasoning, the private production of defense services would occur as a by-product of the elimination of domestic government by an orderly anarchy.

These arguments regarding national defense show the flavor of the argument that people would be better off without government. Orderly anarchy would eliminate the need for government provision of national defense because the risks of invasion would be lower and because the private sector can supply any defense services people want. By considering each activity the government now undertakes, a sub-

---

7. See, for example, Rothbard 1982. Rothbard 1956 lays a foundation for both the ethical and economic arguments against government by reformulating welfare economics to show that market activity is welfare enhancing, whereas government activity, which relies on coercion, is not. Along these lines, Brewster 2002 argues that the state cannot exist if by *state* one means an organization acting in the public interest. People act in their own interests, Brewster argues, and the state is merely designed to appear as if it acts in the public interest. Edelman 1964 lays an interesting foundation for this point of view.

8. This argument is developed further in Hoppe 1998–99, which argues that in the absence of government, insurance companies can provide defense services. This argument is interesting, but it should be noted that companies that offer fire insurance or theft insurance do not provide home security or fire protection services even in areas where such services are not available from government. Note also that typical insurance policies often exclude losses owing to war, even though government provides defense services. In the absence of government, if companies offered insurance against losses from foreign invasion, they might find it cheaper to pay their policyholders for their losses than to provide defense services to protect them.

stantial literature shows that in each case a superior private-sector alternative exists or might be created. Private arrangements can provide public goods, law, and order at any scale. A substantial mainstream academic literature on the inefficiencies of government production and regulation further buttresses the case against government. Thus, the libertarian anarchist position rests heavily on the argument that anything the government does, the private sector can do more effectively and less coercively.

Why Do Governments Exist?

The argument that people should do away with government because everything the government does the private sector can do better would be persuasive if governments were created, as their rationales suggest, to improve their subjects' well-being. In fact, governments are not created to improve the public's well-being. In most cases, governments have been imposed on people by force, and they maintain their power by force for the purpose of extracting resources from subjects and transferring the control of those resources to those in government. Sometimes foreign invaders take over territory and rule the people who live there; more commonly, people already subject to a government overthrow it and establish a new government in its place. Whether government is more or less effective in producing public goods or in protecting property is irrelevant.

A possible exception to this claim is the formation of the U.S. government, which was established to overthrow British rule in the colonies and to replace it with a new government designed to protect the liberty of its citizens. Much of the Declaration of Independence consists of a list of grievances against the king of England, and the American founders wanted to replace what they viewed as a predatory government with one that would protect their rights. One can dispute this story,[9] but for present purposes the point is that even in what appears to be the best real-world case in which government was designed for the benefit of its citizens, it was not designed to produce public goods or to control externalities or to prevent citizens from free riding on a social contract. Its underlying rationale had nothing to do with any of the common economic or political rationales given for government.

The point here is straightforward: despite many theories justifying government because its activities produce benefits to its citizens, no government was ever established to produce those benefits. Governments were created by force to rule over people and extract resources from them. Thus, the argument that citizens would be better off if they replaced government activities with private arrangements and market transactions is irrelevant to the issue of whether an orderly anarchy would be a desirable—or even feasible—replacement for government. The real issue is whether a group of people with no government can prevent predators both inside and outside their group from using force to establish a government.

---

9. See, for example, Beard 1913, which argues that the U.S. Constitution was written to further its authors' interests.

Protection and the State

Without government, people would be vulnerable to predators and therefore would have to find ways to protect themselves. In the anarchy Hobbes described, life is a war of all against all—nasty, brutish, and short. The strong overpower the weak, taking everything the victims have, but the strong themselves do not prosper in Hobbesian anarchy because there is little for them to take. Nobody produces when the product will surely be taken away from them. Even under more orderly conditions than Hobbesian anarchy, predation has a limited payoff because people who have accumulated assets forcibly resist those who try to plunder them, and the ensuing battles consume both predators' and victims' resources.[10]

Disorganized banditry produces Hobbesian anarchy in which nobody prospers because nobody has an incentive to be productive. If the predators can organize, they may evolve into little mafias that can offer their clients some protection. This evolution will create a more productive society, with more income for both the predators and their prey, but the mafias will have to limit their take in order for this outcome to arise. If the mafia can assure its clients that in exchange for payment they will be protected from other predators and allowed to keep a substantial portion of what they produce, output will increase, and everybody's income can rise. Losses from rivalries among mafias will continue to be borne, however, because competing mafias have an incentive to plunder individuals who do not contract with them.

If the mafias become even better organized, they can establish themselves as a state. Predators have every incentive to move from operating as bandits to operating as states because bandits cannot guarantee themselves a long-term flow of income from predation and because if banditry is rampant, people have little incentive to produce wealth. States try to convince citizens that they will limit their take and that they will protect their citizens in order to provide an incentive for those citizens to produce. Governments receive more income than bandits because governments can remain in one place and receive a steady flow of income rather than snatching once and moving on (Usher 1992). In such a situation, citizens gain, too (Holcombe 1994).

Nozick (1974) describes this process in more benign terms. Nozick's protection agencies establish monopolies and evolve into a minimal state, but the evolutionary process is the same. The evolution of predatory bandits into mafias (protection firms) and thence into governments may be inevitable. If not inevitable, it is desirable because governments have an incentive to be less predatory than bandits or mafias. Citizens will be more productive, creating more for predators to take and more for citizens themselves to keep. The predators gain because they need only threaten to use force in order to induce the victims to surrender their property. Citizens benefit

---

10. See Tullock 1967, an article titled "The Welfare Costs of Tariffs, Monopolies, and Theft," which is focused on the welfare cost of monopolies and tariffs, but whose arguments about theft apply here. See also Usher 1992 for a Hobbesian view of life in anarchy. See Bush 1972 for a formal model of the costliness of anarchy and how it leads to government.

because they need not devote resources to using force in defense of their property—the government protects property, except for the share it takes for itself.[11]

Successful predation of this type requires a particular institutional arrangement in which government makes a credible promise to limit its take and to protect its citizens from other predators. Only then do citizens have an incentive to produce much. Government has an incentive to protect citizens in order to protect its own source of income.

The contractarian literature of Rawls (1971), Buchanan (1975), and especially Tullock (1972, 1974) is related to the argument presented here, but it differs in a significant respect. Noting the problems that exist for citizens in Hobbesian anarchy, these writers argue that citizens can gain by forming a government to protect property rights and to enforce contracts. Government is a result of the contract, not a party to it. The argument here is not that government will be created because everyone's welfare will be enhanced by an escape from anarchy, but rather that anarchy will not persist because those with the power to create a government will do so regardless of the desires of those outside of government. The creation of government may enhance everyone's welfare because government has an incentive to protect the source of its income—its citizens' productive capacity—but the "contract" that creates government is not made because everyone agrees to it or because everyone will benefit. Rather, it springs from the capacity of those in government to force their rule on others.

A Potential Problem with Protection Firms

In an orderly anarchy, potential victims of predation can hire protective firms to help them protect their assets, and these protective firms may try to cooperate with each other, as Rothbard (1973) argues. However, with many competing protective firms, potential problems arise. Firms might prey on their competitors' customers, as competing mafia groups do, to show those customers that their current protective firm is not doing the job and thus to induce them to switch protection firms. This action seems to be a profit-maximizing strategy; hence, protection firms that do not prey on noncustomers may not survive. The problem is even more acute if Nozick is correct in arguing that there is a natural monopoly in the industry. In that case, firms must add to their customer base or lose out to larger firms in the competition.

Cowan (1992, 1994) argues that this tendency toward natural monopoly is accentuated because for protection firms to cooperate in the adjudication of disputes, a single arbitration network is required. This network might be established through the creation of a monopoly protection agency, as Nozick suggests, but even if many firms participate, the result will be a cartel whose members have an incentive to act anticompetitively. For the network to work, it must sanction outlaw firms that try to

---

11. Not surprisingly, some people prefer even more protection services, so they hire private protection services to augment the government's. Many people, however, rely entirely on the state's protection of their persons and assets.

operate outside the network. The power to sanction competitors reinforces its monopoly position. As Adam Smith notes, "People of the same trade seldom meet together, even for merriment and diversion, but the conversation ends in a conspiracy against the public" ([1776] 1937, 128). The reasonable argument that protection firms would cooperate to avoid violence and produce justice thus evolves into the argument that such firms would cartelize to use their power for their benefit in a conspiracy against the public.

A more general and therefore more serious threat is that using the assets of a protective firm for both plunder and protection might prove most profitable.[12] A protection firm might use armored vehicles, guns, investigative equipment, and other assets to protect its clients and to recover stolen property or to extract damages from people who violated its clients' rights. The firm might find it more profitable, however, to use its investigative capacity also to locate assets that can be stolen and to use guns and other weapons to rob people who are not its clients. The mafia, for example, does offer protection for a fee, but it also uses its resources for predation. Profit-maximizing firms with these kinds of assets can be expected to employ them in the dual roles of protection and predation. Otherwise, they would not be maximizing their profits, and they would lose market share to firms that do use their resources in this profit-maximizing way.

Much of the time protection firms must have excess capacity in their role as protectors because they need to be able to respond to violations of their clients' rights with sufficient force to return stolen property, collect restitution, and otherwise deal with predators. Most of the time they will need to use their resources only to guard and monitor their clients' property, leaving some of their assets idle.[13] Absent government, protection firms might want to display their excess capacity to use violence conspicuously, in part to reassure their customers and in part to deter aggressors. They also might use these resources, however, in a predatory manner against nonclients.

This line of reasoning further bolsters Nozick's argument that the production of protection is a natural monopoly, and it bolsters Cowan's argument that even if many protection firms remained in anarchy, they would be pushed to cartelize, creating the same result as a monopoly protection firm. If potential customers have to be concerned not only with how well a firm will protect property, but also with the threat that protection firms they do not contract with may take their property, they have even more reason to patronize the largest and most powerful firm. Protection firms do not necessarily offer an escape from Hobbesian anarchy.[14]

---

12. Sutter (1995) argues that in anarchy, power would be biased in favor of protection agencies, which might degenerate into exploitative gangs. Rutten (1999) argues that an orderly anarchy may not always be very liberal because some people or groups might abuse the power they have over others, as the mafia does.

13. Private protection firms under the umbrella of government do not need as much excess capacity because when they detect a violation, their normal response is to call the police to marshal the additional force needed to respond to rights violations.

14. Note also Rutten's (1999) more general argument that protection firms would tend to abuse their power, much like the mafia, sacrificing liberty in any event.

The Special Case of Protection Services

As noted earlier, one conclusion of the libertarian literature on government production is that private providers can provide more effectively all of the goods and services that government now supplies. This conclusion applies to protection services as much as to any government-provided good or service. As with other goods and services, though, it applies to the market provision of protection services within an economy in which government enforces its rules on all market participants, including protection firms. Economic analysis that shows the effectiveness of markets in allocating resources does so within a framework that assumes that property rights are protected and that exchange is voluntary.[15] Economic theorists from Samuelson (1947) to Rothbard (1962) make the assumption that market exchange arises from mutual agreement, without theft or fraud. In the analysis of protection firms, this assumption of voluntary exchange amounts to an assumption that the industry's output is already being produced—as a prerequisite for showing that it can be produced by the market! As a simple matter of logic, one cannot assume a conclusion to be true as a condition for showing that it is true. This problem makes the production of protection services a special case from the standpoint of economic analysis.

The noncoercive nature of market exchange allows competing firms to enter at any time, regardless of incumbents' market share or market power. Protection firms, however, cannot be analyzed on this assumption because they themselves provide the protection that is assumed to exist in a free market and that underlies the ability to enter the market. If they can protect themselves, the assumption is met; if not, the assumption is violated. In the previous section, I explained why the assumption is likely to be violated. The use of force is an integral part of these firms' business activities, and protection firms have an incentive to use their resources for predatory purposes, which includes keeping competitors from entering the market.[16]

In a world dominated by government, how protection firms might behave in the absence of government is a matter of speculation, but in examining the turf wars fought by different mafia families and by rival city gangs, we see a tendency for nongovernmental groups to use force to try to eliminate competitors from the market. Some protection firms might shy away from such activity, but, as noted in the previous section, using the firm's resources for predatory as well as protective activities is a profit-maximizing strategy, and protection firms that are not predatory will tend to lose out in the competition with those that are. If protection firms use predatory means to keep competitors from entering, then one of the fundamental (and usually

---

15. Sutter 1995 shows how asymmetric power can lead to the exploitation of some people in this situation. See also Rutten 1999 on this point.

16. Those who argue that private protection firms would negotiate among themselves to settle disputes are in effect arguing that competitors would not enter the market unless they also entered the dispute-resolution cartel.

unstated) institutional assumptions underlying the demonstration of the efficiency of market activity is violated. This problem makes the provision of protection services different from the provision of most services.

In most industries, firms with market power exercise that power through their pricing decisions, marketing strategies (such as bundling), contractual means (such as exclusive contracts), or other means that involve only voluntary activity on the part of everyone involved. Firms with market power in the protection industry are uniquely in a position to use force to prevent competitors from entering the market or to encourage people to become their customers, simply as a result of the nature of their business.[17] Nozick presents a relatively benign description of how private protective firms might evolve into a minimal state, but in a business where those who are best at using coercion are the most successful, the actual evolution of protection firms into a state may result in a very predatory state.

Government Is Inevitable

In the foregoing arguments, I have maintained that although government may not be desirable, it is inevitable because if no government exists, predators have an incentive to establish one. From a theoretical standpoint, Nozick's argument—that competing protection firms will evolve into a monopoly that then becomes the state—represents one form of the general argument that government is inevitable. Because of the prominence of Nozick's work, I offer no further theoretical defense of it here. More significant, however, as de Jasay notes, "Anarchy, if historical precedent is to be taken as conclusive, does not survive" (1989, 217). Every place in the world is ruled by government. The evidence shows that anarchy, no matter how desirable in theory, does not constitute a realistic alternative in practice, and it suggests that if government ever were to be eliminated anywhere, predators would move in to establish themselves as one by force.[18] One can debate the merits of anarchy in theory, but the real-world libertarian issue is not whether it would more be desirable to establish a limited government or to eliminate government altogether. Economist Bruce Benson notes, "When a community is at a comparative disadvantage in the use of violence it may not be able to prevent subjugation by a protection racket such as the state" (1999, 153). Libertarian philosopher Jan Narveson writes, "Why does government remain in power? Why, in fact, are there still governments? The short answer is that governments command powers to which the ordinary citizen is utterly unequal" (2002, 199–200). Government is inevitable, and people with no government—or even with a weak

---

17. Of course, other types of firms might try to use force as a competitive tool—for example, by saying, "If you don't deal exclusively with us, we will burn your house down." Such actions, however, lie outside the type of market activity normally incorporated into economic analysis, whereas the use of force is an integral part of a protection firm's business activity.

18. Perhaps the most recent examples of areas effectively without government were Bosnia, Somalia, and Afghanistan in the 1990s, which fell well short of being anarchistic utopias.

government—will find themselves taken over and ruled by predatory gangs who will establish a government over them.[19] As de Jasay observes, "An anarchistic society may not be well equipped to resist military conquest by a command-directed one" (1997, 200). People may not need or want government, but inevitably they will find themselves under government's jurisdiction.[20]

Some Governments Are More Predatory Than Others

All governments were established by force and retain their power by force, but some are more predatory than others. Governments can take more from their citizens than can bandits or mafias because of their superior organization, but their advantage in part requires them to be less predatory. Bandits can plunder everything people have, but then nothing more will be left to take, and people will have little incentive to produce more if they believe that another complete plunder awaits them. Bandits must move from victim to victim, using resources to find victims and forcing them to surrender their wealth. Governments can remain in one place, continually taking a flow of wealth from the same people, often with their victims' cooperation and assistance. If governments nurture their citizens' productivity, the amount of their takings can continue to increase over time. It then becomes increasingly important for government to protect its source of income from outside predators, so the production of protection serves the self-interest of those in government as well as the interest of the mass of citizens.

The longer the government's time horizon, the less predatory it will be.[21] If a government takes over by force but believes that it will rule for only a limited time before another gang of predators forces it out, then it has an incentive to take everything it can while it still has the power to do so. This incentive will obtain especially if the rulers are unpopular with the citizens and therefore cannot count on the citizens for support. Governments imposed on people from the outside are likely to be especially predatory, which gives citizens an incentive to form their own government preemptively to prevent outsiders from taking over.

---

19. Much has been made in libertarian literature of the case of Iceland from about A.D. 800 to 1262. For the historical details, see D. Friedman 1979. Yet this example ended nearly 750 years ago, and it existed in a world much different from the modern one. Iceland was remote, given the transportation technology of the day, it was poor, and it had an undesirable climate, making it an undesirable target for predators. Nevertheless, a government was eventually established from the inside.

20. This argument is aimed at libertarians and takes a libertarian perspective. Libertarians should keep in mind, however, that the overwhelming majority of people, if given the choice, would choose government over anarchy, and a substantial number of people would like a bigger and more powerful government than they have today.

21. Levi 1988 discusses the effect of the rulers' time horizon and other factors on the degree to which they act in a predatory manner. Hoppe 2001 argues that monarchy is superior to democracy because political leaders have a longer time horizon.

If a group of outside predators establishes itself as a government, it will have every reason to keep most of the surplus for itself, in part because the people in the predatory group care more about their own welfare than they do about the welfare of the people they rule. Moreover, the conquered group probably will resist takeover by the predators, creating ill will between the conquerors and the conquered. If government is inevitable, and if some governments are better than others, then citizens have an incentive to create and maintain preemptively a government that minimizes predation and is organized to preserve, as much as possible, its citizens' liberty (Holcombe forthcoming).

Can Government Preserve Liberty?

The arguments developed here frame a challenge to the idea that a minimal state can be designed to preserve liberty. If government is simply a matter of the strong forcing themselves on the weak, it should not matter whether citizens want to create a limited government to protect their rights because in the end those who have the most power will take over and rule for their own benefit. That threat is real, and a brief examination of political history shows many examples. One example is the 1917 Russian Revolution that created the Soviet Union. Other examples include China and eastern Europe after World War II and many African nations at the beginning of the twenty-first century. Likewise, limited governments such as the U.S. government created in 1776 and the British government in the nineteenth century became less libertarian and more predatory in the twentieth century. Limited governments may not remain limited, and any government constitutes a standing threat to liberty. A challenge to advocates of a minimal state is to explain how people can create and sustain preemptively a liberty-preserving government.

The historical record also offers some basis for optimism that government's predatory impulses can be controlled. History shows that oppressive governments can be overthrown, as they were in eastern Europe after the collapse of the Berlin wall in 1989, and that even when they are not overthrown, pressures from their citizens can result in less-predatory states. One would not want to hold Russia and China up as examples of libertarian governments, but they do exemplify governments that have reduced their oppression and increased individual liberty. Governments can become less predatory. Even though the U.S. government has been firmly entrenched for two centuries, it is less oppressive than many other governments, notwithstanding that it has become more predatory over time. Thus, the evidence is that the worst thugs do not always seize and maintain power, and even when they do, reversals toward liberty are possible. In light of this experience, it should be possible to identify the factors that make governments less predatory. Such factors fall into two general categories: economic and ideological.

The economic incentives are relatively straightforward. There are net gains from establishing a less-predatory government. Gwartney, Holcombe, and Lawson (1998) have shown that countries with lower levels of government spending have higher incomes and faster economic growth, and in examining economic freedom more broadly Gwartney, Lawson, and Holcombe (1999) have shown that less government interference in all areas of an economy leads to greater prosperity. Olson (2000) examines the political conditions under which less-predatory governments can be established, and a substantial body of work follows up on Olson's ideas to promote less-predatory and more market-oriented governments (Azfar and Cadwell 2003; Knack 2003). If less-predatory governments mean more production, then potentially everyone can gain from replacing more-predatory government with less-predatory government.

Leaders of predatory governments, however, may do better by preserving the status quo, and they may generate sufficient political support by promoting a national ideology (Edelman 1964; North 1981, 1988) or by intimidating potential rivals (Lichbach 1995; Kurrild-Klitgaard 1997) in order to maintain power. As Olson (1965) explains, even if most people believe that they would be better off with a less-predatory government, they have an incentive to free ride on others' revolutionary activities, which limits the possibilities for change. Kurrild-Klitgaard (1997) notes, however, that some incentives for revolutionary action remain. Moreover, revolution is not the only option. Just as government in the United States has grown by small steps, a gradual contraction of government's scope and power also may be brought about. The demise of the eastern European dictatorships after the collapse of the Berlin Wall in 1989 shows that changes can happen with surprising speed. This development points toward the second factor: ideology.

In a famous passage of *The General Theory of Employment, Interest, and Money,* John Maynard Keynes emphasizes the power of ideas: "Indeed, the world is ruled by little else. Practical men, who believe themselves to be quite exempt from any intellectual influences, are usually the slaves of some defunct economist. Madmen in authority, who hear voices in the air, are distilling their frenzy from some academic scribbler of a few years back. I am sure that the power of vested interests is vastly exaggerated compared with the gradual encroachment of ideas" (1936, 383). The American Revolution of 1776 was strongly supported by an ideology of freedom (Bailyn 1992; Holcombe 2002a), as was the fall of the European eastern bloc dictatorships after 1989. At the beginning of the twenty-first century, citizens of governments throughout the world are increasingly coming to accept the libertarian ideas of Mises, Hayek, Friedman, Rothbard, and others.

Together, economic and ideological forces are now creating an environment more conducive to the advance of liberty than the environment of the twentieth century. From an economic standpoint, the connection between freedom and prosperity has become universally recognized. Through most of the twentieth century, the conventional wisdom held that a government-controlled economy would be more productive than a market economy, an idea that persisted until the collapse of the

Berlin Wall in 1989. Economic realities have not changed, but the generally accepted economic view of freedom has. In the twentieth century, the conventional wisdom held that more freedom came at the cost of a less-productive economy. In the twenty-first century, the generally accepted view is that freedom brings prosperity. From an ideological standpoint, the academic scribbler who had the largest influence on the twentieth century was probably Karl Marx, whereas at the beginning of the twenty-first century the ideas of Mises, Hayek, and Friedman have found greater popular acceptance.

A minimal libertarian state would require strong ideological support from its citizens, and both economic and ideological factors are turning in the direction of liberty. As Jeffrey Rogers Hummel says of libertarian ideology, "Although we may never abolish all states, there is little doubt that we can do better at restraining their power if only we can motivate people with the will to be free" (2001, 535).

Government and Liberty

History has shown not only that anarchy does not survive, but also that some governments are better than others. Therein lies the libertarian argument for a limited government. People benefit from an institutional mechanism to prevent their being taken over by a predatory gang. They can provide this mechanism by preemptively establishing their own limited government, in a form they themselves determine, not on the terms forced upon them by outside predators. A government created by the people themselves can be designed to produce the protection they desire while returning to them the bulk of the surplus owing to peaceful cooperation rather than allowing the state to retain it.

Is it really possible to design a limited government that will protect people's liberty? Despite the challenges, it is well-known that some institutional arrangements do a better job of securing liberty and creating prosperity than others. Nations that have protected property rights and allowed markets to work have thrived, whereas nations that have not done so have remained mired in poverty.[22] A libertarian analysis of government must go beyond the issue of whether government should exist. Some governments are more libertarian than others, and it is worth studying how government institutions can be designed to minimize their negative impact on liberty. This proposition is obviously true if one believes that government is inevitable, but even advocates of orderly anarchy should have an interest in understanding how government institutions can be designed to maximize their protection of liberty.

Many writers have noted that limited governments usually tend to expand their scope once established, perhaps suggesting that limited governments, once established, cannot be controlled (Olson 1982, 2000; Higgs 1987; Holcombe 2002a). Neverthe-

---

22. Landes 1998 considers the historical evidence and makes a powerful case for this connection.

less, in the real world, some governments are less oppressive and closer to the libertarian ideal than others. The United States, with one of the oldest governments in the world, remains one of the freest nations, so clearly it is possible to preserve a degree of liberty, even if the situation does not approach the libertarian ideal. In any event, if government is inevitable, there is no real-world libertarian alternative but to work to make government more libertarian. Although ideas have been advanced as to how institutions might be redesigned to lessen government's coercive activities (for example, by Tucker 1990; Anderson and Leal 1991; Holcombe 1995; Holcombe and Staley 2001), there may be no final answer to the question of how to design the ideal government because any innovations in government designed to protect the rights of individuals may prompt offsetting innovations by those who want to use government for predatory purposes. The preservation of liberty will remain a never-ending challenge.

My argument may convince some readers that limited government is necessary to preserve liberty—to protect citizens from being taken over and ruled by a predatory government much worse for their liberty than a government they design themselves. Others may believe, despite the arguments presented here, that libertarian anarchy remains a feasible and desirable alternative. In any event, my arguments point to a different direction for the debate between libertarian anarchists and libertarian minarchists.[23] Both groups agree that government is not necessary to produce public goods or to correct externalities or to get people to cooperate for the public good—that private parties can undertake voluntarily and more effectively all of the activities undertaken in the public sector. The libertarian issue regarding government is whether a society with no government has the means to prevent predators from establishing one by force.

Rothbard (1973) argues that an anarchistic society can resist such predators, whereas Nozick (1974) and de Jasay (1989, 1997) argue that anarchy will not survive. However, most of the arguments supporting a libertarian anarchy have been framed in terms of whether private arrangements can replace government activities. Whether private arrangements are superior to government activity, however, is largely irrelevant.[24] Government is not created to produce public goods, to control externalities, or to enforce social cooperation for the good of all. It is created by force for the benefit of its creators. The libertarian argument for a minimal government is not that government is better than private arrangements at doing anything, but that it is necessary to prevent the creation of an even more predatory and less-libertarian government.

---

23. Although I argue that libertarian anarchy is not a viable alternative, I do not mean to suggest that the libertarian anarchist literature has no merit. In fact, this literature has made valuable contributions in two broad ways. First, it has shown the viability of market institutions in areas where the mainstream literature argues the necessity of government, thus making significant advances in our understanding of both markets and government. Second, it helps promote the libertarian ideology required to rein in the power of predatory government.

24. My argument also suggests that claims that government is immoral (as in Rothbard 1982) are not relevant to the issue of whether people should have government. If government is inevitably imposed on them by force, they have no choice.

References

Anderson, Terry L., and Donald Leal. 1991. *Free Market Environmentalism.* San Francisco: Pacific Research Institute for Public Policy.

Axelrod, Robert. 1984. *The Evolution of Cooperation.* New York: Basic.

Azfar, Omar, and Charles A. Cadwell. 2003. *Market-Augmenting Government.* Ann Arbor: University of Michigan Press.

Bailyn, Bernard. 1992. *The Ideological Origins of the American Revolution.* Enlarged ed. Cambridge, Mass.: Belknap.

Beard, Charles A. 1913. *An Economic Interpretation of the Constitution of the United States.* New York: MacMillan.

Benson, Bruce L. 1989. The Spontaneous Evolution of Commercial Law. *Southern Economic Journal* 55, no. 3 (January): 644–61.

———. 1990. *The Enterprise of Law: Justice Without the State.* San Francisco: Pacific Research Institute for Public Policy.

———. 1998. *To Serve and Protect: Privatization and Community in Criminal Justice.* New York: New York University Press.

———. 1999. An Economic Theory of the Evolution of Governance and the Emergence of the State. *Review of Austrian Economics* 12, no. 2: 131–60.

———. 2001. Knowledge, Trust, and Recourse: Imperfect Substitutes as Sources of Assurance in Emerging Economies. *Economic Affairs* 21, no. 1 (March): 12–17.

Berman, Harold J. 1983. *Law and Revolution: The Formation of Western Legal Tradition.* Cambridge, Mass.: Harvard University Press.

Brewster, Leonard. 2002. The Impossibility of the State. *Journal of Libertarian Studies* 16, no. 3 (summer): 19–34.

Buchanan, James M. 1975. *The Limits of Liberty: Between Anarchy and Leviathan.* Chicago: University of Chicago Press.

Bush, Winston C. 1972. Individual Welfare in Anarchy. In *Explorations in the Theory of Anarchy,* edited by Gordon Tullock, 5–18. Blacksburg, Va.: Center for the Study of Public Choice.

Cowan, Tyler. 1992. Law as a Public Good. *Economics and Philosophy* 8, no. 2 (October): 249–67.

———. 1994. Rejoinder to David Friedman on the Economics of Anarchy. *Economics and Philosophy* 10, no. 2 (October): 329–32.

De Jasay, Anthony. 1985. *The State.* New York: Basil Blackwell.

———. 1989. *Social Contract, Free Ride: A Study of the Public Goods Problem.* Oxford: Clarendon.

———. 1997. *Against Politics: On Government, Anarchy, and Order.* London: Routledge.

Edelman, Murray. 1964. *The Symbolic Uses of Politics.* Urbana: University of Illinois Press.

Foldvary, Fred. 1994. *Public Goods and Private Communities: The Market Provision of Social Services.* Brookfield, Vt.: Edward Elgar.

Friedman, David. 1979. Private Creation and Enforcement of Law: A Historical Case. *Journal of Legal Studies* 8 (March): 399–415.

———. 1989. *The Machinery of Freedom: Guide to a Radical Capitalism.* 2d ed. La Salle, Ill.: Open Court.

Friedman, Milton. 1962. *Capitalism and Freedom.* Chicago: University of Chicago Press.

Gwartney, James, Randall Holcombe, and Robert Lawson. 1998. The Scope of Government and the Wealth of Nations. *Cato Journal* 18, no. 2 (fall): 163–90.

Gwartney, James, Robert Lawson, and Randall Holcombe. 1999. Economic Freedom and the Environment for Economic Growth. *Journal of Institutional and Theoretical Economics* 155, no. 4 (December): 643–63.

Hayek, Friedrich A. 1944. *The Road to Serfdom.* Chicago: University of Chicago Press.

———. 1960. *The Constitution of Liberty.* Chicago: University of Chicago Press.

Higgs, Robert. 1987. *Crisis and Leviathan: Critical Episodes in the Growth of American Government.* New York: Oxford University Press.

———. 2002. Government Protects Us? *The Independent Review* 7, no. 2 (fall): 309–13.

Hobbes, Thomas. [1651] 1950. *Leviathan.* New York: E. P. Dutton.

Holcombe, Randall G. 1994. *The Economic Foundations of Government.* New York: New York University Press.

———. 1995. *Public Policy and the Quality of Life.* Westport, Conn.: Greenwood.

———. 1997. A Theory of the Theory of Public Goods. *Review of Austrian Economics* 10, no. 1: 1–22.

———. 2002a. *From Liberty to Democracy: The Transformation of American Government.* Ann Arbor: University of Michigan Press.

———. 2002b. Political Entrepreneurship and the Democratic Allocation of Economic Resources. *Review of Austrian Economics* 15, nos. 2–3 (June): 143–59.

———. Forthcoming. Why Government? In *Ordered Anarchy: Essays in Honor of Anthony de Jasay,* edited by Aschwin de Wolf.

Holcombe, Randall G., and Samuel R. Staley. 2001. *Smarter Growth: Market-Based Strategies for Land-Use Planning in the 21st Century.* Westport, Conn.: Greenwood.

Hoppe, Hans-Hermann. 1998–99. The Private Production of Defense. *Journal of Libertarian Studies* 14, no. 1 (winter): 27–52.

———. 2001. *Democracy, the God That Failed: The Economics and Politics of Monarchy, Democracy, and Natural Order.* New Brunswick, N.J.: Transaction.

Hummel, Jeffrey Rogers. 1990. National Goods Versus Public Goods: Defense, Disarmament, and Free Riders. *Review of Austrian Economics* 4, no. 1: 88–122.

———. 2001. The Will to Be Free: The Role of Ideology in National Defense. *The Independent Review* 5, no. 4 (spring): 523–37.

Keynes, John Maynard. 1936. *The General Theory of Employment, Interest, and Money.* New York: Harcourt, Brace.

Knack, Stephen, ed. 2003. *Democracy, Governance, and Growth.* Ann Arbor: University of Michigan Press.

Kurrild-Klitgaard, Peter. 1997. *Rational Choice, Collective Action, and the Paradox of Rebellion.* Copenhagen: University of Copenhagen, Institute of Political Science.

Landes, David S. 1998. *The Wealth and Poverty of Nations: Why Some Are So Rich, and Others So Poor.* New York: W. W. Norton.

Levi, Margaret. 1988. *Of Rule and Revenue.* Berkeley and Los Angeles: University of California Press.

Lichbach, Mark Irving. 1995. *The Rebel's Dilemma.* Ann Arbor: University of Michigan Press.

Mises, Ludwig von. 1945. *Omnipotent Government: The Rise of the Total State and Total War.* New Haven, Conn.: Yale University Press.

———. 1979. *Liberalism: A Socio-economic Exposition.* New York: New York University Press.

———. 1998. *Human Action: A Treatise on Economics.* Scholar's ed. Auburn, Ala.: Ludwig von Mises Institute.

Narveson, Jan. 2002. *Respecting Persons in Theory and Practice: Essays on Moral and Political Philosophy.* Lanham, Md.: Rowman and Littlefield.

North, Douglass C. 1981. *Structure and Change in Economic History.* New York: W. W. Norton.

———. 1988. Ideology and Political/Economic Institutions. *Cato Journal* 8 (spring–summer): 15–28.

Nozick, Robert. 1974. *Anarchy, State, and Utopia.* New York: Basic.

Olson, Mancur. 1965. *The Logic of Collective Action.* New York: Shocken.

———. 1982. *The Rise and Decline of Nations.* New Haven, Conn.: Yale University Press.

———. 2000. *Power and Prosperity: Outgrowing Communist and Capitalist Dictatorships.* New York: Basic.

Rawls, John. 1971. *A Theory of Justice.* Cambridge, Mass.: Belknap.

Rothbard, Murray N. 1956. Toward a Reconstruction of Utility and Welfare Economics. In *On Freedom and Free Enterprise: Essays in Honor of Ludwig von Mises,* edited by Mary Sennholz, 224–62. Princeton, N.J.: D. Van Nostrand.

———. 1962. *Man, Economy, and State.* Princeton, N.J.: Van Nostrand.

———. 1973. *For a New Liberty.* New York: Macmillan.

———. 1982. *The Ethics of Liberty.* Atlantic Highlands, N.J.: Humanities.

Rutten, Andrew. 1999. Can Anarchy Save Us from Leviathan? *The Independent Review* 3, no. 4 (spring): 581–93.

Samuelson, Paul Anthony. 1947. *Foundations of Economic Analysis.* Cambridge, Mass.: Harvard University Press.

Smith, Adam. [1776] 1937. *The Wealth of Nations.* Modern Library ed. New York: Random House.

Stringham, Edward. 1998–99. Market Chosen Law. *Journal of Libertarian Studies* 14, no. 1 (winter): 53–77.

Sutter, Daniel. 1995. Asymmetric Power Relations and Cooperation in Anarchy. *Southern Economic Journal* 61, no. 3 (January): 602–13.

Tinsley, Patrick. 1998–99. Private Police: A Note. *Journal of Libertarian Studies* 14, no. 1 (winter): 95–100.

Tucker, William. 1990. *The Excluded Americans: Homelessness and Housing Policies.* Washington, D.C.: Regnery Gateway.

Tullock, Gordon. 1967. The Welfare Costs of Tariffs, Monopolies, and Theft. *Western Economic Journal* 5 (June): 224–32.

————, ed. 1972. *Explorations in the Theory of Anarchy.* Blacksburg, Va.: Center for the Study of Public Choice.

————, ed. 1974. *Further Explorations in the Theory of Anarchy.* Blacksburg, Va.: University Publications.

Usher, Dan. 1992. *The Welfare Economics of Market, Voting, and Predation.* Ann Arbor: University of Michigan Press.

Yeager, Leland B. 1985. Rights, Contract, and Utility in Policy Analysis. *Cato Journal* 5, no. 1 (summer): 259–94.

Acknowledgments The author gratefully acknowledges helpful comments from Bruce Benson, Fred Foldvary, Gil Guillory, Robert Higgs, Hans Hoppe, and two anonymous reviewers of this journal. All arguments presented in the article and any of the article's remaining shortcomings remain the author's responsibility.

Part VII
Dispersed Knowledge and the Limits of Law

Part VII

Dispersed Knowledge and the Limits of Law

[30]

NYU JOURNAL OF LAW & LIBERTY

THE PROBLEM OF MORAL DIRIGISME: A NEW ARGUMENT AGAINST MORALISTIC LEGISLATION

Mario J. Rizzo[*]

This Article applies a theory of rational choice to moral decision making. In this theory, agents act primarily on local and personal knowledge to instantiate moral principles, virtues, and moral goods. The State may seek to prevent them from acting as they independently determine by pre-scribing or proscribing certain conduct by formal legal means. If its pur-pose is to ensure that people act morally or become better persons, we call this "moral dirigisme." Our thesis is that the need to use decentralized knowledge to determine the moral status of an act makes the task of the moral dirigiste well-nigh impossible. The Article models moral agents as ideal-typical utilitarians, Kantians, or natural law adherents. We show that within each of these systems the determination of the morality of an act depends on the "particular circumstances of time and place." Because the State's access to knowledge of the personal and local circumstances of the actor is inferior to the knowledge available to the actor himself, the State does not possess a necessary instrument for the compulsion of mo-rality. It does not have adequate concrete knowledge to know what is good. We conclude that the State cannot make people moral, because even when all members of society accept the same moral framework, it does not and usually cannot have the specific knowledge needed to determine the concrete manifestations of morality.

---

[*] Department of Economics, New York University, Mario.Rizzo@nyu.edu. I am especially indebted to David Harper and Glen Whitman for their comments over a long period of time. I am also indebted to Peter Boettke, William Butos, Eugene Callahan, Neelkant Chamilall, Young Back Choi, Douglas Den Uyl, Richard Epstein, Pierre Garello, David Gordon, Sanford Ikeda, David Kelley, Israel Kirzner, Roger Koppl, Elisabeth Krecké, Chidem Kurdas, Roderick Long, Patricia Marino, Maria Pia Paganelli, Ellen Paul, Jeffrey Paul, Eric Posner, Gerald Postema, Douglas Rasmussen, Arthur Reber, James Sadowsky, Joseph Salerno, Frédéric Sautet, Steven Shavell, and Luc Tardieu. I apologize if I have omitted anyone. I am grateful to the H. B. Earhart Foundation for financial support. Responsibility for errors and for the views expressed is mine alone.

Table of Contents

> "If there are circumstances in which the conduct I should pursue is clear
> to all that know my life, there will always be cases where I alone will
> know what I ought to do, because no one else can know the totality of
> factors my decisions must take into account. That is why, after we have
> given advice, it is reasonable to refrain from judging one who does not
> follow it. One who knows enough to give advice does not know enough
> to tell whether the advice ought to be followed...The incommunicability
> of the prudential judgment sets limits to governing others and provides
> the basic foundation of personal autonomy. An enlightened despotism
> therefore may be a contradiction in terms."[1] –Yves R. Simon

> "Let it be considered, too, that the present inquiry is not concerning a
> matter of right, if I may say so, but concerning a matter of fact."[2]
> –Adam Smith

Introduction

Ethics is not a purely abstract discipline that organizes and gives foundation to our vague moral intuitions.[3] It also involves making practical judgments
and choosing among alternative courses of action.[4] Accordingly, ethical decisions
share many characteristics with decision making in realms of rational choice generally and market systems more specifically.[5] The most important of these charac-

---

[1] YVES R. SIMON, A CRITIQUE OF MORAL KNOWLEDGE 37-8, n.8 (Ralph McInerny trans., 2002) (1934).
[2] ADAM SMITH, THE THEORY OF MORAL SENTIMENTS 152 (Liberty Classics 1976) (1759).
[3] Sometimes a distinction is made between morality and ethics. See, for example, G. H. Joyce, *Morality* in
THE CATHOLIC ENCYCLOPEDIA (Charles G. Heibermann, Edward A. Pace, Conde' B. Pallen, J. Shahan and
John J. Wynne eds.,1913), *available at*: http://www.newadvent.org/cathen/10559a.htm ("Morality is
antecedent to ethics: it denotes those concrete activities of which ethics is the science.") However, the
distinction between morality and ethics is not observed here because our method formalizes moral decision making. See also section V-d, infra.. It is also quite common simply to employ the terms synonymously.
[4] For an emphasis on the practical aspect of ethics, see JOHN FINNIS, FUNDAMENTALS OF ETHICS 3-4 (1983)
("[E]thics is practical because my choosing and acting and living in a certain sort of way . . . is not a secondary . . . objective and side-effect of success in the intellectual enterprise; rather it is *the very object primarily envisaged* . . . [Ethics] has two formal, primary objects (objectives, goods in view); (i) truth about a
certain subject-matter, and (ii) the instantiation of that truth in choices and actions.")
[5] Lionel Robbins was one of the first economists explicitly to recognize the general applicability of a science of rational choice:
"The ends may be noble or they may be base. They may be 'material' or 'immaterial'—if ends can be so
described. But if the attainment of one set of ends involves the sacrifice of others, then it has an economic
aspect . . . . The distribution of time between prayer and good works has its economic aspect equally with

The Problem of Moral Dirigisme   791

teristics is the need to act upon knowledge that is available only in localized settings or contexts, is transient in nature, and may not be amenable to explicit articulation. The thesis of this Article is that recognition of these ubiquitous characteristics of ethical decision making places very strong and narrow limits on the State's ability to dictate moral behavior, even when those under its control are in agreement with its guiding moral principles.[6] We call the attempt or tendency to control certain kinds of moral behavior by formal legal means "moral *dirigisme.*"[7]

Individuals must use their personal and local knowledge when making moral decisions. This knowledge helps satisfy empirical requirements in the application of general moral principles. These requirements appear in different ways in various moral systems. Nevertheless, in each system, knowledge of what F.A. Hayek called, in another context, the "particular circumstances of time and place"[8] is critical to the choice of a specific action in fulfillment of a general rule, maxim, or principle. The argument here will be familiar to economists. It rests on a rough analogy with another kind of decision making: "economic" or market decision making. In market transactions individuals make use of personal or local knowledge in determining the prices and other terms on which they trade. By bringing the agent's knowledge of the particular circumstances of time and place to bear on his decisions, individual knowledge is mobilized for a social purpose.[9] The price system, it is argued, tends to embody knowledge vastly superior to that of any individual to the extent that individual agents are free to act on the basis of their own knowledge. Central economic planning, on the other hand, explicitly replaces the knowledge of the individual with the allegedly superior knowledge of the central planner. What will be shown is that, even outside of market decision making, in most cases, there will be a superior application of general norms when people are free to act on the basis of their own local knowledge than when a "central planner" seeks to compel moral behavior.

The knowledge problem in ethics, as well as in economics, must be both distinguished from and related to incentive problems.[10] The question of the accu-

---

the distribution of time between orgies and slumber." Lionel Robbins, An Essay on the Nature and Significance of Economic Science, 2d ed. 25-26 (1935).

[6] The purpose of this dictation is to increase the moral goodness of individuals or, possibly, of society as a whole (in the sense of a social structure of morally good rules). However, the object is not simply to make people *think* they are engaging in right action and thus to increase their "subjective morality." It is, rather, to compel them to do what is *objectively* right, given a particular ethical framework. It is mistaken, then, to say that people *are* moral or virtuous if they simply *believe* what they are doing is right. To actually be moral one must do what is objectively right *in the framework to which one subscribes.*

[7] The analogy here is with the more conventional term "economic dirigisme" that is, the centralized control of economic affairs by the State.

[8] See Friedrich A. Hayek, *The Use of Knowledge in Society, in* Individualism and Economic Order 80 (1948).

[9] *See generally,* Friedrich A. Hayek, *The Use of Knowledge in Society, in* Individualism and Economic Order 77-91 (1948).

[10] Unfortunately, Hayek does not distinguish between incentive and knowledge problems in his observations on ethical decision making. "Effective" moral responsibility, for Hayek, is the joint outcome of adequate concrete (local and personal) knowledge and adequate incentives to find and act upon a solution to a moral problem. Hayek argues: "The essential condition of responsibility is that it refer to circumstances that the individual can judge, to problems that, without too much strain on the imagination, man can

racy of knowledge upon which moral agents make decisions is, for knowledge acquired as the *byproduct* of other activities, quite separate from the question of whether these agents have the incentive to act morally. We do not make the assumption that simply because agents are able to act upon relatively accurate concrete knowledge that they will do what is morally correct. They could, of course, be ignorant of basic moral norms or general rules. More importantly, however, it is possible for a variety of reasons, such as deficiency of incentives or weakness of will, to know the better yet do the worse. Nevertheless, knowledge of the better is clearly a prerequisite for doing the better. On the other hand, knowledge acquired *deliberately* for the purpose of enhancing the quality of moral decisions obviously cannot be detached from the individual's incentives to act morally.

Yet even in the case of an individual not predisposed to act morally, the local and personal character of the requisite knowledge makes it, at least *a priori*, highly unlikely that this knowledge can be acquired and correctly processed by an external authority seeking to override the individuals' decisions.

In Part One of the Article we introduce the meaning and significance of moral dirigisme. We then examine some conventional arguments against it primarily to distinguish our own theory. In Part Two we both summarize and develop the theory in detail. In Part Three we show how the knowledge problem is present in three classical systems of ethics: utilitarianism, natural law and Kantianism. Part Four first discusses the exceptional case of justice and then examines specific cases of morals laws and compulsory beneficence legislation. Part Five addresses challenges to the theory emanating from the largely illusory idea of moral absolutes as well as the idea of a "moral ecology" or public morality. In last section we draw some conclusions.

PART ONE: THEORETICAL PRELIMINARIES

I.   The Meaning of Moral Dirigisme

Despite his general opposition to what we call "moral dirigisme," John Stuart Mill, in effect, described its core as "interfering with the liberty of action of any...member of a civilised community [for]... [h]is own good, either physical or moral." The moral dirigiste believes that the individual can "rightfully be compelled to do or forbear because it will be better for him to do so, because it would make him happier, because, in the opinion of others, to do so would be wise, or even right."[11] Mill made a fundamental distinction between this largely self-regarding behavior and other-regarding behavior, especially including behavior

---

make his own and whose solution he can, with good reason, consider his own concern rather than another's. . . . In order to be effective, then, responsibility must be so confined as to enable the individual to rely on his own *concrete* knowledge in deciding on the importance of the different tasks, to apply his moral principles to *circumstances he knows*, and to help to mitigate evils voluntarily." In summary, "If what we do is to be useful and effective, our objectives must be limited, adapted to the capacities of our mind and our compassions." FRIEDRICH A. HAYEK, THE CONSTITUTION OF LIBERTY 84 (1960) (emphases added).

[11] JOHN STUART MILL, ON LIBERTY 13 (Stefan Collini ed., 1989) (1859).

that causes "harm" to others. For him the boundary between moral dirigisme and legitimate coercive legislation is the line that separates harm to oneself from harm to others.[12]

Mill's project was to provide a normative justification for coercion, especially in the form of criminal sanctions, for certain classes of conduct. He was concerned with conduct that causes harm or offense to others, on the one hand, and conduct that causes harm to self, and harmless wrongdoing, on the other.[13] In broad terms, Mill's view was that criminalization of the first is justified and, to a limited extent, criminalization of offense could be justified when the offense is grievous, but that harm to self and harmless wrongdoing (moralisms) are not appropriate for criminalization.

Our project, however, is not to determine the proper scope of the criminal law. *In fact, this is not a normative inquiry at all.* It is, rather, a positive analysis of normative issues. In particular, we are interested first, in identifying certain classes of laws supported by moral arguments that incorporate certain prototypical moral purposes, and, second, in determining whether these laws can, in fact, achieve their purposes. These purposes, it must be stressed, are not ours, but those of the dirigiste. Therefore, our object is to determine whether moral dirigisme can attain its *self-imposed* goals.

Accordingly, at the outset, we must address two preliminary questions: (1) What are the characteristics of a *moral* argument in support of a prohibition or command? and (2)What kinds of specific moral purposes do dirigiste laws attempt to serve? Answers to these questions will enable us to identify the types of laws in which we are interested.

First, the difference between a moral argument for the avoidance or commission of some act and a non-moral or "pragmatic" argument is complex. We shall not go into great detail here. However, it is certainly not the case that prag-

---

[12] Mill states the criterion for legitimate coercion, largely in the form of criminal sanctions, as follows: "The only purpose for which power can be rightfully exercised over any member of a civilised community, against his will, is to prevent harm to others." *Id.* at 13. This criterion, however, is not as straightforward as it may seem. Mill's other-regarding behavior does not correspond neatly to the economist's notion of "external effects." This is because the demarcation between self and other-regarding behavior has a large normative component. Behavior can be essentially self-regarding even in the case in which, for example, others are deeply offended by the outward manifestation of an individual's religious beliefs. No one has a duty to suppress his individuality as manifested in such core beliefs and actions for the sake of not giving offense. See, e.g., R. F. Kahn, *J. S. Mill: Ethics and Politics*, in 7 ROUTLEDGE HISTORY OF PHILOSOPHY 62, 68-73 (C.L. Ten ed., 1994). Autonomy of choice is a necessary element in human happiness and so it can act as a trump against the "pains" of offense. On the other hand, drunkenness, for example, although self-regarding in itself, may lead to the violation of familial obligations which is in turn other-regarding. In practice it is hard to separate drunkenness from its further effects since these often follow with extremely high probability. Thus, "the boundaries of self-regarding conduct in specific situations will be marked out on the basis of respecting the rights of others, and acknowledging corresponding duties, regarding the development of individuality." *Id.* at 72.

[13] These are the titles of Joel Feinberg's four volume study: THE MORAL LIMITS OF THE CRIMINAL LAW : HARM TO OTHERS (1984), OFFENSE TO OTHERS (1985), HARM TO SELF (1986), HARMLESS WRONGDOING (1988).

794 Mario Rizzo   2005

matic arguments consider consequences while moral arguments, by definition, do not. Nor is it the case that moral arguments are necessarily restricted to a certain class of consequences, i.e., "moral" harms. What distinguishes the moral case "to do or forbear" is the type of reasons adduced. A moral argument is not simply of the form "*If* we wish to avoid harm X, we must not perform certain actions." In this case a moral argument says, among other things, that every moral agent should (must) want to avoid this harm, whether it is self or other-regarding.[14] A moral argument exhibits disinterestedness in the sense that it claims every agent must avoid the harm as a matter of principle and not simply because he or someone he cares about is the victim. Relatedly, moral arguments are stated in general terms—neither the agents nor patients can be specific, named individuals.[15] Thus, *moral dirigisme is the use of formal legal means, usually criminal sanctions, to compel individuals or groups to avoid or perform actions, primarily to serve certain kinds of moral purposes as supported by moral arguments.*[16]

Second, these moral arguments, which may be of many types, usually refer to moral purposes of particular kinds. These are:

1. Avoiding a purely moral harm or conferring a purely moral benefit to the agent;

2. Avoiding a purely moral harm or conferring a purely moral benefit to others;

3. Avoiding a moralized welfare (physical, psychological, material) harm or conferring a moralized welfare benefit to the agent;[17]

4. Conferring a moralized welfare benefit to others;

---

[14] Subsequently, we do not restrict ourselves to consequentialist moral arguments. *See infra* at section VIII.

[15] Paul Taylor summarizes a very general conception of a moral argument. It is an argument that rests on the acceptance of a norm that is: "general in form and is *intended* (by anyone who adopts it) to apply universally and disinterestedly, is *intended* to take priority over other norms and to be publicly recognized as having such priority, and is *intended* to be substantively impartial in its practical effects when applied to all cases within its specified scope." Paul Taylor, *On Taking the Moral Point of View*, 3 MIDWEST STUDIES IN PHILOSOPHY 35, 38 (1978).

[16] An alternative approach is to say that "judgments" of morality are not based on reason, but on the presence of a particular kind of feeling or impression – say, one of guilt or of virtue. This is roughly David Hume's view as discussed by David Norton: "Imagine, then, that we observe a specific case of intentional killing. As a consequence of confronting this action, we . . . experience certain impressions of sensation . . . . [They may] includ[e] shock or pity, but among these we can expect to find the distinctive impression of moral disapproval or disapprobation. Only if that impression arises will we determine that the killing agent and the killing action are vicious or morally evil. Moreover, we make this determination just because we have this distinctive feeling: we will not need to make use of reason in order to *infer* that moral evil has been encountered." See the Editor's Introduction in DAVID HUME, A TREATISE OF HUMAN NATURE I80 (David Fate Norton and Mary J. Norton eds, 2000). This is also the view apparently taken by Louis Kaplow and Steven Shavell, *Human Nature and the Best Consequentialist Moral System* 1 n. 1 (February 2002) (unpublished article available on Social Science Research Network, http://ssrn.com/abstract=304384). We do not find the Humean approach appropriate because our theory formalizes the moral decision in terms of ideal-typical philosophical systems. Our agents are thinking within an intellectual system, not simply emoting or, at least, acting as if they are.

The Problem of Moral Dirigisme   795

5.   Avoiding a "free-floating" purely moral evil to society as a whole (a "legal moralism").[18]

In a rough way, those laws that require the agent to forbear in order to avoid harm (or, rarely, to convey a benefit) are traditional morals laws. They include both "moral" and "welfare paternalism."[19] Those that require the agent to perform some positive act either to avoid harm or convey a benefit we characterize as compulsory beneficence. While it is true, however, that such laws could be based on an attempt to compel a virtue other than beneficence (for example, obedience to parents or the Church), in contemporary Western law these are not significant.

Our list requires additional clarification. First, by "moral" harm or benefit we mean a consequence that affects a person's character or worth according to some ethical doctrine, without any substantial impact on his welfare in physical, psychological or material terms. There may be very few cases of *purely* moral harm or benefit. Second, by harm or benefit to "others" we mean to some specifically identifiable people other than the moral agent. By "to society as a whole" we mean that the claim is being made that some act or omission is an *intrinsic* evil whether particular individuals are harmed by it. Third, the terms "harms" or "benefits" involve important standard and baseline issues. Moral harm and benefit are relative to the objective or true moral interests, according to the appropriate theory, of the agent or those who are affected by his conduct. Similarly, welfare benefit or harm to the agent is relative to his true welfare interests whether he perceives them or not. Welfare benefits to others are also objective. [20] Harms and benefits are defined relative to the baseline of the individual's entitlements in the (given) background system of abstract rights. Finally, this list is not meant to exhaust all of the logical possibilities but has in view the policies or laws that are or have been important in our society. The list is prototypical in the sense that each purpose is a preliminary model or ideal type. It may be adapted or combined to fit particular empirical cases.

In principle, any law can qualify as "moralistic legislation" because any legally-relevant conduct can be characterized in moral terms. It all depends on how the relevant actors see things.[21] Furthermore, a law can be characterized in more than one way. Thus, a law forbidding shopkeepers from opening on a Sunday may have a moral or quasi-religious aspect (Sabbath observance) as well as an economic aspect (perhaps an increase in leisure time). Whether such a law is consid-

---

[17] A "moralized welfare benefit (harm)" is one for which a moral case or argument is being made.

[18] *See* JOEL FEINBERG, 4 THE MORAL LIMITS OF THE CRIMINAL LAW: HARMLESS WRONGDOING 8 (1988).

[19] *See* Gerald Dworkin, *Paternalism, in* THE STANFORD ENCYCLOPEDIA OF PHILOSOPHY (Edward N. Zalta ed., 2002). Available at http://plato.stanford.edu/archives/win2002/entries/paternalism.

[20] Objective does not mean the same for all people. What promotes a person's well-being depends on his personal and external circumstances.

[21] As Alan Hunt observes: "…'[T]he moral' dimension is not an intrinsic characteristic of the regulatory target, since there is no set of issues that are necessarily moral issues; rather the moral dimension is the result of the linkage posited between subject, object, knowledge, discourse, practices and their projected

ered a "blue law" or some form of economic legislation will depend on a judgment about its main purpose and, perhaps, the rhetoric surrounding advocacy of the law.

We now turn to the *weight* of the moral argument in the overall case for moralistic legislation. When conduct is viewed as enhancing the moral status of agents or as promoting a good society, is that sufficient justification for adopting the relevant moralistic legislation? The strong form of moral dirigisme accepts that the morality or rightness of an action or omission is *sufficient justification* to compel a person to take it or omit it. This strong version is perhaps the earliest form and was expressed by Socrates in Plato's *Republic*:

> ...[I]t's better for everyone to be ruled by what is divine and wise. Ideally he will have his own divine and wise element within himself, but failing that it will be imposed on him from outside so that as far as possible we may all be equal, and all friends, since we are all under the guidance of the same commander....It is clearly the aim...both of the law, which is the ally of all the inhabitants of the city, and of our own governance of our children. We don't allow them to be free until we have established a regime in them, as in a city. [22]

As philosophers in this tradition would later argue, man's natural end is to pursue virtue and the purpose of the state is to ensure that he does so.

A weaker form of moral dirigisme, favored by Thomas Aquinas, has a *prima facie* character. As a first approximation, the king ought, "by his laws and orders, punishments and rewards...restrain the men subject to him from wickedness and induce them to virtuous deeds."[23] This, however, is to be supplemented by prudential qualifications or limitations. Human law, according to Aquinas, "does not lay upon the multitude of imperfect men the burdens of those who are already virtuous."[24] Such considerations as the futility of a prohibition or its productiveness of other, perhaps more serious, wrongs are entirely appropriate and may override the *prima facie* rule. "[H]uman laws do not forbid all vices, from which the virtuous abstain, but only the more grievous vices, from which it is possible for the majority to abstain."[25]

A further development of the Thomistic form of moral dirigisme has been more recently advanced by Robert P. George in *Making Men Moral* in which he recognizes limitations based on the diversity of moral goods and the moral value of free choice, as well as the aforementioned prudential limitations. The State may "legitimately proscribe *only* the fairly small number of acts and practices that are

---

social consequences." ALAN HUNT, GOVERNING MORALS: A SOCIAL HISTORY OF MORAL REGULATION 7 (1999).
[22] PLATO, THE REPUBLIC 310-11 (G.R.F. Ferrari ed., Tom Griffith trans., 2000).
[23] ST. THOMAS AQUINAS, ON KINGSHIP 120 (Gerald B. Phelan trans,1949).
[24] 2 THOMAS AQUINAS, SUMMA THEOLOGICA 1018 (Fathers of the English Dominican Province trans., 1948) (1266-77).
[25] *Id.*

incompatible with *any* morally good life."[26] Despite the reduction of the domain of permissible prohibitions that this entails, George does not seem to appreciate the radical knowledge problems involved in adhering even to his limited form of moral dirigisme.[27]

II.   Conventional Arguments Against Moral Dirigime

It is convenient to classify some of the conventional arguments against moral dirigisme according to the degree to which they approximate the ethical knowledge problem we are seeking to describe. Those least connected with the knowledge problem are based on either the direct or opportunity costs of morals enforcement. For example, suppression of the trade in various drugs or in sexual activity is often associated with violence, black markets and disease. If the cost of these effects is very high, the legal enforcement of drug or sexual morality may be, on the whole, unacceptable.[28] Even if the direct cost of legal enforcement is low, the opportunity cost may be high. In those areas, for example, where the moral standard is too high or difficult for most people to meet,[29] limited enforcement resources may be more productively used in other areas where people are on the margin of appropriate behavior.[30] A related argument is that where the private or informal enforcement of moral norms can be accomplished relatively cheaply, the State should not intervene.[31]

A second group of arguments against moral dirigisme is based on the insufficiency of external acts without intention. These arguments are not to be confused with free-will arguments that we eschew here.[32] David Hume, for example, argued that what the agent directly approves of, in a moral sense, is the state of mind or desire to produce "natural [nonmoral or premoral] good" in himself or in those with whom he has commerce. The external actions per se or the beneficial consequences the actions tend to produce are simply "signs" of evidence of the internal state. This state alone has moral merit.[33] Furthermore, Immanuel Kant distinguishes between "duties of right" (justice) and the "duties of virtue." The former can be enforced by external sanctions because their purpose is simply to en-

---

[26] ROBERT P. GEORGE, MAKING MEN MORAL 40 (1993) (emphases added).

[27] We have more to say about George's form of moral dirigisme in section XIV, infra.

[28] *See* ROBERT P. GEORGE *The Concept of Public Morality in* THE CLASH OF ORTHODOXIES: LAW, RELIGION AND MORALITY IN CRISIS 107-08 (2001).

[29] *See* THOMAS AQUINAS, 2 SUMMA THEOLOGICA 1018 (Fathers of the English Dominican Province trans., 1948) (1266-77).

[30] Economists express this idea by saying that it may be optimal to spend little on punishment when the elasticity (responsiveness) of the activity to legal penalties is low. *See* Gary S. Becker, *Crime and Punishment: An Economic Approach in* ESSAYS IN THE ECONOMICS OF CRIME AND PUNISHMENT 23 (Gary S. Becker and William M. Landes eds., 1974).

[31] *See* Robert Cooter, *Normative Failure Theory of Law*, 82 CORNELL L. REV. 947, 971 (1997).

[32] *See generally,* THE OXFORD HANDBOOK OF FREE WILL (Robert Kane ed., 2002).

[33] "'Tis evident, that when we praise any actions, we regard only the motives that produc'd them, and consider the actions as signs or indications of certain principles in the mind and temper. The external performance has no merit. We must look within to find the moral quality. This we cannot do directly; and therefore fix our attention on actions, as on external signs. But these actions are still consider'd as signs; and the ultimate object of our praise and approbation is the motive, that produc'd them." DAVID HUME, A TREATISE OF HUMAN NATURE 307 (David Fate Norton & Mary J. Norton eds., 2000).

sure the external freedom of all. But the latter are concerned ultimately with a state of mind or the agent's adoption of certain moral rules. Critical to the duties of virtue is the agreement between, in Kant's terms, the *subjective* maxim (or principle) upon which the agent acts and the rational moral law.[34] The agent's subjective maxim, however, is always and only within his control. In neither Hume's general perspective nor Kant's perspective on virtue, then, can legal coercion of external acts make man or society moral.

The final class of arguments against moral dirigisme emanates from the set of views known as "moral pluralism." This class most closely approximates the ethical knowledge problem we are describing. Pluralism claims that among individuals and within a single individual there are conflicting moral and nonmoral values.[35] There are also conflicting ways to produce coherent choices or orderings among those values. None is inherently more reasonable than others. The relevant moral decisions are context-dependent. The context is often one of differing *interpretations* of primary (universal) values or of different *conceptions* of the good life.[36] Since there is no definitive resolution of these conflicts, enforcing or imposing any one value or set of values is arbitrary. This pluralistic argument differs from ours insofar as pluralism stresses the conflicts of values and differing interpretations of basic physiological and psychological "needs," while our view stresses the contingent factual issues or requirements in the application of values *even when the values themselves are not in conflict.*

PART TWO: THE THEORY

III.   Summary of the Theory

This section summarizes our theoretical framework by breaking it down into nine propositions or statements. This will make it easier for the reader to relate the various parts of the Article to each other and to evaluate the logical connections in the overall argument. As a summary, it is meant to be short and assertive rather than comprehensive and demonstrative.

---

[34] "Duties of virtue cannot be subject to external lawgiving simply because they have to do with an end which (or the having of which) is also a duty. No external lawgiving can bring about someone's setting an end for himself (because this is an internal act of the mind), although it may prescribe external actions that lead to an end without the subject making it his end." IMMANUEL KANT, THE METAPHYSICS OF MORALS 31 (Mary Gregor ed. & trans., Cambridge Univ. Press 1996) (1785).

[35] "Moral pluralism is the view that values, obligations, virtues, ideals, or fundamental moral principles are inherently diverse and cannot be reconciled into one harmonious scheme of morality....And values can be incompatible between cultures, between groups in the same culture, between persons, and even within the same person." Virginia Held, *Moral Pluralism, in* 2 THE ENCYCLOPEDIA OF ETHICS 1138 (Lawrence C. Becker & Charlotte B. Becker eds., 2d ed. 2001).

[36] "The primary concern of pluralism is with the relation on which these values [whose realization would make life good] stand in relation to each other; the identity of the values is of interest to pluralist, *qua* pluralists, only insofar as it is relevant to understanding their relations.... Pluralists may disagree with each other and agree with non-pluralists about the identity of the values that warrant our allegiance." JOHN KEKES, THE MORALITY OF PLURALISM 9 (1993).

The Problem of Moral Dirigisme 799

1. Moral choice is not among abstract principles, generic moral goods or virtues but among concrete actions at the margin. Thus, agents do not choose, for example, all instances of beneficence over all manifestations of honesty or vice versa, even when the moral language is one of absolutes.

2. To apply (instantiate) moral principles to (in) particular decisions requires factual knowledge about the state of the world in which the decisions are made, the actions of other individuals, and the interrelated decisions of the agent.

3. The knowledge is concrete, often transient, partial and imperfect. It is relevant to specific decisions at a particular time and place.

4. The knowledge is both deliberately acquired and acquired as a by-product of other useful activity. To the extent that agents have the desire to act morally, they will have the incentive to acquire relevant knowledge and to make use of knowledge already acquired.

5. This knowledge is very often, though not always, unverifiable by external parties or potential enforcers of morality.

6. Given the unverifiability of much of the relevant knowledge, if the State is to enforce morality it must do so with specific prohibitions (or positive commands) that are applicable regardless of (many of) the particular circumstances. This is because of the high enforcement costs associated with ascertaining "unverifiable" conditions.

7. Because of the relative insensitivity of moralistic legislation to "exceptions" based on particular circumstances, agents will have little incentive to discover morally-relevant particular knowledge or to utilize that which they already possess in making the decisions required by the law.

8. Hence, the decisions agents make, in areas covered by moralistic legislation, will not *actually* be moral (except by chance) because they will not take account of the relevant particular circumstances of time and place.

9. This "ethical knowledge problem" (or, from a policy perspective, barrier to effective moral dirigisme) exists across a wide variety of moral philosophies or frameworks. Thus, we suggest, it is a characteristic of ethical action *as such* and not simply of some particular conceptions of it.

IV.   A Theory of Ethical Decision Making

A.   The General Need for Local Knowledge in Moral Decision Making

As a species of pure decision making, moral action requires spatio-temporal knowledge reflecting the contextual nature of all decisions and actions. Any action aims at changing the future state of affairs relative to what it would be in the absence of the action. In a general sense, it aims at some consequence that will be affected by local circumstances. This is easily understood in the context of consequentialist ethics, but even applies in the case of deontological (duty-based) ethics. We shall see this further below. The general idea is that an action "exhibiting" a virtue or following a rule is affected by local circumstances insofar as these *define* or characterize the action. Honesty, for example, is dependent on the local meaning of words, the context of the communication, the expectations of the hearer, and so forth.[37]

The acquisition of relevant knowledge, however, does not necessarily imply the determinacy of moral decisions (although this may be the case in certain forms of utilitarianism). In the Thomistic analysis of rational, voluntary human action, for example, the choices agents make are not rigorously determined by the general or abstract goods that constitute human flourishing (or the "good" for man). The specific actions that ought to be undertaken are informed by the natural law in conjunction with the *knowledge* of the particular circumstances of time and place. But even here this is not a deductive exercise; the decision depends on the application of practical reason—a form of reasoning that does not yield necessary truths.[38] We shall have more to say on this below.

B.   Kinds of Knowledge

This section develops an analysis of different kinds of empirical knowledge relevant to (moral) decision making. Our ultimate purpose is to ascertain the degree to which this knowledge is verifiable by those who seek to act as external enforcers of moral norms. We develop briefly a theoretical account of dispersed or decentralized knowledge.[39]

---

[37] Steven Shavell argues that in contrast to legal rules a "moral[] rule cannot be too detailed and nuanced in character . . . A moral rule against lying [for example] that incorporated too many and too complicated categories of exception would be difficult for children to learn and might challenge the intellect of many . . . If the rule against lying did include numerous exceptions depending on circumstances, a person might have to stop and ponder whether or not to tell the truth; he would not, as often he must, instantly know the answer to his moral obligation." Steven Shavell, *Law versus Morality as Regulators of Conduct*, 4 AM. L. & ECON. REV. 227, 234–35 (2002). This view, putting aside ambiguities associated with the use of words like "too detailed," would be plausible if all morally relevant knowledge had to be acquired explicitly and held explicitly. But this is not true. *See* sec. VI-b, *infra*. Furthermore, it is prima facie implausible once we recognize that children learn the complex grammars of various languages at an extremely young age.
[38] *See* JOHN BOWLIN, CONTINGENCY AND FORTUNE IN AQUINAS'S ETHICS 58-60 (1999).
[39] *See* ALFRED SCHUTZ & THOMAS LUCKMAN, THE STRUCTURES OF THE LIFE-WORLD 304–18 (Richard M. Zaner & H. Tristam Engelhardt, Jr. trans., Northwestern Univ. Press 1973) (1953) (offering a phenomenological approach to the issue of decentralized social knowledge).

Knowledge in any complex society is decentralized in at least two senses. It can be *local*, that is, available only to individuals in a certain geographical location ("the man on the spot") or by virtue of their specific activity. It can also be *personal* in the sense that such knowledge is of the objective or subjective states of the acting individual. In moral action focused on beneficence, for example, the first is exemplified by knowledge of the material or psychological condition of a relative or co-worker. The second is exemplified by knowledge of one's own resources or motives.

Local or personal knowledge can be, in turn, held in two ways. The first is *explicitly* or as knowledge capable, at least in principle, of articulation in propositional form to one's self or to other agents. This articulation and communication is generally costly. On the other hand, the knowledge can be held *tacitly* insofar as it cannot be stated in propositional form and hence is not communicable to others in a direct way. Such knowledge is communicated, if at all, implicitly[40] through personal relationships.

In the case of local knowledge, an individual may have a "sense" of the external situation as when, for example, a benefactor knows that a poor friend has the psychological capacity or will to become self-supporting after a period of financial assistance. Alternatively, the agent may know explicitly that a potential recipient of charitable assistance is willing to undergo training to learn a marketable trade. In the case of personal knowledge, for example, an individual may simply *act* in accordance with a prudent concern for his own physical well-being. On the other hand, he may know explicitly what his mental health requires, including his need for relaxation and diversity of activities.

The means by which local and personal knowledge, whether tacit or explicit, is acquired can shed light on the problem of external ascertainability. This is because the typical means of acquisition are not available to the State as it attempts to determine (and then enforce) moral behavior. To see this, consider that morally relevant empirical knowledge is acquired in three ways. First, it may be deliberately acquired as the individual focuses on specific facts made relevant by general moral rules or aims. These rules or aims determine his framework of fact acquisition. Second, it may be undeliberately acquired as the byproduct of local social or economic interactions quite apart from any effort to behave morally. Finally, it may be undeliberately acquired but as the result of moral action. This would be a case of implicit or tacit learning of the appropriate factual circumstances in which

---

[40] Much applied knowledge and skills are of this type. Knowledge of how to ride a bicycle and swim are good examples. Simply handing a student the mathematical formulae for keeping balance on a bicycle or keeping afloat is ineffective in teaching the skill. *See* MICHAEL POLANYI, *The Logic of Tacit Inference, in* KNOWING AND BEING 144 (Marjorie Green ed., 1969). *See also* H.M. Collins, *What is Tacit Knowledge?, in* THE PRACTICE TURN IN CONTEMPORARY THEORY 107–19 (Theodore R. Schatzki, Karin Knorr Cetina & Eike von Savigny eds., 2001) (discussing this point in the context of the spread of knowledge in a scientific community).

a rule is to be applied.[41] All these means are *presumptively* unavailable to potential external morals enforcers.

Before concluding this section, it should be noted that there are circumstances in which decentralized knowledge may be ascertainable (either tacitly or explicitly) by external enforcers of morality. In general, this will be at a level fairly close to the individual decision makers themselves. For example, family members or friends may possess knowledge of an individual's character—his propensity to benefit, in the long run, from temporary financial assistance. Their knowledge may contain explicitly-held elements, but, more likely, they will have a general impression of him and his likely future. Commercial interactors may be in a good position to ascertain the reliability of individuals, their motives, their propensity for opportunistic dealing, and so forth. When local enforcers of morality have a great deal of relevant empirical knowledge, the case for external pressure or, perhaps, coercion is stronger.[42] To the extent that we are concerned with the knowledge issues alone, then there "should" be external enforcement when the knowledge of the enforcers is high and individual incentives to act morally are low. This is the extreme case when it is possible to "make" men moral.[43]

C. The Explicit Rules Heuristic

We agree with Gilbert Ryle that moral action is not a matter of "avowing maxims and then putting them into practice."[44] It is useful, nevertheless, artificially to construct the dichotomy between maxims, rules, principles, on the one hand, and their application in positive moral action, on the other. This is useful because it grants to the proponents of various forms of moral dirigisme the argument that there is a type of moral knowledge that a central authority can, in fact,

---

[41] We defer until later the question of whether rules, aims, or principles are held tacitly or explicitly. *See* section V-C, *infra*.

[42] Steven Shavell analyzes the factors that determine the optimal domains of morality and law in the enforcement of "moral" rules. In this analysis, the knowledge available to parties other than the moral agents themselves is viewed as one important factor. In some cases the knowledge available to the moral agent will be so superior to all others that, *ceteris paribus*, internal or self-enforcement of rules is optimal. In a second category of cases, external non-governmental enforcers will have sufficiently good knowledge relative to the State that they will be the primary enforcers of moral behavior. In a third category, moral agents and the external enforcers may have knowledge advantages relative to the law only in certain respects (e.g., the precise level of harm a broken promise engenders). Shavell, however, treats the knowledge issues as one among a number of factors, such as the size of the private gain and the social losses due to immoral behavior, that determine or ought to determine the relative advantages of enforcement methods. Our analysis, on the other hand, treats sufficient local and personal knowledge as a missing *necessary* condition for the appropriate legal enforcement of morals. *See* Shavell, *supra* note 37, at 238–40.

[43] Louis Kaplow and Steven Shavell argue that moral rules must be "sufficiently simple (in particular, not requiring information available only to the actor) that other members of society can do their part in enforcing the moral system." Kaplow and Shavell, *supra* note 16, at 12. It is unclear what degree of simplicity they have in mind. Nevertheless, the social (that is, nongovernmental) enforcers of morality are not society-at-large but those who are close to the moral agent—for example, spouses, relatives, friends, and coworkers. What is known to them need not be known to more distant others or to the State. So the social enforcement of moral rules and their complexity are not necessarily in conflict.

[44] GILBERT RYLE, THE CONCEPT OF MIND 46 (1949).

have.[45] This is *general* moral knowledge – the kind that transcends the particular concrete (non-moral, but morally-relevant) circumstances of time and place. Thus it is possible for central authorities to share the moral maxims, principles or rules of the agents but still not be able, concretely, to compel appropriate behavior.

D. Ideal Typical Constructions: Moral Types

To give form and definite content to the ethical knowledge problem, we use the method of ideal-typical constructs. This means we *model* moral agents as either consequentialists (mainly, utilitarians), Kantians, or natural-law agents, primarily, or as moral absolutists or moral ecologists, secondarily.[46] Such agents apply or embody their respective moral philosophy or framework to or in the concrete circumstances they face. Their decisions are a joint application of a certain theory and their perception of the facts the theory determines as relevant. As we have indicated above, for heuristic reasons, we shall assume that agents explicitly hold a moral philosophy, yet their knowledge of the facts may be either explicit or implicit.[47]

Suppose, however, that the moral know-how of the actual or real-world agents amounts to following and applying rules from different, and possibly inconsistent, ethical systems. Should we not examine the decentralized knowledge problem in the amalgamated moral "system" the individuals follow? In the absence of extensive survey or other sociological data describing this (or these) system(s) it is impossible to do so.[48] But it may also be unnecessary for the particular problem we wish to investigate. This is the problem of the need for decentralized knowledge in the application of moral rules. All we wish to demonstrate is that agents require knowledge, much of which is unavailable to others, to make what is, *by their standards*, appropriate moral decisions. These agents may sometimes or in some respects be Kantians or utilitarians, etc. If the unobservable knowledge requirement appears in *all* of these frameworks of moral action, we have made a strong presumptive case that real-world agents also face this requirement.

---

[45] Consequently, our purpose is heuristic and analytical, i.e., to structure an argument, rather than to make an empirical claim.

[46] The first-listed types of moral agents are primary in the sense that they refer to fundamental ethical philosophies. Those secondarily listed (moral absolutists and moral ecologists) are usually embedded in one of the fundamental philosophies, such as natural law theories or Kantianism.

[47] This modeling technique amounts to assuming a "reflective equilibrium," that is, the congruence of general principles with intuitive judgments about specific cases. *See Reflective Equilibrium, in* THE OXFORD COMPANION TO PHILOSOPHY 753 (Ted Honderich ed., 1995).

[48] "[W]e cannot extend our inquiry to cover all of the grounds on which men, even educated men, actually make decisions, or it will degenerate into a catalogue of superstitions." FRANK HYNEMAN KNIGHT, RISK, UNCERTAINTY, AND PROFIT 229 (1921). *See also* Max Weber, *Ideal Types, in* PHILOSOPHIES OF HISTORY: FROM ENLIGHTENMENT TO POSTMODERNITY 212 (Robert M. Burns & Hugh Rayment-Pickard eds., 2000)("[T]hose 'ideas' which govern the behavior of the population of a certain epoch i.e., which are concretely influential in determining their conduct, can, if a somewhat complicated construct is involved, be formulated precisely only in the form of an ideal type, since empirically it exists in the minds of an indefinite and constantly changing mass of individuals and assume in their minds the most multifarious nuances of form and content, clarity and meaning.")

804   Mario Rizzo   2005

E.   The Incentives to Acquire Knowledge

Table I below summarizes our discussion of the types of knowledge, their modes of being possessed and potentially communicated, and their manner of acquisition.[49] The Table has six cells, corresponding to the categories we have introduced. There are three columns and in each column there are two possibilities. In principle, any triplet consisting of one of the two characteristics in each column is possible.[50] Nevertheless, some combinations are more interesting and likely than others. We consider two.

TYPE OF KNOWLEDGE	MODE OF POSSESSION	MODE OF ACQUISITION
personal	tacit	undeliberate
local	explicit	deliberate

TABLE I

First, there is personal and local knowledge that is explicitly possessed (communicated) and deliberately acquired. To understand the nature of the agent's incentives in this case, we need simply to apply a form of the economic theory of search. People will acquire such knowledge by assigning (imagining) an expected value to a marginal unit of time devoted to search. This value is in part the result of an agent's conception of the importance of adhering to a certain moral rule or fulfilling a certain obligation. On the other hand, the agent will also experience costs by engaging in the search for relevant facts. These can be in the form of non-moral goods foregone or the foregone opportunity of attaining other moral goods due to contingent conflicts.

Second, there is personal and local knowledge that is tacitly possessed and not deliberately acquired. We suggest that even in this case agents have a broadly-conceived incentive to acquire it. While, by definition, they do not deliberately search for this kind of knowledge, they can be open to it in varying degrees. People have a tendency to notice or be alert to knowledge that is, in one way or another, useful to them.[51] The more important acting morally is to an individual, the more likely he is to notice those facts that are relevant to the implementation of moral rules, obligations or maxims. This form of alertness is likely to be embedded

---

[49] We are assuming that if knowledge is tacitly possessed, it must be tacitly communicated. And if explicitly possessed, it must be explicitly communicated.
[50] Thus, for example, knowledge may be local, tacitly possessed and potentially communicated, and deliberately acquired.

in certain types of actions in particular kinds of situations. It will be observed as the agents doing the "right thing" in concrete circumstances even if they cannot tell us how or why.[52] Nevertheless, it is true that some relevant knowledge in this category will be a *complete* byproduct of social and economic intercourse. From the narrow point of view of the agent's moral action, its acquisition will be pure luck.

It should be added that what we have said about acquiring relevant knowledge also applies, with the appropriate changes, to the *utilization* of already acquired knowledge. For example, agents will search for opportunities to utilize this knowledge in ways that minimize some combination, depending on their preferences, of moral and non-moral opportunity costs.

We are now in a position to draw several conclusions. First, the incentive deliberately to acquire and utilize morally relevant factual knowledge operates in tandem with the incentive to act morally. Second, this does not imply that the agents will acquire the socially optimal amount of relevant knowledge. This is, in part, due to less than optimal incentives to behave in accordance with the moral law even as the individual sees it.[53] However, this suboptimality is not important for our purposes. Third, what is important is (a) individuals have a greater incentive to acquire accurate relevant knowledge, without purpose of evasion or opportunism, when the problems are "their own" than when they are not and (b) individual agents are in a better position to acquire that knowledge than is the State. Insofar as individuals are the better gatherers of morally relevant knowledge than the State, as we argue, our thesis is supported.

F.   Interdependence in Ethical Decisions

The purpose of this section is to demonstrate that ethical decision making requires something more than taking dispersed, but objective, facts into consideration. It also requires the coordination of (1) the expectations of agents and patients and (2) the various ethical decisions in relation to each other.

The first form of coordination has been alluded to before. It requires mutual understanding with respect to the meaning of actions. Do individuals expect the agent to tell the literal truth about the pleasantness of the evening at the close of the dinner party? Or do they simply expect to hear some expressions of good will? Without common expectations, it is difficult, perhaps impossible, to determine what lying or truth-telling is in a specific context. There is also another, deeper form of mutual understanding. A benefactor may make a donation to a poor person with the expectation that the latter will use the money to become self-supporting. If the beneficiary shares this expectation and has a resolve to "get on

---

[51] Israel Kirzner argues that this is a postulate of the Austrian School of Economics. *See*, ISRAEL M. KIRZNER, *Entrepreneurial Discovery*, *in* THE DRIVING FORCE OF THE MARKET: ESSAYS IN AUSTRIAN ECONOMICS 17 (2000).

[52] *See* ARTHUR REBER, IMPLICIT LEARNING AND TACIT KNOWLEDGE 13–14 (1993) and FRIEDRICH A. HAYEK, *Rules, Perception and Intelligibility*, *in* STUDIES IN PHILOSOPHY, POLITICS AND ECONOMICS 45, 56 (1967).

[53] We mean optimal from the point of view of the rest of society. Others, for example, will want us to be more honest than we would be absent social pressure (or at least we hypothesize).

his feet" then the moral expectations of the parties are, in this sense, coordinated. The parties find it in their mutual interest to adjust their actions to ensure this kind of coordination.

The second form of coordination is the mutual adjustment of the agent's ethical decisions to each other.[54] Ethical decisions of the agent may conflict for purely contingent reasons.[55] To revert to our previous example, a dinner-party guest who had a bad time cannot be both truthful and kind to his host when it expected that he will tell him the literal truth about his evening. The moral agent can decide to be honest or kind, but not both. So a decision to lie must be understood in the context of a decision to be kind, or to be unkind in the context of honesty. The decisions are thus interdependent. Another related aspect of the mutual adjustment of ethical decisions involves tradeoffs in the pursuit of the good or, at a minimum, some basis for the resolution of contingent moral conflicts. In a consequentialist framework, there will inevitably be tradeoffs between honesty and beneficence in the maximization of pre-moral goodness. Each decision has an opportunity cost and the ultimate goal of the moral agent is to maximize the value of the consequences.[56] In a natural law or eudaimonistic framework, the moral agent must balance the satisfaction of various basic or primary goods.[57] Thus, for example, prudence will limit work satisfaction in pursuit of health. Again, the moral decisions of the actors must be understood in the context of other moral aims and decisions. In a Kantian deontological framework, the pursuit of one maxim is limited by the other maxims. So, for example, lying for the purpose of making the host feel good (or even to save a life) is impermissible. Beneficence must be pursued without violating the maxim of honesty. The failure to be beneficent must be understood in the context of the application of an ordinarily unrelated ethical rule.

PART THREE: CONFRONTING THE THEORY WITH CLASSICAL MORAL SYSTEMS

We now turn to the more detailed study of the classical moral systems with the central purpose of demonstrating the importance of local and personal knowledge requirements in the instantiation of moral action. We assume that each moral agent behaves in accordance with one of these frameworks or theories.

---

[54] We do not explore the question of the appropriate balance between moral and non-moral choices.

[55] Ethical decisions may also conflict because of inconsistent principles. This does not concern us here because our method of ideal typical constructs excludes this possibility.

[56] Robert Goodin makes the argument in terms of the moral agent's competing interests: "[T]he good involved in furthering one person's interests can come into conflict with other moral goods, and B's responsibility for protecting A's interests is therefore always susceptible to being overridden by B's other moral responsibilities. These may be responsibilities for B to protect the interests of some other person C. They may be responsibilities for B to protect interests of his own... Finally, these may be moral responsibilities connected with moral ideals rather than with anyone's interests.... Each individual will thus need to balance one set of responsibilities against others." ROBERT E. GOODIN, PROTECTING THE VULNERABLE: A REANALYSIS OF OUR SOCIAL RESPONSIBILITIES 118–19 (1985).

[57] We are putting to the side for the moment those variants of natural law that stress "moral absolutes." *See* sections XI, XII, XIII, *infra*. But even in these approaches not every rule is an absolute. *See* JOHN FINNIS, MORAL ABSOLUTES: TRADITION, REVISION, AND TRUTH 1 (1991) (Moral absolutes "though relatively few . . . are decisively important for conscience, conduct and civilization.").

Thus, individuals can be utilitarians, Kantians, or natural law adherents. For heuristic reasons it is convenient to assume that all individuals in a particular society adhere to the same ethical philosophy; they all make ethical decisions within the same theoretical framework. This enables us to separate the concrete knowledge problem from the problem of knowing the correct moral framework. So, even in a society where there is universal agreement at the level of ethical theory, there will still be a barrier to the central direction of moral action. If, however, we were to be more realistic, then we would have to admit that actual moral codes have elements of the various philosophies combined or that some agents may tend more toward one framework or another. Nevertheless, insofar as there are decentralized concrete knowledge problems in each of the ethical frameworks discussed, and these capture the essence of most actual moral codes, then, as we have previously said, for a hybrid framework, there is a strong presumption that it too will have such problems.

V.   Consequentialism and Utilitarianism

Every moral theory has two components: first, a view of what is good or valuable (i.e., a theory of the *good*); and, second, a view of how individuals and institutions should respond to the good (i.e., a theory of the *right*).[58] While consequentialist theories do not exhibit unanimity of thought regarding the nature of the good, they do command agreement regarding the appropriate response to the good. This response is to promote the good generally throughout society. To see more clearly what this implies, consider the following illustration. It is allowable, or more likely required, from a consequentialist perspective, that an individual lie if that is the only way to promote the good or designated value. The lie itself, or more generally, the dishonoring of the good by one's actions, is not of primary importance. If the contribution of a lie in producing the overall good is greater than the contribution to the good made by telling the truth, then the lie is a perfectly moral act. This is to be contrasted to the anti-consequentialist view that "at least some values call to be honoured whether or not they are thereby promoted . . . [A]ctions [should] exemplify a designated value, even if this makes for a lesser realization of the value overall."[59] .

Utilitarianism is the most highly developed of the modern consequentialist approaches to ethics. The literature is vast and the variations on the basic theme are considerable. Nevertheless, there are enough common themes and methods of analysis that interesting generalizations are possible. Utilitarianism specifies the good or designated value that our broad treatment of consequentialism leaves open. The "good" that utilitarians pursue is "utility"—variously defined as "pleasure," "happiness," "preference satisfaction." or more recently, as "welfare interests."[60] It is obligatory to choose that course of action that produces, or is expected

---

[58] Philip Pettit, *Consequentialism, in* A COMPANION TO ETHICS 230 (Peter Singer ed., 1991).
[59] *Id.* at 231.
[60] Robert Goodin, *Utility and the Good, in* A COMPANION TO ETHICS 242–44 (Peter Singer ed., 1991).

to produce, the greatest surplus of pleasure over pain or the greatest amount of preference satisfaction, and so forth, of all available alternatives.[61]

The utilitarian appears to be in the convenient, but ultimately untenable, position of comparing a myriad of different goals according to a single metric. The utilitarian philosopher need not decide which goods are worth pursuing; *he* need not have a specific theory of the good. It suffices that individuals have goals or desire certain experiences and goods, and that the "social good" consists of an aggregation of these for individuals. The main subject of controversy has been whether the pleasures, happiness, preference satisfactions, or welfare interests can be aggregated across individuals. The aggregation of individual utilities requires two kinds of knowledge that are important from our perspective. First, in order to calculate the hedonic or otherwise-cardinal utility for each individual, the utilitarian moral agent policy maker must know the individual's local and personal circumstances. Consider that providing a certain drug may yield more preference satisfaction to a given individual when there is an outbreak of influenza (local conditions) and when the individual is in poor health (personal conditions) than otherwise. So, if the measurement of individual utility is possible, it is, at best, a contextual enterprise or, as economists say, it is "state dependent."[62] A second kind of knowledge is necessary in order to trade these individual utilities against one another. We must know how characteristics of a potential beneficiary of an act affect his capacity to experience pleasure or satisfaction *relative to others*. Since we cannot really hope to know this, the analysis typically involves the acceptance of a "similarity postulate," that is, "the *assumption* that, once proper allowance has been made for the *empirically given* differences in taste, education, etc. between me and another person, then it is reasonable to assume that our basic psychological reactions to any given alternative will be otherwise much the same."[63] The function of the similarity postulate is to reduce, by assumption, the differences among persons in their capacity to enjoy to certain objectively measurable quantities, and thereby to evade the knowledge problem.

Practically speaking, the interpersonal comparison of utilities must be reduced to *intrapersonal* comparisons: How would I rank experiences if I were in the same objective conditions as another person? To do the job required, the comparing individual must be able to envision himself in a variety of objective local and personal circumstances (perhaps different from what he has ever experienced) and rank his hedonic states accordingly. Assuming the meaningfulness of such rankings of the projected hedonic states of other individuals, by a *given* individual, there is scant reason to suppose that there will be agreement across the different comparing-individuals about these rankings. If there are disagreements, there is nothing in utilitarian moral theory that can settle them. The "social utility maxi-

---

[61] *See Utilitarianism, in* THE OXFORD COMPANION TO PHILOSOPHY 890 (Ted Honderich ed., 1995).
[62] This is admitted by some utilitarians, even if it is not satisfactorily handled by them. *See, e.g.,* John Harsanyi, *Morality and the Theory of Rational Behavior, in* UTILITARIANISM AND BEYOND 50 (Amartya Sen and Bernard Williams eds., 1982).
[63] *Id.* (emphases added).

mum" achieved by utilitarian agents would be an aggregate comprised of inconsistent valuations.

Aside from these fundamental difficulties, a utilitarian would have, at the very least, to recognize that simply as a matter of application of the framework, moral calculations will be more accurate the better his access to local knowledge. "It is easier to know what people *nearby* need, and how best we can help... ."[64]

Jeremy Bentham, in his later work, perceived difficulties for the dirigiste program arising out of the limitations of local and personal knowledge. In *Deontology* he wrote:

> What is good for another cannot be estimated by the person intending to do the good, but by the person only to whom it is intended to be done. The purpose of another may be to increase my happiness, but of that happiness I alone am the keeper and the judge...Refrain, then, from doing good to any man against his will, or even without his consent... .[65]

To the extent that the benefactor cannot know the utility of the potential beneficiary, the act in question, in Bentham's eyes, is not truly beneficence:

> If the notion of serving a man not in the way in which he wishes to be served but in the way he ought to be served or in the way it is best for him to served be carried to a certain length, this is tyranny self-regarding affection, not an act of beneficence for the gratification of the sympathetic or social affection.[66]

In part because of the knowledge problems discussed above, some utilitarians advocate a form known as "rule-utilitarianism." Although it is a minority approach within the school, it is important for our purposes to consider it.[67] Rule-utilitarianism focuses on the rule or a cluster of rules as the unit of evaluation. Thus, "the rightness or wrongness of an action is to be judged by the goodness or badness of the consequences of a rule that everyone should perform the action in like circumstances."[68]

It may seem that the rule-variant substantially reduces the local and personal knowledge problems associated with the application of this philosophy. To the extent that the unit of evaluation is a rule, the agent will simply need confidence that the rule produces consequences that, over a wide variety of cases, are better, or at least as good as the other available rules. He need not know the con-

---

[64] *See* Goodin, *supra* note 63, at 246 (emphasis added).

[65] Cited in HENRY HAZLITT, THE FOUNDATIONS OF MORALITY 89 (1964).

[66] JEREMY BENTHAM, DEONTOLOGY; TOGETHER WITH A TABLE OF THE SPRINGS OF ACTION; AND THE ARTICLE ON UTILITARIANISM 279 (Amnon Goldworth ed., 1983).

[67] *See Utilitarianism, in* THE OXFORD COMPANION TO PHILOSOPHY 892 (Ted Honderich ed., 1995). ("[M]ost present-day utilitarians accept direct [or act-] consequentialism...").

[68] J.J.C. Smart, *An Outline of a Theory of Utilitarian Ethics, in* UTILITARIANISM FOR AND AGAINST 9 (J.J.C. Smart & Bernard Williams eds., 1973).

sequences of his particular act in its concrete context. Thus, it would seem, by its very nature, rule-utilitarianism circumvents the problem of knowing the particular circumstances of time and place. However, this would be largely true only if the set of rules were given to the utilitarian from outside the system. Then the only issue would be whether the circumstances contemplated by the rule are present in the particular case. If the circumstances are very broadly described in the rule, then the knowledge problem would be reduced correspondingly.[69]

The fundamental difficulty is that rule-utilitarianism is wedded to the utilitarian standard of goodness and its prime directive of right conduct—to "maximize utility." The rule-utilitarian, not being a rule fetishist, must be on the lookout for utility-enhancing exceptions or modifications to any given rule. These exceptions come from a finer parsing of the conditions set out in the original rule induced by greater knowledge of the consequences of following the rule under different circumstances. Since utilitarians are under an obligation to do their best, they must always seek greater knowledge and thus better and more particularistic rules. This means that even the rule-utilitarian is a better utilitarian, and hence better moral agent, the greater his knowledge of the particular circumstances of time and place.

As a consequence, if an agent breaks a rule created by the rule-utilitarian dirigiste, there is no simple way of knowing whether he has broken the rule because he does not have adequate incentives to be moral or because he has superior knowledge of what the moral course of action is. Indeed, a rule-utilitarian agent must be encouraged to explore other, possibly better rules for the type of situation in which he finds himself. This may involve a process of trial and error. In any event, all rules must be held tentatively until a more finely-parsed or particularistic rule can be discovered. Without access to the agent's knowledge, the dirigiste does not know whether to encourage or discourage rule breaking.

VI.   Natural Law

To some, it may appear that natural law theories of ethics are non-consequentialist, if not stridently anti-consequentialist, and therefore unlikely to require contingent local and personal knowledge for their application. This impression is fostered by misinterpretation of statements like those of Cicero: "True law is right reason, consonant with nature, spread through all people. It is constant and eternal... ."[70] Nevertheless, in the context of a long tradition, natural law "was not generally understood to be a fixed unalterable set of rules which could be simply applied to human conduct or society irrespective of the circumstances."[71] An important distinction was made between unalterable fundamental principles (the "primary principles") and their application at a particular place and time (the "sec-

---

[69] The more detailed or particularistic the circumstances, the more rule-utilitarianism begins to resemble act-utilitarianism.
[70] MARCUS TULLIUS CICERO, *On the Commonwealth, in* ON THE COMMONWEALTH AND ON THE LAWS 71 (James E.G. Zetzel ed., 1999).
[71] Stephen Buckle, *Natural Law, in* A COMPANION TO ETHICS 166 (Peter Singer ed., 1991).

ondary principles"). [72] More specifically, it would be quite wrong to classify natural-law ethics as non-consequentialist because consequences do matter, albeit a different set of consequences from that which concerns the utilitarian, for example.

Let us begin our analysis by dividing consideration of the natural law into the principles operative at the level of individual life and those operative at the level of society as a whole. These are clearly interrelated because society is obviously composed of individuals and, as we shall see, the individual needs the rest of society for his full development.

Each individual has a natural inclination toward "happiness," by which is meant the flourishing appropriate to himself as a rational creature. The "good" for man consists of some general goods like physical existence, wealth, health, and knowledge of the truth. These are objective goods and not the subjective goods of a utilitarian calculus of pleasure or want satisfaction. Despite their "objectivity" they are not independent of context. A good is good *for* someone in particular spatio-temporal circumstances. It is both "agent-relative" and dependent on local and contingent facts. It advances the *truly* good for an individual, but that is not determinable apart from the context of who he is and where he is.[73] Thus, the contents of the good are not determined by natural law with deductive certainty, but by practical reason in the uncertain circumstances in which the individual finds himself. "But in matters of action, truth or practical rectitude is not the same for all, as to matters of detail, but only as to the same general principles... ."[74] There is no algorithm by which we can combine particular circumstances with the natural law framework and get a single, determinate implication for action. Accordingly, the individual naturally tends toward his own good, but is not compelled by the natural law to pursue, say, health in any particular way at any given time. In fact, he may not pursue it at all in a certain situation where other goods, like the pursuit of truth, may be in conflict. (Consider the great philosopher who compromises his physical health to complete his magnum opus.) The pursuit of moral goods is a "holistic" process whereby conflicts are resolved and balance is established.[75] Practical deliberation, as we have seen, depends on an intelligent grasp of particulars which cannot be superseded by rules.[76] Accordingly, the pursuit of goods requires attention to consequences and necessarily to local knowledge.

Individual flourishing is comprised not only of certain goods, but also of the pursuit or practice of virtues. Virtues, like goods, are contextual. What does a virtue mean in a concrete situation? How is it to be *traded off* against other conflicting virtues? The return of property to its owner, though generically virtuous, is not an instantiation of moral behavior when it is known that this property, say

---

[72] *Id.* at 165-66.

[73] *See* Douglas Rasmussen, *Human Flourishing and the Appeal to Human Nature*, 16 Soc. Phil. and Pol'y 3; 6-10 (1999).

[74] Thomas Aquinas, 2 Summa Theologica 1011 (Fathers of the English Dominican Province trans., 1948) (1266-77).

[75] BOWLIN, *supra* note 38, at 73.

[76] *See* Sarah Broadie, Ethics With Aristotle 203 (1991).

guns, will be used for an evil purpose.[77] The single-minded pursuit of beneficence to a blind, homeless stranger may not be moral under certain circumstances. The requirements for companionship and financial assistance of an injured friend may in a world of scarce time and other resources conflict with helping a stranger.[78] The resolution of these problems depends on the particular circumstances of time and place, including the personal resources, talents and projects of the moral agent.

At the level of the relevant community, the natural law affirms the idea of a social good. Consider for example the oft-quoted statement of Thomas Aquinas that law is "an ordinance of reason for the common good."[79] But what can this "common good" be in light of the contextual nature of the good for individuals? Is there a common moral good for man on earth? There are admittedly two major traditions that deal with this issue. The older one by far is represented by such thinkers as Aristotle and Aquinas. For each of them, in different senses, the common good consists in the right actions of each and all. Accordingly, the state has an obligation to provide the appropriate institutions for the encouragement or promotion of the good and of virtue. It is "for the sake of good actions, and not for the sake of social life, that political associations must be considered to exist."[80] Thus there is a substantive, objective common good for all men by virtue of their generic humanity. Aristotle was clear that coercion could be used to promote this good, while Aquinas in principle agreed, but was worried about the prudence of doing so in particular circumstances.

There is a second strain of thought, more modern and we believe, consistent with the contextual nature of human flourishing. This perspective reached a high level of development in the work of the seventeenth-century philosopher, Samuel Pufendorf. On his view, the precepts of natural law "have a clear utility" directed toward the establishment of "sociality" or what we would today call social cooperation.[81] Human beings are not capable of developing their talents, potential, abilities, or of practicing virtue in isolation. They need both positive assistance and protection from malefactors that association with other human beings affords. But Pufendorf was aware that "the Good can only be defined intersubjectively, as the beneficial outcome of Actions affecting different Persons in society. The needs and wants of those persons change [as we consider the different persons] and therefore the morality that seeks to maximize the Good must alter itself in line with those changes."[82] Therefore, this assistance and protection must have the quality of a *means* to the different ends legitimately pursued by various individuals. We all have a common interest in sociality. In an important sense therefore, Aristotle was wrong to say that the polis exists "for the sake of good actions,

---

[77] *See, e.g.,* BOWLIN, *supra* note 38, at 63; W.T. JONES, THE MEDIEVAL MIND 262 (1969) (2 A HISTORY OF WESTERN PHILOSOPHY).

[78] BOWLIN, *supra* note 38, at 71.

[79] AQUINAS, *supra* note 77, at 995.

[80] ARISTOTLE, THE POLITICS OF ARISTOTLE 120 (Ernest Barker ed. and trans., 1946).

[81] SAMUEL PUFENDORF, ON THE DUTY OF MAN AND CITIZEN 36 (Michael Silverthorne trans., 1991) (1673).

[82] T.J. HOCHSTRASSER, NATURAL LAW THEORIES IN THE EARLY ENLIGHTENMENT 100 (2000).

and *not* for the sake of social life."[83] *There is a deep epistemic problem in determining good actions for others, whereas sociality (social cooperation) is a means of obviating that problem.*

The common good cannot be advanced directly, but through the means or structure provided by society, each individual can more effectively attain his material and moral ends. F. Uberwerg outlined the logic of Pufendorf's argument:

> His interpretation of natural law is essentially defined in relation to Grotius and Hobbes, in that he takes over from the former the principle of sociability, from the latter the interests of the individual, and unites them in the principle that sociability lies in the interest of every individual.[84]

Accordingly, Pufendorf makes the connection between natural law and the promotion of sociality quite strong:

> [T]he fundamental natural law is: everyman ought to do as much as he can to cultivate and preserve sociality. Since he who wills the end wills also the means which are indispensable to achieving that end, it follows that all that necessarily and normally makes for sociality is understood to be prescribed by natural law. All that disturbs or violates sociality is understood as forbidden.[85]

This perspective reconciles the contextual and empirical nature of human flourishing and the existence of a common good for all men by virtue of their humanity. Viewed negatively, it sets "limits on the ways in which each of us could properly pursue our own personal aims."[86] Viewed positively or negatively, it demonstrates that natural law ethics grapples with the knowledge problem in ethical behavior not by prescribing concrete ends, but at least in the Pufendorf variant, by specifying the means by which individuals can potentially fulfill their natural, generic ends more effectively. The actual *solution* to the knowledge problem, as in the determination of concrete ends in the particular circumstances of time and place, is found by the individual who is in possession of local knowledge and is able to cooperate with others for the most effective utilization of that knowledge.

VII. Kantianism

Kant's system of ethics and the modern moral theories which emanate from it are generally understood to be non-consequentialist. In this view, Kantian ethics is a duty-based philosophy and as such may be thought to be without a knowledge problem. For example, if moral agents have a duty simply to tell the truth regardless of the consequences, then the particular circumstances of time and place in which this duty is satisfied would seem to have no role in ethical decision

---

[83] ARISTOTLE, *supra* note 80, at 120 (emphasis added).
[84] Cited in HOCHSTRASSER, *supra* note 85, at 98.
[85] PUFENDORF, *supra* note 84, at 35-36.
[86] THE CAMBRIDGE DICTIONARY OF PHILOSOPHY 520 (Robert Audi ed., 1995)(entry for "natural law").

making.[87] Yet if moral agents' actions are supposed to "honor" a certain value (e.g., truth telling) then they must know whether in a specific context the value is indeed exhibited by the action.[88] Does the "truth" mean something different when your hosts ask you if you enjoyed the dinner party and take your answer at an appropriate discount from what it means when the police want to know where the escaped convicts are? Suppose that we have duty to be loyal or to be humble. Which acts exhibit these traits? Is the broad or narrow social context relevant? The meaning of an action is dependent on contingent facts and our local and personal knowledge of them.

Moreover, any action is *defined* by its actual or intended consequences. "To act is to make a difference to the course of events, and what the act is, is determined by what difference."[89] For example, telling a lie is not immoral because the actor "dislikes" the consequences of deceiving another person. For Kant, it is because lying violates the moral law in the form of the respect we owe all human beings as autonomous ends-in-themselves. A person is treated as mere means to someone else's ends when he is deceived. Accordingly, the consequences of deception are essential to what the particular act of lying *is*. An individual would not be used against his will were he not actually deceived. Analogous arguments could also be made for the importance of consequences in such other violations of morality as theft and murder. So in Kant's ethics consequences are not ignored. It is simply that while consequences are important to the definition of our acts, they are not the *ground* of our moral obligation. "We must not judge the action to be right or wrong according as we like or dislike the consequences. . . . A good man aims at consequences *because* of the law; he does not obey the law merely because of the consequences."[90]

A more comprehensive understanding of the issue can be derived from analyzing our two primary duties according to Kant: the duty to pursue (1) our own perfection and (2) the happiness of others (beneficence).[91] In order to fulfill these general duties, that is to determine which specific actions are in accord with them, we must have personal and local knowledge. In the first case, the individual must know what his "faculties," "capacities," or "natural dispositions" are. These may not be fully known to him, but he is likely to know many things no one else does. This is knowledge of a personal kind. Furthermore, "*capacities* [are] for furthering ends set forth by reason."[92] In other words, these are capacities for action and hence for the attainment of ends, of consequences. Since these consequences are in particular and individual lives, knowledge of local circumstances is critical.

---

[87] *See, e.g.,* Immanuel Kant, *On a Supposed Right to Lie from Philanthropy, in* PRACTICAL PHILOSOPHY 611-15 (Mary J. Gregor ed. & trans., 1996).
[88] Philip Pettit, *Consequentialism, in* A COMPANION TO ETHICS 233 (Peter Singer ed., 1991).
[89] R.M. HARE, SORTING OUT ETHICS 164 (1997).
[90] H.J. PATON, THE CATEGORICAL IMPERATIVE: A STUDY IN KANT'S MORAL PHILOSOPHY 76 (1948) (emphasis added).
[91] BRUCE AUNE, KANT'S THEORY OF MORALS 174 (1979).
[92] KANT, *supra* note 34, at 154.

In the second case, to promote the happiness of another person we must have particular knowledge of him at a given time and place so that we can determine what actually is in his interest. A benefactor must try to understand the concept of happiness held by the potential beneficiary and to "benefit [the latter] only in accordance with *his* concepts of happiness."[93] Although this is so, "it is open to me to refuse them many things that *they* think will make them happy but that I do not."[94] True beneficence makes an effort to enter into the other person's world—his plans, his projects—not simply to give him whatever he thinks he needs or simply wants, but actually to benefit him in his circumstances.

The ethical knowledge problem in Kantianism runs even more deeply. Kant struggled with the resolution of conflicts of moral obligations or in his terms, with conflicting grounds of moral obligation. In his later work he argued that the solution was to be found in limiting "one maxim of duty by another."[95] The duty, for example, to help mankind in general is limited by the similar duty to one's parents. Nevertheless, it is not a simple matter that any duty to one's parents takes precedence over any and all duties to mankind. How exactly such a decision is to be made (and in a world of scarce resources, it must be made) is beyond the scope of analysis here. It is, however, sufficient to say two things. First, the tradeoff between these duties is not perfectly determined by Kantian moral *theory*. Unlike the simpler forms of utilitarianism, there is no algorithm we can apply which in the presence of perfect local and personal knowledge will yield a determinate outcome. Second, although theory will not determine the result perfectly, concrete circumstances will be relevant to the resolution of ethical conflicts and hence will partly determine the outcome. This is the case even on what Mary Gregor calls a "rigoristic" interpretation of Kant's idea that agents have a certain moral "latitude" in fulfilling imperfect duties; in this interpretation latitude is not a license for a genuinely arbitrary decision.[96] "The latitude would be present only because moral philosophy cannot admit sufficient *empirical knowledge of the situation in which we find ourselves* and hence cannot know how much we are capable of doing toward the end and whether an opposing ground of obligation is present which overrides the necessity of acting toward the end here and now or limits the extent to which we must act."[97] Thus, the use of means efficiently adapted to the local situation to fulfill an obligation to help our parents may enable us also to satisfy the otherwise-conflicting obligation to assist a beggar in the street. Furthermore, we are permitted to weigh the grounds of different duties when they do conflict. Surely weighing will make use of the factual details of each situation like the degree of seriousness of the needs of our parents and the strangers, as well as the status relationship between those in need and us. While the seriousness of the one does not relieve us altogether of the obligation to satisfy the other, it may relieve us of that obligation in the existing particular circumstances of time and place.

---

[93] *Id.* at 203.
[94] *Id.* at 151.
[95] MARY J. GREGOR, LAWS OF FREEDOM 104 (1963).
[96] *Id.* at 95-122.
[97] *Id.* at 104-05 (emphasis added).

Even moral decisions that appear "arbitrary" are more correctly viewed as dependent on subjective or personal circumstances. While we do not have a "duty" to pursue our own happiness, we do have a moral right to do so and this will reduce the resources we make available to fulfill our duty to help others. According to Gregor, Kant argues, for example, "that we have no obligation to sacrifice 'our true needs', those satisfactions which are essential to our happiness, in order to promote the well-being of others . . . [a]nd as for what constitutes our true needs, this depends largely on 'our own way of feeling.'"[98]

Simply put, what we are saying is that while Kantian ethics is duty-based, the application of its general maxims requires the particular knowledge of time and place.

PART FOUR: APPLICATIONS TO SPECIFIC LEGISLATION

The previous Part demonstrated the importance of personal and local knowledge in the broad application of classical moral systems. It showed that to be moral or virtuous in any of the major frameworks requires an adjustment of general principles to this knowledge. Sometimes the knowledge is of nonmoral facts, both about oneself and the outside world, while other times, it consists of moral facts, that is, facts about the rest of one's moral behavior.[99] This Part deals with the legal manifestation of dirigiste ideas, some of which can be seen to emanate from aspects of the classical systems. This should not be surprising because the systems formalize and extend features of positive (everyday) morality. We ought not to expect, however, an explicit grounding of the laws in any particular philosophy, although some laws may fit more naturally into one framework rather than another. Without claiming to be exhaustive, we evaluate moral arguments in favor of these laws. Our primary aim is to show that these general proscriptions or prescriptions will not be justified generally, or across the board, by a moral system.[100] The practical implication of this is that, even if the laws are strictly obeyed, they will not make people moral. The commands of the law, understandably, must ignore critical pieces of personal and local knowledge insofar as they do not permit the individual to adjust his behavior to these facts.

VIII.   The Exceptional Virtue of Justice

Before we proceed to examples of moralistic legislation, it is important to eliminate a possible source of misunderstanding. Our thesis is that the State will not be successful in attaining certain kinds of moral goals by compulsion. We have not argued that all laws that have as their purpose the advancement of *any* moral goals will fail to achieve them. Our list of the types of imposed moral ends that

---

[98] *Id.* at 105.

[99] As we have seen, the knowledge individuals have of these circumstances may be explicit or tacit and deliberately or not deliberately acquired. See Section -V-b, *supra.*

[100] This is consistent with the point made by David Richards: "Where public attitudes about morality are, in fact, demonstrably not justified by underlying moral principles, laws expressing such attitudes are morally arbitrary... ." *See* DAVID A.J. RICHARDS, SEX, DRUGS, DEATH, AND THE LAW: AN ESSAY ON HUMAN RIGHTS AND OVERCRIMINALIZATION 96 (1982).

constitute moral dirigisme excludes, most notably, "justice." In its restricted Smithian-Humean sense:

> "[t]he most sacred laws of justice . . . are the laws which guard the life and person of our neighbour; the next are those which guard his property and possessions; and the last of all are those which guard what are called his personal rights, or what is due to him from the promises of others."[101]

Adam Smith calls this "commutative justice" to distinguish it from more encompassing ideas of justice that include, for example, individual or collective beneficence. An important distinction between justice and beneficence is rooted in the ancient idea that the former is a moral duty of perfect obligation while the latter is a moral duty of imperfect obligation. On the basis of some very general principles, the duties deriving from justice are relatively determinate in time, place, person, and manner of implementation. Therefore, the law can enforce these obligations in a relatively cost-effective and definite manner. On the other hand, duties of beneficence, whether individual or collective, are contingent on "so many particulars to be considered in our own circumstances and abilities, and the state of mankind and the world, that we cannot but be in some uncertainty" as to their appropriate determination.[102] The imperfect obligation of beneficence is, for Smith, dependent "on circumstances that are usually too complex for codification."[103]

While Smith refers to the perfect obligations of justice as rules that are "precise," and "accurate," these descriptions may cause some confusion.[104] A better characterization would be to say, as Hume does, that justice consists of "general rules."[105] Generality means that its commands are invariant across a wide range of particular circumstances.[106] For example, in this view and in the traditional common law, the relevant legal description of the circumstances involving a breach of contractual obligation does not include, by and large, the character of the parties, the nature of the goods exchanged, or the price at which they are exchanged. Furthermore, the return of property is demanded by justice even if the owner is a "miser, or a seditious bigot . . . ."[107] Therefore, justice suppresses many facts relating to the particular circumstances of time and place. Compared to beneficence, it is less sensitive to local and personal circumstances.

The second important characteristic of justice is that it is rule-like. Its requirements are predictable given knowledge of the relatively few facts—and their objective character—that relevantly describe the situation at issue. This implies, among other things, that external parties can know what the requirements of jus-

---

[101] ADAM SMITH, THE THEORY OF MORAL SENTIMENTS 163 (Edwin G. West ed., 1976) (1759).

[102] RICHARD PRICE, A REVIEW OF THE PRINCIPAL QUESTIONS IN MORALS 121 (1948) (1787).

[103] ATHOL FITZGIBBONS, ADAM SMITH'S SYSTEM OF LIBERTY, WEALTH, AND VIRTUE: THE MORAL AND POLITCAL FOUNDATIONS OF *THE WEALTH OF NATIONS* 112 (1995).

[104] ADAM SMITH, THE THEORY OF MORAL SENTIMENTS 289-90 (Edwin G. West ed., 1976) (1759).

[105] DAVID HUME, A TREATISE OF HUMAN NATURE 341(David Fate Norton and Mary J. Norton eds., 2000) (1740).

[106] *Id.*

[107] *Id* at 319.

tice are in particular circumstances. Thus, it is possible to impose them on agents at reasonable cost and, most importantly, to do so in a way that reflects the moral requirements of justice.

For Hume, Smith, and us, a society or an individual can be "made" just in this restricted sense without encountering significant epistemic problems in the process. External enforcers can know what is just and unjust behavior on the part of individuals. They can also know, in a general sense, what legal rules and institutions will reflect moral rules of just interpersonal interaction.

While the fundamental difference between the set of moral aims included in our dirigiste list and those that constitute justice lies in their degree of sensitivity to personal and local circumstances, use of general terms like "morality," "moral purposes," and "virtues" may obfuscate this difference. However, our analysis shows that the application of justice is epistemically more economical than is the instantiation of most other moral goods, attributes, or virtues. Justice provides a set of relatively stable expectations that constitute a framework in which agents can pursue, if they choose, the more epistemically-demanding virtues. In the sections that follow, we discuss laws that attempt directly to compel agents to engage in more morally praiseworthy behavior beyond simple justice.

IX.   Illustrations of Moral Dirigisme

We divide our examples of moralistic legislation into two categories: (1) laws that prohibit individual or group behavior that is considered immoral and (2) laws that compel some individuals to aid others for reasons that are largely moral in nature. The first are largely traditional "morals offenses" or "morals laws" while the latter comprise what we call "compulsory beneficence."

A.   Traditional Morals Laws: An Introduction

Traditional morals laws seek to punish immoral character traits and immoral conduct that produce "harm" in a very broad sense of the word. The harms alleged are, and have been historically, quite diverse. While distinct, they are not mutually exclusive because more than one harm can be associated with a specific trait or behavior. There are at least five:

1. Intrinsic Purely Moral Harm to the Agent. This, unlike those that follow, is not, properly speaking, a consequence of a trait or behavior but part of its characterization.[108] Vagrancy, in the sense of not having "a settled home but drift[ing] from one place to another, normally having no regular means of support,"[109] is an example of a crime that has come close to one with intrinsic purely moral harm. While it is usually associated with disorderliness, it is likely that, in itself, "disorderli-

---

[108] *See* Markus Dirk Dubber, *Morals Offenses, in* THE OXFORD COMPANION TO AMERICAN LAW 567 (Kermit L. Hall ed., 2002).
[109] *See* "Vagrancy" *in* THE OXFORD COMPANION TO LAW 1270 (David M. Walker ed., 1980).

The Problem of Moral Dirigisme 819

ness" is little more than an expression of disapproval for unconventional behavior or traits.[110] The law seeks to raise the moral character of those exhibiting these traits.

2. The Purely Moral Harm of Bad Example. This is a negative externality corresponding to the above intrinsic moral harm. In other words, a behavior (or trait) of some individuals, characterized as immoral, may have the effect of leading others to similar behavior. This is because the behavior has an attractive aspect that others can see and by which they may be tempted. Public drunkenness, street solicitation by prostitutes, and open homosexuality are examples of behavior criminalized, in part, because of this harm.

3. Moral Nuisance. This is the offense taken by those who believe others are engaging in immoral behavior.[111] Typically, at least since the early eighteenth century, the law has emphasized the enforcement of laws against "public vice," that is, to immoralities committed in public view.[112] Obviously, public vice is more likely to produce offense than immoral acts committed in private. When the acts are committed in public they constitute "offense to others."[113] Examples of behavior or traits prohibited on this basis are "lewd and disorderly behavior" and violations of the Sabbath, including Sunday drinking and shopping. These are also instances of poor moral example. Sometimes the acts are offensive simply by virtue of their publicness, like public sexual intercourse between a married couple or public defecation. When the acts are committed only in private they are "free-floating," purely moral evils.[114] An example is consensual homosexual acts among adults in private.

4. Ulterior Harms. These are secondary effects of primary conduct that even those who do not believe the latter is immoral would find offensive or harmful. The secondary effects are typically actions that would be prohibited in themselves. An example is operating a house of prostitution that is closely associated with unsanitary conditions, noise, and even rape. Laws treating prostitution as a private or public nuisance especially make use of this connection with secondary harms.

---

[110] We have more to say about vagrancy below.

[111] This has been pointed out by Markus Dubber: "Morals offenses are 'offenses against public sensibilities.' They offend and annoy; they are moral nuisances. And as nuisances, the argument goes, they need to be abated not only to prevent offense to the public, but also to ensure the survival of the moral community." Dubber, *supra* note 112 at 568 (Kermit L. Hall ed., 2002).

[112] *See generally,* ALAN HUNT, GOVERNING MORALS: A SOCIAL HISTORY OF MORAL REGULATION 34-41 (1999).

[113] For a detailed examination *see* JOEL FEINBERG, 2 THE MORAL LIMITS OF THE CRIMINAL LAW: OFFENSE TO OTHERS (1985).

[114] *See* JOEL FEINBERG, 4 THE MORAL LIMITS OF THE CRIMINAL LAW: HARMLESS WRONGDOING 8 (1988).

820　Mario Rizzo　　　　　　　　　　　　　　　　　　2005

5.　Breach of Duty Harms. This refers to those violations of specific duties or status obligations that are associated with primary immorality. An example is a drunken parent who spends his money on alcohol and does not support his children.

While each of these harms are used to buttress the case for prohibiting immoral behavior, only the first two and free-floating moral nuisances can be classified as self-regarding in Mill's framework. Ulterior and breach of duty harms are clearly other-regarding because they go beyond the zone of the justified expression of individuality so critical to Mill's idea of freedom.[115] Thus the arguments in favor of traditional morals laws frequently go beyond the prohibition of self-regarding behavior and, to that extent, the laws are not *purely* morals laws.

1.　Vagrancy

Vagrancy ordinances, now largely viewed as unconstitutionally vague,[116] are instructive as a form of morals legislation that, at its core, attacks certain character traits. Vagrancy is a manifestation of idleness. Consider some of the defining characteristics of vagrancy described by the voided Jacksonville, Florida ordinance. Vagrants are deemed to be:

> persons wandering or strolling around from place to place without any lawful purpose or object, habitual loafers, disorderly persons, persons neglecting all lawful business . . . persons able to work but habitually living upon the earnings of wives or minor children . . . .[117]

In Millian terms this is self-regarding behavior, although it may be associated, in some cases, with behavior that is other-regarding. The moral vice exhibited by vagrancy, in the above quotation, is the perceived failure to embody "respectable" values, to be a productive member of society, and to fulfill the traditional roles of father or husband. It has formed the core of the moralization of the poor and the distinction between industrious and idle poor.[118] Nevertheless, the moral quality of the acts or omissions comprising vagrancy is dependent on the particular circumstances in which the agent finds himself. A person may be habitually "wandering or strolling" because he is an insomniac trying to get tired or because he is looking at the stars and thinking deep thoughts. A man who lives upon the earnings of his wife may be a pillar of the community who has a rich wife. A person who neglects his business and spends his time where alcohol is served may be a member of a country club.[119]

---

[115] The case of "offense" is not entirely straightforward. Clearly, some offenses (sexual intercourse in public) are other-regarding according to Mill, while others (public practice of one's religion) are not. *See* the general discussion in JOEL FEINBERG, 1 MORAL LIMITS OF THE CRIMINAL LAW: OFFENSE TO OTHERS 25-49 (1985).

[116] Papachristou v. City of Jacksonville, 405 U.S. 156 (1972).

[117] Jacksonville Ordinance Code 26-57, *cited in* Papachristou, 405 U.S. at 156 n.1.

[118] *See* ALAN HUNT, GOVERNING MORALS: A SOCIAL HISTORY OF MORAL Regulation 62; 64 (1999).

[119] *See Papachristou*, 405 U.S. at 164 for the above observations and a very clear exposition of the contextual nature of idleness.

The neglect of particular circumstances is especially evident in the conception of the "habitual loafer." This is a person who "idles...[his] time away, typically by aimless wandering or loitering."[120] Now what should he being doing instead? Presumably, he should be working or engaging in serious tasks such as shopping, transporting children to school, doing the laundry or perhaps reading the classics of world literature. A virtuous person may do all or some of these things some of the time, but he need not. The ancient Greeks had a word for people who just walked about without a destination, talking: *peripatētikói* (peripetetics).[121] These were members of Aristotle's school of philosophy who roamed about discussing things. Today there are doubtless individuals who "loaf" because they are troubled, confused, or trying, however imperfectly, to work out their problems of character. None of this is necessarily or presumptively inconsistent with a virtuous life. Whether it is or not depends on the context (local circumstances) and the meaning of the action (personal circumstances).

The case for vagrancy laws, however, has historically gone beyond the character traits discussed above to include possible moral nuisances. The association of idleness with vice[122] means that anti-vagrancy is also anti-gambling, prostitution, drunkenness, lewdness—all of which may manifest themselves in public and give offense to many people. In the limiting case of vagrancy as a pure catchall, its morality is completely derivative of the morality of these other forms of behavior. Furthermore, many of these behaviors produce ulterior harms such as theft, rape, or unsanitary conditions. It is sometimes argued that vagrancy laws provide flexibility[123] such that the police can nip nascent ulterior harms in the bud.[124] All of these associations make an overall evaluation of vagrancy laws difficult since it is not clear which behavior is being targeted.

Vagrancy, however, as an independent ground of morals legislation, rather than as a mechanism for a preemptive strike against conventional crimes or as a catch-all for other morals offenses, disregards morally-relevant circumstances of time and place. As we have seen, character traits are virtuous or vicious only in a specific context.[125]

---

[120] *See* NEW OXFORD AMERICAN DICTIONARY 999 (Elisabeth J. Jewell and Frank Abate eds., 2001).

[121] *See* THE OXFORD DICTIONARY OF ETYMOLOGY 669 (C.T. Onions ed., 1966).

[122] *See* ALAN HUNT, GOVERNING MORALS: A SOCIAL HISTORY OF MORAL REGULATION 62 (1999).

[123] Or "arbitrariness": *See Papachristou*, 405 U.S. at 171 ("the scheme [of vagrancy ordinances] permits and encourages an arbitrary and discriminatory enforcement of the law.").

[124] "A presumption that people who might walk or loaf or loiter or stroll or frequent houses where liquor is sold, or who are supported by their wives or who look suspicious to the police are to become future criminals is too precarious for a rule of law." *Papachristou*, 405 U.S. at 171.

[125] Historically, especially from the fourteenth through seventeenth centuries, but also to some degree into the nineteenth century, vagrancy legislation served social and economic functions, such as preventing the poor from migrating to other areas or attempting to control wages by preventing labor from shopping around. In this respect, vagrancy laws might be viewed only partly as morals legislation, but mainly as legislation designed to alter economic conditions. *See* Arthur H. Sherry, *Vagrants, Rogues and Vagabonds – Old Concepts in Need of Revision*, 48 CAL. L. REV. 557, 560-61 (1960).

2. Prostitution

The criminalization of prostitution has been directed toward the correction of a "public vice" or in the service of public morality rather than as an attempt to prevent illicit sexual relations per se. In other words, the State is interested in "bawdy houses," "houses of ill repute," "street walkers," etc. because of the publicness of these and because of the effect they might have on public morals.[126] Prostitution in its various public manifestations was viewed as a public (or sometimes private) nuisance. The negative impact on public morals, rather than any tangible ulterior harms, constitutes the core of the offense. Prostitutes and houses of prostitution were "disorderly." In practice, this meant of number of things including the corruption of public morals, destruction of female innocence, and upsetting established male-female status roles.[127] Therefore, the attempt to prohibit prostitution has been an endeavor, not so much to make individual men moral, but to make society moral; that is, to ensure the moral atmosphere of public life.[128]

If *public* morality is to be real rather than simply an illusion or façade, it must be (1) reducible to the moral behavior of individuals and (2) directed to the attainment of the least bad or second-best outcome in view of individual preferences as they really are, not as they should be. Laws related to the prohibition of prostitution tend to be broadly applied to sexual behavior of a commercial, or simply public, nature. They ignore the specific circumstances of time and place relevant to the likely alternative behaviors in the presence of such legal proscriptions. The even worse moral offenses likely to be committed in the presence of effective prohibition of prostitution are the center of attention in the writings of Augustine and Thomas Aquinas.

Both Augustine and Aquinas believed that prostitution should be legally tolerated.[129] Their argument is not fundamentally based on the direct enforcement costs of prohibition, although they may be considerable. They believed that prostitution produced certain social goods or advantages in a world of imperfect men. For example, both married and unmarried men would be less likely to have sexual intercourse with the wives of other men or with virgins who were marriageable. The existence of prostitutes reduces the evil and social harm that lust might otherwise produce. In an imperfect world, the common good is sometimes furthered

---

[126] This hypothesis has empirical support. In nineteenth-century America, stress was placed on a bad reputation alone, irrespective of any criminal act, in convicting people of various disorderly offenses. *See, e.g.*, WILLIAM NOVAK, THE PEOPLE'S WELFARE 157-171 (1996). Support can also be found by analysis of the Societies for the Reformation of Manners [SRM] in England in the late and early eighteenth centuries which, through a large system of informers, were alert to immoral behavior that took place in "public" spaces. In general, the "SRM were decidedly less interested in individual or personal immorality; their target was public vice, their goal community virtue and orderliness." *See* ALAN HUNT, GOVERNING MORALS: A SOCIAL HISTORY OF MORAL REGULATION 39 (1999).

[127] *See* WILLIAM NOVAK, THE PEOPLE'S WELFARE 164-67 (1996); ALAN HUNT, GOVERNING MORALS: A SOCIAL HISTORY OF MORAL REGULATION 134 (1999).

[128] *See* section on moral ecology, *infra*.

[129] *See* RICHARDS, *supra* note 100, at 89-90.

The Problem of Moral Dirigisme   823

if evil is not prohibited.[130] From the perspective of human law, men are not made *more* virtuous if prostitution is prohibited. In fact, they are likely to be made *less* virtuous and that, in an important sense, the common morality of the community would deteriorate. *Given* the imperfection of men in regard to the vice of lust, prostitution may be the least bad social outlet. Obviously, however, the actual consequences for the morality of individuals of the legal toleration of prostitution depend on their particular internal circumstances (such as the ability to withstand lustful urges) and external circumstances (such as their opportunities for sexual contact).

The above arguments do not deal, however, with the individual or private morality of prostitution. Immanuel Kant, for example, condemned prostitution in uncompromising terms.[131] Nevertheless, the reasons proffered for this moral conclusion implicitly hinge on contingent facts about the agent's internal and external circumstances, as well as facts about social meaning. If we put to one side Kant's expressions of revulsion against human sexuality per se,[132] we can begin to sort out the relevant factual assumptions in his arguments against commercialized sexual services.

The fundamental ethical premise underlying Kant's position is his Formula for the Dignity of Persons: "Act so that you treat humanity, whether in your own person or in that of any other, always as a end and never as a means only."[133] This is closely related to Kant's view of personhood, specifically, of the moral personality.[134] If we grant Kant's premise that it is *always* wrong to treat others or ourselves as a means only, we can conclude that prostitution is a violation of the moral law if either or both buyer and seller treat each other as means only. This conclusion depends on two general premises, one empirical and the other ethical, as pointed out by David Richards. Paraphrasing Richards, we can summarize the argument in this way:

1.   Prostitution is the sale or alienation of the body, that is, both parties treat the body as a means to income or pleasure without complete commitment.

---

[130] Aquinas formulated a general principle in this respect: "[I]t sometimes happens that the greatest harm comes to a community if an evil is prevented, and so positive law sometimes permits something as an exception lest the community suffer greater disadvantage, not because it is just that the thing permitted be done." THOMAS AQUINAS, ON EVIL 402 (Richard Regan trans., Brian Davies ed., 2003) (1275 – 1280).

[131] *See* IMMANUEL KANT, LECTURES ON ETHICS 157 (Peter Heath and J. B. Schneewind eds., Peter Heath trans., 1997) ("Human beings have no right . . . to hand themselves over for profit, as things for another's use in satisfying the sexual impulse; for in that case their humanity is in danger of being used by anyone as a thing, an instrument for the satisfaction of inclination . . . . Nothing is more vile than to take money for yielding to another so that his inclination may be satisfied and to let one's own person out for hire.").

[132] *Id.* at 377-79.

[133] *See* IMMANUEL KANT, GROUNDWORK OF THE METAPHYSIC OF MORALS 96 (H.J. Paton trans.,1964).

[134] *See* RICHARDS, *supra* note 104, at 109 (1982); *see generally,* ROGER J. SULLIVAN, IMMANUEL KANT'S MORAL THEORY 193-211 (1989).

2.   The alienation of the body alienates the moral personality.[135]

Thus, Kant concludes, since alienation of the moral personality is always wrong, prostitution is always wrong.

However, both of these premises are prima facie incorrect. First, prostitution is generally the sale of sexual *services*. It is no more slavery than any other transaction of labor. Second, the moral personality, in Kant's theory, lies in our ability to choose our own ends in accordance with reason. This ability is not compromised by prostitution unless it is an "irrational" choice. That conclusion would either be question begging or it would be a matter of prudential judgment. In either case, Kant's claim of the universal or intrinsic immorality of prostitution must fail. Prostitution would be immoral, then, only if engaged in imprudently; that is, if the parties leave themselves open to a significant risk of disease or if there will be fatherless children who do not receive proper care, and so forth. These factors rest on the particular circumstances of time and place.[136]

3.   Health Paternalism

Our definition of moral dirigisme includes laws that prohibit individuals from engaging in actions detrimental to their own health. The moralization of health is not of recent origin; it can be traced both to the classical and early Christian philosophers.[137] Temperance, in the sense of moderation in the use of food, alcohol and in the enjoyment of sex is one of the cardinal moral virtues.[138] The current *Catechism of the Catholic Church* views the "reasonable" maintenance of health as a moral obligation.[139]

Historically, the move to sanction legally the "abuse" of various sources of pleasure, particularly alcohol, sexual relations, and drugs, usually occurs when the abuse is associated with the commission of ordinary crimes as well as with the behavior of classes deemed not respectable.[140] To a certain extent, cigarette smoking modifies the pattern. Here the ulterior harms are largely the effects of secondhand smoke and the increased burdens on public healthcare budgets. Nevertheless, the core moral offense in all of these cases is the individual's harm to himself.

---

[135] This is not equivalent to Richards's "The person and the body are the same." RICHARDS, *supra* note 104, at 109. Strictly speaking, his more expansive premise is not required for the conclusion.

[136] Kant explicitly, but mistakenly, rejects this view. *See* IMMANUEL KANT, LECTURES ON ETHICS 157 (Peter Heath and J.B. Schneewind eds., Peter Heath trans., 1997).

[137] *See* Diana Fritz Cates, *The Virtue of Temperance, in* THE ETHICS OF AQUINAS 321 (Stephen J. Pope ed., 2002).

[138] *See* CATECHISM OF THE CATHOLIC CHURCH 495-6 (2nd ed., 1997). ("Four virtues play a pivotal role and accordingly are called 'cardinal'; all the others are grouped around them. They are prudence, justice, fortitude, and temperance.").

[139] *Id.* at 610. ("Life and physical health are precious gifts entrusted to us by God. We must take reasonable care of them, taking into account the needs of others and the common good.").

[140] *See,* generally, David T. Courtwright, *Morality, Religion and Drug Use, in* MORALITY AND HEALTH 237-42 (Allan M. Brandt & Paul Rosin eds., 1997).

And the core argument is that individuals should not be allowed recklessly to injure themselves.[141]

The key moral terms are "excess" and "abuse." These can be defined only relative to a normative standard. In Aquinas, for example, one very important part of the standard is preservation of the individual and the species.[142] Simply promoting the longest possible physical life, however, would be an inappropriate standard. In the broad Aristotelian-Thomist tradition, all moral virtues have the function of moderating the enjoyment of basic goods such as health, wealth, honor, justice, intellectual ability, pleasure, and intellectual and artistic pursuits.[143] Ultimately, this is necessary so that the individual can have a balanced and satisfying life through the enjoyment of an appropriate amount of these goods.[144] This amount, determined by prudence, is at the "mean" *relative to the individual*, between excess and deficiency.[145] Excess may impose burdens directly, such as a drunken hangover, but also indirectly in terms of the other basic goods lost to the individual, such as the intellectual activity he cannot pursue while drunk or hungover. These determinations are highly individual and relative to individual talents, tolerance for alcohol, and other particular internal or external circumstances.[146]

Health paternalism as manifested in legislation, on the other hand, takes a one-size-fits-all approach. It seeks to impose an external, not individually-tailored, standard by which excess or abuse can be ascertained. This is often necessitated by cost of enforcement or the limited-knowledge constraints inherent in legislation. Nevertheless, this characteristic means that paternalistic legislation cannot make men moral.

---

[141] Thus, in a sense "victimless crimes" have victims. *See* Andrew Karman, *Victimless Crime, in* THE OXFORD COMPANION TO AMERICAN LAW 818 (Kermit L. Hall ed., 2002). ("The contention that wagering, commercialized sex, and drug taking are victimless can provoke a number of distinct policy responses... [One] interventionist response arose from...[the] motivation – that members of a compassionate society are indeed 'their brother's keepers.' This paternalistic outlook argues that nonparticipants should not stand idly by as self-destructive adults engage in reckless risk-taking, but should try to save them from destroying themselves.").

[142] *See* THOMAS AQUINAS, 3 SUMMA THEOLOGICA, 1763 (Fathers of the English Dominican Province trans., 1948) (1266-77).

[143] *See* ARISTOTLE, ON RHETORIC: A THEORY OF CIVIC DISCOURSE 64 (George A. Kennedy trans., 1991).

[144] Thus the moral virtues and the appropriate enjoyment of goods are two sides of the same coin. *See* DOUGLAS DEN UYL, THE VIRTUE OF PRUDENCE 206-08 (1991).

[145] *See* ARISTOTLE, THE ETHICS OF ARISTOTLE: THE NICOMACHEAN ETHICS 101-02 (J.A.K. Thomson trans., revised by Hugh Tredennick, 1976). ("I call the mean in relation to the thing whatever is equidistant from the extremes, which is one and the same for everybody; but I call mean in relation to us that which is neither excessive nor deficient, and this is not one and the same for all. ...So virtue is a purposive disposition, lying in a mean that is relative to us and determined by a rational principle, and by that which a prudent man would use to determine it.")

[146] This does not mean that the decision of the individual is "subjective" in the sense of an arbitrary decision. *See* YVES SIMON, THE DEFINITION OF MORAL VIRTUE 106 (Vukan Kuic, ed., 1986). ("The mean has to be relative to us, because it is we and nobody else who have to decide what to do in a given situation. ... It is we who have to decide, but that does not make our decision unqualifiedly subjective. For if we have practical wisdom [prudence], we shall determine what is to be done, and do it, on the basis of a rational principle and *objectively with regard to the circumstances.*" (emphasis added)).

826 Mario Rizzo   2005

The vast and rapidly increasing legal restrictions on smoking[147] do not leave any room for the view that cigarette smoking, in moderation, might have benefits of some kind that offset its risks and harms to the individual's health. It may seem reasonable to infer from legislative and standard medical attitudes that the moral optimum with respect to smoking is zero. There seems to be no recognition that health is not an absolute moral value. Recall, however, the Aristotelian view that the good life is one that is comprised of many generic goods and moral virtues. While at a purely abstract level all of the goods and virtues are compatible with each other, this is not necessarily the case when the individual instantiates these in the context of his life.[148]

There is evidence that cigarette smoking has distinct psychological and cognitive benefits relative to a no-smoking baseline.[149] These are not to be confused with the "benefits" of avoiding nicotine withdrawal by continuing to smoke. The cognitive benefits include "increased concentration, recall, selective attention, productivity, as well as speed, reaction time, and vigilance. Furthermore, it has been demonstrated that smoking diminishes stress, aggressive responses, and reactions to auditory annoyances."[150] How valuable these benefits are to the prudent individual depends on the internal and external circumstances of his life: for example, his talents, interests, and practical constraints.[151] The instantiation of the basic generic goods and virtues in a person's life arises out of a process of matching these to, or situating them in, his circumstances. Thus, an individual may find that smoking increases his concentration and thereby enhances the excellence of his writing or art. Similarly, increased concentration and vigilance due to smoking may enhance prudence which in turn modulates an individual's fear, thus enhancing the attainment of courage. In these situations, the individual is trading off some greater probability of health and long life against an increase in other goods or virtues.[152] Note, however, that this is a tradeoff at the margin. He is not giving up the pursuit of health altogether for the sake of one good or virtue. All the generic goods are compatible in some degree but there is no universally correct degree.[153]

---

[147] *See, e.g.,* Lawrence Gostin, *The Legal Regulation of Smoking (and Smokers): Public Health of Secular Morality?, in* MORALITY AND HEALTH 331 (Allan M. Brandt & Paul Rosin eds., 1997).

[148] DEN UYL, *supra* note 148, at 168 (1991).

[149] *See* J.R. Hughes, *Distinguishing Withdrawal Relief and Direct Effects of Smoking, in* 104 PSYCHOPHARMACOLOGY 409 (1991).

[150] Raquel R. Scheitrum & Emmanuel Akillas, *Effects of Personality Style, Anxiety, and Depression on Reported Reasons for Smoking, in* .7 J. OF APPLIED BIOBEHAVIORAL RESEARCH 57 (2002) (citations omitted).

[151] Den Uyl calls this the individual's "nexus." *See* DEN UYL, supra note 148, at 170 (1991). ("A nexus . . . is that set of habits, endowments, circumstances, talents, interests, histories, beliefs, and the like which *descriptively* characterize an individual and which he brings to a new situation.").

[152] In the admittedly special case of a man making sacrifices for the sake of good friends or country, Aristotle says, "For he [the man of good character] would rather have intense pleasure for a short time than quiet pleasure for a long time: rather live finely [morally] for one year than indifferently for many; rather do one great and glorious deed than many petty ones." *See* ARISTOTLE, *supra* note 145, at 302-03.

[153] Additional individuating circumstances may include the age at which one starts smoking (most smoking-related diseases take years to develop), the presence of diseases like depression and schizophrenia (the symptoms of which may be alleviated by smoking), and, more controversially, the number of cigarettes smoked per day. The problem of any single standard was amusingly presented in a rather dated

The Problem of Moral Dirigisme   827

4.   Hate or Bias Crimes

There have been many attempts at justification of bias crime laws, including the claim that bias crimes spread fear throughout a specific community. From here the inference is made that they have a greater negative impact on society as a whole than the same crime committed without bias. Nevertheless, two persistent and related moral rationales for the increased punishment associated with such crimes are first, the greater blameworthiness of the perpetrators and second, the need to send a message to the public about the inherent evil of discriminatory *motivation*, quite apart from the harm of underlying criminal acts.[154] Thus, the *incremental* punishment is for an attitude, a state of mind or even a character trait deemed immoral. Bias crimes single out "bias" as opposed to "greed, power, lust, spite, desire to dominate and pure sadism" as worse reasons for the requisite criminal intent in the underlying behavior.[155] This class of motives is being punished because of its greater immorality. In effect then, bias crime legislation embodies a certain formal hierarchy of moral values. The hierarchy is purely "formal" because it is independent of context, that is, the particular circumstances of time and place. It is hard to conceive, however, of any plausible hierarchy in which bias, independent of context, is *always* worse than greed, power, etc. as a motivation for crime.

5.   Sodomy Laws and *Lawrence v. Texas*

In *Lawrence v. Texas*,[156] the U.S. Supreme Court struck down all state sodomy laws as a violation of the liberty interest of individuals protected by the Due Process Clause of the Fourteenth Amendment to the Constitution. The Court struck down a Texas statute that applied only to homosexuals as well as, in overruling *Bowers v. Hardwick*,[157] a Georgia statute that applied to both homosexuals

---

story by the moral philosopher Yves Simon. *See* SIMON, *supra* note 146, at 129. The following is taken from a lecture given at the University of Chicago in the fall quarter, 1957:

> I read recently in Time magazine, in the "Religion" section, how some theologians hold that as long as you do not smoke three packs of cigarettes a day, there is no sin involved. I find that absolutely ludicrous. It is true that, if you consume three packs a day, you may face a problem not only of health and temperance but also of justice in the use of wealth. ... But what I do not understand is how anyone can even pretend to deal with such a contingent matter by offering a specific, uniform, quantitative advice to millions of readers. How much a person smokes depends [or should depend] on an infinite variety of circumstances. Thus if you have an examination next week, and if smoking helps you to concentrate, or at least keeps you awake, exceeding your usual quota may even be a matter of justice toward your parents who paid for your tuition and expect you to do your best in school. Again, it is not that there are no objective standards of temperance, or courage, or justice; it is only that there is no single standard for all.

[154] JAMES B. JACOBS & KIMBERLY POTTER, HATE CRIMES: CRIMINAL LAW & IDENTITY POLITICS 79–81, 90 (1998).

[155] *Id.* at 80. Criminal law requires that acts be accompanied by an appropriate state of mind (criminal intent); hate or bias crime legislation goes to the motives or rationale underlying the intent. In other words, the criminal *intends* to kill a black person *because* he hates black people and not, for example, because the person betrayed his confidence. Bias crime legislation does not change the underlying definition of a crime.

[156] 539 U.S. 558 (2003).

[157] 478 U.S. 186 (1986).

and heterosexuals. Obviously, this decision is first and foremost a statement and interpretation of Constitutional law. However, we consider it from a moral perspective. Underlying the decision is an appreciation of the idea that moral goods cannot be defined primarily by physical behavior. In criticizing *Bowers*, the Court said:

> To say that the issue in *Bowers* was simply the right to engage in certain sexual conduct demeans the claim the individual put forward, just as it would demean a married couple were it to be said that marriage is simply about the right to have sexual intercourse.[158]

For human beings, sexual behavior has meaning: "When sexuality finds overt expression in intimate conduct with another person, the conduct can be but one element in a personal bond that is more enduring."[159] The precise content of this meaning varies with the particular circumstances of time and place. The State, however, is not entitled to supply this meaning.[160] The laws in *Bowers* and in *Lawrence* "purport to do no more than prohibit a particular sexual act."[161] In effect, and insofar as these are *morals* laws, however, the State is supplying a moral meaning equivalent to the least valuable form that persons engaged in such behavior might intend, such as casual sex with strangers or sex with a prostitute.[162] All of a type of behavior is characterized by a particular least-good instantiation. This is a perversion of the use of time and place considerations in the determination of the moral character of an action.

On the other hand, in an effort to reconcile the Court's decision with *Einsenstadt v. Baird*,[163] which protects the privacy of unmarried heterosexual sex, some proponents of upholding the Texas law used the "inverse" of the least-good argument. The amicus brief filed by the Family Research Council, for example, argued:

> Physically similar sexual acts [that is, sodomy] between married persons are constitutionally protected. Physically similar acts between unmarried persons of different sexes occur within relations

---

[158] *Lawrence*, 539 U.S. at 567.

[159] *Id.*

[160] *Id.*

[161] *Id.* For example, the Georgia statute read: "A person commits the offense of sodomy when he or she performs or submits to any sexual act involving the sex organs of one person and the mouth or anus of another." GA. CODE ANN. § 16-6-2 (1984). The Texas statute defined deviate sexual intercourse as "(A) any contact between any part of the genitals of one person and the mouth or anus of another person; or (B) the penetration of the genitals or the anus of another person with an object." TEX. PENAL CODE § 21.01 (1) (2002).

[162] *See* Stephen Macedo, *Against the Old Sexual Morality and of the New Natural Law*, in NATURAL LAW, LIBERALISM, AND MORALITY 27, 35 (Robert P. George ed., 1996). Here, Macedo is criticizing an argument by John Finnis, but the criticism is more generally applicable. *See infra* note 169.

[163] 405 U.S. 438 (1972).

which Texas may wish to encourage, either as valuable in themselves, *or because they could mature into marriage, or both*.[164]

Thus, heterosexual sodomy is to be (or can be) judged by its "best" instantiation, that which leads to marriage, while homosexual sodomy is to be judged by its "worst" instantiation, that which is promiscuous or masturbatory.[165] The Council is implicitly conceding that sexual behavior is to be judged by its deeper meaning. There is no way to ascertain meaning except by reference to the local and personal knowledge (intentions) of the agents. The statutes, however, completely abstract from meaning or context. They seek to moralize physical behavior when, however, moral acts are acts of meaning.[166]

B. Compulsory Beneficence Laws: An Introduction

Duties of beneficence are duties to enhance the well-being of one or more persons whose current condition is the result of something other than the wrongful actions of the potential benefactor. Therefore, we do not distinguish cases in which people are living lives of "average" well-being with the potential of improvement, or who have had a low level of well-being due to a birth defect or a slow acting disease acquired later in life from those in which people have been subject to a sudden misfortune requiring urgent assistance (as in most Good Samaritan legislation). A duty to convey a benefit or prevent harm caused by nature or other human beings is, in our framework, a duty of beneficence.[167] The baseline for beneficence is a person's current position or likely future position where there is no violation of any other duty (that is, other than the putative duty of beneficence) by the potential benefactor to that person.[168]

The following two sections discuss the Americans with Disabilities Act and the Good Samaritan Principle as examples of compulsory beneficence.

---

[164] *See* Brief Amicus Curiae for the Family Research Council and Focus on the Family at 3, Lawrence v. Texas, 539 U.S. 558 (2003) (emphasis added). The prior sentence elaborates this idea: "The critical difference . . . is not the raw physical behavior but the relationships: same-sex deviate acts can never occur within marriage, during an engagement to marry, during a courtship prior to engagement, or within any relationship that could ever lead to marriage." *Id.* at 3. .

[165] *See* John Finnis, *Is Natural Law Theory Compatible With Limited Government?*, *in* NATURAL LAW, LIBERALISM, AND MORALITY 1, 15 (Robert P. George ed., 1996). The argument is unambiguous: "So [homosexuals'] genital acts together cannot do what they may hope and imagine . . . Reality is known in judgment, not in emotion, and in reality, whatever the generous hopes and dreams with which some same-sex partners may surround their genital sexual acts, these acts cannot express or do more than is expressed or done if two strangers engage in such activity to give each other pleasure, or a prostitute gives pleasure to a client in return for money, or (say) a man masturbates to give himself a fantasy of more human relationships after a grueling day on the assembly line." *Id.*

[166] The outlawing of physical acts per se would make sense from the standpoint of the individual's own morality if they were always and everywhere immoral. *But see* Part Five, *infra*.

[167] For a discussion of the duty to prevent harm as distinct from the duty to confer a benefit, see Liam Murphy, *Beneficence, Law and Liberty: The Case of Required Rescue*, GEO L.J. 605, 627-30 (2002).

[168] This is also the criterion for the absence of a duty to rescue as proposed by Lord Macaulay. THOMAS BABINGTON MACAULAY, *Notes on the Indian Penal Code*, *in* MISCELLANEOUS WORKS OF LORD MACAULAY 253-54 (Lady Trevelyan ed., 1880).

1.   Americans with Disabilities Act

The Americans with Disabilities Act of 1990 (ADA) prohibits discrimination against "qualified individual[s] with disabilities."[169] The Act covers both applicants for positions and current employees. It includes both physical and mental impairments that substantially limit major life activities such as seeing, hearing, speaking, walking, learning, performing manual tasks, and so forth, in fairly open-ended fashion. Employers must "reasonably" accommodate these disabilities before determining whether the person is qualified for the job at issue. Thus, if a person confined to a wheel chair could perform the job of receptionist just as well as those without a walking disability if an inexpensive ramp were built to allow access to the office, then he would be considered qualified under the Act.

There are two major rationales for the ADA, each of which has important moralistic aspects. The first is the idea that the ADA is part of welfare reform and the second is that it is an anti-discrimination law for the disabled.

a)   The ADA as Welfare Reform Legislation

As welfare reform, the central idea is that the ADA is a less expensive method of conveying benefits to the disabled than traditional welfare legislation. This was certainly the way the legislation was sold to President George H.W. Bush and to Republicans in general. From an economic perspective, the burden of redistribution can be reduced by increased production on the part of the disabled. In other words, the cost of the traditional transfer seems to be the foregone opportunity of this production. But the foregone opportunity to society as a whole is the *net* marginal product of the worker – net of the accommodation costs. As long as some disabled persons become employed because of the Act and stop receiving transfer payments, they are reducing the cost of their "welfare" by their net marginal product. Whether this is a significant savings depends on the number of people going off transfer payments. Nevertheless, there are other less obvious costs aside from the direct costs of accommodation. We discuss them in the next section.

The possible cost-reducing aspect of the ADA should not blind us to the ultimate fact that it was promoted as a less costly form of *welfare*, that is, of providing benefits to those in need. In our framework, this is still compulsory beneficence legislation.

b)   Reducing Patterns of Subordination and Discrimination

Another moralistic rationale for the Act is as an extension of anti-discrimination legislation for the disabled. In effect, this means helping the disabled to live more fulfilling lives, with more options and possibilities to be productive. The ADA may also have the consequence of changing attitudes toward the disabled, for example, in increasing the level of respect shown to them. The current state of affairs, according to some who hold this view, consists of a pattern of subordination and discrimination that may, to a certain unknown extent, be self-

---

[169] 42 U.S.C. §§ 12101, 12111 (1990).

The Problem of Moral Dirigisme   831

reinforcing. The disabled are viewed as unproductive, and by internalizing this view, they tend to perform less well than they are actually able. Employers simply take this level of productivity as given. Furthermore, even aside from self-reinforcing factors, a "rational discrimination" against the disabled, that is, one based on their true, lower productivity, still traps them in a framework of subordination. Employers have, it is claimed, a moral obligation to weaken this social framework or pattern.[170]

The elimination or reduction of the pattern of subordination may be viewed as a moral obligation of beneficence.[171] "We" have an obligation to make life better for the disabled. The "we" are not so much employers but consumers, owners of other factors of production (including workers, who supply their labor), and owners of capital upon whom the costs of nondiscrimination fall.[172] The law compels them, in effect, to forfeit a certain part of their potential income, or in the

---

[170] This is the thrust of Samuel Bagenstos's view: "[T]he well-entrenched prohibition of rational discrimination [in racial and other areas] is best justified as resting on the notion that employers who have a choice between participating in a subordinating system and working (at reasonable cost) against such a system have a *moral obligation* to respond in a way that reduces subordination. [Disability] accommodation rests on the same notion." Samuel Bagenstos, *"Rational Discrimination," Accommodation and the Politics of (Disability) Civil Rights,* 89 VA. L. REV. 825, 838 (2003) (emphasis added). And, again, "[a]lthough antidiscrimination law is plainly moralistic, its moralism inheres not in an effort to punish individuals who act on bad thoughts, but on the large-scale project of eliminating subordination and segregation and of enforcing a principle of equal membership in society." *Id.* at 839.

[171] There is a technical point about whether the obligation is one of beneficence or of justice. Mark Kelman argues that the reasonable accommodation requirement of the ADA is not a strong "entitlement" but a "colorable 'claim' on social resources that competes with a variety of other claims on such resources." *See* Mark Kelman, *Market Discrimination and Groups,* 53 STAN. L. REV. 833, 834 (2001). It is a distributive claim because, in effect, the baseline in a market setting is the *net* marginal value contribution that workers make in the context of their employment. It is fair to judge all potential employees by the same standard. *Id.* at 835, 837. This is consistent with our analysis.
For an opposing point of view, that the obligation is one of justice, see, Bagenstos, *supra* note 174 at 862. ("For if a distribution reflecting intentional discrimination is unjust and hence an improper baseline for determining whether redistribution has occurred, why can we not say the same thing about a distribution reflecting the creation of institutions inaccessible to people with disabilities (i.e., one reflecting the lack of accommodation)? By this account accommodation requirements (like antidiscrimination requirements) simply restore a just distribution; they do not 'redistribute.'").

[172] The ADA requires that, for the qualified disabled, the wage equal the gross marginal product of labor rather than the net marginal product. In effect, the law places a tax equal to the accommodation costs on disabled labor. Normally, if a tax is imposed on a factor of production, the quantity demanded will fall as firms substitute away from the taxed factor. The ADA, however, makes this substitution effect illegal. This is because the firm is not supposed to treat accommodated labor any differently from non-accommodated labor with respect to wages, hiring, or firing. Therefore, the firm will experience losses on the marginal units of disabled labor. The losses incurred will induce the firm to reduce total output by more than it would in the case of a simple tax with no prohibition against substitution. From this output effect, there will be a decline in the demand for all factors of production: capital, nondisabled labor, and disabled labor. In summary, the overall effects will be: (1) a rise in the price of the product (assuming all firms in the industry are affected by the ADA tax); (2) a fall in output that is larger than if substitution were permitted; and (3) a decline in demand and price of disabled labor and other inputs. From this analysis, it is clear, at least in general terms, where the burdens of the ADA's compulsory beneficence lie. Consumers will pay higher prices and nondisabled labor and the owners of other inputs will receive lower remuneration. However, some disabled labor will also be unemployed who otherwise would have had jobs at lower "discriminatory" wages. It is suggested by Thomas DeLeire that the latter have been the "less- experienced and less-skilled workers with mental disabilities, which generally are more difficult to accommodate than physical disabilities." *See* Thomas DeLeire, *The Unintended Consequences of the Americans with Disabilities Act,* 23 REGULATION 21, 24 (2000).

case of consumers to pay higher prices, to benefit the qualified disabled. The Act also imposes burdens on the unlucky disabled who will become unemployed because of cutbacks in the output of affected firms.

Obviously, the Act makes no exceptions for those non-disabled who have heavy family financial obligations, those who give significant resources to the poor, those who behave beneficently toward the disabled outside of the employment context, those who make employment accommodation to disabled not qualified under the Act, and especially for the unemployed qualified-disabled the Act is ostensibly designed to help.[173] Thus, the Act cannot make reasonable accommodation to the morally-relevant facts.

2. The Good Samaritan Principle

The Good Samaritan Principle can be understood, especially from a utilitarian perspective, as a manifestation of a general principle of beneficence. Accordingly, there is no need to restrict it to emergency rescue situations or to those of low costs to the rescuer-benefactor.[174] As a moral principle, it can be stated rather broadly:

> *Individuals have a moral duty to provide positive assistance to strangers whenever the costs to them of doing so are less than the benefits to the strangers.*

This "optimizing principle"[175] is a straightforward implication of the "Benthamite" maxim: Everybody is "to count for one, nobody for more than one," combined with the utilitarian imperative to maximize the "happiness" of society.[176]

The concrete knowledge problems inherent in trying to follow this version of the Principle are enormous. First, the benefactor must have knowledge of what, in fact, would benefit the stranger in the short or long run and in the conditions in which he finds him. Secondly, the benefactor has a problem of moral balance. There are other "demands" for his beneficence, the attainment of his other moral goods, or the instantiation of other virtues. A law that attempted to compel this form of beneficence in specific cases as they arose would not survive the knowledge-test. The dirigiste could not know what is truly moral in the circumstances.

---

[173] Some of the disabled persons will be unemployed as a result of the Act and so they bear some of the costs of beneficence to the other disabled. Since the former tend to be the more severely disabled, see note 172, *supra*, it seems unjust, by the standard adopted in the Act, to require them to be beneficent to the more abled.

[174] Indeed, the low-cost restriction is not present in the original version in the New Testament. In this story, the Samaritan came across a man who had been mistreated by robbers and he "bandaged his wounds, having poured oil and wine on them. Then he put him on his own animal, brought him to an inn, and took care of him. The next day he took out two denarii, gave them to the innkeeper, and said, 'Take care of him; and when I come back, I will repay you whatever more you spend.'" *Luke* 10:29, 34-36, THE NEW OXFORD ANNOTATED BIBLE (3d ed. (2001) (New Revised Standard Version)).

[175] See the discussion in Murphy, *supra* note 167, at 650-52.

[176] Actually, the Benthamite maxim is due to Mill. *See* JOHN STUART MILL, UTILITARIANISM AND OTHER ESSAYS 336 (Alan Ryan ed., 1986).

He would simply compel agents to engage in certain objectively-defined behaviors irrespective of the agent's personal and local knowledge.

The optimizing Good Samaritan Principle can be restricted along a number of dimensions. Each of these restrictions is likely to ease the knowledge problem. They are: (1) the range of persons taken into the purview of beneficence; (2) the scope of situations in which potential beneficiaries require assistance; and (3) the depth or amount of assistance benefactors are required to render. The broad utilitarian version does not restrict the range to those who just happen to be nearby; presumably the agents have some cost-justified obligation to look for persons in need. It also does not restrict its scope to those in urgent or emergency need. Finally, it does not specify a maximum of assistance so long as the costs to the benefactor are lower than the gains to the beneficiary.

Consider now the Good Samaritan Principle as it normally manifests itself in legislation. These laws are normally restricted across the three dimensions. The range comprises those persons who happen to be in the view of the potential benefactor-rescuer. The scope is limited to one in which emergency or urgent aid is needed. The depth of assistance is constrained both by the utilitarian cost-benefit principle and by a "low" maximum level of costs to the benefactor.

Each of these restrictions reduces the knowledge problem in this form of compulsory beneficence. If we are not required to look for people in need, we are less likely to misidentify the existence of cases of need. If we are only required to deal with emergencies, we are more likely to be in a position to know the cause and remedy of the problem (for example, the child is drowning in a pool and so it is obvious that his immediate need is for lifeguard services). Finally, and most importantly, the pecuniary and time expenditure, as well as the risk to life and limb, incurred by the potential rescuer must be low. This ensures that no major sacrifice of other moral goods or instantiations of other moral virtues is likely to be suffered. So the agent's internal moral balance reflecting the appreciation of his unique circumstances is not substantially threatened.

Good Samaritan laws, restricted in the ways we have discussed, are not *in themselves* subject to the very significant knowledge problems that generally arise in compelling virtue. The knowledge objections to moral dirigisme in this case are likely to be weak. Nevertheless, there are two further related considerations. First, the restricted form of the Good Samaritan Principle is likely to be followed whether or not there is legislation. The social and moral incentives for low-cost rescue are great: praise, blame, feelings of virtue and of guilt. No one wants to be characterized by his own conscience or by others as a "moral monster."[177] Accordingly, in itself, it is not an important case of moral dirigisme when such laws exist. Second, and more importantly, the assertion of a legally-enforceable Good Samaritan Principle, even of a relatively restricted form, might lay the groundwork for the growth of such duties beyond the cases where knowledge problems are small,.

[177] For a discussion, see Murphy, *supra* note 167, at 608.

This is because the barriers between more restricted and less restricted Good Samaritan duties are porous. The continuity in the various dimensions of range,
scope, and depth, create the possibility of a slippery slope.[178] This continuity has
been illustrated by the nineteenth-century essayist, lawyer, and historian, Thomas
Babington Macaulay. Range, according to Macaulay, brings up the matter of prox-
imity to the potential beneficiary which is a continuous variable. Scope refers to
the degree of urgency in the need experienced – again a continuous variable. Finally, the depth of assistance or cost that the Samaritan is expected to sustain is
also continuous.[179]

In conclusion, restricted Good Samaritan laws will usually prove superfluous; their "unrestricted" form runs afoul of important local and personal
knowledge requirements; and the restricted form has some tendency to expand
through a slippery slope process. Accordingly, from the perspective of this Article,
it seems best to avoid imposing such duties in law.

PART FIVE: CHALLENGES TO THE THEORY

X.   Moral Absolutes

A fundamental challenge to the perspective we have advanced here is the
strand of moral thinking, based on the natural law approach of Thomas Aquinas,
that takes the view there are moral proscriptions of an absolute nature. In other
words, it is argued that there are a relatively small number of actions that are always and everywhere immoral.[180] It may seem that, on this view, there is no ethical knowledge problem. The concrete circumstances of time and place must be
irrelevant if indeed certain acts ought never to be done. This conclusion, however,
would be mistaken.

The issues are complex but it seems possible to isolate four factors that
make absolute proscriptions only "relatively-absolute." [181] These are:

1.   Moral absolutes are defined in terms of acts and not mere behaviors;

2.   The moral quality of acts are affected by the empirical context in
     which they take place;

3.   Certain acts have foreseeable, but unintended, bad consequences.
     Whether these are morally acceptable is a matter of personal, but not

---

[178] *See, generally,* Mario J. Rizzo & Douglas Glen Whitman, *The Camel's Nose is in the Tent: Rules, Theories and Slippery Slopes, in* 51 UCLA L. REV. 539, 557-60 (2003).

[179] *See* MACAULAY, *supra* note 172, at 253–55. It is interesting to note here that at one point in his life, Macaulay was "impoverished by his devotion to philanthropy." See the entry "*Macaulay, Thomas Babington, 1st Baron Macaulay*", *in* CAMBRIDGE BIOGRAPHICAL DICTIONARY 932 (Magnus Magnusson, KBE, ed., 1990).

[180] *See* Finnis, *supra* note 57, at 1–9.

[181] *See* FRANK H. KNIGHT, *The Rights of Man and Natural Law, in* 2 SELECTED ESSAYS BY FRANK H. KNIGHT 239 (Ross B. Emmett ed., 1999).

arbitrary, judgment. A judgment of acceptability may make evil consequences permissible;

4.   Certain acts are impermissible because they run counter to the basic goods that all people must pursue. However, the greater the degree of individuation permitted in the pursuit of basic goods, the greater the variety of acceptable lifestyles.

First, it is important to recognize that the proscriptions of moral absolutists are against acts and not physically-described behaviors. All action involves intentions, both intended outcomes and, ipso facto, intended means. Thus, for example, it is not possible to evaluate a decision to obtain a hysterectomy as such. To make a moral evaluation we must situate the physical behavior of removing the uterus in the context of a plan. Suppose cancer is present in the uterus and the agent wishes to have her uterus removed to stop the cancer from spreading. The immediate or proximate object of her decision is to stop the cancer. This is her direct intention. The further fact that she is now unable to be become pregnant and that the procreative function of her sexuality is impeded does not render her act immoral.[182] It is a foreseeable and accepted, but not directly intended, outcome. The same physical behavior – removal of a uterus – is a different act if cancer is not present because the proximate intention of the agent must be different. In this case, the immediate intention (the object) of removing the uterus may be impeding procreation. If so, the act is correctly described as sterilization. In the first case, the act is more appropriately described as removing or stopping the spread of cancer.

In this framework the kind of action a behavior is depends on the particular circumstances of time and place. What the actor directly intends is crucial to the true description of the action, and her intentions are only indirectly related to the objective circumstances in which the decision takes place, that is, the presence of cancer and the likelihood of halting its spread. Thus, there are two categories of relevant personal or local facts: first, and primarily, those relating to what the actor means by the decision; and, second, the outward facts of the particular situation. We have seen how the first category consists of a subjective decision. The second is also susceptible to a personal judgment. Even where cancer has been shown objectively to be present, a woman can directly intend sterilization, especially if she accepts that she has little likelihood of stopping the spread of the disease.

For our purposes the important question is whether these facts are likely to be available to a central moral decision maker? If agents are to be compelled to make choices that are objectively right, given the absolutist perspective, the compeller must have the appropriate knowledge of the agent's choice-act. This, however, is not objective in the sense of, for example, the verifiable consequences of behavior or simply the observable physical conditions in which the behavior is

---

[182] We are assuming here, of course, that to intend directly to impede the procreative function is immoral.

initiated. It involves the direct intentions of the actors and their assessment of outward conditions.[183]

Second, the conditions antecedent to an act can affect its moral quality. Consider the prohibition against adultery which, at a certain level, is fairly clear. There are, of course, issues regarding the validity of a particular marriage. Putting those aside, suppose that a husband has been lost in a war.[184] He is missing in action and presumed dead by the military authorities. So his wife remarries. But now rumors surface that the previous husband is still alive. Must the woman and her new husband immediately separate? Assuming that they are of good will and want honestly to do the right thing, how much credence should they place in these rumors? There isn't a single right answer to these questions because the degree of confidence one "should" have in rumors is not determined by logic or deduction but by prudence. To a certain, perhaps large extent, this is a "subjective disposition"[185] — a disposition built up over time by individual practice and experience in moral decision making coupled with a general desire to make honest decisions. So there is a range of appropriate moral decisions depending on particular local and personal circumstances.

Third, an act may be "absolutely" prohibited when its good or morally neutral proximate intention is not sufficiently important to warrant the foreseeable, but unintended, evil consequences. Simply because these consequences are not directly intended, it does not follow that the agent can ignore them. They must be minimized as when an individual uses force to repel force.[186] Whether this action is properly described as self-defense will depend, in part, on the degree of discrimination the agent uses in the application of force. If he uses far more than is necessary, it will be implausible to argue that the action has a moral object. Similarly, if the likelihood that the use of force will save the agent is reasonably expected to be very low, then a sufficiently grave reason for causing an evil will not be present. Individual judgment in awareness of local and personal facts will be

---

[183] Consider the formulation of an advocate of this view, Pope John-Paul II:

> "The morality of the human act depends primarily and fundamentally on the 'object' rationally chosen by the deliberate will . . . In order to be able to grasp the object of an act which specifies the act morally, it is therefore necessary to place oneself in the perspective of the acting person . . . By the object of a given moral act, then, one cannot mean a process or an event of the merely physical order, to be assessed on its ability to bring about a given state of affairs in the outside world. Rather, that object is the proximate end of a deliberate decision which determines the act of willing on the part of the acting person." Pope John-Paul II, Encyclical Veritatis Splendor ch. II, Part IV, ¶ 78 (1993), available at
> http://www.vatican.va/edocs/ENG0222/_P8.HTM.

This is quoted more fully in GERMAIN GRISEZ & JOSEPH BOYLE, *Response to Our Critics and Our Collaborators*, *in* NATURAL LAW AND MORAL INQUIRY: ETHIICS, METAPHYSICS AND POLITICS IN THE WORK OF GERMAIN GRISEZ 221--22 (Robert P. George ed., 1998). Importantly, Grisez and Boyle immediately add, "This analysis makes it clear that the exceptionless moral norms that the Church teaches (and we defend) are not the 'merely behavioral norms' that proportionalists posit as the target of their attack on moral absolutes." *Id.* at 222.

[184] This example is taken from SIMON, *THE DEFINITION OF MORAL VIRTUE*, *supra* note 146, at 109-10.

[185] *Id.* at 111.

[186] *See* Aquinas, *supra* note 146, at 1465 .

determinative in such cases. In the last forty years, some writers in the Roman Catholic tradition have become even more explicit about the importance of balancing good and bad effects. Peter Knauer, for example, has argued that even an evil means may be tolerated if there is a proportionately good effect to counterbalance it. In these cases the agent's "moral intention" goes only to the good and not the evil.[187]

The final factor responsible for the real contingency of moral absolutes is the agent-contextuality of the pre-moral goods that individuals do and should seek to attain. Natural law theories usually posit a limited number of such goods, such as life, friendship, knowledge and play.[188] These goods are viewed as basic or constitutive of human flourishing rather than as instrumental toward it. In some accounts each of these basic goods must be respected in every act.[189] Of course, this can produce problems of conflict to which mental gymnastics must be applied. The critical and related problem is the degree of individual flexibility or variation permitted in the concrete instantiation of basic goods. For example, if procreation is a value for human beings generically, must it be a value for all human beings and in every act that metaphysically may be related to it? The Roman Catholic Church teaches that non-coital sexual relations between married individuals are "counter-life" even where the woman is physically unable to conceive due to age.[190] Such activities, it is argued, do not demonstrate respect for the basic good of life. Natural law principles, however, cannot generate a universally correct set of individuated basic goods against which acts can be determined to embody respect for basic goods. The fundamental idea of flourishing, as we have seen above, is agent-specific.[191] There is significant diversity in the specific characteristics of human beings due to personal variations and differences in culture. The more the natural-law agent accepts individuated basic goods, the more moral absolutes will be actual-agent specific or in our terminology, contingent on the particular circumstances of time and place.

XI. Unhinged Absolutes

Before concluding our theoretical discussion of moral absolutes, let us consider a world in which people simply believe in absolutes, absolutely. In other words, they accept strict prohibitions or very specific positive commands not embedded in any general framework or philosophy. In this case, it may seem that the "wiggle room" identified and discussed above would not be present. A person might accept these as a matter of moral culture or religious faith. In a society of

---

[187] *See* CHRISTOPHER KACZOR, PROPORTIONALISM AND NATURAL LAW TRADITION 32 (2000).

[188] *See* Stephen Buckle, *Natural Law, in* THE BLACKWELL COMPANION TO ETHICS 170-71 (Peter Singer ed., 1991).

[189] *Id.* at 171.

[190] POPE PAUL VI, ENCYCLICAL HUMANAE VITAE, Chap. I, para.11 (1968), available at http://www.vatican.va/holy_father/paul_vi/encyclicals/documents/hf_p-vi_ene_25071968_humanae-vitae_en.html

[191] If the relevant agent is not the concrete individual acting in particular circumstances, then which characteristics, potentials and dispositions must the appropriate agent embody?

such people, can legislation make them moral? To answer this question, let us consider three important sets of factors.

1. The level of abstraction characteristic of the prohibition or command is highly relevant. If, for example, people are absolutely commanded to be beneficent, the precise form this takes is still subject to particular circumstances. At the very least, this would have to be the case when there are two or more absolute commands that may come into conflict with each other in a particular context. Instantiations of honesty and beneficence may sometimes conflict, even if these virtues do not conflict generically.

2. The roles of faith and reason or argument are often not entirely separate, but are intertwined. In the ethics writings of Thomas Aquinas, for example, the positions of the Roman Catholic Church are interpreted and argued for within the framework of his neo-Aristotelian natural law philosophy. Aquinas does not consider it sufficient to issue dicta on moral questions. Human reason and revelation are ultimately compatible because they stem from the same source: divine intelligence.[192] Thus, insofar as agents engage in Thomistic moral reasoning (or act as if they do), the apparent exceptions to moral absolutes discussed in the previous section[193] would continue to have relevance to persons of faith.

3. People often do not really hold moral absolutes, absolutely. Therefore, compulsion will not make them moral by the moral framework that is actually held in a society. In this respect we must consider what people say and what they do.

    (a) *What People Say*: American Catholics, for example, by large majorities say that "artificial" birth control and abortion to save the life of the mother are morally justified.[194] So Catholics, whom one might expect to hold absolutes, absolutely, do not. Their actual moral system is

---

[192] This point is emphasized by Servais-Théodore Pinckaers: "Thomas does not separate the two principles sources, revelation and reason, theology and philosophy, as would be done later. On the contrary, one can see in him a very close collaboration in the use of authorities between the content of faith and reason, the Gospel and Aristotle. While discerning perfectly the difference between these two different kinds of light, Thomas endeavors to show their convergence, which rests on a fundamental harmony . . . . There exists, therefore, a close coordination between theological and philosophical sources in Thomas's moral works. It is based upon the fundamental harmony between revelation and reason, each of which, according to its own level and its own method, flows from divine truth." Servais-Théodore Pinckaers, O.P., *The Sources of the Ethics of St. Thomas Aquinas* (Mary Thomas Noble, O.P. trans.) *in* THE ETHICS OF AQUINAS (Stephen J. Pope ed., 2002).

[193] *See supra.,* section XI.

[194] In the U.S. 61% of Catholics disagree with the Church's teaching on contraception and 87% believe that abortion is morally acceptable if the pregnancy poses a serious threat to the woman's health.) See the compilation of surveys in Catholics for Free Choice, A WORLD VIEW: CATHOLIC ATTITUDES ON SEXUAL BEHAVIOR AND REPRODUCTIVE HEALTH 12, 17 (2004), available at http://www.catholicsforchoice.org/activepubs/sexandr/worldview2004.pdf.

more like what we have described above: principles accommodated to time and place considerations.

(b) *What People Do*: Moral systems, especially including the moral absolutes held, often change when people are confronted with the costs or consequences of their decisions. This is particularly the case during periods of social and economic transition. Changes in behavior may be characterized as violations of moral rules due to weakness or they may be characterized as changes in the moral rules themselves. There is no simple way to distinguish these.[195] Some possibilities of distinguishing rest on whether such deviations are widespread, violators feel guilty, informed moral authorities begin to change their preachments, and so forth. The point for our purposes is that the de facto violation of any absolute may mark the beginning of a change in the moral system adhered to by the agents. Thus, "[m]any of those who believe that homosexual acts should not be criminalized do not see themselves as being lax about the immorality of homosexuality; they simply do not think it is immoral at all."[196] Under these circumstances, moral dirigisme may simply be retarding moral evolution and not creating a better or more virtuous society.

In summary, the possible existence of moral absolutes does not require any major adjustment to our thesis that moral behavior requires, in general, detailed attention and adaptation to the particular circumstances of time and place.

XII.   Moral Absolutes: The Case of Sodomy

There is no doubt that the Supreme Court's decision in *Lawrence v. Texas*[197] is important both from the perspective of the statutes it invalidated and for the future of morals laws and moralistic legislation as they are related to sexuality. Many of those who argued for upholding sodomy laws believe that homosexual sodomy is always and everywhere immoral.[198] They appear to base that position, insofar as it can be distinguished from one exclusively founded on Biblical injunctions that they *choose* to accept[199], on the general idea that homosexual acts are unable to participate either actually or potentially in the objective good of marriage.[200] Marriage is defined, in this account, as the *type* of relationship that is in-

---

[195] This a Wittgensteinian point. *See, e.g.*, BRIAN BIX, JURISPRUDENCE: THEORY AND CONTEXT 149, n.17 (2d ed. 1999).

[196] *Id.* at 149.

[197] 539 U.S. 558 (2003).

[198] *See, e.g.* FINNIS, *supra* note 57, at 8-9 (1991).

[199] Some Biblical injunctions enjoy widespread acceptance, while others are ignored or downplayed. Frank Knight provides one reason: "…[T]he Christian who thinks he believes that certain things are right because they are ordered or sanctioned by the divine will as revealed in the Bible (or by his church), actually believes these things to be divinely ordered because on other grounds he believes them to be right and good, and because he believes on other grounds that the teachings of his religion ordain what is good." *See* FRANK H. KNIGHT, *Liberalism and Christianity, in* THE ECONOMIC ORDER AND RELIGION 33-34 (Frank H. Knight and & Thornton Merriam eds., 1945).

[200] *See* FINNIS, *supra* note 165 at 15.

trinsically related to the procreation and rearing of children. So homosexual acts, in effect, are choices against a basic, universal, and objective good.

The argument has three constituent ideas: (1) A decision against a basic good is being made; (2) It is never moral directly to tradeoff one basic good against another; and (3) A relationship may be justified completely at the generic level, that is, it may be morally justified because it is of the same type as another, but not justified because it is of a different type. Each of these constituents ignores morally-relevant circumstances of time and place.

The first argument confuses generic goods with their instantiation in time and place. For many people, procreation is not possible: for example, for the sterile and the old. Thus, they are not trading off a real possibility. Furthermore, for homosexual persons procreative acts may not be a good at all. And simply to engage in these acts and to feign marriage for the sake of a putative common or universal good does not seem advisable.[201] Therefore, no choice against a good is being made under these particular circumstances.

Second, a choice against one good for another good is not immoral under any reasonable interpretation of the natural law. In fact, it is inevitable in a world of conflicts and scarcity.[202] Consider, for example, the case in which a heterosexual married couple decides not to choose against procreation and leaves all of their sexual acts open to it. Under normal conditions, they will have many children and this will put stress on other aspects of their marriage. Other goods, like opportunities for mutual growth, friendship, intimacy and, possibly, the full education of the children, will have to be sacrificed. Prudence demands a careful consideration of the facts of each case in order to achieve a balance of goods.

The third proffered argument may be an elaborate form of question begging. To define "marriage" as a type of relationship open to procreation is, at best, to mistake a temporal category for an analytical or moral category. Does a sterile marriage properly belong to the category of an intimate sexual relationship intended to be long lasting that is open to procreation? The word "open" is being used in a value-laden or, perhaps, metaphysical way that *presupposes* the answer to what type of relationship sterile marriage is. (It is certainly not being used in any physical sense.) If this is the case, then to exclude all homosexual relations from the same category as sterile marriage is also question begging. When the circumstances of time and place are considered, it will be seen that sterile or advanced

---

[201] *See, e.g.,* Richard Sparks, What the Church Teaches about Homosexuality, CATHOLIC UPDATE (July, 1999). Available at http://www.americancatholic.org/Newsletter/CU/ac0799.asp ("[T]he Church calls all homosexual persons, like their single heterosexual counterparts, to be chaste, that is, sexually appropriate for their uncommitted, unmarried state in life.").

[202] See, for example, the criticism of absolutism from an "economic" point of view in KNIGHT, *supra* note 199, at 52 ("The moral problem is one of right balance between conflicting values, valid goods, not one of choosing the good instead of the bad or choosing 'either' one 'or' another of opposed standards or norms.").

age marriage are no more open to procreation than same sex relationships. Either both are sodomy or neither are.

XIII. The Moral Ecology

John Finnis and Robert George have each put forward minimalist forms of moral dirigisme.[203] In these approaches, the State does not seek to proscribe vices and prescribe virtues for the sake of the morality of the coerced agents. It coerces individuals primarily to create a good public morality, that is, a social structure conducive to virtue and hostile to vice To be more specific, we consider George's concept of "public morality."[204] Reduced to its essentials, the publicness of good moral behavior is comprised of three factors: preventing bad example that might affect the unthinking, educating people about moral right and wrong, and preserving (creating) a good social environment free of immoral temptations.[205] The social benefit is independent of whether the directly targeted individuals abstain from immoral behavior solely because of legal sanctions. They are not the intended beneficiaries of the public good. The beneficiaries are people who generally desire to act morally, but who might be overwhelmed by bad example, moral ignorance, or temptations to do otherwise. Relatedly, they may be confused or discouraged by the breakdown of a shared moral and social consensus about the nature of "objective" moral goods or institutions, such as marriage. This could lead them to undervalue or misconstrue such goods.

The public-morality view is completely derivative of the proper identification of immoral and moral actions. Thus, to create a good moral ecology with all of its putative advantages, it is necessary to determine what actually damages or helps the moral framework of society. Since morality can be instantiated only relative to particular circumstances of time and place, the Finnis-George moral dirigiste must solve the knowledge problem before a favorable public morality is created.

George recognizes that there are a plurality of ways to attain basic moral goods and exhibit virtue. Nevertheless, both he and Finnis believe that there are a number of actions that are always and everywhere immoral and thus are not consistent with any conception of the morally good life.[206] Among these are homosexual activity, the production, sale, and use of pornography, prostitution, and drug abuse. Thus, if consensual homosexual activity in private is legal (as it is now), those who are not now engaging in such activity may think it is morally acceptable

---

[203] *See* ROBERT P. GEORGE, MAKING MEN MORAL: CIVIL LIBERTIES AND PUBLIC MORALITY (1993); FINNIS, *supra* note 165, at 1–26 (Robert P. George ed., 1996).

[204] *See, generally,* ROBERT P. GEORGE, *The Concept of Public Morality, in* THE CLASH OF ORTHODOXIES: LAW, RELIGION, AND MORALITY IN CRISIS 93-109 (2001).

[205] George adds a fourth aspect: "...preventing the (further) self-corruption which follows from acting out a choice to indulge in immoral conduct." *See* GEORGE, *supra* note 203, at 1 (1993). This is inconsistent with an emphasis solely on public morality and constitutes a small area of disagreement with John Finnis. For a discussion of their disagreement, see Robert P. George, *Forum on Public Morality: The Concept of Public Morality,* 45 AM. J. JURIS. 17, 28-31 (2000).

[206] *See* GEORGE, *supra* note 203, at 38-40; 191-192 (1993).

and so people will be miseducated while others will be given a bad example that they may follow without much thought or be tempted to have homosexual relations. Further, since pornography tends to demean the sexual act according to George, then its circulation will portray bad role models and give people, especially the young, the idea that such depicted acts are morally acceptable.[207] In both the above cases, as some people will indulge in these intrinsic evils, the social consensus about the purpose of sexuality and the nature of the institution of marriage will dissolve. This will cause doubts about what is expected of people in relationships and thus people will lose the security and moral good of marriage.

If, however, we are correct that moral absolutes, the sense of concrete proscriptions and prescriptions that are invariant with respect to particular circumstances, do not exist in any of the major ethical frameworks, then the idea of a general public morality is deeply problematic. If "good" public morality teaches people that reading pornography is always and everywhere immoral then we suggest the wrong lesson is being taught. Furthermore, costs would be imposed upon those individuals who in fact are engaging in moral behavior in their particular circumstances. They would be coerced by the State into attaining a lesser good or engaging in immoral conduct. In addition, to the extent that individuals' particular circumstances are known to families, neighbors, associates, and others, they would be giving bad example by providing a warped illustration of the use of prudence to make moral decisions. Instead of making it easier to pursue virtue or avoid vice, the moral ecology would be filled with misinformation and perverse incentives.

Conclusion

This Article makes two separable contributions. First, we apply a rational choice theory with a strong emphasis on decentralized knowledge to moral decision making. This approach stresses the importance of tacit, as well as explicit, local and personal knowledge in the application of moral principles to concrete actions. We also show that particular moral decisions are adjusted to the other moral, as well as nonmoral, decisions of the agent.

Second, we apply this technique of analysis to the problem of moral dirigisme, or the attempt to make the actions of people moral through coercion. We show that the attempt founders on the phenomenon of decentralized social knowledge. Most moral decisions require the particular knowledge of time and place that is usually available only to the individual decision maker. This knowledge is often the byproduct of local economic and social relations; other times it is specifically sought after by those who have the incentive to be moral in the context of problems they have made their own. Equally important, as mentioned above, is the ineradicably personal, but not arbitrary, reconciliation or integration of individual moral decisions. In a world of scarce resources, including the time of the agent, the good or virtuous life is one in which particular decisions form a whole that conduces either to utility, flourishing, or the establishment of a kingdom of

---

[207] GEORGE, *supra* note 204, at 93.

rational ends. Each of the classical moral systems, in its own way, requires local and personal knowledge for the effective pursuit of morality. The unavailability of this knowledge to the dirigiste condemns his plans for the moral improvement of humanity to moral incoherence and irrationality. Central planning is chaotic in the moral as well as in the economic world.